PEARSON

ALWAYS LEARNING

Looking At Us

An Interdisciplinary Study of Human Behaviors

Custom Edition for Saint Leo University
SSC 101

Taken From:

Cross-Cultural Psychology: Critical Thinking and Contemporary Applications,
Fourth Edition
by Eric B. Shiraev and David A. Levy

Anthropology, Second Edition
by Barbara Miller

Contemporary Society: An Introduction to Social Science, Twelfth Edition
by John A. Perry and Erna K. Perry

Sociology Now
by Michael Kimmel and Amy Aronson

Essentials of Sociology: A Down-to-Earth Approach, Eighth Edition
by James M. Henslin

Cover photograph courtesy of Saint Leo University.

Taken from:

Cross-Cultural Psychology: Critical Thinking and Contemporary Applications, Fourth Edition
by Eric B. Shiraev and David A. Levy
Copyright © 2010, 2007, 2004 by Pearson Education, Inc.
Published by Allyn & Bacon
Boston, Massachusetts 02116

Anthropology, Second Edition
by Barbara Miller
Copyright © 2008, 2006 by Pearson Education, Inc.
Published by Allyn & Bacon

Contemporary Society: An Introduction to Social Science, Twelfth Edition
by John A. Perry and Erna K. Perry
Copyright © 2009, 2006, 2003, 2000 by Pearson Education, Inc.
Published by Allyn & Bacon

Sociology Now
by Michael Kimmel and Amy Aronson
Copyright © 2009 by Michael Kimmel and Amy Aronson
Published by Allyn & Bacon
Boston, Massachusetts 02116

Essentials of Sociology: A Down-to-Earth Approach, Eighth Edition
by James M. Henslin
Copyright © 2009 by James M. Henslin
Published by Allyn & Bacon

Printed in the United States of America

4 5 6 7 8 9 10 v092 16 15 14 13 12

000200010270771655

MT/CM

ISBN 10: 1-256-14548-3
ISBN 13: 978-1-256-14548-6

Contents

chapter 9

■ Social Groups and Formal Organizations 199

Section V: Deviance and Social Control

chapter 10

■ Deviance and Crime 222

chapter 11

■ Psychological Disorders 253

chapter 17

■ Readings 393

Preface

The Human Behavior Perspective course introduces Saint Leo University students to a study of human behavior via the scientific lenses of anthropology, psychology, and sociology. This textbook was compiled by Saint Leo University faculty from popular secondary sources within each of the three disciplines. Our primary goal was to create a comprehensive textbook written from the perspective of each respective discipline. Given that vast area of knowledge in each discipline, we felt it was important to draw from the respected and established authors of textbooks in each of three different fields. We feel that this textbook will enhance instruction and learning in the Human Behavior Perspective course because the sources included are current, well written, engaging, and relevant. Our hope is that students will develop an appreciation of the different as well as the complementary interpretations and explanations of human behavior offered by anthropology, psychology, and sociology.

Special thanks to Dr. David Krahl (sociology), Dr. Susan Pappas (anthropology), and Dr. Patricia Campion (sociology) for your dedication and hard work on this project. Also special thanks to the Pearson representatives, Nicole McHam and Julie McBurney, who made this possible for our instructors and students.

Happy Learning,

Dr. Leilani Goodmon
Assistant Professor
Department of Psychology and Social Sciences
Saint Leo University

chapter 1

Through the Lens of Science

IN THIS CHAPTER, YOU WILL LEARN

- *of the existence of the external world, which we inherit, and the social world, which we create;*
- *that the analysis of the social world with the tools of science is a fairly recent innovation;*
- *the basic differences between the social and the natural sciences;*
- *the elements and steps of the scientific method;*
- *which disciplines constitute the social sciences;*
- *the various research methods used in the social sciences.*

Life on our planet has undergone tremendous changes since its beginning, both in the natural world into which we are born, and the social world we have created and to which each generation contributes. What do we mean by the **natural** and the **social** worlds? Clearly, at birth all living things enter a physical world that is not of their own making. Plants and animals either adapt to this ready-made environment or die out. They cannot change the nature of their habitat, for on planet Earth all living organisms exist in an environment shaped by forces and governed by laws that are only partially and imperfectly understood and only minimally amenable to change or control. Early humans did not understand this world and attributed many phenomena to spirits and supernatural beings. Today, the natural world is studied by the methods of science in such disciplines as biology, physics, chemistry, ecology, and so on. These disciplines are the so-called exact sciences and are not within the realm of our inquiry in this text.

Each newly born **human** being, however, also enters a social world that has been shaped by those born previously and is continually reshaped by each new generation. The existence of this **social** world, while taken for granted by the majority of people, is of tremendous importance to humans. It is what distinguishes them from other animals. Animals, aside from certain biological adaptations to new environments or climates, retain an essentially unchanged lifestyle from the moment of their emergence. Humans, on the other hand, have manipulated their social world to the point of affecting their lifestyles dramatically (although their biological and physical characteristics have scarcely changed in the last 20,000 years). This social world was not always well understood, either, but in the last 200 years, disciplines have originated with the goal of examining it with the same scientific methodology that the exact sciences use. These disciplines are collectively called the **social sciences**.

The social sciences were born in a period of social turmoil, when new ideas and beliefs were causing conflict and fragmentation in European societies. They represented an attempt to make sense of a social reality that had become too difficult to grasp with the old tools. They offered the hope that the social world could also be examined in a dispassionate, objective way that would yield specific rules of behavior for people to follow to improve their individual and collective lives. Perhaps the expectations for the social sciences were too high: in spite of efforts, few grand theories have been developed or secrets of social life have been uncovered. Nonetheless, the social sciences and their methodology remain effective—and probably unique—tools for rationally examining our social world.

Contemporary Society: An Introduction to Social Science, Twelfth Edition
by John A. Perry and Erna K. Perry

The Social Sciences

The purpose of the social sciences is to study systematically all aspects of the human condition and of human behavior, using a methodology borrowed from the physical sciences wherever possible. This insistence on systematic and methodical study is what distinguishes the social sciences from philosophy, art, and literature, which also comment and reflect on all facets of the human condition. In fact, insights into the nature of human behavior and the characteristics of societies have been expressed by artists, poets, and philosophers since time immemorial. Artists, poets, and philosophers avail themselves of such tools as intuition, imagination, authority, tradition, rational thought, and common sense, tools available to all of us and which we still use every day. Unfortunately, however, these tools have a major shortcoming: they are not always accurate and thorough, and they are often colored by individual or societal prejudices. For instance, for centuries people believed that the earth was flat and, thus, one could fall off its edge. That was a reasonable deduction if one used only one's senses: the earth does look flat when we look only as far as our eyes reach. It was also accepted knowledge that the earth was the center of the universe and the sun went around it, and that too was a logical conclusion if all one did was look with the naked eye. However, when instruments were invented that could measure and see beyond the human senses, the knowledge that up to then had been accepted as truth needed to be modified; and that did not happen without a fight. The Polish astronomer Nicolaus Copernicus (1473–1543) and the Italian Renaissance astronomer Galileo Galilei (1564–1642) were ostracized and nearly lost their lives when they tried to convince their compatriots that it was the earth that circled the sun, not the other way around, thus challenging the ancient wisdom of such authorities as Aristotle and the Catholic Church. These astronomers had not trusted their senses alone but attempted to arrive at the truth by using a new tool of inquiry: science.

The Social World Seen through the Lens of Science

Science may be briefly defined as a method using a system of rational inquiry dependent on the empirical testing of facts. It is this method, rather than a particular body of content, that gives scientists a unique way of looking at things. The purpose of the scientific method is to obtain evidence that is verifiable and subject to replication and to make no judgment about even the most seemingly obvious "facts" until original suppositions are overwhelmingly supported by proof.

The social sciences emerged when some social philosophers determined to use the scientific method to study specific aspects of human behavior in the social world. Initially, social philosophy differed little from philosophy in general, but certain ideas prevalent in the eighteenth century, during the era commonly called the Enlightenment, led to the division of social philosophy into a number of separate disciplines. This historical period was characterized by an increase in people's faith in the power of reason. Scholars and philosophers became convinced that, just as universal laws of nature had been discovered by natural scientists through the use of the scientific method, similar laws would become apparent if human behavior could be examined by the same approach. Once the principles of social life were uncovered, they theorized, a more perfect society could be attained.

Technology marches on! Social scientists have another tool at their disposal—the ubiquitous computer—to help them in researching how people interact even in the remotest societies.

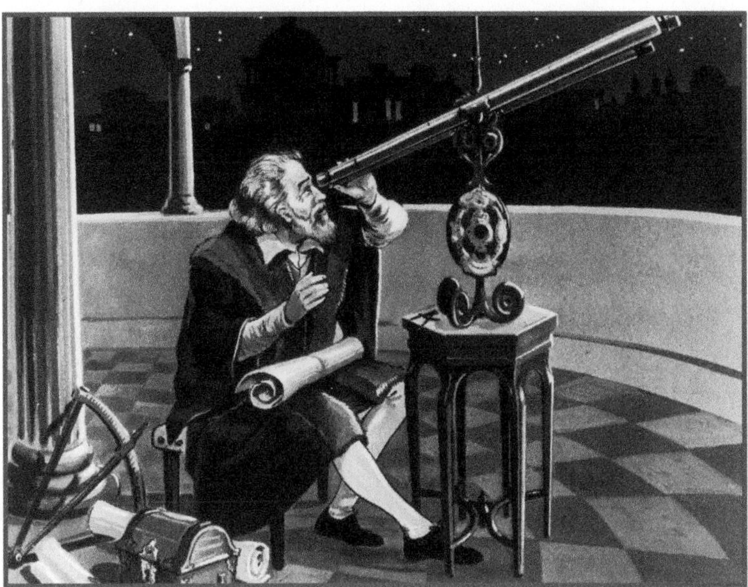

Galileo Galilei, an Italian astronomer and physicist (1564–1642) theorized, after looking at the sky with a telescope, that it was the earth that moved around the sun, and not the other way around as was commonly believed in his time. Many theories in the social sciences also dispel some widely held, but incorrect, beliefs.

As usually happens, the need for a new approach to the analysis of human social behavior was prompted by dramatic societal changes. The conditions brought about by the Industrial Revolution and the movement of people to cities encouraged thinkers to seek solutions to the many new problems faced by individuals in these changed societies. With the rise of industry, in fact, two new social classes emerged: the owners of manufacturing machinery and the industrial workers who operated it. There were vast discrepancies in the standards of living between these two social classes, with the workers laboring for long hours in difficult conditions and suffering frequent layoffs. As people kept moving to cities in search of factory jobs, cities became places in which conditions of overcrowding and lack of hygiene were rampant. Soon, cities became breeding grounds of poverty and crime. It was primarily these problems that the early social scientists attempted to address by applying the scientific method to human behavior, in this way giving rise to the social sciences. These include cultural anthropology, economics, geography (including demography and ecology), political science, psychology, sociology, and those dimensions of history that go beyond the strictly narrative recounting of events.

What do the social sciences study today? Following are some examples of what contemporary social science examines. An economist at Georgetown University is one of four authors of a report that concludes that childhood poverty costs the United States about $500 billion a year because poor children become less productive adults, earn less money, commit more crimes, and have more health problems that are paid for by taxpayers. Consequently, the authors suggest that the United States would be well served to invest significant resources to poverty reduction (Eckholm, 2007, A15).

A physicist at the University of Maryland, who calls himself an "econophysicist," maintains that present patterns of economic inequality are "as natural, and unalterable, as the properties of air molecules in your kitchen" (Shea, 2005, 67). Econophysicists use the tools of physics to study markets and other economic phenomena. Thus, in studying wealth distribution in the United States, these researchers maintain that the dispersion of income is similar to the distribution patterns of the energy of atoms in gases that are at thermal equilibrium. Moreover, this is a pattern that many closed, random systems tend to follow.

Stanford University psychologists and economists designed a study to find out which part of the brain is active when a person decides to spend money at a shopping mall, and what produces the urge to buy (Tierney, 2007, D1). A Columbia University sociologist tries to decode social interactions to discover why people give themselves reasons for actions and attitudes (Gladwell, 2006, 80).

Finally, more and more the social sciences are combining with the exact sciences to discover findings in the areas of medicine and climate, findings that will affect and possibly benefit people and societies.

In defining the social sciences, the key words are *systematically* and *methodically*. Because the social world is subjected to scientific scrutiny, the knowledge that has accumulated about how humans live in their world is organized according to definite concepts, theories, and research and not according to random, subjective, and possibly biased observation.

The Scientific Method

Although the social sciences are considered scientific disciplines, they cannot employ exactly the same methodology as the natural or physical sciences. They do, however, share with all sciences the use of the scientific method. The basic technique of the scientific method is a special kind of observation called *scientific observation.* This kind of observation differs from simply looking around. Those of us who have the use of our vision look at things all the time, but we seldom arrive at scientific conclusions. We obtain evidence from our senses, but for such evidence to be reliable, it must first be confirmed by the scientific method. That is, scientific observation must proceed *systematically.* Scientists must select and define a problem and then make an organized plan for collecting data. Scientific observation must be *accurate and precise.* In collecting data, scientists must subject them to careful checking, rechecking, and cross-checking, as well as to careful measurement. Scientific observation should take place under *controlled conditions,* although that is frequently impossible. Researchers should be able to make particular features of the environment remain constant, so that when other features change, they can be sure which specific cause is determining which effect. This requirement is difficult to achieve in the social sciences, because research on people cannot always be performed in a laboratory. Control is difficult even in the natural sciences, because many phenomena can only be observed at a distance. Finally, scientific observation must be made by a *trained observer.* Only such a person knows which data are relevant and which are only peripherally important. The vocabulary of science includes concepts, theories, and research.

Concepts

Concepts are generalized, abstract ideas that symbolize whole categories of people, objects, and processes. They are ways of classifying things that are in the same category. For instance, the concept of "chair" includes all those objects made for people to sit on, although there is an infinite variety of such objects, from gilded Louis XIV antiques to the chrome-and-vinyl kitchen variety. Concepts are used to simplify the way people think and communicate. Society, nation, art, education, and voting are only some examples of concepts.

Concepts are used by social scientists to generalize about some aspects of human inter-action. They are guidelines that direct the interpretation and analysis of reality. Concepts are the technical vocabulary of the social sciences, and they have precise meanings that may differ considerably from the generally understood versions.

Theories

Theories are sets of concepts and generalizations so arranged that they explain and predict possible relationships among phenomena. In the social sciences, theories are formulations of principles of behavior through which scientists try to increase their knowledge of human interaction. Theories are founded on observation and analysis using the vocabulary of concepts. Without theories, the accumulation of knowledge would be impossible, just as the formulation of theories would be impossible without concepts. A theory does not have the force of a law. A law is an explanation of unchanging relationships among events. According to the law of gravity, an object always falls in the same direction under given conditions. The social sciences have no laws because they deal with people rather than with inanimate objects, and people have intelligence and will that are not subject to unchangeable laws. Theories are always open to change and even to total rejection if new evidence is presented to challenge them. Finally, when people speak of "theory" in casual conversation, they mean nothing more than a guess. In scientific terminology, a theory carries much more weight because it is based on supporting evidence.

Research

Research tests and bolsters, or refutes, theories. Research may be defined as systematic scientific inquiry conducted under controlled conditions in which data are carefully observed for the purpose of determining the relationship between one factor (for example, income) and one or more other factors (for example, child-rearing techniques).

Variables. The factors whose relationship social scientists try to uncover are called *variables.* These are characteristics that differ (vary) in each individual case—from person to person, from group to group, from time to time, from place to place, and from situation to situation. In explaining what variables are, one social scientist adds that "A variable is a name for something that is thought to influence (or be influenced by) a particular state of being in something else...in addition, [it is] a special kind of concept that contains within it a notion of degree or differentiation" (Hoover & Donovan, 1995, 21–22). Age, educa-

Marie Curie, a French-Polish physicist and chemist and the first woman scientist to win a Nobel Prize, working in her laboratory. Scientific research is conducted systematically, under strictly controlled conditions in which data are carefully observed and accurately noted, to be able to determine relationships between one factor and one or more other factors.

tion, income, religion, and political affiliation are some of the most frequently used variables in social scientific research. Social scientists use measurements, usually of a statistical nature, to determine the value of a variable in a specific case.

Variables, then, are concepts that vary, and they are used in the social sciences to uncover how change in one phenomenon can explain change in another one. Variables are of two kinds: *independent* or *dependent*. **Independent** variables are those that exert influence on **dependent** variables. The relationship between variables may be one of **cause and effect**, in which case the independent variable is the cause and the dependent variable receives its effect. The relationship between variables may also be one of **correlation**, meaning that two or more variables are simply related in some way. Correlation and causation are distinct phenomena and should not be confused. *Correlation* occurs purely by chance and the variables change together, whereas in *causation*, one phenomenon is responsible for another. Sometimes the correlation among two or more variables turns out to be *spurious*, meaning that it is false—that in reality the association is caused by another factor that scientists have not even considered and did not intend to measure. It is, therefore, imperative that scientific research be carefully controlled. Variables must be clearly stated and must be measurable; the relationship between variables must be equally clear and measurable; and the pursuant hypothesis (that the variables are related) must be testable (Hoover & Donovan, 1995, 35).

Steps of the Scientific Method

The steps in the scientific method, illustrated in Figure 1.1, may be summarized as follows.

Selecting and Defining a Topic. First, an investigator must have a clearly defined idea of what should be investigated. A topic for investigation is usually prompted by curiosity; thus, it tends to be in the form of a question. For instance, are children of first-generation immigrants more successful in attaining upward mobility than children of native-born citizens? The researcher should also specify whether a causal relationship is suspected (one variable causing the occurrence of another). Because it is difficult to prove causal relationships and distinguish cause from effect, researchers are often satisfied with proving that a correlation between two or more phenomena exists.

Reviewing the Literature. After selecting the topic, the researcher must review all the existing literature on the subject to ensure that it has not already been investigated. If it has, the researcher might have to alter the topic, perhaps focusing on a facet of it that has not been investigated previously. A review of the literature is an important step in the scientific method. It connects new research with old, allows the accumulation of ideas, and directs scientists to the right variables to pursue. Libraries are now equipped with computerized systems that make the job of reviewing books and articles much less time consuming than it was in the past.

Forming a Hypothesis. The hypothesis is a tentative statement of the selected topic that is subject to testing and verification. The hypothesis must, in clearly expressed terms, predict a relationship between two or more variables. Hypotheses may be based on a researcher's mere hunch or educated guess; for instance, a researcher may speculate that religion influences the way a person votes. The remaining steps of the scientific method may prove the hypothesis valid (yes, religion affects voting behavior), may cause it to be reformulated (yes, but only if the voter is in a specific age bracket), or may contradict it altogether (no, religion has nothing to do with voting behavior). A hypothesis may also derive from common-sense deductions, curiosity, or traditional wisdom; it may emerge from existing theories and previous research; or it may originate from a review of the literature on an issue that interests a researcher.

Developing a Research Design (Collecting, Classifying, and Analyzing Data). The research plan that is developed after the hypothesis is stated must specify from what group(s) and in what manner data are to be collected. Decisions must also be made about how best to obtain the data (direct observation, questionnaires, interviews, or a combination of research methods).

After data have been systematically collected, the researcher must classify, organize, and record them. Data must also be made public so that others may have access to both the findings and the procedures. In most scientific disciplines, including the social sciences, computers are used to classify and organize data.

The data are then analyzed. In this step, the researcher subjects the previously classified data to various statistical methods to see whether relationships are substantial or so small that they may be due to chance. Statistical computation determines whether the data support the hypothesis.

Verifying. Because most research is subject to error—of which the researcher may or may not be aware—another important step in the scientific method is verification. This step consists of repeating the research project (replication) and may be done either by the scientist who conducted the original research or by another scientist. For research to be considered successful, it must be capable of being repeated by another scientist with the same results.

Generalizing. Finally, conclusions must be drawn from the analysis of data. Do the data substantiate the original hypothesis? Do they refute it? Are alterations to the hypothesis in order? A cautious researcher tends to make undergeneralizations, which may keep his or her research from being useful to others. An overconfident researcher tends to make overgeneralizations, which may lead to false hypotheses and wrong conclusions.

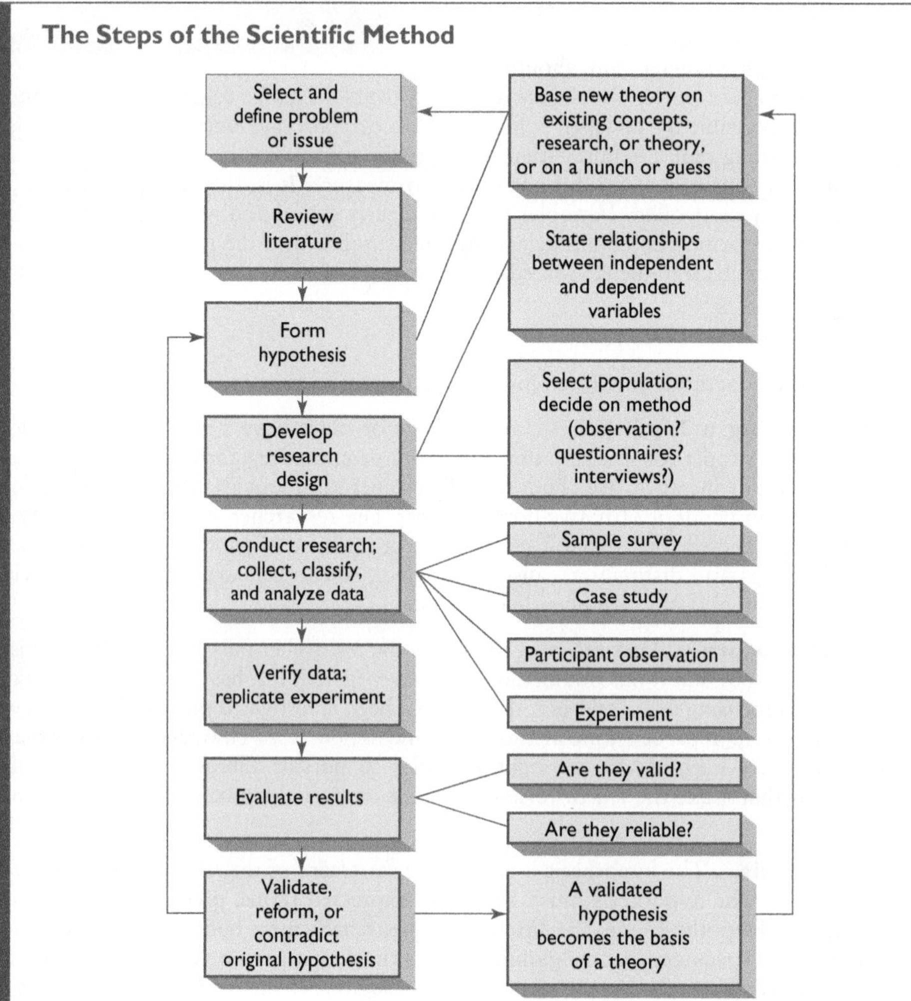

FIGURE 1.1 Science includes the method by which information is obtained. Scientists in all scientific disciplines, therefore, must follow the steps of the scientific method with rigor and objectivity.

Conclusions are usually summarized in reports, sometimes published in professional journals or as monographs. The researcher attempts to relate the conclusions to existing theories or current research and makes suggestions about the necessity of altering some accepted theoretical assumptions or the need for new hypotheses that have emerged from the research.

The Scientific Spirit: Skepticism, Objectivity, Relativity

Underlying the scientific method is an attitude best described as the *scientific spirit*. The most important principle of the scientific spirit is that scientists approach everything with great *doubt and skepticism*, taking nothing for granted. This attitude must be displayed even with regard to their own findings, which are always subject to change after further analysis.

Another principle is that of *objectivity*. Scientists must try to rid themselves completely of personal attitudes, desires, beliefs, values, and tendencies when confronting data intended to support a finding. They must try to be totally dispassionate, allowing no individual biases to affect their judgment. Of course, such a degree of objectivity is only an ideal to which scientists aspire; no human can be objective all the time. The issue of objectivity has been especially polemical in the social sciences, which deal with the relationships and behavior of people.

Closely related to objectivity is the third principle of the scientific spirit: *ethical neutrality*. According to this principle, scientists must not make value judgments about their findings; they must not pronounce their conclusions to be good or bad, right or wrong. They must be concerned only with whether the findings are true or false.

Finally, scientific conclusions must never be considered final, absolute, or universal truths. Rather, they should be considered as *relative* to the time and place in which they are obtained and always subject to change or revision.

The Social Science Disciplines

The boundaries among the social sciences are artificial in the sense that they all study the same thing: human behavior in the social environment. Each discipline, however, focuses on specific facets of that world and behavior, in effect allowing social scientists to specialize. Social scientists are aware of the overlapping nature of their disciplines, and they often borrow from one another. The differences, in short, are a matter of emphasis.

Anthropology

Anthropology combines a natural science—biology—and information gathered from the social sciences to uncover the relationships between human biological traits and traits acquired socially, that is, by living in groups. The discipline is divided into *physical anthropology*, which is concerned principally with human biological origins and the variations in the human species, and *cultural anthropology*, which has traditionally dealt with the study and comparative analysis of preliterate societies.

Physical anthropologists deal with traits that appear in specific populations and with characteristics that populations develop as a result of adaptation to particular environments. The variety of "racial" groupings among human populations is a subject of research for anthropologists, as are fossil studies and research on living primates. Additionally, physical anthropologists use *genetics*, the science that analyzes heredity, in an attempt to uncover how the genes of living organisms determine the characteristics of their offspring. Genetics is particularly useful to social scientists as they try to untangle the complex issue of how much of human behavior is learned and how much is inherited. Another way of putting it is that physical anthropology is divided into three branches that frequently overlap: *paleoanthropology*, meaning the study of fossils, of hu-

Anthropological research includes much dirty work as researchers dig and sift through many layers to find the fossils that provide clues to the history of the human race.

man and of related species; *primatology*, or the study of primates; and *genetics*, or the study of modern human variability and adaptability.

Cultural anthropology concerns itself with all facets of human culture: kinship forms, linguistics, material artifacts, economic structures, music, and folklore. In addition, cultural anthropologists today are likely to include the study of subgroups within contemporary societies and apply their methodology to new settings. An examination of the gay and lesbian community in a large metropolitan area, for instance, or a description of the lifestyles of prostitutes or the homeless are examples of studies that could be carried out by cultural anthropologists.

Anthropologists have developed a gamut of theories, some of which are discussed in the text. For an overview of these theories, see the Web site of the University of Alabama, **http://www.as.ua.edu/ant/faculty/murphy**, and of Indiana University, **http://www.mnsu.edu/emuseum/cultural/anthropology/theories/html.**

Anthropology also includes the field of *archeology*, which is concerned with unearthing fossilized bones and artifacts of humans and other species to furnish dates and historical data about past societies, both those that left no written records and those whose records may have been lost or are incomplete. Anthropological concepts are used to describe the physical development of humans as well as to delineate their chief feature, culture.

Psychology

Psychology focuses on the forces that shape and motivate individuals, forming their minds and personalities. The discipline, especially in its medical form, *psychiatry*, draws on the natural sciences for information concerning the physical structure of humans, their nervous system, their physical development and maturation, and other physical processes. It draws on the social sciences for input in the areas of behavior that originate from social interaction. Because psychology deals with human beings, who are complex mixtures of biological and social elements, the discipline is wide-ranging and the most experimental of the social sciences. Psychologists must be familiar with human biology as well as with social processes and their effects. For instance, in trying to explain the human capacity to blush, psychologists must understand how the body undergoes certain biologically caused organic changes—blood rushes into the veins and capillaries of our face and chest area. They also must be aware of the social pressures that trigger these changes—someone stares at us, or compliments us, or, on the contrary, scolds us in front of someone whose respect we crave. The embarrassment we feel is expressed by blushing.

Social psychologists specialize in studying socialization, emotions, memory, perception, and intelligence. They also examine such issues as language acquisition, motivation, learning, adjustment and maladjustment, the effects of heredity and environment, problem solving, and others. The Encyclopedia of Psychology online offers more than 2,000 links on psychological subjects: **http://www.psychology.org**.

Sociology

Sociology is the newest of the social sciences, having emerged long after the other social science disciplines were already established. Contemporary sociology may be defined as the systematic and scientific study of human social relationships and of all the social systems that such relationships engender. In more popular terms, sociology is said to be the study of human groups in interaction, or the scientific study of human society and human group behavior. While psychology also analyzes human behavior, its focus is the individual. The focus of sociology, on the other hand, is the individual in interaction with others or as he or she moves in the social environment.

The climate for a science to study human groups did not arise until nearly the middle of the nineteenth century, when the French philosopher Auguste Comte coined the name "sociology" in his *Positive Philosophy* (1838). In this treatise, Comte repudiated authority and speculation in favor of systematic observation and classification as the bases of all scientific inquiry. He was followed most notably by the French social philosopher Emile Durkheim. Durkheim demonstrated the use of scientific methodology in the new discipline by outlining how he studied suicide by planning a research design, collecting masses of data on suicide rates in a number of societies, and using the data to derive a theory suggesting that social factors—conditions of upheaval in society and the extent of integration of people in the social order—affect even such personal choices as committing suicide (*Suicide*, 1897).

Today, sociology studies an enormous variety of subjects, in particular human groups of every stripe, organizations, and institutions. The discipline looks at the environment, religion, politics, the economy, deviance, criminality, change, demography, industry, technology, medicine, urban and rural areas, and so on. It focuses especially on the organization of complex industrial societies, such as the United States, analyzing data and events through a number of theoretical models, the foremost of which are functionalism, conflict theory, and symbolic interactionism. In addition, research is undertaken within the framework of newer theories, such as feminism, exchange theory, and postmodernism. Most of the social sciences share some of these theoretical approaches.

Box 1.1 Psychology: How Much of a Science?

Researchers in the social sciences, because they deal with human behavior in a variety of circumstances, cannot avail themselves of the scientific method to the same extent as researchers in the exact sciences do. Humans are characterized by intelligence and will, and do not follow exact rules of behavior—they are influenced by numerous variables, both biological and social. In spite of this, adopting the scientific method has advanced enormously our knowledge about what makes humans tick.

One of the most glamorous of the social sciences has been psychology (and its medical portion, psychiatry, which depends on medical research for its findings). Psychology has appealed to large numbers of people because it delves into the mysteries of human behavior. Why are some people antisocial? Why do some become mass murderers and others become people of good will, engaged in service to others? What makes some marriages happy and others full of conflict? Why do some parents raise children who become respectful and respected citizens, and others raise children who grow up to be juvenile delinquents? These and myriad other, similar questions have been tackled by psychologists, beginning with the famous Viennese researcher Sigmund Freud, who developed theories of the unconscious mind and childhood stages of development.

More recent theories and methods of treatment have depended on the Rorschach inkblot test to explain some facets of personality, have assumed the existence of multiple personalities, have theorized about repressed memories of sexual abuse, have posited that some individuals are subject to sexual addiction, have accused members of an addict's family of facilitating that individual's behavior by codependency, and have used such therapies as "critical incident" debriefing for trauma victims, as well as eye-movement desensitization and reprocessing techniques. Some of these theories have created conflicts between practicing psychologists and academic psychologists (those who do research). The latter have accused mental health practitioners of using faddish, unproved techniques that on occasion may be harmful and have challenged them to prove that such treatments are valid. The conflict stems from the academics' dependence on controlled trials and other statistical methods to determine whether a specific treatment works, whereas mental health practitioners tend to base their techniques on clinical experience, and sometimes intuition, instead of scientific evidence.

Some academic psychologists—a number of whom have split from the dominant professional organization, the American Psychological Association, and have formed a separate organization—claim that clinical psychologists have been out of touch with scientific research findings. They cite surveys that show that many clinical psychologists, busy with patients, fail to read even one scientific journal article a month and that many doctoral programs in clinical psychology do not require research training. Such failures allow untested and possibly damaging treatments to be used, according to the academics, who have founded journals with the specific mission to use "objective investigation of controversial and unorthodox claims in clinical psychiatry, psychology, and social work."

Clinical practitioners are not taking this criticism lying down. Some maintain that their work with troubled patients cannot be based on experimental trials and that science has little relevance in the consulting room. They say that problems presented by some of their patients are much more complex than anything researchers have studied. Such conflicts in the discipline bode well for its future because they will eventually force clinicians to become more aware of what science has to offer and will soften the attitudes of academic researchers to accept the notion that sometimes science is not the only answer (Goode, 2004, D1 and D6).

The patient on a couch and the therapist sitting behind him or her with a notebook has been a symbol of psychology ever since Sigmund Freud used it. It has also been ridiculed and used as a source of humor by comedians. However, psychologists use many other situations to help patients.

Economics

The economy is a human institution, that is, an ingrained habit through which people have attempted to facilitate their survival in the face of scarcity of resources. Economics is the discipline that studies the systems that societies construct to help them in this endeavor. Economists attempt to understand the activities of people in the production, distribution, and consumption of goods and services necessary to sustain life. They examine the value of work, of natural resources, and of money as a medium of exchange; they define the concepts of supply and demand, savings and investments, cost and price, and economic fluctuations; and they describe the principles used by political systems to justify their methods of distribution of goods and services.

Economics attempts to explain some social processes (such as "who gets what and why"), the origins of some social problems (such as poverty), the importance of work as a source of identity, occupational status, increases or decreases in the standard of living, the effects of rising expectations, and so on.

Economists, too, have availed themselves of a number of theories—classical, neoclassical, Keynesian, monetarist, and others—that will be addressed in upcoming chapters. Two Web sites that offer clear descriptions of both the theories and the scholars who espoused them are: **http://www.bized.ac.uk/virtual/economy/library/theory** and **http://www.frbsf.org/publications/education/greateconomists**.

Geography

Geography is primarily a natural science concerned with the planet we inhabit, that is, the land, bodies of water, mountains, valleys, types of vegetation, and animal habitats. These subjects are in the area of physical geography, which draws most of its knowledge from the disciplines of astronomy, botany, ecology, geochemistry, geology, meteorology, oceanography, and so on. However, geography is also concerned with the ways in which people use the natural environment: why they settle in some locations rather than others, which types of land are good for agriculture and which for mining, what routes of transportation people choose to follow and why, and where people establish their industrial centers. These matters are in the realm of human/cultural geography and depend on information obtained from such social sciences as anthropology, history, political science, psychology, sociology, urban studies, and so on. Of special importance to the social sciences are several disciplines that are offshoots of geography. *Demography* is the study of populations, including increases and decreases in size, composition, age grouping, and future trends. *Ecology* is the science that studies the relationship between all living organisms and their natural environment. It includes *biodiversity*, or the study of the variety and interdependence of species. Geography and its related fields are clearly described online at **http://en.wikipedia.org/wiki/geography**.

History

History is not universally considered a social science, because its primary objective is to record human events for future generations. In fact, historians often cannot use the scientific method. The discipline, however, does attempt to study systematically a sequence of related events—or a number of such sequences—for the purpose of learning about, verifying, and establishing meaningful relationships among them. Because history provides a context in which to study human relationships systematically, it may be considered a social science. Historical facts are interspersed in discussions of every facet of the social sciences, because it is impossible to interpret the present and speculate about the future without reference to the past.

Political Science

The chief concern of political science is the study of power. The discipline probes the need for an institution to maintain order, make decisions, and provide for defense. It also analyzes the forms the institution takes and the processes that emerge. The discipline includes such concepts as the state, politics, power, and ideology. Historically, political science has had a strong philosophical, legal, and administrative orientation. More recently, the discipline has taken a turn toward the social sciences in that it is concerned with the effect of government and its processes on individuals and groups in society. An important part of political science is *international relations*, which tries to uncover patterns of behavior among the nations of the world. The University of Michigan website contains a wealth of resources on the subject: **http://www.lib.umich.edu/govdocs/polisci/html**.

Box 1.2 Fur or Nakedness, Tools or Diet?

Have you ever wondered why almost all animals have some kind of furry covering and humans, who are also animals, are naked? Or whether it was what we ate in the early stages of human existence that caused our brains to develop to a greater complexity than those of other animals? Or what came first, the chicken or the egg?

These are not the primary concerns of anthropology, but they are subjects of research in paleoanthropology. This discipline, a subfield of anthropology, is seldom mentioned in the media, and the results of its research are often considered esoteric and of interest only to other researchers in the same discipline. Yet, the findings are not only fascinating in themselves, but they also tell us much about our ancient forebears, about our ancient environment, about how we, as well as many of our traditions, have evolved through the millions of years of our existence on planet Earth.

Because mammals need to keep warm, most of them have fur or hair. Some mammals lost their fur as their environment changed; thus, whales and walruses lost it when they began to live in the sea. Elephants and rhinoceroses developed a very thick skin and, besides, are very big, so they do not lose much heat during cold nights. But humans continue to live in climates that are very cold; why did they lose their furry covering? A number of theories try to answer this question.

First, some researchers believe that when hominids split from the common ape ancestor, some five million years ago, they became bipedal. This allowed them to walk out of the dense forests they had inhabited earlier and be subject to the hot sun on the treeless African savannah. To keep a bit cooler, they gradually lost their hairy or furry covering.

This explanation is not totally convincing, however, because naked skin would not have been ideal in the heat of the day or in the cold of the night. Other researchers have proposed a different theory, which seems to be a better explanation for the mystery of human hairlessness. They maintain that humans lost their fur to rid themselves of external parasites—blood-sucking lice, fleas, and ticks—that not only tormented them but also transmitted a number of diseases. Moreover, these scientists add, once hairlessness had evolved through natural selection, it became a method of sexual selection, that is, it became a sign that the individual was free of parasites, therefore sexually attractive. Why are men hairier than women? Because there is more pressure on women to be sexually attractive to men than vice versa. Why have we retained pubic and armpit hair? Because those are humid areas replete with sweat glands, which give off pheromones, or airborne hormones, which in turn are thought to send sexual signals in mammals. Complete hairlessness in the climate of Africa led to the acquisition of dark skin. Studying the evolution of a gene that determines skin color, researchers determined that humans became hairless about 1.2 million years ago.

Unfortunately, the planet was in the grip of an ice age from 1.6 million years ago to only 10,000 years ago. This meant that people had to cover themselves. And how did scientists determine the date of this event? They studied the DNA of human head and body lice, which evolved from the original louse as soon as humans began to use body coverings. It seems that people have been wearing clothes since between 42,000 and 72,000 years ago. Finally, the invention of clothing probably was a factor in the spread of humans around the globe, especially in the colder northern climates. So, by researching a seemingly frivolous subject, we discover many facts of human history (Wade, 2003, D1 and D4).

Similarly, researchers have found the earliest known stone tools, mixed with fossilized animal bones. They have dated this find to almost 2.6 million years ago and have deduced from this combined find that the primal technology was used to butcher animal carcasses for meat and marrow. Such an enriched, high-protein diet probably led to a larger brain, which in turn enabled these hominids to adapt to their environment better—to make better tools, to find better shelter, to hunt more or bigger animals (Wilford, 2003, D3).

As to which came first, the chicken or the egg, that has not been resolved yet!

Research Methods in the Social Sciences

In the search for meaningful facts to test and bolster their hypotheses, leading to valid theories, social scientists use a number of research methods (Table 1.1).

These methods may be *historical*—that is, they may include a perusal of documents such as public records, newspapers, legal codes, court records, minutes of various committees, and annual reports of corporations; they may be comparative and *cross-cultural*, in which comparisons of different societies—or specific segments of them—are made for the purpose of tracing cultural patterns to determine either their universality or their uniqueness (these methods are especially used in anthropology); or they may be *mathematical*, based on complicated calculations using mathematical and statistical principles to express ideas. In fact, the mathematical and quantitative approaches in the social sciences have been gaining ground. In the last several decades, the computer has become a staple in social scientific research. Frequently, a combination of methods as well as sources is used: public and private documents are analyzed, the artistic output of a specific historical period is scrutinized, the literature is studied, and statistical information—birth and death rates, for instance—is compiled. Most social scientists shy away from research methods that are subject to personal interpretation. They prefer methods that appear to be more objective, that is, in which personal biases are kept out as much as possible. This does not mean that descriptive, subjectively interpreted work is not being produced, nor that such work lacks meaning. The research methods most commonly used by social scientists today are as follows.

TABLE 1.1 Common Methods of Social Science Research

Method	Subject of Research	Procedure	Used for	Criticism
Sample survey	Statistically valid sample of a population.	Collect data; have sample fill out questionnaires; conduct personal interviews; obtain factual information; probe attitudes; establish relationships among variables.	Establishing facts.	Not always 100% accurate in reflecting attitudes and opinions.
Case study	Total behavior of a particular unit of people.	Gain confidence of members; obtain biographies of members; learn each member's views; establish hypothesis or relationships that can be tested by other means.	Studying a particular unit (family, gang, ethnic group) in depth or several units for comparison.	Most useful when events under consideration are rare; often cannot be used as a basis for generalization; expensive and difficult to compute quantitatively.
Participant observation	Members of a specific group.	Researchers take part in life of group members, sometimes without revealing their identities.	Studying all or some aspects of a group's culture from the inside out.	Depends on personality of researcher; researchers may be biased; researcher may try to overgeneralize.
Experiment	In the laboratory, people volunteer or are paid to be subjects. In the field, researcher studies an existing group.	Subjects undergo a number of tests, and their responses are recorded. Researchers control or hold constant one variable and systematically observe or measure the results.	Establishing facts that cannot be established in any other way.	Very expensive if many people are involved; physical safety and dignity of people must be considered; people change their behavior when they know they are being observed.

Sample Survey

The sample survey research design consists of two separate features, the sample and the survey. The researcher decides to study a specific group, which is called the *population*, a statistical concept referring to the totality of the phenomenon under investigation. For example, the population might consist of middle-aged professionals, newly registered voters, or college students enrolled in four-year private schools. Because it is impossible to study every individual who is a member of the chosen population, researchers select a statistically valid sample. There are procedures that allow researchers to select such a sample. Only if the sample is truly representative of the total population can generalizations about the results of research be made.

The next step is to survey the sample population. Surveying involves collecting data by means of questionnaires, personal interviews, statistical information, or probing of attitudes. Most important, relationships among variables are analyzed. If a broad spectrum of the population is being surveyed at a specific point in time, the study is called *cross-sectional.* Preelection polls are a familiar example. Major magazines and news organizations are constantly polling people to probe their attitudes on current events.

If the survey continues over a longer period, engaging in contrasts and comparisons, it is referred to as a *longitudinal* study.

The sample survey is a useful research design, yielding accurate results for some investigative questions but not for others. It is comparatively easy to establish factual information with the sample survey technique, but there is a greater margin for error in surveying attitudes and opinions.

Case Study

The case study research design is especially helpful when it is necessary to study a particular unit in depth or to study several units for purposes of comparison. The unit may be a person, a family, a group of residents of a retirement community, employees of a particular corporation, members of a religious movement, and so on. The researcher must obtain a complete, detailed account of the behavior of the unit under consideration. In the case study, the entire population of the unit is surveyed.

Case studies are most valuable not so much because of their accuracy, but because they often suggest hypotheses that can then be tested by other methods. They are most valuable when the unit being analyzed is relatively rare, such as a group of brainwashed prisoners of war or a group of converts to an authoritarian religion.

Box 1.3 Consilience

Scientific knowledge has expanded so rapidly that today any lay person knows much more about how things work than a nineteenth-century physician did. Harvard naturalist Edward O. Wilson believes that such expansion of knowledge is due to the scientific method. Moreover, Wilson argues in his book, *Consilience: The Unity of Knowledge*, that human behavior and human affairs can only be interpreted through biology and the other natural sciences. He maintains that social scientists, by ignoring the natural sciences, have handicapped their efforts at expanding the knowledge of their own disciplines. The reason for the success of the natural sciences, according to Wilson, is consilience, by which the author means a linking of insights from a number of different disciplines into a system of explanation that is coherent. As an example, modern medicine is based on the knowledge gathered from molecular and cell biology, which in turn are based on genetics, which ultimately obey the laws of physics. The social sciences, on the other hand, often seem to operate as if they inhabited a separate universe. Wilson insists that to gain self-awareness, "we must accept that human life is a physical phenomenon, generated and sustained by the same principles as bugs, trees and fishes" (Cowley, 1998, 59).

These ideas are not new. In a preceding book, *Sociobiology: The New Synthesis*, Wilson posited that certain tendencies in human behavior—status seeking, altruism, nepotism—have a biological basis. A number of critics on the left, however, panned the book, accusing its author of social Darwinism (because life is competitive, winners are superior and rise to the top, and losers are inferior and eventually disappear). Nonetheless, the author continued to elaborate on sociobiology, and today a number of psychologists and sociologists are beginning to test his idea that human behavior has a biological component. For example, psychologists and neuroscientists have shown that the mind—a social concept—is the product of the brain—a physical organ. Because the brains of contemporary humans have evolved in the process of natural selection (see the next chapter), certain aptitudes, biases, and abilities of humans that affect their behavior exist because they facilitated survival in some previous environment. In fact, studies have shown that people everywhere have an innate ability to acquire language, to recognize faces and the meaning of facial expressions, and that they avoid incest. It turns out that many of these abilities are located in specific areas of the brain, which neuroscientists are now tracing. Neuroscientists are also beginning to understand what dreams are, and here too they have found that certain areas of the brain are responsible for them. In the same way, Wilson believes that some day, using the combination of natural and social sciences, social scientists will find the reasons for war, inflation, and religion. They could settle the question of which social arrangements best accommodate the universal features of human nature, or which environmental conditions bring out the best or the worst in human beings.

Ultimately, Wilson hopes that through consilience, humans, who have become the greatest destroyers of life, will come to realize how dependent they are on other earthbound organisms. In Wilson's own words, "Most of the issues that vex humanity daily—ethnic conflict, arms escalation, overpopulation, abortion, environmental destruction, and endemic poverty, to cite several of the most persistent—can be solved only by integrating knowledge from the natural sciences with that from the social sciences and the humanities. Only fluency across the boundaries will provide a clear view of the world as it really is, not as it appears through the lens of ideology and religious dogma, or as a myopic response solely to immediate need. . . . A balanced perspective cannot be acquired by studying disciplines in pieces; the consilience among them must be pursued" (Wilson, 1998, 62).

Wilson's ideas are being followed by other scientists. As noted earlier, some economists are beginning to use some tools of physics to study markets and other economic phenomena. These so-called econophysicists point out that incomes and wealth behave very much like atoms. The distribution pattern of upper-middle-class incomes (approximately $150,000) in the United States, in fact, follows a pattern called "exponential," which is the same pattern of the energy of atoms in gases that are at thermal equilibrium. This pattern is also one that is used by many other random systems. The incomes of the wealthiest 3 percent follow what is called in physics a *power law:* a very long distance between their high income and the income of the next layer. Most other developed nations follow a similar pattern of income distribution. Therefore, the econophysicists say, even though individuals have a will and governments try to redistribute wealth, neither will succeed because "large, complex systems have their own statistical logic that trumps individual, and state, decisions" (Shea, 2005, 67).

Behavioral economists, teamed with psychologists, have also developed a "Tightwad-Spendthrift" scale intended to predict whether a person will spend a lot of money on things they do not necessarily need, or forgo the purchase and keep the cash. They positioned volunteers in an MRI machine, gave them an amount of money they could spend, and showed them images of a variety of objects. When a subject saw something of interest, one specific area of the brain lit up, showing activity there. If the object held no interest for the volunteer, another area of the brain became active. It was thus possible for the researchers to see, before the volunteers made their decision, whether they were going to buy the object or not (Tierney, 2007, D1 and D6).

Participant Observation

Somewhere between the case study and the sample survey techniques, we find a method called *participant observation.* Here the researcher tries to take part in the lives of the group members being studied. The researcher associates with group members as closely as possible and attempts to share in their experiences and lifestyles, sometimes without revealing his or her purpose. A number of sociologists and anthropologists have used this technique, developed by anthropologists to study preliterate cultures, to analyze ethnic and black street-corner cultures.

The participant observation technique has its shortcomings. Much depends on the personality of the researcher, who must develop trust in, and friendship with, the subjects. Thus, there is the danger of the researcher becoming too involved with the subjects and thereby losing objectivity, as well as the danger of overgeneralizing in the belief that the findings obtained from the group studied are true of all similar groups. At the same time, this method, like the case study, has given researchers many useful insights that can be tested and verified later by more quantitative techniques.

The Experiment

The experimental method is used in all scientific disciplines. In the social sciences, the experiment may take place either in a laboratory or in the field. In the laboratory experiment, people are recruited to serve as subjects who can be volunteers or paid by the researcher. The scientist conducts a number of tests and records the subjects' responses. In the field experiment, the researcher goes out among the people instead of bringing them to the laboratory. In both the field and the laboratory, one variable is controlled (by setting up control groups), and the results are systematically observed and measured. Every scientific experiment consists of (1) keeping all variables constant except one, (2) changing that one variable, and (3) discovering what happens.

Obviously, experimentation under controlled conditions is not possible in all social science disciplines and is also subject to shortcomings. Wide-ranging experiments in which thousands of people are involved are very expensive and difficult to organize. The physical safety and the dignity of people must be safeguarded. It is impossible to force people to act as subjects in an experiment, and the ethics of tricking them into acting as experimental subjects are certainly questionable. Finally, when people are aware that they are the subjects of an experiment, their behavior tends to change from the usual. This tendency can ruin the experiment and make results invalid. Experiments on people are most reliable when the subjects are not aware of the true goals of the experiment but do know that some type of experiment is being conducted. Nevertheless, even harmless deception sometimes leads to intellectual dishonesty in interpreting results, and so the technique is not widely used.

Statistical Analysis

By whatever method data are gathered by social scientists, one of the most favored manners of analyzing them is with statistics. **Statistics** are methods in the form of numbers used to process the information obtained by research. Statistics simplify the communication of information and help researchers make decisions about the meaning of their research. Statistics that communicate information in a clear manner are called *descriptive* statistics. Descriptive statistics convey the *central tendency*—what is typical—of a group of numbers by calculating the mean, the median, and the mode.

The **mean** is obtained by adding all of the figures and dividing them by the number of cases. This is what an instructor does when she reports on the average exam grade obtained by students. If the mean is 95, it is assumed that the central tendency of that particular population (class of students) is to study very hard. Central tendency can also be measured by the **median**, which is the number in the middle of the distribution of scores (so that roughly half of the students would have higher scores than the median, and half would have lower scores). Although it is the least frequently used measurement, central tendency can be measured with the **mode**, the number that appears most frequently in a group of numbers—in this case, the one single score obtained by the largest number of students.

Statistics are also *inferential*, providing techniques researchers use to decide whether they can make valid statements about a specific population based on a particular sample of it. Statistical tests exist that allow researchers to calculate percentage statements of probability; the higher the percentage of probability, the more assurance that what was true of a sample is true of the population at large.

Box 1.4 Collecting Data with a Human Face

Certain subjects do not lend themselves easily to social science research. People who have undergone traumatic experiences, whether in a war, in a revolution, during a famine, or in other disasters, are not always willing to talk about the pain they experienced. Yet, the insights social scientists gather from such experiences are invaluable in showing how humans respond to specific situations.

The experiences of European Jews who survived the Holocaust are especially difficult to extract without causing psychological harm to the victim. One social scientist who specializes in interviewing Holocaust survivors describes his methodology:

> *After almost 25 years of interviewing survivors of the Holocaust, my own technique has evolved through a series of variations. I began using an interview schedule—a questionnaire—that was divided into four sections: prewar life, life during the war and Holocaust, postwar experiences, and later experiences. That worked fairly well, but I found myself veering off from the questionnaire because it was not only confining but also distracting to some interviewees. From the beginning I tried to do as much research as possible. In a preliminary phone conversation I would learn the hometown or city of the survivor and where he or she was during World War II. Eventually, I would bring street maps of the cities and the ghettos and even maps of some of the camps and initiate the interview (after, "Please tell me where you are from and where you were during the war") with "Can you show me the street where you lived," and then ask questions about where the schools were, the synagogues, places of work, and so forth. Questions about religion, family life, frequently get as specific as food on the Sabbath, soccer games, school schedules and curricula, to relationships with non-Jews and details about daily routines. Over the years, I have found it productive to engage in the interview to the point of asking clarifying questions, depending on the flow of the narrative, and interrupting as surreptitiously as possible to explicate more carefully. Critical to a productive interview were gaining trust and conveying a sense of at least basic knowledge of the history and geography of the Holocaust. (Survivors frequently seem convinced that an American barely knows where Poland is, much less Lodz or Rosisz.) It is fundamental, then, that the interviewer subtly conveys a sense of familiarity with that history and geography. There is no question that survivors believe that no interviewer can completely understand or appreciate the nature of the experience of the Holocaust. They are correct, of course, and yet somehow an interviewer must convey at least a minimal sense of that appreciation and a knowledge of that vital stumbling block. Perhaps the most significant and painfully problematical element of many survivor interviews has to do with silence. Elie Wiesel once noted that "the silences also speak." My feeling about this has remained from the start: the silences must be allowed to persist, even if they are accompanied by tears. It behooves the interviewer to permit the silence to be resolved by the interviewee, if only to protect the survivor's integrity. What is happening during those silences? Is the survivor searching for a correct word? Overwhelmed with the memory? Wondering why he or she is revealing these anguished stories? Convinced that no language can properly convey the real meaning or a thorough description of the experience? Is there a language that can completely communicate what went on from minute to minute in a place like Auschwitz? Is there an Auschwitzese to convey to an outsider the simultaneous internal and external actions of those times and places? Such questions of simultaneity and the difficulties of serial language to describe it have plagued writers from James Joyce to Sigmund Freud, from Louis Carrol to Franz Kafka, from Primo Levi to Thaddeus Borowski. The literary questions assume horribly depressing consequences in survivor testimonies and produce frustration and silence. A good interviewer ought to be aware of such seemingly esoteric yet central issues.*

(*Source*: Personal communication with Sidney Bolkosky, William E. Stirton Professor in the Social Sciences, Professor of History; Director, Honors, University of Michigan.)

The Scientific Method in the Social Sciences

In summary, none of the research methods available to social scientists is 100 percent effective or error proof. Conducting research is difficult in all sciences, but in the social sciences the difficulty is compounded by the problems of subjectivity, logistics, and the unpredictability of human behavior, and by the great number of variables that must be controlled.

As a result, social scientists often use whatever technique seems to best fit the needs of their research designs. The *historical* or *impressionistic* study, which consists of describing and analyzing observations according to informal but coherent and purposeful guidelines, is still popular. The *demographic* method is also used with good results. This is the method used by the Census Bureau to report population and urbanization trends. Demographers, sociologists, and economists all look at demographic facts and come to some conclusions as to what they indicate.

It should be stressed again that in spite of the use of the scientific method, social scientists have more difficulty obtaining verifiable data than do physical scientists. Examining fossil remains in the laboratory is very different from examining people as they relate to one another. Not only do people not lend themselves to many of the experiments that can be performed on the inert fossil, they also evoke a reaction from the researcher, which the fossil does not. Researchers cannot help reacting to people—they find an individual likable or disagreeable, good-looking or ugly, intelligent or dense—whereas in analyzing a fossil such judgments do not even enter the researchers' minds. Much as they wish to further objectivity, the conclusions of social scientists may be tinged by bias. In the social sciences, then, there are no absolute conclusions and no absolutely objective interpretations.

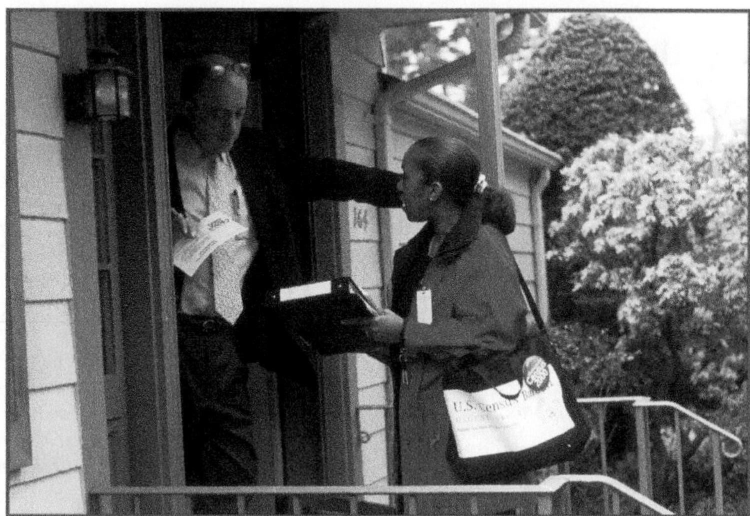

The methods of science have become essential in contemporary postindustrial societies. In analyzing scientific research, statistics are a dominant tool. The decennial census that counts individuals residing in the nation provides a multitude of other information.

The Chapter in Brief

Social science disciplines evolved from social philosophy to study scientifically how people behave in the social world that is of their own making (as opposed to the physical world into which they are born). The disciplines are fairly new, although their subject matter has occupied philosophers for thousands of years. What is really new about the social sciences is that they attempt to use the scientific method to formulate generalizations and theories about human behavior in society.

The social sciences use the scientific method as a tool for theory building. The scientific method implies that researchers do their work with a set of attitudes that includes doubt, objectivity, and ethical neutrality. The scientific method also involves a specific technique based on precise and systematic observation and recording of data. This technique includes the selection and definition of problems and a plan for the collection of data; a statement of hypothesis; the actual collection of data, their classification, analysis, and verification (replication); and generalization. Controlled conditions and trained observers are also essential. The scientific method uses concepts (abstract ways of classifying things that are similar), theories (sets of concepts arranged so as to explain and predict possible and probable relationships among phenomena), and research (which tests and bolsters theories or refutes them).

Social scientific research includes the following methods: the sample survey, the case study, participant observation, and field and laboratory experiments. In addition, the historical or impressionistic methods and the demographic method are used.

The scientific method, although it is vastly superior to gathering information by superficial observation, insight, or other traditional methods, is especially difficult to apply in the social science disciplines because of the need for objectivity, skepticism, and ethical neutrality.

Terms to Remember

case study A method of research consisting of a detailed, long-term investigation of a single social unit.

concept A generalized idea about people, objects, or processes that are related to one another; an abstract way of classifying things that are similar.

cross-section A survey of a broad spectrum of a population at a specific point in time.

ethical neutrality An attitude of the scientific method in the social sciences, requiring that scientists not pass moral judgment on their findings.

experiment A method of research in which the researcher controls and manipulates variables in one group to test the effects of an independent variable on a dependent variable.

hypothesis A tentative statement, in clearly defined terms, predicting a relationship between variables.

longitudinal A survey that continues over a long period, engaging in contrasts and comparisons.

objectivity A principle of the scientific method, especially in the social sciences, requiring researchers to divest themselves of personal attitudes, desires, beliefs, values, and tendencies when confronting their data.

participant observation A method of research in which researchers try to take part in the lives of the members of the group under analysis, sometimes without revealing their purposes.

population In the social sciences, a statistical concept referring to the totality of phenomena under investigation (e.g., all college students enrolled in four-year private universities).

research An aspect of scientific methodology that bolsters and complements theories. In the social sciences, four fundamental formats are used: the sample survey, the case study, the experiment, and participant observation.

sample survey A method of research consisting of an attempt to determine the occurrence of a particular act or opinion in a particular sample of people.

theory A set of concepts arranged so as to explain and/or predict possible and probable relationships.

variables Factors whose relationships researchers try to uncover; characteristics that differ (vary) in each individual case.

Suggested Readings

Babbie, Earl. 2001. *The Practice of Social Research*, 9th ed. Belmont, CA: Wadsworth. How research in the social sciences is done—a comprehensive and readable text.

Best, Joel. 2001. *Damned Lies and Statistics: Untangling Numbers from the Media, Politicians, and Activists.* Berkeley: University of California Press. This book suggests how statistics can be misused by politicians, administrators, the media, and other activists for their own agendas.

Ericksen, Julia A. 1999. *Kiss and Tell: Surveying Sex in the Twentieth Century.* Cambridge, MA: Harvard University Press. An evaluation of the methodology used by social scientists in the many surveys of human sexuality.

Hoover, Kenneth, and Todd Donovan. 1995. *The Elements of Social Scientific Thinking*, 6th ed. New York: St. Martin's Press. A concise introduction to the vocabulary, concepts, and methods of the social sciences. Mainly jargon-free, this small book leads students through the complex path of social scientific thinking.

Ross, Dorothy. 1991. *The Origins of American Social Science.* Cambridge, NJ: Cambridge University Press. A historical look at the development of the social sciences in the United States.

Tilly, Charles. 2006. *Why?* Princeton, NJ: Princeton University Press. A Columbia University scholar attempts to decode the structure of social interactions. Why do we give the reasons we do to explain our behavior? According to the author, people rely on four categories of reasons: conventions, stories, codes, and technical accounts. An interesting sociological argument.

Web Sites of Interest

http://www.academicinfo.net/subsoc.html
Offers descriptions and definitions of the various social sciences and links to other sites of interest.

http://en.wikipedia.org/wiki/social_sciences
Another source of information about the social sciences.

http://www.abacon.com/sociology/soclinks/mega.html
Allyn and Bacon's own sociology Web site.

http://www.top20sociology.com
Links to the top 20 sociology sites.

In addition to these sites, each individual social science has sites on the Internet.

■ Studying Contemporary Humanity

Each of anthropology's four fields may involve study of contemporary people, but the field that is exclusively devoted to living people is cultural anthropology. For example, archaeologists sometimes conduct ethnoarchaeological research, biological anthropologists who study contemporary human variation work with living people, and many linguistic anthropologists conduct research that is similar to that of cultural anthropologists. All of these endeavors involve *fieldwork*. For a cultural anthropologist, the *field* is anywhere that people are: a village far from the anthropologist's home, or a clinic or school in the anthropologist's own country.

participant observation: a method of studying contemporary humans in which the researcher lives with and studies the people for an extended period of time.

When cultural anthropologists are in the field, their main method is **participant observation,** a way of learning about culture in which the researcher lives in and studies a culture for an extended period of time. The method was invented by cultural anthropologists and is still their primary means of learning about living people.

Learning about Contemporary Culture through Fieldwork

This section explores how cultural anthropologists learn about culture through fieldwork and the overarching fieldwork tool, participant observation. It describes the process of fieldwork from the first step of getting an idea for a research project, to entering the field, leaving the field, and writing up the results.

The first step is to choose a research topic. One may find a topic by doing library research to see what has already been done and identify a gap in current knowledge to date. Historical events often prompt new research ideas. The appearance of the HIV/AIDS virus has stimulated substantial research interest. Conflict situations in Ireland, Rwanda, the former Yugoslavia, and other places have prompted cultural anthropologists to ask what keeps states together and what inspires internal violence (Harris 1992). Following the 9/11 attacks on the United States, many cultural anthropologists devoted effort to studying international conflict. The rising number of immigrants worldwide has stimulated research into migrants' adaptation patterns.

Unanticipated events can lead to a research topic. Spanish anthropologist Maria Cátedra stumbled on an important discovery during exploratory fieldwork in Asturias, northern Spain (see Map 1.1, p. 19). A person committed suicide in a hamlet in the mountains near where she was staying. She learned that the area had an extremely high rate of suicide and that the local people did not consider suicide strange. She decided to conduct her research on the social dynamics and meaning of suicide in the area.

Another approach is to conduct a *restudy*, in which an anthropologist goes to a previously studied site to look at the same topic again at a later period to see what has changed, or to look at a different topic in the same location (see the Critical Thinking box).

Selecting a research location may go hand in hand with deciding on the topic, as in Maria Cátedra's study. In the early days of cultural anthropology, over a 100 years ago, there was a definite preference for locations far from North America and Europe, such as Pacific islands and remote regions of Africa and Latin America. Another early preference was to study small groups with the goal of gaining a comprehensive view of the culture. An underlying goal was to study cultures that were "uncontaminated" by the outside world and

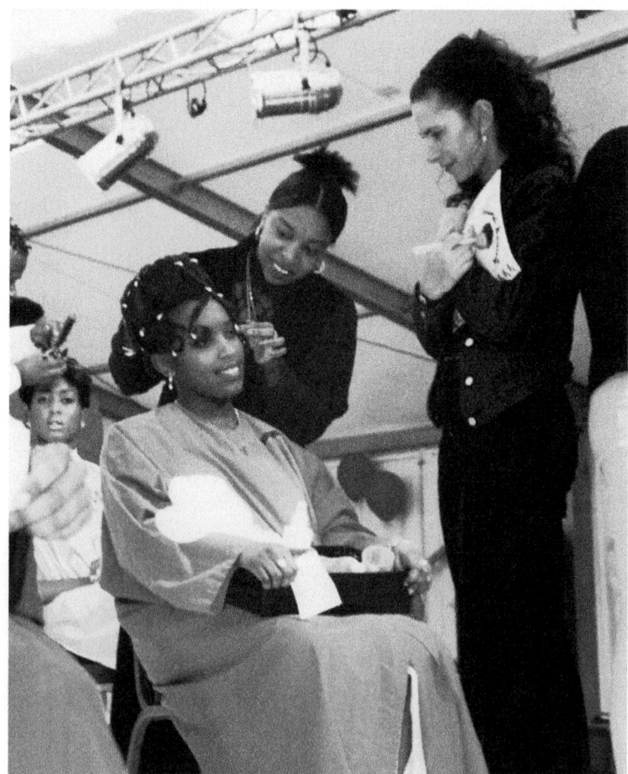

Lanita Jacobs-Huey's fieldsites include hairstyling competitions throughout the United States and London, England. Here, a judge evaluates the work of a student stylist at the Afro Hair & Beauty show in London, England. ■ (Source: Lanita Jacobs-Huey)

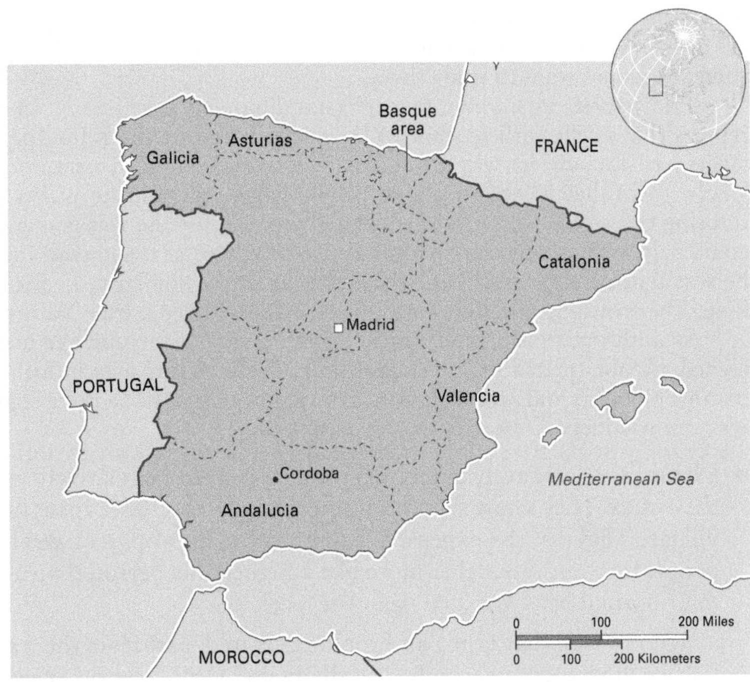

MAP 1.1 Spain. The Kingdom of Spain is the largest of the three countries occupying the Iberian Peninsula. The geography is dominated by high plateaus and mountain ranges. Spain's population exceeds 40 million. Spain's administrative structure is complex, including autonomous communities, such as Andalucia and Catalonia, and provinces. The central government is granting more autonomy to some of the localities, including the Basque area.

thus represented "primitive" society. Things are much different now. Although many cultural anthropologists still conduct research in remote (to those of us in North America) places, many others conduct research in urban areas worldwide, in international institutions such as the United Nations, and in their own countries.

Depending on the host country's rules, a visa or other kinds of permits may be required. Some countries restrict research in particular regions within their boundaries or on particular topics. China only recently relaxed the restrictions it imposes on American researchers, and Russia's policies changed even more recently.

Many countries now also require that researchers follow official guidelines for *protection of human subjects*. In the United States, since the 1990s, universities and other institutions that support or conduct research with living people must establish *institutional review boards (IRBs)* to monitor all research with living humans to make sure that it conforms to ethical principles. IRB guidelines follow a medical model designed to protect people who participate as "subjects" in medical research, often involving trial drugs, and are thus quite formal and restricting. Institutional review boards require informed consent, in writing, of the research participants. **Informed consent** is a feature of research ethics requiring that the researcher clearly informs participants of the intent, scope, and possible effects of the study and then seeks their agreement to participate. In many anthropology research projects, such formal and written consent is feasible, but in many instances it is not, especially in oral-based cultures where most people are not literate. Institutional review boards vary in terms of their rules, and they often change. So, if you are considering a research project, check with your relevant IRB. At many institutions, student research projects are "excluded" from IRB review, so long as they conform to ethical principles as approved by a faculty mentor.

informed consent: a feature of research ethics requiring that the researcher clearly informs participants of the intent, scope, and possible effects of the study and then seeks their agreement to participate.

Research equipment may include data-collection tools such as a laptop, cameras, and audio recorders. Special clothing may be required, such as long-sleeved garments for women researchers in the Middle East. Health preparations may involve a series of shots for immunization against contagious diseases such as yellow fever. A well-stocked medical kit may be essential if the research project is located far from a clinic or hospital. Safety in the research locale has to be given serious thought.

A researcher who is not fluent in the local language must pursue intensive language training before undertaking fieldwork. Even with substantial language training in advance, many cultural anthropologists have found that they need to learn a local dialect of the standard version. Many researchers rely on the assistance of local interpreters.

Establishing Rapport

Acceptance of the anthropologist by the people is crucial for successful research in cultural anthropology. A primary goal of the anthropologist is to establish **rapport**, or a trusting relationship between the researcher and the study population. The basic foundation of rapport is an open and honest presentation of goals by the anthropologist. When entering the field area, anthropologists should attempt to explain their

rapport: a trusting relationship between the anthropologist and the study population.

interest in learning about the people's lives. This seemingly simple goal may be incomprehensible to the local people, especially those who have never heard of cultural anthropology and who cannot imagine why someone would want to study them.

Many stories exist about misunderstandings and *false role assignments*. For example, Richard Kurin reports that in the earliest stage of his research among the Karan people in northwest Pakistan, the villagers first thought he was a spy from the United States, Russia, India, or China (1980). After he convinced them that he was not a spy, the villagers thought he was a teacher of English because he was tutoring one of the village boys, next a doctor because he was giving out aspirin, and then a lawyer who could help them in negotiating local disputes because he could read court orders. Finally, they decided that he was a descendant of a local clan—thanks to the similarity of his last name to that of their ancestral king. The crowning touch for him was being considered a true "Karan."

An anthropologist's class, "race" or ethnicity, gender, and age may affect how she or he will be welcomed and interpreted by the local people. These factors may influence the success of fieldwork by paleoanthropologists and archaeologists, but they are likely to be more significant for cultural anthropologists who are conducting research among living people.

- Class. Cultural anthropologists often appear to be relatively wealthy and powerful to the people they study. They know that the anthropologist must have spent hundreds of dollars to travel to their village. They see the expensive equipment. This apparent wealth differential may mean that the people treat the researcher more like a high-status person than an average person or that they alter their normal behavior as a sign of respect.

  Laura Nader has urged anthropologists to depart from the tradition of studying people who are less wealthy and powerful by "studying up" (1972). In other words, she advocates doing research on the cultures of business elites, political leaders, policy makers, and government officials. In such situations, cultural anthropologists may find it difficult to get their prospective participants to talk with them. Research on the high-fashion industry of Japan placed a cultural anthropologist in touch with many members of the Japanese elite (Kondo 1997). These influential people made it clear to her that they would take her to court if they felt she wrote anything defamatory about them.

- "Race" and ethnicity. For most of its history, cultural anthropology has been dominated by Euro-American, White researchers who have studied people who are most often non-Euro-American and non-White. The effects of "Whiteness" on role assignments range from the anthropologist being labeled as a god or ancestor spirit to his or her being reviled as a representative of a colonialist past or imperialist present.

  While doing research in rural Jamaica, Tony Whitehead learned how perceptions of his "race" interacted with social class and status. An African American born in a family of poor sharecroppers, Whitehead thought that his background would lead to solidarity and rapport. Instead, the people assigned him to a high social position and referred to him as a "pretty talking man" because of his North American English. They also referred to him as "brown"—not on the basis of his skin color but because of his assumed high status. The status assignment did not impede Whitehead's fieldwork, but it did give him food for thought about the complexities of "race," class, and social status.

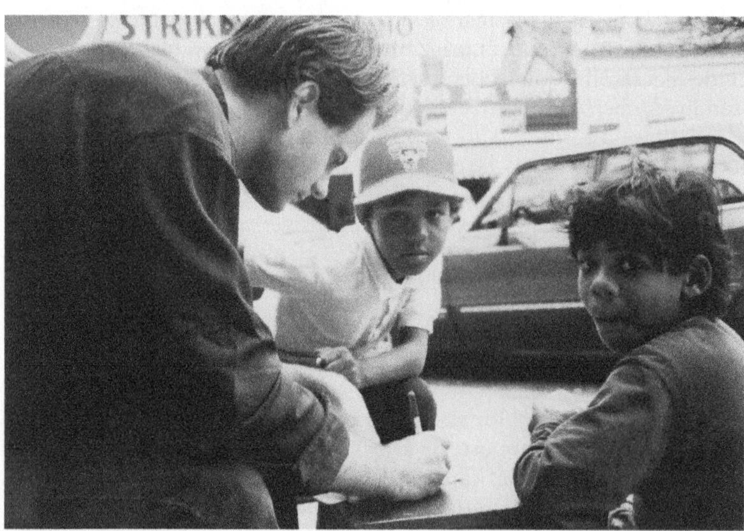

Tobias Hecht plays a game with some of the street children in his study in Rio de Janeiro, Brazil. ■ (Source: Isabel Balseiro)

Box 1.5 Critical Thinking

Missing Women in the Trobriand Islands

A lasting contribution of Bronislaw Malinowski's ethnography, *Argonauts of the Western Pacific* (1961 [1922]), is its detailed examination of the kula, a trading network linking many islands in the region in which men have long-standing partnerships for the exchange of everyday goods such as food as well as highly valued necklaces and armlets.

More than half a century later, Annette Weiner (1976) traveled to the Trobriand Islands to study wood carving. She settled in a village less than a mile from where Malinowski had done his research. She immediately began making startling observations: "On my first day in the village, I saw women performing a mortuary [death] ceremony in which they distributed thousands of bundles of strips of dried banana leaves and hundreds of beautifully decorated fibrous skirts" (xvii). Nowhere in Malinowski's voluminous writings did these women's activities appear. Weiner was intrigued and decided to change her research project to investigate women's goods, exchange patterns, and prestige.

Men, as Malinowski showed, exchange shells, yams, and pigs. Women, as Weiner learned, exchange intricately made skirts and bundles of banana leaves.

Power and prestige derive from both exchange networks. Reading Malinowski alone informs us about the world of men's status systems and describes them in isolation from half of the islands' population: women. Weiner's book, *Women of Value, Men of Renown* (1976), provides an account of women's trading and prestige activities as well as how they are linked to those of men. Building on the work of her predecessor, Weiner shows how a full understanding of one gender domain requires knowledge of the other.

Critical Thinking Questions

- Can you think of an explanation for why Malinowski overlooked women's exchange systems?
- Do Annette Weiner's findings simply provide another one-sided view? Explain.

Trobriand men's coveted trade goods include this shell necklace and armlet. ■ (Source: Irven Devore/Anthro Photo)

A Trobriand girl wears a valued skirt at a dance in honor of the ancestors on Kiriwina Island. She and other female participants coat their skin with coconut oil and herbs and wear decorative flowers. ■ (Source: © Albrecht G. Schaefer/CORBIS)

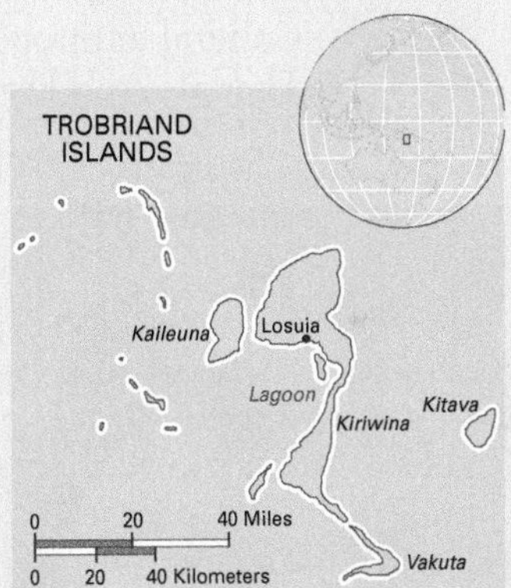

MAP 1.2 Trobriand Islands, Papua New Guinea. Also known as the Kiriwina Island, these islands are an archipelago of coral atolls lying off the eastern coast of the island of New Guinea.

- Gender. Depending on the culture, gender roles and spatial boundaries may have a serious impact on research access. The very arrival of a young, unmarried woman may raise problems. A woman on her own may be considered weird or even unacceptable. On the other hand, where a public–private divide exists, some women researchers have been able to gain access to both men's public worlds and women's domestic worlds because they are assigned a gender-neutral role. In general, it is easier for men to gain rapport with men and for women to gain rapport with women. A woman researcher who studied a secretive gay community in the United States found that she could conduct research in settings dedicated to sociability and leisure, such as family gatherings, parties, and bars (Warren 1988:18). But she was not able to observe in domains dedicated to sexuality, such as homosexual bath houses.

- Age. Typically, anthropologists are adults, and they may therefore find it difficult to gain rapport with members of other age groups. Margaret Mead once commented that the ideal research team would consist of a three-generation family including children trained to understand what they are experiencing (1986:321). She knew that this ideal would not be practical. The best that researchers can do is to be aware of their limits and use imagination in establishing rapport across age groups. This challenge may require learning to understand and use age-specific language.

Culture Shock

culture shock: deep feelings of uneasiness, loneliness, and anxiety that may occur when a person shifts from one culture to another.

Culture shock consists of the deep feelings of uneasiness, loneliness, and anxiety that often occur when a person has shifted from one culture to another. Culture shock can affect any anthropologist who conducts fieldwork, not just cultural anthropologists. It can involve negative reactions to the new culture's food, language, and social rules about privacy, for example. Food differences were a major source of adjustment difficulties for a Chinese anthropologist who came to the United States (Huang 1993). He could never get a "full" feeling from American food. Salads were especially unsatisfying. An American anthropologist who went to a Pacific island named Pohnpei found that her lack of fluency in the local language was the most serious cause of anxiety for her (Ward 1989). She bemoaned the fact that even the dogs of Pohnpei understood more than she did.

Sooner or later, depending on the researcher's adaptability and the nature of the challenges in the new context, culture shock usually passes. In time, the new culture becomes so familiar that the end of fieldwork and the return home may result in *reverse culture shock*. An anthropologist from California who spent a year in South India experienced reverse culture shock when he returned home (Beals 1980:119). Trust and warmth seemed to be replaced by inhumanity and coldness. He could not understand why people moved so quickly. He could not understand the babble on the television set, and he missed the soft sound of lowing cattle. Everything seemed wrong.

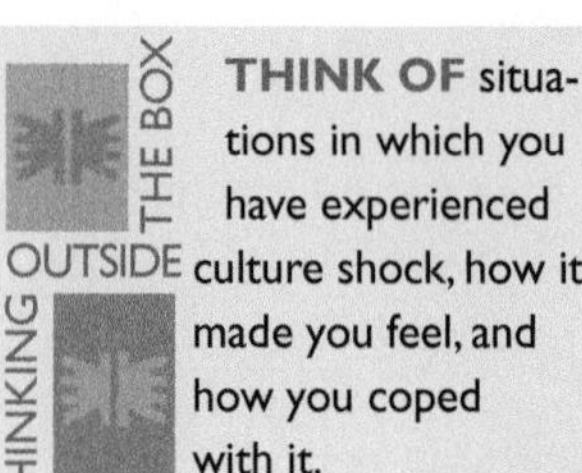

THINK OF situations in which you have experienced culture shock, how it made you feel, and how you coped with it.

Data-Collection Methods

Cultural anthropologists rely on participant observation as their cornerstone method. They also rely heavily on asking people questions either formally or informally. In addition, a range of other methods allow for more specialized data collection.

American cultural anthropologist Liza Dalby in full geisha formal dress. ■ *Besides learning to dress correctly, what other cultural skills did Liza Dalby probably have to learn?* (Source: Liza Dalby)

Participant Observation

The basic fieldwork technique of participant observation provides insights about the regular patterns that characterize the daily, weekly, and seasonal round of life, as well as about special events such as celebrations and about irregular, unexpected events such as arguments or intergroup violence. Being a participant means that, as much as possible, the anthropologist adopts the lifestyle of the people, living in the same kind of housing, eating the same food, speaking the local language, and participating in the study group's activities. Long-term participation is critical to the quality of the data. It improves the likelihood that the people in the study will not alter their behavior in response to the presence of the anthropologist. A minimum of a year is typical, because that period allows the anthropologist to see how the pattern of life changes over the seasons.

While participating in the culture, a cultural anthropologist seeks to observe carefully what is going on: who lives with whom, who interacts with whom, who the leaders are, and what seems important to people. The range of topics is vast, and a single anthropologist cannot hope to observe everything.

Asking Questions

Observation needs to be supplemented by asking questions. The most informal way to ask questions is through conversations with people while conducting participant observation. A more formal method is an **interview**, which is the gathering of verbal information through questions. Interview questions are often open-ended, which means that the respondent is asked to reply without any limits set on the response. These questions provide information that is **qualitative**, or descriptive. In contrast, **surveys**, or questionnaires, may be administered in a written format. Either the anthropologist or the person being questioned fills in answers on a paper form. Surveys often use closed-ended questions, which means, for example, that respondents must answer a question about whether they eat fish by saying "never," "rarely," "sometimes," or "often." Closed-ended questions provide **quantitative** or numeric data. Each of these kinds of data-collecting methods may be appropriate, depending on the context and kind of information sought. Cultural anthropologists tend to favor more open-ended formats because these provide what are called *emic* (insiders') views rather than *etic* (outsiders') views. Surveys, if used at all, should be carefully tested before use to be sure they make sense within the cultural context.

American cultural anthropologist Marjorie Shostak (*right*) during fieldwork among the Ju/wasi of Botswana in 1975. Shostak focused her research on women's lives and wrote *Nisa*, a life history of a Ju/wasi woman. ■ (Source: © Mel Konner/Anthro-Photo)

interview: the gathering of verbal information from living people through questions.

qualitative: descriptive.

survey: a means of data collection among living people that consists of the administration of a set of written questions that are either open-ended or closed-ended.

quantitative: numeric.

Like anthropologists studying humanity's past through site excavation, cultural anthropologists may employ sampling techniques because they realize they cannot talk to everyone in their field site or observe every activity. Random sampling may, in some contexts, be an appropriate and effective way to add breadth to one's study. For example, the anthropologist might visit and interview members of one household on each city block in a given zone, and that household would be determined in random fashion (say, the third house on the left side of the street). Cluster sampling is also used to provide more targeted information. Thus the anthropologist might visit 20 households in a poorer neighborhood and the same number in a richer neighborhood. A special kind of nonrandom sampling that cultural anthropologists often use is called *snowball sampling* (Bernard 1995). In this method, the sample grows through having research participants suggest other people who would be useful to interview. Although it is less scientifically representative than a random sample, using a snowball sample is often the only feasible way to proceed and will provide qualitative findings of value.

Three Specialized Methods

Several specific methods can be used to provide in-depth information on certain aspects of culture.

- A method that provides quantitative data about people's behavior is called *time allocation study*. Recording, or asking the people themselves to record, daily activities provides rich insights into what people do (Gross 1984). Daily time allocation data about people's work, leisure, and special activities have shown, for example, how the patterns of men's and women's lives differ. Anthropologists using this method have sometimes been surprised at how much activity (such as hunting parties on moonlit nights, certain rituals, and social activities of a private nature) goes on at night.
- Another specialized method is the *life history*. A life history, is a detailed narrative of a single person's life experience as told to the researcher. It provides the most "micro" view of a culture. In the earlier days of the discipline, anthropologists who used this method tried to choose a "typical" or representative person. But since no single person is ever representative (in the scientific sense) of an entire culture, anthropologists now focus on people who are particularly interesting. A study of four Hindu ascetics in Sri Lanka found that their long, matted hair had deep connections with their life history (Obeyesekere 1981). The ascetics say that their matted hair is a sign of a deity's presence. The anthropologist saw that they had all experienced psychological, personal afflictions, including sexual anxieties in their married life. In his interpretation, their matted hair symbolizes this suffer

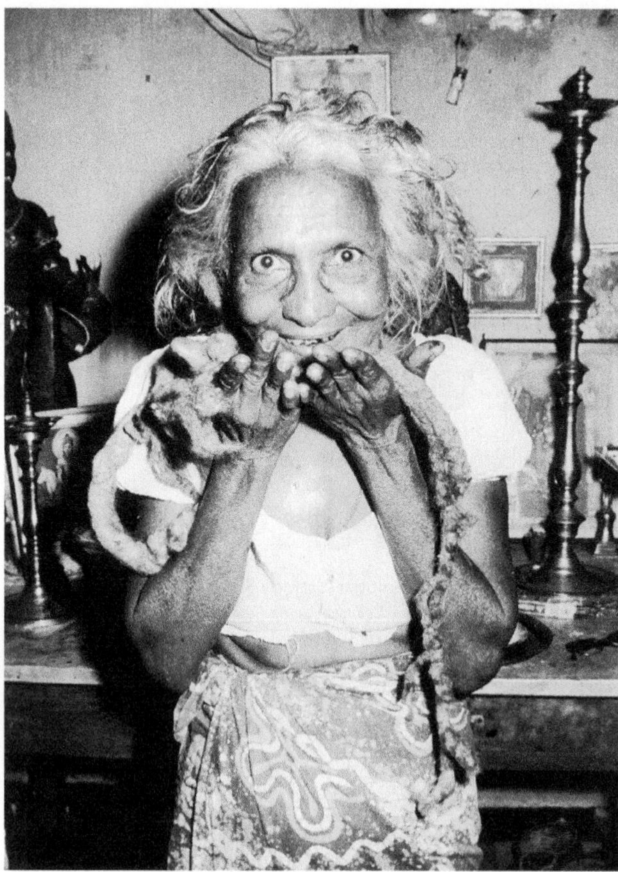

A Sri Lankan woman whose life story Gananath Obeyesekere analyzed. A priestess to the deity Kataragama, she stands in the shrine room of her house, holding her long matted hair. ■ *Think of how hairstyles in a culture that you know express a person's religion, marital status, or sexual preferences.* (Source: Gananath Obeyesekere)

ing and provides them with a special status as holy and, thus, beyond the rules of married life and sexual relations.

■ Cultural anthropologists also use texts and historical archives. The category of *texts* includes written or oral stories, myths, plays, sayings, speeches, jokes, and recordings of **discourse**, or language in use. In the early twentieth century, Franz Boas collected thousands of pages of texts from Native American groups of the Northwest Coast of Canada. This collection has proved valuable to contemporary tribal members as a repository of now-forgotten stories, songs, and rituals.

Teamwork

It is clear that a single anthropologist faces a major challenge in trying to participate, observe, ask, and otherwise learn about a huge range of topics. Whereas paleoanthropologists and archaeologists usually work in teams, cultural anthropologists have generally worked alone. Increasingly, though, cultural anthropologists are participating in team projects either with other anthropologists or with professionals in other specialties.

Recording and Analyzing Contemporary Culture

Cultural anthropologists must record their findings carefully and thoroughly, keeping track of dates, context, personal impressions, and queries. Care must be taken to keep fieldwork records secure from damage, loss, or possible theft.

Field Notes

The primary method for recording findings that cultural anthropologists have used, for over a 100 years, is the taking of field notes. In earlier times, field notes were handwritten in journals by kerosene light on a crude wooden table in an "exotic" setting. Today, cultural anthropologists sometimes record their observations in handwritten notes, but more often in computer files, tape recordings, and video recordings. The age-old rule that "sooner is better" in recording observations and events still applies. Daily recordings are essential because human memory is so frail. Many anthropologists make "scratch notes" during the day, on small pieces of paper kept in a shirt pocket, to enhance their memory. Even a relatively uneventful day may result in dozens of pages of notes.

Audio Recording and Photography

Various recording methods are important supplements to handwritten and computerized notes. These recording techniques require ethical care. They must be protected from improper use—perhaps kept in a locked trunk or closet. The recording of individual voices on tape or faces on film must not proceed without the permission of the people themselves. Film recording is useful in all of anthropology's fields.

Crossing the Fields: Visual Anthropology

Visual anthropology encompasses a variety of methods such as still photography, film, and hypermedia. In the early years of anthropology, still photography was the only method available, and equipment was large and cumbersome. Now, increasing technological capabilities offer far more potential for using visual methods for collecting, analyzing, and presenting anthropological evidence. As noted earlier in this chapter when we considered methods for studying humanity's past, aerial photography aids in site location and can help pinpoint excavation work to make it more effective and less destructive.

discourse: language in use.

Past, present, and potential uses of visual media vary across the four fields of anthropology, given the fields' differing objectives and sources of data. Yet similarities exist as well. We invite you to discover examples of past, present, and potential uses of visual media in the four fields. To spark your thinking, here are a few examples.

Using still photography and film for data collection has long been a core method in cultural anthropology. Early in the twentieth century, Franz Boas was a pioneer in filming rituals of Native American peoples as a *salvage anthropology* project. Later, his student Margaret Mead used film as a way of collecting data and documenting cultural practices in everyday life. One of her best-known film-making projects was the recording of how mothers bathed their babies in several cultures. These short films provided her with material for comparing child care and psychological development of children across cultures.

New forms of computer software allow data analysis and representation of archaeological evidence through simulations and reconstructions (Forte and Siliotti 1997). A recently developed graphics language called Virtual Reality Mark-up Language (VRML) can describe three-dimensional objects and allow the user to move into three-dimensional space via hypermedia links. Information and objects can be rotated and observed from any angle. Computer simulations can generate reconstructions of temples and cities from their architectural remains and reconstructions of whole fossils from fragments.

Analysis, Interpretation, and Representation of Findings

Most cultural anthropologists return from the field with more data than they will ever be able to write up completely. Most also have collected a variety of types of data—written and visual, qualitative and quantitative. It is often daunting to contemplate analyzing the richness of the fieldwork experience.

Qualitative data include descriptive field notes, narratives provided by research participants such as myths or life histories, and video recordings of events. No set guidelines exist for the analysis and representation of qualitative data; this is an area where the "art" of cultural anthropology comes to the fore. One procedure is to search, either by hand or with the aid of a computer, for recurrent themes in the data. The anthropologist becomes immersed in the data, poring over it, until patterns of words and actions emerge that are then taken to be keys to understanding the culture under study. New forms of software allow for thematic searching, but this method depends, first, on computerizing all the data and, second, on devising a good coding scheme to guide the search.

Analysis of quantitative, or numeric, data is usually done with the aid of a computer. For example, in a study of household expenditure patterns using a sample of 120 households in Jamaica, the weekly expenditure data collected over a year were entered into a computer (Miller and Stone 1983). The data were sorted into urban and rural groups and, within those groups, into three expenditure groups (lower, medium, higher). The last step was to compute and compare mean (average) expenditures on food, housing, and transportation for the various social groups (see Figure 1.2).

Fieldwork results are usually written up in an **ethnography**, a book-length description of a culture or cultures studied for an ex-

ethnography: a book-length description of a culture or cultures based on extended fieldwork among living people.

A computer reconstruction of the Great Temple at Tenochtitlan (Mexico City), Mexico. Computers are proving to be invaluable in many areas of research in anthropology, including architectural reconstructions such as this one. ■ (Source: © Photoservice Electa)

FIGURE 1.2 Mean Weekly Expenditure Shares (percentage) in Eleven Categories by Urban and Rural Expenditure Groups, Jamaica, 1983–1984

	Urban				Rural			
Item	Group 1	Group 2	Group 3	Total	Group 1	Group 2	Group 3	Total
Number of Households	26	25	16	67	32	30	16	78
Food	60.5	51.6	50.1	54.7	74.1	62.3	55.7	65.8
Alcohol	0.2	0.4	1.5	0.6	0.5	1.1	1.0	0.8
Tobacco	0.8	0.9	0.9	0.9	1.1	1.7	1.2	1.4
Dry Goods	9.7	8.1	8.3	8.7	8.8	10.2	14.3	10.5
Housing	7.3	11.7	10.3	9.7	3.4	5.7	3.9	4.4
Fuel	5.4	6.0	5.0	5.6	3.7	3.9	4.1	3.9
Transportation	7.4	8.2	12.4	8.9	3.0	5.3	7.6	4.9
Health	0.3	0.6	0.7	0.5	1.5	1.4	1.7	1.5
Education	3.5	2.8	3.1	3.2	1.2	2.1	3.0	1.9
Entertainment	0.1	0.9	1.1	0.6	0.0	0.1	0.3	0.2
Other	5.2	8.3	6.9	6.8	2.1	6.0	6.9	4.6
Total*	100.4	99.5	100.3	100.2	99.4	99.8	99.7	99.9

*Totals may not add up to 100 due to rounding.

Source: From "Social Patterns of Food Expenditure Among Low-Income Jamaicans" by Barbara D. Miller in *Papers and Recommendations of the Workshop on Food and Nutrition Security in Jamaica in the 1980s and Beyond,* ed. by Kenneth A. Leslie and Lloyd B. Rankine, 1987.

tended period of time. Ethnographies vary in style and content. In *realist ethnographies*, the anthropologist presents the findings of the study in a scientific way, adopting an objective view of the culture and incorporating little first-person voice. These ethnographies focus on the culture and its members' practices and beliefs. Most classic ethnographies, such as those by Margaret Mead and Bronislaw Malinowski, are realist ethnographies, and many contemporary ethnographies fit in this category, too.

In contrast, *reflexive ethnographies* tell the story of the research interaction between the anthropologist and the members of the culture studied. The word *reflexive* refers to the position of the ethnographer as constantly reflecting on his or her role in affecting the very findings of the project. Reflexive ethnographies explicitly seek to present a personalized account, with the anthropologist squarely in the picture. An example of such an ethnography is Vincent Crapanzano's book *Tuhami*, which explores the life history of a Moroccan man who believed he was possessed by spirits (1980). Crapanzano interweaves the effects of his presence in Tuhami's life and thinking, showing how cultural anthropology research is an iterative (two-way) process. As Crapanzano notes, "As Tuhami's interlocutor, I became an active participant in his life history. . . . Not only did my presence, and my questions, prepare him for the text he was to produce, but they produced what I read as a change of consciousness in him. They produced a change of consciousness in me, too" (p. 11).

Many of the newest ethnographies strike a balance between realism and reflexivity. Cultural anthropologists know very well that no one can spend a long period of time immersed in a culture without affecting it and also being affected by the experience. They realize that their research does not conform completely to the traditional scientific method, nor can it because they study living people in their everyday lives. Instead of the observation-hypothesis-observation conducted in a laboratory situation, good cultural anthropology requires sensitivity to the researcher's position and impact in the field and honest reporting about these matters.

Cultural anthropologists also write short articles for scholarly journals. Just like anthropologists who study humanity's past, cultural anthropologists share their findings with the public through radio, television, the Internet, and articles in popular magazines. Many cultural anthropologists work in museums creating exhibits for public education. In this work, they seek to build collaborations with the people whose culture is being represented in order to avoid possible misinterpretations.

A multidisciplinary team comprising anthropologists, engineers, and agricultural experts from the United States and Sudan meet to discuss a resettlement project in the Sudan. ■ *Have you ever carried out research as part of a team? If so, what are the pros and cons?* (Source: Michael Horowitz)

chapter 2

Anthropology: The Study of Humanity

THE BIG QUESTIONS

- *WHAT is anthropology?*
- *WHAT do the four fields of anthropology cover?*
- *WHAT are examples of anthropology in the "real world"?*

Anthropology, Second Edition
by Barbara Miller

Old bones, buried treasure, *Indiana Jones and the Temple of Doom*, intrigue, and even danger: These popular impressions of anthropology from movies and television depict anthropologists as adventurers, heroes, and heroines. Many anthropologists do have adventures. Some do discover ancient pottery, hidden tombs, medicinal plants, and jade carvings. But most of their research is not glamorous.

THINKING OUTSIDE THE BOX

WHAT ARE your impressions of anthropology? Make notes of these impressions and then review them at the end of the course.

■ Introducing Anthropology

Anthropology is the study of humanity, including our prehistoric origins and contemporary human diversity. Compared to other disciplines that study humanity (such as history, psychology, economics, political science, and sociology), anthropologists consider a greater span of time and a broader range of topics. Anthropology is a unique discipline because it takes both a deep and a broad view of humanity.

Some anthropologists spend years in difficult physical conditions searching for the most ancient fossils of our ancestors. Others live among, and study firsthand, contemporary residents of Silicon Valley, California, trying to document and understand how people work, organize family life, and adapt to a situation that is permeated by modern technology. Some anthropologists are skilled in conducting laboratory analyses of the contents of tooth enamel to reveal where an individual once lived. Others pore over ancient pottery designs and attempt to understand the meanings of symbols. Others observe chimpanzees in the wild to learn how they find and share food, communicate with each other, care for their offspring, and resolve conflict.

The breadth of anthropology includes methods that range from the more scientific to the more humanistic. Some anthropologists consider anthropology to be a science: a form of inquiry that involves the formulation of a hypothesis, or hunch, about the way things work and then observation or testing to see whether the hypothesis is correct. A scientific approach tends to rely on quantitative, or numeric, data. Other anthropologists pursue a **humanistic approach:** a subjective attempt to understand humanity through the study of people's art, music, poetry, language, and other forms of symbolic expression. This approach avoids working from a pre-set hypothesis but instead seeks insight through culturally informed understanding. The humanistic approach tends to be qualitative, relying on verbal description or other forms of representation of themes and patterns. Both the scientific approach and the humanistic approach are valued in anthropology because both provide insights about humanity, and this book provides both views, as appropriate.

This chapter first provides an overview of the discipline of anthropology. We then discuss four themes that are important in the discipline's history and that serve as organizing principles for much of the material in this book. The second section offers a brief overview of each of anthropology's four fields, followed

anthropology: the study of humanity, including the prehistoric origins of humans and contemporary biological, cultural, and linguistic variation.

science: a form of inquiry based on hypothesis formation and hypothesis testing.

humanistic approach: a form of inquiry through understanding of subjectivity and meaning.

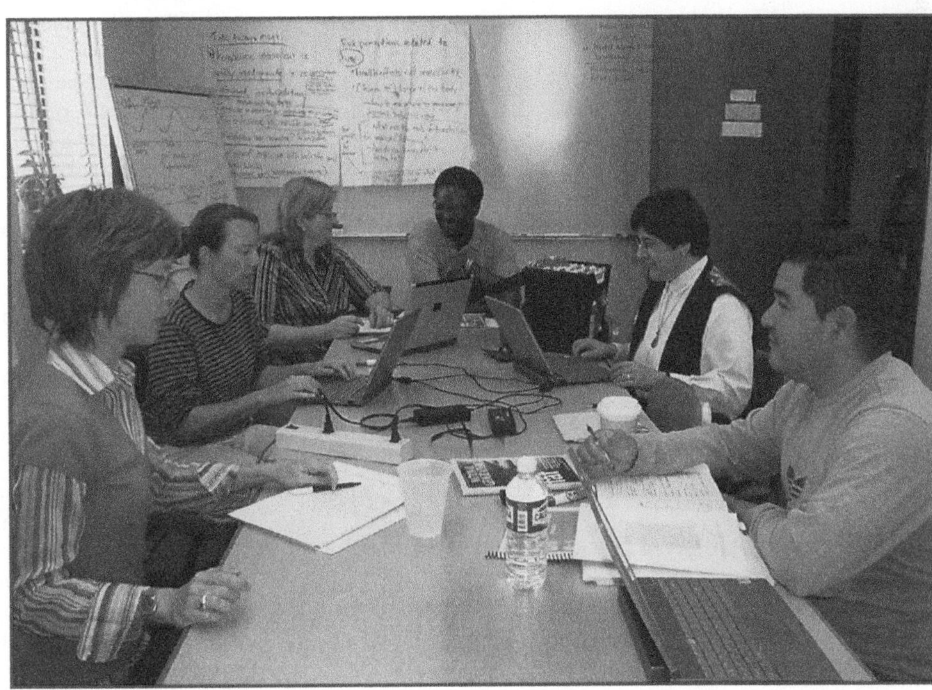

One hundred years ago, cultural anthropologists conducted research in places considered "exotic." Here, a team of anthropologists and student researchers discuss their research project on Silicon Valley culture. (*Source:* J. A. English-Lueck, Cofounder Silicon Valley Cultures Project)

A technician from Pakistan dons an anticontaminant suit at Intel's facility in Santa Clara, California. He works to make silicon computer chips, the Silicon Valley's most famous product. *How many computer chips are produced annually in the world and from what are they made?*
(*Source:* Bob Sacha/Corbis)

by an example of how the four fields fit together to create a "whole greater than the sum of its parts." The chapter's third section considers what anthropologists do and the relevance of anthropology to everyday life.

Conceptual Foundations

Anthropologists raise, and seek to answer, serious questions about humanity: What are humans? How do humans differ from other animals? Where did humans come from? Are all humans the same? Why do humans behave the way they do? Why do humans have language? How can we explain conflict among humans? How are humans changing? One of the most exciting things about anthropology is that new findings continue to shed light on these questions. A recent discovery in the Alps of a frozen corpse, first thought to be a lost hiker, provides insight into the life and death of a man who probably died from an arrow wound while trying to flee from enemies.

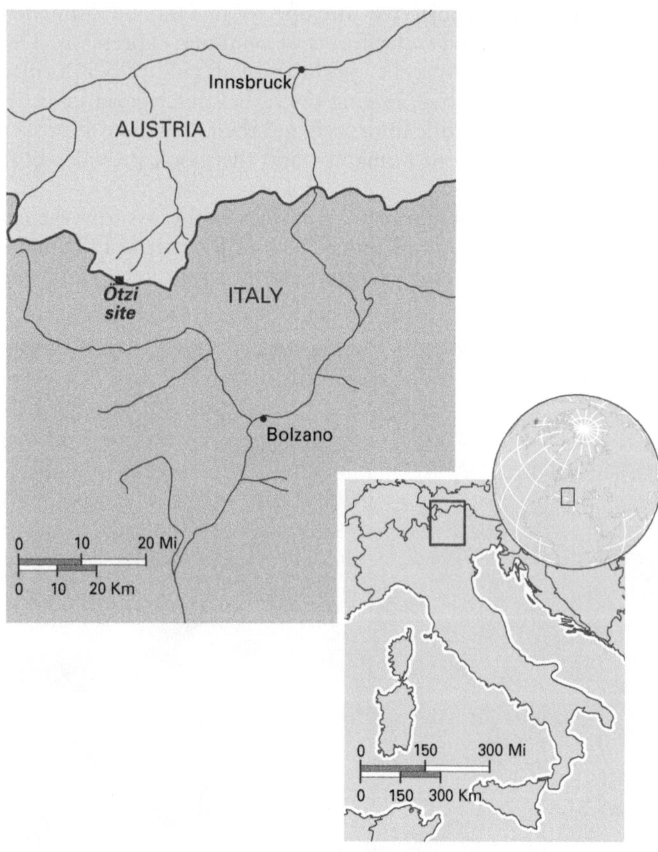

MAP 2.1 Site of Discovery of Ötzi in Italy. Ötzi was discovered near the border of Austria and Italy. After a period of dispute between the two countries about which should have custody of the mummified remains, Ötzi is now housed in the South Tyrol Museum of Archaeology in Bolzano, Italy.

The discipline of anthropology, according to available written records, arose in Europe. If you have studied Western philosophy, you know that thinkers such as Plato (fifth century BCE) and his student, Aristotle (fourth century BCE), pondered many of the same questions about humanity that concern us today: What makes humans different from animals, and how did humans come to be the way they are? (*Note:* BCE stands for "Before the Common Era," which is a secular transformation of BC, or "Before Christ." Similarly, CE stands for "Common Era" and is used in place of AD, which stands for the Latin phrase that means "Year of the Lord.") It is highly likely, though, that the classical Greek philosophers were not the first people to wonder about humanity. They were the first, however, to have provided enduring written evidence of their thinking.

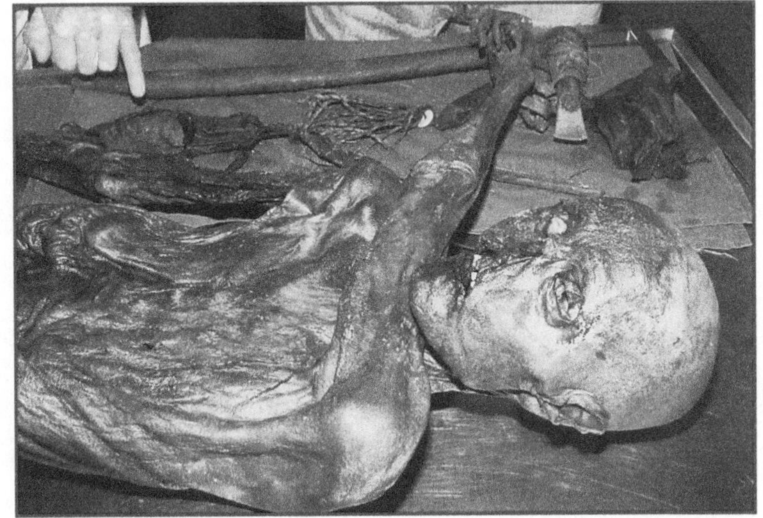

In 1991, a couple hiking along a ridge in the Alps discovered a frozen corpse in a melting glacier. Since then, research on Ötzi, or the "Iceman," has provided information about how he died, where he lived, what he ate, and what he was wearing at the time of his death about 5,000 years ago. *On the Internet, review sources on Ötzi and choose one that appears to provide the most scientific information about these findings.*
(*Source:* © Bettmann/CORBIS)

A prominent feature of anthropology's classical heritage today is the existence of two basic ways of knowing about humanity. The tradition of Aristotle supports the scientific approach, which says that we can learn about humanity through careful observation. The humanities approach owes more to Plato, who was skeptical about knowledge gained through observation. He said that knowledge is better gained through understanding (see Figure 2.1).

The major animating force of early anthropological thinking was an awareness of "the other"—especially "other" people but also "other" beings, such as apes and chimpanzees, or "monsters," as represented by the fossil evidence of extinct creatures. Long-distance wars of conquest were a major way in which Europeans gained exposure to "other" peoples. The Greeks colonized the entire Mediterranean region and thus had interactions with many non-Greek peoples. The ambitious explorer and conqueror, Alexander the Great, extended the boundaries of his empire from Greece to India during the fourth century BCE and thus expanded Europeans' exposure to distant lands and peoples. Later on, the Romans went even further and encountered Celtic people in Britain.

The Greek writer, Herodotus, chronicler of the Persian Wars during the fifth century BCE, is considered by many to have been the first anthropologist, though a self-trained one (historians claim him as the first historian, too). Herodotus recorded astute descriptions of the diverse peoples he met during his travels. In what we now consider good reporting, he is often careful to distinguish between what he witnessed firsthand and what was hearsay.

Other travelers, explorers, and conquerors added to early awareness of peoples and places beyond the known world. But most ordinary people's experience, during the many centuries before the development of ocean-going ships in the fifteenth century, was limited to what they could see in roughly a 25-mile radius from their place of birth (Brace 1997). Roads were poor, there was no public transportation, and little printed material was available outside cities. Human appearance, language, and behavior within that 25-mile radius would have been quite similar.

During the Middle Ages (the sixth to fourteenth centuries), Christianity was widespread in Europe, and most people accepted the Bible's explanation of the origin of humanity and why humans appear to differ in culture and language. During this period, the classical Greek heritage of human reasoning and questioning was abandoned in favor of faith-based explanations about the origin and characteristics of humanity.

The European Enlightenment, beginning in the fifteenth century, ushered in dramatic changes to the prevailing views of humanity. It led to controversial questioning of the biblical narrative. Once again,

Plato, fifth century BCE	Skeptical of observation-based knowledge	Humanistic approach in anthropology
Aristotle, fourth century BCE	Believed that knowledge can be gained from observation	Scientific approach in anthropology

FIGURE 2.1 Classical Roots of Two Ways of Knowing in Anthropology

This fifteenth-century European depiction of indigenous peoples of the New World includes views of brutality and cannibalism. *One interpretation of such primitivist depictions is that they justified the conquest of people considered to be little more than animals. Five hundred years later, how has the world's understanding of "the other" changed, and what accounts for such change?* (*Source:* © Leonard de Selva/CORBIS)

people began asking "Who are we?" and "Where did we come from?" Two important factors underlay the European Enlightenment. The first factor is Islamic science and philosophy. Through the Crusades, many Europeans became aware of Islamic accomplishments in the Middle East. In addition, the Moorish (Arabic) conquerors of Spain in the fourteenth century brought with them a scientific tradition of learning. The second major factor was the increased rate of contact with "other" people through European explorations in Africa, Asia, and the Americas. Exposure to Islamic learning and contact with non-European peoples and places led to scholars' questioning of biblical explanations about humanity.

The early explorations and colonization also produced the first classifications of "other" people. European descriptions of "others" emphasized their physical characteristics, including skin color and facial features, dress (or lack of dress), and practices that struck European observers as bizarre or even odious, such as worship of non-Christian deities and human sacrifice and cannibalism, as some reports claimed. In the New World, one of the first important distinctions that Europeans made was between "Christians" (the Europeans) and "non-Christians" (the Native Americans). Distinctions based on skin color emerged later. In the New World colonies, the terms *White* and *Black* first corresponded to legal differences between people who had rights, "White" people, and those who did not, the enslaved "Black" people (Orser 2004:7).

In the second half of the nineteenth century, the scientific approach to studying natural and social phenomena began to gain acceptance among Europeans and Euro-Americans. Its rise influenced the emerging discipline of anthropology. In its formative years, anthropology was dominated by the concept of **evolution**, a term that refers to the process of gradual and cumulative change in the characteristics of species, populations, and culture. Early anthropologists wrote about the evolution of the human species, social organization, and languages, and all their models showed an upward path of change from "savagery" or "barbarism" to "civilization." Civilization, defined in terms of European criteria, was the culmination of human evolution.

evolution: inherited and cumulative change in the characteristics of species, population, and culture.

Anthropology has changed substantially since the late 1800s. Its knowledge base has expanded, its theories have developed, and modern research methods would astound the founding figures in the discipline. The number of anthropologists has increased, along with the emergence of many specialties. Anthropology is no longer carried out only by Europeans and North Americans. It is global. Departments of anthropology now exist worldwide, from Argentina to Kenya to Japan. Anthropology in different countries and regions takes on particular characteristics that respond to the cultural context in which it is found. For example, in Latin American countries, social inequality and human rights are prominent topics of study.

In spite of these positive changes, power inequalities still exist in anthropology—and in other disciplines, too. Global inequalities shape funding opportunities and the sheer ability of students to be able to study anthropology (Kuwayama 2003). European and North American countries have the most money to support anthropological research, data collections, and museums. Far more Euro-Americans can afford to become anthropologists than can people in poorer countries. Globally, the power of the English language places Euro-Americans in a central position; writings published in other languages are less likely to gain worldwide attention. Within the wealthy nations, social inequalities also exist in terms of who becomes an anthropologist. In the United States and Canada, although numbers are rising somewhat, ethnic minorities are severely underrepresented in anthropology.

Four Enduring Themes

During the history of anthropological thought, four themes recur: the effects of environment and landscape in shaping humanity, how humanity changes, culture as key to humanity, and the unity and diversity of humanity (see Figure 2.2).

Environment and landscape	Like all living things, humans have been shaped by a wide range of environments. Humans have also exerted significant effects on the environment.
Changes	Throughout human prehistory and history, humanity has changed biologically and culturally.
Culture	Learning that is transferred from generation about shared beliefs and behavior.
Unity and diversity	Humanity is one species, yet cultures differ, enhancing adaptation to different environments.

FIGURE 2.2 Four Enduring Themes in Anthropology

Environment and Landscape Shape Humanity. Early thinkers often explained differences found around the world in people's lifestyles and physical appearance as the result of environment and climate. They associated cold, dark regions with light skin and associated hot, bright regions with dark skin. Some anthropologists still seek explanations for variations in human biology by considering environmental factors. Explanations for aspects of the human evolutionary past, such as the transition to bipedalism (walking on two feet) as opposed to swinging in trees, often take the natural environment and landscape into account as explanations. For example, one theory of why early human ancestors began to walk on two feet is that global climate changes reduced the amount of rainforests and increased open grasslands, prompting early human ancestors to abandon the trees for the ground. Such changes in response to external conditions that contribute to the survival of the species are called **adaptations**.

Humans act to transform, and sometimes destroy, the environment and landscape in which we have evolved. We refer to human-created changes in nature as **anthropogenic**, or caused by humans. Deforestation is a powerful, anthropogenic source of environmental change. Mass clearing of forests began only a few thousand years ago, with the invention and spread of agriculture. In those few thousand years, a dramatic reduction in forest coverage has been accompanied by a decline in biodiversity, including plants, animals, and the human life that depended on forests. The increased food production from farming has had high costs in terms of the environment. Changes that involve trade-offs between positive and negative effects are called **adaptive compromises**. In other words, some things are gained while others are lost. We shall encounter many examples of adaptive compromises in this book.

adaptation: a change in response to external conditions that contributes to the survival of a species.

anthropogenic: an effect caused by humans.

adaptive compromise: a change that involves trade-offs between positive and negative effects.

Change. Change in humanity is constantly taking place. Some adaptations may be responses to changes in the environment and landscape, such as the emergence of bipedalism (walking on two feet) during human evolution. As people learned how to produce new forms of tools, they were able to adapt to more challenging environments. Among contemporary humans, people who move from rural areas to a city often experience heightened blood pressure (Hackenberg et al. 1983). Cultural transformations in diet affect human biology. When people consume more protein, they tend to grow taller. When they eat more sugar and fats, they are likely to become obese.

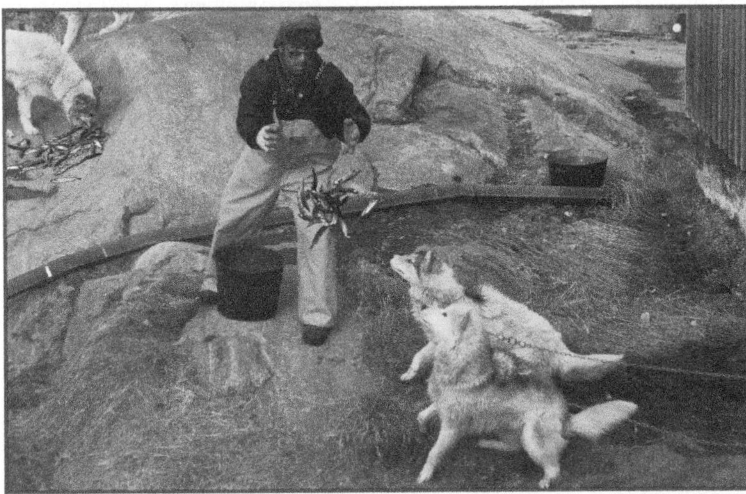

In Aasiaat, central West Greenland, keeping sledge dogs has long been an important feature of Inuit culture, and one that requires a great deal of work to provide food for the dogs. Since the 1990s, the extent of sea ice has decreased markedly and the time window in which dogs can be used to pull sledges has become shorter each year. Sledge dogs are now becoming scarce in Aasiaat. (*Source:* Carsten Egevang/ARC-PIC.com)

The Berber people live in North Africa and the Middle East. Most make their living herding animals, though many are now settled farmers and urbanites. (*Source:* Nik Wheeler/CORBIS) (Left) A Berber girl takes part in a group engagement ceremony in Imilchil, Morocco. (Right) A young woman of the Kabylie, a Berber group of Algeria, wears a headband that signifies mourning during a public march to protest the government's denial of human rights to the Kabylie. *Provide two images of people in your culture that illustrate intracultural variation.* (*Source:* © Tiz/CORBIS SYGMA)

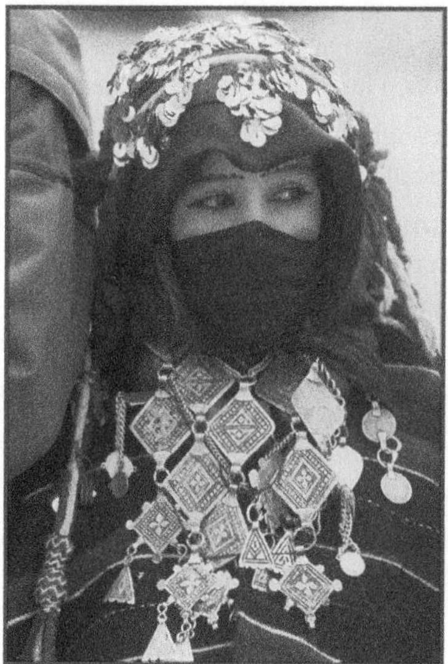

globalization: a contemporary process of cultural change related to dense and rapid linkages of trade, communication, population movement, and other forms of international and transnational contact.

culture: learned and shared ways of behaving and thinking.

symbol: an object, sustance, or concept that stands for something else.

Are biological and cultural changes making people more alike promoting greater diversity? Some contemporary thinkers say that **globalization**, a contemporary process of cultural change related to dense and rapid linkages of trade, communication, population movement, and other forms of international and transnational contact, will obliterate local cultural differences and create a global mono-culture. Others say that even though globalization brings about greater unity in some respects—the spread of English and Spanish as dominant languages, for example—new localized versions of these mega-cultural patterns are emerging, such as "World Englishes" (local variants of English).

Anthropologists are tracking the effects of globalization on human biology. For example, the distribution of vaccines against infectious diseases will bring an end to polio. On a less positive note, it is possible that the spread of American-style fast food may bring with it the spread of obesity.

Culture. The story of humanity—how we became human and why we are the way we are now—is mainly about the increasing importance of human culture as our primary means of adapting to our wider environment and to environmental change. The concept of culture is one of the most complicated in the English language (Williams 1990). We propose this basic working definition: **culture** consists of learned and shared ways of living and thinking. By saying that culture is learned, we mean that culture is not biologically transmitted through genes or any kind of "hard wiring." Culture is passed down through the generations by learning. Saying that culture is shared excludes idiosyncratic and highly individualized ways of living or thinking. One person alone cannot have a culture. Culture is bigger than any one of us.

Anthropologists have long taken culture to be a distinguishing feature separating humans from other animals. Scholars who study human evolution throughout prehistory search for evidence of the beginnings of culture such as tool-making or symbolic behavior such as art or language. Culture relies heavily on the use of symbols. A **symbol** is an object, substance, or concept that stands for something else. Most symbols are "arbitrary"; that is, there is no logical or necessary relationship between a symbol and that for which it stands. Some nonhuman primates can understand symbols, and recent research shows that a culture-based boundary between humans and nonhuman primates is not clearly defined. Chapter 5, on the nonhuman primates discusses the evidence that some nonhuman primates have some features of culture.

Unity and Diversity. All living people belong to one species, yet anthropologists also recognize the existence of human diversity. Anthropologists attempt to define and study "difference" and face the challenge of saying what constitutes a real and significant difference as opposed to a superficial difference. From the fifteenth century on, European colonizers referred to the peoples they met in Africa, Asia, and the Americas as "primitive," "non-Christian," and less than human (Jahoda 1999). Their definitions of difference as equivalent to primitive, pagan, and not quite human served the interests of the colonial powers by legitimizing their intrusion into people's lives and lands, the promotion of Europeanization, and the often ruthless enslavement of non-Europeans for labor. Given this history, anthropologists take a cautious position when it comes to defining and describing difference, because such definitions may play into the interests of the more powerful over the less powerful and may stigmatize specific groups.

Sometimes, anthropologists agree that certain differences, which appear to be negative, cannot be dismissed. For example, if a particular genetic pattern is linked to a greater likelihood of having a life-threatening illness, then this difference is important and is something that health researchers and care providers should address. The sickle-cell trait, and associated anemia and other health problems, is a case in point revealing how important the links are between patterns of genetic variation and their social consequences. The sickle-cell trait in hemoglobin, within the red blood cells, is the result of a genetic mutation that occurred thousands of years ago in parts of Africa, the Mediterranean, and southern Asia (see Map 2.2). In those regions, children born with the sickle-cell trait had a survival advantage in the face of malaria.

Where malaria is not a problem, however, the sickle-cell gene provides no survival advantage and can cause impaired health, including anemia, pain, fatigue, and eye problems in some people. In the United States, sickle-cell anemia is the most common inherited blood disorder, affecting mainly people whose ancestors lived in the areas where the gene first emerged. The highest frequency occurs among African Americans, but sickle-cell disease also afflicts people of other ethnic groups, including Latinos and Arab Americans. In addition to health concerns, people with sickle-cell disease have experienced various kinds of discrimination, in the job market for instance. The sickle-cell trait is a clear example of a biological "difference" that has both health effects and social effects.

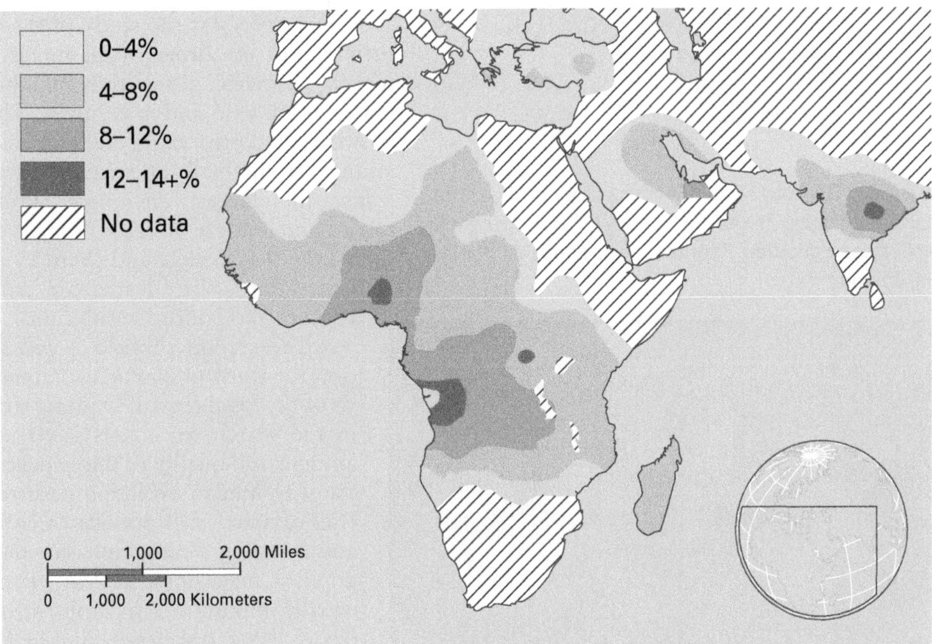

MAP 2.2 Distribution of the Sickle-Cell Trait in Africa and Eurasia. The sickle-cell trait is a condition in which there is one gene for the formation of sickle hemoglobin and one for the formation of normal hemoglobin. The trait appears to have evolved as an adaptation against malaria.

■ Anthropology's Four Fields

In North America, anthropology is divided into four fields (see Figure 2.3) that focus on separate, but connected, subject matter related to humanity:

- *Biological anthropology* (or physical anthropology): the study of humans as biological organisms, including their evolution and contemporary variation.
- *Archaeology* (or prehistory): the study of past human cultures through their material remains.
- *Cultural anthropology* (or social anthropology): the study of living peoples and their cultures, including variation and change. Culture refers to people's learned and shared behaviors and beliefs.
- *Linguistic anthropology:* the study of human communication, including its origins, history, and contemporary variation and change.

Some anthropologists argue that a fifth field, *applied anthropology*, should be added. **Applied anthropology** (also called practicing anthropology or practical anthropology) is the use of anthropological knowledge to prevent or solve problems and to shape or achieve policy goals. The authors of this book

applied anthropology: the use of anthropological knowledge to prevent or solve problems and to shape or achieve policy goals. Also called *practicing anthropology* and *practical anthropology*.

take the position that the application of knowledge, just like theory, is an integral part of each of the four fields and should be integrated within each of them. Thus, this book treats applied anthropology as an intrinsic part of all four fields.

biological anthropology: the study of humans as biological organisms, including their evolution and contemporary variation. Also called *physical anthropology.*

BIOLOGICAL ANTHROPOLOGY
CULTURAL ANTHROPOLOGY
ARCHAEOLOGY
LINGUISTIC ANTHROPOLOGY
Applied — Theory — Applied — Theory — Applied — Theory — Applied — Theory — Applied — Theory — Applied — Theory — Applied — Theory — Applied — Theory

FIGURE 2.3 The Four Fields of Anthropology (*Source:* From p. 6 in *Cultural Anthology* 3rd ed. By Barbara Miller. Copyright © 2005 by Pearson Education. Reprinted by permission of Allyn & Bacon, Boston.)

Biological Anthropology

Biological anthropology, or physical anthropology, is the study of humans as biological organisms, including their evolution and contemporary variation. It encompasses three subfields. The subfields rely on different kinds of data, but they share an interest in the relationship between morphology (physical form) and behavior.

Primatology is the study of the nonhuman members of the order of mammals called primates. Primatologists study nonhuman primates in the wild and in captivity. The category of nonhuman primates includes a wide range of animals from small, nocturnal creatures to gorillas, the largest members. Primatologists record and analyze how the animals spend their time, how they collect and share food, their social groups, their leadership patterns, and conflict and conflict resolution.

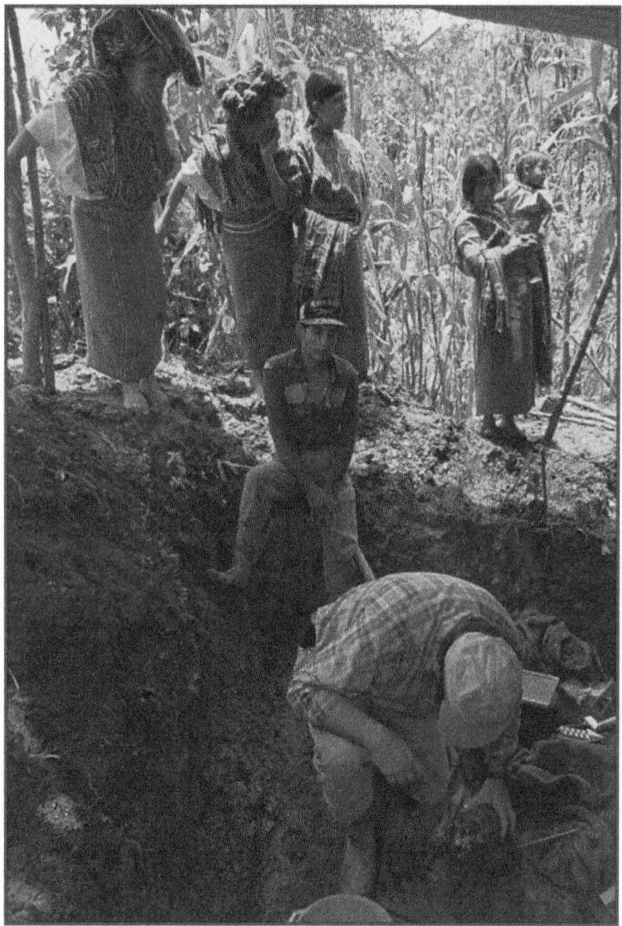

Maya people watch as forensic anthropologist Francisco de Leon conducts an exhumation of more than 50 bodies in a highland Guatemalan village in 1997. (*Source:* AP/Wide World Photos)

The second subfield is *paleoanthropology*, the study of human evolution on the basis of the fossil record. One important activity in the search for fossils is to increase the amount and quality of the evidence related to the way human evolution occurred. Discoveries of new fossils provide "a-ha!" moments and arresting photographs for the covers of popular magazines. A less glamorous but equally important activity in paleoanthropology is dating and classifying new fossils.

The third subfield is the study of *contemporary human biological variation.* Anthropologists working in this area define, measure, and seek to explain differences in the biological makeup and behavior of contemporary humans. In the past, biological anthropologists defined what they perceived as significant differences across modern humans as "racial" (quotation marks indicate that the meaning of this term is contested). Early anthropologists in the late nineteenth and early twentieth centuries used the term "race" to refer to social categories defined on the basis of skin color, hair texture, head shape, and facial features. These biological markers were supposedly associated with inborn ways of behaving and thinking. The controversial book, *The Bell Curve: Intelligence and Class Structure in American Life* (Herrnstein and Murray 1994), is an example of such thinking in the United States in its assertion that "race" determines intelligence and class position.

In fact, DNA evidence clearly demonstrates that "races," defined on the basis of external physical features, are not scientifically valid categories. They lack internal consistency and clear boundaries. Anthropologists do, however, recognize the reality of racism and that many people treat people differently on the basis of this thinking. At the same time, some groups now consciously adopt a social identity tied to "race" and find positive feature in such group identity.

Several areas of biological anthropology are amenable to applied work. Applied primatologists help provide data to support primate conservation projects (see Lessons Applied box). Biological anthropologists who study contemporary human variation provide knowledge relevant to social welfare programs based on their research about how health and nutrition change when people migrate to cities or about growth patterns of children in refugee camps. Programs can then more effectively target their resources to those most in need. *Forensic anthropology* is another applied area of biological anthropology. It uses laboratory analysis to identify human remains; to provide information about the context of the death, time of death, and cause of death; and to identify victims' age, sex, and ethnic heritage. In addition to lab work, forensic anthropologists may also provide expert testimony in courtrooms. They often join the efforts of international humanitarian aid organizations in identifying the victims of natural disasters such as earthquakes and the victims of political violence and genocide.

Archaeology

Archaeology means, literally, the "study of the old" but "old" is limited to human culture. Therefore, the time-depth of archaeology goes back only to the beginning of *Homo sapiens* (around 200,000 years ago). Archaeology encompasses two major areas: *prehistoric archaeology*, which concerns the human past before written records, and *historical archaeology*, which deals with the human past in societies that have written documents. This distinction makes sense because archaeological interpretation in the absence of written records faces the challenge of having only material objects to study. Prehistoric archaeologists often identify themselves with broad geographic regions, studying, for example, *Old World archaeology* (Africa, Europe, and Asia) or *New World archaeology* (North, Central, and South America).

archaeology: the study of past human cultures through their material remains.

Another set of specialties within archaeology is based on the context in which the archaeology takes place. One such specialty is underwater archaeology, the study and preservation of submerged archaeological sites. Sites may be under water because of rising water levels over time or because of an accident such as a shipwreck. Underwater archaeological sites may be from either prehistoric or historic times. Some prehistoric sites include early human settlements in parts of Europe, such as household sites discovered in Switzerland that were once near lakes but are now submerged. Prominent historic contexts include shipwrecks.

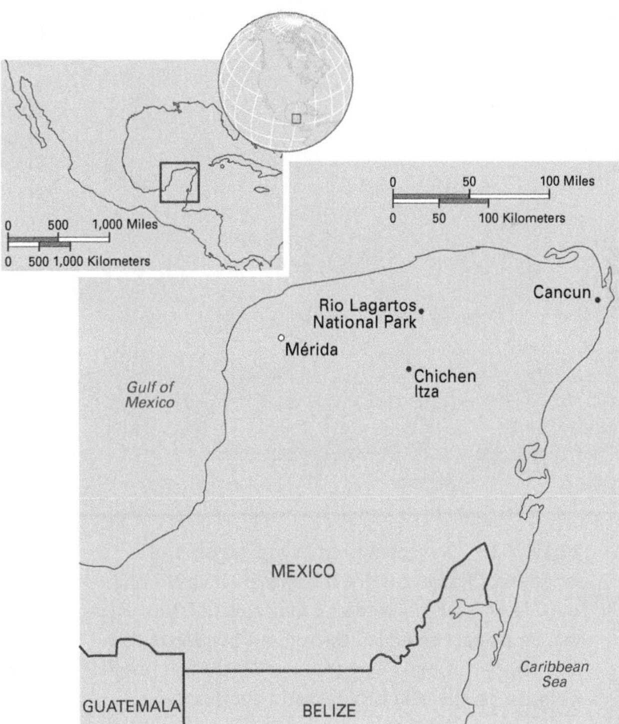

MAP 2.4 Yucatan Peninsula, Central America. The Yucatan peninsula, the location of many Maya archaeological sites, includes parts of eastern Mexico, northern Belize, and northern Guatemala. The boundary area between these states contains the largest tropical rainforest in Central America, now endangered because of extensive deforestation. Tourism is the basis of the region's economy.

An ongoing, six-year project in underwater archaeology is being carried out on the Yucatan peninsula of Mexico (Pilar 2003, Vesilind 2003; see Map 2.4). This research provides insight into Maya funerary and religious practices dating from hundreds of years ago. Throughout the region are deep holes filled with water, created by a meteor crash around 65 million years ago. These pools are called cenotes (pronounced sen-OH-tays), from the Maya word for "abyss." Most cenotes are so deep and difficult to enter that the archaeologists undergo special diving training. The cenotes are an important part of the cultural heritage of Mexico, but they are endangered. Their contents are being disturbed by the activities of sports divers. As many as 10,000 sports divers a year enter the

Box 2.1 Lessons Applied

Orangutan Research Leads to Orangutan Advocacy

Primatologist Biruté Galdikas (pronounced Beer-OO-tay GAL-dee-kas) first went to Indonesia to study orangutans in 1971 (Galdikas 1995). She soon became aware of the threat to the orangutans from local people who, as a way of making money, capture them for sale to zoos around the world. The poachers separate the young from their mothers, often killing the mothers in the process. Sometimes local police locate and reclaim the captured orphans. They try to return them to the rainforest, but the transition into an unknown niche is extremely difficult, and many do not survive.

Orangutan juveniles are highly dependent on their mothers, maintaining close bodily contact with them for at least two years and nursing until they are age 8. Because of this long period of orangutans' need for maternal contact, Galdikas set up her camp to serve as a way station for orphans, and she became the maternal figure. Her first "infant" was an orphaned orang, Sugito, who clung to her like its own mother for years.

The survival of orangutans on Borneo and Sumatra (their only habitats worldwide) is endangered by massive commercial logging and illegal logging, population resettlement programs, plantations, and other pressures on the forests where the orangutans live.

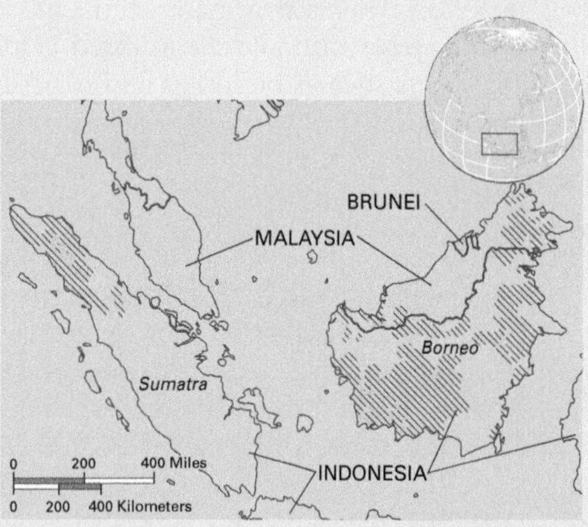

MAP 2.3 Orangutan Regions in Malaysia and Indonesia. Orangutans are the only great apes living outside Africa. Fossil evidence Indicates that their habitats in the past extended throughout Southeast Asia and southern China. They are now limited to pockets of forest on the islands of Sumatra and Borneo.

Galdikas is focusing her efforts on orangutan preservation. She says, "I feel like I'm viewing an animal holocaust and holocaust is not a word I use lightly. . . . The destruction of the tropical rainforest is accelerating daily" (Dreifus 2000:D3). Across all ranges, it is estimated that during the twentieth century the orangutan population experienced a huge decrease, from 315,000 in 1900 to 44,000 in 2000 (IUCN/SSC Conservation Breeding Specialist Group 2004). Aerial surveys (Ancrenaz et al. 2005) and DNA analysis of living orangutans (Goossens et al. 2006) confirm recent and dramatic declines that, if not halted, will lead to extinction in the next few decades.

Biruté Galdikas in Indonesia. She has been studying orangutans for over three decades and is an active supporter of conservation of their habitat. Learn about her work and the status of wild orangutans by searching on the Web. (*Source:* @ Spooner/Redmond-Callow/Gamma Press)

Galdikas has studied orangutans longer than anyone else. She links her knowledge of and love for the orangutans with applied anthropology and advocacy on their behalf. Since the beginning of her fieldwork in Borneo, she has maintained and expanded the Camp Leakey field site and research center (named after her mentor, Lewis Leakey, who inspired her research on orangutans). In 1986, she cofounded the Orangutan Foundation International (OFI), which now has several chapters worldwide.

She has published scholarly articles and given public talks around the world on her research. Educating the public about the imminent danger to the orangutans is an important part of her activism. Galdikas and other orangutan experts are lobbying international institutions such as the World Bank to promote forest conservation as part of their loan agreements.

Camp Leakey employs many local people in diverse roles, including anti-poaching guards. The OFI sponsors

cenotes along the coast alone. Therefore, the team of professional archaeologists is working with some urgency to survey and document as many cenotes as possible.

Another specialty is *industrial archaeology,* which focuses on changes in material culture and society during and since the Industrial Revolution. Although it is pursued worldwide, industrial archaeology is especially active in Great Britain, home of the industrial revolution. There industrial archaeologists study such topics as the design of iron bridges, the growth and distribution of china potteries, miners' housing, and cotton mills. An important role of industrial archaeology is the conservation of industrial sites, which study tours to Borneo for international students and opportunities for them to contribute to conservation efforts.

The success of Galdikas's activism depends on her deep knowledge of orangutans. Over the decades, she has filled thousands of notebooks with her observations of orangutan behavior, along with such details about their habitat as the fruiting times of different species of trees. A donor recently gave software and funding for staff to analyze the raw data (Hawn 2002). The findings will indicate how much territory is needed to support a viable orangutan population. In turn, these findings will facilitate conservation policy and planning.

Food for Thought

- Some people claim that science should not be linked with advocacy because it will create biases in research. Others say that scientists have an obligation to use their knowledge for good causes. Where do you stand in this debate and why?

are more likely to be neglected or destroyed than are sites that have natural beauty or cultural glamour attached to them.

The archaeology of the recent past is another important research direction. An example is the "Garbage Project" conducted by archaeologists at the University of Arizona at Tucson (Rathje and Murphy 1992). The "Garbage Archaeologists" excavated part of the Fresh Kills landfill on Staten Island, near New York City. Its mass is estimated at 100 million tons and its volume at 2.9 billion cubic feet. Thus, it is one of the largest human made structures in North America. Excavation of pop-top can tabs, disposable diapers, cosmetics containers, and telephone books reveals much about recent consumption patterns and how they affect the environment. One surprising finding is that the kinds of garbage people often blame for filling up landfills, such as fast-food packaging and disposable diapers, cause less serious problems than paper. Newspaper, especially, is a major culprit because of sheer quantity. This information can help improve recycling efforts throughout the world. The Fresh Kills landfill continues to grow rapidly due to everyday trash accumulation and other, less common, sources of debris, such as the remains from the World Trade Center in Manhattan following the 9/11 attack.

In archaeology, applied work is growing. Since the 1970s, in the United States a major impetus to this involvement has been the national policy of *cultural resource management* (*CRM*). This policy requires an archaeological survey of "cultural resources" that may be affected whenever a major new construction project, such as a highway, is planned. It also requires plans for preservation of the affected cultural resources. The phrase *cultural resources* includes properties and objects such as buildings and structures, sacred places, historic and modern landscapes, historic documents, museum collections, and individual artifacts (Bergman and Doershuk 2003). The requirement for CRM surveys led to major growth in employment opportunities for archaeologists. About one-third of the professional (nonacademic) archaeologists in the United States are currently involved in CRM work. Internationally, such survey work is not always mandated, and valuable sites and artifacts are destroyed by bulldozers in the name of progress—for example, building an airport or road. Internationally, archaeologists are increasingly active in providing knowledge that can help improve the lives of people in poor countries.

Ironbridge, England, is an important site of industrial archaeology. Considered the "birthplace of industry," the site includes the world's first iron bridge and remains of factories, furnaces, and canals.
Take a virtual tour of the site by going to www. ironbridge.org.uk. (*Source:* Barbara Miller)

Cultural Anthropology

cultural anthropology: the study of living people and their cultures, including variation and change.

Cultural anthropology is the study of living peoples and their cultures, including attention to variation and change. Cultural anthropologists learn about culture by spending extended periods of time with the people they are studying.

Areas of specialization in cultural anthropology include economic anthropology, political anthropology, medical anthropology, psychological anthropology, and development anthropology (the study of the effects and patterns of international development policies and plans in cross-cultural perspective). In all these areas, cultural anthropologists explore cross-cultural variation in behavior and beliefs. The prefix *ethno* is often applied to an English term to suggest a cross-cultural view of whatever topic is being considered. For example, *ethnobotany* is the cross-cultural study of people's knowledge about and use of various plants in their environment. This is urgent research because many of the world's plants and their uses are still undocumented, many are being lost through development projects and deforestation, and much of the knowledge about their uses is dying out.

Cultural anthropologists also study and document contemporary cultural change. Cultural anthropologists are studying the effects of globalization on all aspects of cultures worldwide. For example, research on the use of the Internet sheds light on changing patterns of consumption and trade. It can also reveal how communication via the Internet helps members of migrant groups stay in touch with distant relatives or share information about their cultural identity with people they have never met. In this way, cultural anthropologists see how contemporary people create, maintain, and transform their cultures in a new, virtual world.

Since the 1980s, several important developments in cultural anthropology have raised new questions and generated new data that have transformed the field. *Feminist anthropology*, or a perspective in anthropology that emphasizes the need to study female roles and gender-based inequality, is a major area of interest. Feminist anthropology has moved beyond cultural anthropology into the other fields of anthropology where it has also had a transformative effect. Another new area is *gay and lesbian anthropology*, or *queer anthropology*, which focuses on the study of gay and lesbian sexuality and culture.

Applied anthropology is a vigorous part of cultural anthropology. Several professional associations in the United States and elsewhere reflect that importance. These include NAPA (National Association of Practicing Anthropologists) and WAPA (Washington Association of Professional Anthropologists) and Internet groups such as Anthropology in Action, based in the United Kingdom. Applied cultural anthropologists provide input to such activities as needs assessment, project design, social impact analysis, social marketing, and project evaluation. Cultural anthropologists have helped design HIV/AIDS prevention programs by making their messages more culturally relevant. Cultural anthropologists have documented environmental destruction by mining companies and helped the affected villagers protest that destruction and gain redress. They have also helped prevent the construction of large dam projects that would have displaced thousands of local people. In addition, cultural anthropologists have done social surveys of malnutrition in famine areas to help aid agencies provide food most effectively. In health care settings in the United States, they have served to enhance cross-cultural understanding between medical doctors and members of immigrant populations.

Stephen Lubkemann is trained as a cultural anthropologist and an underwater archaeologist. He is documenting the remains of the hull of DRTO-036, a vessel that wrecked in the Dry Tortugas in the mid-nineteenth century. It lies within Dry Tortugas National Park in the Florida Keys. (*Source:* Photo by Richard Gould)

Cultural anthropologists also contribute to policy formulation, analysis, and critique. For example, they contribute to framing policy objectives to alleviate rural poverty in Nepal—an effort that will address social inequality. They critique policies related to international trade. A growing set of experiences now points to "best practices" in terms of how culture can and should be taken into account in projects and policies. Many decades of experience show how ideas imposed by uninformed but well-meaning outsiders have damaging effects or are simply a waste of effort. It is clear that one of the main problems in international relations and aid is that people in the "first world" lack knowledge about "other" people and their values, needs, and lifestyles. Cultural anthropologists help fill that knowledge gap by sharing their findings with policy makers and program designers.

Linguistic Anthropology

Linguistic anthropology is devoted to the study of communication, mainly (but not exclusively) among humans. Linguistic anthropology has three subfields: *historical linguistics*, the study of language change over time and how languages are related; *descriptive linguistics* or structural linguistics, the study of how contemporary languages differ in terms of their formal structure; and *sociolinguistics*, the study of the relationships among social variation, social context, and linguistic variation, including nonverbal communication.

linguistic anthropology: the study of human communication, including its origins, history, and contemporary variation and change.

Serpent Mound, Ohio, is a prehistoric monument stretching over more than a quarter of a mile. It is uncertain who built the mound, when it was built, and what the serpent shape signified. Today, the mound is situated within a state park and is accessible to the public. *Do some research to find out more about this and other serpent-shaped mounds. (Source:* © Tony Linck/ Superstock, Inc.)

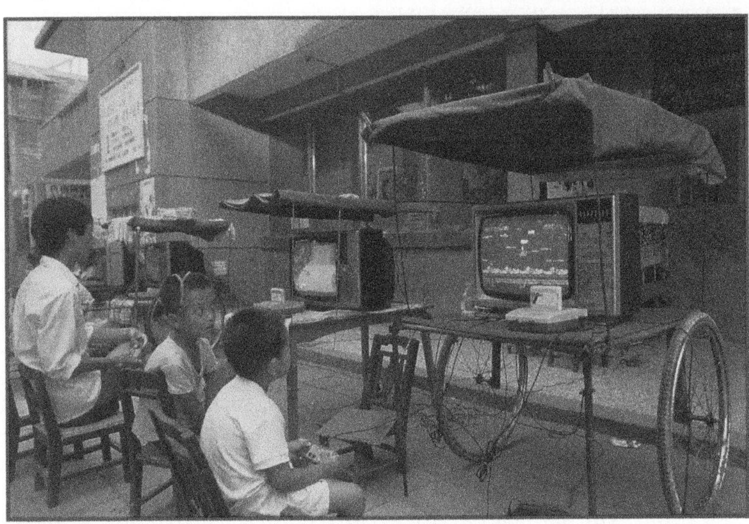

Children playing video games in southern China in 1991. Since 2004, China's Ministry of Culture screens foreign games in terms of how their content relates to Chinese national interests and the possible effects of sexual and violent material on young people. *What is your position on the role of governments in censoring video games? (Source:* © Michael S. Yamashita/ CORBIS)

THINK OF what you know about your home country in terms of the subject matter of anthropology's four fields. Do you know more in some of the fields than in others? What might account for that difference?

Several new directions connect linguistic anthropology to important real-world issues. First is a trend to study language in everyday use, or discourse, and how it relates to power structures at local, and international levels (Duranti 1997a). In some contexts, powerful people speak more than less powerful people, whereas sometimes the more powerful people speak less. Power relations may also be expressed through intonation, word choice, and such nonverbal forms of communication as posture and dress. Second is increased attention to the role of information technology in communication, especially the Internet and cell phones. Third is attention to the increasingly rapid extinction of indigenous languages worldwide.

Linguistic anthropologists play important roles in applied research and policy advising. For example, they consult for educational policy makers in North America about language teaching in schools and how to meet the needs of multilingual populations. They conduct research on classroom dynamics—student participation and teachers' speech patterns—and ask whether there are practices that could be changed to alter gender or ethnic inequalities. Internationally, linguistic anthropologists are promoting the rights of indigenous peoples to use their own language as an aspect of cultural rights. Their documentation of dying languages of the past has proved useful to indigenous people who wish to revive their ancestral language.

The Four Fields: What Do They Add Up To?

Anthropology's four fields are now highly specialized, and no individual anthropologist has expertise in the entire discipline. The authors of this book continually strive to gain insights from the other fields, through four-field conferences, discussion, and the very process of writing a textbook together. As one illustration of how all four fields contribute important knowledge to a particular issue, consider the question "What is Europe?"

Crossing the Fields

What Is Europe?

The European Union (EU), created in 1992, succeeds the six-member European Commission that was founded in 1957. As of 2007, the EU comprises 27 countries. Bulgaria and Romania, joining in 2006, are the newest members. Several others, such as Croatia and Turkey, are candidates. Morocco applied for membership but was rejected. Norway and Switzerland declined to apply for membership.

The EU, with its nearly 5 billion people, constitutes a political and economic entity that plays a more powerful role in global affairs than could any single European country. Its leaders, however, are increasingly concerned that excessive enlargement will weaken the organization. They are faced with two major challenges: defining boundaries for membership and creating a sense of citizenship and belonging. These political questions raise the deeper issue of: What is Europe? What are its geographic boundaries? What is its cultural identity? What ties join its people together? Research in the four fields of anthropology sheds light on why the EU's attempts to define the EU as "Europe" and to provide internal homogeneity have been elusive (Rathgeb 2002).

Biological anthropology reveals that the population of Europe has been formed through thousands of years of immigration from diverse origins. Most biological anthropologists accept that all modern humans (*Homo sapiens*) originated in Africa and then spread throughout the world (Stringer and Andrews 1988). The earliest modern humans arrived in Europe around 40,000 years ago. Their ancestors originated in Africa, with descendant populations migrating to the Middle East and Asia before venturing west into Europe where Ice Age conditions prevailed (Cavalli-Sforza 1997; Chickhi et al. 1998). Since then, many immigrant waves have contributed to the genetic variation found among contemporary Europeans (Sokal 1991). Because of this long-standing pattern of immigration and subsequent population mixing, no genes are distinctively "European." The European genome is a patchwork quilt made of many genetic bits and pieces (Barbujani and Bertorelle 2001). Genetic strains from the Middle East and Africa are predominant.

Archaeological data mirror the biological evidence because the many population movements into what is now called Europe brought with them distinct forms of material culture, such as preferred foods, pottery, house style, public architecture, tools, and weapons. The mainstays of "European" diet today—pork, beef, goat, wheat, barley, beer, and wine—all came from the Middle East.

Furthermore, elements of "European" culture extended much further than what we think of as Europe today. For example, Celtic civilization, with its heartland currently in western Ireland, Scotland, Wales, and northwest France, extended into northern Africa. Thus early European cultures were not restricted to "Europe."

Standing stones at Mzoura, Morocco. This circle is similar to many stone circles in Europe, illustrating prehistoric Celtic connections between Europe and Africa. (*Source:* Barbara Miller)

In terms of culture, the EU is also a patchwork, and an increasingly complex one as immigrants continue to arrive, especially from Africa, the Middle East, and Asia, bringing their lifeways and values with them. They also bring their language, and Europe is now the home to thousands of speakers of Han Chinese, Vietnamese, Hindi, Arabic, Turkish, Kurdish, Wolof, and more. What is Europe?

Just as research in the four fields shows that there is internally homogeneous "Europe," it is just as clear that aspects of "Europe" extend far beyond what one might think of as its geographic boundaries. Centuries-old patterns of trade, migration, and other forms of communication mean that "Europe" exists in Africa, Asia, and even the New World. Some people use the term *Eurasia* to indicate the shared features between the two continents (Goody 1996). The term *Euro-Americans* is commonly used to designate people of the United States and Canada of European descent. No one, though, has proposed the term *Eurafrica*, though many strong reasons for doing so exist, including genetic, archaeological, cultural, and linguistic ties. Part of Europe's identity may lie in its denial of links with Africa.

The second problem the EU faces is the creation of a sense of shared identity among its members states. The challenge of choosing an official language arose early on and still poses problems. The EU chose English as the language for policy making and for communication among member nations. This choice overlooks 10 other official national languages and more than 100 other languages spoken in EU member countries. The EU has two different categories for nonofficial languages. It recognizes Irish and Basque, for example, as "regional minority" languages and has drafted legislation to promote their use as important "heritage" languages. The EU classifies "immigrant minority" languages, such as Arabic and Chinese, as languages of "foreigners." This differentiation may reflect a wish to mute subordinate immigrant groups and bring them into a more "European" identity through linguistic change.

The EU has attempted to create "European" symbols such as a flag, currency, an anthem, and cultural heritage sites (Shore 1993). Although most such attempts have been unsuccessful to date, many people who live in EU states appreciate the convenience of a single EU passport and currency. Perhaps these two highly functional items will form a more coherent sense of unity than any other symbols.

Findings from anthropology's four fields suggest that it is erroneous and probably futile for European Union policy makers to attempt to forge a vision of a homogeneous Europe. Doing so would require the erasing of thousands of years of prehistory, history, and recent patterns of immigration. Rather than ignoring the rich diversity of its peoples and its dynamic international relationships, EU leaders might instead take a boldly pluralistic view of EU identity and build on that rich foundation.

Visit the EU's website to learn about current efforts to promote intercultural dialogue: http://ec.europa.eu/culture.

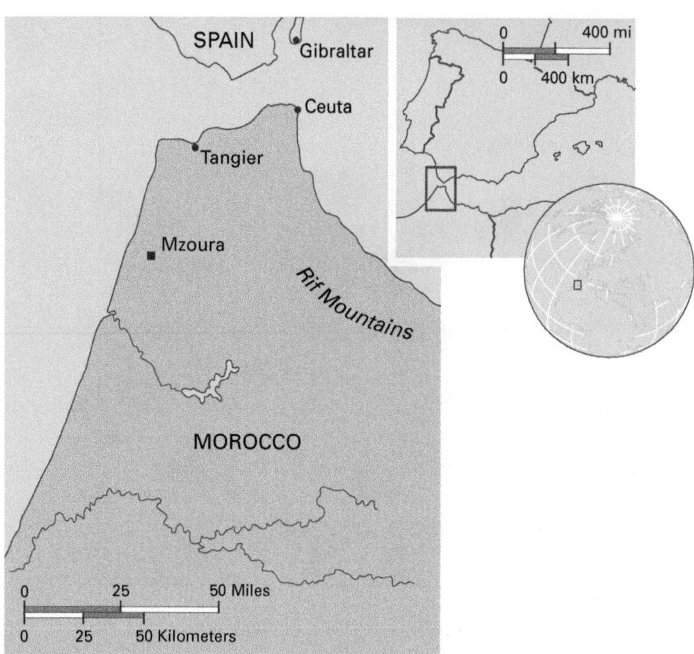

MAP 2.6 Northern Morocco. Morocco is separated from the southernmost tip of Spain by the Strait of Gibraltar, a distance of 8 miles (13 km.). A tunnel to connect the two countries is in the planning stages.

Ethics, Relevance to the Public, and Careers

This section covers three topics: research ethics, the relevance of anthropology to the public, and what anthropology can contribute to your career.

Ethics

Ethics comprises rules of conduct about what is right and wrong in terms of both motives and actual behavior. These issues were not prominent in the early phases of anthropology, but they are extremely important now. When the earliest archaeologists opened an ancient tomb, removed the contents and put them on display in museums in their home countries, they were not thinking about the ethical implications of their actions. The earliest anthropologists who encountered isolated tribal groups were not aware that they might spread diseases among people who had no resistance. Now, however, ethics, relevance, and responsibility are high on the agendas of all anthropologists.

Starting in the 1950s and 1960s, often heated discussions about ethics in anthropology arose in the United States, surrounding the possibility that the U.S. government was using anthropologists as spies conducting secret research in Latin America and then in Southeast Asia during the American–Vietnam war. These cases were never resolved, and claims and counterclaims went largely unproven. Accusations included the possibility that such research had been used by the U.S. government to kill suspected enemies and destroy villages where the anthropologists had done research. The possibility that anthropologists might have consciously gathered data that would later be used against the people they studied horrified most anthropologists. Some anthropologists, though, said that when one's country is at war, it is a citizen's duty is to do everything possible to aid that effort, even if it means posing as an anthropologist to gain information about the enemy.

The first formal statement on anthropological ethics was issued in 1971 by the American Anthropological Association (AAA). It was revised in 1986 and again in 1998. The code of ethics has three major sections: research, teaching, and application (see Figure 2.4). Under research, the anthropologist's first responsibility is to avoid doing anything that would harm the people, animals, and materials they study.

In terms of teaching, the 1998 code sets down principles that apply to good teaching in any field: treating all students equally and fairly, being responsive to students' needs and interests, and acknowledging student assistance in research and publications. The single point about ethical teaching specifically related to teaching anthropology is that professors should engage students in the discussion of ethical issues and discourage students from participating in ethically questionable projects.

The ethical principles for conducting research also guide anthropologists who undertake applied work. The code suggests that anthropologists should carefully consider the ethical implications of any such involvement before getting involved. Further, the code says that inaction or even noncooperation with certain projects may be ethically justifiable.

Anthropology and the Public

Contemporary anthropologists are concerned that anthropology should be relevant to public education. Archaeology has taken the lead in this effort. Archaeologists have provided guidelines and examples of how to incorporate archaeology into middle school and high school education curricula, and into college education at both the undergraduate and graduate levels. The goal of public education is normally to produce knowledgeable citizens, and that of archaeology is normally to preserve the archaeological record and develop awareness of the significance of archaeological resources. These two goals can fit together well. Citizens should know about their country and its history and prehistory, and that of the wider global world. Teaching about archaeology can fill that need, expanding on the range of what is normally taught in history and social studies classes.

> **THINKING OUTSIDE THE BOX**
>
> **WHAT OTHER** courses that you have taken included discussion of ethics? Should ethics be part of every academic discipline or only of some? Be prepared to explain your position.

An archaeologist working in Florida once examined his daughter's eighth-grade social science textbook and was dismayed to see that the discussion of the history of the United States began with Jamestown and the Pilgrims (Milanich 2001). The 12,000 or more years in which Indians had lived in Florida were not mentioned, nor were the Spanish missions and French settlements. Nearly 15 years later, he received an email from a school in St. Petersburg mentioning that the fourth-grade class was doing a project on famous Floridians, and one girl had selected Cacique María. The teacher was seeking some advice on how to help find information for the student's project. The archaeologist was impressed at the change. The Florida Department of Education now mandates that social studies courses emphasize Florida history in the fourth and eighth grades. Standards require that students learn about "early Spanish settlements" and "loss of Native American homelands." Educators are collaborating with archaeologists to prepare lesson plans. Archaeologists are helping by writing texts for fourth- and eighth-graders that cover topics such as changing climatic conditions at the end of the last Ice Age, the state's first inhabitants, native chiefs, and Spanish colonialism.

Incorporating archaeological knowledge into grade-school texts is a good way to share it with a wide public. Such textbooks provide a more accurate and richer story of the past, help build interest in and respect for the past, and thus enhance public stewardship of the past.

Anthropology and Careers

For those who are not interested in majoring in anthropology, anthropology can be an excellent minor or double major. Anthropology complements almost any other area of study by adding greater time depth and a cross-cultural perspective. If you are majoring in music, complementary study in the music of the world will greatly enrich your primary interest. The same applies to subjects as different as interior design, psychology, and criminal justice.

For students interested in pursuing a major in anthropology (or in one of its fields, depending on what your college or university has to offer), we recommend that you make this choice with your eyes wide open. A B.A. in anthropology, just like a B.A. in most other liberal arts subjects, is not a professional degree. Like degrees in history, psychology, and sociology, it is a "good liberal arts degree." It provides a solid background relevant to many career directions that are likely to require further study: law, law enforcement, medicine, social services, education, and business, for instance. The emphasis in anthropology on cross-cultural awareness, understanding of connections among aspects of humanity, and awareness of the dynamics of change are all intellectual assets and skills that employers value (see inside back cover).

Not many of you will decide to go on to pursue a master's degree (M.A.) or doctorate degree (Ph.D.) in anthropology, but we have some advice for those who do: Be passionate about your interest, pay attention to the ethical aspects of your involvement, and be aware that full-time jobs as professors are rare and highly competitive, as are full-time jobs as professional anthropologists. It is often wise to combine a "professionalizing" skill with anthropology, such as a law degree, an M.A. degree in project management, a Master's of Public Health (M.P.H.), a certificate in disaster relief, or attendance at a training program in conflict prevention and resolution.

Useful skills in a variety of areas can be gained to complement each of anthropology's four fields. In biological anthropology, it may be your knowledge of anatomy that helps you get a job teaching anatomy in a medical school or working in a forensics lab. In archaeology, it may be your experience on a summer dig that helps you find a job with the CRM people in your home state. In cultural anthropology, your interviewing skills may land you a position with a marketing company. In linguistic anthropology, your knowledge of bilingualism means that you can help design a more effective program for teaching English to refugees.

Studying anthropology makes for smart people and people with breadth and flexibility. In the United States, current college graduates are likely to change careers (not just jobs, but careers) several times in their lives. You never know where you are going to end up working or in what endeavor—so it pays to be smart, broadly informed about the world, and flexible. Anthropology will help you to ask original and important questions about humanity and to provide original and important answers.

Research

1. Primary ethical obligations are to the people, species, and materials they study and to the people with whom they work. These obligations can supersede the goal of seeking new knowledge:
   - Avoid harm or wrong, understanding that the development of knowledge can lead to change, which may be positive or negative for the people or animals worked with or studied.
   - Respect the well-being of humans and nonhuman primates.
   - Work for the long-term conservation of the archaeological, fossil, and historical records.
   - Consult actively with the affected individuals or group(s), with the goal of establishing a working relationship that can be beneficial to all parties involved.
2. Ensure that anthropological research does not harm the dignity or privacy of the people with whom they conduct research, or harm the safety, well-being, and survival of animals with which they work.
3. Determine in advance whether human research participants wish to remain anonymous or receive recognition. Informed consent of persons being studied must be obtained in advance. Informed consent does not necessarily imply or require a written or signed form, but involves the quality of consent that is provided on the basis of a clear understanding of possible effects of participation in the research.
4. Recognize their obligations to individuals, groups, and host institutions that participated in or otherwise facilitated the research.

Responsibility to Scholarship and Science

1. Anticipate possible ethical dilemmas and raise these issues in their research proposals.
2. Assume responsibility for the integrity and reputation of the discipline and abide by general moral rules of science:
   - Do not deceive.
   - Do not knowingly misrepresent.
   - Do not prevent reporting of misconduct.
   - Do not obstruct the research of others.
3. Preserve opportunities for future fieldworkers.
4. Use findings in an appropriate fashion and, whenever possible, disseminate findings to the scientific and scholarly community.
5. Consider all reasonable requests for access to data and ensure preservation of data for posterity.

Responsibility to the Public

1. Make findings appropriately available to sponsors, students, decision-makers, and other nonanthropologists and ensure that such information is well understood and properly utilized.
2. It is possible to move to a position of advocacy, but this is an individual decision rather than an ethical responsibility.

Teaching

1. Do not discriminate on the basis of sex, marital status, "race," social class, political convictions, disability, religion, ethnic background, national origin, sexual orientation, age, or other criteria irrelevant to academic performance.
2. Strive to improve teaching, availability, counseling, and helping students obtain professional placement.
3. Impress upon students the ethical challenges in every phase of anthropological work.
4. Publicly acknowledge student assistance in research and preparation of work and compensate students justly for their participation in all professional activities.
5. Avoid sexual liaisons with students for whose education they are in any way responsible.

Application

1. Follow the same ethical guidelines in all anthropological work, be open with funders, and make carefully considered decisions about what types of work in which to be involved.
2. Be honest with employers about qualifications, capabilities, and aims and do not accept conditions contrary to professional ethics.
3. Be alert to dangers of compromising anthropological ethics and understand that contributions to public or private sector actions and policies may include both proactive participation and noncooperation, depending on circumstances.

Note: The AAA code does not dictate behavior or include sanctions. It is designed to promote discussion and provide general guidelines for ethically responsible decisions.

Source: Reproduced by permission of the American Anthropological Association from the Code of Ethics of the American Anthropological Association, approved June 1998.

FIGURE 2.4 The Code of Ethics of the American Anthropological Association, 1998

The Big Questions Revisited

WHAT is anthropology?

Anthropology is the study of humanity, including the prehistoric origins of humans, our nonhuman primate relatives, contemporary human biological and cultural variation, and human communication past and present. Anthropology's roots go back at least to the time of the classical Greek and Roman philosophers, who raised questions about humanity's origins and diversity. During the Middle Ages, the Bible was the source of explanations about humanity in most of Europe, but after the European Enlightenment of the seventeenth and eighteenth centuries, the biblical view began to be displaced by a scientific view.

Since the latter half of the nineteenth century, anthropology has emerged as a formal academic discipline. Throughout its history, four enduring themes in anthropology have been how environment and landscape shape humanity, change over time, culture as the key to humanity, and unity and diversity.

WHAT do the four fields of anthropology cover?

North American anthropology is divided into four fields: biological anthropology, archaeology, cultural anthropology, and linguistic anthropology. These fields contain distinct but related subject matter.

Biological anthropology, or physical anthropology, is the study of humans as biological organisms. It includes the subfields of primatology, paleoanthropology, and contemporary human variation. Archaeological anthropology, or archaeology, is the study of past human cultures through their material remains. It contains two subfields: prehistoric archaeology and historical archaeology, and several other domains (such as underwater archaeology and industrial archaeology) based on characteristics of the sites involved. Cultural anthropology, or social anthropology, is the study of living people and their cultures and of variation and change therein. Cultural anthropology contains many subfields, including economic anthropology, political anthropology, psychological anthropology, medical anthropology, and more. Linguistic anthropology is the study of human communication—its origins, history, and contemporary variation and change. Most linguistic anthropologists study contemporary communication among humans and are thus closely linked to cultural anthropology.

Applied anthropology is sometimes put forward as a possible fifth field in the discipline. This book takes the perspective that application of knowledge, just like theory, is an integral part of each of the four fields and should be studied as such, not as a discrete field.

WHAT are examples of anthropology in the "real world"?

Anthropology is not just an academic discipline populated by professors in universities. One aspect of anthropology's public role is its concern with ethics in all its activities, from research to teaching to applied work. Ethics are rules regarding what is right and what is wrong in motives and behavior. Anthropological ethics about research state that the anthropologist's primary responsibility is to protect the well-being of people, sites, species, and materials involved in his or her research. Ethics about teaching involve principles that apply to teaching in any field, such as treating all students fairly, but also include the specific goal of engaging students in discussion of ethical principles. Anthropologists who undertake applied work should abide by the principles governing research as well as by additional guidelines about honesty in dealing with sponsors and not taking on any work that is ethically questionable. Applied work is an important way in which anthropologists can share their expertise with the public.

Anthropology is relevant to many kinds of careers. As a minor or double major, it complements and strengthens many other disciplines by adding greater time depth and cross-cultural breadth of understanding. As a B.A. major, it is an excellent foundation for future professional study—for example, in legal, business, and health fields. In M.A. programs, a professional degree in anthropology can lead to careers in many areas. At the Ph.D. level, it prepares anthropologists for teaching in colleges and universities and for research and policy roles in organizations such as governments and international organizations.

Key Concepts

adaptation, p. 33
adaptive compromise, p. 33
anthropogenic, p. 33
anthropology, p. 29
applied anthropology, p. 35
archaeology, p. 37
biological anthropology, p. 36
cultural anthropology, p. 40
culture, p. 34
evolution, p. 32
globalization, p. 34
humanistic approach, p. 29
linguistic anthropology, p. 41
science, p. 29
symbol, p. 34

Suggested Readings

Patrick Brantlinger. *Dark Vanishings: Discourse on the Extinction of Primitive Races, 1800–1930*. Ithaca, NY: Cornell University Press, 2003. This book documents Victorian and post-Victorian rhetoric in Europe that viewed the extinction of "primitive races" as inevitable, given prevailing Darwinian views of the "survival of the fittest." The author shows how this narrative plays out in North America, Australia, New Zealand, and Ireland. In the last case, the discourse justified inadequate government action in the case of the potato famine.

James Deetz. *In Small Things Forgotten: An Archaeology of Early American Life*. New York: Doubleday, 1996. Deetz argues that understanding past cultures is best accomplished through studying everyday things such as gravestones, doorways, musical instruments, and pottery shards. The updated version of this classic study includes more material on women and African Americans.

Jane Goodall. *Reason for Hope: A Spiritual Journey*. New York: Warner Books, 1999. Primatologist Jane Goodall provides her memoirs, including recollections of her childhood in London during World War II, Louis Leakey's mentorship when she was a young fieldworker, and her long-term fieldwork in Tanzania with chimpanzees. She also reflects on the ethical implications of animal research.

Cori Hayden. *When Nature Goes Public: The Making and Unmaking of Bioprospecting in Mexico*. Princeton, NJ: Princeton University Press, 2003. The exchange of plants for corporate promises of royalties or community improvement projects is studied from the perspective of cultural anthropology. Using the results of in-depth research at several sites in Mexico, the author considers who stands to win and lose, how companies should pay, and to whom.

Gustav Jahoda. *Images of Savages: Ancient Roots of Modern Prejudice in Western Culture*. New York: Routledge, 1999. The author examines the historic roots of prejudice in Western thinking, tracing such beliefs as monstrous cannibals, wild men of the woods, and ape-like savages. These beliefs peaked in the nineteenth century, when many of them gained scientific respectability. Some of these themes persist today in descriptions of people perceived as "other," including the poor and the mentally ill.

Richard J. Perry. *Five Concepts in Anthropological Thinking*. Upper Saddle River, NJ: Prentice-Hall, 2003. After a brief introduction on theory in anthropology, the author discusses the following concepts: evolution, culture, structure, function, and relativism. A final chapter provides a summary and a discussion of "unsettled issues."

Adriana Petryna. *Life Exposed: Biological Citizens after Chernobyl*. Princeton, NJ: Princeton University Press, 2002. A cultural anthropologist considers the aftermath of the disaster and how the people affected face their new lives of disability and uncertainty.

Hugh Raffles. *In Amazonia: A Natural History*. Princeton, NJ: Princeton University Press, 2002. This book provides a wide view of the region and its people.

Anthony J. Regan and Helga M. Griffin, eds. *Bougainville before the Conflict*. Canberra: Pandanus Books, 2005. Twenty-eight chapters address the archaeological evidence about the settlement of Bougainville island in the South Pacific, the genetic evidence about the people, language history and variation, and contemporary cultural variation on the island. Several chapters describe the problems caused by European colonialism, especially the Panguna mine, which played a pivotal role in the eventually successful movement of Bougainville for independence from Papua New Guinea.

W. Richard Stephens. *Careers in Anthropology: What an Anthropology Degree Can Do for You*. Boston: Allyn and Bacon, 2002. Sixteen profiles of careers in, and related to, anthropology, provide insights about career options and paths to a career in anthropology. The mini-biographies include people working in cultural resource management, international development, computer engineering, coroner's investigation, the administration of not-for-profit organizations, and more.

chapter 3

Culture and Diversity

THE BIG QUESTIONS

- *WHAT is culture?*
- *WHAT are some bases of cultural diversity?*
- *WHAT do anthropologists debate about culture?*

Anthropology, Second Edition
by Barbara Miller

I can't pass a rock
like you
without being mystified
or hypnotized

I have heard stories
of rocks
and have known some
rocks personally

They represent the
world by their presence
wisdom has no
relationship to size

One time, perhaps many times
a man became a rock
thinking that a fine way
to gain immortality

This Native American poem of the Wintu people of California refers to a rock formation called the "Bag of Bones" (Theodoratus and LaPena 1994:24–25). It also expresses a message about the connectedness between humans and natural sites. Today, however, many people have replaced a connectedness to stones, streams, and mountains with a connectedness to technology and to modern monuments such as the Eiffel tower, satellite dishes, and huge shopping malls.

Culture now seems less connected to nature, but perhaps that is an overgeneralization. One of anthropology's goals is to study the relationship between nature and culture and how each shapes humanity's past, present, and future.

The Concept of Culture

As noted earlier, this books' definition of culture is that it is learned and shared behavior and beliefs. Paying in-depth attention to it is a necessary step before going further in the exploration of humanity. Many scholars agree that although biology was the major actor in humanity's earliest evolution, culture is now the key shaper of humanity.

Definitions of Culture

The question of how to define culture has intrigued anthropologists for over a century. Even now, spirited discussions take place between animal scientists and cultural anthropologists about whether nonhuman animals have culture and, if so, how it resembles or differs from human culture. This section reviews some important differences in how anthropologists define culture, then considers some characteristics of culture, and, last, discusses ethnocentrism and cultural relativism.

Because culture is a core concept in anthropology, it seems likely that anthropologists would agree about what it is. This may have been the case in the early days of the discipline in the nineteenth century, when there were far fewer anthropologists. But by the middle of the twentieth century, an effort to collect definitions of culture produced 164 different ones (Kroeber and Kluckhohn 1952).

The earliest definition of culture was proposed by British anthropologist Edward Tylor in 1871: "Culture, or civilization ... is that complex whole which includes knowledge, belief, art, law, morals, custom, and any other capabilities and habits acquired by man as a member of society" (Kroeber and Kluckhohn 1952:81). The phrase *that complex whole* has been the most durable feature of Tylor's definition. Three other features have not stood the test of time. First, most anthropologists now avoid using *man* to refer to all humans and instead use generic words such as *humans* and *people*. One might argue that the word *man* can be used generically according to its linguistic roots, but studies indicate that this usage can be confusing. Second, most anthropologists no longer equate culture with civilization. The term *civilization* implies a sense of "highness" versus noncivilized "lowness" and sets up an invidious distinction placing "us" (the so-called civilized nations of Europe and North America) in a position superior to "them"—the other societies. Third, many anthropologists now think that culture is also found in some nonhuman primates in which observed variations in behavior are not determined genetically but are learned and shared (McGrew 1998).

Contemporary views about the question "What is culture?" fit into three perspectives: **idealism**, **behaviorism**, and **holism** (see Figure 3.1). These views differ in terms of whether they conceive of culture as consisting mainly of internalized meanings, or mainly of observable behavior, or both.

- The idealist view, also called symbolist and interpretivist, is that culture consists of learned and shared beliefs, thoughts, meanings, and symbols.
- The behaviorist view is that culture consists of learned and shared ways of behaving.
- The holistic view is that culture consists of learned and shared beliefs, meanings, and symbols *as well as* learned and shared ways of behaving. In reality, most anthropologists would agree that beliefs and behavior are both important and are interrelated aspects of culture.

Idealism

Behaviorism

Holism

FIGURE 3.1 Three Views of Culture

idealism: the view that culture consists of ideas and beliefs.

behaviorism: the view that culture consists of learned and shared patterns of behavior.

holism: the view that culture consists of both behavior and beliefs and how they are interrelated.

microculture: distinct patterns of learned and shared behavior and ideas found in localized regions and among particular groups. Microcultures include ethnic groups, genders, and age categories. Also known as *local culture*.

macroculture: learned and shared ways of behaving and thinking that cross local boundaries, such as a sense of national culture that some governments seek to promote to enhance unity, or the global consumer culture that pervades upper-middle-class and upper-class groups transnationally.

Culture is found universally among human beings, and thus it exists in a general way as something everyone has, a kind of culture with a capital "C." Culture also exists in a more specific way. The term **microculture**, or local culture, refers to distinct patterns of learned and shared behavior and ideas found in localized regions and among particular groups. Microcultures include ethnic groups, racial groups, genders, and age categories. The term **macroculture** refers to learned and shared ways of behaving and thinking that cross local boundaries, such as the sense of national culture that some governments seek to enhance unity, and the global consumer culture that pervades upper-middle-class and upper-class groups around the world.

Anthropology's Focus on Culture: Past and Present

Three fields of general anthropology are most directly concerned with the study of culture: archaeology, linguistic anthropology, and cultural anthropology. This section provides an abbreviated intellectual history of these three fields.

Archaeology and Culture of the Past The study of culture in the human past has been a topic of popular and scholarly interest for centuries (Trigger 1989). The Greeks and Romans revered the past, and they collected relics and fossils unearthed from construction sites. The biblical age also envisioned the ancient past as a golden age—the time of Adam and Eve in the Garden of Eden. The biblical description of human prehistory, though, was shaken during the early centuries of European colonialism. Europeans were especially perplexed about the existence of people in the New World, because the Bible never mentioned them. When the Spanish arrived in Mexico and saw the advanced cities and massive wealth of the Aztec empire, it became clear there was a flaw in the Eurocentric vision of Europe as the only civilized region and of European people as the only people capable of civilization.

In the 1600s, the Danes established the first museum of antiquities, or "ancient objects" (Bahn 1996). The seventeenth and eighteenth centuries saw increased interest in antiquities in Europe and among Europeans in the American colonies. Collectors at this time were called *antiquarians*, untrained people who collected and studied relics of the ancient past as a hobby. Early antiquarians, however, laid the basis for contemporary archaeological methods. Thomas Jefferson, in 1784, undertook the first recorded excavation to be conducted in North America (Patterson 2001). With the goal of learning about the origins of Native Americans, his project is now recognized as an early example of the scientific method: He had a research goal and a method to achieve that goal. The method involved careful excavation and detailed recordkeeping of several mounds on his Virginia estate at Monticello.

During the mid-nineteenth century, antiquarianism began to evolve into archaeology, a formal area of study with science defining its goals and methods. A Danish scholar, Christian Jurgen Thomsen, was an important figure in this transition period. He devised a three-age system of prehistory based on the evolution of tools: the Stone Age, the Bronze Age, and the Iron Age. He introduced the concept of *association* by which non-tool artifacts are dated on the basis of their association in the site with tools made of stone, bronze, or iron. He organized the Danish museum's collections in accordance with this principle and, in 1836, published a major book on his findings called the *Guide to Northern Archaeology*. In 1843, another Dane, Jens Worsaac, published an account of Danish prehistory entitled *Primeval Antiquities of Denmark*, which established his career as a full-time professional archaeologist and his being recognized as the father of modern archaeology (Bahn 1996:90).

Daniel Wilson, active during the mid- and later nineteenth century, coined the term *prehistory* and popularized it in Britain and North America through his several publications. Born poor in Edinburgh, Scotland, he migrated to Canada where he undertook excavations in the Great Lakes region. At a time when the prevailing European sentiment was that Native Americans were "savages," he recognized the existence of civilization among non-Western peoples and claimed that all humans can be civilized. In 1857, he taught an honors course in archaeology at the University of Toronto, probably the first formal course taught on archaeology anywhere.

A panel of the so-called Elgin marbles, a collection of marble friezes and other sculptures originally located at the Acropolis in Athens, Greece, now housed in the British Museum in London. Over the centuries, countless objects were taken from their original sites and displaced into private collections or museums. Many of these objects are the focus of heated debates about whether they should be returned to their place of origin. ■ *Learn more about the Elgin marbles as "contested" and take an informed position in the debate as to whether they should remain in London or be returned to Athens. (Source: British Museum, London, UK/Bridgeman Art Library)*

Important Old World sites excavated during this period include Athens and Troy. Excavations in the Indian subcontinent, led by the British archaeologist Sir Mortimer Wheeler, focused on the major monuments there and produced rich documentation of early Buddhist and Hindu temples. The first European archaeological expedition to China was led by a Swede, Sven Hedin, in 1895. Japan was the first Asian country to adopt archaeology. Japan pioneered a cultural properties protection law in 1876 and launched its first excavation a year later. Archaeology was first taught in Japan in 1907 at Kyoto University.

In 1871 in Africa, a German geologist discovered the site of Great Zimbabwe, capital of the fourteenth-century Shona kingdom. This discovery prompted a heated debate in Europe about who had built such an impressive and large settlement, with clear distinctions between the elite who lived inside the walls and the commoners who lived outside. The prevailing Eurocentrism denied an indigenous African heritage for the site, whereas archaeologists insisted on its African origins.

In the New World, archaeologists have been drawn to Maya sites in Mexico and Central America since the late 1800s. Temple sites and hieroglyphics provided rich material for collection and interpretation. In 1911, a Yale University historian, Hiram Bingham, discovered the remains of an ancient Incan city, Machu Picchu, located high in the Andes mountains in Peru (see the photograph on p. 234). This discovery generated great excitement in New World archaeology and once again prompted questions about what "civilization" consists of and who has it.

processualism: the theory that environment and other material factors determine certain kinds of cultural changes.

postmodernist archaeology or **postprocessual archaeology:** a perspective that rejects general theories of the human past and objective interpretations of sites and artifacts in favor of rich descriptions of particular cases and intuitive interpretation of evidence.

A major theoretical change since the 1960s in North America was a move away from the earlier emphasis on simply providing detailed descriptions of particular sites. American archaeologist Lewis Binford was influential in pushing for theory building and generalization across sites. He launched **processualism**—the theory that environment and other material factors determine certain kinds of cultural changes. Processualists ask "why" questions and seek to find general principles to explain changes over time, such as the emergence of cities and states. For example, processualists would ask why the Maya state emerged when and where it did, and they would search for environmental influences such as the availability of critical natural resources (water, for example). This approach still characterizes most archaeological research worldwide.

Since the 1980s, however, **postmodernist archaeology,** or **postprocessual archaeology,** has gained followers (Hodder 1996). This perspective rejects the search for general theories as ways of understanding the human past and instead emphasizes the rich description of particular cases and the intuitive interpretation of evidence. Postmodernist archaeology says that objective interpretations of sites and artifacts are not possible because the interpreter is inevitably biased by his or her position and perspectives (as male or female, middle-class, or White). Postmodernist archaeology is closely associated with Ian Hodder, for-

The site of Great Zimbabwe in southeastern Africa has generated intense speculation among archaeologists since its discovery by European explorers in the nineteenth century. British archaeologist Gertrude Caton-Thompson conducted excavations there in the 1920s and reported that Bantu people built the monuments several centuries earlier. ■ *Assume that the Government of Zimbabwe has just hired you to construct a website about Great Zimbabwe, and you have one week to accomplish this task: what information will you include? (Source: © Robert Holmes/CORBIS)* merly of Cambridge University and now at Stanford University in the United States. Hodder urges archaeologists to study meaning and symbols in archaeological remains and to search for the role of individuals and creativity. Such archaeologists link their attempts to understand, for example, gender-related symbols, cosmology (ideas about the universe), and sacred sites with the work of cultural anthropologists, thereby demonstrating the value of greater integration between these two fields (Robb 1998).

THINKING OUTSIDE THE BOX

CONSIDER the garbage you create within a typical week and make a list of its contents. What would a processual model say about your garbage? What would a postmodernist (or postprocessual) perspective say? Compare your results with those of other students.

Linguistic Anthropology and the Study of Language as Culture
Linguistic anthropology as a professional area of research and teaching emerged in the United States in the later nineteenth century when researchers began to document disappearing Native American languages. As with the other fields of anthropology, its intellectual roots extend much further back than thought. Within European history, in the early pre-Christian era, Greek philosophers thought that the earliest humans were distinguished from modern humans by their lack of language. Later, biblical writings said that language began when God, through Adam, named the animals (Patterson 2001:10). The Bible also explained why languages differ: In order to punish the people who built the Tower of Babel, God scrambled their language and scattered them around the globe. The Christian view that God alone could have invented words, grammar, and writing retained a prominent position in Western thinking into the nineteenth century (Harris 1968:57).

The European Enlightenment inspired study of non-Western languages. In the United States, George Washington and Thomas Jefferson supported the collection of Native American vocabularies over several decades of the 1700s (Patterson 2001:11). Comparisons of the word lists of many languages convinced some people that all Native American languages must have come from a single language and that they were related to European languages. Both Washington and Jefferson were interested in demonstrating the shared humanity of Native Americans and Europeans.

At about this time, the *comparative method* in language study was established. By comparing features of contemporary languages, one could reconstruct language history. A major advance based on the comparative method occurred in 1786 when Sir William Jones proposed that Greek, Latin, Celtic, and Sanskrit (the classical language of India) had a common origin. This discovery also supported the view of the unity of humankind by showing the close connections between Europeans and the people of India.

The mid-nineteenth century was a major watershed in the emergence of a scientific approach to the cross-cultural study of language. The reasons are similar to those discussed earlier: colonialism's encounters with non-Western peoples, the rise of evolutionary theory in the mid-1800s, and the decline of the biblical model. Edward Tylor, a founding figure of cultural anthropology, paid considerable attention to language (Lounsbury 1972). Tylor was interested in origins and in the "progress" toward "civilization"—issues that had been pursued in the preceding century but were given a new impetus and a much longer timeframe by writers such as Darwin. He and others moved the question of origins from the supernatural domain to the natural domain. Language was now seen as part of humanity's natural endowment rather than as God-given.

A key question of Tylor's time was whether the ideas necessary for language are innate within the human mind or are acquired through experience. Prominent theories stated that verbal language started with the natural cries of animals or through imitating the sounds of nature. Another question was why people have language in the first place. Is it primarily for psychological self-expression or to serve social purposes?

Another concern of the late nineteenth and early twentieth centuries was the question of differences among languages and the significance of such differences (Lounsbury 1972). By the early twentieth century, most linguistic anthropologists had abandoned the idea that languages differ because their speakers are at different stages of evolution. This change was largely due to the contributions of Franz Boas (discussed in the following section on cultural anthropology). In contrast to his contemporaries, Boas argued that the structure of a language could not hinder thought and could not (if different from English or French) be a marker of a less psychologically advanced people. He said that languages are adapted to the circumstances of life but are not limiting. Boas invented the concept of **linguistic relativism**, the idea that all languages are equally sophisticated and competent. Further, Boas insisted that one cannot understand another culture without knowing its language (Duranti 1997:53).

Edward Sapir, the founding father of linguistic anthropology, followed the relativist lead of Boas by saying that languages could differ in structure (grammar) but still have equally sophisticated content and competence. Writing in the 1920s and 1930s, he argued that language is a prerequisite for the development of culture. He also believed that languages have the power to train people into certain ways of thinking, and that languages thereby actually create different "thought worlds" for their speakers.

A later approach called **structuralism**, which originated in France, attracted attention in the United States in the 1960s. Structuralism is a theoretical perspective prominent in both linguistic and cultural an-

linguistic relativism: the idea that all languages are equally valid and must be understood in their own terms.

structuralism: an approach in cultural anthropology that emphasizes the role of large, powerful structures in society (such as the economy, social and political organizations, and ideological systems) in shaping people's behavior and beliefs.

Claude Lévi-Strauss, French cultural anthropologist, is most noted for his contribution to structural anthropology, or the study of underlying patterns in culture especially through the analysis of themes that recur in myths and rituals. ■ (*Source:* © Sophie Bassouls/CORBIS SYGMA)

thropology. Its premise is that meaning in language and other aspects of culture emerges from the relationships between and among various elements of a language or culture (Barnard 2000:120). For example, meaning does not come from individual sounds or words but, rather, depends on how sounds or words are placed in relation to each other. The French cultural anthropologist Claude Lévi-Strauss is the leading figure of structuralism. He claimed that all human thinking is based on binary oppositions: two opposed factors such as male and female, culture and nature, or raw food and cooked food. These oppositions, he says, reflect the deep problems that human thought and culture must deal with—major issues such as the difference between people and animals, for example, or between life and death. He found, in his study of 813 myths from North and South American indigenous peoples, that these basic binary oppositions are always mediated by a third, middle-ground element, which then forms a kind of solution to the basic problem of duality. Mediating elements are often categorically ambiguous, or crossovers (such as the Sphinx, which is part human and part animal, and rotten food, which is neither raw nor cooked). French structuralism emphasizes the symbolic meanings and relationships of cultural elements. Currently, French structuralism is not accepted in its pure form by many anthropologists. But certain features are still influential, especially the idea that the true meaning of language lies beneath the surface and can be discovered only through symbolic analysis and the appeal of binary oppositions in interpreting linguistic, textual, and social data.

The latter half of the twentieth century, from the 1980s to the present, brought a new vitality to linguistic anthropology with an emerging emphasis on *discourse* (language in use) in the context of social roles and power relations. Many contemporary anthropologists use a blended theoretical approach that sees language and other forms of communication, especially mass communication, as shaped by the material realities of life and, in turn, as shaping those realities (Duranti 1997).

THINKING OUTSIDE THE BOX

SELECT A folktale or story such as "Cinderella" or "Star Wars," and apply a structural analysis to it, including the drawing of a formal diagram of key elements and their relations. See whether a nature/culture, good/evil, or other dichotomy fits, and then see whether you can find a mediator, or third element.

Cultural Anthropology and the Study of Human Culture The history, goals, and findings of cultural anthropology are linked with those of the other fields of anthropology. An early landmark is Charles Montesquieu's book, *The Spirit of the Laws*, published in 1748 (Barnard 2000:22ff). Based on library research, this book discusses the temperament and government of people around the world. Montesquieu's explanation for differences among various people was the environment, not biology or mental ability. He stated that nature and climate dominated "savages" more than the Romans, Chinese, or Japanese.

By the mid-nineteenth century, the concept of evolution began to gain ground among Western thinkers. Herbert Spencer published works about cultural evolution a few years before Darwin's publications emerged (Harris 1968). He attempted to devise an evolutionary scheme for all components of culture, including the family, the economy, and language. Like other thinkers of this period, Spencer relied on reports about non-European cultures from explorers and missionaries, and thus his schemes relied on faulty and often fanciful examples. However, it may be that another thinker of the time, Karl Marx, was more influential than either Spencer or Darwin in shaping ideas about cultural evolution. Marx's contributions to the emerging field of cultural anthropology include a focus on material aspects of culture, such as the *mode of production* as the basic feature of cultures and emphasis on the role of social conflict as the major force driving cultural change. Marx was also a founding father of the study of social inequality, and he may be one of the first policy-oriented social scientists, as demonstrated by his statement: "The philosophers have *interpreted* the world in various ways: the point however is to *change* it" (quoted in Harris 1968:219). The Marxist model of cultural evolution exhibits striking parallels to Darwin's in that both view progress as achieved through competition and struggle. Marxism was the basis of anthropology in the former USSR and China.

Three men, considered the founding fathers of cultural anthropology and all writing in the late eighteenth and early nineteenth centuries, were Sir Edward Tylor and Sir James Frazer in England and Lewis Henry Morgan in the United States. All three proposed evolutionary models for culture and for particular features of culture, such as kinship systems and religion. Early forms of kinship were said to be centered on women, with inheritance passing through the female line, whereas more evolved (European) forms centered on men, with inheritance passing through the male line. Magic was said to precede religion, which was said to precede science.

The early cultural anthropologists were predominantly "armchair" anthropologists whose research involved reading reports written by others. Tylor, working in this mode, proposed the first definition of culture in 1871. Frazer's multivolume publication *The Golden Bough* (1970 [1890]) is a compilation of myths, rituals, and symbols from around the world organized thematically. It includes sections on sacred trees, deities related to corn, and harvest rituals, for example. Morgan, a lawyer in Rochester, New York, abandoned the armchair to conduct field research over several years with the Iroquois of central New York (Patterson 2001:26). Morgan was interested in the main question of the time: whether living humans are all related to each other or are descended from different roots and therefore unrelated. He compared Native American kinship terms with Asian kinship terms and concluded that they were similar. On these grounds, he argued that Native Americans and Asian people were related, thus supporting the position that humanity is biologically and culturally one.

Polish-born Bronislaw Malinowski is generally considered the father of *participant observation*, the cornerstone research method of cultural anthropology. For his first research project, he spent many months living with people of the Trobriand Islands, off the east coast of Papua New Guinea, learning their language, eating their food, and trying to gain a comprehensive picture of all aspects of their culture from sexual behavior to canoe magic to musical instruments (Barnard 2000:66ff). By learning the local language, he was able to dispense with interpreters and thereby gain a much more direct understanding of Trobriand culture. Malinowski's work established a theoretical perspective called **functionalism** wherein a culture is viewed as similar to a biological organism with various parts working to support the operation and maintenance of the whole. Thus a culture's kinship system or religious system contributed to the functioning of the culture of which it was a part. The medical specialty of anatomy inspired this model.

Another landmark figure in cultural anthropology, whose impact extended to the discipline of anthropology as a whole, is Franz Boas. Born in Germany and educated there in physics and geography, Boas came to the United States in 1887 and played a major role in establishing anthropology in the United States during the first half of the twentieth century (Patterson 2001:46ff). He brought with him a skeptical view about Western science gained from a year's study with the Inuit of Baffin Island (see Map 3.1) where he learned that a physical substance such as "water" can be perceived very differently in different cultures. Boas recognized the plural validity of different cultures and is considered the father of the key concept **cultural relativism,** or the position that each culture must be understood in terms of the values and ideas of that culture and should not be judged by the standards of another. Accordingly, no culture is any more "advanced" than another. Boas thus launched an enduring critique of evolutionism in cultural anthropology.

Boas rejected comparison and theory-building and promoted **cultural particularism,** an emphasis on the uniqueness of each culture and on the need for detailed study and description of individual cultures within their own historical contexts. Boas built the discipline of anthropology in the United States through his role as a professor at Columbia University, where he trained many prominent students. He was an activist anthropologist and was inspired by a politically progressive philosophy to promote social justice, racial equality, and gender equality in the United States. Once he was commissioned by President Theodore Roosevelt to study the effects of the U.S. environment on immigrants and their children (Patterson 2001:49). He and his research team measured 17,821 people and concluded that head size responds quickly to environmental change and that, therefore, bodily form is not "racially" determined. His report was dismissed by the U.S. Immigration Commission and the Congress, which passed the Immigration Restriction Act in 1924. Boas was outraged and called the act racist and xenophobic (Patterson 2001:49).

In the 1950s, *environmental determinism,* the theory that environment shapes culture, arose in the United States as a prominent challenge to cultural particularism. This movement was led by two American anthropologists: Julian Steward and Leslie White. Although Steward's and White's theories differed in certain details, both gave primacy to material, environmental factors in shaping culture. In comparison to earlier, unilineal views of evolution (which says that all societies have to pass through the same stages), their model allowed for multilineal evolu-

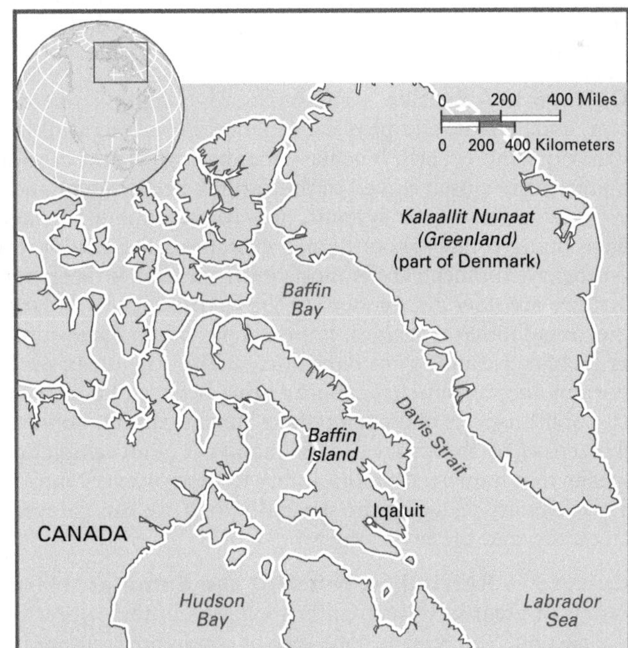

MAP 3.1 Baffin Island, or Inuktituk, Canada. The largest island in the Canadian territory of Nunavut, Inuktituk has a population of 11,000. Iqaluit, the capital of Nunavut province is located on the island.

functionalism: the view, established by Malinowski, that a culture is similar to a biological organism, with various parts supporting the operation of the whole.

cultural relativism: the view that cultures must be understood in terms of their own values and beliefs and not judged by the standards of another culture; the assumption that no culture.

cultural particularism: the view that each culture is unique and should be studied and described within its own historical context.

Franz Boas is considered the father of North American anthropology. He promoted the concept of cultural relativism, rejected the notion of biological "race," and supported a four-field approach to understanding humanity. ■ (*Source:* © Bettmann/CORBIS)

tion, with different stages occurring in different environmental contexts. Beginning in the 1960s, a related perspective emerged. **Cultural materialism** emphasizes examining the material aspects of life, such as the environmental context and how people make a living within particular environments. Marvin Harris is the anthropologist most closely associated with this perspective. This approach parallels processual theory in archaeology.

Another theoretical position, which also began gaining prominence in the 1960s, is **interpretive anthropology** or symbolic anthropology. This perspective emphasizes understanding culture by studying people's ideas, their interpretations of their lives, and the meanings that are important to them. Interpretive anthropology is an idealist view as opposed to the more behaviorist view (review Figure 3.1, p. 51). It emphasizes what people think as the most important part of culture. Leading proponents of the interpretivist/symbolic view are Clifford Geertz and Mary Douglas.

Characteristics of Culture

This section outlines some important characteristics of the elusive concept of culture. Culture is learned, adaptive, related to nature but not the same as nature, based on symbols, integrated, and always changing.

Culture Is Learned Culture is learned, not innate. Cultural learning begins from the moment of birth, if not before (some people think that an unborn baby takes in and stores information through sounds heard from the outside world). Much of people's cultural learning is unconscious, occurring as a normal part of life through observation and imitation. Schools, in contrast, emphasize formal learning, although much informal learning occurs in schools, too—through peer pressure, for example. Throughout most of humanity's prehistory and history, children learned appropriate cultural patterns by receiving guidance from elders, hearing stories, and watching performances. The learning of one's culture through a combination of direct and indirect means is referred to as enculturation.

cultural materialism: a technical approach to culture that emphasizes the material aspects of life, such as the environmental context and how people make a living in particular environments.

interpretivism or interpretive anthropology: a theoretical approach to culture that emphasizes what people think about, their explanations of their lives, and the meanings that are important to them. Also known as *symbolic anthropology*.

Primatologists' studies of culture in nonhuman primates point to two kinds of learning that differ in some ways from learning among humans (Alvard 2003). First is *imitation*, or learning through behavioral duplication. Young chimpanzees watch their mother using a stick to get termites out of a termite mound, and they repeat the action. The second form of learning is called *local enhancement*, or stimulus enhancement. This term refers to the increased probability that individuals will learn a trait on their own when they are exposed to the conditions that make the acquisition of the behavior likely. In this view, young chimpanzees learn to use sticks to collect termites not because they watch their mother and imitate her. Instead, given the proximity of sticks and termites, they are likely to learn on their own that using the sticks is an effective way to get food.

Culture Is Adaptive The story of humanity is one of adaptation and change in both biology (body size, body shape, and physical capabilities such as walking and talking) and culture (learned and shared behaviors and beliefs). It is likely that biological and cultural adaptations during the early evolution of humanity were closely linked to the natural environment and climate at the time.

Human economic systems, or ways of making a living, are basic elements of cultural adaptation that have changed throughout human evolution. The earliest ways of making a living were directly dependent on the environment: If the most preferred fruit is there, eat it; if not, go for second best. Many economic systems are now independent of the environment to a large extent and therefore reflect modern humans' greater adaptive capacities. For example, a computer software specialist can make a living while residing in Dublin, Ireland, or in Bangalore, India. As human evolution proceeded, culture became the most important adaptive mechanism mediating between humans and their environment (see Figure 3.2).

Some aspects of contemporary human culture, however, may be nonadaptive in that they are actually dangerous to the survival of humanity. The development and spread of weapons of mass destruction means that humans have the ability to destroy everyone on the planet. Now, as never before, our cultural capacities are changing more rapidly than we can foresee the costs and benefits to humans, other living creatures, and the environment.

Culture Is Related to, But Not the Same as, Nature The relationship between nature and culture is of great interest to anthropologists in their quest to understand people's behavior and thinking in the past and the present. One way of seeing how culture is related to, but diverges from, nature is to consider that basic "natural" demands of human life are met in different ways in different cultures. Take, for example, the biological functions that everyone must perform to stay alive: eating, drinking, sleeping, and eliminating (requirements for shelter and clothing vary, depending on the climate, and procreation is not necessary for individual survival). Living people have to perform these functions; otherwise, they would die. But it is impossible to predict how, when, or where these functions will be fulfilled. That is because culture plays a major role in defining how people eat, drink, sleep, and eliminate. Thus these functions are to a large extent arbitrary: They involve culturally shaped meanings.

FIGURE 3.2 A Reconstruction of an Upper Paleolithic Dwelling with Mammoth Bones as the Framework. Remains of such houses are found in Ukraine and central Asia.

Eating The human body requires certain nutrients for survival, but these nutrients can be provided in many ways. For example, eating meat is not necessary for survival. People living in vegetarian cultures have survived quite well without eating meat of any sort for centuries. Culture shapes what one eats, how one eats, and when one eats, and it affects ideas about eating.

Preferences about what tastes good vary markedly, and many examples exist of foods that are acceptable in one culture and not in another. In China, most people think that cheese is disgusting, but in France, most people love cheese. Another distinction exists between eating animals that are alive and animals that are dead. In a few cultures, consumption of live (or nearly live) creatures is considered a gourmet specialty; for example, one Philippine dish includes ready-to-be-born chicks. In many cultures where hunting and fishing are dominant ways of procuring food, people believe that the freshness of the catch is important. They consider canned meat or fish highly undesirable. Food and how it is consumed convey symbolic meaning about social status, gender, and age. For example, upper-class people in England eat dinner in a specific set of courses. Middle-class people are more likely to have fewer courses. In the United States, one stereotype is that "real men" do not eat quiche. Older people and younger people in the United States often go to different types of restaurants when they are eating out, not just because of the kind of food served but also because of ambience and social context.

Ethiopian women dining at an Ethiopian restaurant. The main meal consists of several meat and vegetable dishes, cooked with special spices and laid out on injera bread, a soft, flat bread that is torn into small pieces and used to wrap bite-sized bits of meat and vegetables. The entire meal can be eaten without utensils. ■ *How does this dining scene resemble or differ from a recent meal that you have had in a restaurant? (Source:* © Michael Newman/PhotoEdit)

Taste categories, too, are culturally constructed. Although anthropologists and other scientists have attempted to delineate universal taste categories into four basic types (sweet, sour, bitter, and salty), cross-cultural research disproves these four as universals. Among the Weyéwa people of the highlands of Sumba (see Map 3.2), an island in eastern Indonesia, the flavors recognized are sour, sweet, salty, bitter, tart, bland, and pungent (Kuipers 1991).

How to eat is another important aspect of food behavior. Rules about eating are one of the first things one confronts when entering another culture. Proper dining manners in India require that a person eat using only the right hand, because the left hand is reserved for cleaning oneself after elimination. A clean right hand is believed to be the purest dining implement, because silverware, plates, and glassware that have been touched by others, even though they have been washed, are never truly clean.

Drinking The cultural elaboration of drinking is as complex as that of eating. Every culture defines what is appropriate to drink, when to drink, and with whom. In French culture, it is normal to drink wine, not water, with lunch and dinner. In the United States, water typically accompanies lunch and dinner, although children are supposed to drink milk. In India one drinks water only after the meal is finished, not during the meal itself.

Different social categories of people drink different beverages. Particular drinks and the style of serving and drinking them, like food, have different meanings. If you were a guest and the host offered you a glass of water when you arrived, you might think it odd (just as you would if the host offered you a peanut butter and jelly sandwich for dinner). If your host explained that it was "sparkling water from France," you might be more impressed. In cultures where alcoholic beverages are consumed, men tend to consume more than women. Social drinking, whether the beverage is coffee, beer, or vodka, creates and reinforces bonds. Beer-drinking "rituals" of American college fraternities are a dramatic example. In a brief ethnographic film entitled *Salamanders*, made at a university in the northeastern United States, during parties the brothers run to various "stations" in the fraternity house, downing a beer at each (Hornbein and Hornbein 1992). At one point, the film shows us a brother who chugs a beer, turns with a

A Maya vessel from Belize, Central America, contains residues of cacao dated around 600 BCE. Documents from the time of the Spanish conquest indicate that liquid chocolate was poured from one pot to another to produce foam. The foam was the most desirable part of the drink. ■ *Compare this technology to ways of preparing and serving preferred hot drinks in your culture.* (*Source:* © Terry G. Powis/Photo courtesy of Thomas R. Hester)

stagger toward the next station, and then falls flat on his face and passes out. (Most of our students, as they watch the film, laugh when he falls down.) The movie also documents a drinking ritual in which both young men and women at some fraternity parties swallowed live salamanders, sometimes two or three at a time, with large gulps of beer.

Sleeping Common sense might say that sleep is the one natural function that is not shaped by culture, because people tend to do it every twenty-four hours, everyone shuts their eyes to do it, everyone lies down to do it, and almost everyone sleeps at night. Going without sleep for an extended period would eventually lead to insanity and even death.

There are, however, many cultural aspects to sleep, including the question of who sleeps with whom, how much sleep a person should have, and sleep disorders. Across cultures, marked variation exists in rules about where infants and children should sleep: with the mother, with both parents, or by themselves in a separate room? Among indigenous peoples of the Amazon region of South America, mothers and babies share the same hammock for many months, and breastfeeding occurs whenever the baby is hungry.

Culture often shapes the amount of time a person sleeps. In rural India, women sleep fewer hours than men because they have to get up earlier to start the fire for the morning meal. In fast-track, corporate North America, "type A" males sleep relatively few hours and are proud of that fact—to sleep too much is to be a wimp. A new disorder in Japan, called *excessive daytime sleepiness* (EDS), is especially common in Tokyo and other cities (Doi and Minowa 2003). Excessive sleepiness is correlated with more accidents on the job, more absenteeism, decreased productivity, deteriorated personal and professional relationships, and increased rates of illness and death. Women are almost twice as likely as men to experience EDS, and married women are especially vulnerable.

Eliminating Given its basic importance in cross-cultural experience, it is ironic that elimination receives little attention (in print) from anthropologists. Anyone who has traveled internationally knows that there is much to learn about elimination when in an unfamiliar context.

The first question is where to eliminate. Differences emerge in the degree to which elimination is a private act or can be done in more or less public areas. In many European cities, public options include street urinals for males but not for females. In most villages in India, houses do not have interior bathrooms. Instead, early in the morning, groups of women and girls leave the house and head for a certain field where they squat and chat. Men go to a different area. Everyone carries, in their left hand, a small brass pot full of water with which they splash themselves clean. Think about the ecological advantages: This system adds fertilizer to the fields and leaves no paper litter. Westerners may consider the village practice unclean and unpleasant, but village-dwelling people in India would think that the Western system is unsanitary because using toilet paper does not clean one as well as water, and they would find the practice of sitting on a toilet less comfortable than squatting.

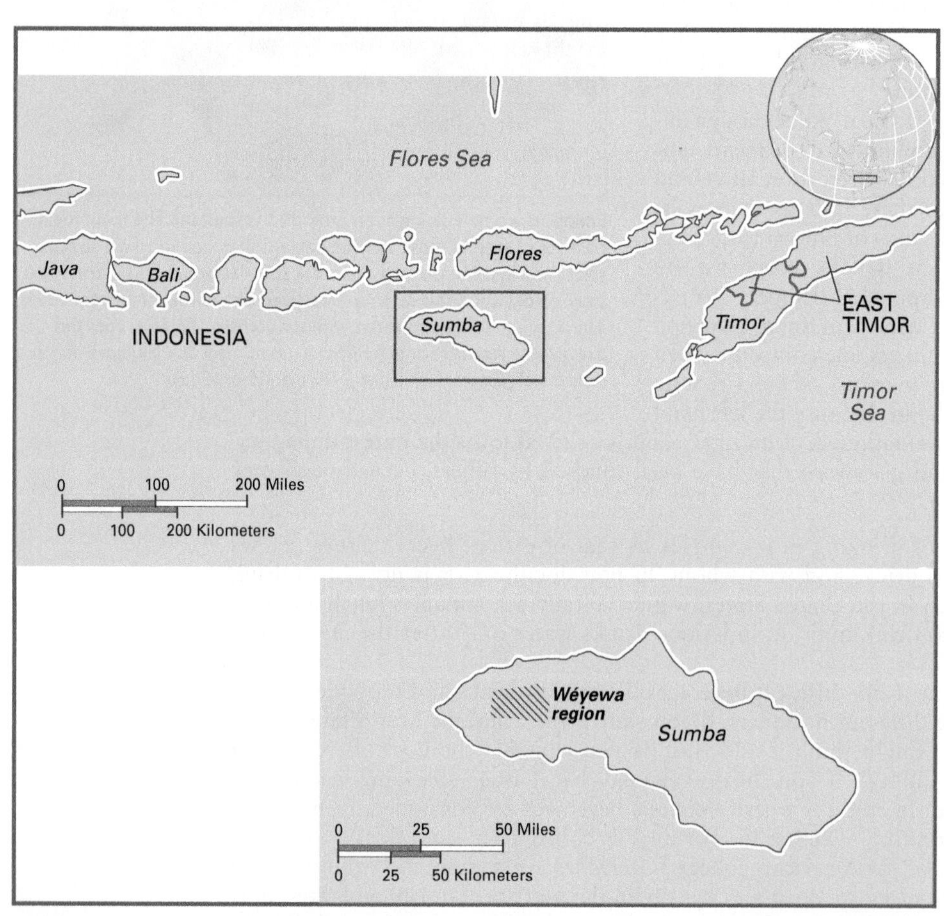

MAP 3.2 Sumba, Indonesia. One of the Lesser Sunda Islands, Sumba has a population of about 400,000. The ancestry of the Sumbanese is a mixture of Malay and Melanesian, and the indigenous languages are varieties of Austronesian.

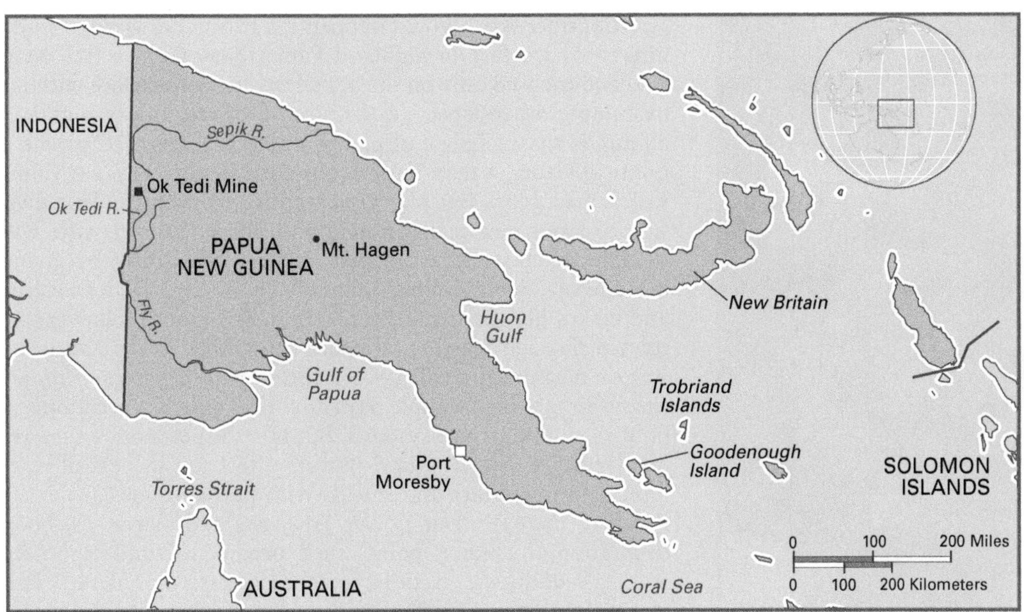

MAP 3.3 Papua New Guinea. The Independent State of Papua New Guinea gained its autonomy from Australia in 1975. Mostly mountainous with coastal lowlands, PNG is richly endowed with gold, copper, silver, natural gas, timber, oil, and fisheries. Its population is around 5,700,000. Port Moresby, the capital, has a high rate of HIV/AIDS infection among the working-age population.

In many cultures, the products of elimination (urine and feces) are considered polluting and disgusting. Among some groups in Papua New Guinea (see Map 3.3), people take great care to bury or otherwise hide their fecal matter for fear that someone will find it and use it for magic against them. A negative assessment of the products of elimination is not universal, however. Among some Native American cultures of the Pacific Northwest region of Canada and the United States, urine, especially women's urine, was believed to have medicinal and cleansing properties and was considered the "water of life" (Furst 1989). In some death rituals, it was sprinkled over the corpse in the hope that it might rejuvenate the deceased. People stored urine in special wooden boxes for ritual use, including for a baby's first bath (the urine was mixed with water for this purpose).

Culture Is Based on Symbols Our entire lives—from eating breakfast to greeting our friends, making money, creating art, and practicing religion—are based on and organized through symbols. A *symbol* is an object, word, or action with a culturally defined meaning that stands for something else with which it has no necessary or natural relationship. Symbols are arbitrary (bearing no necessary relationship to that which is symbolized), unpredictable, and diverse. Because symbols are arbitrary, it is impossible to predict how a particular culture will symbolize something. Although one might assume that people who are hungry would have an expression for hunger involving their stomach, no one could predict that in Hindi, the language of northern India, a colloquial expression for being hungry says that "rats are jumping in my stomach." The linguistic history of Barbara—the name of the author of this book—reveals that originally, in the Greek, it referred to people who were outsiders, "barbarians," and, by extension, uncivilized and savage. On top of that, the Greek term referred to such people as "bearded." The symbolic content of the American name Barbara does not immediately convey a sense of beardedness in its current context because symbolic meaning can change. It is through symbols that culture is shared, stored, and transmitted over time.

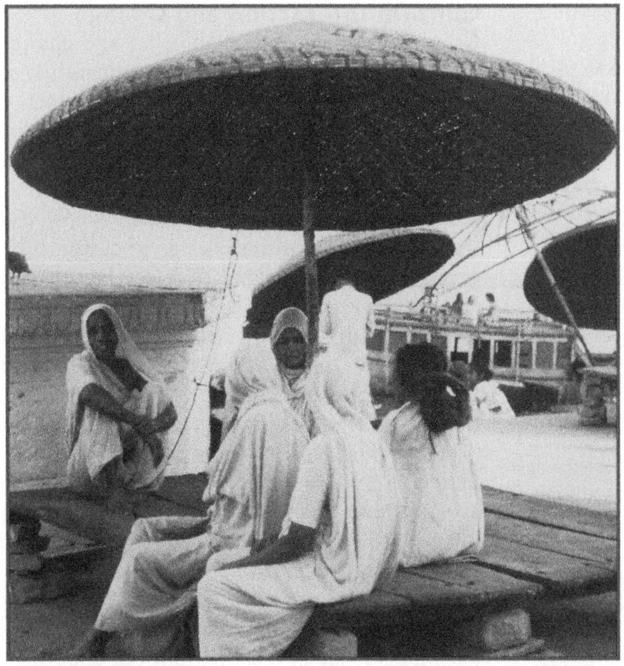

In India, a white sari (women's garment) symbolizes widowhood. ■ *What might these women think about the Western custom of a bride wearing white? (Source:* Barbara Miller)

Cultures Are Integrated To state that cultures are internally integrated is to assert the principle of holism. Thus, studying only one or two aspects of culture provides understanding so limited that it is more likely to be misleading or wrong than more comprehensive approaches.

Aymara women of the Andean highlands in South America wear distinctive clothing, including rounded hats made of felt and multicolored shawls. In the cities, this distinctive clothing is giving way to more cosmopolitan styles and the abandonment of the hat and shawl. ■ *What clues do you gather about people's culture from the clothing they wear? (Source: ©Wolfgang Kaehler/CORBIS)*

Consider what would happen if a researcher were to study intertribal warfare in highland Papua New Guinea (see Map 3.3) and focused only on the actual practice of warfare without examining other aspects of culture. A key feature of highland culture is the exchange of pigs at political feasts. To become a political leader, a man must acquire many pigs. Pigs eat yams, which men grow, but pigs are cared for by women. This division of labor means that a man with more than one wife will be able to maintain more pigs and rise politically by giving more feasts. Such feasting enhances an aspiring leader's status and makes his guests indebted to him. With more followers attracted through feasting, a leader can gather forces and wage war on neighboring villages. Success in war brings gains in territory. So far, this example pays attention mainly to economics, politics, and marriage systems. But other aspects of culture are involved, too. Supernatural powers affect the success of warfare. Painting spears and shields with particular designs is believed to increase their power. At feasts and marriages, body decoration (including paint, shell ornaments, and elaborate feather headdresses) is an important expression of identity and status. Looking at warfare without attention to its wider cultural context yields an extremely narrow view.

Cultural integration is relevant to applied anthropologists interested in proposing ways to promote positive change. Years of experience show that introducing programs for change in one aspect of culture without considering their effects in other domains is often detrimental to the welfare and survival of a culture. For example, Western missionaries and colonialists in parts of Southeast Asia banned the practice of head-hunting. This practice was connected to many other aspects of the people's culture, including politics, religion, and psychology (a man's sense of identity as a man sometimes depended on the taking of a head). Stopping head-hunting might seem like a good thing, but its cessation had disastrous consequences for the cultures in which it was practiced.

globalization: a contemporary process of cultural change related to dense and rapid linkages of trade, communication, population movement, and other forms of international and transnational contact.

localization: cultural change that occurs when global changes are received and transformed through interaction with existing cultures.

Cultural Interaction and Change

Cultures interact with each other and change each other through contact. Trade networks, international development projects, telecommunications, education, migration, and tourism are just a few of the factors that affect cultural change through contact. **Globalization**, the process of intensified global interconnectedness and movement of goods, information, and people, is a major force of contemporary cultural change. It has gained momentum through recent technological change, especially the boom in information and communications technologies (Pieterse 2004).

Globalization does not spread evenly, and its interactions with and effects on local cultures vary substantially from positive change to cultural destruction and extinction. Four models of cultural interaction capture some of the variation (see Figure 3.3). The *clash of civilizations* argument says that the spread of Euro-American capitalism and lifeways throughout the world has created disenchantment, alienation, and resentment among other cultural systems. This model divides the world into the "West and the rest."

The *McDonaldization* model says that, under the powerful influence of U.S.-dominated corporate culture, the world is becoming culturally homogeneous. "Fast-food culture," with its principles of mass production, speed, standardization, and impersonal service, is taken to be at the center of this new global culture.

Hybridization or *syncretism* is the third model. It occurs when aspects of two or more cultures are mixed to form something new—a blend. In Japan, for instance, a grandmother might bow in gratitude to an automated banking machine. In the Amazon region and in the Arctic, indigenous people use satellite imagery to map and protect the boundaries of their ancestral lands.

The fourth pattern of change is called **localization**. It refers to cultural change that occurs when global changes are received and transformed through interaction with existing cultures. There is no doubt that fast-food culture can now be found in many parts of the world, but anthropologists also provide strong evidence of localization. For example, in many countries, people resist the pattern of quick eating, insisting on leisurely family gatherings. The McDonald's managers in these contexts alter the pace of service in their restaurants to allow for this much slower turnover of tables.

Ethnocentrism and Cultural Relativism

Most people grow up thinking that their culture is the only way of life and that other ways of life are strange and inferior—and other people less than human. Anthropologists label this attitude **ethnocentrism:** judging other cultures by the standards of one's own culture rather than by the standards of those other cultures. Ethnocentric views have fueled centuries of efforts to change other people in the world, sometimes in the guise of religious missionary proselytizing, sometimes in the form of colonial domination.

The European colonial expansion that began in the fifteenth century was intended to extract wealth from the colonies. In addition to plundering their colonies, the Europeans ethnocentrically imposed their culture on indigenous groups. The British poet Rudyard Kipling reflected the prevailing view when he said that it was "the white man's burden" to spread British culture throughout the world. Christian missionaries played a major role in transforming non-Christian cultures.

Many contemporary Western powers exhibit similar attitudes, making foreign policy decisions that encourage the adoption of Western economic, political, and social systems. There is much that is good about many Western institutions, including democratic political processes, but the notion that these same institutions can work everywhere and should be transplanted to different contexts without modification is testimony that ethnocentrism is alive and well in the world today.

The opposite of ethnocentrism is cultural relativism, the idea that all cultures must be understood in terms of their own values and beliefs and should not be judged by the standards of another culture. Cultural relativism assumes that no culture is better than any other. How does a person gain a sense of cultural relativism? Besides living with other peoples, the best ways to develop a sense of cultural relativism include traveling (especially extended periods of study abroad), taking a course in cultural anthropology, eating different foods, listening to music from Appalachia or Brazil, reading novels by authors from other cultures, making friends who are "different" from you, and exploring the multicultural world on your campus. In sum, exposure to "other" ways, with a sympathetic eye and ear to understanding and appreciating differences, is the key.

One way in which some anthropologists have interpreted cultural relativism can be termed **absolute cultural relativism**, the conviction that whatever goes on in a particular culture must not be questioned or changed because no one has the right to question any behavior or idea anywhere—it would be ethnocentric to do so. But absolute cultural relativism can lead in dangerous directions. Consider the example of the Holocaust during World War II, in which millions of Jews and other minorities in much of Eastern and Western Europe were killed as part of the German Nazis' Aryan supremacy campaign. To be consistent with its own logic, the absolute cultural relativist position must maintain that, because the Holocaust was undertaken in accordance with the values of the culture, outsiders have no business questioning it.

Critical cultural relativism offers an alternative view that poses questions about cultural practices and ideas in terms of who accepts them and why, and who they might be harming or helping. In terms of the Nazi Holocaust, a critical cultural relativist would ask, "Whose culture supported the values that killed millions of people on the grounds of racial purity?" Not the cultures of the Jews, Gypsies, and other victims. It was the culture of Aryan supremacists, who were one subgroup among many. The situation was far more complex than a simple absolute cultural relativist statement takes into account, because there was not just one culture and its values involved. Rather, it was a case of *cultural imperialism*, in which one dominant group claims supremacy over minority cultures and proceeds to impose its will and exploit the situation in its own interests and at the expense of other cultures. Critical cultural relativism avoids the trap of adopting a homogenized view of complexity. It recognizes internal cultural differences and acknowledges the existence of winners and losers, oppressors and victims. It pays attention to different interests of various power groups. Beyond the clear case of the Nazi Holocaust, critical cultural relativism can be applied to illuminate many recent and contemporary conflicts, such as those in the former Yugoslavia, Rwanda, and Iraq.

A growing number of cultural anthropologists seek to critique the behavior and values of groups from the standpoint of some set of generally agreed-upon human rights. (Here *critique* means to probe underlying power interests, not just to make negative comments as in the general usage of the term *criticism.*) But even these anthropologists recognize how difficult it is to generate a universally agreed-on list

ethnocentrism: judging another culture by the standards of one's own culture rather than by the standards of the other culture, usually resulting in a negative view of the other culture.

absolute cultural relativism: the view that no one has the right to question any cultural behavior or idea anywhere because it would be ethnocentric to do so.

critical cultural relativism: the view that all cultures' practices and ideas should be examined in terms of who accepts them and why, and whom they might be harming or helping.

Clash of civilizations	Conflict model
McDonaldization	Takeover and homogenization model
Hybridization or syncretism	Blending model
Localization	Local cultural remaking and transforming of global culture

FIGURE 3.3 Four Models of Cultural Interaction

of values and principles different cultures view as good and right. Clearly, no single culture has the answer, and none has the right to dictate to others. As French anthropologist Claude Lévi-Strauss commented, "No society is perfect" (1968:385). While considering the "imperfections" of any and all cultures, anthropologists should examine and discuss their own biases and then try to view all cultures objectively. This means critiquing all cultures—one's own and "others"—on an equal basis.

This pre-Hispanic Maya calendar in stone was more accurate than European calendars, which required the Gregorian Reform to eliminate 11 days in 1572. It relies on a base-20 mathematics and a celestial cycle of 18,980 days. Western ethnocentrism often led to overlooking scientific achievements embedded in non-Western modes of thinking. ■ *In math and science classes you have taken, how much have you learned about non-Western ideas? (Source: ©* Otis Imboden/National Geographic Image Collection)

■ Multiple Cultural Worlds

Many microcultures exist within larger cultures (see Figure 3.4). A particular individual is likely to be a member of several microcultures. Microcultures may overlap or may be related to each other hierarchically in terms of power, status, and rights.

The contrast between *difference* and *hierarchy* is important. People and groups can be considered different from each other on a particular criterion, but may or may not be unequal. For example, people with blue or brown eyes might be recognized as different, but this difference does not entail unequal treatment or status. In other instances, such differences do become the basis for inequality.

Class
"Race," ethnicity, and indigeneity
Gender and sexuality
Age
Institution

FIGURE 3.4 Some Bases of Microcultures

Class

Class is a social category based on people's economic position in society, usually measured in terms of income or wealth and exhibited in terms of lifestyle. Class societies may be divided into upper, middle, and lower classes. Separate classes are, for example, the working class (people who trade their labor for wages) and the landowning class (people who own land on which they or others labor). Classes are related in a hierarchical system, with upper classes dominating lower classes. Class struggle, in the classic Marxist view, is inevitable as those at the top seek to maintain their position while those at the bottom seek to improve theirs. People at the bottom may attempt to improve their class position by gaining access to resources and by adopting aspects of upper-class symbolic behavior, such as speech, dress, and leisure and recreation.

class: a social category based on people's economic position in society, usually measured in terms of income or wealth and exhibited in lifestyle.

"race": a group of people defined in terms of selected biological traits, usually phenotypical features; now discredited as lacking scientific validity.

Class is a recent social development in human history, extending back in time for only 12,000 years or more, and still not found in many local cultures. Among the few relatively undisturbed groups of indigenous peoples, everyone has equal wealth and sharing food and other resources among the group is expected.

"Race," Ethnicity, and Indigenous Peoples

Race refers to groups of people with supposedly homogenous biological traits. The term "race" is extremely complicated as it is used in diverse ways in different parts of the world and among different groups of people. Therefore, it makes sense to put the word in quotation marks in order to highlight its multiple meanings. In South Africa, as in the United States, "race" is mainly defined on the basis of skin color. In pre–twentieth-century China, body hair was the key biological basis for racial classification (Dikötter 1998). The "barbarian" races had more body hair than the "civilized" Chinese people. Chinese writers referred to bearded, male missionaries from Europe as "hairy barbarians." Into the twentieth century, some Chinese anthropologists divided humans into evolutionary stages on the basis of amounts of body hair.

Anthropological and other scientific research demonstrates that biological features do not explain or account for a person's behavior or lifestyle. Boas proved this point a century ago, and studies continue to pile up evidence. Rather than being a biological category, racial classifications are cultural constructions. They are often associated with discrimination against and cruelty toward those "races" considered less worthy by those in power. Examples are numerous. A notion of racial purity justified Hitler in his program of exterminating Jews and others who were not of the Aryan "race." Racial apartheid in South Africa denied citizenship, security, and a decent life to all those labeled "Black." In the United States, although racism is denied politically, it exists in many domains. African American political scientist Andrew Hacker states that race is the most important criterion of social difference in the United States (1992). In his book, *Two Nations: Black and White, Separate, Hostile, Unequal*, he writes that no one who is White in the United States can truly understand what it is like to be Black.

Ethnicity refers to a shared sense of identity among a group based on a heritage, language, or culture. Examples include African Americans and Italian Americans in the United States, the Croats of Eastern Europe, the Han of China, and the Hutu and Tutsi of Rwanda. This sense of identity is sometimes expressed through political movements to gain or protect group rights and recognition or more quietly stated in how one lives one's daily life. It can be a basis for social ranking, for claims to resources such as land or other property, and for social identity. Among many Native American groups in South and North America, ethnicity is an important basis of cultural revival.

A view into the yard of a house of a low-income neighborhood of Kingston, Jamaica. ■ *Why do you think people in these neighborhoods prefer the term low-income to poor?* (*Source:* Barbara Miller)

Compared to the term "race," ethnicity appears to be a more neutral, less stigmatizing term. But it, too, has been, and still is, a basis for discrimination, segregation, and oppression. The "ethnic cleansing" campaigns conducted in the early 1990s by the Serbs against Muslims in the former Yugoslavia are an extreme case of ethnic discrimination. In China, Han ethnic domination over minority ethnic groups has been a reality for centuries. Han political repression of the Tibetan people prompted thousands of Tibetans to flee their homeland. Living in exile, they struggle to keep their ethnic heritage alive.

Indigenous peoples, following guidelines laid down by the United Nations, are defined as groups who have a long-standing connection with their home territory predating colonial or other societies that prevail in their territory (Sanders 1999). They are typically a numerical minority and often have lost the rights to their original territory. The United Nations distinguishes between indigenous peoples and *minority ethnic groups* such as the Roma, the Tamils of Sri Lanka, and African Americans. This distinction is more useful in some contexts than others (Maybury-Lewis 1997b). Many indigenous groups are now taking active steps to recover their lost lands, to revive their forgotten languages and rituals, and to build a new and stronger future for themselves through various forms of organization and resistance to negative outside forces. Often, anthropologists have been able to support these efforts through their research (see Lessons Applied box.)

ethnicity: a sense of group affiliation based on a distinct heritage or worldview as a "people."

indigenous peoples: a group with a long-standing connection with a home territory that predates colonial or outside societies prevailing in the territory.

gender: culturally constructed and learned behaviors and ideas associated with masculinity, femininity, or a "third," or blended, gender. Gender is contrasted to sex, which uses biological markers to define categories of male and female.

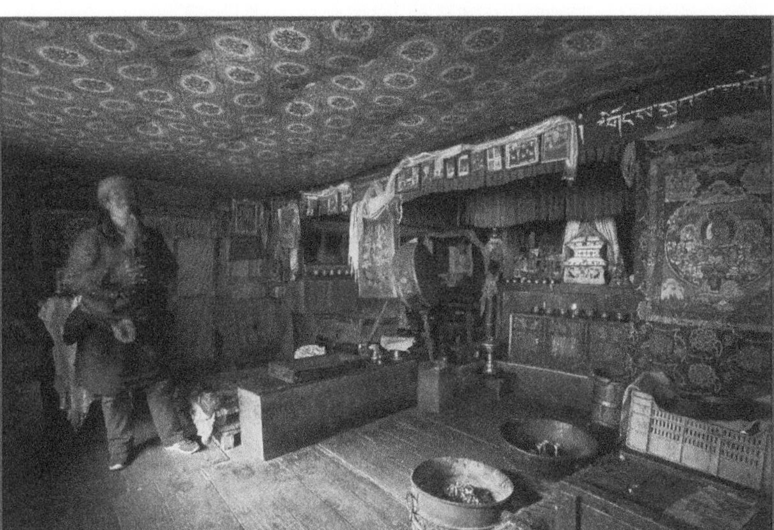

Many Tibetans have left their homeland as refugees since China took control of the region. Most live in India and Nepal. This scene is the inside of a Tibetan Buddhist monastery in Nepal. ■ *Do some Internet research to learn about current policies in Nepal toward Tibetan refugees.* (*Source:* © Galen Rowell/CORBIS)

Box 3.1 Lessons Applied

Historical Archaeology and the Story of the Northern Cheyenne Outbreak of 1879

The Northern Cheyenne long resisted the takeover of their native lands in Montana, first by Euro-American settlers in the latter half of the nineteenth century and then, since the mid-twentieth century, by energy companies (McDonald et al. 1991). They have also resisted the dominant culture's telling of their history. The Cheyenne collaborated with historical archaeologists from the University of South Dakota Archaeology Laboratory to document their version of an incident in their resistance to domination, the Cheyenne "Outbreak" from Fort Robinson, Nebraska, in the winter of 1879.

For several generations, some Cheyenne have accepted the White version of the Outbreak. The story begins with the signing by several chiefs in 1867 of a treaty they did not fully understand. The treaty provided for the relocation of Cheyenne people from Montana to "Indian Territory" in present-day Oklahoma. Once this condition was understood, a party of chiefs traveled to Washington, DC, to inform President Grant of their desire to remain in their homelands. Grant allowed them to stay, temporarily. After the Custer Massacre at Little Big Horn, the Cheyenne chiefs feared reprisals, even though the Cheyenne were not involved in the battle. Over the next few years, the U.S. military attacked Cheyenne settlements, destroying their food supply, killing their horses, and driving them from their homes. Under the leadership of Chief Dull Knife, the Cheyenne agreed to move south on what they considered to be a trial basis. Many fell ill and died during the difficult 70-day journey.

Two years later, the U.S. military told Dull Knife that his group would be relocated again. On the way to the new location, some of the Cheyenne tried to escape but were recaptured, locked into barracks, and told they had to move south. Dull Knife refused to return to the "land of sickness." Their food and water supplies were cut off in order to force their submission. With only a few guns, Dull Knife's people broke out from the barracks on an evening in January 1879. Nearly half of them were killed in the ensuing battle, but the survivors fled via an escape route toward home. They were recaptured after 11 days; most of them were killed.

The controversy between White and Cheyenne accounts of the Outbreak concerns the escape route. The White narrative designates Area C, a long, barren ridge. The Cheyenne version, has the route going through Areas A and B. Archaeological fieldwork was conducted to check the accuracy of each version. Representatives of the Northern Cheyenne tribes provided geographic information. They also ensured the spiritual integrity of the project by incorporating prayers and story-telling into the research, a practice that expressed reverence for the land and artifacts. Methods included visual inspection, random shovel testing, and use of metal detectors. Most of the artifacts were spent ammunition. No artifacts of any kind were found in Area C, whereas a number of artifacts likely to have been deposited during the Cheyenne Outbreak were found in Areas A and B. With no firm evidence that they went into Area C it is more likely, then, that they chose a route through terrain that provided natural cover. The deeper significance of this controversy lies in the fact that if Area C was the escape route, then Dull Knife and his people made a serious mistake, taking a route that would expose them as easy targets on what was a brightly moonlit night. The collaboration between the Northern Cheyenne and the archaeologists helped the Cheyenne validate their version of their history. It demonstrated the

Gender

Gender refers to culturally constructed and learned behaviors and ideas attributed to males, females, or sometimes a blended or "third" gender. Gender can be contrasted to sex, which uses biological markers to define categories of male and female. Cultural anthropology shows that a person's biological makeup does not necessarily correspond to gender. Only a few tasks, such as nursing infants, are tied to biology.

Cross-culturally, gender differences vary from societies in which male and female roles and worlds are similar or overlapping to those in which genders are sharply differentiated. In much of rural Thailand, males and females are about the same size, their clothing is similar, and their agricultural tasks are complementary and often interchangeable (Potter 1977). In contrast, among many groups in highland Papua New Guinea, extreme gender segregation exists in most aspects of life, including the kinds of food men and women eat (Meigs 1984). The men's house physically and symbolically separates the worlds of men and women. Men engage in rituals that purge them of female substances: nose or penis bleeding, vomiting, tongue scraping, sweating, and eye washing. Men possess sacred flutes, which they use of archaeology to support indigenous people's resistance to dominant cultural narratives. It also showed that the different interests of Native Americans, who seek knowledge of their cultural history and identity, and of archaeologists, who seek data about land and materials controlled by the tribes, are both served through collaboration and mutual respect.

Food for Thought

- Go to the Web and learn about Dull Knife Memorial College and the current status of the Cheyenne Outbreak Trail.

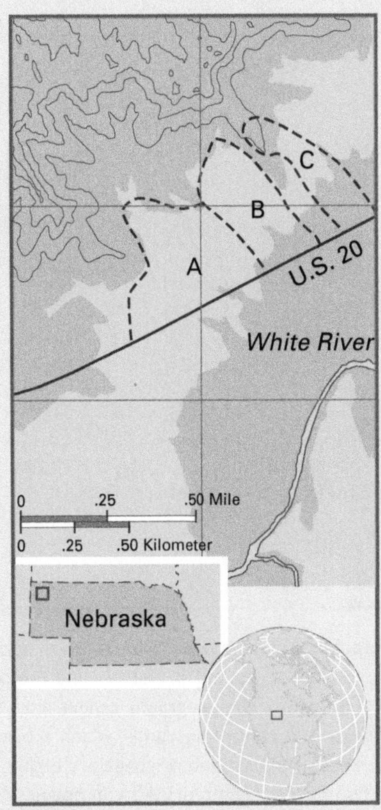

MAP 3.4 Northern Cheyenne Survey Project, Nebraska, United States. The Cheyenne version of the Outbreak involves sectors A and B, which is confirmed by archaeological evidence. (Source: *Adapted from p. 69, "The Northern Cheyenne Outbreak of 1879: Using Oral History and Archaeology as Tools of Resistance" by J. Douglas McDonald et al. In The Archaeology of Inequality, ed. by Randall H. McGuire and Robert Paynter. Cambridge, MA: Basil Blackwell, 1991.)*

parade though the village from time to time. If women dare to look at the flutes, men traditionally had the right to kill them.

Age

The human life cycle, from birth to old age, takes people through cultural stages for which appropriate behavior and thinking must be learned anew. In many African herding societies, elaborate age categories for males define their roles and status as they move from being boys with few responsibilities and little status, to young men who are warriors and live apart from the rest of the group, to adult men who are allowed to marry, have children, and become respected elders. "The Hill," or the collective members of the United States Senate and the House of Representatives, is a highly age-graded microculture (Weatherford 1981). The Hill is a *gerontocracy* (a group ruled by senior members) in which the older politicians dominate younger politicians in terms of amount of time for speaking and how much attention a person's words receive. It may take a junior member between ten and twenty years to become as effective and powerful as a senior member.

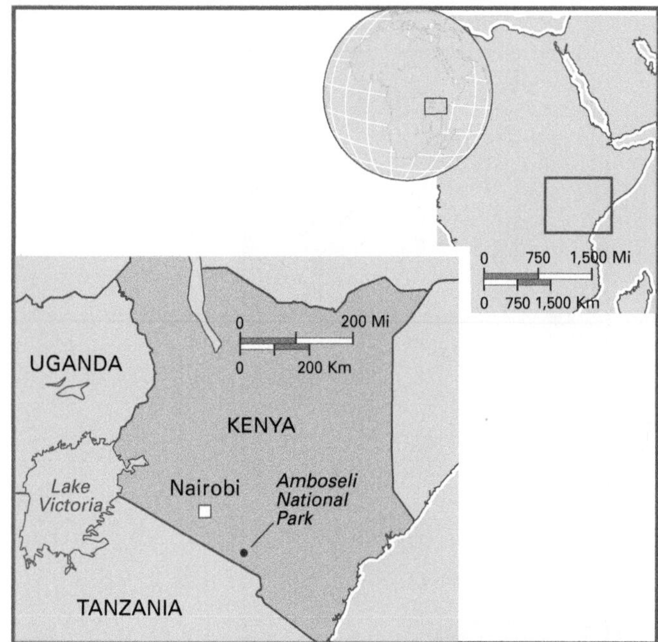

MAP 3.5 Kenya. The Republic of Kenya has a population of about 35 million people. The capital and largest city is Nairobi and the official languages are Swahili and English. The geography ranges from the Indian Ocean coastal region to the central highlands, which are split by the Great Rift Valley. Ethnicity, religion, and language are highly diverse. One of the most famous contemporary African novels, *Weep Not Child*, was written by a Kenyan, Ngugi wa Thiong'o; it is about life in Kenya during the British occupation.

■ Crossing the Fields

Elderly Females Take the Lead in Baboon Societies

Beginning in 1971, several decades of observation of baboons in Amboseli National Park, southern Kenya, reveal a pattern in which an elderly female serves as a leader at critical times in group movements (Altmann 1998). Adult males are usually in the forefront during actual fights with predators or other baboon groups. In such instances, each individual seems to decide for itself whether to threaten the intruders, hang back, or flee.

The decisive role of elderly females appears at controversial points in group movements when the question is which route to take. An elderly female typically makes the choice that is followed. The researchers wonder why the "opinions" of these females carry so much weight. It is not necessarily because of social rank: Elderly females of high, middle, and low social rank have been observed to take the lead. A more promising explanation lies in the number of female offspring an elderly female has. Among baboons, females are the permanent members of the group, whereas males move to another group at maturity. An elderly female with many female offspring has a large following. This explanation works in most cases, but there are some elderly female leaders who have few offspring and some females with many offspring who do not assume leadership roles.

Another possible explanation is the size of an individual female's social network beyond her offspring. Bearing offspring is a time when social networks are extended and affirmed as relatives and acquaintances cluster around the infant and mother. These ties are reinforced through grooming. For males, social relationships are less enduring—though of broader range—given the fact that they leave their birth group, have to establish themselves in another group, and may change groups several times.

Food for Thought

- Think about what your microculture involves in terms of residence during adulthood. How does staying in or near one's home area, or moving away from it, affect friendship and other ties?

Mother baboons and offspring, Kenya. (*Source:* © Joe McDonald/CORBIS)

Native American dancers perform at the annual Gateway Pow Wow in Brooklyn, New York. ■ *Are there examples in any of your microcultural experiences of attempts to revitalize aspects of the culture? (Source:* © CRDPHOTO/CORBIS)

Institutions

Institutions, or enduring group settings formed for a particular purpose, have their own characteristic microcultures. Institutions include hospitals, boarding schools and universities, and prisons. Anyone who has entered such an institution has experienced a feeling of strangeness. Until you gain familiarity with the often unwritten cultural rules, you may do things that offend or puzzle people, that fail to get you what you want, and that make you feel marginalized and insecure.

Relationships of power and inequality exist within institutions and between different institutions. These relationships cut across those of other microcultures, such as gender. Schools, like hospitals and prisons, have their own institutional cultures. Anthropologists who study educational institutions show that schools often replicate and reinforce stereotypes, power relations, and inequalities of the wider society. A study of middle schools in the southwestern Rocky Mountain region of the United States found a situation in which teachers marginalized Mexican immigrant girls (Meador 2005). In this school, Mexican immigrant students are labeled as ESL (English as a second language) students because they are not fluent in English and take special courses designed to improve their English. So, from the start, language and labeling are problems for these students. In addition, the teachers' mental model of a "good student" is a student who is:

- Motivated to do well in school and gets good grades
- An athlete
- Popular and has good students as friends
- Comes from a stable family

It is impossible for Mexican immigrant children to conform to this image. Mexicana girls are especially disadvantaged because most are not interested in, or good at, sports. The few Mexicana girls who are motivated to try to get good grades are consistently overlooked by the teachers who instead call on students who are confident, bright, and popular, and who sit in front of the classroom and raise their hands eagerly.

Valuing and Sustaining Diversity

Most anthropologists value and are committed to cultural diversity just as environmentalists value biological diversity and are committed to sustaining it. Thus cultural anthropologists deeply regret the decline and extinction of different cultures. Anthropologists contribute to the preservation of cultural diversity by describing cultures as they have existed, as they now exist, and as they change. Many cultural anthropologists have become advocates or activists in the area of cultural survival. An organization called Cultural Survival has been helping indigenous peoples and ethnic minorities deal as equals in their interactions with outsiders. Cultural Survival's guiding principle is:

> We insist that cultural differences are inherent in humanity; protecting this human diversity enriches our common earth. Yet in the name of development and progress, native peoples lose their land, their natural resources, and control over their lives. The consequences often are disease, destitution, and despair—and war and environmental damage for us all. The destruction is not inevitable. (www. culturalsurvival. org)

Cultural Survival sponsors programs to help indigenous peoples and ethnic minorities help themselves in protecting and managing natural resources, claiming land rights, and diversifying their means of livelihood (see inside front cover of this book).

Contemporary Debates about Culture

Within anthropology, enduring theoretical debates both divide the discipline and give it coherence. Three important contemporary debates, discussed here, will resurface throughout the book. Each is concerned with the basic question of how people behave and think and why they behave and think the way they do.

Biological Determinism versus Cultural Constructionism

biological determinism: a theory that says genes and hormones shape human culture.

cultural constructionism: a theory that says learning shapes culture.

agency: the ability of an individual to make choices and exercise free will.

Biological determinism seeks to explain why people do and think what they do by considering biological factors such as people's genes and hormones. Thus, biological determinists search for the gene or hormone that might lead to behavior such as homicide, alcoholism, or adolescent stress (see Critical Thinking box). They examine cultural practices in terms of how these contribute to the "reproductive success of the species," or how they contribute to the gene pool of subsequent generations by boosting the number of surviving offspring produced in a particular population. Behaviors and ideas that have reproductive advantages are more likely than others to be passed on to future generations. Biological determinists, for example, have provided an explanation for why human males apparently have "better" spatial skills than females. They say that these differences are the result of evolutionary selection because males with "better" spatial skills would have an advantage in securing both food and mates. Males with "better" spatial skills impregnate more females and have more offspring with "better" spatial skills.

Cultural constructionism, in contrast, maintains that human behavior and ideas are best explained as products of culturally shaped learning. In terms of the example of "better" male spatial skills, cultural constructionists would provide evidence that such skills are passed on culturally through learning, not genes. They would say that parents and teachers socialize boys and girls differently in spatial skills and are more likely to promote learning of certain kinds of spatial skills among boys. Anthropologists who favor cultural construction and learning as an explanation for behaviors such as homicide and alcoholism point to childhood experiences and family roles as being more important than genes or hormones. Although most cultural anthropologists are cultural constructionists, many connect biology and culture in their work.

Interpretivism versus Cultural Materialism

The two perspectives considered here, interpretivism and cultural materialism, differ in terms of how culture should be studied and understood. Interpretivism focuses on understanding culture by studying what people think about, their explanations of their lives, and the meanings that are important to them. Thus interpretivists largely have an idealist view of what culture is, and this view shapes their approach to studying culture. Cultural materialism, in contrast, seeks to explain beliefs and behavior in terms of how they are related to questions of making a living and other "material" aspects of life.

A famous example of this debate concerns India's many cows. To interpretivists, this phenomenon is best understood by paying attention to Hindu beliefs about cows as sacred animals that must not be killed and that must be protected in their old age. On the other side, cultural materialists maintain that there are many cows in India because they are important economically. Cows, even when scrawny-looking to a Wisconsin farmer, are worth more alive than dead (Harris 1974). They can be used for plowing fields and are less costly than motorized equipment to the farmer and to the environment, because fossil fuel is not needed to run them. As they wander along village lanes and city streets, they consume trash (including wet garbage such as orange peels and dry materials such as paper and cast-off clay drinking cups), which they transform into dung. The dung is collected and used as farm fertilizer or, after being mixed with straw and dried as patties, as cooking fuel. For these reasons, cultural materialists would say that the sacredness of cows among Hindus provides a form of religious protection against the killing of these economically useful animals.

THINKING OUTSIDE THE BOX

IMAGINE THAT you are on a debating team. The issue is cars in the United States. Prepare to support both an interpretivist and a cultural materialist position about how to understand why people in the United States have so many cars.

Individual Agency versus Structurism

This debate concerns the question of how much individual will, or agency, affects the way people behave and think, compared with the power of major forces, or "structures," that are beyond individual control. Western philosophical thought gives much emphasis to the role of **agency**, the ability of individuals to make choices and exercise free will. In contrast, structurism holds that free choice is an illusion because choices are structured by forces such as the economy, social and political organizations, and ideological systems.

Box 3.2 Critical Thinking

Adolescent Stress: Biologically Determined or Culturally Constructed?

Margaret Mead, one of the first trained anthropologists of North America, went to Samoa in 1925 to study child-rearing patterns and adolescent behavior. She sought to answer these questions (1961:24):

- Are the disturbances that vex adolescents in the United States due to the nature of adolescence itself or to the culture?
- Under different cultural conditions, does adolescence vary?

Mead observed and interviewed fifty adolescent girls of three different villages. Her conclusion, published in the famous book *Coming of Age in Samoa* (1961 [1928]), was that Samoan children grew up in a relaxed and happy atmosphere. As young adolescents, their transition to adulthood was sexually free and unrepressed. These findings had a major impact on thinking about child rearing in North America, prompting more relaxed forms of child rearing in the hope of raising less stressed adolescents.

In 1983, five years after Mead's death, Australian anthropologist Derek Freeman published a critique of Mead's work, saying that that her findings on adolescence were wrong. Freeman, a biological determinist, believes that adolescents everywhere are driven by hormonal changes that cause social and psychological upheavals. He pointed to two flaws in Mead's work. First, he says her fieldwork was inadequate because she spent a short time in the field (nine months) and had insufficient knowledge of the Samoan language. Second, he believes that her theoretical bias against biological determinism led her to overlook evidence that was contrary to her interests.

Freeman also marshals statistical evidence against Mead's position. He compares rates of adolescent delinquency in Samoa and England and finds that they are similar. In sum, he argues that sexual puritanism and social repression characterized Samoan adolescence and that adolescence is universally a difficult time.

Freeman's critique prompted a vigorous response from several cultural anthropologists in defense of Mead. One of these is Eleanor Leacock, an expert on how colonialism affects indigenous cultures. She claims that Freeman's position fails to take history into account: Mead's findings apply to Samoa of the 1920s, whereas Freeman's data are from the 1960s. By the 1960s, Samoan society had undergone radical cultural change because of World War II and intensive exposure to Western influences, including Christian missionaries. Freeman's data, in Leacock's view, do not contradict Mead's findings because they are from a different period.

Critical Thinking Questions

- Mead felt that finding one "negative case" (the absence of adolescent stress in Samoa) was sufficient to disprove the view that adolescent stress is a cultural universal. Do you agree that one negative case is sufficient?
- If an anthropologist found that a practice or pattern of behavior was universal, does that necessarily mean that it is biologically driven?

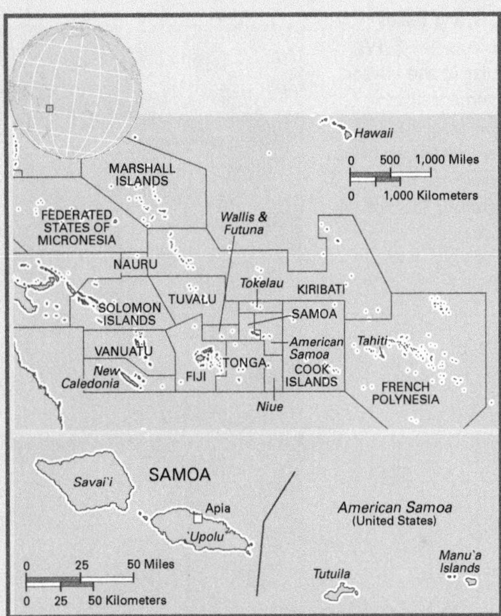

MAP 3.6 Samoa, American Samoa, and the South Pacific. Samoa, or the Independent State of Samoa, was known as German Samoa (1900–1919) and Western Samoa (1914–1997) until recognized by the United Nations as a sovereign country. Its population is around 177,000. American Samoa, or Amerika Samoa in Samoan English, is a territory of the United States with a population of about 57,000. During World War II, U.S. Marines in American Samoa outnumbered the local population and had a strong cultural influence. Unemployment rates are now high and the U.S. military is the largest employer.

(Top) Traffic in the city of Varanasi (Banaras), in northern India. Foreign visitors to India have often commented that the presence of wandering cows is a sign of wastefulness and inefficiency. ■ (*Source:* © Jack Fields/CORBIS)

(Bottom) SUVs, trucks, and buses share the road in Los Angeles. SUVs are increasingly popular in the United States even as environmentalists criticize them for their poor gas mileage. ■ *If you were an energy policy maker, what lessons would you draw from these two photographs? (Source:* AP/Wide World Photos)

For example, explaining why people are poor, unemployed, or on welfare in the United States has been approached from both positions by anthropologists and others. Those who emphasize agency in explaining behavior and ideas say that people are poor, unemployed, or on welfare by their own (direct or indirect) choice. If they wished, they could choose to be otherwise. Structurists would say that the poor and unemployed are trapped by structural forces and cannot escape these traps. They would argue that the people at the bottom of the economic ladder have little opportunity to exercise choice about being elsewhere than at the bottom.

Beyond the Debates: Holists at Heart

Some anthropologists emphasize people's ideas as the most important feature of humanity and human culture, whereas others look first to how people make their living and organize themselves in groups.

Besides having different theoretical positions, some anthropologists apply the findings of their research to solving or preventing real-world problems, whereas others stick more to academic pursuits. In spite of the diversity among anthropologists, anthropologists are deeply interested in just about everything having to do with humanity, including its past, its present, and its future. Anthropologists are all, more or less, holists at heart.

The Big Questions Revisited

WHAT is culture?

Culture is a central concept of anthropology. Archaeologists devote their efforts to studying cultures of the past, and cultural anthropologists study cultures of the present. Much of linguistic anthropology looks at the cultural aspects of communication. Biological anthropologists consider the intersections between people's biological heritage and their culture.

Although anthropologists disagree about how to define culture, they agree that it is learned and shared. Idealists say that culture consists of learned and shared beliefs, ideas, and motivations. Behaviorists maintain that culture is learned and shared behavior. Holists, taking a comprehensive view, say that culture is both learned and shared beliefs and behavior. Most anthropologists are more likely to be holists than to be pure idealists or behaviorists.

Because culture is so difficult to define, anthropologists sometimes refer instead to its characteristics: It is learned, adaptive, related to (but not the same as) nature, based on symbols, integrated, and ever-changing.

Anthropologists coined the terms *ethnocentrism* and *cultural relativism*. Opposites of each other, the first refers to a position that judges other cultures by the standards of one's own culture. Cultural relativism is the idea that cultures can be understood only in terms of their own values. The terms *absolute cultural relativism* and *critical cultural relativism* add complexity and depth to these issues.

WHAT are some bases of cultural diversity?

Cultures exist at different levels, macro and micro, and are based on several social factors, including class, "race," ethnicity and indigenous status, gender, age, and institutional context. These factors are sometimes associated with inequality and discrimination. The Crossing the Fields section shows how gender and age affect status and decision making among a baboon population in southern Kenya, thus demonstrating the importance of these factors among nonhuman primates as well as among humans.

A general anthropological principle is that diversity (as distinct from inequality) is valuable because different cultural "blueprints for life" offer possibilities for human sustainability into the future.

WHAT do anthropologists debate about culture?

Anthropology has a rich history of theoretical approaches and changing topics. Three enduring debates about culture exist in the discipline of anthropology. The first is the debate between biological determinism and cultural constructionism. In biological determinism, biology is more or less destiny. Genes, hormones, and chromosomes determine human behavior and thinking. In cultural constructionism, learning, or enculturation, is the more powerful factor shaping the way people act and think. Margaret Mead's research among adolescents in Samoa in the 1920s supports a constructionist view of adolescence.

In the second major debate, interpretivists say that emphasis should be placed on studying people's beliefs and ideas, whereas cultural materialists emphasize studying economic and other material aspects of life.

In the third debate, the position that speaks for human agency says that individuals have substantial choice and power in shaping what they do and believe, whereas the structurists feel that, although human agency does exist, powerful structures such as economics, the media, and governments shape human culture and limit human choices.

In spite of these spirited debates, anthropologists agree that it is important to study humanity's past, present, and future; they are holists at heart.

Key Concepts

absolute cultural relativism, p. 61
agency, p. 68
behaviorism, p. 51
biological determinism, p. 68
class, p. 62
critical cultural relativism, p. 61
cultural constructionism, p. 68
cultural materialism, p. 56
cultural particularism, p. 55
cultural relativism, p. 55
ethnicity, p. 63
ethnocentrism, p. 61
functionalism, p. 55
gender, p. 64
globalization, p. 60
holism, p. 51

idealism, p. 51
indigenous peoples, p. 63
interpretism or interpretive anthropology, p. 56
linguistic relativism, p. 53
localization, p. 60
macroculture, p. 51
microculture, p. 51
postmodernist archaeology, p. 52
postprocessual archaeology, p. 52
processualism, p. 52
"race," p. 62
structuralism, p. 53

Suggested Readings

John J. Bodinger de Uriarte. *Casino and Museum: Representing Mashantucket Pequot Identity*. Tucson: University of Arizona Press, 2007. The Mashantucket Pequot Museum and Research Center and Foxwoods is the largest casino in the Western hemisphere. This book explores how Mashantucket generates economic benefits as well as legitimizes the tribe's identity.

Chip Colwell-Chanthaphonh. *Massacre at Camp Grant: Forgetting and Remembering Apache History*. Tucson: University of Arizona Press, 2007. This book weaves together archival evidence, narratives, and ethnographic research to shed light on the 1871 massacre of over 100 Apache men, women, and children who had surrendered to the U.S. Army near Tucson, Arizona. It shows how historical trauma and painful memories live on in people's collective memories.

Charles E. Orser Jr. *Race and Practice in Archaeological Interpretation*. Philadelphia: University of Pennsylvania Press, 2004. The author makes a case that historical archaeologists have an obligation to study "race"-based inequalities that existed in the past. He discusses conceptual differences between "race" and ethnicity, probes how to read "race" in archaeological materials, and provides an in-depth examination of "the practice of race" in nineteenth-century Ireland.

Jan Nederveen Pieterse. *Globalization and Culture: Global Mélange*. New York: Rowman and Littlefield, 2004. This book provides an overview of arguments about how globalization affects culture, paying special attention to three major paradigms: the clash of civilizations, McDonaldization, and hybridization. The last two chapters focus on hybridization and antihybridization backlashes.

Colin Samson. *A Way of Life that Does Not Exist: Canada and the Extinguishment of the Innu*. New York: Verso, 2003. Colonial assimilationist policies are apparent in the living conditions of Innu communities of Davis Inlet, Labrador. Each chapter in this book focuses on how a Euro-Canadian institution (housing, education, law, religion, and health) has been imposed on a people who have never signed a treaty or given their permission to be ruled by the Canadian state.

Richard A. Shweder. *Why Do Men Barbecue? Recipes for Cultural Psychology*. Cambridge, MA: Harvard University Press, 2003. This collection of essays provides a cultural relativist's view on topics such as whether and how long infants sleep with their parents, morality and suffering, emotions, women's roles, science, and religious beliefs.

4 chapter

Science, Biology, and Evolution

THE BIG QUESTIONS

- *WHAT is the scientific view about humanity?*
- *HOW does the concept of evolution explain humanity?*
- *HOW does evolution work?*

In 1842, Charles Darwin moved to a village southeast of London. The village, given its location near London, had a good postal service—a fact that was important to Darwin in his research. Each day he wrote to breeders of domestic animals asking them for information about their breeding practices and outcomes. By accumulating such information, he subsequently concluded that the coats of the ancestors of domesticated horses were likely to have been striped. Such information about artificial selection was crucial to his development of the theory of natural selection as the key process driving evolution.

This chapter first provides historical context for the scientific view of how humanity emerged and changed through evolution. The second section describes the development of the scientific concepts of evolution, natural selection, and heredity. The last section considers how evolution works in terms of humanity.

Science and the Tree of Life

This section focuses on European thinking about evolution. Philosophies and religions from other parts of the world, such as Hinduism in India and Islam in the Middle East, had their own theories about humanity, but these are not part of the scientific approach that anthropology adopted.

Before Science

The classical Greeks and Romans were the first to put their thoughts about humanity into writing. Centuries later, the spread of Christianity throughout Europe led to the decline of Greco-Roman ideas and to the rise of biblical explanations for the origin of humanity and humanity's place in nature. We briefly discuss these two phases in Western thinking as background to the later emergence of science and its views about humanity.

Greco-Roman Thinking about Humanity The earliest recorded ideas about the origin of humanity are contained in the writings of Greek thinkers such as Plato and Aristotle in the fifth and sixth centuries BCE (see Figure 4.1). They developed the concept that all the components of the natural world are parts of one system. Another aspect of their thinking was that universal laws govern the natural world, including humans. Humans, in classical Greek philosophy, were part of, not separate from, the natural world, and scholars wrote that animals and humans shared a common origin in natural processes.

Several hundred years after the time of Plato and Aristotle, a Roman philosopher named Lucretius, writing in the first century BCE, proposed that the earliest humans differed from contemporary Romans. He suggested that they were brutish (animal-like), lived alone in caves, ate berries, and lacked tools and language. Both classical Greek and Roman thinkers viewed the ability to make tools, the use of fire, and verbal language as crucial steps in the ascent of humanity from its bestial state (Cole 1990). Thus the basic elements of a view of humanity as changing from an earlier, primitive form to later, more complex forms was established early in Western thought.

The Early Christian Perspective The collapse of the Roman Empire in the fifth century brought a radical change in how Western thinkers, nearly all Christian by that time, viewed humanity and its origin. The account given in the Old Testament of the Bible largely replaced Greco-Roman ideas. According to the biblical view, the Judeo-Christian God created humans—first in the form of a man, Adam, and then in that of a woman, Eve. As a result of humanity being God's work, the first people were fully equipped with language, a rational and cultured mind, and the ability to live together in societies. All their mental and moral capacities placed humans apart from and superior to other animals (Goodrum 2002).

Most Western philosophers living in and immediately after the periods described as the Dark Ages (the fifth to twelfth centuries) and the Middle Ages (twelfth to fifteenth centuries) held to a literal biblical explanation of human origins. For them, the Bible provided a true and accurate explanation for human origins and their place in nature. According to the book of Genesis, all creatures had been created at one time, about 6,000 years earlier, and they continued to exist in the form in which they had been created. There was no understanding of the earth's great age, of extinct species, or of the transformation of humanity over time.

During the Dark and Middle Ages, faith replaced reason in Europe, and Greco-Roman insights were abandoned. Islamic scholars, in the Middle East, read the classical Greek texts and translated them into Arabic. When Christian armies drove the Muslims from Spain in the twelfth and thirteenth centuries, these texts were left behind and translated by curious Medieval Christian scholars into Latin. Some of these translated texts dealt with animal and human origins (Lindberg 1992). In the thirteenth century, the noted Christian philosopher Thomas Aquinas integrated elements of Greek ideas about humanity with biblical interpretations (Ruse 2003). Despite his writings and those of

6th–5th century BCE	Greek philosophers consider humans part of the natural world.
1st century BCE	Lucretius suggests human ancestors were brutish cave dwellers.
5th century CE	Biblical narrative predominates in Europe through to the nineteenth century.
11th–12th century CE	Islamic scholars build on Greco-Roman ideas about the natural world.
13th century CE	Aquinas reconciles Greek ideas with the biblical narrative.
16th century CE	Vesalius writes the first detailed and accurate description of the human body.
17th century CE	Bacon sets out the basic elements of the scientific method. Ussher and Lightfoot calculate the time of the biblical creation using "begats."
18th century CE	Linnaeus assembles the first comprehensive taxonomy of living things. Cuvier establishes the principles of scientific paleontology. The Great Chain of Being metaphor predominates. Malthus writes about competition among individuals for scarce resources.
19th century CE	Lamarck proposes that existing species arise independently and are then transformed through the inheritance of acquired characteristics. Lyell establishes geology as a science. Amateur archaeologists discover fossils of extinct animals in association with stone tools. Wallace and Darwin suggest that evolution through natural selection best explains the Tree of Life. Darwin publishes *On the Origin of Species* and provides compelling evidence that natural selection drives evolution. Mendel presents the results of his experiments on heredity.
20th century CE	The words *genetics* (1906) and *gene* (1909) are first used. Avery et al. show that DNA carries genetic messages (1943). Watson and Crick publish findings on DNA (1953). Two international teams of scientists sequence the human genome (2001).

Note: BCE = Before the Common Era, and CE = Common Era. In the text, we use the BCE abbreviation but dispense with CE. Thus any date in this text without the letters BCE refers to the Common Era.

FIGURE 4.1 Timeline of Western Thought about Humanity and Evolution

other philosophers of the time, the prevailing explanations in Europe about the origin of humanity remained biblically based throughout the Middle Ages.

Science Emerges

Science is a form of knowledge seeking that involves a set of steps called the **scientific method**. The first step of the scientific method is making observations of a particular phenomenon. These observations then lead to a hypothesis, or possible explanation, to account for what was observed. Next comes the testing of the hypothesis by performing experiments or making new observations that lead to the confirmation, amendment, or rejection of the hypothesis. The scientific method, overall, involves a repeated pattern of hypothesis—testing—hypothesis. Each round of hypothesis generation and testing should be informed by the previous round. This continuing process is needed because the goal of science transcends simple description, or knowing that things happen. Science seeks to know why things happen.

scientific method: a form of knowledge-seeking that entails making observations, formulating an explanatory hypothesis, testing the hypothesis, and confirming, amending, or rejecting the hypothesis.

The Renaissance and the Scientific Method The foundation of the scientific method lies in the European Renaissance, which ushered in the revival of art, architecture, and literature in Italy in the fifteenth century. Over time, the influence of the Italian Renaissance spread to other parts of Europe.

Its impact on the development of science as a way of thinking was especially strong in England, where Francis Bacon, in the early seventeenth century, developed the basic ideas of how scientific investigations should be pursued. His contribution can be summed up as follows: Instead of reading

The Judeo-Christian narrative of human origins is set out in the Bible. It says that all living things are unchanged since they were made by God, and it traces all people back to Adam and Eve, who were also created by God. (*Source:* © Bettmann/CORBIS)

about something in a book, go out and observe the phenomenon for yourself. Then investigate its causes by devising your own explanation (hypothesis) and then testing it.

Scientific Bases of Human Evolution Emerge Three major advances in the understanding of the earth and its creatures, generated during and after the Renaissance, led to a new way of thinking about human origins and to the foundation of the scientific study of human evolution.

First, the foundations of scientific anatomy, the study of the human body, were established in the sixteenth century by Andreas Vesalius, a scholar from the Low Countries, or what is now Belgium. He realized that the textbooks used by his professors were based on a confusing and inaccurate mixture of human and monkey anatomy. The illustrations, he knew, were not derived from or checked against careful dissections. Once again, it was the classical Greeks who had, 10 centuries before, dissected human bodies for the purpose of studying how the body works. But after that time, and into the Dark Ages, the practice of dissection was abandoned. Vesalius decided to do his own dissections and to write his own, accurate human anatomy book. His efforts ensured that, from then on, scientists would have access to reliable information about the structure of the human body.

Just as the structure and working of the human body were confused and shrouded in mystery by nonscientific thinking, so too was thinking about the age of the earth and the living creatures that inhabit it. In 1650, James Ussher, then Archbishop of Armagh in Ireland, used the number of "begats" in the Book of Genesis to calculate the precise year of the act of Creation. According to his arithmetic, the act of Creation took place in 4004 BCE. A little later, a theologian at Trinity College, John Lightfoot, calculated that the act of Creation took place at 9 a.m. on October 23 in 4004 BCE.

Second, in the eighteenth century, a new science devoted to studying the earth arose: geology. Its development received much impetus in the nineteenth century, with the beginnings of industrialization. The excavations required to build canals and railroads gave people an opportunity to see rock formations that previously had been accessible only by looking at seaside cliffs and riverbanks.

A Scottish scientist named Charles Lyell is considered the father of geology. In 1830, he provided a scientific version of the history of the earth in his book *The Principles of Geology*. A major contribution is the importance of **stratigraphy**, the study and description of a vertical series of sediment or rock layers

stratigraphy: the study and description of a vertical series of sediment or rock layers that have accumulated over time.

fossils: the preserved remains of a plant or animal of the past, usually a bone, a tooth, or an impression such as a footprint or leaf impression.

The Mezquita (mosque) in Córdoba, Spain. Córdoba was the capital city of Islamic Spain. Construction of the Mezquita began in the early eighth century, and it soon became a center of Muslim worship and scholarship. The Christians retook Córdoba in the thirteenth century and converted much of the Mezquita into a church. Later additions during the Renaissance brought an even more hybrid appearance. A distinctive Islamic feature that remains is the mihrab, the octagonal structure with high arched windows. Research the significance of this feature of Islamic architecture. (*Source:* © Patrick Ward/CORBIS)

that have accumulated over time. Lyell pointed out that *strata* (layers) increase in age the further down they are in any geological sequence. This principle also applies to **fossils** (preserved remains of an animal or plant from the past) or stone tools contained within the strata. In other words, the lower in a sequence of rocks a fossil is, the older it is likely to be. Lyell recognized that certain factors could disrupt this rule, such as upheavals in the earth's surface due to natural causes or deliberate burial, which places an object beneath the level where it would be found naturally.

The implications of the new science of geology were profound. First, it provided a scientific alternative to the biblical explanation for the earth's appearance, which is based on the story of the great flood during which Noah built his ark. Second, it raised serious questions about the biblical view of the earth's age by providing evidence that the earth had to be much older than 6,000 years.

Third, the existence of fossils caused a serious conceptual problem for biblical scholars because the story of the flood and Noah's ark makes it impossible for any life forms to have existed from before the flood. Starting in the eighteenth century and increasing in the nineteenth century, stone tools were discovered in England and France, in association with fossils of extinct animals such as mammoths. Scientists began to accept that fossils were the remains of extinct animals and plants. Their association with evidence of humans further called into question the theory of the Big Flood. A growing number of reports about human fossils found in association with stone tools provided evidence that humans were much older than the biblical story said.

Science and Classification

The goal of scientific classification schemes is to group similar things together in increasingly broad, or inclusive, categories. The classification system of Swedish scientist Karl von Linné, first proposed in 1758, is still used by scientists today. Called the *Linnaean system* after its founder, it originally included seven major levels for all living things, from the most inclusive category to least inclusive: kingdom, phylum, class, order, family, genus, and species. Linnaeus's original system was later expanded by adding the new category tribe, between the genus and family, and by introducing the prefix *super-* above a category and the prefixes *sub-* and *infra-* below it. These additions increase the potential number of categories below the level of order to a total of 12 (8 of the categories that apply to modern humans are displayed in Figure 4.2).

The principles of Linnaean classification are important in many areas of biological anthropology, especially primatology and paleoanthropology. Anthropologists use the term **taxon** (plural, *taxa*) to refer to any group named at any level in the Linnaean hierarchy. A taxonomy, then, is a classification scheme that shows how various taxa are related to each other. The **Linnaean taxonomy**, a hierarchical structure for classifying all organisms, is a binomial system. Two categories, genus and species, make up the Latinized name for all species, extinct or living. For example, *Homo sapiens* is the genus and species of modern humans. According to convention, scientists can abbreviate the name of the genus, but not that of the species. Thus, we can write *H. sapiens* but not *Homo s.* The reason for this rule is that a species name,

taxon: any group recognized at any level in the Linnaean hierarchy (plural, taxa).

Linnaean taxonomy: a hierarchical structure for classifying living creatures that was introducted by Linnaeus in 1758; its basic unit is the species.

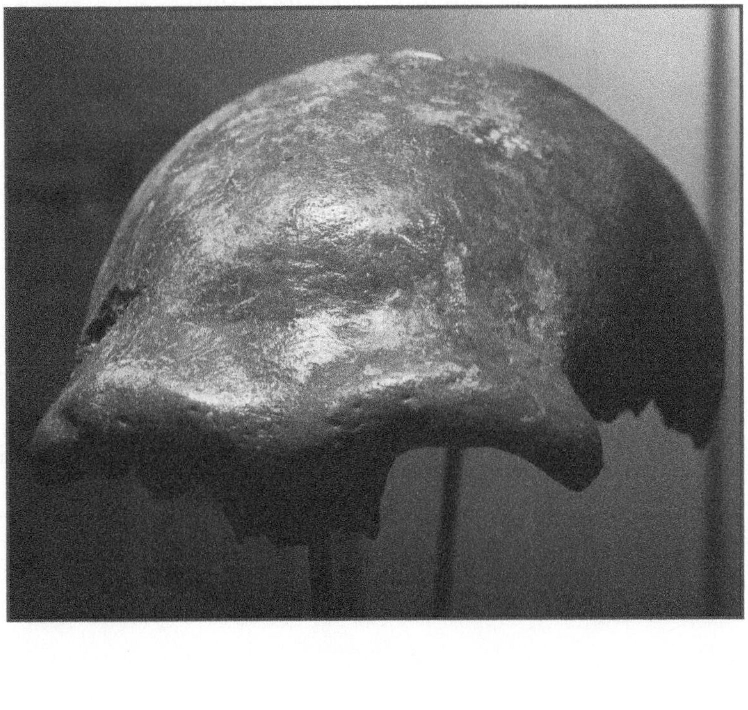

This Neanderthal skull cap was recovered in 1856 by quarry workers in a cave exposed by erosion from the Neander River, Germany. It took nearly a decade for scientists to appreciate its significance. *Consider what happened between the time of its discovery and 1864 that may have influenced this change.* (Source: © Giraudon/Bridgeman Art Library)

THINKING OUTSIDE THE BOX

CONSIDER the category of running shoes. What features do all running shoes have in common that make them running shoes and not some other category of footwear? What are the major subcategories within the category of running shoes?

Linnaean Category	Modern Humans
Kingdom	Animal
Phylum	Chordate
Class	Mammal
Order	Primate
Family	Hominid
Tribe	Hominin
Genus	*Homo*
Species	*Homo sapiens*

FIGURE 4.2 Modified Linnaean Categories

within its genus, is unique. If the species name were abbreviated, and there were more than one species in the genus with the same first letter, confusion would result.

species: a group of interbreeding organisms reproductively isolated from other such groups.

Biological anthropologists must place any new fossil evidence about human prehistory into the most appropriate species. Members of the same species should be more like each other, in *morphology* (the size, shape, and appearance of an organism) and in behavior, than they are like the members of another species. The prevailing definition of a **species**, according to the biological species concept, is a group of interbreeding organisms that are reproductively isolated from other such groups. Thus members of a species can produce fertile offspring only with each other and not with members of any other species. Such interbreeding keeps members of a species looking more like each other than like individuals that belong to other species. This definition, however, is problematic for paleoanthropologists who study human evolution. They have no information about the breeding patterns of extinct taxa. Instead, they identify species in the fossil record on the basis of morphology as a proxy for information about the individual's breeding pattern. The working assumption is that fossils that look similar are from animals that were capable of interbreeding. Another analytical challenge is deciding what degree of difference to allow within species and when to decide that a fossil is different enough that it almost certainly belongs to a separate species.

Evolution Explains the Tree of Life and Humanity's Place on It

THINKING OUTSIDE THE BOX

WHAT IS the prevailing view of human origins and evolution in your cultural background? Does it reject or accept the Darwinian view, or does it provide some kind of accommodation with it?

This section discusses the scientific approach to understanding humanity that involves evolution and the three processes that evolution requires: variation, heredity, and natural selection. Evolution is a process of cumulative change in the characteristics of organisms or populations, occurring in the course of successive generations related by descent. It usually is a slow process, and it tends to lead to a more complex animal evolving from a less complex predecessor.

Evolution and the Tree of Life

Individuals within the same species are more closely related to each other than they are to an individual from another species. Likewise, species within the same genus are more closely related to each other than they are to a species from another genus. And so on, up to the highest levels in the Linnaean hierarchy. Scientists use the same classification system for all living animals because they have concluded that all living animals ultimately share a common ancestor.

DNA: abbreviation for deoxyribose nucleic acid, a molecule containing the genetic instructions that guide the development and functioning of all living organisms.

At first, scientists determined relationships morphologically—by comparing animals in terms of anatomical features that are visible to the naked eye or with a conventional light microscope. The assumption was that the larger the number of shared structures, the more closely related the animals. Then, beginning with pioneering studies in the early 1900s, scientists became able to compare and classify animals using the morphology of molecules. Now they determine the relationships among taxa by comparing their **DNA**, or deoxyribonucleic acid, a molecule containing the genetic instructions that guide the development and functioning of all living organisms. Over time, it became apparent that animal species similar in morphology also had similar molecules and similar genetic codes. Even though the wing of an insect and the arm of a primate look different, the same basic genetic instructions guide their development (Carroll et al. 2001) (see Figure 4.3).

FIGURE 4.3 Genetics. The wing of a bird and a human arm are structurally different, but the signaling genes involved in their development are the same. Birds and modern humans must have inherited these genetic instructions from a distant (millions of years ago) common ancestor.

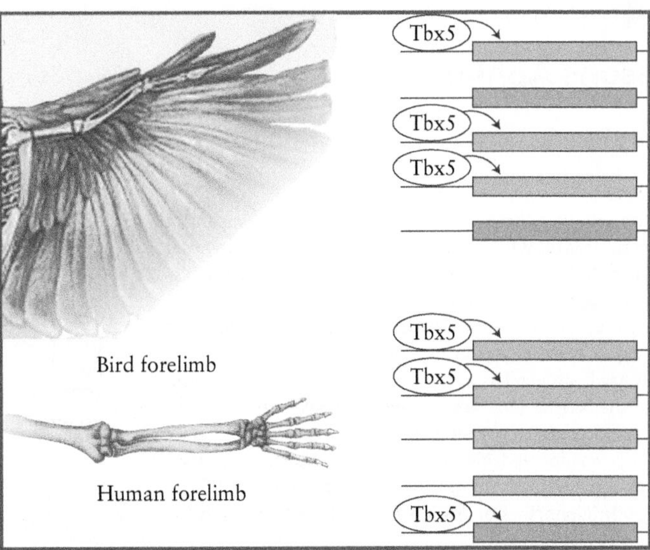

Prior to Darwin, the dominant metaphor for humanity and its relationship to other animals was the *Great Chain of Being* (see Figure 4.4). According to this image, a single chain links primitive animals with more advanced forms of life. Introduced by Medieval Christian philosophers, it persisted into the nineteenth century. According to the Great Chain of Being metaphor, modern humans are at the top end of the chain, and their superior position means that they are dominant over the creatures below them. In some renditions of the Great Chain of Being model, creatures are placed at different heights corresponding to their order in boarding Noah's ark. In contrast, increasing amounts of genetic data indicate that all living things are connected through common descent within a single *Tree of Life*, or *TOL* (see Figure 4.4). The metaphor of a tree with many branches is now the prevailing image that scientists have for all living creatures, including humans.

The TOL metaphor gained prominence in the latter part of the nineteenth century. The branching pattern of the tree reflects the way scientists think the plants and animals within the TOL are related. The tree model emphasizes complexity, with many branches and sub-branches. The branches have different lengths and run in different directions. Some become dead ends and die out.

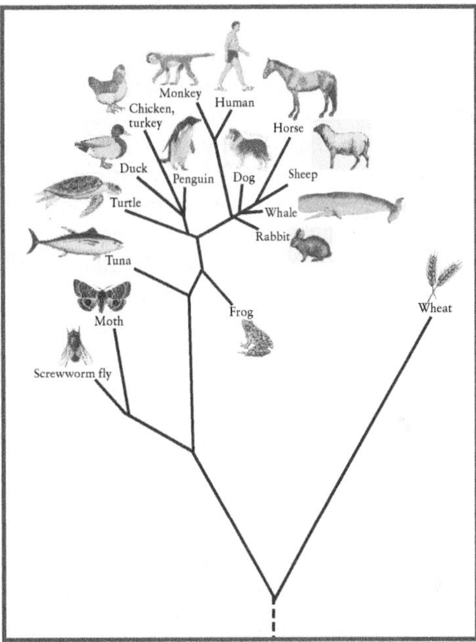

FIGURE 4.4 Metaphor Comparisons. (Left) The Great Chain of Being, the Judeo-Christian view, depicts all living creatures in a sequence with humans occupying the place closest to God. (Right) The scientific model sees all forms of life, living and extinct, as part of a tree-like structure. Modern humans are located on the end of one of the many branches connected to the vertebrate part of the Tree of Life.

Box 4.1 Lessons Applied

Applying Science to the Ethical Treatment of Nonhuman Primates

DNA evidence reveals that the genomes of humans and chimpanzee genomes overlap substantially. In addition, recent research shows many similarities between their cognitive processes that further blur the distinction between modern humans and chimpanzees (Gallup et al. 1977; Miyamoto et al. 1988). These findings are being used in two different areas: by animal rights activists and by medical researchers.

This research has been used as a rationale by animal rights activists in many parts of the world. One area of vigorous activity is in New Zealand, where an organization called the Great Ape Project New Zealand (GAPENZ) was formed. Members of the group lobby for special protection for the living animals closest to modern humans (Cavalieri and Singer 1993). Supporters of GAPENZ seek three basic rights for the great apes (Taylor 2000):

- not to be deprived of life
- not to be subjected to torture or to cruel, degrading, or disproportionately severe treatment
- not to be subjected to medical or scientific experimentation where it is not in the best interests of the individual

The close biological link between modern humans and chimpanzees strengthens the case for great ape protection, but it also increases pressure from medical researchers to use chimpanzees as surrogates for humans in medical research. The New Zealand Animal Welfare Act of 1999 included no "rights" for nonhuman primates, but it does prohibit research on them unless it is in their own "best interests."

Food for Thought

- What are the protections in place for nonhuman primates in your home country? Do you think they are adequate? Why or why not?

genomes: the totality of genetic information encoded in the DNA of an individual.

natural selection: the process by which organisms better adapted to the environment reproduce more effectively compared with less well adapted forms.

genotype: a set of alleles an organism possesses.

All current evidence—including evidence from anatomy, molecules, and DNA—says that modern humans and chimpanzees/bonobos shared the same small branch of the TOL until around 8 million years ago, after which the branch split. Research into primate **genomes** (a genome is the totality of genetic information encoded in the DNA of an organism) shows substantial overlap between humans and chimpanzees/bonobos. This finding has important implications for the treatment of chimpanzees and bonobos (see Lessons Applied box above).

Natural Selection

By the mid-1800s, the concept of evolution was gaining acceptance in spite of often strong negative reactions from biblical literalists—and in spite of the fact that no one yet understood how evolution worked. Charles Darwin and Alfred Russel Wallace both, independently, came up with a key concept in understanding species change: natural selection. **Natural selection** is the process by which organisms that are better adapted to the environment reproduce more effectively and increase in numbers faster than less well-adapted forms. Natural selection accounts for both the diversity and the branching pattern of the TOL. It is the main driving force behind evolution.

Although Darwin is often considered the originator of the concept of evolution, he is more appropriately acknowledged as providing a coherent theory about the way evolution works with his landmark contribution of developing the concept of natural selection. Working in parallel to Darwin was another English scientist, Alfred Russel Wallace. Wallace was a natural historian who spent much time in what is now Malaysia, studying wild plants and animals. In 1858, Wallace submitted a paper about natural selection to the Linnaean Society of London. Other British scientists were aware that Darwin was also writing a book about natural selection. Friends of Darwin urged him to summarize his ideas and send them at once to the Linnaean Society. Thus a paper entitled "On the Tendency of Species to Form Varieties, and on the Perpetuation of Varieties and Species by Natural Means of Selection," co-authored by Darwin and Wallace, was presented at a meeting of the Linnaean Society, in London, in July 1858. The realization that he was not alone in understanding the importance of natural selection stimulated Darwin to finish his book. On November 24, 1859, the first edition of his groundbreaking book, *On the Origin of Species by Means of Natural Selection*, was published.

Natural selection suggests that because resources are finite, and because of random variation, some individuals will be better than others at accessing those resources. That variant will then gain enough of an advantage that it will produce more offspring than the other individuals belonging to the same species. Biologists refer to this advantage as an increase in an animal's *fitness*, or the probability that an animal of a particular **genotype**, or set of alleles an organism possesses, will survive and reproduce. Darwin's notebooks are full of evidence about the effectiveness of the type of artificial selection used by animal and plant breeders. Darwin's genius was to think of a way in which the same process could occur naturally—a natural kind of "breeding" that would lead to improvements in a species over time.

(Left) After his five-year journey around the world on the HMS Beagle, Charles Darwin became a laboratory scientist, using his house and garden as his lab. He collected evidence for his theory of natural selection from his own observations and through correspondence with people who bred plants and animals. *(Source:* © Bettmann/CORBIS) (Right) The naturalist Alfred Russel Wallace is less well-known than Darwin, but he also realized, independently, that natural selection was the mechanism driving evolution. *Do online research to find out where Wallace made his observations that led to his ideas about natural selection.* *(Source:* © Hulton Archive/Getty Images)

Variation

Darwin also recognized the significance of the observation that no two individual animals are exactly alike: There are no perfect copies, or clones. Differences, even small ones such as leg length or strength, can be crucial in determining whether an individual can escape from a predator. The individuals that do escape survive to reproduce, passing on their genes to the next generation. The ones that do not survive make no genetic contribution to succeeding generations. Before Darwin, philosophers and scientists thought that each species had an optimum size and shape and that any variation was an unproductive deviation from the perfect form. Darwin recognized that the small differences among individuals within a species provide the raw material on which natural selection operates.

Heredity

Artificial selection works only if the offspring of a mating faithfully inherit the feature or features desired by the breeder. In natural selection, it works only if the offspring inherit the feature that confers greater fitness. Darwin understood that heredity existed, but he did not understand the mechanism for it. Nor did he realize that variation and heredity were part of a single genetic system.

While Darwin was finishing his book, a Catholic monk named Gregor Mendel was painstakingly working out the essential rules of inheritance in a monastery garden in Brno, in what is now the Czech Republic. The discipline of genetics, the field of biology that deals with heredity, was established on the basis of his deductions based on breeding experiments conducted on collections of artificially bred plants. In 1865, Mendel presented the results of his research to the Natural Science Society in Brno. His findings are summarized in two propositions known as Mendel's laws. We will discuss them in the next section when we consider how evolution works.

Mendel deduced the basic rules governing heredity, but he had no means of investigating what determined the color and texture of the peas, or the color of the flowers produced by the pea plants, in his monastery garden. The word **gene**, which is a DNA segment that carries genetic information, was not coined until 1909, several years after Mendel's pioneering experiments came to the notice of scientists. Mendel was, however, fortunate that his peas provided several examples of a simple one-to-one link between a gene and a trait, which is called a single-gene, or monogenic, effect. We now know that most traits are controlled by more than one gene; that is, they are *polygenic effects*. In addition, many genes, under different circumstances, can have more than one effect, and these are called *pleiotropic effects*. These nineteenth-century advances in scientific thought carved out a new direction for thinking about humanity's past and present.

gene: a DNA segment that carries genetic information.

The twentieth century heralded the contributions of scientists working at ever smaller levels of evidence—from cells to chromosomes and then to DNA. This new evidence, especially evidence from DNA, provided new insights into how humanity has come to be what it is and about the relationship of humanity to other living creatures.

How Evolution Works

microevolution: evolutionary changes that operate at the level of the individual and over short periods of time.

macroevolution: large-scale events that take place during the evolutionary history of a group of organisms, including adaptive radiations, speciation, and extinction.

phenotype: an organism's size, shape, appearance, or internal structure; also morphology.

This section discusses how evolution works at two levels. The first is **microevolution**, the evolutionary processes that operate at the level of the individual and over short periods of time. It includes all the short-term genetic changes (over hundreds of years) that have occurred and still occur, generation-by-generation, within local populations. The second level is **macroevolution,** evolutionary processes that operate at large scale and over long periods of time. It includes long-term genetic changes (over hundreds of thousands of years) that have occurred in human evolutionary history. Microevolution is more relevant to understanding human origins, and so more attention is devoted to it.

Microevolution

The section describes the molecular mechanisms that are involved in sexual reproduction and small-scale evolution. Much of this discussion is rooted in Mendelian genetics.

Mendel's Two Laws We now return to Mendel and his peas in order to understand the scientific view of microevolution. Mendel began his work with the important observation that the pea plants in his garden produced pods containing either yellow or green peas. He set out to understand the "rules" that determined traits such as pea color. First, he selected plants that produced either green or yellow peas. Then he bred within each pea color until all the cross-pollinations, or crosses, were producing plants that produced all yellow peas or all green peas. Next he crossed the plants that faithfully produced yellow peas with plants that faithfully produced green peas. Mendel found that all the plants of the first cross produced yellow peas; none of the plants produced green peas, nor did any exhibit a mixture of yellow and green peas. Finally, Mendel took the plants that produced yellow peas and bred them with each other; this is called the second cross. This time, for every three plants with yellow peas, there was one that produced green peas. Mendel was painstaking. His notebooks show that the 3:1 yellow/green ratio was based on 6,022 plants with yellow peas and 2,001 plants with green peas.

Mendel reached two important conclusions. First, pea color is *discrete*. Mendel's plants produced peas that were either yellow or green; no plants produced peas that were shades in between. Mendel reasoned that a single mechanism could explain the dominance of yellow over green and the subsequent 3:1 yellow-to-green ratio. He suggested that a trait such as pea color was controlled by two sets of instructions, one inherited from the male parent plant and one from the female parent plant. Mendel proposed that his results could be explained if one of these sets of instructions is dominant and the other recessive. He suggested that for pea color, the instructions for yellow (Y) are dominant and those for green (y) are recessive. Mendel reasoned that if, in an individual plant, at least one of the two sets of instructions is the dominant version (YY or Yy), then that plant will produce yellow peas. The only circumstance under which a plant will produce green peas is when it has inherited recessive versions of the instructions from both parents (yy).

Mendel conducted similar experiments with the flowers of the pea plants. In this case he showed that purple flowers were dominant and white flowers recessive. The combination of two recessive instructions appears in only a quarter of the crosses (see Figure 4.5). The fact that pea and flower colors are discrete, and that they do not blend together, is known as Mendel's First Law, or the *Law of Segregation* (see Figure 4.6).

Mendel's experiments also showed that there is not always a one-to-one correspondence between an organism's **phenotype** (or morphology, meaning its size, shape, appearance, or internal structure)—in this case the

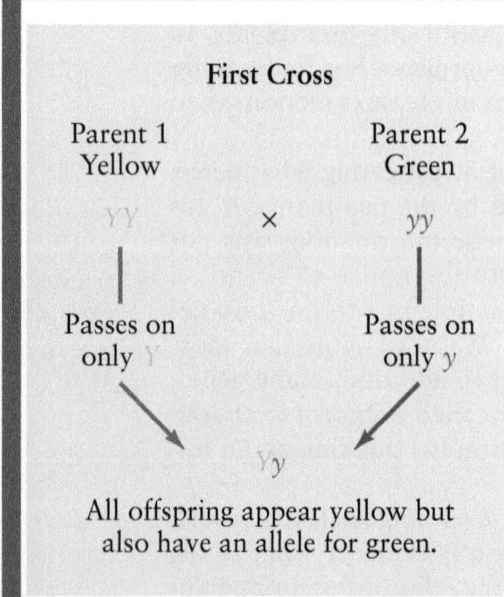

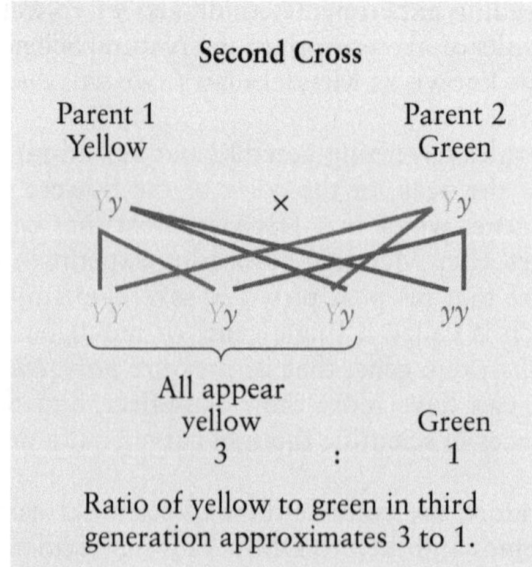

Y = yellow y = green

FIGURE 4.5 Mendel's Experiments. The results of Gregor Mendel's experiments convinced him that pea color was determined by two sets of instructions, one dominant and one recessive.

Law of Segregation	Consequence
Each parent has a pair of genes (alleles) for traits such as pea color and flower color, but each gamete (egg or sperm) has only one of the two versions.	The appearance of the offspring depends on which of each pair of genes it inherits from its parents.

Law of Independent Assortment	Consequence
During the formation of gametes, chromosomes and the genes they carry are distributed randomly.	Traits on different chromosomes, such as pea color and flower color, vary independently.

FIGURE 4.6 Mendel's Laws

color of peas or pea flowers—and its genotype (the genetic basis of a trait). Sometimes, different genotypes can produce the same phenotype. For example, plants that produce only purple flowers, the purple phenotype, can be either PP or P*p*. However, the plants that produce white flowers, the white phenotype, can be only the genotype *pp*. Mendel found that other traits, such as the texture of the surface of the peas (smooth or wrinkled) behaved in the same way.

When Mendel studied pea and flower color, he was dealing with dichotomies of yellow/green or purple/white, which are called *discontinuous* traits. Most of the characteristics with which biological anthropologists work, however, are not *dichotomous*. Paleoanthropologists studying fossils deal with *continuous* traits, such as the size of a tooth or the thickness of a limb bone. These features have smooth, continuous distributions. Biological anthropologists who study contemporary human variation deal with continuous traits such as body weight and level of hormones in the blood. How do you get continuous curves if traits are discrete? There are two explanations. The first is that, unlike pea and flower color, many genes are involved in determining the size of a tooth or the thickness of a limb bone. What looks like a continuous curve really reflects the combination of the effects of many genes (see Figure 4.12, p. 88). The second is that nongenetic factors such as nutrition also contribute to making a smooth curve.

The results of Mendel's experiments demonstrate that genes may come in several versions called alleles. The genotype of an individual is made up of its own particular combination of alleles. If the **alleles**, or any one of a number Gf DNA codings That occupies a given position on a chromosome, for any trait inherited from the individual's parents are the same, then the genotype of that individual is described as *homozygous*. If the alleles are different, the individual is described as *heterozygous*. Each allele has an effect, but as Mendel discovered, some effects are stronger than others. In homozygous individuals, such as Mendel's *PP* and *pp* plants, there is no trial of strength between the alleles; the instructions they give are the same. However, in heterozygous individuals, one allele, the dominant allele, exerts the decisive influence on the phenotype. The allele whose effect is masked is the recessive allele. Remember Mendel's peas and his demonstration that what look to be similar versions of the same dominant phenotype, a purple flower color, can be produced by either of two combinations of alleles (*PP* and *Pp*), whereas the recessive phenotype, a white flower color, always has the same pair of alleles (*pp*). The form a particular animal or plant takes, which is called its overall *phenotype*, is the sum of the biological effects of all the genes in that individual, combined with the environmental effects the animal encounters during and after its development.

What carries the message? Genes do not exist in cells as individual units. Most genes exist in packages called **chromosomes;** a chromosome is a single macromolecule of DNA in a cell—it contains many genes. Mammalian cells are composed of a dense nucleus and clear cytoplasm. The nucleus is dense because the chromosomes it contains are made up of a mixture of proteins and nucleic acid. Except for the male and female sex cells that unite at fertilization, the nuclei of modern human cells have 23 pairs of chromosomes. Twenty-two of these pairs, called autosomes, are common to both sexes. The pair of chromosomes that brings the total number of chromosomes up to 46 consists of the two sex chromosomes. Females have a pair of X chromosomes, whereas males have one X chromosome and one Y chromosome.

Every human being starts out as a single cell, the fertilized egg. How does a single cell become an organism consisting of literally millions and millions of cells? The answer is the process called **mitosis,** whereby one somatic cell with 46 chromosomes divides into two cells, during which time each strand of the genetic material replicates itself so that each daughter cell also has 46 chromosomes. In this way, mitosis maintains the number of chromosomes in the daughter cells. A different process, called **meiosis** or reduction division, is the process by which sex cells, or gametes, are produced. Meiosis reduces the number of chromosomes in the daughter cells by half. Thus, when two sex cells combine at the time of fertilization to form the zygote, the new individual will have the same number of chromosomes, 46, as the parents. At

allele: any one of a number of DNA codings that occupies a given position on a chromosome.

chromosome: a single macromolecule of DNA in a cell; it contains many genes.

mitosis: the process whereby one somatic cell with 46 chromosomes divides into two cells, during which time each strand of the genetic material replicates itself so that each daughter cell also has 46 chromosomes.

meiosis: the process by which sex cells, or gametes, are produced. Also called *reduction division* because the number of chromosomes is reduced from 46 to 23.

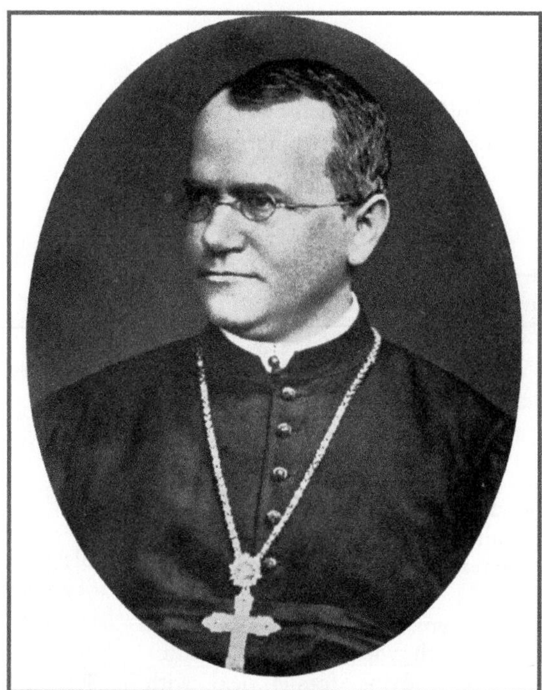

Gregor Johann Mendel is recognized as the first geneticist. His laboratory was the garden of the monastery of which he became the Abbott. His painstaking breeding experiments established that the properties of plants and animals do not blend but come in discrete packages that are transmitted from generation to generation. (*Source:* © Image Select/Art Resource, NY)

James Watson's and Francis Crick's deductions about how DNA carries the genetic code depended heavily on evidence about the structure of DNA, much of which came from Rosalind Franklin's pioneering interpretations of the patterns produced when she shone X-rays through DNA crystals. (*Source:* National Portrait Gallery, London)

fertilization each parent provides one of each of the 22 pairs of autosomes, and either an X or a Y chromosome.

At the time of meiosis, the chromosomes that go into the sex cells (a process called *sorting*) do so independently. Thus, because modern humans have 23 pairs of chromosomes, there are 223 (over 8 million) possible combinations of chromosomes in the sex cells produced by one parent. This finding, known as Mendel's Second Law, or the *Law of Independent Assortment*, explains the independence of traits, and it is also the main reason why siblings of the same parents differ genetically.

DNA Enters the Scene We now turn to the question of where genes are located. Genes in the nucleus must be in either one or the other of the two molecules, proteins and nucleic acids, that make up the chromosomes. Proteins are mostly large molecules with complex shapes that fulfill important functions in cells. Nucleic acids are made up of units called nucleotides. Each nucleotide consists of three components: a sugar, a phosphate group, and a base (see Figure 4.7). There are two types of nucleic acids: DNA and RNA. The sugar in DNA is deoxyribose, and that in RNA is ribose—hence their different names. The type of nucleic acid found in chromosomes is DNA.

In the early years of genetic research, most scientists thought that genes were in the protein component of the chromosomes, for it was clear that the genes had to be in some sort of code, and proteins seemed to be more complex (and thus more likely to carry a code) than nucleic acids. But a series of experiments conducted in the 1940s using bacteria showed conclusively that genetic information was encoded in the nucleic acid component of the chromosomes. Even though scientists had shown that DNA was the site of the genetic code, there was still much to explain. How is the genetic message encoded in the nucleic acids, and how is the code translated into instructions for the machinery that makes proteins? How do the genes make copies of themselves when cells divide?

The puzzle of how DNA copies itself was solved in the 1950s when American scientist James Watson and British scientist Francis Crick worked out the details of the structure of DNA. They reasoned that only the bases were variable enough to carry a coded message. There are two sorts of base: purines and pyrimidines. Each of these comes in two forms. At any one location on your DNA you have one purine (adenine, A, or guanine, G) or one pyrimidine (cytosine, C, or thymine, T) base. Experiments using extracts of DNA had previously shown that the amount of A always matched that of T, and the amount of G always matched that of C.

When X-rays were directed at crystals made from DNA molecules, the images suggested that DNA was made of two ribbons, or strands, lying side by side and arranged in the form of a helix of constant width. Pyrimidines are larger molecules than purines, so pairings made either of two pyrimidines or of two purines did not fit the X-ray crystallography data; such a helix would have been wider across pairs of the pyrimidine bases and narrower across the places on the helix where smaller purine molecules linked the two strands of DNA. Accordingly, Watson and Crick reasoned that a purine was paired with a pyrimidine, and vice versa. Thus A was always paired with T, and G with C (not A with C, or G with T) (see Figure 4.8).

In 1953, Watson and Crick sent a one-page letter to the science journal *Nature,* in which they announced their ideas about how the sequence of bases in DNA carry the genetic code. The

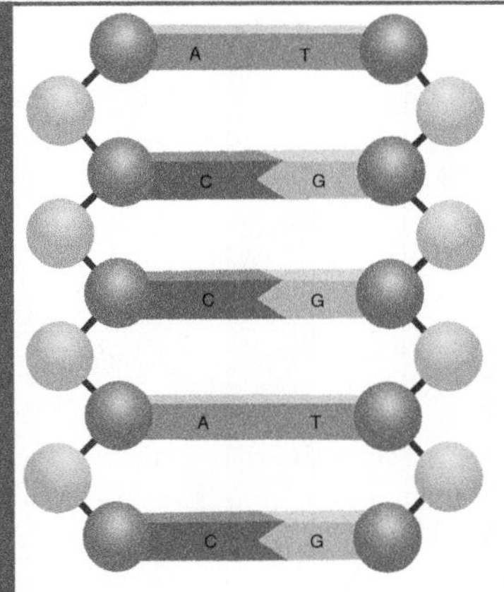

FIGURE 4.7 A Short Section of DNA. This diagram shows how two strands of nucleic acids are held together by chemical bonds between pairs of complementary bases.

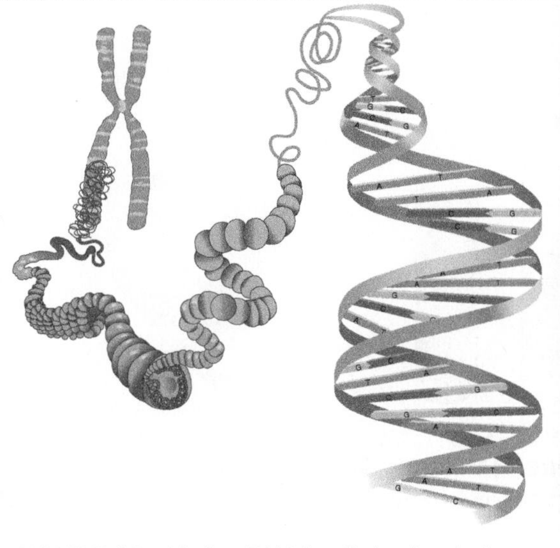

FIGURE 4.8 Nuclear DNA is coiled and packed tightly with proteins to form the chromosomes in each nucleus.

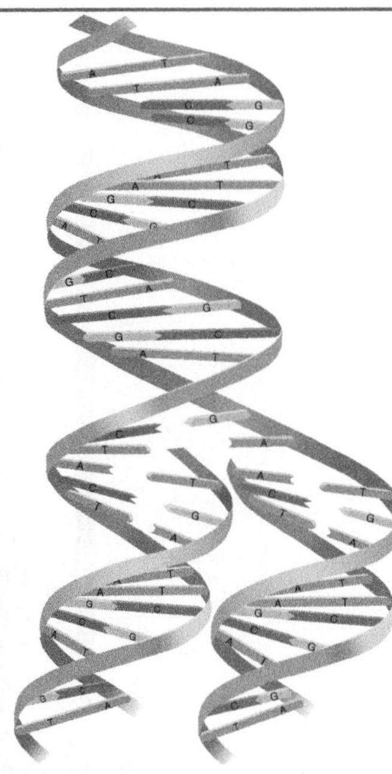

FIGURE 4.9 Unzipped DNA. As soon as the parental DNA is unzipped into single strands, complementary DNA is assembled to make two double-stranded daughter DNA molecules.

elegance of their solution was that if the two component strands of DNA were peeled apart, as they are in cell division, then each one provides a template that, because of the A:T and G:C rule, will specify the correct order for the base pairs in any DNA copies. But how does the copying work? How is the genetic information in a single human fertilized egg copied again and again so that each of the billions of cells in our bodies has its own copy of our genetic code? When a cell divides, be it the fertilized egg, or a sex cell, or one of the cells in your skin, the DNA in each of the two daughter cells is a faithful copy of the DNA of the parent cell. The process that makes the DNA copies in the two daughter cells is known as *DNA replication.*

DNA replication works as follows. First, special proteins move down the double helix, unzipping it in much the same way as a closed zipper parts when you pull down the handle. Then the bases exposed on the now single strands of parental DNA specify the bases that are assembled to make the complementary strand of DNA. Wherever the parental strand has an A, the cell's machinery will insert a T into the growing strand. Wherever there is a G, a C will be inserted. This A:T and G:C assembly "rule" means that each of the two daughter cells should have a perfect copy of the DNA in the parental cell (see Figure 4.9).

DNA replication, like all processes, is not completely reliable. Occasionally, the wrong base is added to the daughter DNA molecule. If the dividing cell is a skin cell, then there is always a risk that the single-base change will affect the behavior of the daughter cell such that it lacks the means to respond to the message to stop dividing. When this happens the cell becomes malignant, and the result is a potentially life-threatening cancer. When a replication error occurs in a sex cell, it does not always have a negative effect. In fact, most **mutations** (errors made when DNA is copied at the time of cell division) are neutral, and some are positive. If a sex cell bearing a positive mutation is involved in fertilization, then the offspring will have a slight advantage over others belonging to the same species. Geneticists refer to this advantageous behavior in the offspring as conferring greater genetic fitness on that individual.

mutation: an error made when DNA is copied at the time of cell division.

Mutations occur constantly but not randomly. Most mutations occur in "hot spots" on chromosomes. Most have no effect on an individual's genetic fitness; these are called *neutral mutations*. Because mutations occur at a constant rate, the amount of accumulated genetic difference caused by mutations reflects how much time has elapsed since two daughter species evolved from an ancestral species. This is the principle of what scientists call the molecular clock. Mutations in sex cells, or gametes, are one source of the evolutionary novelties referred to as *genetic variation*. The other reason why "daughter" DNA may be subtly different from that of the parent is the recombination that occurs during sexual reproduction.

During meiosis, each of a component pair of chromosomes should remain intact. But sometimes, a section of a chromosome becomes detached and switches from one member of the pair to the other, a

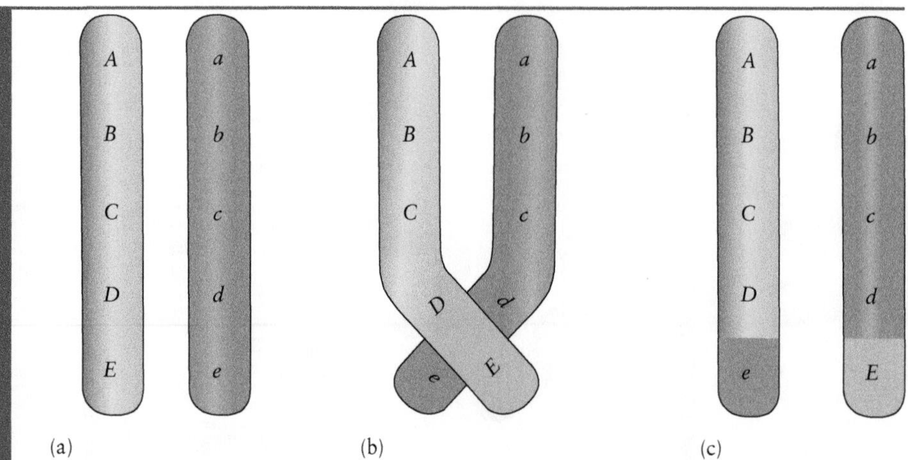

FIGURE 4.10 The Recombination Process. Recombination, the exchange of short pieces of parental chromosomes during meiosis, is one of the reasons why offspring differ genetically from their parents.

process called *recombination* (see Figure 4.10). The result of recombination is that offspring in the new generation have chromosomes that are not seen in either parent. The chances that the pieces switched between chromosomes would be the same in two offspring of the same parents are extremely small. This means that two offspring of the same parents are unlikely to have exactly the same chromosomes. These small differences do not necessarily have any effect on phenotype. But in some situations they lead to subtle, adaptively important phenotypic differences among the offspring. Of the two sources of genetic variation, mutations and recombinations, the latter provide most of the variation on which natural selection operates.

There is another reason why offspring of the same parents are different. Recall Mendel's Second Law, the Law of Independent Assortment, which says that when offspring inherit one of their 22 pairs of autosomal chromosomes from their parents, they do so randomly. The likelihood that this mix will be exactly the same in any two offspring of the same parents is extremely small. Thus the independent assortment of chromosomes is yet another reason why offspring of the same parents differ. But unlike mutations and recombinations, which endure from generation to generation, the differences due to the independent assortment of chromosomes are ephemeral. Imagine shuffling two sets of 22 colored playing cards. The chances that you will end up with same combination the next time you shuffle them are very small. So it is with chromosomes. When they are reshuffled in the next generation, the chromosome combinations will be different. The genetic variation due to independent assortment has no staying power.

Linking Genes with Phenotypes Selection, natural and artificial, acts on the phenotype. But you inherit your parents' genes, not their ability to see further, or to hear danger before others do, or to flee more rapidly from predators. How does the genetic message of an individual get translated into its phenotype? The short answer is that the genetic message and the phenotype are linked by proteins. Proteins are the components of the cellular machinery that constructs other molecules, such as sugars and fats, and ultimately the tissues that make up our bodies, such as muscles, nerves, bones, and teeth. Proteins consist of sequences of 20 types of amino acids. Although Watson and Crick's proposals for the structure of DNA explained how DNA could be replicated, they did not explain how the order of the nucleotide bases in a ribbon of DNA could provide blueprints for all the protein molecules that each of us can make.

A code in which two nucleotides coded for an amino acid (for example, AA, AT, AG, AC, TA) would not work. It would provide for only 42, or 16, of the 20 amino acids. But a code based on three nucleotides (for example, AAA, AAT, AAG, AAC, TAA), which is called a *triplet code*, would provide more than enough specificity, for it would result in 43, or 64, available combinations. In 1966, little more than a decade following Watson and Crick's letter to *Nature*, scientists confirmed that the genetic code is a triplet code. Sixty-one out of a possible 64 triplets, or triplet codons, specify an amino acid. The code is not ambiguous, because each triplet codes for only one amino acid (for example, GAA codes only for glutamic acid). However, it is redundant, for some amino acids are specified by more than one codon (for example, GAA and GAG both code for glutamic acid, so a switch from GAA to GAG would be a neutral mutation).

Thus the base component of a nucleotide is what makes it distinctive. A sequence of three nucleotides, or a triplet codon (for example, GAA or GAG), determines the type of amino acid, and the order of the amino acids determines the nature of the protein. This is the essence of the genetic code. The first part of the journey from DNA to a protein is called *transcription* because the DNA is read, or transcribed, into a type of ribonucleic acid, or RNA, called *messenger RNA* (see Figure 4.11). Then comes *translation*, when the messenger RNA moves to another part of the cell where its sequence of bases is translated into a string of amino acids that makes up the protein specified by that particular gene.

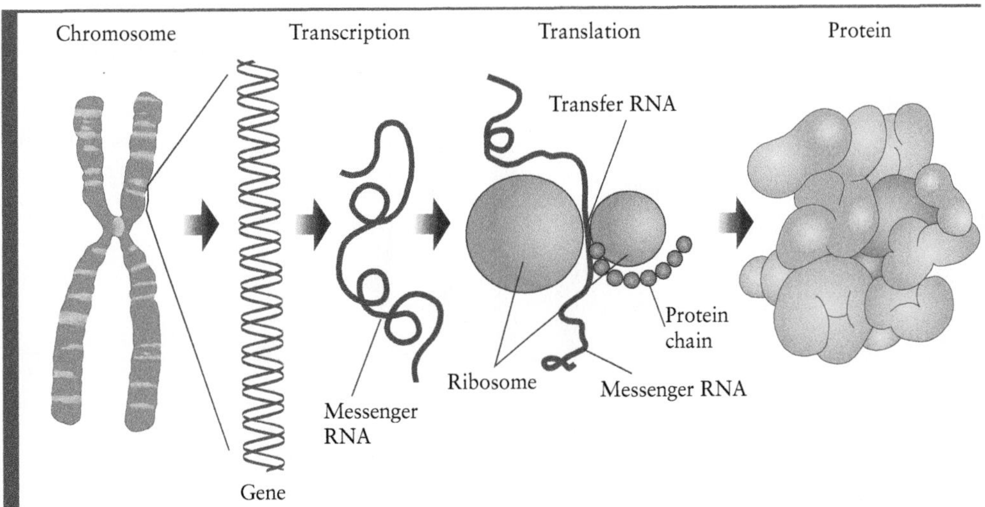

FIGURE 4.11 Protein Production. Proteins are produced within a cell by a combination of transcription and translation.

The scale of the system devoted to carrying the genetic code is awesome. Human nuclear DNA consists of 3 billion (3.109) complementary pairs (called base pairs) of nucleotides (for example, A matched with T, or G with C). In modern humans, nuclear DNA is arranged in 23 pairs of DNA molecules that vary in length by a factor of five. Each of these DNA molecules is a double helix that consists of two strands of DNA joined at each pair of complementary bases by chemical bonds. The shortest of these long and highly coiled DNA molecules contains 50 million (5.106) base pairs, the longest 250 million (250.106) base pairs. Together with its protein superstructure, each pair of these helical DNA molecules makes up one of our chromosomes. The DNA in a mammalian cell contributes barely 0.25 percent of its total weight, yet the total length of the uncoiled DNA in the longest chromosome would be close to 4 inches. A typical animal cell contains more than a yard of tightly coiled DNA. However, only about 5 percent of our DNA codes for genes. The function of the remaining 95 percent is largely unknown, but scientists do know that some of it is involved in controlling when genes are switched on and off.

Each nucleated cell in the body, except for a sperm or an egg, no matter whether it is in the brain or in the skin, has a complete set of nuclear genes called the *nuclear genome*. What type of cell it becomes, and what functions it subsequently carries out, however, are determined by the particular mix of genes activated in that cell. Active genes are those that are switched on, or expressed, in that cell. Genes are turned on and off during development, and the functions of an adult cell can also be switched on and off by some of the non-gene DNA.

Male sperm cells consist almost entirely of chromosomes from the nucleus, whereas the egg contains chromosomes and some cytoplasm. The importance of this difference emerges when we consider the inheritance of the portion of the DNA that is found in small organelles, called *mitochondria*, within the cytoplasm of all cells, including the egg. Scientists call this *mitochondrial DNA*, or mtDNA, to distinguish it from the DNA in the nucleus, which is called nuclear DNA. There are many more maternal mitochondria in the egg than paternal mitochondria in the sperm, so mtDNA is essentially inherited entirely via the maternal line.

Unlike nuclear DNA, mtDNA is not bound to proteins. It exists in the form of small loops that are only about 16,800 base pairs in length. Each mitochondrion has between 5 and 10 of these loops, and each cell may have as many as 1,000 mitochondria, yet mtDNA still makes up only about 1 percent of the total DNA within a cell. The genes in mtDNA mostly specify proteins involved in the basic activities that are required for the care and maintenance of any cell, no matter what its special function is. The functioning of mtDNA seems to be resistant to minor differences in the sequence of the bases, so this makes mtDNA a good place to look for variations in DNA sequences that accumulate purely as a function of time, with little or no selection effect.

A gene determines the nature of a particular protein molecule. Genes occupy discrete segments of DNA, either on a chromosome or in the mtDNA. These segments are referred to as a gene's *locus*, or place (plural, *loci*). In the nuclear genome, chromosomes come in pairs, so nuclear genes have two loci. Mitochondrial genes have a single locus. Human beings are estimated to have about 25,000 to 30,000 genes. Some, called *structural genes*, code for proteins that are the components of things such as muscle and bone. Others, called *regulatory genes*, code for proteins that control processes. Genes vary in size from fewer than 20 base pairs to many thousands of base pairs. Sometimes there is a simple one-to-one link between a gene and a biological effect; such an arrangement is called a *single-gene*, or *monogenic, system.*

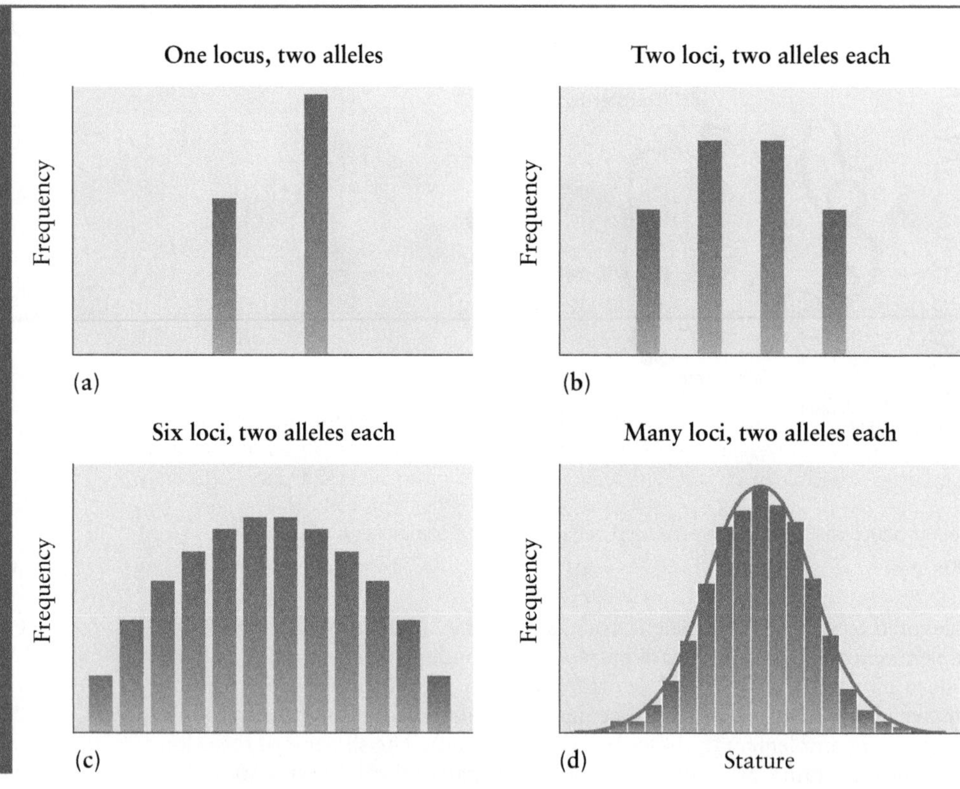

FIGURE 4.12 Traits. A plot of the expressions of a trait that is determined by many genes, such as stature, produces a smooth curve.

Most of the traits that vary among individual modern humans, such as stature, are controlled by many genes and hence are called *polygenic systems* (see Figure 4.12).

DNA is central to animal and plant life. It determines the nature of the proteins, and proteins determine what types of cells we have in our bodies and also, to a large extent, control what size and shape we are. The environment, including culture, influences human growth and development, but many of those influences are mediated by DNA.

DNA is also the basis of heredity. Offspring resemble their parents because each parent contributes half of the offspring's DNA. DNA is the thread that runs through and connects generations of the same family. It also connects us to the rest of the Tree of Life. Modern humans share approximately 99 percent of their DNA with a chimpanzee, 90 percent with a mouse, and 40 percent with a banana. Why? The reason is that all of us (even the banana!) shared a common ancestor in the distant past.

Genes located near each other on the same chromosome tend to change, and to be selected for, as a group rather than individually. These are called linked genes. A group of genes that consistently appears together is called a haplogroup, and organisms that share the same groups of genes are said to have the same haplotype (see Box 4.2, p. 90).

Evolution within Populations This section considers how evolution works at the level of a *population*, defined as a group of potentially interbreeding individuals within a species, and the subject area of population genetics. What matters within populations is the frequency and distribution of individuals with particular versions of genes.

In theory, it is possible for a population to be in a steady state with respect to evolution. In other words, the frequency of alleles does not change over time. This state is called the *Hardy-Weinberg equilibrium*. Such a steady state would exist if the alleles did not change (that is, there were no mutations), if individuals in the population mated randomly, if there were no selection, if the population were large enough to be theoretically infinite, *and* if no alleles were lost or gained. This ideal steady state, though, never exists in reality. Variation is regularly and randomly introduced into the system by mutations, which alone have little impact unless they spread within a population. Two processes encourage the spread of mutation: selection and genetic drift.

Selection can be artificial or natural. In artificial selection, breeders accelerate the pace of evolution by deliberately bringing about the opposite of random mating. Think of the trouble that breeders of prize animals take to ensure that their strain of dog, cat, or horse is strengthened by choosing the right mate. Stallions that sire champion racehorses are sold for millions of dollars because their genes have a high probability of producing a race-winning phenotype.

Natural selection is a process that constantly screens new and existing genetic variation. It cannot, by itself, generate novel variation; only mutations and the recombination of genes can do that. Natural selection works because "fitter" individuals are selectively advantaged, with the result that their pattern of alleles is represented in greater numbers in subsequent generations. Fitness, in this technical sense, is the probability that animals of a particular genotype will survive and reproduce. For example, if the expression of the A molecule in the ABO blood group system increases genetic fitness, then both the AA and AO genotypes should be equally favored by natural selection. Natural selection cannot discriminate between different genotypes if they result in the same phenotype.

Natural selection does not always result in the characteristics of the population shifting away from the average. For example, one version of natural selection, *stabilizing selection*, consists of selection against the extremes of the range of values for that species. Stabilizing selection is probably the mechanism that maintains stasis in one of the two varieties of macroevolution (discussed in the next section), called the *punctuated equilibrium model.*

Not all evolution within a population is due to selection, either natural or artificial. Much is due to chance, and chance is particularly important in small groups. When an epidemic or famine, for example, causes a population to decline in number, some genotypes, by sheer chance, will survive in larger numbers than others. If the population subsequently expands, these survivor genes will occur at a higher frequency than before. This process is called the *bottleneck effect* (see Figure 4.13). A similar change in gene frequency occurs when a small part of the original population becomes isolated. Again by chance, some genes will occur at higher frequency in these isolates than in the original population. **Genetic drift** is the effect on a population caused by chance through which some alleles, over generations, become more frequent or more rare.

genetic drift: the effect on a population caused by chance through which some alleles, over generations, become more frequent or more rare.

Crossing the Fields

Breeding and Culture in "the Sport of Kings"

For over 300 years, the English racehorse has been selectively bred to produce the fastest breed of horse in the world over any distance greater than one-quarter of a mile. Descended from three imported Arabian stallions and some domestic mares, the present generation is the result of "selective breeding"; every mating since 1791 has been recorded in the *General Stud Book.* Along with this process, English racing society emerged and evolved as well.

Cultural anthropologist Rebecca Cassidy conducted fieldwork related to thoroughbred breeding and racing in Newmarket, England, the center of British thoroughbred racing. She comments, "Riding across Newmarket Heath on some shiny specimen of thoroughbred perfection I often thought to myself, 'I must be the luckiest anthropologist ever'" (Cassidy 2002:vi).

Cassidy learned about the thoroughbred world by participating in it in diverse ways: as a guest of an owner at events, as a trainer's assistant, as a "lass" (jockey), and as a lowly hand in the stable yard. She recalls that as she was mucking out a stall one cold morning, covered with various kinds of horse secretions and wondering why she was there in the first place, her boss yelled, "Rebecca! Get your anthropological arse out here!" (p. ix).

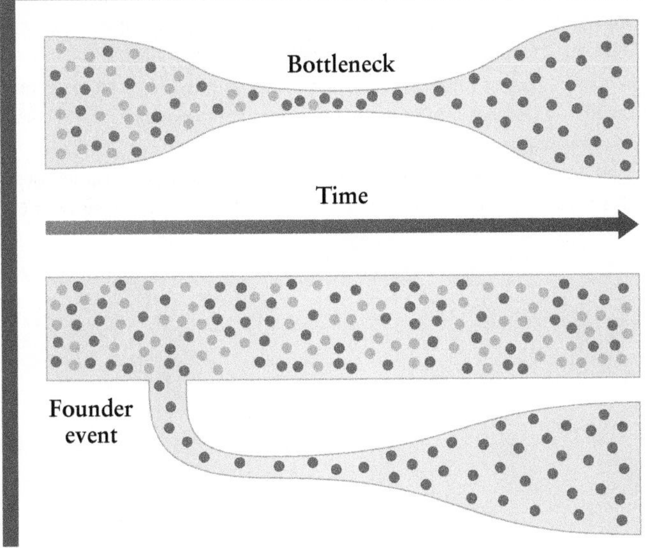

FIGURE 4.13 Bottleneck Effect. When a population declines dramatically, the genes that make it through the bottleneck are not a random sample. The same process applies, when a small number of individuals are separated from the main population through a founder event.

Box 4.2 Methods Close-Up

Using DNA Evidence to Reconstruct the Origin of the Indigenous People of the Andaman Islands

THE ANDAMAN ISLANDS are a string of islands in the Bay of Bengal that belong to India. Available archaeological data do not provide clear evidence of when modern humans first settled there. For unknown numbers of centuries, though, many of the islands were inhabited by people who fished, gathered, and hunted for their livelihood. In the early stages of European exploration and colonization, descriptions of the indigenous people of the Andamans included mention of their having tails and being cannibals who would kill and eat anyone who landed on their islands.

In 1789, when the British made their first attempt to establish a settlement, the total indigenous population was estimated at about 6,000 people, and the islands were theirs alone (Miller 1997). Now, more than 200 years later, over 400,000 people live on the islands, migrants from the Indian mainland. The total number of indigenous people is about 400. This dramatic decline is the direct and the indirect result of British colonialism, which brought contagious diseases, led to increased violence among indigenous groups, and involved outright killing by the British of Andaman people who resisted their land being taken from them.

From the time of earliest observation of Andamanese people by outsiders, they have been objects of curiosity because of their physical appearance. They are much shorter than the majority populations of neighboring South and Southeast Asia. In addition, their hair forms small, tight curls close to their head. They look more like members of indigenous populations of southern Africa and of remote and hilly regions of southern India and Southeast Asia, including Malaysia and the Philippines.

Only four surviving clusters of indigenous Andamanese exist. The smallest group, just a few dozen people, is made up of the last members of the "Great Andamanese" populations. They live on a small island near Port Blair and in what is essentially a reservation area. North and Middle Andaman Islands were formerly populated by several different groups of "Great Andamanese" peoples, but there are no indigenous peoples on these islands any more. The Jarawa, numbering perhaps 200, live in a reserved area on the southwest portion of South Andaman. The Onge, around 100 in number, live in one corner of Little Andaman. Another 100 people or so live on North Sentinel Island, and they are called the Sentinelese. No one from the outside has gotten much closer than arrow-range of their shore in the past century.

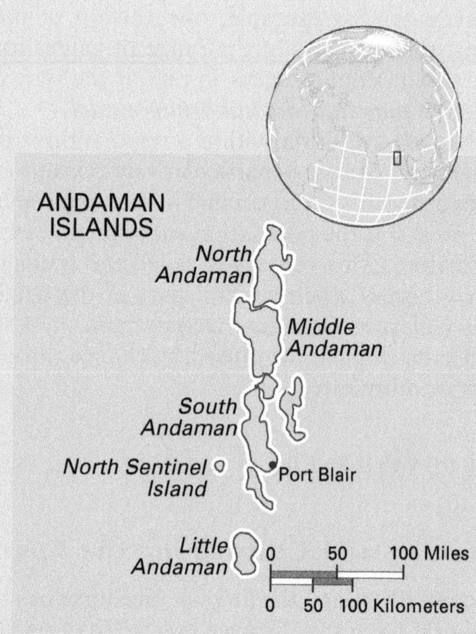

MAP 4.1 The Andaman Islands, India. The 576 islands are geographically part of Myanmar and Southeast Asia. The British Empire controlled them until India's independence in 1947.

Anthropologists have recently used genetic evidence to trace the spread of modern humans out of Africa throughout the rest of the world (the topic of Chapter 8). An intriguing part of this story is the settlement of the Andaman Islands. Where, anthropologists ask, do the Andamanese people fit into the picture of modern humanity's global migrations? Is their similarity in appearance to southern African indigenous peoples due to a shared recent common ancestor or was it independently acquired?

Some nineteenth-century anthropologists collected skeletons of the Andamanese, and the remains of more than fifty individuals are in the Natural History Museum in London. Scientists selected eleven relatively well-preserved Andamanese skeletons from this collection for analysis (Endicott et al. 2003). They examined the teeth from these skeletons to see whether there was sufficient DNA to enable them to be compared with the DNA from living populations. They concentrated on two parts of the mitochondrial genome (mtDNA), the hypervariable (HRV1) and the protein-coding regions.

The findings indicate that the islands were initially populated through a single migration event no earlier than 40,000 years ago. The evidence points to the origin of the settlers in eastern India.

Another study used blood samples of living Andamanese people from the Great Andamanese group and the Onge people (Thangaraj et al. 2002; Thangaraj et al. 2005). These results revealed two distinct sequences, named M31 and M32, which the authors claim have no overlap with known sequences in either India or Southeast Asia. They attribute this finding to a process called *genetic drift* (see p. 89), which is likely in such small populations. Thus any resemblance to African populations is the result of independent evolution.

An even more recent study, however, examined mtDNA for some "tribal" populations of eastern India and found strong similarities with the M31 sequence (Endicott et al. 2006). This study puts the approximate time of migration to the islands at around 30,000 years ago, a time of low sea levels, which would have facilitated access to the archipelago from the mainland.

Because mtDNA analysis is highly complicated, it can lead to errors in interpretation and scientific disagreements about interpretation of results. Analytical methods are, however, improving yearly. Researchers working to reconstruct ancient population movements into Asia are also hampered by lack of data, especially for tribal populations in India and for the population of Myanmar as a whole, which is closed to outside scientists. Scientists, though, continue to find value in museum collections and to increase DNA datasets for living populations.

One of the many uninhabited islands in the Andamans, with typically dense coverage of mangrove trees. The Indian government is encouraging people from the mainland to settle in the Andamans. One result is widespread deforestation. *Visit the web site www.andaman.org for information on the Andaman Islands.* (*Source:* Barbara Miller)

Ethnographic research in the early twentieth century often involved photography. This girl wears the skull of her deceased sister. Indigenous people of the Andamans revere the bones of their dead relatives and would not want them to be taken away, studied, or displayed in a museum. (*Source:* A. R. Radcliffe-Brown, *The Andaman Islanders.* Cambridge: Cambridge University Press, 1992 [1922])

Cassidy learned about how people's perceptions of the "nature" of horses was related to their breeding, the process of training and racing thoroughbreds, bloodstock auctions, and the huge industry of betting on horses. In addition, it involved a particular social class system consisting of owners, breeders, trainers, racing administrators, lads, farriers (blacksmiths), stud-workers, and work-riders.

A pervasive explanation for ability or talent in both horses and people is breeding and pedigree. Breeding and pedigree explain a successful horse—it has "good blood." They explain a well-bred horse's failure—it was an accident, a flaw, even too much fine blood perhaps requiring more "rough" blood in future matings.

The social aristocrats of the racing world are the owners, and their position is thought to be based on superior blood and breeding. But not everyone born into an elite racing family is considered a member of the racing community. If a person fails to maintain a connection to racing, blood relatives draw a line through his or her place on the family tree. The explanation for this failure would be found in blood: an accident, a flaw, or too much fine blood.

This system of blood explanations for both horses and humans is now being challenged. In terms of horses, the possibility of cloning may destroy the traditional concept of pedigree, because individual horses would no longer be unique. In terms of the human aristocracy of horse owners, the increasing trend toward ownership by foreigners, especially wealthy oil sheikhs from the Middle East, also threatens the meaning and stability of blood as the explanation for human success or failure.

Macroevolution

Macroevolution is the large-scale evolutionary history of any group of organisms. This section briefly discusses three examples of macroevolutions: speciation, adaptive radiation, and extinction.

speciation: a form of macroevolutionary change in which new species are produced either by the splitting of an existing species into two new species or by the transformation of an existing species into a different descendant.

Speciation Speciation is the macroevolutionary process in which new species are produced either by the splitting of an existing species into two new species or by the transformation of an existing species into a different descendant. Among mammals, including primates, a new species can be generated in two ways: *allopatric* and *parapatric* speciation. In allopatric speciation, a small part of an existing species undergoes so much microevolution—usually with the help of some isolating mechanism such as a change in the course of a large river or a change in climate that eliminates forests between the isolated population and the main population—that it eventually becomes distinct from the parent species. In parapatric speciation, speciation occurs at the boundary between two distinct regional populations. Although interbreeding occurs within the boundary zone (the resulting offspring are called hybrids), on either side of the boundary each group behaves as if it were a reproductively isolated species.

Some researchers think that new species are the result of gradual change involving the whole population. This point of view is the *phyletic gradualism model* of evolution, and the form of gradual speciation associated with it is termed *anagenesis*. Others see speciation as being due to bursts of rapid evolutionary

A horse race at Ascot, England, attended by members of the elite. Rebecca Cassidy's research shows parallels between English perceptions about breeding and quality in race horses and in humans. (*Source:* © 2004 Getty Images)

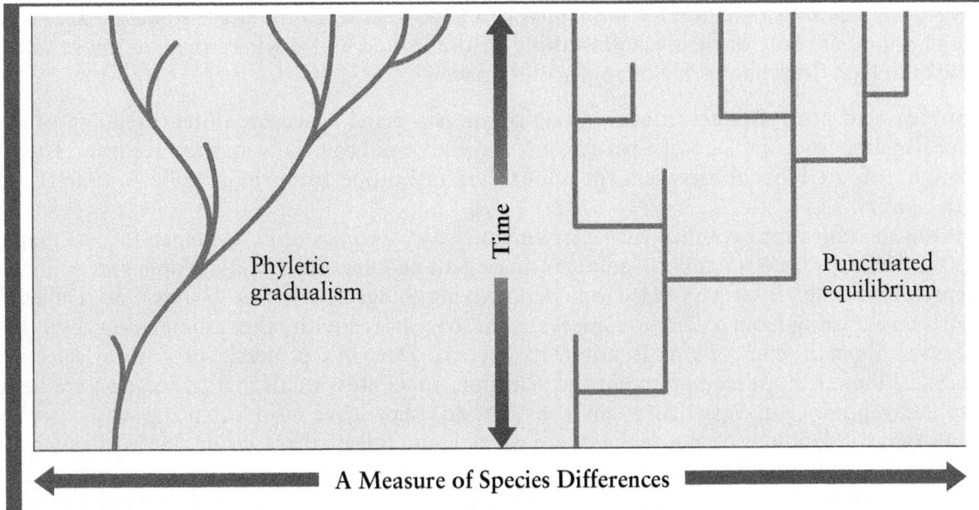

FIGURE 4.14 The Phyletic Gradualism and Punctuated Equilibrium Models for Evolution

change concentrated in a subset of the population. In this model, most morphological evolution occurs at the time of allopatric speciation. This rapid-change model also suggests that between these bursts of evolution there should be no sustained trends in the direction of morphological evolution, just "random walk" fluctuations in morphology (see Figure 4.14).

The term *stasis* is used to describe these periods of morphological stability. The pattern of long periods of stasis separated by episodes of species generation is called the *punctuated-equilibrium model.* Species formation in the rapid-change model is called *cladogenesis*—literally, "speciation by splitting." In some circumstances, speciation may be due to large-scale changes in the genotype brought about by rearrangements in the chromosomes. Researchers think that such large-scale changes may have occurred when modern humans split off from the other apes (Navarro and Barton 2003).

Adaptive Radiation One way in which taxa differ is in whether their members are *generalists* or *specialists.* Generalists use and tolerate a wide range of environments, and they eat a variety of foods. Specialists are restricted to a narrow range of habitats, and their diet is usually limited to certain kinds of foods, such as leaves or fruits. Given these differences, generalists and specialists are likely to have different evolutionary histories. When climate change affects the habitat, specialist taxa, occupying their narrow niches, are more likely to become extinct, yet they are also more likely to respond to changes in the paleoenvironments by speciating. Generalist lineages tend to speciate less.

During evolutionary history, some groups of taxa have undergone periods of intensive speciation and diversification. The term **adaptive radiation** refers to the macroevolutionary process of rapid speciation of one or a few species as an adaptation to a new ecological niche. Adaptive radiations appear to be associated with an opportunity to exploit a new environment, such as when another group declines in number or goes extinct and an opportunity opens up in an existing environment.

adaptive radiation: the macroevolutionary process of rapid speciation of one or a few species as an adaptation to a new ecological niche.

Extinction **Extinction** is the macroevolutionary process when a living species ceases to exist. In the fossil record, paleoanthropologists assume that a species is extinct when they can no longer find fossil evidence for it. All species, including ours, will ultimately become extinct. What is at issue is whether the causes of a species's extinction are to be found within its microevolutionary history or whether extinctions are determined by external events such as changes in the environment. This question can be studied in the laboratory by varying the conditions under which rapidly evolving organisms such as fruit flies are kept. It can also be investigated by comparing changes in the fossil record with evidence about past climates.

extinction: a form of macroevolutionary change that occurs when a living species ceases to exist or, in paleoanthropology, when one no longer finds fossil evidence of a species.

Later, we will discuss examples of species of early human ancestors that are now extinct. We will also consider the possible role of humans in leading to the extinction of other animals, especially large game animals. The topic of extinction connects to the biblical narrative discussed earlier in the chapter. According to the Bible, God would not have created animals that would become extinct. The fact of species extinction, established in the nineteenth century, was one more reason why doubt was cast on the biblical narrative about the origin of humanity.

Alternative Explanations for Human Origins

This chapter has presented scientific explanations for human evolution. It does not address or make judgments about matters of religious faith held by people who, for one reason or another, are opposed to a scientific, evolution-based explanation for humanity. It is important to consider the so-called anti-evolutionists through a look at some of their manifestations in the United States where they are most active. This section looks only at Christian forms of anti-evolutionism.

creationism: the Bible-based belief that all species date from the Day of Creation and have always been the way they are now.

Creationism and Neo-Creationists **Creationism** is a belief based on a literal reading of the Bible that all species date from the Day of Creation and have always been the way they are now. The roots of creationism are in the biblical literalism that flourished in Europe from the Middle Ages until the mid-nineteenth century.

Creationism comes into conflict with Darwinian theory and scientific evidence in two major ways (Scott 2004). First, it rejects a common ancestry among all peoples and among people and animals. A literal interpretation of the Bible says that God created living things as separate "kinds." So, Darwin's view of humans as originating from a common ancestor, and one shared with other animals, suggests that what the Bible says about human origins is not true. Second, Darwin's principle of natural selection goes against biblical literalism. According to natural selection, some individuals in a population are better able to survive and reproduce in a particular environment, and they leave more offspring who carry on their genes. Thus many individuals do not make it, are wasted, and fall by the wayside. How can such a wasteful process be the result of a benevolent God (Scott 2004:xxiii)? In the view of the creationists/anti-evolutionists, a benevolent God would not allow such waste. Since such a benevolent God exists, natural selection cannot be valid.

Creationism has many historical and contemporary manifestations. William Paley, mentioned earlier in this chapter, published a book in 1802 entitled *Natural Theology*, a defense of the biblical version of creation. Paley suggested that an elaborate outcome, such as a watch, means that there must have been a watch designer and a watch maker in the past. Something as complex as a watch could not be the result of a series of accidents over time. An example from the living world is the complex eye of mammals. Because the mammalian eye is so complex, there must have been a designer and maker of it in the past. This approach is called an *argument from design*, or *intelligent design* (Ruse 2003).

THINKING OUTSIDE THE BOX

DO SOME RESEARCH to find out why the practice of dissection was abandoned in Europe at the same time that Christianity became the dominant religion.

The argument from design, and against scientific evolution, has changed its focus and now frames itself as scientific. Intelligent Design Creationists (IDCs) claim that intelligent design is a scientific theory that should be placed alongside, and even displace, evolution as the best explanation for human origins. Supporters of intelligent design emphasize a principle called *irreducible complexity*. They suggest that some parts of life are so complex that they would not function unless all the parts were present at once. Irreducible complexity means that a process such as evolution, which depends on chance events, could not have resulted in a sophisticated structure like the mammalian eye. The IDCs claim that their view deserves equal time in schools with that of human evolution, on the principle of "fairness," a principle that all sides should be heard (Scott 2004:xxiii). Disputes in the United States are ongoing about educational content.

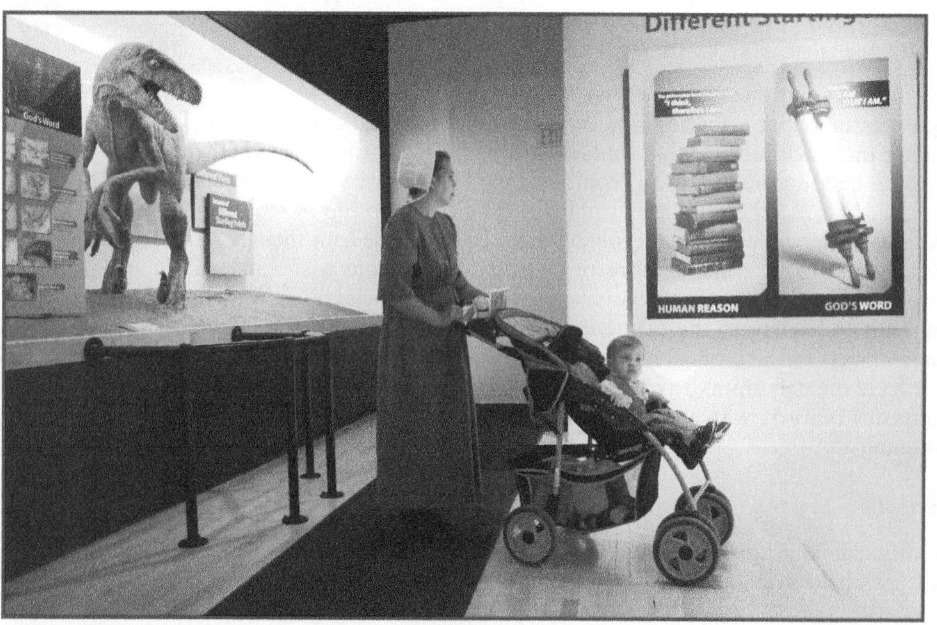

An Amish mother and her child from Ohio view an exhibit at the Creation Museum in Petersburg, Kentucky. The museum opened in May 2007. (*Source:* Mark Lyons/Corbis).

The Response from Science Biological anthropologists and others who accept the scientific approach agree that organisms are complex. They say, however, that the fossil record indicates that organisms did not become complex instantly. Instead, organisms accumulated complexity over time—even immense periods of time—under the influence of natural selection. Natural selection, they say, is sufficient to explain the diversity and complexity of modern humanity. The natural world, including humanity, did not need a designer.

In the United States, the IDCs and other supporters of what is called creation science claim that it provides a *scientific* alternative to evolutionary interpretations of human origins. No one doubts the religious sincerity of creation scientists, but their explanations are not science. Science relies on data; creationism relies on belief and rejects data. Evolution is consistent with evidence; creationism is consistent with belief.

The Big Questions Revisited

WHAT is the scientific view about humanity?

The links between humanity and the rest of the natural world have been recognized at least since the time of the classical Greek and Roman philosophers, but the scientific evidence for this view has accumulated largely in the past two centuries.

In Europe, a literal interpretation of the Bible was the predominant view between the fifth and nineteenth centuries. Humanity was thought to have arisen through divine creation, and humans were viewed as being at the top of the Great Chain of Being. This view made no allowance for extinct creatures or for any evolutionary change within species.

The Renaissance and the age of exploration provided the foundation for scientific thinking, which relies on observation, hypothesis formation and revision, and further observation in order to understand phenomena. From the fifteenth century onward, accumulating evidence led scientists to question the validity of an explanation for human origins that relied on a literal interpretation of the biblical narrative.

HOW does the concept of evolution explain humanity?

By the middle of the nineteenth century, substantial evidence had accumulated to support the theory of evolution. Evolution needs three things: natural selection, variation, and heredity.

Variation occurs because mutation and recombination ensure that no two individuals are exactly alike. Mendelian genetics provided the basic rules about heredity and the inheritance of variation. The mechanism of inheritance is the genetic code that is encrypted within DNA.

The extent to which modern humans and other animals share the same DNA provides the best evidence that humanity is part of the Tree of Life. The genomes of a modern human and a chimpanzee are more similar than those of a chimpanzee and a gorilla. Thus, just as DNA is the thread that connects different generations of the same animal, it also connects humanity to the rest of the natural world.

HOW does evolution work?

Evolution works at two levels: microevolution and macroevolution. Microevolution works at the level of the individual and includes short-term changes within local populations. Macroevolution consists of long-term processes that have occurred in evolutionary history, such as the emergence of new species, adaptive radiations, and extinction.

Starting in the 1950s, discoveries about DNA showed how small changes in the structure and function of molecules can produce changes in the structure and function of an animal. These small changes in the structure of DNA, when reflected in the phenotype, provide the differences in performance upon which natural selection can act.

Not everyone accepts the Darwinian model of human evolution that argues for the roots of humanity in earlier animal ancestors and for the process of natural selection as the key determinant of adaptation and change over time. Especially in the United States, neo-creationism is an increasingly popular alternative to explaining human origins through a literal interpretation of the Bible. Neo-creationists, especially the Intelligence Design Creationists, argue that life is so complex that it requires an intelligent designer (God) who created it all at once; in their view, complexity could not have evolved through something as random as natural selection.

Key Concepts

allele, p. 83
adaptive radiation, p. 93
chromosome, p. 83
creationism, p. 94
DNA, p. 78
extinction, p. 93
fossil, p. 76
gene, p. 81
genetic drift, p. 89
genome, p. 80
genotype, p. 80
Linnaean taxonomy, p. 77
macroevolution, p. 82
meiosis, p. 83
microevolution, p. 82
mitosis, p. 83
mutation, p. 85
natural selection, p. 80
phenotype, p. 82
scientific method, p. 75
speciation, p. 76
species, p. 78
stratigraphy, p. 63
taxon, p. 77

Suggested Readings

Robin M. Henig. *The Monk in the Garden*. Boston: Houghton Mifflin, 2000. This book is based on careful research about Mendel and his famous experiments. The second half of the book deals with how Mendel's work was rediscovered and became the basis for modern genetics.

Mark Issak. *The Counter-Creationism Handbook*. Berkeley: University of California Press, 2005. This book presents anti-evolutionist arguments and counter-arguments. Chapters are organized into philosophy and theology, biology, paleontology, geology, astronomy and cosmology, physics and mathematics, and history, linguistics, and folklore. Two chapters address biblical creationism and intelligent design (ID).

Horace F. Judson. *The Eighth Day of Creation*. New York: Simon and Schuster, 1980. This book traces the discovery of the basis for the genetic code. Judson interviewed many of the leading scientists, and the book provides a detailed account of the research that preceded the unraveling of the structure and function of DNA.

Evelyn Fox Keller. *The Century of the Gene*. Cambridge, MA: Harvard University Press, 2000. Keller chronicles the history of the research that culminated in the discovery of the chemical basis for genes. The book assumes some knowledge of science.

Ernst Mayr. *What Evolution Is*. New York: Basic Books, 2001. This text, which assumes some knowledge of biology, provides an introduction to the principles of, and evidence for, evolution.

John A. Moore. *Science as a Way of Knowing*. Cambridge, MA: Harvard University Press, 1993. A history of how biological thinking and research developed, this book begins with the Greeks and then sets out the major developments in biological research.

John A. Moore. *From Genesis to Genetics*. Berkeley, CA: University of California Press, 2002. This book explains the controversy between scientific evolution and creationism. The author encourages science and religion to do the work for which each is uniquely qualified.

Mark Pagel. *Encyclopedia of Evolution*. Oxford: Oxford University Press, 2002. This encyclopedia contains short articles about the main elements of evolution. It covers all the major topics, including Mendelian and population genetics, natural selection, and micro- and macroevolutionary mechanisms.

Robert T. Pennock, ed. *Intelligent Design: Creationism and Its Critics*. Cambridge, MA: MIT Press, 2002. The author presents the arguments for and against Intelligent Design Creationism.

Mark Ridley. *Evolution*. Oxford: Blackwell, 2003. This includes both evolutionary theory and the evidence for evolution.

Michael Ruse. *The Darwinian Revolution*. Chicago: Chicago University Press, 1999. This history of evolutionary thought begins by describing ideas about evolution before Darwin. Then it reviews the impact of Charles Darwin's ideas about evolutionary mechanisms on his contemporaries and those who followed.

Michael Ruse. *Can a Darwinian Be a Christian? The Relationship between Science and Religion*. New York: Cambridge University Press, 2001. The author says "yes," and presents arguments on the following topics: the origin of life, the soul, design, miracles, pain, and ethics. He explores the complexity of the issues and how a particular standpoint might be reached.

Eugenie C. Scott. *Evolution vs. Creationism: An Introduction*. Berkeley: University of California Press, 2004. Scott provides a comprehensive and balanced survey of the debate in the United States about teaching evolution in schools. The book discusses diverse religious points of view, relationships between religious beliefs and science, and the scientific evidence of human evolution. The volume concludes with references for further exploration.

P. Tort. *Darwin and the Science of Evolution*. New York: Abrams, 2001. This short, illustrated book provides an introduction to Darwin's life and explains how he developed the ideas that shape current scientific thinking about evolution.

Christopher P. Toumey. *God's Own Scientists: Creationists in a Secular World*. New Brunswick, NJ: Rutgers University Press, 1994. A cultural anthropologist reports on the results of his long-term research project among contemporary Christian creationists in North Carolina in the 1980s. The book includes historical context on reactions to evolutionary theory in the United States during the nineteenth and early twentieth centuries. Most of the book focuses on the variety of creationist groups and thinking in North Carolina and includes disputes with schools about the teaching of evolution.

5 chapter

Human Development and Socialization

Man is born a barbarian, and only rises himself above the beast by culture.

BALTASAR GRACIAN (1601–1658)—
SPANISH WRITER AND JESUIT PRIEST

He who opens a school closes a prison.

VICTOR HUGO (1802–1885)—
FRENCH POET AND NOVELIST

As Lynn headed out to go shopping, she already knew her four-year-old son was in a bad mood. All that day he had been doing all that he could to frustrate her. First, he chose not to eat breakfast and then he spilled apple juice all over the carpet. He categorically refused to put on his red jacket and continuously tried to unbuckle his seatbelt in the car. Since they had arrived at the shopping mall, he had been whining continuously for 20 minutes and demanding they go to the toy store immediately. The mother's patience finally ran out when her son ran away and started picking up coins from the fountain. Lynn pulled him out of the fountain and spanked him three or four times. The son reacted first with a brief and silent pause of embarrassment and then filled the shopping mall with a high-pitched scream. A couple of crystal tears rolled down his cheeks. "This is horrible. You cannot treat your child like this," a woman passerby said loudly as she pointed at Lynn. "You shouldn't do that, ma'am," uttered another woman. "At least not in a public place." Lynn could not understand why these strangers reacted in this way. She had arrived two years ago, as a Cambodian refugee, and thus far had had nothing critical said to her. What had she done to upset these people? Cambodian child-rearing practices allow spanking. Moreover, this type of physical punishment is a major component of the child's learning process in her home country, where parental authority in the family is absolute and may not be challenged. Most parental behavior is supported by the extended family, the local community, and the Buddhist religion. True, child spanking is common around the world. However, if a parent grew up in a different culture, what rule should he or she follow: tradi-

Cross-Cultural Psychology: Critical Thinking and Contemporary Applications,
Fourth Edition, by Eric B. Shiraev and David A. Levy

tional ethnic or contemporary American, which denounces spanking? What if the parent chooses spanking? If we tell a parent what to do, will this violate the parent's freedom of choice? We know that spanking as a custom can change. Perhaps education will stimulate such a change: Around the world, middle-class parents believe less in physical punishment than working-class parents do. Hopefully, an open competition of ideas will deem spanking the least effective method of upbringing. However, this is only a wish. The competition of ideas continues. So does spanking of children.

Development and Socialization

Psychologists distinguish between human development and socialization. **Human development** is viewed as the changes in physical, psychological, and social behavior that are experienced by individuals across the life span—from conception to death. **Socialization** is the process by which an individual becomes a member of a particular culture and takes on its values and behaviors. Neither human development nor socialization stops at age 18 or even 25. It is a lifelong process with accelerations and delays, changes in direction, sudden transitions, and long-term conversions. Human development is not only growth, but also decline and modification. In a small village in China or in a big city in South America, people change their attitudes and acquire new beliefs. They may lose skills in one area while developing expertise in other fields. A writer or an actor can become president. Presidents become writers. People go through life changes both positive and negative, migrate, or stay in one place. Regardless of who you are, you may change your career and lifestyle when you are 20, 40, or 60 years old.

We begin with an overview of the impact of culture on development and socialization and then—before describing specific life span stages—turn attention to several specific psychological theories of development.

Quality of Life and the Child's Development

The overall quality of life—availability of food and other products, type of living conditions, quality of education and health care, presence or absence of violence in the child's life, and a number of other factors—significantly affects the child's development. Countries vary in overall density of population and number of immediate family members. A unit of two adults living with their own children is common in Western societies, such as Canada, Sweden, or the United States, whereas the large extended family in which parents, children, grandparents, cousins, and even some distant relatives live in one household is common in non-Western countries, such as Pakistan, Rwanda, or Indonesia. Technological advancements and socioeconomic improvements may affect the composition of the family (Berry, 1997).

A study of 799 students in Greece, Cyprus, the Netherlands, Great Britain, and Germany examined the relationship of family bonds to family structure but did not find substantial differences among families in the sampled countries in terms of emotional closeness, geographic proximity to relatives, and frequency of telephone contacts (Georgas et al., 1997). However, when the extended families were analyzed, differences were found between generally wealthy individualist countries in the sample (the Netherlands, Great Britain, and Germany) and predominantly collectivist countries (Greece and Cyprus). The extended families in the latter sample were emotionally and geographically closer to each other than the families from the individualist sample.

Not only family size but also specific aspects of family relationship can correlate with industrial and financial advancement. For instance, second- and third-generation Mexican American children showed decreasing frequency of altruistic behavior compared to their first-generation Mexican American peers, who are less advanced economically (Knight & Kagan, 1977).

Access to resources and educational opportunities are likely to provide an advantageous environment for the developing child. Vygotsky (1932) established that guided interaction with a more knowledgeable partner should advance the intellectual development of the child. Middle-class parents answer children's questions with more elaborate explanations than do parents of a lower social class, who are generally less educated than middle-class families. It was shown in one study that Mexican mothers from low-socioeconomic status groups—contrary to mothers from other families—used tactile interaction, such as a touch and push, with their children more frequently than they used verbal means (Zepeda, 1985). In many working class communities in the United States, as well as in preindustrial communities in Africa and the Pacific, parents have low willingness to instruct their children themselves and tend to assume that children can learn things on their own (Rogoff, 1990).

Poverty may directly affect relationships within the family. In preindustrial and economically underdeveloped societies, partly because of limited access to resources, close cooperation within families becomes an economic necessity.

Norms, Customs, and Child Care

The child's development and socialization depend on the people with whom the child interacts, the places where they spend time together, and the roles children play (Whiting & Whiting, 1975). Adults assign children to some roles and disallow others. For example, cross-cultural differences in the behavior of boys and girls may be partially due to different roles assigned to them by adults. Girls are more apt to stay close to home and are more involved in child-care activities than are boys (Whiting & Edwards, 1988). Rough-and-tumble play is a common child's activity across cultures. However, in traditional Muslim countries, girls are seldom encouraged by their parents to engage in such games (Ahmed, 2002).

There are similarities in patterns of social support from children, spouses, relatives, and friends. However, comparative studies identify plenty of national and cultural differences. For example, rocking or thumb-sucking in children would be considered wrong by white South African mothers. For native African mothers such behavior is absolutely normal. U.S. mothers respond more favorably to their babies' requests when the infants are playing with physical objects. Japanese mothers, on the other hand, are more responsive when their babies are engaged in play with them. Japanese parents, unlike U.S. parents, rarely leave their children with baby-sitters. These children learn how to interact with other adults, and this may explain why Japanese children display a higher rate of anxiety than U.S. boys and girls do when the parents are not present (Bornstein & Tamis-LeMonda, 1989). Studies on parent–child communication show that French and Italian parents and children are more interactive than German pairs (Best, 1994). An exaggeration in one's gratitude is considered normal and is even expected in Arab cultures (Triandis, 1994). "Thank you" letters are commonly sent by U.S. boys and girls to their birthday guests. This tradition is practically unknown in Ukraine, Armenia, and many other countries.

Cultural traditions of collectivism are positively correlated with the authoritarian style of parenting, which is based on strict demands, behavioral control, and sanctions (Rudy & Grusec, 2001). In other words, in predominantly collectivist cultures more parents practice authoritarian methods than they do in individualist cultures. Of course, we should understand that besides collectivism, many societal factors contribute to authoritarian methods, including political authoritarianism, lack of education, social instability, and educational traditions. For instance, Russian adolescents perceived parents and teachers as more controlling than did U.S. students (Chirkov & Ryan, 2001). Russian elementary and secondary education and parenting styles are seen by observers as more authoritarian than the styles practiced in the United States.

Findings from a comparative study of white, Mexican American, and Mexican parents revealed that white parents reported less authoritarian parenting than Mexican Americans. However, no differences were found in authoritarian parenting style between white and Mexican parents (Varela et al., 2004).

Box 5.1 Cross-Cultural Sensitivity

Are there any words that a teacher is not supposed to use in a multicultural classroom? Of course, profanities should be out. What about other words? Let us discuss a story in which good intentions are not always supported by the appropriate knowledge.

For example, if you were a teacher in a New York public school and all students in your class are black or Hispanic, would you choose to read them multicultural books? When Ruth Sherman, a 27-year-old teacher, read a story to her class about Brenda, a little black girl from Haiti, the students liked the reading very much. They really enjoyed the teacher's funny voice and good acting. They enjoyed it so much that some students asked Ms. Sherman to make a few copies of the story so that they could read it at home. This is where the controversy begins. No, it is not about the copyright law. The photocopy of the story caught some parents' eye and sparked their angry reactions (Clementson, 1998). The problem was in the title of the story: *Nappy Hair*. *Nappy* is a colloquialism for curly African hair. What is wrong with it? Unfortunately this word is sometimes used as a put-down or disrespectful expression. Some parents, therefore, believed that this title should not have been used in class because it ridicules people with a certain type of hair. Others suggested that the words were not the problem. The problem was the teacher—because she was white she had no business to use such words with black children.

When we asked our colleagues to comment on this story, some of them—and they all were college professors and researchers of different backgrounds—emphasized to us that it always creates an unpleasant feeling when someone mentions anything about your body height, shape of your eyes, size of your nose, skin color, and texture of your hair in connection with your ethnicity or origin. As mentioned earlier, to be sensitive, one should develop empathy—the ability to understand and appreciate other people's feelings. The teacher in this story did nothing illegal. However, as a teacher, she touched a very sensitive string of people's identity and emotions attached to it.

Adoptive parents of children with different ethnic backgrounds are likely to use similar strategies of adoption disclosure, caring above all about whether the truth about adoption causes a psychological trauma in the child, and whether it is done at the appropriate time and under favorable circumstances (Alexander et al., 2004).

Once a norm is established, it may be passed on from one generation to the next. In most traditional African cultures, obedience is a highly desired pattern of behavior for children, a pattern that is crucial for the child's survival in harsh living conditions (Klingelhofer, 1971). Most Western concepts of child-rearing judge obedience critically and condemn most forms of adult–child coercion.

The parents' age must be remembered both for joy and anxiety.

CONFUCIUS (551–479 B.C.E.)—CHINESE PHILOSOPHER

Parental Values and Expectations

Parents typically have their own developmental timetables: they expect their children to acquire particular characteristics (such as walking, talking, or reasoning) at certain ages. Research shows that despite large individual variations, there are some cultural patterns in such expectations (Super & Harkness, 1997). In one study, for example, Israeli mothers of European background expected their children to develop certain cognitive skills earlier than did mothers of non-European origin (Ninio, 1979). U.S. mothers had earlier expectations of their children's assertiveness than Japanese mothers, and Japanese mothers had earlier expectations about their children's ability to control their emotions and express courtesy (Hess et al., 1980). According to Levy (1996), in societies that are small, egalitarian, and with little occupational specialization, children are expected to learn "on their own," whereas in industrialized democratic societies there are explicit expectations about what, with whom, when, and how children should learn.

Parents' particular beliefs are translated into behavior that, in reverse, influences other beliefs. Japanese mothers generally view autonomy of the child as her ability to interact with other children. For many Israeli mothers, the child's independence is the ability to perform certain instrumental tasks, such as answering the phone and setting the table (Osterweil & Nagano, 1991).

Parents from different cultural groups may hold different views on the formal education of their children and their role as parents in this process. Chao (1996) asked a sample of 48 immigrants of Chinese origin (Taiwan) and 50 European American mothers of preschool age children to indicate their views on the role of parenting in the child's school success. The Chinese mothers expressed a greater interest in education and suggested that they were willing to sacrifice for the sake of the children to a greater extent than their U.S. counterparts. On the contrary, European American mothers stressed the importance of building their children's self-esteem and expressed less motivation regarding their children's education. Why did these differences occur? Most of the Taiwanese immigrants to the United States who were studied came from a middle-class stratum and most of them emigrated from Taiwan for economic reasons. This might suggest a high level of achievement motivation in this group.

Parents who are afraid to put their foot down usually have children who stepped on their toes.

CHINESE PROVERB

In a 2001 study, parental concepts of desirable and undesirable behavior were compared across two samples: 30 Japanese and 30 U.S. mothers. The women were asked to describe the behavioral characteristics they found most desirable and undesirable in children and to choose one characteristic in each list that they considered most highly positive or negative. In describing desirable characteristics, mothers in both cultures tended to emphasize social cooperativeness and interpersonal sensitivity. Comparisons of negative behaviors revealed cultural contrasts. U.S. mothers were far more likely than Japanese mothers to designate aggressive and disruptive behaviors as negative, whereas Japanese mothers tended to highlight social insensitivity and uncooperativeness (Olson et al., 2001).

Consider another illustration. A study asked 175 mothers from India, Japan, and England to indicate the age at which they expect their child to achieve confidence in 45 different activities, including education, compliance, interaction with other children, emotional control, and environmental awareness (Joshi & MacLean, 1997). It was found that competence was expected at an earlier age in Japan than it was in England. Indian mothers expected competence at a later stage than mothers in both England and Japan. However, the expectations of Indian mothers were considerably different from the expectations of the other two groups on all items except environmental competence, where they were "later" than Japanese

Box 5.2 Critical Thinking

Look at the Samples

The authors of the three-country study mentioned below suggested that the differences among the samples could not be attributed to socioeconomic factors because all the samples were taken from suburban areas and the income was approximately the same in terms of its purchasing power. However, such direct comparisons can be misleading. Even though a family in country A can purchase the same amount of food as a family in country B, the quality of purchased food could be dramatically different. If two families in two countries have access to medical care, the quality of care in country B could be significantly higher than the quality in country A. In the case studied previously, the scope and depth of the problems that India faces—overpopulation, infectious diseases, corruption, environmental problems, to name a few—can only remotely resemble the daily problems of average U.S. and Japanese citizens.

but "earlier" than English mothers. Why did such differences occur? The subjects from Japan and England were taken from urban areas. Children in those regions live primarily in small families and the mother—who is likely to have a job—is expected to encourage her child's independence at an early age. In contrast, the Indian mothers may not be under such pressure to encourage their child's independence early. Indian children from the sample lived mainly in large extended families, with many relatives representing two or three generations in one household. Even though one might expect that Japanese and Indian societies share similar cultural characteristics such as collectivism and the priority of family values, such similarities may be overshadowed by particular socioeconomic factors such as quality of life, availability of diversified information, and access to computers and advanced technologies.

Erikson's Stages of Psychosocial Development

American psychologist Erik Erikson (1950) theorized that all humans pass through a series of eight developmental stages that stretch from birth to death. Each stage is characterized by a developmental conflict, problem, or crisis. If the crisis has a positive resolution, the person's ego is strengthened by gaining a virtue that results in greater adaptation and a healthier personality. But if the crisis has a negative resolution, the ego loses strength, resulting in inhibited adaptation and an unhealthier personality. For instance, if a young girl's conflict between a desire to go and play on the street (an independent decision, initiative) and fear of retribution from parents (guilt) has a positive resolution, she will emerge with the virtue of purpose; negative outcome, however, would result in a sense of unworthiness (see Table 5.1).

Erikson thus defined the healthy or mature personality as one that possesses the eight virtues (namely hope, will, purpose, competence, fidelity, love, care, and wisdom) that emerge from a positive resolution at each stage of development. It was Erikson's belief that the outcome of every crisis resolution is reversible. The goal in his approach to psychotherapy, therefore, was to encourage the growth of whatever virtues the person was missing to achieve happiness (Erikson, 1968).

TABLE 5.1 Developmental Stages According to Erikson

Stage	Ego Crisis	Age	Positive Outcome
1	Basic trust versus mistrust	0–1	Hope
2	Autonomy versus shame and doubt	2–3	Will
3	Initiative versus guilt	3–5	Purpose
4	Industry versus inferiority	5–12	Competence
5	Ego identity versus role confusion	Adolescence	Fidelity
6	Intimacy versus isolation	Young adult	Love
7	Generativity versus stagnation	Adulthood	Care
8	Ego integrity versus despair	Maturity	Wisdom

Source: Based on Erikson (1950).

According to a comprehensive analysis (Gardiner et al., 1998), this theory could be applicable in a wide variety of cultural settings. However, as was the case with Maslow's theory, Erikson has been criticized by psychologists for mixing objective description with subjective prescription. Specifically, the virtues he uses to define the healthy individual are clearly in accordance with Western, Judeo–Christian ethics, values, and social institutions. In other words, Erikson, like many social theorists, may have been describing what he believes should be, rather than what is. We wish to emphasize that it is not our intention to impugn the value judgments implicit in the theory of Erikson; in fact, we find ourselves closely aligned with many of his beliefs. However, values and veracity are not synonymous. Further, we must remember that our perceptions of the world are inescapably colored by our own personal beliefs, and that the distinction between description and prescription frequently is a jumbled one, indeed.

In Erikson's theory, the stages indicate a very general sequence that cannot always be paralleled in other countries. For most adults in economically developed societies, healthy and financially independent retirement is one of the prime areas of concern. Monetary savings and investments became a source of either elation or frustration for millions of individuals in the United States, Germany, Japan, and other countries. At the same time, billions of human beings have absolutely no money to save in the bank. Hunger, civil and ethnic wars, violence and oppression imposed by authorities, chronic ecological problems, and other cataclysms are the permanent focus of these people's daily concerns. Various unpredictable disturbances present a wide range of unpredictable problems, and the sequence of these problems is not as linear as it appears in Erikson's classification. Therefore, in many cases, more immediate strategies of survival may dominate people's lives. Studies of immigrants to the United States show that identity concerns can occupy people's minds during adulthood, long after the period Erikson had proposed in his classification (Birman & Trickett, 2001).

In industrialized, wealthy democracies people can exercise a relative freedom of choice. They have available to them the choice of different foods, places to live, schools to attend, job opportunities, ideologies, lifestyles, and even religions. However, and this is a paradox, the process of individual development may be stressful in countries in which people are confronted with a wide variety of choices. Conversely, in many other cultures many people's identities and lifestyles are prescribed at birth. They accept a particular religion, political ideology, occupation, and place to live. People have fewer choices, and therefore their transition from one stage to another may be "smoother" than for people in the Western cultures, which have more choices. In other words, Erikson's theory could be more applicable to societies with so called *broad socialization* practices that emphasize independence and free self-expression, than in countries with *narrow socialization* that prescribes an ideology that strictly identifies both right and wrong behaviors.

It is important to note that in some cultures, social maturation is not associated with increased independence, as Erikson believed, but rather with increased interdependence. In some cases, for example, Buddhism, isolation may be rewarding and should not necessarily be avoided. Intimacy may occur at earlier life stages in some ethnic groups. Moreover, role confusion may not be typical for individuals from traditional cultures but becomes significant for immigrants from these countries.

In general, when applying Erikson's theory to specific cultural conditions, try to analyze how each culture views each life crisis—assuming, of course, that the crisis takes place—and what is generally expected of an individual to perform, believe in, or reject to solve the crisis.

■ Piaget's Stages of Cognitive Development

Swiss psychologist Jean Piaget (1963) was primarily interested in how children develop the process of thinking about themselves and the world around them. According to Piaget, the child's cognitive growth is a stage-by-stage process, consisting of four stages. In stage one, the *sensorimotor* stage, infants learn about their interaction with their immediate environment. During stage two, the *preoperational* stage, children develop the foundation for language acquisition. Here children do not comprehend that other people may see things differently (*egocentrism*). At the third stage of *concrete operations*, children learn logic and realize that volume, amount, and weight may stay the same despite changes in the object's physical appearance (the process is called *conservation*). The final stage, *formal operations*, is when adolescents develop the ability to think abstractly.

Do children from all over the world move through these stages? Summarizing results from a handful of studies, Dasen (1994) suggested that the stage sequence—preoperational—operational–abstract thinking—appears to be universal across cultures. Children move from one stage to another as Piaget has predicted. Nevertheless, other psychologists were more cautious in their cross-cultural assessments of Piaget's findings (Gardiner et al., 1998). Most of the critical comments are related to the methodology and procedures used by Piaget and his colleagues. For instance, researchers who conducted earlier cross-cultural studies of language development using Piaget's theory had only limited knowledge of the language studied. Maybe because of this, researchers often used standardized tests that did not require the child to have language proficiency.

Moreover, accurate birth dates of many children were not commonly available so that the actual age of the child studied was not always known.

Piaget's theory does a good job of explaining how children deal with conservation of volume, weight, and amount. Our everyday thinking, however, and ability to make practical decisions in a maze of daily circumstances are not explained well by this theory (Goodnow, 1990). Critics also pointed out that Piaget provoked a temptation to interpret some developmental stages as more "valuable" than others. This, in turn, leads to further categorizations. In reality, though, social success, satisfaction, or adaptation strategies, as well as certain activities and professions, do not require that the individual function on the level of formal operations. It is also questionable whether the formal operational stage is achieved by all adolescents in all societies. In both Western and non-Western settings there are many healthy, happy, and successful individuals who basically fail on formal operational tasks (Byrnes, 1988).

> A man may not transgress the bounds of major morals, but may make errors in minor morals.
>
> *Confucius* (551–479 B.C.E.)—CHINESE PHILOSOPHER

Stages of Moral Development According to Kohlberg

American psychologist Lawrence Kohlberg (1981) described six stages of moral development in which children and adults are able to make several types of moral judgments. In brief, people go from lower stages of reasoning, where they prefer to avoid punishment for wrongdoing, to the higher stages, where they choose social contract and then universal principles to guide moral actions (see Table 5.2).

Snarey (1985) examined 45 empirical studies of moral judgment development conducted in 27 countries and suggested that the first four stages appear to be universal in the subjects of all cultures studied. However, some critics express skepticism about cross-cultural validity of this theory. Why?

The methodology used in cross-cultural studies on moral development was based on hypothetical stories about moral choices that were related well only to U.S. subjects (Shweder et al., 1990). For example, in one such story a woman is suffering from an illness. She is prescribed an expensive drug that may save her life; however, the pharmacist in the story charges an excessive amount of money for the prescription. The woman's husband does not have the money. The moral predicament in this vignette is whether it is moral to steal the drug.

It looks like a story that makes sense and the situation described is not unusual. However, in many countries, medicine is under government control, and pharmacists cannot charge patients market prices. Some items are in short supply and briberies in these cases are common ways to get the prescription. Moreover, in some countries, physicians themselves—and not pharmacists—have access to medication and distribute it to their patients.

Another point of criticism is that the developmental stages are closely linked to values of Western liberalism and individualism based on moral choice. Liberal individualism, however, cannot always represent moral principles that are applicable to all cultures and peoples. In many cultures moral judgment is based mostly on existing traditions, and not necessarily on free will and choice. For certain religious groups, certain types of moral behavior are strictly prescribed in the Bible, Torah, or other religious scriptures. Other studies point out that the individual's moral judgments are caused by circumstance and are

TABLE 5.2 Kohlberg's Stages of Moral Development

Stage 1.	Preconventional level: Judgments about what is right and what is wrong are based on fear of punishment.
Stage 2.	Preconventional level: Moral conduct produces pleasure, whereas immoral conduct results in unwanted consequences.
Stage 3.	Conventional level: Any behavior is good if it is approved by significant others.
Stage 4.	Conventional level: The existing laws determine what is moral and immoral.
Stage 5.	Postconventional level: Moral behavior is based on individual rights and underlying social circumstances.
Stage 6.	Postconventional level: Moral conduct is regulated by universal ethical principles that may rise above government and laws.

not necessarily based on a certain level of the person's moral development (Matsumoto, 1994; Vassiliou & Vassiliou, 1973).

An interesting cross-cultural examination of Kohlberg's theory was conducted by Ma and Cheung (1996), who compared moral judgments of more than 1,000 Hong Kong Chinese, English, and U.S. college and high-school students. The test consisted of four stories and each story contained a description of a moral problem. The subjects were asked to make judgments about the possible solutions to the problem. It was found that Chinese tended to emphasize the importance of the stage 3 judgments and considered stage 4 judgments as more similar to stage 5 and 6 judgments. The English and U.S. subjects tended to regard stage 4 judgments as more similar to stage 2 or 3 judgments.

The authors argue that moral judgments of the Chinese person are reinforced by traditional norms and regulated by conformity to primary groups. Chinese see issues, such as concerns for social order, consensus, and abiding by the law, from a collectivist perspective. A strong orientation to perform altruistic acts for the sake of close relatives and friends is part of Chinese culture. According to the authors, Chinese are also influenced by the Confucian concept of the five cardinal relationships, which emphasizes the harmonious connection between sovereign and subject, father and son, husband and wife, brother and brother, and friend and friend. Social order, consensus, and law-abiding behavior are attached to the Chinese collective mentality. On the contrary, Western people are concerned primarily with individual rights and their interests being protected by the law. In the West, people easily sue each other because the law mediates interpersonal relationship. Chinese tend not to resolve their conflicts in legal institutions. They prefer instead to resolve their conflicts by using interpersonal contacts. This practice, however, can become a double-edged sword. On one hand, it may appear that interpersonal orientation is more humane and appealing than the law-based system. (Indeed, it seems healthier to settle a conflict than seek legal help.) On the other hand, an emphasis on an interpersonal system of communications may stimulate nepotism and corruption—two serious problems that Hong Kong officials themselves recognize very well.

Developmental Stages

It is widely understood that human development takes place in stages. Typically, birth and physical death—as the initial and final points of physical existence—are present in developmental classifications. Beliefs in reincarnation and immortality promote the understanding of the life span as a cycle. Views on the beginning of a child's life (i.e., when does it start, at conception or at a certain later stage?) vary cross-culturally and are based on people's educational background, religion, and other ideological values.

Birthdays, initiation rituals, weddings, graduations, job promotions, the birth of children and grandchildren, retirement, and other significant life events mark the most important points of human transition. Several biological, behavioral, and physiological changes are also recognized cross-culturally as indicators of particular life stages. Among these natural events are emergence of permanent teeth, first words, first menstruation and menopause in women, and intensive growth of facial hair in young men. Gray hair is commonly viewed as a sign of maturity despite tremendous individual variations of hair pigmentation. There are also age categorizations based on nonscientific beliefs or particular developments and life events. Such events may symbolically identify either the beginning or ending of a particular life stage. One's first intercourse could be seen as a confirmation of one's "manhood" or "womanhood." Reaching the drinking age—that is 21 in the United States and 18 in the Ukraine, for example—could also be interpreted as a sign of legal maturity.

Books on human development distinguish several common stages within the life span: prenatal period, infancy, childhood (divided into early and middle childhood), adolescence, and adulthood, which is, in turn, subdivided into three stages: early adulthood, middle adulthood, and late adulthood (see Table 5.3).

There can be slightly different categorizations of the life span, however. For example, according to

TABLE 5.3 The Periods of Human Development

Prenatal period	Infancy	Childhood	Adolescence	Adulthood
From conception to birth: It takes approximately 266 days in every ethnic, racial, or social group.	From birth to 2 years: the child acquires initial motor, cognitive, and social skills.	From 2 to 11–12 years: the child acquires language and learns about the most important social skills.	From 11–12 to 19–20 years: the child has reached sexual maturity but has not yet taken on rights and responsibilities of the adult status.	From 20 years onward: the individual has achieved adult status as prescribed by the norms and laws of a particular society.

Hindu tradition, infancy, early childhood, and middle childhood are not separate stages (Valsiner & Lawrence, 1997). Moreover, in more than half of the societies studied by Schlegel and Barry (1991), there was no special term for adolescence.

Life before Birth: Prenatal Period

In London and in Beijing, as well as in any other part of the planet, the **prenatal period**—typical time between conception and birth—is 38 weeks. From the beginning, the developing embryo in a mother's womb can be exposed to either favorable or unfavorable conditions. For instance, the natural environment around the mother could be stable or unstable, safe or dangerous. Across the world, environmental problems and perilous conditions, such as hunger, violence, excessive radiation, exposure to chemicals, air and water pollution, to name a few, can cause various complications in pregnancy and serious birth defects. The availability or lack of professional prenatal care is also a crucial factor affecting the unborn child's development. There are many common cognitive and behavioral trends related to pregnancy. Studies show, for instance, that in most countries, when a family expects a child, boys are desired more than girls (Hortacsu et al., 2001) and cross-nationally, teen pregnancies are more common in rural than in urban populations (Barber, 2001).

The fetus's life can be interrupted by a mother's decision to terminate her pregnancy. Nearly 50 million abortions are performed in the world each year. Almost 60 percent of them take place in developing countries, where close to 90 percent of the over 20 million illegal and unsafe abortions are performed each year. This is despite the fact that in many cases abortion in developing countries is restricted by law and condemned by religion. The risk of death from an unsafe, or illegal, abortion in a developing country is 15 times higher than the risk in developed countries. Each year 70,000 women die as a result of such procedures (WHO Press Release WHO/28, May 17, 1999). Countries vary in terms of frequency of abortions performed. For instance, in the 1990s, there were 206 legal abortions per 100 births in Russia; in comparison, Sweden has a ratio of 30–100, Austria 17–100, and the Netherlands 10–100.

Attitudes toward pregnancy also differ. In traditional collectivist countries, such as Malaysia, Singapore, Indonesia, Philippines, and Thailand, pregnancy is more family centered with active participation and guidance from family (Gardiner et al., 1998). In individualist societies, childbirth tends to be a rather private affair. However, one should be careful and try not to make stereotypical judgments. Many foreign exchange students, for example, mentioned to us how open many Americans are about their pregnancies: people make official statements, inform relatives and friends, and throw parties to spread the word about their condition. (An entire "episode" of a popular television series in the 1990s was devoted to such events in the life of the show's main characters.) However, in Russia—a collectivist society—pregnancy is commonly kept secret until the changes in the woman's body become obvious. Husbands are not only absent when their wives give birth but are also prohibited from entering birth clinics and may be escorted out by the police if they dare to go inside the facility. Tradition and law often go hand in hand (see Table 5.4).

> Infancy conforms to nobody; all conform to it.
>
> *Ralph Waldo Emerson* (1803–1882)—U.S. POET AND PHILOSOPHER

TABLE 5.4 A List of Selected Customs Followed by Some Immigrant Women in Families in the Maternity Ward in the United States

Region of the World	Custom Followed by Some Immigrants from that Region
Russia	A child is not supposed to be seen by strangers for at least one month so that he or she is protected from the "evil eye."
Vietnam	A new mother should not be exposed to cold because it disrupts the equilibrium that is believed crucial to good health.
Muslim countries	Examination or delivery must be done by female health workers only.
Some African countries	The tradition is to take the placenta home and bury it.
Latin American countries	Women do not breast-feed the child in the first couple of days after delivery.

Source: Aizenman (2002).

First Steps: Infancy

Infancy is period from birth to two years when the child acquires initial motor, cognitive, and social skills. A newborn child needs total care. It is obvious that environmental and social conditions in which the new life begins have a crucial impact on the child's life, health, and perhaps his or her personality traits. Infant mortality, for example, varies greatly from country to country and depends on the socioeconomic and political conditions of each particular nation. For example, infant mortality in Afghanistan is 155 deaths per 1,000 live births, and it was the highest in the world in 2008. Infant mortality in Niger is 175, and in Chad it is 100. In Turkey, the child mortality is 37 per 1,000. In Mexico it is 19, in China it is 21 and in India it is 32. Economically developed countries have the lowest rates. For instance, in Kuwait it is 9, in the United States the rate is 6.3, and in Canada it is 5.1. The lowest rates are in Japan, which is 2.8, and in Sweden, which is 2.75 (*The World Factbook*, 2000).

The child's **temperament**, or personality traits present in infancy, presumably has a genetic basis (Buss & Plomin, 1985). Temperament may also be influenced by environmental factors. Parents respond differently when their child is crying. There are adults who easily neglect their children when they cry, and there are those who respond immediately. An immediate or delayed response to the child's crying may stimulate or inhibit certain emotions and other behavioral reactions in the infant. There are individual and cultural variations in such responses. For example, in one of the projects on cross-cultural similarities and differences in mother–infant communications, rural Kenyan and middle-class Bostonian mothers were compared. There were many similarities between the samples studied. Mothers in both locations would eagerly touch, hold, or talk to a child if he or she was crying. However, the U.S. mothers communicated more with words and less with physical contact than did Kenyan mothers (Berger, 1995).

Ask a mother who has raised a healthy infant, and she will probably tell you that her son or daughter was able to recognize human faces very early. Indeed, most infants feel calm when they see familiar faces and show signs of worry when they see a stranger's face near them. A study conducted in several countries showed that most infants develop a form of attachment around their seventh month of life (Kagan et al., 1978). Such attachment patterns in a strange situation are universal and can be divided into three categories (Gardiner et al., 1998):

1. anxious and avoidant [children do not pay much attention to their parent(s)];
2. anxious and resistant [children tend to stay very close to their parent(s) and worry about his/her/their whereabouts];
3. securely attached [children are not threatened by a stranger in the presence of the parent(s)].

Some researchers found that the prevalence of the anxious-and-avoidant type is relatively higher in West European countries, whereas the anxious-and-resistant type is more prevalent in non-Western countries, such as Israel and Japan (Van Ijzendoorn & Kroonenberg, 1988). Consistent with attachment theories, findings of a comparative U.S.–Japanese study indicated that a clear majority of mothers in both countries perceive children with desirable characteristics as secure and children with undesirable characteristics as insecure (Rothbaum et al., 2007).

Right-handedness appears prevalent in all cultures and, as studies show, this function is most likely genetic (Coren, 1992). However, different cultural practices and beliefs were found to affect the behavior of millions of children around the world. In many countries, for example, left-handedness was resisted, and both teachers and parents attempted to change this "anomaly" as they would call it, by forcing children to unlearn many of their skills that required the use of the left hand. Environmental factors also influence the ways children develop their motor activities. As an example, motor skills of African infants develop several months before they develop in white children: parents use different training strategies when they teach their children to walk (Gardiner et al., 1998).

Box 5.3 A Case in Point

Customs in Parental Behavior

It is an East European custom—well maintained in the twenty-first century—not to show a newborn child to anyone except close relatives during the first month of the baby's life. Reasons? This isolation is considered by many Russians a necessary precaution against an "evil eye." In other words, the child remains relatively deprived of other people and new experiences for some 30 days of his life.

Question: Do you think that this practice—that is exercised, perhaps, by millions of parents and leads to a relative isolation of the child during the first 30 days of her life—may somehow affect the child's psychological development?

Societal changes shape patterns of parental behavior. For example, frequency of breast-feeding and the level of a nation's industrial development are negatively correlated. In other words, breast-feeding declines the more the nation becomes industrialized and that causes further societal changes. The availability of baby formula and other foods, changes in women's occupation and social status, a general change in public attitudes, and other factors all promote freedom of choice for women to decide whether to breast-feed.

Infants are constantly surrounded by a complex system of sounds that represents a particular language. Children make important sound distinctions at a very early age and this may explain some linguistic differences that people experience when they learn a foreign language. For example, our mutual colleague from Japan has difficulties pronouncing the *L* when he speaks English (likewise, many Americans cannot pronounce the typically hard German *R*, the *KH* in Hebrew, or *GH* in the Ukrainian language). Japanese infants typically do not notice the difference between *L* and *R* because there is no *L* sound in the Japanese language and their parents do not use such sounds in their conversations. English-speaking infants are able to detect this difference, even if they cannot talk themselves. Perhaps our pronunciation difficulties have deep roots in our infancy, when we began to recognize and memorize sounds. For example, many Russians could not distinguish the difference between sounds *i* (in *bit*) and *ee* (in *beat*). In the Russian language, there is no distinction between these two sounds. Some linguists suggest that the Danish language is especially difficult to speak because it contains so many unfamiliar sounds that non-Danish people were not exposed to as infants.

> Life's aspirations come in the guise of children.
>
> *Rabindranath Tagore* (1861–1941)—BENGALI POET AND NOVELIST

Discovering the World: Childhood

Mencius, an ancient Chinese philosopher, wrote that a great person is one who does not lose his childhood heart. Children are great because they are sincere and emotional. **Childhood** is a period of continuous growth, learning, and development. During early childhood children's thinking is wishful and fantastic. Young children are often uncertain about the difference between reality and fantasy and they often mix them together. They constantly check their thinking against the reality but still believe in the magical power of their ideas. During middle childhood, which lasts from approximately age 6–12 years,

Box 5.4 Critical Thinking

On Labeling of Dependency

It is frequently emphasized that people in Japan are more interdependent and emotionally attached to each other than people in Western societies. There are many explanations and interpretations of this assumption. Some of them refer to early socialization experiences. According to one view people in Japan develop a pattern called amae that makes people interdependent (Doi, 1989). Amae is described as the tendency of the self to merge with the self of another person. This tendency becomes part of everyday life in Japan and is especially encouraged in the early mother–child relationship (Yamaguchi, 2004). In the United States, security is seen as leading primarily to autonomy, self-esteem, and self-expression. In Puerto Rico, security is seen as leading primarily to respect, obedience, and calmness. Finally, there are differences in perceived antecedents of attachment, with Anglo mothers placing greater emphasis on autonomy fostering and Puerto Rican mothers placing greater emphasis on controlling behavior (Carlson & Harwood, 2003). How different is the Japanese *amae* from dependency, a concept known in Western psychological schools? (Dependency is a need for comfort, approval, or attention and may be described at the behavioral level as a child crying, clinging, following the mother, and other behaviors that encourage attention from caregivers.) To compare the meanings of both concepts, Vereijken and colleagues (1997) evaluated descriptions given by Japanese experts to *amae* and descriptions given by Western experts to dependency. The experts used a Q-sort method for the evaluation. First they were given 90 cards that each contained a written description of a particular behavior that characterizes the mother-and-child relationship. Then the experts were asked to arrange the cards in a certain order so that the cards chosen at the beginning would present the most salient behaviors, typical for *amae* (Japanese experts) and dependency (Western experts). The researchers found, despite predictions, a striking similarity between the behavioral definition of *amae*, given by Japanese experts, and the behavioral definition of dependency as provided by experts in the United States (r = 0.77). It is quite possible that in different cultures, certain universal behavioral patterns are labeled differently. In reality, different labels may describe similar behaviors.

children continue to develop thinking and social skills. Abstract thinking begins to play a greater role in their daily events. Still, the child's thinking is primarily based on observations and direct experiences. If something is tangible or observable, it is easily comprehended and interpreted. As an example, several studies involving English, Japanese, and Norwegian children suggest that they develop elaborate conceptions of war earlier than they do of peace. The conceptions of war focus primarily on aspects such as killing, fighting, and the use of weapons. Conflicts are pervasive and have concrete aspects that can be observed. Peace, however, is a less tangible and notable phenomenon. It may not register in interpersonal experience early in life to the extent that violence and aggression do (Rosenau, 1975).

Look at pictures that children draw. Some complex and colorful, some schematic and simple, they reflect what children see or wish for. Children see the reality around them and reflect it in their thoughts and fantasies. For example, 700 stories generated by 160 Chinese and U.S. elementary-school students were analyzed. Chinese stories showed greater concern with authority, greater concern with moral rectitude, fewer instances of physical aggression, and greater salience of the role of natural forces and chance than the U.S. sample did (Domino & Hannah, 1987). If children's drawings reflect reality, could adults make any suggestions about a child's life by discovering that themes of victimization constantly appear in drawings of Palestinian children living in Israel (Kostelny & Garbarino, 1994)? Could we explain why in U.S. children's drawings, boys were pictured as more powerful than girls (Rubenstein, 1987)?

In practically all cultures—with the exception of regions that suffer severe food shortages—mothers try to coax their children into eating. They use various methods: from punishment to reward for good eating, from persuasion to feeding games (Dettwyler, 1989). Eating habits and food preferences of an adult person are generally linked to early-age feeding practices (Schulze et al., 2001). Eating preferences show great variability among countries and families. Bread and many types of fruit and vegetables are common in most cultures; however, there are products that children begin to eat during childhood that are considered inappropriate for other children living in other cultures. Muslim children do not eat pork, Hindu boys and girls may never try beef, and Europeans stay away from dog's meat.

If attempts to feed children appear to be similar across different countries, cosleeping, or the practice of allowing the child to sleep in one bed with the parents, usually varies from country to country. Typically, cosleeping is resisted by U.S. parents or at times allowed in some limited way. U.S. and Western mothers commonly put their children in separate bedrooms. This practice is largely uncommon among Indian Mexicans (Morelli et al., 1992). One should note, however, that cosleeping is practiced in some countries, in part, because of living conditions: parents simply cannot afford a separate bedroom for each child in the family.

Many elements of social identity are formed during childhood. Children between the second and fourth grade are able to clearly identify themselves with their ethnic group, nationality, and social class (Dawson et al., 1977). At this stage, both Arab and Jewish schoolchildren in Israel were significantly different in their flag preference, clearly divided along the Arab–Jewish origins (Lawson, 1975). The arrival of television in many developing areas indicates the beginning of a new chapter in the lives of people living there. However, the impact of television can be different in every culture. In a longitudinal research conducted in northern Manitoba, it was shown that children who were already eager to explore the Western world through television became more aggressive and out-group oriented. Children who were trying to avoid a relationship with the West became less aggressive and more in-group oriented than the other group (Granzberg, 1985).

Anyone can say without conducting research that children around the world love to play. There are some functions of play that are universal across cultures, such as teaching children about interaction patterns, cooperation, sharing, and competition (Farver et al., 2000). Despite these similarities, different cultural practices may develop different behavioral traits. In a study conducted in the early 1970s, playing children in North America appeared to be more competitive than children in many other societies studied (Madsen, 1971). These results, however, should be verified in contemporary conditions. Why? In the United States today, for example, a mother who signs her son or daughter up for a little league soccer team will perhaps get a note from the league explaining, very politely and cautiously, that the main purpose of the game is participation, not necessarily winning. In many contemporary children's sports leagues in the United States (i.e., baseball, football, basketball, soccer, ice hockey, and others), there are serious attempts made to emphasize a more nonachievement focus. For instance, in the fall of 1999, one of the local youth soccer leagues in Ohio prohibited parents from screaming and cheering on the sidelines because it may offend and disturb some of the children playing in the game—especially those who are losing.

Is there evidence that societal norms restricting children's behavior in many ways may cause children to become aggressive and rebel? According to the suppression–facilitation hypothesis, behaviors that are discouraged in a culture will be seen infrequently in mental health facilities. For example, if parents punish children for being violent, there should not be many violent mental patients in this country's mental facilities. The suppression–facilitation model also assumes that behaviors that are rewarded will be seen excessively. From the standpoint of another hypothesis, the adult distress threshold hypothesis, the behaviors that were discouraged in childhood will be seen in clinics more often than "acceptable" behaviors. Weisz and his colleagues (1987) tested this model in a cross-cultural study that involved Thai and U.S. children. Buddhist traditions of Thailand are different from the U.S. cultural norms. The former emphasizes nonaggression, politeness, modesty, and respect for others. Parents are very intolerant toward impulsive, aggressive, and "undercontrolled" behavior in their children. As the first hypothesis predicted, "overcontrolled" problems (aloofness, withdrawal) were reported more frequently for Thai children than they were for U.S. children. Problems such as violence and disorderly behavior were reported more frequently for U.S. children. Thus the suppression–facilitation hypothesis received some empirical support.

A boy becomes an adult three years earlier than his parents think he does, and about two years after he thinks he does.

LEWIS HERSHEY (1893–1977)—U.S. GENERAL

■ Major Rehearsal: Adolescence

John and Jorge are two 16-year-old neighbors and friends of different ethnic backgrounds. At the same time, they are so much alike. They both wear adult-size clothes, both have a shadow of a mustache on their upper lip, both play computer games for many hours a day, both contemplate getting a summer job, and both think of attending a local college in two years. As adolescents, they both have reached sexual maturity but have not yet taken on the rights and responsibilities of the adult status.

Adolescence is viewed not only as a developmental stage but also as a cultural phenomenon. For instance, extended schooling in many developed countries stretches the period from childhood to adulthood. On the contrary, many nonindustrialized cultures encourage their members to take on adult roles as early as possible. Thus, the adolescent stage becomes almost indistinguishable. In some countries, such as Sudan and Brazil, many children begin to work full time and take care of other family members as early as age 12 and sometimes even earlier. In other societies such as India, a girl can marry in her early teens and move to her husband's home to accept the roles of wife and mother. Cultural conditions can determine the recognition of an entire developmental stage.

The rapid changes in weight and height are important characteristics of adolescence. Cross-culturally, girls mature as much as two years earlier than boys. Since the beginning of observations in the 1800s in Europe and North America, girls have been maturing earlier than previously studied age groups of girls, approximately several months per every 10 years. For example, from 1850 to the 1950s, the average age of first menstruation in girls has decreased 5 years and became close to 12 years. This trend has significantly slowed in the second half of the twentieth century and was apparently not observed in less-developed non-Western countries (Frisch & Revelle, 1970). One possible explanation for this earlier maturation is the improved health care, nutrition, and living conditions of most citizens of the developed regions of the world.

Formal thinking at this developmental stage replaces concrete thinking, and moral judgments are often made on the basis of the individual's values (Piaget, 1963). At the same time, adolescent thinking could be full of contradictions, unpredictable assumptions, and sudden turns. Despite their ability to make ethical judgments and their tremendous cognitive reserves, adolescents do not have the vision or wisdom often found at a more mature age. Altruism and selfishness, enthusiasm and withdrawal, tolerance and impatience may easily exist together in the same individual at the same time. If the child's perception of the world is generally naive and trustful, adolescence is often associated with the development of cynicism (Sigel, 1989). Cynicism—which is the belief that people generally and repeatedly violate prescriptive moral standards for their behavior—can become salient in adolescence because of the young person's tendencies to grow increasingly independent and critical, or because of an increasing amount of discouraging information about society that one receives in late adolescence, especially in the countries where political scandals became a common practice (Schwartz, 1975). However, we should anticipate a lack of publicly expressed cynicism in countries in which ideological and political homogeneity is strictly reinforced by the government. In such cases, an adolescent may develop cynical views without exposing them to pollsters or social scientists (Gozman & Edkind, 1992). For more than a century, many Western psychological sources have been discussing the issue of teenage rebelliousness and defiance as an anticipated period of every young person's life (Glad & Shiraev, 1999; Hall, 1916; Kon, 1979). Psychologists and sociologists try to understand whether or not various antisocial fads associated with "youth culture" have deep psychological roots in the young person's desire for independence (Petersen, 1988). "Gangs" in North and Central America, "hooliganism" in Russia, or "ladette culture" of British girls (a behavioral pattern of "acting like boys" and involving in smoking, swearing, fighting, drinking, and being disruptive in school) are just a few examples of such antisocial trends among the adolescents. Prevalence of young people among violent groups in non-Western cultures has been documented as well. Yet, it is quite doubtful that psychological reasons alone could explain why the young join various rebellious groups. Obviously, there are specific socioeconomic and political factors that must be taken into consideration. For example, there are scores of documented cases in Africa involving young adolescents and children being forced to join rebellious militant groups against their will (Beah, 2008).

Social and political conditions play a significant role in individual socialization. In a study conducted in Israel, children of North American and Soviet immigrants showed significantly different patterns of behavior in the classroom. Students from North America were peer-group oriented. Students from the Soviet Union were teacher oriented (Horowits & Kraus, 1984). The Soviet system of education, compared with the U.S. system, had a very strong emphasis on student discipline and obedience. Moving into a new cultural environment, Soviet adolescent immigrants did not change their obedience-oriented behavioral pattern. In another study conducted in Israel, Soviet-educated adolescents were significantly more realistically oriented in their moral judgments than the Israelis who grew up in Israel (Ziv et al., 1975). Perhaps many years of personal humiliation and the struggle against the communist government for an opportunity to emigrate from the Soviet Union have contributed to the development of realistic and pragmatic attitudes (Kliger, 2002). Social and political factors affect adolescent's cultural identity. A study of Palestinian Arab Christian adolescents in Israel showed that most of them tend to maintain their ethnic and religious distinct identity. However, when compared to Muslim Arabs, they expressed more willingness to adopt elements of the Jewish society. They also feel stronger assimilation pressures coming from Israeli Jews. Christian Arabs are commonly viewed as a "double minority" because they are Arabs, and the majority of Arabs are Muslims and, in addition, they live in a predominantly Jewish country. The stronger willingness of Palestinian Christian Arabs to engage in social and cultural contact with Israeli Jews may reflect a desire to gain more access to important resources such as education and work. In addition, Palestinian Christian Arabs tend to distinguish themselves historically as a more Westernized cultural group (Horenczyk & Munayer, 2007).

Overall, social and political conditions in a particular country may affect attitudes and motivation of the young (Bronfenbrenner, 1970). For example, in the 1980s young people in Poland—a socialist country at that time—reported more aggression in their attitudes than young people in Finland (Fraczek, 1985). For several years, Poles lived under a state of emergency and violence initiated by the government and this could have triggered more violence on an interpersonal level.

In another study, 1,500 highschool students from Finland and Estonia were asked to imagine themselves in three hypothetical situations (Keltikangas-Jaervinen & Terav, 1996). For example, if one of your classmates is repeatedly teased by some of your other classmates, what would you do? If one of your classmates continues to be the target of a blackmailing, what would you do? If you see someone stealing money from one of your classmates, what would you do? The students then were offered several alternative solutions to these situations: aggressive, prosocial, social responsible, and avoiding. As a result, several tendencies were revealed. Estonian adolescents were more aggressive and less socially responsible in their answers than their Finnish counterparts. Moreover, avoidance was shown to be the most typical way of solving problems for Estonian students. How can one interpret the differences? The countries studied are very close geographically and share many elements of culture and history. The authors explain the results by referring to social and political factors. For more than 40 years, Estonia was a part of the Soviet Union, whereas Finland remained an independent country. Western values of individualism were persistently emphasized in child socialization in Finland. On the contrary, in Soviet Estonia, public education and socialization promoted the mantra of collectivism, obedience to authority, loyalty to the homeland, and a sense of social responsibility. Here comes some confusion in the interpretation: as far as we know, the system promotes loyalty, responsibility, and collectivism in socialist countries. Why did the actual attitudes of the young people in this study reveal the presence of aggression, avoidance, and lack of responsibility? The authors of the study suggest that despite the communist government's efforts, most young people in Estonia simply rejected the main values promoted by the authorities. However, other factors could also have contributed to the socialization of Estonian youth of the 1990s. The unprecedented political and ideological struggle in the country after it gained independence, rapid growth of crime and corruption, increasing social inequality, a virtual loss of guaranteed social security—these factors could have triggered a sense of disappointment and frustration in the population. Perhaps these negative developments of the most recent times, and not only the experiences of the early 1980s, affected the attitudes of Estonian youth revealed in this study.

Collectivist and individualist norms influence individual behavior and perceptions. Elbedour and colleagues (1997) compared perceptions of intimacy in the relationships among Israeli Jewish and Israeli Bedouin adolescents. More than 600 students, from grades 7 to 11, completed questionnaires in which students were asked to rate statements describing same-sex adolescent friendship on a four-point scale ranging from low (1) to high (4). Statements such as, "To what extent does the following statement characterize the relationship with a close friend?" were asked. Characteristics such as emotional closeness, control, conformity, and respect for the friend were studied. Each of these characteristics was measured with the help of eight questions. The results showed that Jewish adolescents (more individualist than collectivist), as opposed to Bedouin adolescents (more collectivist than individualist), expressed less of a need to control or to conform to their friends. The Bedouin adolescents tended to emphasize both control of and conformity to friends.

> Men are more like the time they live in than they are like their fathers.
>
> *ALI IBN-ABI-TALIB* (600–661)—FOURTH CALIPH OF MUSLIMS

Adulthood

In all cultures, **adulthood** represents maturity, responsibility, and accountability. This period is typically divided into three stages: early adulthood, middle adulthood, and late adulthood (Levinson, 1978). The early adulthood stage is usually linked to formative processes, whereas the middle and late adulthood stages are associated with accomplishments of various kinds. However, the line separating these periods is unclear. Many adults have been and are able to accomplish great things at a very young age. For example, George Washington became an ambassador to France at 21. He won his first battle as a colonel at 22. Luther was 29 when he started his religious reformation of Christianity. Fidel Castro became a Cuban leader at 32. Einstein published his famous theory of relativity at 26. Joan of Arc was only 17 when she led the French troops to a miraculous victory over the English in 1429. She was put to death at 19.

Although some psychological functions decline with age, the individual's socialization during adulthood continues. Two models—the **persistence** and the **openness**—attempt to explain this process (Renshon, 1989). According to the first model, persistence, adults acquire attitudes and learn behaviors early in life and tend not to change them later. For example, if a child grows up in a religious family in Morocco, he or she will likely be religious no matter where he or she lives as an adult. The other model, openness, states the opposite: people do change their attitudes and behavior because they have to adjust to changing situations and the transformations can be substantial. In other words, early childhood and adolescent experiences do not necessarily determine who the person is today. Despite the fact that some students of socialization are intrigued by the persistence approach, most analysts agree that socialization does not stop at the age of 18 or 20. It was confirmed that socialization continues in the adulthood stage and many transitions in the individual's opinions and behavior take place during this developmental stage (Sigel, 1989).

Adulthood experiences vary across cultures and depend on age, gender, socioeconomic status, occupation, family structure, and a variety of life events. Violence, economic hardship, and hunger may affect the lives of an entire generation. As an example, social and political developments in Afghanistan during the last 25 years of the twentieth century were marked by a series of devastating developments. Among them were the revolution and dismissal of the king, the Soviet invasion in 1979, the war against the occupation, and the seemingly endless civil war that took tens of thousands of lives. An adult who was born in 1950, for example, during practically all stages of his adult life, was exposed to continuous stress, poverty, traumatic events, and fear for his life. At the same time, a person born in 1950 in a small Norwegian town could have lived a life absolutely free of cataclysms, significant events, and unexpected turns.

In adulthood, most people develop their sense of **identity**, the view about themselves as individuals and members of society. Identity formation cannot be understood outside of its cultural context. In traditional societies, for example, people accept their identity in the systematic and coherent environment. The society is supposed to provide a sense of security for its individuals. The individual constantly refers to others for evaluation (Kagitcibasi, 1985). Individuality is especially restricted on the level of ideology or religion. People learn about their roles and acquire them while gradually moving from one life period to another. In Western industrialized societies, the performance of social roles is more open to individuals because the roles are not strongly formalized. Individuals take membership in a wide variety of diverse subgroups (Camilleri & Malewska-Peyre, 1997). Western societies, compared with non-Western ones, offer individuals a wide range of options. Individuals are not only given options; they are also encouraged to choose.

In the contemporary world, the amount of education required for young people to prepare for many jobs is expanding. As these people pursue education for longer periods, they also postpone transitions into adult roles. Moreover, when the power of traditional authority weakens and young people increasingly gain control over their own lives, they generally choose to wait longer to start families. The median ages for these adult transitions are in the late 20s in every industrialized society and rising rapidly in developing countries (Arnett, 2002). The fact that transitions into adult roles have become somewhat delayed in many societies has led to the spread of a new period of life, called *emerging adulthood*, that extends from the late teens to the mid-twenties and is characterized by self-focused exploration of possibilities in love, work, and worldviews. Young people in industrialized societies now go through this period, and it is growing in prevalence among young people in developing countries as well (Arnett, 2000).

> I not only use all the brains I have but all I can borrow.
>
> *WOODROW WILSON* (1856–1924)—TWENTY-EIGHTH U.S. PRESIDENT

In people's minds adulthood is linked to wisdom. The more mature a person is, the wiser he or she is expected to be. Societal expectations affect our perception of adult intelligence. For instance, quickness of thinking is linked to *fluid intelligence*, the ability to form concepts, think abstractly, and apply knowledge to new situations. *Crystallized intelligence* is the individual's accumulated knowledge and experience. In Western societies, speed of thinking is highly valued and fluid intelligence is interpreted as an indicator of success. In many non-Western societies, speed of operations is valued less, because experience, or crystallized intelligence, is perceived as more important that quickness (Gardiner et al., 1998). There are many mediating individual circumstances and social factors that affect crystallized intelligence. For example, a 60-year-old Iranian father can be a perfect mentor for his son who starts a business in a small town near the Caspian Sea. The same father could be less efficient and knowledgeable after his family immigrates to another country.

In some cultures of the nonindustrialized world, the concept of middle age is indistinct. For instance, a person may be described as "young woman" or "old man," but not "a middle-aged person." Similarly, some view midlife crisis as a stage for those who have the time and money to afford it.

> The wine of life keeps oozing drop by drop, the leaves of life keep falling one by one.
>
> *OMAR KHAYYAM* (TWELFTH CENTURY)—PERSIAN POET AND ASTRONOMER

Late Adulthood

When do people get old? Is aging a physical wearing and decline that takes place without a substantial change of attitudes? When do people slow down? Aging is a biological process. Although biologists haven't found conclusive explanations about universal characteristics of aging (Cox, 1988), most people of old age suffer from similar diseases (such as cancer, dementia, and arthritis), their skin becomes less elastic, and their hair loses its pigmentation. The muscles begin to atrophy, the bones become more brittle, and the cardiovascular system becomes less efficient. Most psychological functions decline too. Hearing and visual impairments are common. Memory may deteriorate while there tends to be a decrease in reaction time. However, human beings defy the "rules" of nature. Goethe, a great German poet, completed his *Faust* when he was 80. Lamark

Box 5.5 A Case in Point

Counselor Yola Ghammashi (personal interview, April 2008) is developing a concept of a *frozen culture* to describe the lives and experiences of many adult immigrants within their new homelands. Some immigrant adults after they settle in a new country continue to maintain most of the customs, speech patterns, beliefs, and emotional attachments similar to what they had before immigration. They deliberately speak their old language, maintain most cultural habits, and resist learning or adapting to different cultural norms. Their home country, meanwhile, transforms over time. Customs, fashion, and speech patterns might change. Yet these immigrants continue to live in a self-created culture of the past. They think they do not belong to their new culture. Yet their "old" culture no longer exists in the form they remember. Do you know of such individuals? What can you tell about the elements of their "frozen cultures"?

completed his great zoological book, *The Natural History of Invertebrates,* when he was 78. Ronald Reagan became president when he was 70. Mahatma Gandhi reached the peak of his popularity when he was 75. Mother Teresa did not slow down her charitable work before she died at 87.

In many countries, the **late adulthood** period begins with retirement, when a person formally quits her job. If a person does not work outside the home, this period begins perhaps when the individual gives up his major family responsibilities. There are common national "deadlines" for formal retirement, which vary greatly. In Russia, a woman can retire at age 55 and men can do so five years later. In the United States, the common retirement age is 65. Norwegians push their retirement age up to 70. It is expected that so long as life expectancy goes up, the retirement age will go higher.

Countries vary greatly regarding their population's life expectancy. Japan and Switzerland have a life expectancy close to 80. Poverty, natural disasters, and chronic political and economic problems keep the life expectancy of some countries (Nigeria, Bangladesh, and Chad, for example) at the age of 60, 50, and even lower. This is at least 10 years or more below the average life expectancy in the developed countries (*The Word Factbook,* 2002).

In collectivist cultures, the elderly usually occupy a high social status. In individualist societies young people enjoy the greatest status, whereas the elderly can often be isolated and even rejected. Indeed, studies show that respect for the elderly is higher in Japan and China than it is in the United States (Yu, 1993). As in other Western countries, the parent–child relationship in the United States is more voluntary than it is, for example, in Asian countries, especially when the child reaches adulthood (Hsu, 1985; Tolbert, 2000). In most African and Asian societies, intergenerational families are the norm, and the younger family members customarily take care of older relatives (Gardiner & Kosmitzki, 2008). Asian and Latin American families in the United States come from cultural traditions that place great importance on the role of children to support, assist, and respect the family (Chilman, 1993; Uba, 1994). Changes in a sense of obligation to assist, support, and respect the family were examined among an ethnically diverse group of 745 U.S. individuals as they began to move from secondary school into young adulthood. A sense of family obligation increased for all young adults, with slight variations depending on ethnic and financial backgrounds. Young adults from Filipino and Latin American families reported the strongest sense of familial duty during young adulthood, as compared to people of other ethnic backgrounds (Fuligni & Pedersen, 2002). Some studies have observed greater familial support among teenagers from families experiencing economic crises (Elder & Conger, 2000). Gender can also shape family obligations, with traditional gender roles often urging girls, more so than boys, to provide more assistance to the family.

French author and historian Andre Maurois (1967) wrote that growing old is no more than a bad habit that a busy man has no time to form. Age and aging are strongly related to an individual's time perspective. In turn, this time perspective may affect an individual's attitudes (Cutler, 1975). In early childhood the dominant perception is that time is virtually limitless. Early adulthood brings the realization that time is a scarce resource. Middle age and later stages lead to the perception that time becomes seriously limited. Gergen and Black (1965) pointed out that among public policy attitudes, orientations toward solutions to international problems are linked to one's perception of personal future time: senior people have a sense of urgency and tend to settle conflicts, whereas the young may display stubbornness. Renshon (1989) argued that in the arts, the phenomenon of late-age creativity and boldness occurs often in different cultures. The last works of Shakespeare, Rembrandt, Verdi, Beethoven, and Tolstoy might suggest that the final stages of the life cycle can bring release from conventional concerns and free the artist to make major creative statements that represent a culmination of the person's vision.

Box 5.6 A Case in Point

Culture and Perception of Aging

There is a trend in many Western cultures to hide the signs of aging. In contemporary U.S. society people often refrain from saying "old," and prefer to use a more neutral "senior" label. People surgically eliminate wrinkles on their faces and bodies, buy expensive cremes to keep their skin elastic, wear toupees and chignons, and try different "magic" colors to eliminate the natural gray of their aging hair. Do adults really dislike how they look when they get older? Do they believe that they become less attractive and therefore want to change their appearance to boost self-esteem? There is no evidence that this is actually true. Moreover, some studies suggest that self-esteem and personal "attractiveness" are not correlated (Kenealy et al., 1991).

Question: Do you think that the cosmetic industry and plastic surgeons—to boost their sales and get more clients—are interested in creating the "younger image" hype?

Exercise 5.1

Develop Critical Thinking Skills Working with Original Sources

Kim (2002) generalized comparative data on verbal communications between children and adults in several Asian countries and the United States. Japanese middle-class mothers speak much less frequently to their young children than do their U.S. counterparts. Moreover, Chinese preschool teachers see quietness as a means of control, rather than passivity, and appreciate silence more than U.S. teachers. Consequently, East Asian children tend to be not as verbal as their European American counterparts. Japanese children produce significantly fewer utterances per turn than North American children, and they use verbal expression to communicate emotions less frequently than do U.S. children.

Find this article:

Kim, H. (2002). We talk, therefore we think? A cultural analysis of the effect of talking on thinking. *Journal of Personality and Social Psychology, 83(4),* 828–842.

Answer these questions:

What were the research data selected in this study? What were the samples selected for this study? In your view, were these samples representative (did they resemble the population of children in the studied countries)? What was the main method used in this study? How substantial were the differences found in this study? What conclusions does the author make? What explanations does the author offer? Could you give your own explanations?

Chapter Summary

- Since ancient times, many of the world's thinkers considered human development a result of the interaction between environment and natural individual predispositions. Contemporary theories of human development emphasize the meaning of both individual and cultural factors of socialization. However, many classical developmental theories were ethnocentric and failed to take into account the richness of human diversity.
- In the interdependent families commonly found in rural traditional societies, the family structure is characterized by interdependency on both dimensions: between parents and their children and among children themselves. In independent families—the typical middle-class nuclear family in most European and North American countries—the family structure is characterized by independence on both dimensions.
- The developing child is seen as an individual with inborn dispositions and skill potential. The child's environment is a part of a larger cultural system. Both the environment and the individual are seen as open and interchanging systems. The power of the culturally regulated environment comes from the coordinated action of the three elements of the niche. They relate to each other, to outside forces, and to the developing individual.
- According to Erikson, a developing individual moves through a series of psychological crises. Each crisis, or conflict, grows primarily out of a need to adapt to the social environment and develop a sense of competence. Once a crisis is resolved, the individual moves further. This theory, with some amendments, is applicable in a wide variety of cultural settings. However, Erikson has been criticized for mixing objective description with subjective prescription. Specifically, the virtues he uses to define the healthy individual are clearly in accordance with Western, Judeo–Christian ethics, values, and social institutions.
- Studies suggest that the stage sequence (preoperational, operational, abstract thinking) and reasoning styles described by Piaget appear to be, with some limitations, universal across cultures. The limitations refer to the methodology and some procedures used by Piaget and his colleagues that are viewed as ethnocentric. Moreover, the Piaget theory explains how children deal with conservation of volume, weight, and amount. However, everyday thinking and the ability to make practical decisions in particular cultural settings are not well explained by this theory.
- According to Kohlberg, there are six stages of moral development in which children and adults are able to make several types of moral judgments. In brief, people go from lower stages of reasoning, where they prefer to avoid punishment for wrongdoing, to the higher stages, where they choose social contract and then universal principles to guide moral actions. This theory may be

applied to different cultural settings. Yet, the methodology used in the cross-cultural studies on moral development was based on hypothetical stories about moral choices that were related mainly to U.S. subjects. Another point of criticism is that the developmental stages are closely linked to values of Western liberalism and individualism based on moral choice, values which are not shared universally around the world.

- Cross-culturally, human development is understood as taking place in stages. Specialists refer to particular cultural norms and biological, behavioral, and physiological changes, which are identified cross-culturally with a particular life stage. Most books on human development distinguish several common stages within the life span: prenatal period, infancy, childhood (divided into early and middle childhood), adolescence, and adulthood, which is also divided into three stages: early adulthood, middle adulthood, and late adulthood.
- During the prenatal period, the developing embryo in the mother's womb can be exposed to either favorable or unfavorable conditions. One's access to resources and professional prenatal care along with a stressful social and psychological environment are crucial factors affecting the unborn child's development. Attitudes about pregnancy, abortion, and childbirth vary from culture to culture and are linked to local traditions and laws.
- Each culture provides a particular set of norms regarding parent–child relationships. Cross-culturally, the child's thinking is wishful. Each child's developmental niche includes social practices, values, and demands conveyed to him or her from parents and care-givers.
- Adolescence is viewed not only as a developmental stage but also as a cultural phenomenon rooted in social and economic conditions. Many nonindustrialized cultures encourage their members to assume adult roles as quickly as possible, almost skipping the adolescence stage. Adolescence marks the beginning of sexual maturation. Despite their ability to make ethical judgments and their tremendous cognitive reserves, adolescents do not have the vision or wisdom often found at a more mature age.
- In all cultures, adulthood represents maturity, responsibility, and accountability. This period is divided into stages of early, middle, and late adulthood. Early adulthood is usually linked to formative processes and middle adulthood is associated with accomplishments. In adulthood, individuals generally form their sense of identity, which is the view of themselves as individuals and members of society. The fact that transitions into adult roles have become somewhat delayed in many societies has led to the recognition of a new period of life, called *emerging adulthood*, that extends from the late teens to the mid-twenties and is characterized by self-focused exploration of possibilities in love, work, and worldviews.
- In many countries, the late adulthood period begins with retirement, when a person formally quits his or her job or gives up his or her major responsibilities. Late adulthood is linked to the physiological process of aging. Life expectancy, general socioeconomic conditions, individual psychological and physiological characteristics, and societal attitudes toward the elderly comprise the individual's final developmental niche.

Key Terms

Adolescence The period from 11–12 to 19–20 years. The child has reached sexual maturity but has not yet taken on the rights and responsibilities of the adult status.

Adulthood The period from 20 years onward. The individual has achieved the adult status prescribed by norms and laws of a particular society.

Childhood The time from 2 to 11–12 years. The child acquires language and learns about the most important social skills.

Identity The view of oneself as an individual and a member of society.

Infancy The period from birth to two years when the child acquires initial motor, cognitive, and social skills.

Late Adulthood The period of physical wearing and decline.

Human Development The changes in physical, psychological, and social behavior as experienced by individuals across the life span from conception to death.

Persistence Model The theoretical view that suggests that adults acquire attitudes and behaviors early in life and tend not to change them later.

Openness Model The theoretical view that suggests that adults change their attitudes and behavior to adjust to changing situations.

Prenatal Period The time between conception and birth, which lasts approximately 38 weeks.

Socialization The process by which the individual becomes a member of a particular culture and takes on its values, beliefs, and behaviors.

Temperament Personality traits (presumably of a genetic basis) present in infancy.

Personality, Morality, and Emotions

Our personality, morality, and emotions are vital aspects of who we are. Let's look at how we learn these essential aspects of our being.

Freud and the Development of Personality

Along with the development of our mind and the self comes the development of our personality. Sigmund Freud (1856–1939) developed a theory of the origin of personality that has had a major impact on Western thought. Freud, a physician in Vienna in the early 1900s, founded *psychoanalysis*, a technique for treating emotional problems through long-term, intensive exploration of the subconscious mind. Let's look at his theory.

Freud believed that personality consists of three elements. Each child is born with the first element, an **id**, Freud's term for inborn drives that cause us to seek self-gratification. The id of the newborn is evident in its cries of hunger or pain. The pleasure-seeking id operates throughout life. It demands the immediate fulfillment of basic needs: food, safety, attention, sex, and so on.

The id's drive for immediate gratification, however, runs into a roadblock: primarily the needs of other people, especially those of the parents. To adapt to these constraints, a second component of the personality emerges, which Freud called the ego. The **ego** is the balancing force between the id and the demands of society that suppress it. The ego also serves to balance the id and the **superego**, the third component of the personality, more commonly called the *conscience*.

The superego represents *culture within us*, the norms and values we have internalized from our social groups. As the *moral* component of the personality, the superego provokes feelings of guilt or shame when we break social rules or pride and self-satisfaction when we follow them.

The id and the superego are always in conflict. When the id gets out of hand, pleasure rules. We break society's norms, and get in trouble. When the superego gets out of hand, we go in the other direction. Becoming overly rigid in following society's norms, we end up wearing a straitjacket of rules that inhibit our lives. In the emotionally healthy individual, the ego succeeds in balancing these conflicting demands. In the maladjusted individual, however, the ego fails to control this conflict between the id and the superego. Either the id or the superego dominates this person, leading to internal confusion and problem behaviors.

Sociological Evaluation Sociologists appreciate Freud's emphasis on socialization—his assertion that the social group into which we are born transmits norms and values that restrain our biological drives. Sociologists, however, object to the view that inborn and subconscious motivations are the primary reasons for human behavior. *This denies the central principle of sociology:* that factors such as social class (income, education, and occupation) and people's roles in groups underlie their behavior (Epstein 1988; Bush and Simmons 1990).

Feminist sociologists have been especially critical of Freud. Although what we just summarized applies to both females and males, Freud assumed that what is "male" is "normal." He even said that females are inferior, castrated males (Chodorow 1990; Gerhard 2000). It is obvious that sociologists need to continue to research how we develop personality.

Sports are a powerful agent of socialization. That sumo wrestling teaches a form of masculinity should be apparent from this photo. What else do you think these boys are learning?

Socialization into Emotions

Emotions, too, are an essential aspect of who we become. Sociologists who research this area of our "humanness" find that emotions also are not simply the results of biology. Like the mind, emotions depend on socialization (Hochschild 1975, 1983; Wang and Roberts 2006). This may sound strange. Don't all people get angry? Doesn't everyone cry? Don't we all feel guilt, shame, sadness, happiness, fear? What has socialization to do with emotions?

Global Emotions At first, it may look as though socialization is not relevant, that we simply express universal feelings. Paul Ekman (1980), an anthropologist who studied emotions in several countries, concluded that everyone experiences six basic emotions: anger, disgust, fear, happiness, sadness, and surprise. He also observed that we all show the same facial expressions when we feel these emotions. A person from Zimbabwe, for example, could tell from just the look on an American's face that she is angry, disgusted, or fearful, and we could tell from the Zimbabwean's face that he is happy, sad, or surprised. Because we all show the same facial expressions when we experience these six emotions, Ekman concluded that they are built into our biology, "a product of our genes."

Expressing Emotions The existence of universal facial expressions for these basic emotions does *not* mean that socialization has no effect on how we express them. Facial expressions are only one way in which we show emotions. Other ways vary with gender. For example, U.S. women are allowed to express their emotions more freely, while U.S. men are expected to be more reserved. To express delighted surprise, for example, women are allowed to make "squeals of glee" in public places, even to jump a bit as they hug one another. Men are not. Such an expression would be a fundamental violation of their gender role.

Then there are culture, social class, and relationships. Consider culture. Two close Japanese friends who meet after a long separation don't shake hands or hug—they bow. Two Arab men will kiss. Social class is also significant, for it cuts across many other lines, even gender. Upon seeing a friend after a long absence, upper-class women and men are likely to be more reserved in expressing their delight than are lower-class women and men. Relationships also make a big difference. We express our emotions more openly if we are with close friends, more guardedly if we are at a staff meeting with the corporate CEO. A good part of childhood socialization centers on learning these "norms of emotion"—how to express our emotions in a variety of settings.

What We Feel The matter goes deeper than this. Socialization not only leads to different ways of expressing emotions but even affects *what* we feel (Clark 1997; Shields 2002). People in one culture may even learn to experience feelings that are unknown in another culture. For example, the Ifaluk, who live on the Caroline Islands of Micronesia, use the word *fago* to refer to the feelings they have when they see someone suffer. This comes close to what we call sympathy or compassion. But the Ifaluk also use this term to refer to what they feel when they are with someone who has high status, someone they highly respect or admire (Kagan 1984). To us, these are two distinct emotions, and they require separate words to express them.

Research Needed Although Ekman identified only six emotions that are universal in feeling and facial expression, I suspect that other emotions are common to people around the world—and that everyone shows similar facial expressions when they experience them. I suggest that feelings of helplessness, despair, confusion, and shock are among these universal emotions. We need cross-cultural research to find out whether this is so. We also need research into how culture guides children to feel and express emotions.

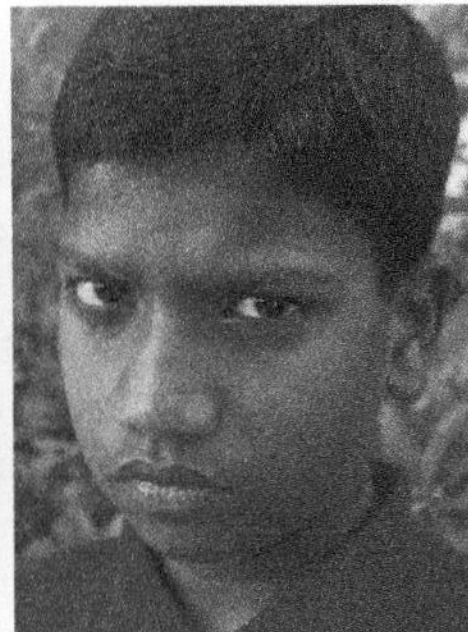

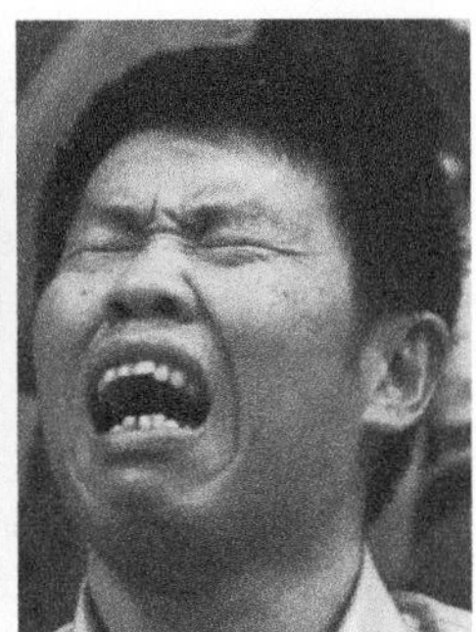

What emotions are these people expressing? Are these emotions global? Is their way of expressing them universal?

Society Within Us: The Self and Emotions as Social Control

Much of our socialization is intended to turn us into conforming members of society. Socialization into the self and emotions is an essential part of this process, for both the self and our emotions mold our behavior. Although we like to think that we are "free," consider for a moment just some of the factors that influence how we act: the expectations of friends and parents, of neighbors and teachers; classroom norms and college rules; city, state, and federal laws. For example, if in a moment of intense frustration, or out of a devilish desire to shock people, you wanted to tear off your clothes and run naked down the street, what would stop you?

The answer is your socialization—*society within you.* Your experiences in society have resulted in a self that thinks along certain lines and feels particular emotions. This helps to keep you in line. Thoughts such as "Would I get kicked out of school?" and "What would my friends (parents) think if they found out?" represent an awareness of the self in relationship to others. So does the desire to avoid feelings of shame and embarrassment. Our *social mirror,* then—the result of being socialized into a self and emotions—sets up effective controls over our behavior. In fact, socialization into self and emotions is so effective that some people feel embarrassed just thinking about running nude in public!

In Sum: Socialization is essential for our development as human beings. From interaction with others, we learn how to think, reason, and feel. The net result is the shaping of our behavior—including our thinking and emotions—according to cultural standards. This is what sociologists mean when they refer to "*society within us.*"

Socialization into Gender

Learning the Gender Map

For a child, society is unchartered territory. A major signpost on society's map is **socialization into gender.** As we learn what is expected of us *because* we are a male or a female, we are nudged into different lanes in life, into contrasting attitudes and behaviors. We take direction so well that, as adults, most of us act, think, and even feel according to this gender map, our culture's guidelines of what is appropriate for our sex.

The significance of gender is emphasized throughout this book. For now, though, let's briefly consider some of the "gender messages" that we get from our family and the mass media.

Gender Messages in the Family

Our parents are the first significant others who show us how to follow the gender map. Their own gender orientations have become embedded so firmly that they do most of this teaching without being aware of what they are doing. This is illustrated in a classic study by psychologists Susan Goldberg and Michael Lewis (1969), whose results have been confirmed by other researchers (Fagot et al. 1985; Connors 1996).

> Goldberg and Lewis asked mothers to bring their 6-month-old infants into their laboratory, supposedly to observe the infants' development. Covertly, however, they also observed the mothers. They found that the mothers kept their daughters closer to them. They also touched their daughters more and spoke to them more frequently than they did to their sons.
>
> By the time the children were 13 months old, the girls stayed closer to their mothers during play, and they returned to their mothers sooner and more often than the boys did. When Goldberg and Lewis set up a barrier to separate the children from their mothers, who were holding toys, the girls were more likely to cry and motion for help; the boys, to try to climb over the barrier.

Goldberg and Lewis concluded that mothers subconsciously reward daughters for being passive and dependent, and sons for being active and independent.

These lessons continue throughout childhood. On the basis of their sex, children are given different kinds of toys. Boys are more likely to get guns and "action figures" that destroy enemies. Girls are more likely to get dolls and jewelry. Parents also subtly encourage the boys to participate in more rough-and-tumble play. They expect their sons to get dirtier and to be more defiant, their daughters to be daintier and more compliant (Gilman 1911/1971; Henslin 2007). In large part, they get what they expect. Such experiences in socialization lie at the heart of the sociological explanation of male–female differences.

We should note, however, that some sociologists would consider biology to be the cause, proposing that Goldberg and Lewis were simply observing innate differences in the children. In short, were the mothers creating those behaviors (the boys wanting to get down and play more, and the girls wanting to

Frank and Ernest

The *gender roles* that we learn during childhood become part of our basic orientations to life. Although we refine these roles as we grow older, they remain built round the framework established during childhood.

be hugged more), or were they responding to natural differences in their children? It is similarly the case with toys. In an intriguing experiment with monkeys, researchers discovered that male monkeys prefer cars and balls more than do female monkeys, who are more likely to prefer dolls and pots (Alexander and Hines 2002).

Gender Messages from Peers

Sociologists stress how this sorting process that begins in the family is reinforced as the child is exposed to other aspects of society. Of those other influences, one of the most powerful is the **peer group,** individuals of roughly the same age who are linked by common interests. Examples of peer groups are friends, classmates, and "the kids in the neighborhood."

As you grew up, you regularly saw girls and boys teach one another what it means to be a female or a male. You might not have recognized what was happening, however, so let's eavesdrop on a conversation between two eighth-grade girls studied by sociologist Donna Eder (2007). You can see how these girls are reinforcing images of appearance and behavior that they think are appropriate for females.

CINDY: The only thing that makes her look anything is all the makeup . . .
PENNY: She had a picture, and she's standing like this. (Poses with one hand on her hip and one by her head)
CINDY: Her face is probably this skinny, but it looks that big 'cause of all the makeup she has on it.
PENNY: She's ugly, ugly, ugly.

Boys, of course, also reinforce cultural expectations of gender (Pascoe 2003). When sociologist Melissa Milkie (1994) studied junior high school boys, she found that much of their talk centered on movies and TV programs. Of the many images they saw, the boys would single out sex and violence. They would amuse one another by repeating lines, acting out parts, and joking and laughing at what they had seen.

If you know boys in their early teens, you've probably seen behavior like this. You may have been amused or even have shaken your head in disapproval. As a sociologist, however, Milkie peered beneath the surface. She concluded that the boys were using media images to develop their identity as males. They had gotten the message: "Real" males are obsessed with sex and violence. Not to joke and laugh about murder and promiscuous sex would have marked a boy as a "weenie," a label to be avoided at all costs.

Gender Messages in the Mass Media

Also guiding us in learning our gender map are the **mass media,** forms of communication that are directed to large audiences. Let's look at how their images reinforce **gender roles,** the behaviors and attitudes considered appropriate for our sex.

Television Television reinforces stereotypes of the sexes. On prime-time television, male characters outnumber female characters. Male characters are also more likely to be portrayed in higher-status positions (Glascock 2001). Sports news also maintains traditional stereotypes. Sociologists who studied the content of televised sports news in Los Angeles found that female athletes receive little coverage (Messner et al. 2003). When they do, they are sometimes trivialized by male newscasters who focus on humorous events in women's sports or turn the female athlete into a sexual object. Newscasters even manage to emphasize breasts and bras and to engage in locker-room humor.

Stereotype-breaking characters, in contrast, are a sign of changing times. In comedies, women are more verbally aggressive than men (Glascock 2001). The powers of the teenager *Buffy, The Vampire Slayer,* were remarkable. On *Alias,* Sydney Bristow exhibited extraordinary strength. In cartoons, Kim Possible divides her time between cheerleading practice and saving the world from evil, while, also with tongue in cheek, the Powerpuff Girls are touted as "the most elite kindergarten crime-fighting force ever assembled." This new gender portrayal continues in a variety of programs, such as *Totally Spies.*

The gender messages on these programs are mixed. Girls are powerful, but they have to be skinny and gorgeous and wear the latest fashions, too. Such messages present a dilemma for girls, as this is almost impossible to replicate in real life.

Video Games One of the hallmarks of today's society is video games. Even preschoolers are involved: One-fourth of 4- to 6-year-olds play them for an average of an hour a day (Rideout and Vandewater 2003). You've probably noticed that college students, especially men, relieve stress by escaping into video games. The first members of the "Nintendo Generation," now in their thirties, are still playing video games—with babies on their laps.

Sociologists have begun to study how the sexes are portrayed in video games, but their influence on the players' ideas of gender is still unknown (Dietz 2000; Berger 2002). Because these games are on the cutting edge of society, they sometimes also reflect cutting-edge changes in sex roles, the topic of the Mass Media in Social Life box on the next page.

Anime *Anime* is a Japanese cartoon form targeted at children. Because anime crosses boundaries of video games, television, movies, and books (comic), we shall consider it as a separate category. As shown below, perhaps the most recognizable feature of anime is the big-eyed little girls and the fighting little boys. Japanese parents are concerned about anime's antisocial heroes and its depiction of violence, but to keep peace they reluctantly buy anime for their children (Khattak 2007). In the United States, the mass media aimed at children often depict violence—so, with its cute characters, anime is unlikely to bother U.S. parents. Anime's depiction of active, dominant little boys and submissive little girls leads to the question, of course, of what gender lessons it is giving children.

In Sum: "Male" and "female" are such powerful symbols that learning them forces us to interpret the world in terms of gender. As children learn their society's symbols of gender, they learn that different behaviors and attitudes are expected of boys and girls. First transmitted by the family, these gender messages are reinforced by other social institutions. As they become integrated into our views of the world, gender messages form a picture of "how" males and females "are." Because gender serves as a primary basis for **social inequality**—giving privileges and obligations to one group of people while denying them to another—gender images are especially important to understand.

Anime is increasing in popularity—cartoons and comics aimed at children and pornography targeted to adults. Its gender messages, especially those directed to children, are yet to be explored.

MASS MEDIA in SOCIAL LIFE

Lara Croft, Tomb Raider: Changing Images of Women in the Mass Media

The mass media reflect traditional and changing roles of women. Amidst the portrayals of women as passive, as subordinate, or as mere background objects, a new image has broken through. This new image, as exaggerated as it is, illustrates a fundamental change in gender relations. Lara Croft is an outstanding example of this change.

Like books and magazines, video games are made available to a mass audience. And with digital advances, they have crossed the line from what are traditionally thought of as games to something that more closely resembles interactive movies. Costing an average of $10 million to produce and another $10 million to market, video games have intricate subplots and use celebrity voices for the characters (Nussenbaum 2004).

Sociologically, what is significant is that the *content* of video games socializes their users. As they play, gamers are exposed not only to action but also to ideas and images. The gender images of video games communicate powerful messages, just as they do in other forms of the mass media.

Lara Croft, an adventure-seeking archaeologist and star of *Tomb Raider* and its many sequels, is the essence of the new gender image. Lara is smart, strong, and able to utterly vanquish foes. With both guns blazing, she is the *cowboy* of the twenty-first century, the term cowboy being purposefully chosen, as Lara breaks stereotypical gender roles and dominates what previously was the domain of men. She was the first female protagonist in a field of muscle-rippling, gun-toting macho caricatures (Taylor 1999).

Yet the old remains powerfully encapsulated in the new. As the photo on this page makes evident, Lara is a fantasy girl for young men of the digital generation. No matter her foe, no matter her predicament, Lara oozes sex. Her form-fitting outfits, which flatter her voluptuous physique, reflect the mental images of the men who fashioned this digital character.

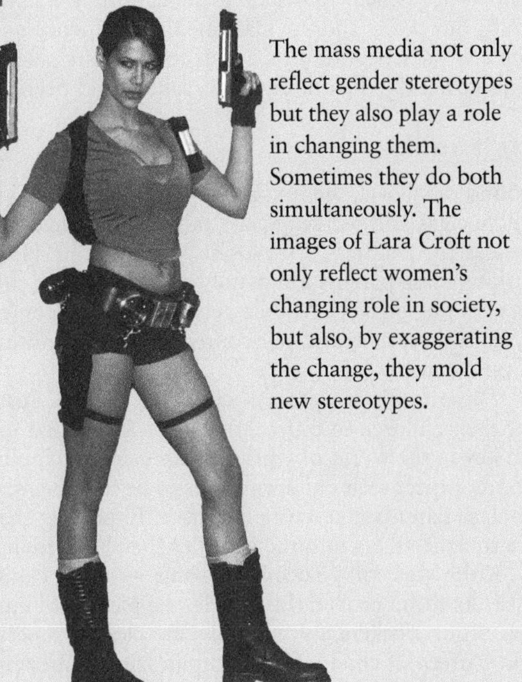

The mass media not only reflect gender stereotypes but they also play a role in changing them. Sometimes they do both simultaneously. The images of Lara Croft not only reflect women's changing role in society, but also, by exaggerating the change, they mold new stereotypes.

Lara has caught young men's fancy to such an extent that they have bombarded corporate headquarters with questions about her personal life. Lara is the star of two movies and a comic book. There is even a Lara Croft candy bar.

For Your Consideration

A sociologist who reviewed this text said, "It seems that for women to be defined as equal, we have to become symbolic males—warriors with breasts." Why is gender change mostly one-way—females adopting traditional male characteristics? To see why men get to keep their gender roles, these two questions should help: Who is moving into the traditional territory of the other? Do people prefer to imitate power or weakness?

Finally, consider just how far stereotypes have actually been left behind. For completing certain tasks, the reward is to see Lara in a swimsuit or lingerie.

Agents of Socialization

People and groups that influence our orientations to life—our self-concept, emotions, attitudes, and behavior—are called **agents of socialization.** We have already considered how three of these agents—the family, our peers, and the mass media—influence our ideas of gender. Now we'll look more closely at how agents of socialization prepare us to take our place in society. We shall first consider the family, then the neighborhood, religion, day care, school and peers, and the workplace.

The Family

Around the world, the first group to have a major impact on us is our family. Sociologists have found that middle-class and working-class families socialize their children differently, a process with lifelong consequences for children. Sociologist Melvin Kohn (1959, 1963, 1976, 1977; Kohn et al. 1986) found that working-class parents are mainly concerned that their children stay out of trouble. They also tend to use physical punishment. Middle-class parents, in contrast, focus more on developing their children's curiosity, self-expression, and self-control. They are more likely to reason with their children than to use physical punishment.

These findings were a sociological puzzle. Just why would working-class and middle-class parents rear their children so differently? Kohn knew that life experiences of some sort held the key, and he found that key in the world of work. Bosses usually tell blue-collar workers exactly what to do. Since blue-collar parents expect their children's lives to be like theirs, they stress obedience. At their work, in contrast, middle-class parents take more initiative. Expecting their children to work at similar jobs, middle-class parents socialize them into the qualities they have found valuable.

Kohn was still puzzled, for some working-class parents act more like middle-class parents, and vice versa. As Kohn probed this puzzle, the pieces fell into place. The key was the parents' type of job. Middle-class office workers, for example, are closely supervised, and Kohn found that they follow the working-class pattern of child rearing, emphasizing conformity. And some blue-collar workers, such as those who do home repairs, have a good deal of freedom. These workers follow the middle-class model in rearing their children (Pearlin and Kohn 1966; Kohn and Schooler 1969).

The Neighborhood

As all parents know, some neighborhoods are better than others for their children. Parents try to move to those neighborhoods—if they can afford them. Their commonsense evaluations are borne out by sociological research. Children from poor neighborhoods are more likely to get in trouble with the law, to become pregnant, to drop out of school, and even to have worse mental health in later life (Brooks-Gunn et al. 1997; Sampson et al. 2001; Wheaton and Clarke 2003; Yonas et al. 2006).

Sociologists have also found that the residents of more affluent neighborhoods watch out for the children more than do the residents of poor neighborhoods (Sampson et al. 1999). This isn't because the adults in poor neighborhoods care less about children. Rather, the more affluent neighborhoods have fewer families in transition, so the adults are more likely to know the local children and their parents. This better equips them to help keep the children safe and out of trouble.

Religion

How important is religion in your life? You could be among the two-thirds of Americans who belong to a local congregation, but what if you are among the other third? Why would religion be significant for you? To see the influence of religion, we can't look only at people who are religious. Even in the extreme—people who wouldn't be caught dead near a church, synagogue, or mosque—religion plays a powerful role. Perhaps this is the most significant aspect of religion: Religious ideas so pervade U.S. society that they provide the foundation of morality for both the religious and the nonreligious. For many Americans, the influence of religion is more direct. This is especially true for the two of every five Americans who report that during a typical week they attend a religious service (Gallup Poll 2007; *Statistical Abstract* 2007:Tables 73, 75). Through their participation in congregational life, they learn doctrine, values, and morality, but the effects on their lives are not limited to these obvious factors. For example, people who participate in religious services learn not only beliefs about the hereafter but also ideas about what kinds of clothing, speech, and manners are appropriate for formal occasions. Life in congregations also provides a sense of identity for its participants, giving them a feeling of belonging. It also helps to integrate immigrants into their new society, offers an avenue of social mobility for the poor, provides social contacts for jobs, and in the case of African American churches, has been a powerful influence in social change.

Day Care

It is rare for social science research to make national news, but occasionally it does. This is what happened when researchers published their findings on 1,200 kindergarten children they had studied since they were a month old. They observed the children multiple times both at home and at day care. They also videotaped and made detailed notes on the children's interaction with their mothers (National Institute of Child Health and Human Development 1999; Guensburg 2001). What caught the media's attention? Children who spend more time in day care have weaker bonds with their mothers and are less affectionate to them. They are also less cooperative with others and more likely to fight and to be "mean." By the time they get to kindergarten, they are more likely to talk back to teachers and to disrupt the classroom. This holds true regardless of the quality of the day care, the family's social class, or whether the child is a girl or a boy (Belsky 2006). On the positive side, the children also scored higher on language tests.

Are we producing a generation of "smart but mean" children? This is not an unreasonable question, since the study was designed well, and an even larger study of children in England has come up with similar findings (Belsky 2006). Some point out that the differences between children who spend a lot of time in day care and those who spend less time are slight. Others stress that with several million children in day care (*Statistical Abstract* 2007:Table 564), slight differences can be significant for society. The researchers are following these children as they continue in school. The most recent report on the children, when they were in the 6th grade, indicates that these patterns are continuing (Belsky et al. 2007).

The School and Peer Groups

As a child's experiences with agents of socialization broaden, the influence of the family decreases. Entry into school marks only one of many steps in this transfer of allegiance and learning of new values. The Cultural Diversity box on the next page explores how these new values and ways of looking at the world sometimes even replace those the child learns at home.

When sociologists Patricia and Peter Adler (1998) observed children at two elementary schools in Colorado, they saw how children separate themselves by sex and develop their own worlds with unique norms. The norms that made boys popular were athletic ability, coolness, and toughness. For girls, popularity was based on family background, physical appearance (clothing and use of makeup), and the ability to attract popular boys. In this children's subculture, academic achievement pulled in opposite directions: For boys, high grades lowered their popularity, but for girls, good grades increased their standing among peers.

You know from your own experience how compelling peer groups are. It is almost impossible to go against a peer group, whose cardinal rule seems to be "conformity or rejection." Anyone who doesn't do what the others want becomes an "outsider," a "nonmember," an "outcast." For preteens and teens just learning their way around in the world, it is not surprising that the peer group rules.

As a result, the standards of our peer groups tend to dominate our lives. If your peers, for example, listen to rap, Nortec, death metal, rock and roll, country, or gospel, it is almost inevitable that you also prefer that kind of music. It is the same for clothing styles and dating standards. Peer influences also extend to behaviors that violate social norms. If your peers are college-bound and upwardly striving, that is most likely what you will be; but if they use drugs, cheat, and steal, you are likely to do so, too.

The Workplace

Another agent of socialization that comes into play somewhat later in life is the workplace. Those initial jobs that we take in high school and college are much more than just a way to earn a few dollars. From the people we rub shoulders with at work, we learn not only a set of skills but also perspectives on the world.

Most of us eventually become committed to some particular line of work, often after trying out many jobs. This may involve **anticipatory socialization,** learning to play a role before entering it. Anticipatory socialization is a sort of mental rehearsal for some future activity. We may talk to people who work in a particular career, read novels about that type of work, or take a summer internship in that field. Such activities allow us to gradually identify with the role, to become aware of what would be expected of us. Sometimes this helps people avoid committing themselves to an unrewarding career, as with some of my students who tried student teaching, found that they couldn't stand it, and then moved on to other fields more to their liking.

An intriguing aspect of work as a socializing agent is that the more you participate in a line of work, the more the work becomes a part of your self-concept. Eventually you come to think of yourself so much in terms of the job that if someone asks you to describe yourself, you are likely to include the job in your self-description. You might say, "I'm a teacher," "I'm a nurse," or "I'm a sociologist."

Cultural Diversity in the United States

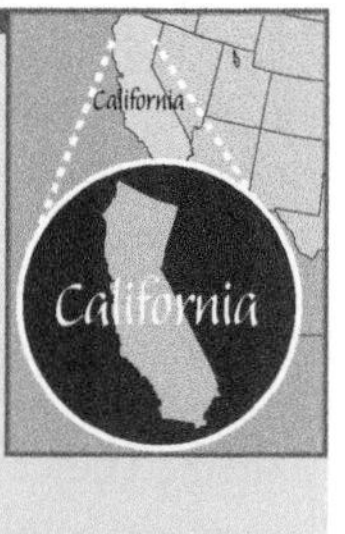

Caught Between Two Worlds

It is a struggle to learn a new culture, for its behaviors and ways of thinking may be at odds with ones already learned. This can lead to inner turmoil. One way to handle the conflict is to cut ties with your first culture. Doing so, however, can create a sense of loss, perhaps one that is recognized only later in life.

Richard Rodriguez, a literature professor and essayist, was born to working-class Mexican immigrants. Wanting their son to be successful in their adopted land, his parents named him Richard instead of Ricardo. While his English-Spanish hybrid name indicates the parents' aspirations for their son, it was also an omen of the conflict that Richard would experience.

Like other children of Mexican immigrants, Richard first spoke Spanish—a rich mother tongue that introduced him to the world. Until the age of 5, when he began school, Richard knew only fifty words in English. He describes what happened when he began school:

> The change came gradually but early. When I was beginning grade school, I noted to myself the fact that the classroom environment was so different in its styles and assumptions from my own family environment that survival would essentially entail a choice between both worlds. When I became a student, I was literally "remade"; neither I nor my teachers considered anything I had known before as relevant. I had to forget most of what my culture had provided, because to remember it was a disadvantage. The past and its cultural values became detachable, like a piece of clothing grown heavy on a warm day and finally put away.

As happened to millions of immigrants before him, whose parents spoke German, Polish, Italian, and so on, learning English eroded family and class ties and ate away at his ethnic roots. For Rodriguez, language and education were not simply devices that eased the transition to the dominant culture. Instead, they slashed at the roots that had given him life.

To face conflicting cultures is to confront a fork in the road. Some turn one way and withdraw from the new culture—a clue that helps to explain why so many Latinos drop out of U.S. schools. Others go in the opposite direction. Cutting ties with their family and cultural roots, they wholeheartedly adopt the new culture.

Rodriguez took the second road. He excelled in his new language—so well, in fact, that he graduated from Stanford University and then became a graduate student in English at the University of California at Berkeley. He was even awarded a Fulbright fellowship to study English Renaissance literature at the University of London.

But the past shadowed Rodriguez. Prospective employers were impressed with his knowledge of Renaissance literature. At job interviews, however, they would skip over the Renaissance training and ask him if he would teach the Mexican novel and be an adviser to Latino students. Rodriguez was also haunted by the image of his grandmother, the warmth of the culture he had left behind, and the language and thought to which he had become a stranger.

Richard Rodriguez represents millions of immigrants—not just those of Latino origin but those from other cultures, too—who want to be a part of life in the United States without betraying their past. They fear that to integrate into U.S. culture is to lose their roots. They are caught between two cultures, each beckoning, each offering rich rewards.

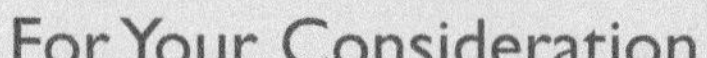

For Your Consideration

I saw this conflict firsthand with my father, who did not learn English until after the seventh grade (his last in school). German was left behind, but broken English and awkward expressions remained for a lifetime. Then, too, there were the lingering emotional connections to old ways, as well as the suspicions, haughtiness, and slights of more assimilated Americans. His longing for security by grasping the past was combined with his wanting to succeed in the everyday reality of the new culture. Have you seen anything similar?

Sources: Based on Richard Rodriguez 1975, 1982, 1990, 1991, 1995.

Resocialization

What does a woman who has just become a nun have in common with a man who has just divorced? The answer is that they both are undergoing **resocialization;** that is, they are learning new norms, values, attitudes, and behaviors to match their new situation in life. In its most common form, resocialization occurs each time we learn something contrary to our previous experiences. A new boss who insists on a different way of doing things is resocializing you. Most resocialization is mild—only a slight modification of things we have already learned.

Resocialization can also be intense. People who join Alcoholics Anonymous (AA), for example, are surrounded by reformed drinkers who affirm the destructive effects of excessive drinking. Some students experience an intense period of resocialization when they leave high school and start college—especially during those initially scary days before they find companions, start to fit in, and feel comfortable. To join a cult or to begin psychotherapy is even more profound, for this immerses people in views that conflict with their earlier socialization. If these ideas take, not only does the individual's behavior change but he or she also learns a fundamentally different way of looking at life.

Total Institutions

Relatively few of us experience the powerful agent of socialization that sociologist Erving Goffman (1961) called the **total institution.** He coined this term to refer to a place in which people are cut off from the rest of society and where they come under almost total control of the officials who are in charge. Boot camp, prisons, concentration camps, convents, some religious cults, and some military schools, such as West Point, are total institutions.

A person entering a total institution is greeted with a **degradation ceremony** (Garfinkel 1956), an attempt to remake the self by stripping away the individual's current identity and stamping a new one in its place. This unwelcome greeting may involve fingerprinting, photographing, shaving the head, and banning the individual's *personal identity kit* (items such as jewelry, hairstyles, clothing, and other body decorations used to express individuality). Newcomers may be ordered to strip, undergo an examination (often in a humiliating, semipublic setting), and then put on a uniform that designates their new status. (For prisoners, the public reading of the verdict and being led away in handcuffs by armed police are also part of the degradation ceremony.)

Total institutions are isolated from the public. The walls, bars, gates, and guards not only keep the inmates in but also keep outsiders out. Staff members closely supervise the day-to-day lives of the residents. Eating, sleeping, showering, recreation—all are standardized. Inmates learn that their previous statuses—student, worker, spouse, parent—mean nothing. The only thing that counts is their current status.

No one leaves a total institution unscathed, for the experience brands an indelible mark on the individual's self and colors the way he or she sees the world. Boot camp, as described in the Down-to-Earth Sociology box on the next page, is brutal but swift. Prison, in contrast, is brutal and prolonged. Neither recruit nor prisoner, however, has difficulty in pinpointing how the institution affected the self.

Socialization Through the Life Course

You are at a particular stage in your life now, and college is a good part of it. You know that you have more stages ahead of you as you go through life. These stages, from birth to death, are called the **life course** (Elder 1975; 1999). The sociological significance of the life course is twofold. First, as you pass through a stage, it affects your behavior and orientations. You simply don't think about life in the same way when you are 30, are married, and have a baby and a mortgage, as you do when you are 18 or 20, single, and in college. (Actually, you don't even see life the same as a freshman and as a senior.) Second, your life course differs by social location. Your social class, race–ethnicity, and gender, for example, map out distinctive worlds of experience.

This means that the typical life course differs for males and females, the rich and the poor, and so on. To emphasize this major sociological point, in the sketch that follows I will stress the *historical* setting of people's lives. Because of your particular social location, your own life course may differ from this sketch, which is a composite of stages that others have suggested (Levinson 1978; Carr et al. 1995; Quadagno 2007).

Down-to-Earth Sociology

Boot Camp as a Total Institution

Resocialization is often a gentle process. Usually we are gradually exposed to different ways of thinking and doing. Sometimes, however, resocialization can be swift and brutal, as it is during boot camp in the Marines. This private at Parris Island is learning a world vastly unlike the civilian world he left behind.

The bus arrives at Parris Island, South Carolina, at 3 A.M. The early hour is no accident. The recruits are groggy, confused. Up to a few hours ago, the young men were ordinary civilians. Now, as a sergeant sneeringly calls them "maggots," their heads are buzzed (25 seconds per recruit), and they are quickly thrust into the harsh world of Marine boot camp.

Buzzing the boys' hair is just the first step in stripping away their identity so that the Marines can stamp a new one in its place. The uniform serves the same purpose. There is a ban on using the first person "I." Even a simple request must be made in precise Marine style or it will not be acknowledged. ("Sir, Recruit Jones requests permission to make a head call, Sir.")

Every intense moment of the next eleven weeks reminds the recruits, men and women, at Parris Island that they are joining a subculture of self-discipline. Here pleasure is suspect and sacrifice is good. As they learn the Marine way of talking, walking, and thinking, they are denied the diversions they once took for granted: television, cigarettes, cars, candy, soft drinks, video games, music, alcohol, drugs, and sex.

Lessons are bestowed with fierce intensity. When Sgt. Carey checks brass belt buckles, Recruit Robert Shelton nervously blurts, "I don't have one." Sgt. Carey's face grows red as his neck cords bulge. "I?" he says, his face just inches from the recruit. With spittle flying from his mouth, he screams, "'I' is gone!"

"Nobody's an individual" is the lesson that is driven home again and again. "You are a team, a Marine. Not a civilian. Not black or white, not Hispanic or Indian or some hyphenated American—but a Marine. You will live like a Marine, fight like a Marine, and, if necessary, die like a Marine."

Each day begins before dawn with close-order formations. The rest of the day is filled with training in hand-to-hand combat, marching, running, calisthenics, Marine history, and—always—following orders.

"An M-16 can blow someone's head off at 500 meters," Sgt. Norman says. "That's beautiful, isn't it?"

"Yes, sir!" shout the platoon's fifty-nine voices.

"Pick your nose!" Simultaneously fifty nine index fingers shoot into nostrils.

The pressure to conform is intense. Those who are sent packing for insubordination or suicidal tendencies are mocked in cadence during drills. ("Hope you like the sights you see/Parris Island casualty.") As lights go out at 9 P.M., the exhausted recruits perform the day's last task: The entire platoon, in unison, chants the virtues of the Marines.

Recruits are constantly scrutinized. Subperformance is not accepted, whether it be a dirty rifle or a loose thread on a uniform. The subperformer is shouted at, derided, humiliated. The group suffers for the individual. If a recruit is slow, the entire platoon is punished.

The system works.

One of the new Marines (until graduation, they are recruits, not Marines) says, "I feel like I've joined a new society or religion."

He has.

For Your Consideration

Of what significance is the recruits' degradation ceremony? Why are recruits not allowed video games, cigarettes, or calls home? Why are the Marines so unfair as to punish an entire platoon for the failure of an individual? Use concepts in this chapter to explain why the system works.

Sources: Based on Garfinkel 1956; Goffman 1961; Ricks 1995; Dyer 2007.

Childhood (from birth to about age 12)

Consider how different your childhood would have been if you had grown up in another historical era. Historian Philippe Ariès (1965) noticed that in European paintings from about 1000 to 1800 A.D., children were always dressed in adult clothing. If they were not depicted stiffly posed, as in a family portrait, they were shown doing adult activities.

From this, Ariès drew a conclusion that sparked a debate among historians: He believed that during this era in Europe, childhood was not regarded as a special time of life. He said that adults viewed children as miniature adults and put them to work at very early ages. At the age of 7, for example, a boy might leave home for good to learn to be a jeweler or a stonecutter. A girl, in contrast, stayed home until she married, but by the age of 7 she was expected to assume her share of the household tasks. Historians do not deny that these were the customs of that time, but some say that Ariès' conclusion is ridiculous. They say that other evidence of that period indicates that childhood was viewed as a special time of life (Orme 2002).

Having children work like adults did not disappear with the Middle Ages. It is still common in the Least Industrialized Nations, where children still work in many occupations—from blacksmiths to waiters. They are most visible as street peddlers, hawking everything from shoelaces to chewing gum and candy. The photo on the upper left of page 189 not only illustrates different activities, but it also reflects a view of children remarkably different from the one common in the Most Industrialized Nations.

Child rearing, too, was remarkably different. In earlier centuries, parents and teachers considered it their moral duty to terrorize children to keep them in line. They would lock children in dark closets, frighten them with bedtime stories of death and hellfire, and force them to witness gruesome events. Consider this:

> A common moral lesson involved taking children to visit the gibbet [an upraised post on which executed bodies were left hanging from chains], where they were forced to inspect rotting corpses hanging there as an example of what happens to bad children when they grow up. Whole classes were taken out of school to witness hangings, and parents would often whip their children afterwards to make them remember what they had seen. (DeMause 1975)

In contemporary Western societies such as the United States, children are viewed as innocent and in need of protection from adult responsibilities such as work and self-support. Ideas of childhood vary historically and cross-culturally. From paintings, such as this 1642 British portrait by the Le Nain brothers, *A Woman and Five Children*, some historians conclude that Europeans once viewed children as miniature adults who assumed adult roles at the earliest opportunity.

Industrialization transformed the way we perceive children. With children having the leisure to go to school, they came to be thought of as tender and innocent, as needing more adult care, comfort, and protection. Over time, such attitudes of dependency grew, and today we view children as needing gentle guidance if they are to develop emotionally, intellectually, morally, even physically. We take our view for granted—after all, it is only "common sense." Yet, as you can see, our view is not "natural." It is, instead, rooted in geography and history.

In Sum: Childhood is more than biology. Everyone's childhood occurs at some point in history and is embedded in particular social locations, especially social class and gender. *These social factors are as vital as our biology, for they determine what childhood will be like for us.* Although a child's *biological* characteristics (such as being small and dependent) are universal, the child's *social* experiences (the kind of life the child lives) are not. Because of this, sociologists say that childhood varies from culture to culture.

Adolescence (ages 13–17)

Adolescence is not a "natural" age division. It is a social invention. In earlier centuries, people simply moved from childhood into young adulthood, with no stopover in between. The Industrial Revolution brought such an abundance of material surpluses, however, that for the first time in history, millions of people in their teens were able to remain outside the labor force. At the same time, education became a more important factor in achieving success. The convergence of these two forces in industrialized societies created a gap between childhood and adulthood. In the early 1900s, the term *adolescence* was coined to indicate this new stage in life (Hall 1904), one that has become renowned for inner turmoil.

To ground the self-identity of children and mark their passage into adulthood, tribal societies hold *initiation rites*. In the industrialized world, however, adolescents must "find" themselves on their own. As they attempt to carve out an identity that is distinct from both the "younger" world being left behind and the "older" world that is still out of range, adolescents develop their own subcultures, with distinctive clothing, hairstyles, language, gestures, and music. We usually fail to realize that contemporary society, not biology, created this period of inner turmoil that we call *adolescence*.

Transitional Adulthood (ages 18–29)

If society invented adolescence, can it also invent other periods of life? As Figure 5.1 illustrates, this is actually happening now. Postindustrial societies are adding a period of extended youth to the life course, which sociologists call **transitional adulthood** (also known as *adultolescence*). After high school, millions of young adults go to college, where they postpone adult responsibilities. They are mostly freed from the control of their parents, yet they don't have to support themselves. Even after college, many return home, so they can live cheaply while they establish themselves in a career—and, of course, continue to "find themselves." During this time, people are "neither psychological adolescents nor sociological adults" (Keniston 1971). At some point during this period of extended youth, young adults gradually ease into adult responsibilities. They take a full-time job, become serious about a career, engage in courtship rituals, get married—and go into debt.

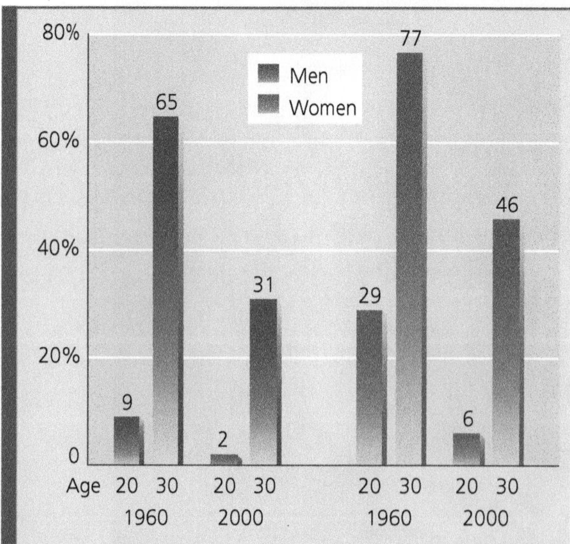

FIGURE 5.1 Transitional Adulthood: A New Stage in the Life Course Who has completed the transition? The data show the percentage who have completed the transition to adulthood, as measured by leaving home, finishing school, getting married, having a child, and being financially independent. (*Source:* Furstenberg et al. 2004.)

The Middle Years (ages 30–65)

The Early Middle Years (ages 30–49) During their early middle years, most people are more sure of themselves and of their goals in life. As with any point in the life course, however, the self can receive severe jolts. Common in this period are divorce and losing jobs. It may take years for the self to stabilize after such ruptures.

The early middle years pose a special challenge for many U.S. women, who have been given the message, especially by the media, that they can "have it all." They can be superworkers, superwives, and supermoms—all rolled into one. The reality, however, usually consists of conflicting pressures—too little time, too many demands, even too little sleep. Something has to give, and attempts to resolve this dilemma are anything but easy.

In many societies, manhood is not bestowed upon males simply because they reach a certain age. Manhood, rather, signifies a standing in the community that must be achieved. Shown here are 10- to 12-year old Aboriginal boys in Australia, prepared for their initiation circumcision ceremony. Except for their loin cloths, their "clothing" has been painted on their bodies.

The Later Middle Years (ages 50–65) During the later middle years, health issues and mortality begin to loom large as people feel their bodies change, especially if they watch their parents become frail, fall ill, and die. The consequence is a fundamental reorientation in thinking—*from time since birth to time left to live* (Neugarten 1976). With this changed orientation, people attempt to evaluate the past and come to terms with what lies ahead. They compare what they have accomplished with what they had hoped to achieve. Many people also find themselves caring not only for their own children but also for their aging parents. Because of this set of burdens, which is often crushing, people in the later middle years sometimes are called the "sandwich generation."

Life during this stage isn't stressful for everyone. Many find late middle age to be the most comfortable period of their lives. They enjoy job security and a standard of living higher than ever before; they have a bigger house (one that may even be paid for), drive newer cars, and take longer and more exotic vacations. The children are grown, the self is firmly planted, and fewer upheavals are likely to occur.

As they anticipate the next stage of life, however, most people do not like what they see.

The Older Years (about age 65 on)

In industrialized societies, the older years begin around the mid-60s. This, too, is recent, for in agricultural societies, when most people died early, old age was thought to begin at around age 40. Industrialization brought about improved nutrition and public health, which prolonged life. Today, people in good health who are over the age of 65 often experience this period not as old age, but as an extension of the middle years. People who continue to work or to do things they enjoy are less likely to perceive themselves as old (Neugarten 1977). Although frequency of sex declines, most men and women in their 60s and 70s are sexually active (Denney and Quadagno 1992).

Because we have a self and can reason abstractly, we can contemplate death. Initially, we regard death as a vague notion, a remote possibility. But as people see their parents and friends die and observe their own bodies no longer functioning as before, the thought of death becomes less abstract. Increasingly during this stage in the life course, people feel that "time is closing in" on them.

Are We Prisoners of Socialization?

From our discussion of socialization, you might conclude that sociologists think of people as robots: The socialization goes in, and the behavior comes out. People cannot help what they do, think, or feel, for everything is simply a result of their exposure to socializing agents.

Sociologists do *not* think of people in this way. Although socialization is powerful and affects us all profoundly, we have a self. Established in childhood and continually modified by later experience, the self is dynamic. Our self is not a sponge that passively absorbs influences from the environment, but, rather, a vigorous, essential part of our being that allows us to act on our environment.

Indeed, it is precisely because individuals are not robots that their behavior is so hard to predict. The countless reactions of other people merge in each of us. As the self develops, each person internalizes or "puts together" these innumerable reactions, producing a unique whole called the *individual.* Each individual uses his or her own mind to reason and to make choices in life.

In this way, *each of us is actively involved in the construction of the self.* For example, although our experiences in the family lay down the basic elements of our personality, including fundamental orientations to life, we are not doomed to keep those orientations if we do not like them. We can purposely expose ourselves to groups and ideas that we prefer. Those experiences, in turn, will have their own effects on our self. In short, although socialization is powerful, we can change even the self within the limitations of the framework laid down by our social locations. And that self—along with the options available within society—is the key to our behavior.

chapter 6

Cognition: Sensation, Perception, and States of Consciousness

We do not see things with our eyes; we see them through our eyes and with our minds.

ANONYMOUS

As a rule, what is out of sight disturbs men's minds more seriously than what they see.

JULIUS CAESAR (100–44 B.C.E.)—
ROMAN STATESMAN

At the end of class Albert raised his hand and asked a question: "Do cross-cultural psychologists acknowledge important differences between Europeans and non-Europeans in America?" He then contended that for centuries, the ancestors of the former group relied mostly on visual perception. Europeans, he said, must see, verify, measure, and then rationalize their impressions. They do not feel or believe a priori; they must experience everything before their own eyes. Africans, he said, referring to his own ancestors, were different because of environmental conditions that caused them to rely mostly on hearing and touch. They felt objects and vibrations through their skin, could masterfully express themselves through their voices, and did not always need visual verifications. Albert concluded that due to such perceptual differences between European and African ancestors, European Americans are more likely to succeed in engineering, science, and writing, whereas African Americans tend to excel at playing music, singing, and other nonvisual arts. "Do you have any evidence to support your idea?" one of the students replied. "You see, you need verifications. I do not have them. I simply feel this way," responded Albert, laughing at his own answer.

Was Albert right when he daringly suggested the differences between Africans and Europeans? Are there any significant sensory differences among people of various cultures? Or maybe people see, hear, and feel the physical world in the same way? If not, what particular characteristics of vision, smell, touch, or taste have the strongest cultural roots? On a more "practical" side, should fashion designers pay attention to certain colors either liked or disliked by particular ethnic or national groups? Do pilots in all countries prefer to scan the control board in front of them from left to right? Can people in Brazil enjoy the sound of music liked by people in China? Do people see similar dreams? We will try to address these and other questions throughout this chapter. First let us begin with a brief review of the most basic principles underlying human cognitive processes.

Cross-Cultural Psychology: Critical Thinking and Contemporary Applications, Fourth Edition, by Eric B. Shiraev and David A. Levy

Sensation and Perception: Basic Principles

The process by which receptor cells are stimulated and transmit their information to higher brain centers is called **sensation**. You see a blue star in the evening sky or feel a dull pain in your arm—all sensations begin from an environmental stimulus, either external or internal, in the form of energy capable of exciting the nervous system. Sensation converts external energy into an internal neurophysiological process, which "results" in a particular psychological experience: we see the star and feel the pain. Do we feel all environmental stimuli? Obviously not, because certain stimuli are not experienced at all.

The minimum amount of physical energy needed for an individual to notice a stimulus is called an **absolute threshold**. The **difference threshold** is the lowest level of stimulation required to sense that a change in the stimulation has occurred. **Sensory adaptation** is the tendency of the sensory system to respond less to stimuli that continue without change. We can adapt, for example, to particular conditions, such as heat or cold, the presence or absence of air pollution, and spicy food. Residents of a small resort town in Spain are less likely to attend to the air they breathe, whereas a tourist visiting this town from a polluted Mexico City or Los Angeles is likely to notice the incredible freshness of the air.

For each of the five senses (vision, hearing, smell, touch, and taste), discrete neural pathways normally carry sensory information, a signal, to specific regions in the brain. The nature of sensation depends on the area of the brain that is activated by a signal. For example, electrical stimulation of the primary visual cortex, which is located in the occipital lobes of the brain, produces visual sensations, whereas stimulation of the auditory complex in the temporal lobes is experienced as sound. Color sensation is a process based on the functioning of three different types of cones in the eye's retina. Each cone responds to wavelights, but fires most persistently at a particular point on the spectrum. Thus short-wavelight cones are responsible for the sensation of blue, middle-wavelight cones produce the sensation of green, and long-wavelight cones produce red sensations. Mixing these three primary colors together, most individuals detect as many as 1,000 color shades (Brown & Wald, 1964). When a person detects a smell, information from the receptors travels directly to the primary olfactory complex in the frontal lobes. Taste receptors consist of two paths. The first path is connected to the primary gustatory cortex in the brain, which allows people to detect tastes. The second path is connected to the brain's limbic system, which can generate immediate emotional and behavioral responses to tastes. Several receptors in the skin feed into a single sensory neuron that is connected to the spinal cord. This allows for immediate reflexive action, such as the quick movement after touching something hot.

The process that organizes various sensations into meaningful patterns is called **perception**. Physiologists assert that perception involves activation of association areas in the cortex, thus integrating prior knowledge with current sensation. Three colored vertical stripes—blue, white, and red—displayed in sequence on a piece of material will have little meaning for a boy from Bangladesh or Northern Ireland. However, for a French adult, this sequence of colors would be associated with the French national flag. When one of us takes a guitar and plays the first cords of the song *Stairway to Heaven*, many U.S. or British students identify it as a classic-rock ballad written by Led Zeppelin. However, those who grew up outside the Western tradition of rock music interpret these notes as nothing more than a "melody."

Sensation and perception are two basic processes first studied in psychological laboratories more than 100 years ago in several countries, including Germany, France, Russia, Great Britain, and the United States. Comparative analysis of the data obtained by these laboratories shows remarkable quantitative and qualitative similarities in both sensory and perceptual processes in people of different countries (Yaroshevski, 1996). However, in most experiments, psychologists studied sensation using a "standard"—for psychological research in the 1800s—sample of subjects: the researchers themselves, their academic assistants, and, of course, the students. Therefore, the data in such studies were obtained mainly from highly educated, white male subjects. Cross-cultural investigation of sensation began with the research conducted by Rivers (1901) and associates, who selected their subjects in Europe and Torres Strait Islands, a territory near Australia. Rivers examined a popular assumption about the extraordinary visual sharpness of non-Europeans. The assumption was disproved: the vision of the Torres Strait Islanders was not found to be outstanding.

How Culture Influences What We Perceive

Our experience with the environment shapes our perception by creating perceptual expectations. These expectations, known as a **perceptual set**, make particular interpretations likely to occur and increase both the speed and efficiency of the perceptual process. Perceptual sets common in people of a particular culture—and most relevant to their experience—are not necessarily developed in individuals from other cultures.

Personal experience influences one's sensation and perception. If many individuals from a particular group share such experiences, there should be some common group-related sensory or perceptual patterns. For example, we are usually aware of the aroma outside a restaurant when we are hungry, yet we are much less sensitive to it when our stomach is full. In general, if we need something, we pay attention to the stimuli that are linked to the gratification of the need. But what if a person is constantly deprived of food or water, like millions of people on earth are? In one study, researchers examined the effects of food and water deprivation on word identification (Wispe & Drambarean, 1953). The deprived participants perceived the need-related words (words standing for food and drinks) at shorter exposure times than the nondeprived subjects. In another study, researchers compared the perceptual experiences of children from poor and wealthy families (Bruner & Goodman, 1947). They asked children to adjust the size of a circle of light to match the sizes of various coins: a penny, a nickel, a dime, and a quarter. Children from wealthier families tended to see the coins as smaller than they actually were, whereas children from poor families overestimated the size of the coins. The investigators argued that the need for money among children from poor homes influenced their perception of the coins. This interesting finding has been reproduced in Hong Kong with similar results (Dawson, 1975).

Environmental conditions affect sensation and perception in many ways. Studies have shown that hunter and gatherer cultures have a lower rate of color blindness among their members than societies practicing agriculture. Indeed, from an evolutionary standpoint, not many color-blind hunters could have survived because of their inability to distinguish details, colors, and contours, a skill critical in hunting or gathering activities (Pollack, 1963). Another example refers to the level of noise in the surrounding environments. People who live in deserts do not suffer hearing loss to the extent that city dwellers do (Reuning & Wortley, 1973). In deserts the level of noise is significantly lower than it is in urban areas and this could explain, in part, the difference in hearing problems.

The absence of experience can become a significant factor that affects perception. For example, researchers raised kittens in complete darkness except for several hours each day. During these brief periods, the kittens were placed in a cylinder with either horizontal or vertical stripes (Blakemore & Cooper, 1970). The animals could not observe their own bodies and the only object they saw were the stripes. Five months after the beginning of the experiment, the kittens reared in "horizontal" environments were unable to perceive vertical lines. Their brains lacked detectors responsive to vertical lines. Similarly, the kittens reared in "vertical" environments were unable to perceive horizontal lines. The animals' brains adapted to either "horizontal" or "vertical" worlds by developing specialized neuronal pathways. Similar results were obtained in studies of individuals who were born blind but obtained sight after a surgical procedure later in life (Gregory, 1978). Most of these people could tell figure from ground, detect colors, and observe moving objects. However, many of them could not recognize objects they previously knew by touch. The absence of a visual experience affected these people's cognition after sight was gained!

Box 6.1 CRITICAL THINKING

Origin and Sensory Preferences

This chapter opened with an episode in which Albert raised a question about basic cultural and psychological differences between African Americans and European Americans. His hypothesis resembles the so-called compensation hypothesis: Africans are likely to excel in auditory (hearing) tasks, whereas Europeans deal more effectively with visual (seeing) stimuli. In other words, Africans may prefer to communicate through the auditory modality whereas white Europeans might favor written communications. If Africans, compared to Europeans, appear to have difficulty with the study of mathematics, this can be "compensated" by a high facility for learning languages and a good sense for rhythm and music (McLuhan, 1971). According to Shade (1991), one of the important features in African American perceptual style is the preference of auditory, aural, and tactile perceptions, as compared with predominantly visual perceptions common in European Americans. African Americans are trained to concentrate on people rather than abstract ideas and nonhuman objects. A similar suggestion was extended to the field of art. Auditory and tactile sensations and perceptions were proposed as being specifically African and quite different from the visual culture of the Europeans. Some authors propose the existence of verve, a special element of African psychology. This is an energetic, intense mental set or preference to be simultaneously attuned to several sensory stimuli rather than singular events or a linear set of stimuli (Boykin, 1994).

These hypotheses are intriguing; however, there is very little empirical data to support assumptions about substantial sensory differences between Africans and Europeans. Empirical studies have also come up short in supporting the hypothesis of physiological differences between visual and auditory transmission of information among different cultures. No evidence was found to back a hypothesis about the superiority of black students in auditory judgments and white students in visual judgments. Empirical evidence on the prominence of auditory, tactile, or kinesthetic cues for Africans is also very limited.

On the whole, environmental conditions, as well as activities and experiences, determine culture-related differences and similarities in sensation and perception. Children learn to pay attention to certain stimuli, ignore others, and develop particular cognitive preferences for some culture-related images, smells, tastes, and sounds (Shiraev & Boyd, 2001).

How People Perceive Pictures

Draw a person on a piece of paper. Make sure you draw the head, the body, the hands, and the legs. Do not skip the ears and the mouth. No matter how well or how poorly you draw, the immense majority of people around the world should identify what you drew as a picture of a person.

Perception of pictures is linked to a person's educational and socialization experience or the lack thereof. In a study conducted among the Mekan—a remote group in Ethiopia with limited access to formal schooling and little exposure to pictures—scientists used detailed drawings of animals. With few exceptions the subjects identified the animals, but only after some time and with obvious mental effort (Deregowski et al., 1972). Hudson (1960), who studied how South Africans perceived and interpreted safety posters and signs, provided another demonstration of the links between educational experience and perception. The number of misinterpretations of the posters was much lower for urban and more educated subjects than for rural and less educated individuals. Numerous experiments have demonstrated that people generally have more difficulty in judging pictures of faces of other ethnic groups compared to faces of their own group (Meissner & Brigham, 2001). In one such study, two samples of Turkish-born and Austrian children living in Europe were asked to look at the photographs of Turkish and German faces and match photographs of faces in frontal and angled views. Turkish children were faster in matching Turkish faces than were Austrian children. There was no difference in perception of German faces: both groups matched them equally fast. Most likely, as this research suggests, the Turkish-born children have had more frequent interpersonal contact with Germans than the Austrian kids with Turkish groups (Sporer et al., 2007).

There is evidence that scanning patterns are subject to some cultural variations. The most significant finding is that the direction we examine pictures—from left to right, from right to left, or from top to bottom—is linked to our reading habits (Goodnow & Levine, 1973). For example, it is likely that people in England, Argentina, or Canada, who read from left to right, also have a left–right scanning pattern; Arab and Hebrew readers, who read from right to left, should demonstrate a right–left scanning pattern; and Japanese readers, who read from top to bottom, should have a top–bottom pattern of picture scanning. However, there are exceptions from this rule. For example, in a test on the copying of geometric figures, Hebrew subjects showed a left–right preference. How did the researchers explain this finding? Both Hebrew and English scripts require mainly left-to-right strokes for single letters. In comparison, in the Arab language, the right-to-left direction is required for the writing of individual letters. Therefore, from a practical standpoint, it is always useful to examine not only reading but also writing patterns of a particular culture. These findings can raise interesting assumptions about how some professionals (i.e., pilots, operators, etc.) of different cultural backgrounds scan signals from monitors and other visual indicators.

Box 6.2 CASE IN POINT

Picture Interpretation and Access to Media

Liddell (1997) reported that children in South Africa were less skilled interpreters of pictures than their European counterparts, and this tendency was first noticed as early as in the 1960s. The differences between the samples were larger for African children from rural areas. The mistakes in picture interpretation included making mistakes in depth perception, identification of face blemishes, and interpretation of motion markers. Also, South African children had more difficulties than children in the European sample in creating narrative—short descriptive—interpretations of the pictures. Do these results suggest that because pictures may be a relatively poor source of organizing the South African children's knowledge, the authors of school textbooks should limit the usage of pictures?

We want you to think about the results from a different perspective. The children in the examined samples, despite recent progress in communications, still face a tremendous lack of opportunities compared with their European, Asian, or North American peers. Limited access to television and movies, inability to use personal computers at home, limited access to computers at school, lack of pictorial materials at home, and many other poverty-related problems can contribute to the significant limitations in the child's use of pictures. Make your call now. Should you suggest limiting the number of pictures in South African textbooks or should you rather insist that the child have better access to pictorial materials outside the classroom?

Visual scanning is related to writing and drawing. Take, for instance, the drawing of circles. The differences between cultural groups are perhaps based on the way people learn to write in their native language. If writing requires more clockwise movement, then the child is more likely to make his or her circles in the same manner. In a comparative Japanese–U.S. study the direction of circle drawing for U.S. students and Japanese students was compared. Results showed that with advancing grade, U.S. students increasingly drew circles in a counterclockwise direction whereas the Japanese increasingly drew them in a clockwise direction (Amenomouri et al., 1997). Another study showed that children who speak Hebrew tend to draw circles in a clockwise direction more often than the other two groups studied, whose language was French or English (Zendal et al., 1987).

Studies also show that people, including residents of big cities, are substantially faster and more accurate at visually detecting animals compared to nonliving objects such as moving cars (New et al., 2007). Ian Spence and his colleagues (Spence et al., 2006) found differences in men's and women's ability to distinguish objects that appear in their field of vision. Such differences were not overwhelming; yet, it was found that men were generally better at remembering and locating general landmarks in pictures, while women were better at remembering and locating food.

■ Perception of Depth

Depth perception refers to the organization of sensations in three dimensions, even though the image on the eye's retina is two dimensional. Look at the drawing of the famous Devil's tuning fork (below). Now we challenge you to draw the fork by memory, without looking at the picture. Why is it difficult? The picture is two dimensional with several confusing depth cues. However, the brain, because of our experience with depth cues, interprets this object as three dimensional. It is interesting that many people without formal schooling or previous exposure to three-dimensional pictures do not find this particular picture confusing (Deregowski, 1974; Hudson, 1960). Those who are not familiar with how to interpret depth cues—usually due to environmental conditions, extreme poverty, and lack of formal schooling—will perceive them as two dimensional. Some non-Western subjects experience difficulty with pictorially presented depth stimuli. However, according to several studies, education and training can significantly improve depth perception (Leach, 1975; Nicholson et al., 1977).

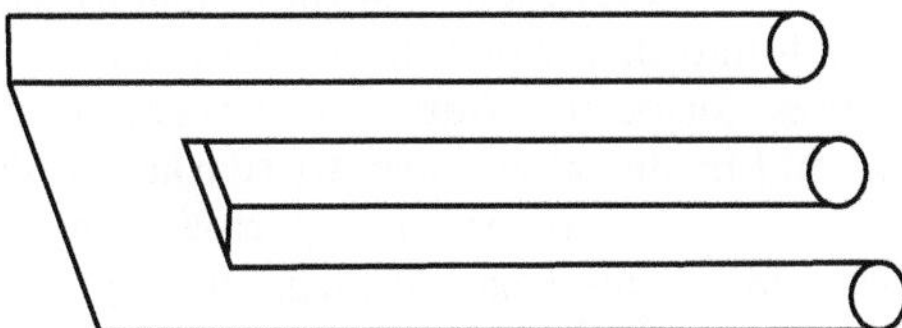

Altogether, picture perception is a combination of cognitive skills. Some national, regional, or culture-specific conditions determine which skills improve in individuals and which skills remain underdeveloped.

> Beware in case you lose the substance by grasping at the shadow.
>
> AESOP (SIXTH CENTURY B.C.E.)—GREEK FABULIST

■ Are People Equally Misled by Visual Illusions?

Look at the pictures below. They represent famous visual illusions. In the Müller–Lyer illusion, the line on the left appears shorter than the line on the right. In the Ponzo illusion, the upper line appears larger than the one at the bottom. In the horizontal–vertical illusion, the vertical line appears to be larger than the horizontal one. The vast majority of us are susceptible to these illusions; even though we know that the lines are equal in length, they appear unequal to us. However, such susceptibility is not common in all individuals and there are some cultural variations in how people perceive visual illusions.

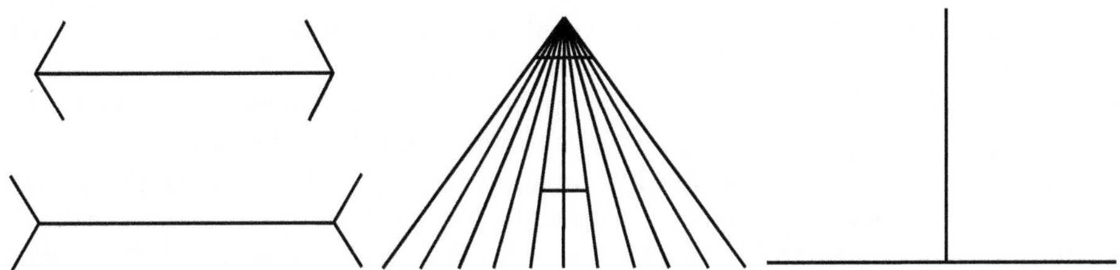

For example, a study of receptiveness to the Ponzo illusion in the United States and Guam suggested that non-Western and rural subjects showed less susceptibility to the illusion than the individuals from either Western or urban areas (Brislin, 1993). Likewise, on both the Müller–Lyer and horizontal–vertical illusions, the Western samples, living primarily in industrial urban environments, were more illusion-prone than any of the non-Western samples. Subjects from regions with open landscapes were more susceptible to the horizontal–vertical illusion than subjects from regions in which such views are rare (Segall et al., 1966).

How can we interpret such perceptual differences? As suggested earlier in the chapter, if certain groups differ in their visual perception, such differences may be influenced by the different experiences of the members of these groups. According to a popular "carpentered world" hypothesis (Segall et al., 1966), people who are raised in an environment shaped by carpenters—most of us live in rectangular houses with rectangular furniture and similar street patterns—tend to interpret nonrectangular figures as representations of rectangular figures seen in perspective. They also have a tendency to interpret the lines in the horizontal plane that look as if they are moving away from an observer as appearing to be shorter than the lines that cross the viewer's line of vision (the horizontal–vertical illusion).

Virtually, all people who had formal schooling got used to converting two-dimensional pictures into three-dimensional images even though pictures on computer screens and photographs in magazines are displayed on a flat surface. Certain perceptual sets (see the beginning of the chapter) allow people to see "flat" objects as if they actually exist in "volume" (Segall et al., 1990).

Some Cultural Patterns of Drawing

Individuals with no formal schooling, young children, and early artists a few thousand years ago did not acquire the ability to convert three-dimensional perceptions into two-dimensional paintings or sketches. In some cultural groups, their paintings often display objects, details, and surroundings independently of one another. For instance, Australian Aborigines usually depict the trunk of a crocodile as seen from above, while the head and the tail are drawn as being seen from the side (Dziurawiec & Deregowski, 1992). Beveridge (1940) and Thouless (1932) found that African drawings available to them were less affected by visual cues than European drawings were. With the lack of perspective in African pictures, objects were depicted as they were in reality rather than how they actually appear to the observer.

Perceptual distortions are easily found in various forms of drawings. For instance, in many national art traditions a linear perspective does not occur. Numerous perceptual distortions are found in modern art, as well as in ancient Egyptian, and medieval Spanish art (Parker & Deregowski, 1990). The polydimensional representation of space has been used at some period in most cultures. In much of ancient Egyptian and Cretan painting, for instance, the head and legs of a figure were shown in profile, but the eye and torso of a figure were drawn frontally. In Indian and early European paintings, created before the seventeenth century, figures and other vertical forms were represented as if seen from ground level, whereas the horizontal planes that figures and objects stood on were shown as if viewed from above. Paul Cezanne (1839–1906), a famous French artist, represented things on his paintings as if seen from different directions and at varying eye levels. Cubism, one of the prominent schools in modern art, aimed to give the viewer the time experience of moving around static forms in order to examine their volume and structure. In cubist pictures, the viewer is specifically encouraged to examine the surfaces of depicted objects from every possible angle.

Perception of Color

Color has three universal psychological dimensions: hue, brightness, and saturation. Hue is what people mean by color, brightness refers to a color's intensity, and saturation indicates a color's purity. If there are similar underlying physiological mechanisms of color perception, does this mean that perception of color has very little cultural variation? Are culturally sanctioned activities able to influence color perception?

According to so-called language-related theories of color perception—that emphasize the role of language in the identification and labeling of colors in each and every language—there are words that are linked to various units of the visible spectrum (Berry et al., 1992). The developing child learns these words and starts to use them in order to identify colors. It is interesting that even though the vast majority of healthy individuals are able to detect the same range of colors, there are languages that lack certain words for particular colors. For example, the color red is always represented by a separate word, whereas the colors green and blue are sometimes not distinguished linguistically. An explanation for this finding is based on an assumption that due to environmental conditions, the less vivid colors were less salient to non-Europeans and for that reason less likely to be identified and labeled with a separate word (Ray, 1952).

There were other attempts to explain such a perceptual confusion between the colors green and blue. Some studies stress physiological differences between racial groups in terms of their color perception. For instance, Pollack (1963) demonstrated that certain visual perceptual skills might be related to factors such as retinal pigmentation. He found that persons with denser retinal pigmentation had more difficulty detecting contours and showed relative difficulties in perceiving the color blue. Studies of color preferences showed that women across countries tend to choose and like reddish hues, such as pink. On the other hand, men had a preference for greenish-blue colors. The researchers suggest that the differences in color preferences may be connected to the evolutionary ability of the female brain to deal with gathering of food products such as fruits, while men's brains tend to be "wired" to be better hunters in green and lush environments (Hurlbert and Ling, 2007). However, physiological and evolutionary explanations of cultural differences in the detection of color did not gain as much popularity as the theories that emphasize the importance of learning experiences and linguistic norms of perception.

The subjective social and individual psychological meaning of color can be crucial to our understanding of color perception. There are strong universal trends in people's feelings about colors. In one prominent study, data from 23 countries revealed stable cross-cultural similarities. The concept "red" was perceived as being quite salient and active. "Black" and "gray" were considered bad, whereas "white," "blue," and "green" were considered good. "Yellow," "white," and "gray" were persistently seen as passive (Adams & Osgood, 1973).

The history of human civilization gives many examples about other trends in color interpretation. Take, for example, the color red. In many nations it became a political symbol of violence, revolution, and revolt. In totalitarian China and the Soviet Union, government officials made red banners the official flags of their countries. The official flag of Nazi Germany was also red. Rebellious students in Europe waved red flags during mass violent demonstrations in the 1960s. A red flag was also raised by radical guerrilla fighters in South and Central America, in Southeast Asia, and in South Africa. In the 1970s, one of the most notorious left-wing terrorist groups in Italy carried the name Red Brigades. Yet in Japan, the red color stood for philanthropy and vitality and the red circle on the national flag represents the sun.

In Druze culture, a religious community living primarily in Lebanon, Syria, and Israel, colors are associated with five cosmic principles. These principles are represented by the five-colored Druze star: reason (green), soul (red), word (yellow), precedent (blue), and immanence (white). In big cities, people tend to give directions in geometric terms (for example, "move down for three blocks and then take a right turn on the Seventh Street and pass two traffic lights"). In small communities, people tend to use landmarks and feel more comfortable giving directions this way (Roland, 2006).

Another interesting set of facts is related to human perception of black and white. More than two decades ago, researchers found that preschool children in the United States from various racial groups tended to prefer light- to dark-skinned people on pictures and photographs and to favor the color white over black. European children also displayed a tendency toward the positive evaluation of light-skinned figures relative to dark-skinned ones (Best et al., 1975). Moreover, cross-cultural research has established that people associate the color white with more positive feelings than black and that this bias seems to emerge by the preschool years. Subsequent research has shown that native African children share the same color bias (Williams & Best, 1990). The association of the color white with something "good," "pure," and "familiar" and black as primarily "negative," "unclean," and "unknown" is common in many cultures. The investigators speculate that the pan-cultural preference for light over dark may reflect a generalization from light and dark cycles of the day. Light is generally associated with certainty and safety, whereas darkness is more likely to represent danger and uncertainty. Nature may have endowed humans with a tendency to dislike the dark, just as it has endowed them with a susceptibility to a fear of snakes and spiders. Sea pirates raised black banners over their ships as a symbol of intimidation. In Christianity, angels are white and demons are black. In the Islamic context, the color white is symbolic of purity and equality of all people. As in many places on the earth, a typical Bulgarian bride would be dressed in white on her wedding. However, the bride's bouquet would never consist of white roses, as the white rose is indicative of death, according to Bulgarian folk beliefs. In addition, people from various religious backgrounds wear black clothes when they are mourning. In the English language, definitions of the word "black" include "without any moral light or goodness," "evil," "wicked," "indicating disgrace," and "sinful." Definitions of "white" include "morally pure," "spotless," "innocent," and "free from evil intent." In 1993, during a period of economic recession, when a newspaper asked Russians what color they associated with their lives, 42 percent said gray and 21 percent said black. Most of them felt as though they entered into "darkness" when things were extremely difficult (Kelley, 1994).

Studies of young children exposed to drastically different cultural environments show that despite differences in visual environment, language, and education, the children tend to display similar patterns of color term acquisition. It is remarkable that kids from rural areas having limited contact with the world and children from contemporary urban and suburban areas both learn how to name colors slowly and with great individual variation (Robertson et al., 2004).

Box 6.3 CASE IN POINT

A Few Color–Related Idioms in Several Languages

In English and in Serbian people may say that they "feel blue," which stands for sadness. In Portuguese, "everything is blue" stands for "everything is well." However, if a German is "blue," this person is intoxicated. In contrast, in Arabic, having a "blue day" may stand for having a bad day. In Russian, if you called a man "blue," you must have implied that he is gay. However, "blue" in Russian can be also referred to a cherished dream. In German, to "see red" means the same that it does in English. The "white lie" denotes the same in Arabic and in English. In German, distant and indefinite future is gray. The expression "rose-colored glasses" has the same meaning in Russian, German, and English. The expressions "pink elephants" and "yellow press" have the same meaning for people in New York, London, and Belgrade. People can turn "green," which indicates "being extremely angry" in many languages. Similarly, "blue blood" stands for aristocracy in dozens of tongues. "Yellow eye" stands for envy in Arabic, and "yellow smile" stands for embarrassment in Brazil. "Brown" in Russian may indicate fascist beliefs, and "gray" stands for boredom.

Information for this case was provided by Mirjana Simic, Walid Abdul-Jawad, Manal Alafrangi, Pedro DeAraujo, Fahad Malik, Makoto Tanaka, and Denitza Mantcheva.

In summary, it appears that there is a significant degree of similarity in the way color terms are used in different cultures. Verbal labels, if they are not available in the lexicon of a language, can be readily learned. Systematic formal schooling and the availability of various informational sources—such as books, television, and computers—can play a significant role in such learning.

Other Senses

So far in this chapter, our attention has been directed at vision, the most systematically studied modality in cross-cultural psychology. There is significantly less information concerning other types of sensation or perceptual cross-cultural processes. Let us consider some relevant data.

Hearing

Psychology textbooks emphasize the universal nature of human auditory sensation and perception processes. Most variations in hearing are based on individual physiological differences, which are related to age, education, professional training, environmental conditions, and general experience. The most important differences are related to the meanings attached to particular sounds in different cultures. During childhood and the following periods of socialization, individuals get used to particular voices, sounds, and even noises, and subsequently interpret them according to the norms established in their culture.

Taste

People across the world respond to four basic tastes: sweet, sour, bitter, and salty. It has been shown that individuals of different cultures vary only insignificantly in their ability to detect these four primary tastes. However, as might be expected, there are tremendous cross-cultural variations in taste preferences and beliefs about basic flavors (Laing et al., 1993). For example, people in the regions closer to the equator generally prefer spicier foods, compared with their counterparts living farther to the north or south. Therefore, Italians will be likely to consider Scandinavian cuisine as dull, whereas many people in Sweden or Denmark will refer to Italian food as spicy. Across the globe, human beings have learned to avoid rotten or spoiled foods. Tastes associated with such products are typically described as very unpleasant. However, because of certain customary food practices passed on from one generation to the next, people in various parts of the world eat and enjoy a wide range of decayed or fermented foods (Rozin & Fallon, 1987). The smell and taste of such products tend to be extremely unpleasant to individuals unfamiliar with them. However, for those people who have eaten these foods since childhood, because of the adaptation process, their taste and smell are enjoyable. As an example, cheese is liked in many parts of the world. However, people who primarily eat cheese produced out of cow milk are likely to find cheeses made out of goat milk objectionable. Yogurt as a fermented milk product is widely consumed in some parts of the world. Don't ask people who are not familiar with yogurt to try it: only few would dare. Many people in China enjoy decayed eggs. Would you try one if you are not from China? Can you come up with other examples?

Smell

Even though researchers today understand the physiology of the olfactory sense, our knowledge about how smell affects behavior is very limited. There are data suggesting that exposure to a substance (underarm secretion) may affect the menstrual cycle in women (Cutler et al., 1986). In another study, investigators examined the positive impact on safe driving of having a pleasant odor in the car (Baron & Kalsher, 1996). However, data on cross-cultural variations in olfactory perception are mostly anecdotal and focus mainly on cross-cultural differences in odor preferences and prevailing odors.

Touch

The sense of touch is a combination of at least three qualities: pressure, temperature, and pain. The last one has received the most attention from cross-cultural psychologists. Many individual and situational characteristics (for example, skin texture, age, social status, presence or absence of other people, and level of individual motivation) can determine perception of pain. Passively experienced anxiety can increase pain. Fear, anger, or stress can inhibit it. Love and pride can cause some people to hide even the most excruciating pain.

Some specific cultural norms and expectations influence people's experience of pain (Morse & Park, 1988). For example, subjective reports of labor pain are lower in societies where childbirth is not considered to be a defiling event and where little help or comfort is offered to women in labor. Differences in the ability to endure pain are often a function of the circumstances in which the perception of pain is occurring. People exposed to harsh living and working conditions may become more stoical and less susceptible to pain than those who live and work in comfortable conditions (Clark & Clark, 1980). People without adequate access to health care may use a higher threshold to define unbearable pain, compared with those with guaranteed medical care (Halonen & Santrock, 1995).

Across cultures, people appear to place a high value on clothing previously worn by loved ones. Touching (and often wearing) a loved person's garments is commonly accompanied with positive emotional experiences. However, people in most circumstances tend not to touch objects worn by a stranger, especially if these clothes contain body residues such as hair or moisture (Rozin & Fallon, 1987). Proprioceptive sense helps people register body position and movement. Individual variations in our ability to detect and then coordinate body position can be significant. The evidence of cultural differences and similarities is mostly anecdotal. Some well-known facts about a few Romanians who are good in gymnastics, some Russians who are superb in ballet, and certain East Asians who are excellent in martial arts should not encourage anyone to make any valid generalizations.

Box 6.4 CROSS–CULTURAL SENSITIVITY

You perhaps know that police—in order to subdue the most violent suspects—occasionally use pepper spray. It causes some eye and skin irritation and is considered to be a quite effective preventive force. Now read how stereotypes may affect professional judgment. A Massachusetts training police officer in an interview with a local newspaper, the *Cambridge Chronicle*, suggested that members of ethnic groups accustomed to eating spicy foods are less susceptible to the use of pepper spray against them. Members of ethnic groups who have consumed cayenne peppers from the time they were small children, the officer explained, might have a greater resistance to the spray. Among these "high-resistance-to-pepper-spray" groups are Mexican Americans, Pakistanis, and members of Louisiana's Cajun population. Fortunately, the Cambridge Police commissioner later corrected his subordinate and said that there is no scientific evidence to support any statements about the pepper spray susceptibility of certain ethnic groups (Police Apologize for Spice Remark. *Reuters*, August 16, 1999). Medical studies have shown that any person's single exposure to pepper spray causes immediate changes in mechanical and chemical sensitivity of the eye that persist for a week (Vesaluoma et al., 2000).

Nothing really belongs to us but time, which even he has who has nothing else.

BALTASAR GRACIAN (1601–1658)—SPANISH WRITER AND JESUIT PRIEST

Perception of Time

Talk to several people who have traveled or lived abroad. They could tell you how people in different cultures perceive and treat time guidelines. One of our colleagues from the Caribbean recently said that on his island people are generally not in a hurry compared with people from the United States, who usually are. Indeed, it is believed that Westerners tend to define punctuality using precise measures of time: 1 minute, 15 minutes, an hour, and so forth. In other cultures time can be treated differently. According to Hall (1959), before the informational revolution, the Mediterranean Arab culture had only three standard sets of time: *no time at all, now* (which is of varying duration), and *forever* (too long).

In other studies published over an extended period (Abou-Hatab, 1997; Meleis, 1982), researchers paid attention to this interesting aspect of Arab culture: its less-structured time orientation than one developed in most individuals in Western cultures. For example, individuals of Arab descent in traditional settings may display a tendency to be more interested in and focused on events or circumstances that are present or occur "now" and may pay less attention to those expected or scheduled to happen sometime in the future. Some experts suggest that this tendency in perception of time may have an impact on how patients or clients of Arab descent perceive their tasks during therapy. Some of them may need extra effort from the therapist to accept a particular timetable for behavioral or cognitive changes (Erickson & Al-Timimi, 2001). It is also important, though, to be cautious and not overgeneralize: Being Arab American does not mean to have a certain predetermined perception of time.

There are different ways of arranging time in a definite order known as calendars. Most people on earth use the Gregorian calendar, which has religious origin and, since its adoption in the sixteenth century, counts years since the incarnation of Jesus. Other major religions also have their own calendars. The first year of the Islamic calendar, for example, is the year when Mohammed moved from Mecca to Medina. In North Korea today, the official calendar starts at the birthday of the late communist leader Kim Il-sung in 1912. The official calendar of Taiwan also starts in 1912, the year of the founding of the Republic of China.

Akbar (1991), who compared perceptions of time in European American and African cultures, also acknowledged the Westerners' emphasis on precise measurement of time. He suggested that time in the European and North American cultures is treated as a commodity or product that can be bought and sold as any other item for consumption, whereas in the African system, time is not viewed as a commodity.

The African time concept is very elastic and includes events that have already taken place, those that are taking place right now, and even those that will happen. Time can be experienced through one's own individual life and through the life of the tribe to which each individual belongs (Nobles, 1991). In Swahili—the language widely used in Eastern and Central Africa—there are two words that indicate time: *sasa* and *zamani.* The first one stands for the present and generates a sense of immediacy. The second word indicates the past, but not merely as a "warehouse" of time. It is also a connector of individual souls. Most African peoples perceived human history in the natural rhythm of moving from *sasa* to *zamani.* The life cycle is renewable. After physical death, as long as a person is remembered by relatives and friends who knew her, this person would continue to exist in the *sasa* dimension. When the last person who knew the deceased also dies, that means the end for that individual.

Hamermesh (2003) conducted a cross-cultural analysis of affluent people in the United States, Germany, Australia, Canada, and South Korea. Hamermesh discovered that across cultures, people express dissatisfaction about the lack of time they experience as their incomes rise. As people's wealth increases so do the number of opportunities available to them. As this demand increases, however, the "supply" of time does not grow. Therefore, time becomes more valuable, and people become increasingly frustrated about the lack of it.

Did you know that age and aging might be related to an individual's perspective of time, at least in people of the industrial world? In turn, this changing individual time perspective may impact many other personal attitudes (Cutler, 1975). Perhaps for most people, in early childhood, the dominant perception is that time is limitless. Early adulthood brings the realization that time is a scarce resource. Middle age and later stages lead to the perception that time becomes seriously limited. As Gergen and Black (1965) pointed out, orientations toward problem solving in international politics are substantially related to one's psychological perception of personal future time: older politicians may be in a "hurry" to resolve conflicts. Renshon (1989) also argued that in the arts, the phenomenon of late-age creativity and boldness occurs relatively often. The last works of Shakespeare, Rembrandt, Verdi, Beethoven, Tolstoy, and Picasso all suggest that the final stages of the life cycle often bring release from conventional concerns and free artists to make major creative statements that represent a culmination of their vision.

Various authors have reported about a seemingly cross-cultural tendency: People notice an apparent accelerating of self-reflected time flow experienced with age. In diaries, self-observations, personal recollections, and other sources, many older people notice that time runs faster now than it did when they were younger. These observations, however, are subjective and were not verified in experiments. Laboratory studies that measured the impact of age on perception of time intervals, however, were few and inconsistent in their results (Wearden et al., 1997).

> Culture opens the sense of beauty.
>
> RALPH WALDO EMERSON (1803–1882)—AMERICAN POET AND PHILOSOPHER

> Beauty is nothing other than the promise of happiness.
>
> STENDAHL (1783–1842)—FRENCH NOVELIST

Perception of the Beautiful

The song "Let It Be" performed by the Beatles or a Mexican folk song, a dress designed by Versace or a Peruvian picturesque poncho, a Persian rug or a Nigerian ivory statuette, the Taj Mahal palace or a Chinese porcelain vase—these creations can be enjoyed by anyone and everyone on the planet. The term **aesthetic experience**, or perception of the beautiful, is used to identify the feeling of pleasure evoked by stimuli that are perceived as nice, attractive, or rewarding. Researchers suggest that aesthetic responses are underpinned by the amount of cortical arousal produced by some stimuli in the brain (Berlyne, 1960, 1974). People seek certain stimuli because the activity of dealing with them is pleasant. Others consider aesthetic appreciation as curiosity and stimulus-seeking activities. Berlyne (1971) found that the characteristics of a stimulus that generally evoke curiosity, joy, and appreciation are those such as novelty, ambiguity, incongruity, and complexity.

Several common perceptual mechanisms lead to similarities across cultures in aesthetic appreciation. For example, there are empirical studies in which subjects from different cultures displayed similarities in their evaluation of different works of art, primarily paintings (Child, 1969). Many similarities in perception and appreciation of beauty were found in different cultural groups despite socioeconomic differences among them (Berlyne, 1974; Ross, 1977). For instance, in a survey conducted by Nasar (1984), both Japanese and U.S. subjects were asked to evaluate videotapes and slides of urban street scenes in each country. An examination of preference scores revealed that both Japanese and U.S. subjects preferred foreign scenes to native ones. In both groups, the scenes of orderly and clean streets with very few vehicles on them were more often preferred.

Beware though. There are tremendous inconsistencies in how people see and interpret both beautiful and ugly creations. For instance, in the history of Western painting, impressionism as a new artistic genre was publicly ridiculed and rejected. Many years later it became an internationally acclaimed style and collectors began to pay huge sums of money for impressionist paintings. When the Eiffel tower was first erected in Paris, most people condemned this grandiose landmark. Today, who can imagine Paris without the Eiffel tower?

Box 6.5 CRITICAL THINKING

As Beautiful as ...Your Money Can Buy

Beautiful things sell. Art collectors and art dealers around the world know this well. Today many classical paintings change hands, not for thousands, but millions of dollars! However, does the price tag on a painting or sculpture determine how beautiful the creation is? Why are the smallest paintings by Cezanne or pencil sketches by Leonardo almost priceless, whereas a beautiful original colorful landscape could be purchased for $20 from a street artist in Rome? Do you agree that sometimes people first assign and attach value to particular pieces of art and only then do they begin to evaluate this object from the standpoint of aesthetic perception? If a sculpture is considered "famous" or a song "popular" by most members of our society, are we likely to consider the sculpture as "beautiful" and the song as "nice"? Do you think that our evaluation of a song, painting, fashion style, or dance changes according to how well or how poorly it is advertised or promoted?

What is considered tasteful and beautiful is not confined within geographic regions or among particular ethnic groups. Many national patterns become international, captivating the minds and influencing the behavior of millions of people. To illustrate, consider *kawaii*, a Japanese artistic style of design. Rooted in the celebration of youthfulness and cuteness, conveyed by neat stories and playful designs of bright colors, kawaii has become popular outside of Japan and can even be seen influencing street fashion in Europe, the United States, and many other countries. Another Japanese school of flower arrangement called *ikebana* has received wide international acclaim and found scores of followers around the world (Faiola, 2003).

Cultural aesthetic standards can be numerous and widely defined; they can also be limited in appearance and narrowly defined. For example, in the countries in which governments or ideological institutions control the media, and therefore restrain the free flow of information, such standards of beauty and ugliness are typically precisely defined. Because of the lack of available information, scarcity of products, and ideological pressures, people's choices are limited and certain items—clothing, music, or even hairstyles, for example—quickly become dominant (Sears et al., 2003; Shiraev & Bastrykin, 1988).

Perception of Music

The traditional music of different cultures may fluctuate in notion and harmony. For instance, conventional Western harmony is different from Japanese and Indian styles (Sadie, 1980). In many non-Western traditions the idea of the note as a stable, sustained pitch is foreign. Some Indian and Japanese musical intervals—or tonal dyads differing only slightly in frequency ratio—are perceived as extreme dissonance in the West and are usually avoided by composers and musicians. However, these intervals appear to be beautiful and are used freely in the classic music of these two countries (Maher, 1976).

Contemporary Western music notation reflects the underlying general perception of beauty developed in Western culture. Perceptual problems that can cause displeasure in the Western listener—born and raised in Sweden, Italy, or Ukraine—may occur because of the different scales, intervals, and rhythmic patterns used in Western and non-Western music. In non-Western cultures—for example, in Middle Eastern Islamic countries—classical music for the most part is not written down in advance, as is the practice in Europe and America. Notwithstanding the fact that written notations are found in many cultures around the world, in many non-Western countries, classical music is usually improvised on framework-like patterns. In fact, in these societies many types of music exist mostly in performance. One should not exaggerate, nevertheless, cultural differences in musical perception. Contemporary mass media, global trade, and interpersonal contacts provide unique opportunity for many people to learn, understand, and appreciate different musical styles.

Let us make some preliminary conclusions. As we have learned, most psychologists share the contemporary belief that sensory differences among cultures are insignificant and their impact on human behavior is minimal. In general, the universal similarity in the anatomy and physiology of human sensory organs and the nervous system seems to suggest that sensory impressions and their transmission through the perceptual system are basically the same across cultures. Despite similarities, however, people may see beautiful and ugly things differently, and there is a substantial weight of cultural factors in our aesthetic perception.

Most of the time, healthy adults are aware of their sensations and perceptions. A street vendor in Spain or a teacher in Pakistan can describe what they see or hear and are able to separate the "objective" reality from thoughts about it. No matter what we do, either paying careful attention to some events or **daydreaming** about others, we are aware of our subjective experiences.

The ultimate gift of conscious life is a sense of mystery that encompasses it.

LEWIS MUMFORD—TWENTIETH-CENTURY U.S. HISTORIAN AND CRITIC

Suffering is the sole origin of consciousness.

FYODOR DOSTOYEVSKY (1821–1881)—RUSSIAN NOVELIST

Consciousness and Culture

Culture is an inseparable attribute of human **consciousness**—the subjective awareness of one's own sensations, perceptions, and other mental events. It is a process that has several stages or states. The "normal" flow of consciousness may consist of periods of full attention and concentration or relative detachment from the outside events. Periods of wakefulness are altered by periods of sleep. Under various circumstances, the normal flow of consciousness can be altered by meditation, psychoactive substances, trance, or hypnotic suggestion. However, the very concept of consciousness is elusive, thus making its cross-cultural examination particularly difficult.

From the dawn of scientific exploration of mental life, ancient thinkers were aware of consciousness. Major ideas about human consciousness were developed within the Christian, Muslim, Jewish, Hindu, Buddhist, and other theological schools of thought (Smith, 1991). They developed fundamental ideas about the soul as immortal, divine, and separable from the body. With further development of philosophy and science, two types of fundamental views on consciousness were established. One view was held by the monists, who believed in the inseparability of the body and soul. The second view was held by the dualists, who recognized an independent existence of body and soul. Both philosophical platforms still affect many people's personal views on consciousness.

The idea of individual consciousness as dependent on socialization experiences and other cultural factors was developed throughout the twentieth century by a number of psychologists (Piaget, 1963; Vygotsky, 1932; Wundt, 1913). According to psychological anthropologist Hallowell (1955), people live within a **behavioral environment**, a mental representation of time, space, and the interpersonal world. Specific cultural beliefs and practices shape the individual's behavioral environment. For example, among the Ojibwa Indians studied by Hallowell, their behavioral environment included the self, other people, their gods, existing relatives, and deceased ancestors. Thus, when considering an action with moral consequences, the Ojibwa take into account possible impacts of the action on spirits and relatives.

Consciousness directs human behavior in ways that are adaptive in particular physical and social environments. People tend to focus on things that are important for survival or the accomplishment of a goal. A motorist in New York will definitely pay attention to traffic reports on the car radio, whereas his guest from South Africa may not attend to them at all. Consciousness devotes extra cognitive resources to information that may be particularly meaningful for individual adaptation. For instance, the contents of the consciousness of Ifaluk, a people of Micronesia in the Pacific Ocean, reflect the way their culture structures reality: people are aware of their immediate location at all times because life depends on successful navigation of the surrounding ocean (Lutz, 1982).

There are popular opinions about the main attributes of Western consciousness as being linear, pragmatic, and rational (Jackson, 1991). If this is the case, these elements of consciousness should be overwhelmingly present in various forms of Western art. If consciousness is rational, it should be reflected in "rational" forms of artistic expression. However, the history of Western art (literature and painting, for example) shows numerous examples of nonlinear, mystical, multidimensional, and irrational views reflected by the writer's pen or the artist's paintbrush. Existentialism and symbolism in literature, cubism and primitivism in painting, and modernism in music are all examples of irrational and nonlinear perception and reflection of reality by Western artists. Perhaps one of the best illustrations of a nonlinear perception of life is the literary world of Gabriel García Marquez, one of the most significant writers of the twentieth century. A Colombian native, he spent most of his life in Mexico and Europe as a journalist and writer. Take, for example, his most famous novel, One Hundred Years of Solitude. The main characters in the book live within several time dimensions. It seems that they are not concerned with time at all. Occasionally, the past is diminished into a single moment, and then the future becomes present and twisted in a mysterious way. The dead return home and those who are alive disappear in the skies without a trace. Consciousness becomes circular and brings back memories and transfers individuals in time and space. Analyzing Marquez's work, one can find elements of Catholic religious doctrine, Spanish cultural tradition, and Native Indian beliefs. Perhaps such a mixture of different influences reflected in the author's mind and in his literary works reveals many fascinating aspects of human consciousness. Please read One Hundred Years of Solitude by Marquez. Will you find it difficult to confine human consciousness within the simplistic boundaries of Western or non-Western labels?

Sleeping is no mean art: For its sake one must stay awake all day.

FRIEDRICH NIETZSCHE (1844–1900)—GERMAN PHILOSOPHER

In the drowsy dark cave of the mind dreams build their nest with fragments dropped from day's caravan.

RABINDRANATH TAGORE (1861–1941)—BENGALI POET AND NOVELIST

Sleep and Cultural Significance of Dreams

At this moment, about a third of the world population is sleeping. **Sleep** is a nonwaking state of consciousness characterized by general unresponsiveness to the environment and general physical immobility.

During sleep, responsiveness to external, and particularly visual, stimulation is diminished, but it is not entirely absent (Antrobus, 1991). There are tremendous individual variations in how "wakeful" we are when sleeping. In addition, cultural practices, sleeping arrangements, and general environmental conditions can influence people's responsiveness to external stimulation during sleep. There are also significant individual variations in terms of duration of sleep. In every country around the world, some individuals sleep for five or six hours, whereas others need nine or ten hours. Duration of sleep may vary from culture to culture. As an illustration, in a study of the sleep–wakefulness cycle in Mexican adults, Taub (1971) found that the average duration of sleep in Mexican subjects was longer than in other Western countries.

Since the dawn of their existence, humans have wondered about both the nature and significance of **dreams**, storylike sequences of images occurring during sleep. McManus and coauthors (1993) make a distinction between two types of cultures in terms of their interpretation of dreams. *Monophasic* cultures value cognitive experiences that take place only during normal waking phases and do not incorporate dreams into the process of social perception and cognition. Dreams are regarded as indirect indications of the dreamer's concerns, fears, and desires (Bourguignon, 1954). *Polyphasic* cultures value dreams and treat them as part of reality. The first type of culture is typically associated with a materialistic worldview on psychological experience. The second type of culture is associated with the spiritual or traditional view.

For many years, people considered dreams as experiences accumulated by the dreamer's traveling soul or revelations conveyed to the dreaming individual from the spiritual world. This polyphasic view on dreams can be found in contemporary cultural groups. Moss (1996) describes several core elements in the traditional dream practice of Iroquois, a Native American tribe. Dreams are perceived as flights of the soul, which leaves the body and travels in space and time. Therefore, dreams are real events and should be taken literally. Dreams demand action because they indicate something that the person has failed to perform while awake. For Iroquois, dreams also yield information about future events. Similarly, Araucanos in Chile believe that dreams help to communicate with other people and are related to future events (Krippner, 1996). Among many native peoples in Australia, it is believed that one can travel in his or her dreams for particular purposes. Among some African tribes there is a conviction that both the living and deceased relatives can communicate with the dreamer. Dreams can be transmitted from one person to another and some people can do so with malicious purposes. Some Zambian shamans imply they can diagnose a patient's illness through information contained in this person's dreams (Bynum, 1993).

Traditional psychological theories of dream interpretation—including psychoanalysis—pay most attention to the latent, hidden content of dreams. Usually therapists would try to interpret the meaning of the dream, something that is not obvious to the dream-teller, who is actually a person who receives psychological counseling. Less attention in most Western therapies is given to the manifest content, that is, to the sequence of events reported by the dream-teller. In polyphasic cultures, people typically consider dreams as a source of individual guidance; dreams are readily shared with others and the meanings of these dreams is discussed (Murray, 1999). Studies of dream interpretations in traditional societies show that the actual content of the dream—the story told by the person—is often interpreted literally by individuals and may serve as an important process that initiates adaptive behaviors (Pratt, 2000).

Contemporary science develops several views on the nature of human dreams. Some physiologists, for example, suggest that dreams are pure biological phenomena with no psychological meaning (Crick & Mitchison, 1983). Others theories suggest (Hobson, 2002) that during this altered state of consciousness, the brain stem is activating itself internally. This activation does not contain any ideas, emotions, wishes, or fears. The forebrain produces dream imagery from "noisy" signals sent to it from the brain stem. As this activation is transmitted through the thalamus to the visual and association zones of the cerebral cortex, the individual tries to make sense of it. Because the initial signals are essentially random in nature, the interpretations proposed by the cortex rarely make complete logical sense. However, the issues most relevant to the individual enter dreams in some way because the incoming signals are compared with the dreamer's existing knowledge and attitudes (Cartwright, 1992; Foulkes, 1985). In other words, experiences should influence our dreams (Kern & Roll, 2001).

A study of a sample of Zulu South Africans (aged from 25 to 92 years old) showed substantial differences between urban and rural subjects. Less educated and less affluent individuals from the country tended to consult with dream interpreters and act in response to dreams much more often than the urban participants. Moreover, subjects with less education were more likely than others to report the specific impact of dreams on their lives. More older than younger respondents experienced dreams as a direct communication with ancestors and were more likely than others to respond to dreams with prayer and rituals (Thwala et al., 2000).

Despite significant differences in the manifest content of dreams (i.e., the actual content of the recalled dream), the latent content (the dream's meaning) is believed to be cross-culturally comparable. The similarities in the way people describe the content of their dreams were demonstrated in a Japanese–U.S. study (Griffith et al., 1958). Students in both groups reported having dreams about falling, eating, swimming, death, snakes, finding money, examinations, being unable to move, and various sexual experiences.

Dream scenarios are personal, but they are enacted within the stage set by the dreamer's sociocultural reality (Roll et al., 1976). Take, for example, a study in which the dreams of more than 200 Finnish and Palestinian children were compared (Punamaki & Joustie, 1998). Half the subjects were selected from working-class and middle-class Finnish suburbia and half were taken from two areas in the Middle East. One represented the Gaza Strip, an area with frequent military confrontations. The other area was not known for any violent outbursts. Children in both groups were asked to report their dreams daily during a seven-day period. The recorded dreams were content analyzed. It was found that life in a violent environment was linked to a greater extent to dream content than the culture and other personal factors. The Palestinian children who lived in the violent social environment reported having predominantly intensive and vivid dreams, which incorporated aggression and persecution as main themes, more often than the other children studied did. It was also found that in Arab children's dreams there were predominantly external scenes of anxiety that typically involved fear. In Finnish children, dreams contained anxiety scenes that involved mostly guilt and shame. The authors interpreted the results by referring to social and cultural conditions in the studied samples. The Finnish society is considered to be more individualistic than the Palestinian society and therefore more oriented toward the experiences directed into individuals themselves. The Finnish children are less interdependent than Arab children. Also, according to the established cultural traditions, the Finnish understanding of dreaming is based predominantly on Freudian influences that emphasize the importance of individual psychological reality. According to the Arab tradition, dreaming is mainly understood as an external message from forces to guide the dreamer.

Keep in mind one important difference between these two cultures. Finland is an economically advanced and democratic European country with one of the highest incomes per capita in the world. Palestinian people for many years have experienced poverty, injustice, and have suffered from constant struggles between various political groups for influence and power. It is plausible to propose that everyday stressful experiences can contribute to dream content.

Substantial gender differences were found in other cross-cultural studies of dreams, according to which women are likely to experience dreams in which the dream character is abused and attacked (Cartwright, 1992). One finding reported by Munroe and Munroe (1972) in an East African sample showed that both males and females express roughly equal amounts of aggression in the reported dreams. Subsequent analysis revealed that a high proportion of aggression in female dreams was linked to situations in which the women were victims of attack and abuse, a concern that reflects reality.

Specialists in Turkish folklore identify a typical theme in dreams reported by males: the quest, both physical and spiritual, for the most gorgeous and beautiful woman in the world. According to one explanation (Walker, 1993), this preoccupation may be linked to the tradition of arranged marriage. According to this practice, many Turkish men cannot see their brides before the time of the wedding. This emotional deprivation creates a state of secret admiration and fascination of the future wife. Another explanation, however, can be offered. Because the relatives of the bride and groom commonly arrange many Turkish marriages, most men's relationships with women lack the important elements of romanticism and adventure. As a result, men "compensate" in their dreams for this missing romantic activity and experience.

Tedlock (1987) suggested that people's reports about their dreams include more than the dream report. She implied that what one tells about a dream is based on a particular cultural concept of the dream and culturally sanctioned ways of sharing dream content. Using particular rules of communication, we may report some elements of our dream and delete others. In short, our culture may change our experience of dreams and therefore our dreams are loaded with cultural elements that include not only dream content but also the ways in which dreams are communicated (Ullman & Zimmerman, 1979).

Imagine now somebody from a different country is sharing with you a recent dream. Can you interpret its contents? Some people claim that they can interpret any dream right after hearing it. We seriously doubt such propositions. Besides hidden psychological factors, there are numerous contextual influences that affect not only the dream but also the way it is recalled, shared, and interpreted. These are some questions that you perhaps have to ask when you listen to someone's dream. What motivates the person to recall and tell a dream? (Is it a teacher's assignment, your request, or a spontaneous conversation?) Under what circumstances is the dream recalled? Who is present during the dream recollection? What is the relationship between the dream-teller and the listener? How is dreaming understood in the teller's culture? How is dreaming understood in the listener's culture? What meaning do certain dream symbols carry in the studied culture?

Box 6.6 **CRITICAL THINKING**

Can Dreams Predict Anything?

There are popular stories about famous discoveries taking place during sleep. The famous benzene ring and the periodic system of chemical elements were allegedly "discovered" by their authors when they were dreaming. In many famous fairy tales, literary works, and film creations, heroes and heroines read important life forecasts in their sleep. We all know that in every country, there are people who believe that dreams can predict the future or may be considered an omen of something to come. It is a belief in Turkey that if one discloses a dream about receiving a favor before the favor is offered, then the event foretold in the dream may end in disaster (Walker & Uysal, 1990). A 2009 Russian calendar of dreams predicted that a tooth lost in one's dream will mean a misfortune for this person in the future. Around the world, books are written and manuals published on how to interpret each particular dream. Why do so many people maintain such an attitude toward dreams? We have to take into consideration how powerful people's superstitions are as regulators of behavior. We follow them often without a conscious attempt to think critically. Meanwhile, some dreams may be rationalized. Imagine a person has a dream about a car accident. When the dream content does not coincide with an actual car accident the day after the dream, the content of the dream can be easily forgotten. If an accident really happens, he or she is likely to refer to the dream: "I knew this was going to happen." Similarly, when dream content coincides with a conscious attitude, we tend to hold an opinion about the possible motivational power of dreams. In general, knowledge about dreams and critical thinking abilities can diminish an individual's dependency on dreams as predictors of the future.

No matter how psychologists explain dreams, researchers can provide plenty of interesting facts about the interaction between culture and the psychological experiences of dreams (Roll, 1987). Dreams not only reflect our private world of hopes, fears, and concerns but also mirror the environment in which people live.

> The supernatural is the natural not yet understood.
>
> ELBERT HUBBARD (1856–1915)—AMERICAN AUTHOR

Beyond Altered States of Consciousness

Altered states of consciousness (ASC) is the general name for phenomena that are different from normal waking consciousness and include mystic perceptual and sensory experiences, such as meditation, hypnosis, trance, and possession (Ward, 1994). Like Cinderella in the famous fairy tale—a neglected outcast daughter in her stepmother's family—ASC are not highly regarded by Western academic psychologists. The rapid development of empirical research based on the pragmatism and positivism of European science coupled with the skepticism encouraged by the Enlightenment era contributed to the lack of scholarly attention to ASC. Under the influence of the Protestant tradition and in Western Europe, ASC were considered mostly as abnormal phenomena. Similarly, many mental disorders were commonly interpreted as supernatural developments (Warner, 1994).

Meanwhile, ASC is a widely reported phenomenon across the globe. The different forms of ASC are identified in the majority of societies and may be viewed as a special form of human experience (Laughlin et al., 1992; Ward, 1994). Let us consider several ASC.

Trance is a sleeplike state marked by reduced sensitivity to stimuli, loss or alteration of knowledge, and automatic motor activity. Trances are often induced by external sources, such as music, singing, and direct suggestion from another person. Trances may provide a sense of protection, wisdom, and greatness. For the group, it can provide a sense of togetherness and unity. Mass religious ceremonies, collective prayers, rock concerts, political gatherings, and other collective actions can induce a trance in the participants. There is a difference between a visionary trance, when a person is experiencing hallucinations, and a possession trance, when a person reports that his body is invaded or captured by a spirit or several spirits. The possession experience is usually, but not always, recalled with fear and hesitation because of its traumatic significance. Trancelike and possession experiences are described as parts of religious practices in many cultures (Bourguignon, 1976; Rosen, 1968). According to one survey, visionary or possession trance states were reported in 90 percent of the countries in a large world sample (Bourguignon, 1994).

Several religious groups consider trances as part of their regular religious experience (Taves, 1999). Incidences of visionary trances are more common among men than in women and in hunter–gatherer societies. Possession trance is more typical among women and those who are not from hunter–gatherer cultures (Bourguignon, 1976; Gussler, 1973; Lee & Ackerman, 1980). Some psychologists develop a view that many shamanic practices involving ritualistic trance affect the brain's serotonin and opioid neurotransmitter systems—all affecting an individual's emotional states, behavioral responses, and even the belief system (Winkelman, 2000). The same way as Prozac or Xanax (alprazolam) can change mood and anxiety manifestations, many shamanic practices affect other people's experiences. However, many of these individuals are not aware of this effect and continue to believe that shamans are capable of supernatural or magic healing. Many cultural groups today continue to practice self-induced trance as a form of "purification" from evil and emotional healing. For example, some Jewish groups in the Middle East practice Stambali—a trance-inducing ritual used for the promotion of personal well-being and as a form of crisis intervention (Somer & Saadon, 2000).

There have been attempts to evoke trance states and similar experiences in laboratory settings. One of the most significant studies on this topic was conducted by neurophysiologist Michael Persinger. The subjects in this study reported trance experiences when the temporal lobes in their brains were stimulated artificially with a weak magnetic field. Specifically, they reported feelings of great and "eternal" presence, omnipotence, serenity, and wisdom. According to a theory, trance is associated with the release of opiates in the body, which induces a temporary state of elation, euphoria, and excitement (Persinger, 2003). Such experiences are interpreted in a variety of ways ranging from "divine" to "weird." These interpretations are contingent on the context in which the trance takes place, as well as the cultural background of those experiencing it: religious subjects would talk about spiritual experiences, while skeptics would mention sensory disturbances.

Possession is explained better when it is evaluated simultaneously from the observer's standpoint, the victim's point of view, and from the perspective of the community at large (Lee & Ackerman, 1980). In this context, there are several scientific explanations related to the previous case and other similar episodes of "demonic possession." One explanation appeals to the stress accumulated by victims from job dissatisfaction, work conflicts, and economic hardship. Individuals who claim possession are provided with culturally acceptable outlets for their previously restrained frustration (Halperin, 1996).

Beliefs about possession are also documented in many Slavic, German, and Scandinavian folk tales. In Morocco, as in many other Islamic countries, folk beliefs about possession include the concept of demons or *jinni*. These demons like wetness and prefer to live near water, under old trees, in washrooms, old ruins, as well as in cemeteries and waste dumps. If disturbed, these creatures get enraged, possess someone's body, and take revenge on this person's psyche. Many individuals who experienced symptoms of possession say they can identify the time and the place in which the possession took place. Some claim to have stepped on a demon while walking in the garden at night. Others believe they disturbed a demon who lived in the bathroom pipes or in nearby bushes.

Similar beliefs in demonic possession as the cause of particular mental disorders are found among people in many cultural and religious groups. The best-selling novel by William Peter Blatty (known to most people as *The Exorcist*, in a Hollywood movie version) is a literary case of a wealthy mother in the United States who, unable to find effective medical treatment for a child who suffers from severe and disturbing psychological symptoms including possession trance, turns to religious healers (see Exercise 6.2).

In 2005, a Romanian monk and four other people were charged in the death of a 23-year-old nun during an apparent exorcism. The woman was allegedly left without food for three days and died due to dehydration, exhaustion, and lack of oxygen. The monk, who belongs to the Orthodox branch of the church, reportedly explained that his actions were an attempt to rid the woman of the devil inside her.

Nowhere can man find a quieter or more untroubled retreat than his own soul.

MARCUS AURELIUS (112–180)—ROMAN EMPEROR AND STOIC PHILOSOPHER

Box 6.7 A CASE IN POINT

Mass Hysteria and Possession as Altered States of Consciousness

Lee and Ackerman (1980) documented and analyzed an interesting case of mass possession at a small college in West Malaysia. The incident involved several, mostly female, students who manifested various physical symptoms and bizarre behaviors, such as difficulty breathing, convulsive muscular contractions, and screaming. The victims were oblivious of their surroundings, went through dance frenzies, reported demonic possessions, and complained about seeing strange creatures. The possessed claimed that they became other beings, because of the spirits that had taken over the body. Bomohs or traditional Malai healers were called to help. They treated the possessed individuals by sprinkling them with holy water, sacrificing a small animal in an attempt to pacify the offended spirits, and giving victims talismans to protect them from evil spirits. Notably, when the healers confirmed the existence of spirits in the victims' bodies, it provoked further incidents of possession. Moreover, most people in the area believed that the symptoms of this altered state of consciousness were contagious.

Meditation is a quiet and relaxed state of tranquility in which a person achieves an integration of thoughts, perceptions, and attitudes. Usually, this state is attained with the cooperation of a special principle or belief. People who meditate often describe their experience as leading to liberation from the self or an expansion of conscious awareness. In Buddhism, for example, it is believed that meditation leads to a deepened and clearer understanding of reality (Ornstein, 1977). During meditation, a special state of consciousness can be achieved in which obstacles of private desire are completely consumed.

Meditation can be highly therapeutic because it might reduce stress (Collings, 1989). Contrary to contemporary scientific principles of psychotherapy, which require control over the outcome of one's actions, in many types of meditation principles of detachment from others are valued. A meditating person withdraws the senses from objects of pleasure or hardship. If the complete state of detachment is reached, then the individual is able to feel tranquility, serenity, and love. Those trained in detachment are far less subject to the stresses and strains of life, compared with people who do not practice meditation.

The contemporary psychological evidence suggests that the most fundamental mechanisms of sensation, perception, and the main states of consciousness, including both the normal flow of consciousness and its altered states, are universal across cultures. In all, the important differences are primarily concerned with the specific content of these experiences and the ways people process information according to both overt rules and covert practices of their countries and communities. With the development of technologies and human interaction, different human experiences are rapidly learned by various cultural groups through television, movies, art, the Internet, interpersonal contacts, and many other forms of communication. People learn more about each other by revealing their dreams and religious experiences and through understanding different mental realities. Still, we know little about our diverse cognitive world and the cultural backgrounds underlying it.

Exercise 6.1

A Cross-Cultural Psychoanalytic Interpretation of Dream Content

Clarissa P. Estes (2003) rightfully suggests that there are many dreams that reflect both immense and extensive feelings that the dreamer, in real life, is unable to cry about. In short, dreams release our suppressed concerns. Please read some of the author's interpretations of several common dreams. They, as Estes believes, are typical in women of all cultural and social backgrounds.

In this dream, a woman is helping an old person to cross the street. Suddenly, the old person smiles diabolically and "melts" on her arm, burning her deeply (or harms her in some other way). The dream sends a message that malevolent things are disguised as benevolent things. The woman tries to avoid threatening facts, but the dream shouts a warning to her: stay away from somebody and be careful in your current relationships.

In the "scary dark man" dream, a frightful intruder appears in the woman's apartment or house. She can feel his presence, his breath. The woman experiences horror and helplessness. She cannot scream for help or dial an emergency number. This dark man may appear as a thief, Nazi, rapist, terrorist, and so forth. The meaning of the dream is that the woman should awaken and reconsider her life again: something frightening is going on inside her. This is a dream of a woman who is "drying out," who is deprived of her creative function, and so far makes no effort to help herself.

In the "injured animal" dream, a woman sees an injured or wounded animal. This dream could represent a serious violation of the woman's freedom and other basic rights. Being unable—due to cultural censorship—to understand why her rights are violated, the woman accepts this safe way of symbolic expression of her concerns. An injured animal dream appears especially often in women in cultures in which they are deprived of their rights, abused, and discriminated against.

If a disembodied voice is heard in the dream (the voice that does not belong to a particular person or creature), this could mean that the woman's life is coming to an extreme. It could be a sign that she has "too much positive stimulation" or "too many responsibilities," and so forth. The woman is either "overloved" or "underloved," either "overworked" or "underworked." Bottom line, she must reevaluate her current life.

Assignment

Write your critical comments regarding each of these interpretations. Could you agree with some of these explanations? What interpretations do you disagree with? Explain why.

Exercise 6.2

Watch the classic movie *The Exorcist,* which you can rent in any video store. Answer the following questions.

What kind of altered states of consciousness can we recognize in the main character of the movie: visionary trance or possession trance?

There is a tradition found in many tribes around the world, such as in Mission Indians in California, to assign special duties of communicating with the spirit world to a medicine man (Caprio, 1943). In the movie, who was given the duty to negotiate and eventually expel the spirit from the girl's body?

Please summarize and generalize the diagnoses given to the girl by various doctors. What other cultures were mentioned in the conversations or can be seen in the movie? Try to give your opinion of why the theme of possession is still very popular among educated people.

Chapter Summary

- Our experience with the environment shapes our perception by creating perceptual expectations. These expectations, known as a perceptual set, make particular interpretations more likely to occur. They allow people to anticipate what they will encounter and, therefore, increase both the speed and efficiency of the perceptual process.
- There are several factors that may contribute to differences in people's sensation and perception. There are physical and environmental conditions, genetic factors, socialization norms, and acculturation practices.
- Studies on cross-cultural differences in the perception of simple patterns showed only small variations. Cross-cultural similarities in the drawing of visual patterns suggest the presence of a common mechanism for perceptual processes. Shape constancy of perception is significantly influenced by learning experiences. Culturally specific conditions determine which skills will improve in individuals in a particular culture and which skills will remain underdeveloped.
- Psychologists offer several hypotheses that explain cultural differences in illusion susceptibility. The carpentered world hypothesis postulates a learned tendency among people raised in an environment shaped by carpenters to interpret nonrectangular figures as representations of rectangular figures seen in perspective.
- There is a strong degree of similarity in the way color terms are used in different cultures. Moreover, verbal labels, if they are not available in the lexicon of a language, can be readily learned. Education, travel, interpersonal contacts, and the media can play a significant role in the development of color recognition and labeling.
- There are perhaps common perceptual mechanisms that lead to similarities across cultures in the perception of time and in aesthetic appreciation. Many similarities in perception of the beautiful were found in different cultural groups despite apparent socioeconomic differences among them. Because the traditional music of different cultures may differ in notion and harmony, there are some cultural differences in the perception of musical harmony.
- The universal similarity in the anatomy and physiology of human sensory organs and the nervous system seems to make it likely that sensory impressions and their transmission through the perceptual system are comparable across cultures.
- Consciousness is a process, which has several stages or states. The "normal" flow of consciousness may consist of periods of full attention and concentration or relative detachment from the outside events. Periods of wakefulness are altered by periods of sleep. Under various circumstances, meditation, psychoactive substances, trances, or hypnotic suggestion can alter consciousness. The understanding of consciousness is based on general cultural views of mental life and the relationship between body and soul.
- From a cultural standpoint, the normal flow of consciousness directs our behavior in ways that are adaptive in particular physical and social environments. Individual consciousness is dependent on socialization experiences, which, in turn are based on cultural factors, collective forms of existence, or shared collective experiences. Human consciousness develops together with the development of both physical and social environments. Increasing knowledge of the world at the same time broadens consciousness.
- Both duration and patterns of sleep may vary individually and from culture to culture. Despite significant differences in the manifest content of dreams, the latent dream content is believed to be generally similar in people living in different cultures. Dreams not only reflect our private world, but also mirror the environment in which we live. The dreaming individual's brain organizes and retrieves various images in a "culturally ascribed" manner.
- Phenomena such as meditation, trance, hypnosis, and near-death experiences during coma are very common in practically every culture. Analyzing them, a specialist should take into consideration personal characteristics of the studied individuals, their educational level, and position within the society. Specialists should also notice that certain life circumstances can influence individual experiences. Another set of conditions is a predominant cultural attitude toward altered states of consciousness expressed in the media, people's everyday conversations, or public opinion (if data are available).

Key Terms

Absolute Threshold The minimum amount of physical energy needed for the observer to notice a stimulus.

Aesthetic Experience A term used to identify the feeling of pleasure evoked by stimuli that are perceived as beautiful, attractive, and rewarding. The term also refers to displeasure evoked by stimuli that are perceived as ugly, unattractive, and unrewarding.

Altered States of Consciousness (ASC) The general name for phenomena that are different than normal waking consciousness and include mystic experiences, meditation, hypnosis, trance, and possession.

Behavioral Environment A mental representation that orients people to dimensions such as time, space, and the interpersonal world.

Consciousness The subjective awareness of one's own sensations, perceptions, and other mental events.

Daydreaming Turning attention away from external stimuli to internal thoughts and imagined scenarios.

Depth Perception The organization of sensations in three dimensions, even though the image on the eye's retina is two dimensional.

Dreams Storylike sequences of images occurring during sleep.

Difference Threshold The lowest level of stimulation required to sense that a change in the stimulation has occurred.

Meditation A quiet and relaxed state of tranquility in which a person achieves an integration of emotions, attitudes, and thoughts.

Perception The process that organizes various sensations into meaningful patterns.

Perceptual Set Perceptual expectations based on experience.

Sensation The process by which receptor cells are stimulated and transmit their information to higher brain centers.

Sensory Adaptation The tendency of the sensory system to respond less to stimuli that continue without change.

Sleep A nonwaking state of consciousness characterized by general unresponsiveness to the environment and general physical immobility.

Trance A sleeplike state marked by reduced sensitivity to stimuli, loss or alteration of knowledge, rapturous experiences, and the substitution of automatic for voluntary motor activity.

7

chapter

Intelligence

The means by which we live have outdistanced the ends for which we live. Our scientific power has outrun our spiritual power. We have guided missiles and misguided men.

MARTIN LUTHER KING, JR. (1929–1968)—
AMERICAN CIVIL RIGHTS LEADER

Time has a way of demonstrating—the most stubborn are the most intelligent.

YEVGENY YEVTUSHENKO (1933–)—
RUSSIAN POET AND WRITER

Our friend Charles Wiley—a journalist who has visited almost every country in the world—showed us a photo that he took in the People's Republic of China. We were at Charles's house and his guests took turns staring at the photo. On the picture, there was an entrance to Jinan University in Guangzhou. The large sign at the entrance read (as Charles translated to us): "Be loyal to the country, be faithful to your friends, persevere with your mission, be respectful to your parents and teachers." "You see," said one of the guests. "This is why the Chinese have such great test scores. They learn about discipline and hard work from early childhood. Look at their IQ numbers. They are ahead of everybody and it's no wonder. I wish I could send my two teenagers to China. Maybe there they would learn something useful." Everybody laughed and the conversation quickly switched to football. Two months later, one of us—who got a copy of the photo—showed it to a colleague who was born in Beijing. "You know," he replied, "you are asking me whether loyalty and respect are prime educational and cultural values in China. I do not want to disappoint you. It looks fine on the paper but in reality things are different. Do you think that *all* people there are just puppets who do whatever the government tells them to do? Do you think that *all* people there are loyal to their friends?" "No, but we're talking about the overall relationship between self-discipline and high test scores." "Oh, self-discipline. . . . It's family pressure," the friend replied with a mysterious smile. "You have to understand the Chinese family. Intelligence is a result of family influence."

Cross-Cultural Psychology: Critical Thinking and Contemporary Applications,
Fourth Edition, by Eric B. Shiraev and David A. Levy

Defining Intelligence

First of all, what is **intelligence?** Ask psychology professors at your college or university. If you ask 10 of them, you will receive nine different definitions. Just nine? What about the tenth teacher? (If you are asking this question now you are already revealing curiosity, an important feature of your intelligence.) The tenth professor will simply refer you to the introductory psychology textbook currently in use.

A quick glance through several introductory psychology textbooks published in the 2000s would reveal the same diverse picture: intelligence is defined in a variety of ways. For example, intelligence may be described as a set of mental abilities; the capacity to acquire and use knowledge; problem-solving skills and knowledge about the world; the ability to excel at a variety of tasks; or as a skill that allows us to understand, adapt, learn, reason, and overcome obstacles. Which point of view should we choose? First, most definitions include the word "knowledge." Intelligence is knowing and understanding the reality. Then, most definitions draw attention to problem solving, which leads to an assumption that intelligence is a set of mental skills that helps individuals to reach goals. Intelligence is also an ability to use knowledge and skills in order to overcome obstacles. And finally, intelligence helps in the adaptation to changing conditions.

Such an inclusive understanding of intelligence can be useful for cross-cultural psychologists because it allows them to incorporate the cultural factor in the discussion of intelligence. Indeed, people live in different environments and acquire knowledge and skills necessary to pursue goals and adapt to different cultural settings.

Intelligence is also inseparable from **cognition,** a diversified process by which the individual acquires and applies knowledge. It usually includes processes such as recognition, categorization, thinking, and memory.

There are several scientific approaches to intelligence. Let us consider them briefly, using the previous vignette as a starting point for discussion.

Some researchers, especially during the earlier stages of intelligence testing at the beginning of the twentieth century, suggested the existence of a general factor—or central cognitive function—that determines a certain level of performance on a variety of cognitive tasks (Spearman, 1927). The existence of this central cognitive function was evidenced by a set of positive correlations among performances on verbal, spatial, numerical, and other assessment problems. People with high academic ranking tended to score well on measures such as general knowledge, arithmetic ability, and vocabulary. On the contrary, people with low scores on verbal tasks were likely to have low scores on other tests.

Over the years, the idea of "one factor" that determines intellectual functioning has been frequently challenged. One such critic, Thurstone (1938), proposed the existence of not only one but rather three intellectual skills: verbal, mathematical, and spatial.

Sternberg (1985, 1997) also supported a hypothesis about a multidimensional structure of intelligence and suggested the existence of three fundamental aspects of intelligence, that is, analytic, creative, and practical. According to his arguments, most intelligence tests measured only analytic skills. Analytic problems in the test are usually clearly defined, have a single correct answer, and come with all the information needed for a solution. On the contrary, practical problems are usually not clearly defined. The person has to seek additional information and offer various "correct" solutions to the problem under consideration. To solve these problems successfully, the person would need to have accumulated everyday experiences and be motivated enough to find the solution.

Studying the diversity of human behavior and achievement, Gardner (2007) argued that along with logical, linguistic, or spatial intelligence measured by psychometric tests, there are other special kinds of musical, bodily kinesthetic, and personal intelligence a person's ability to understand himself or herself, or other people). However, as you may see, the ability to plan, evaluate a particular situation, and make useful decisions about the situation is essential for human survival and well-being. Then again, skills such as musical and body kinesthetic—in most cases—are not necessarily essential for human endurance and adaptation.

From the beginning of the empirical studies of intelligence, culture was claimed to be its important "contributor." For example, Piaget (1972) argued that intelligence has similar cross-cultural developmental mechanisms. On one hand, children in all countries assimilate new information into existing cognitive structures. On the other hand, these cognitive structures accommodate themselves to the changing environment. Vygotsky, a Russian psychologist, (1978) believed that intelligence could not be understood without taking into consideration the cultural environment in which the person lives.

In psychology, most attention has been given to the so-called **psychometric approach to intelligence.** This view is based on an assumption that our intelligence can "receive" a numerical value (Wechsler, 1958). This approach is also probably the most controversial one because of an ongoing debate about how accurately these values can be assigned and interpreted.

From an introductory psychology class you perhaps remember that typically, most intelligence tests contain a series of tasks. Each test contains several subtests that measure various cognitive skills. When you take the test, you are asked to solve verbal and nonverbal problems, make perceptual judgments, solve puzzles, find word associations, explain pictures in your own words, memorize sequences of words or numbers, and so on. After your answers are checked, your score is converted into a special score. Then your score is compared with the average score of your peers—presumably, and in most cases, this includes people of the same nationality and age group as you are. In fact, the comparison will yield your actual intelligence quotient, or for short, IQ. Approximately 95 percent of the population have scores on IQ tests within two standard deviations of 15. That means IQs of most people—95 out of 100—will be somewhere between 70 and 130.

There has long been intense controversy about the validity of measures and interpretation of intelligence test scores, and there are at least two major points in debates about intelligence testing:

1. What do intelligence tests actually measure?
2. How can it be proven that the test score was not influenced by factors such as the attitudes, motivation, or emotional states of test takers?

Critically important for those who attempt to interpret cultural differences on intelligence scores are (1) the distinction between cognitive potential, (2) cognitive skills developed through interaction with cultural environment, and (3) scores on a particular test. The problem is that the standard tests may not provide for the direct assessment of cognitive skills shaped by a particular cultural environment. Unless intelligence tests accommodate the activities that people perform in their day-to-day life, the tests created in one culture will continue to be biased against other cultural groups. This means that the test performance may not represent the individual's cognitive potential (Vernon, 1969). Moreover, factors such as language, test content, and motivation reportedly contribute to an individual's performance on tests (Sternberg, 2007). For example, there are many aspects of human intelligence, such as wisdom and creativity, that many tests are simply not designed to measure.

By nature, men are nearly alike; by practice, they get to be wide apart.

CONFUCIUS (441–479 B.C.E.)—CHINESE PHILOSOPHER

Intelligence cannot be meaningfully understood outside its cultural context. As an example, cross-cultural research conducted over a few decades shows that intelligence is understood differently in various cultural contexts. Studies also reveal that children have advanced practical skills that are not recognized on academic tests. In addition, the child's physical health may affect the child's performance on intelligence tests (Sternberg, 2004).

Another major point of most discussions is how to interpret the numerical value of intelligence. If 12-year-old boys and girls in a northern part of a city scored 90 on a test, whereas boys and girls from a southern part of the city scored 105 on the same test, what does this mean? The most fired debates take place when intelligence value is assigned to ethnic or national groups. Apparently, some significant differences in body size, shape, and skin color do not evoke such heated discussions and, as a result, we have misunderstanding rather than detailed interpretations of group differences between intelligence scores.

Before we continue our analysis, let us express one concern. As we suggested earlier, there are perhaps very few issues in psychology that have become as divisive as the concept of intelligence. Around the world the debates about intelligence are often motivated by a variety of political, ideological, and group interests (Helms, 2006). In some cases, a particular political agenda comes first and psychology serves as a provider of data. Scientific arguments are often overshadowed by emotional rhetoric. We accept, of course, that people who want to advance their particular views could use cross-cultural psychology for this purpose. Therefore, the goals of cross-cultural psychology perhaps will be better served if these views are not rejected outright but are critically analyzed.

Ethnic Differences in IQ Scores

Most of the questions that cross-cultural psychology attempts to address are concerned with a set of measurable similarities and differences among different cultural, ethnic, and national groups. Are ethnic groups characterized by a particular pattern of intellectual ability? For example, can one prove that Italians, in general, are more creative than Germans, but that the German mode of thinking is more "precise" than the Brazilian mode? Do some cultural groups have a "better" memory than others? Do poverty and other devastating social problems influence intelligence? Is systematic formal schooling the key to human intellectual equality? Is such equality achievable in principle?

In the United States, early attempts to measure IQs were targeted at minorities and new immigrants arriving in this country. For example, in 1921 the National Academy of Sciences published the results of one of the first massive national studies on intelligence. The results allowed the organizers of this study to rank newly arrived immigrants according to their IQ scores. This is how the "intellectual" order of the immigrants looked: England, Holland, Denmark, Scotland, Germany, Canada, Belgium, Norway, Austria, Ireland, Turkey, Greece, Russia, Italy, and Poland. In addition, the data showed the first evidence that blacks generally scored lower than whites on those tests. It was also reported that the Polish in this study did not score significantly higher than the blacks did (Kamin, 1976).

Today various tests show differences in intelligence scores among large cultural groups. For example, in the United States, Asian Americans (of East Asian origins) score the highest, followed by European Americans, Hispanics, and lastly African Americans. Thus, on the average, African American schoolchildren score 10–15 percent lower on a standardized intelligence test than white schoolchildren do. Similar results were reported for adults (Rushton & Jensen, 2005; Suzuki & Valencia, 1997). For better comprehension of the differences between some of the groups, just imagine that the average white person tests higher than about 80 percent of the population of blacks and an average black person tests higher than about 20 percent of the population of whites. According to studies, some racial-group differences in IQ appear in early childhood. For example, on the Differential Aptitude Battery, by age 6, the average IQ of East Asian children was 107, compared with 103 for white children and 89 for black children (Lynn, 1996). The size of the average black–white difference does not change significantly over the developmental period from three years of age and beyond.

The mean intelligence test scores for Latino groups are usually between those of blacks and whites. If we divide U.S. citizens along their religions, we will find that Jews, and specifically Jews of European origin, test higher than any other religious group in the United States. Studies of Korean and Vietnamese children adopted into white homes in the United States show that they tend to grow to have IQs 10 or more points higher than their adoptive national norms (Rushton & Jensen, 2005). Even though it is established that Americans of Japanese, Chinese, and Korean ancestry have higher scores than American whites, there is no consistency in research findings. The differences in scores that do occur are usually in the low single digits. The average difference between black and white IQ scores is established at every level of the socioeconomic ladder. In other words, upper-class blacks have lower test scores than upper-class whites, and lower-class whites have higher test scores than lower-class blacks. Cultural disparities in cognitive performance are found around the world. In India, members of the higher castes obtain higher mean scores and examination marks than do those of the lower castes. In Malaysia, members of the Chinese and East Indian minority communities have higher mean scores than those of the majority Malay population. In South Africa, members of the white, East Indian, and colored population groups obtain higher mean scores than members of the indigenous black African majority (Lynn & Vanhanen, 2002).

Some groups are found to have higher scores on certain scales and lower scores on others. For instance, the verbal intelligence scores of Native Americans were found to be lower than these same scores were for other ethnic groups. However, some studies showed the existence of high visual-spatial skills in Native American groups (McShane & Berry, 1988). East Asians score slightly higher than whites on nonverbal intelligence and equal or slightly lower on verbal intelligence. Moreover, studies suggest that the visual and spatial abilities of East Asians are superior to their verbal abilities, despite substantial political and socioeconomic differences among East Asian countries (Herrnstein & Murray, 1994).

It is not enough to have a good mind; the main thing is to use it well.

RENÉ DESCARTES (1596–1650)—FRENCH PHILOSOPHER AND MATHEMATICIAN

Explaining Group Differences in Test Scores: Intelligence and Intelligent Behavior

In an attempt to explain some group differences on intelligence test scores, Sternberg (1997) suggested distinguishing between intelligence and intelligent behavior. Intelligence, from his standpoint, is a mental process that may or may not result in particular behavioral responses. These behaviors vary from culture to culture. Something considered intelligent among members of one culture may not be viewed as such in other cultures. If a Washingtonian knows how to negotiate the conditions of a three-year lease with a car dealer, this skill may not be—and likely will not be—very useful at a farm market in Istanbul or Helsinki. Dealing with different cultural contexts, people develop different cognitive skills and acquire dissimilar

Box 7.1 CROSS–CULTURAL SENSITIVITY

Because of stereotyping some people may believe that all members of a group—or at least most of them—have either high or low IQ scores. However, the overall ethnic or national differences say little about diversity within particular groups. It is important to mention stereotyping because it may have an indirect impact on school performance and perhaps other activities. How? Imagine, for instance, a teacher knows there are five Hispanic and three black children in her class. Making a stereotypical judgment, the teacher would assume that these children should have lower intelligence test scores and, therefore, are less capable of learning than other children in class. This stereotype may create an expectation and attitude that result in the teacher, having only good intentions, giving "easier" assignments to these children, and not challenging them in their educational effort.

ways of thinking and learning that are useful in their particular cultural environment. Take, for example, the way people use categories to describe their experience. Traditionally, among navigators in Southeast Asia, the word "south" is often used to refer only to "seaward," which can be any side of the horizon (Frake, 1980). This centuries-old understanding of directions is inappropriate and confusing to visiting foreigners.

However, people may share some general understandings about what intelligence is because the underlying psychological mechanisms of intelligence are expected to be quite similar in all individuals. Among these processes are abilities to understand a problem, identify its type, prepare a solution, find resources to solve the problem, manage the process of solution, and, finally, evaluate the outcome of behavior. Nevertheless—and this is a key element in the understanding of intelligent behavior—the specific content of such behavior in each of these stages is determined by the specific environment in which the individual lives (Farhi, 2007). A chess master in India uses these strategies to make particular moves on a chessboard, whereas a farmer in Bosnia, using the same psychological mechanisms, secures a good deal buying a new tractor.

Reasoning that is causal, scientific, and based on empirical facts is not applicable in all cultures all the time (Shea, 1985). A ritualistic dance of a Brazilian tribesman may be considered "unintelligent" behavior by many people in London or Tokyo: "Look at him, he is dancing to stop the rain," some taunt sarcastically. These same taunting individuals, however, go every week to their temples and churches and, by doing this, commit themselves to similar ritualistic acts. Moral? People develop cognitive skills best adapted to the needs of their lifestyle (Dasen et al., 1979).

Do Biological Factors Contribute to Intelligence?

According to the **nativist view**, most cognitive phenomena are inborn. They unravel as a result of biological "programming," and environmental perception requires little active construction by the organism. Hypothetically, according to this view, a boy in Nepal or a girl in Venezuela are both expected to develop some elements of conceptual thinking by approximately the age of seven. No one can make these children think conceptually when they are four years old. This view argues that hereditary factors determine both the depth and scope of our intellectual skills.

These are not just the empty statements of a handful of researchers. In the 1980s, two scientists asked more than 1,000 scholars to give their opinion about IQ, in particular about the differences in IQ scores among ethnic groups. Even though only 1 percent suggested that the differences are always caused by genetic factors, almost 45 percent of the professionals reported that the differences are the product of both genetic and environmental variations (many could not or did not want to give a definitive answer). Remarkably, of all those interviewed only one in seven said that the difference is entirely due to environmental factors (Snyderman & Rothman, 1988). French neuroscientist Stanislas Dehaene (2002) maintains that the mathematical ability of humans may be imbedded in the brain and could be generally independent of memory and reasoning. Moreover, an individual's learning experience, school programs, and even spoken language (like French) may even suppress the development of certain inborn mathematical skills. Dehaene also argues that some languages, like Chinese, may be more helpful to develop a person's basic natural mathematical abilities.

Further support to the assumption that an individual's ability to be successful on cognitive tests is somehow biologically "programmed" and may be less dependent on this person's educational effort comes from a study conducted by Derek Briggs (2001). He found that young people who take preparation courses for college admission tests (such as the SAT in the United States) show only a small improvement in their scores. In other words, whether people study for this test or not, the results of these two groups are likely to be the same. Although some critics reasoned that the conclusions of this study simply pointed out the little effectiveness of the preparation courses, others suggested that certain cognitive skills cannot be improved over a short period of time, which indicates the existence of "deeper" roots of these skills.

There is evidence that heredity plays an important role in human intelligence. For example, the intelligence scores of identical twins raised either together or apart correlate almost +0.90 (Bouchard et al., 1990). One study of 543 pairs of identical twins and 134 pairs of nonidentical twins in Japan reported a substantial heritability of 0.58 for IQ (Lynn & Hattori, 1990). About two dozen studies conducted using magnetic resonance imaging (MRI) to measure the volume of the human brain have found an overall correlation with IQ (Vernon et al., 2000). Twenty-five percent of cases of mental retardation are caused by known biological defects (Grossman, 1983). Moreover, the intelligence scores of adopted children strongly correlate with the scores of their biological parents, whereas there is only a weak correlation between scores of adoptive parents and adopted children (Munsinger, 1978). The correlation between the IQ scores of two biologically unrelated individuals, who were raised together, is also relatively low: +0.20 (Bouchard & McGue, 1981). It is also known that vocabulary size, or the number of words a person remembers and uses in his or her communications, may depend on genetic predispositions. However, even though various data suggest high correlations between parents and children and brothers and sisters in terms of their intellectual skills, these data tell little about what would happen to people's IQ scores if they lived in a different social context than the one in which they actually grew up. Moreover, genetic links for individual differences and similarities do not imply that group differences—on the national level, for example—are also based on genetic factors (Sternberg, 2004). The fact that the heritability of IQ is high does not mean that individual differences in intellectual functioning are permanent. It shows that some individuals are probably genetically predisposed to be more teachable, more trainable, and more capable of learning skills than others, under current conditions and within specific cultural contexts (Lynn & Hattori, 1990).

Besides genetic factors, cross-cultural psychologists examine how particular environmental conditions affect human physiology and whether such biological changes influence cognitive skills. It was found, for instance, that the presence or absence of a particular chemical in a specific geographic region might have affected the overall cognitive performance of the population living in that territory. To illustrate, iodine-deficient areas are found in some regions of Indonesia as well as in Spain. Clinicians report that substantial iodine deficiency in the human body can cause severe mental and neurological abnormalities (see Bleichrodt et al., 1980). In accordance with predictions, cognitive test scores obtained from children living in iodine-deficient areas of Spain and Indonesia were much lower than the scores obtained from children residing in neighboring areas where the water contained sufficient amounts of iodine.

We now turn to a discussion of recent studies related to cognitive processes in order to illustrate how and to what extent they are shaped by cultural and social factors.

Incompatibility of Tests: Cultural Biases

Our friend Roberto, a psychologist from Miami, designed a test to measure the decision-making skills in small-business managers. Could he use this test in Colombia, Chad, or any other country? Yes, he can try. But will his assessments of decision making in these countries be accurate? Earlier, we learned about equivalency, one of the important requirements of any comparative research. If a test were designed for a particular ethnic group, the test questions or tasks may not have similar meaning for other cultural groups. Many specialists (Berry, 1988; Mishra, 1988; Poortinga & Van der Flier, 1988) emphasize the importance of such issues as "culture fairness" and "test transfer."

Theoretically, cognitive processes are believed to be similar in virtually all healthy individuals of different groups. However, these processes are applied to various, person-specific environmental, social, psychological, and cultural circumstances (Cole et al., 1971). People develop dissimilar cognitive skills because they are shaped by different contexts. A girl who goes to a private school in Paris, stays with her 45-year-old single mother, and has her own bedroom and personal computer lives in an environment that is quite different from that of a North Korean boy who shares his room with two siblings, attends public school, does not have a personal computer, and has very young parents who work in a shoe factory. A test may adequately measure some elementary cognitive skills in these two children, but at the same time it can be of a little use in terms of measuring other, culture-specific cognitive skills.

Most intelligence tests benefit specific ethnic groups because of the test vocabulary—words and items used in the test questions. For instance, tests may contain internal bias because they use words that are familiar only to some groups. As a result, members of these groups receive higher scores than those who do not belong to these groups. For example, try to solve the following problem.

Find the odd man out: Rose Tulip Forget-me-not Basil

The correct answer is "basil" because all the other words stand for flowers, and basil is not a flower. The critics of this type of question argue that unless the subject knows something about different flowers and plants, it will be very difficult for him to find the right answer. Those of us having access to flowers will benefit in this situation. Moreover, one may assume that there are more girls who are familiar with the names of flowers than there are boys. Therefore, girls will probably give more correct answers than boys.

Cultural experience may affect test scores and some test designs demonstrate this. For example, in one study, British children were found to solve test problems more creatively than Asian students from Hong Kong, Indonesia, and Malaysia. One explanation for this finding is that the subjects were required to give numeric verbal responses to the test items, something that is not a typical problem-solving task for Asian cultures (Wright et al., 1978). Another example illustrates how a test can benefit members of a particular group. A culturally oriented vocabulary test unique to the African American community was given to kids of different ethnic groups. Black kids scored around a mean of 87 out of a possible 100; however, white children's mean score was only 51 (Williams & Mitchell, 1991). In general, black youths perform better than white young people on free-word recall tasks when the categories (words) are related to African American daily experience (Hayles, 1991).

Commenting on overall differences in black–white intelligence scores, some critics imply that in intelligence tests there are many words and expressions that some black kids would not understand or are likely to misinterpret. For example, how would a child who grew up in a ghetto and was deprived of many sources of information understand words such as "composer," "symphony," or "regatta"?

He who does not know one thing knows another.

KENYAN PROVERB

A Word about "Cultural Literacy"

Most verbal intelligence tests contain sections on general knowledge. Obviously, our "general knowledge" is based on events that took place in a particular cultural environment. Most U.S. kindergartners possess knowledge about George Washington. Later comes information about Benjamin Franklin, the Great Depression, Titanic, *Gone With the Wind*, Liberty Bell, Watergate, Fidel Castro, Michael Jordan, Nelson Mandela, hip-hop, and Alex Rodrigues. For a young Italian man, some of these words are likely to sound unfamiliar. His cultural knowledge is based on other facts, events, and developments that are different from those one can experience in the United States. For example, words and names such as Mussolini, Andreotti, Fiat, Brigate Rosse, Juventus, and Adriano Celentano would be identified in Italy with almost no difficulty. Could you identify all these names? The answer is "no" unless you have lived in Italy or possess great knowledge of Italian history, politics, soccer, and music.

Our literacy is culture based. There is no doubt that 2 + 2 = 4 in all countries. An antonym for "death" is "life" in virtually every literate community regardless of its cultural heritage or nationality. However, beyond these universal categories—at least they sound universal for most of us—there is always culture-specific knowledge. Could you come up with your own examples of culture-specific knowledge in the United States or any other country?

Those who disagree with the existence of bias argue that IQ scores can more or less accurately predict future success at school—high test scores are positively correlated with high scores on intelligence tests. The specialists who believe that IQ tests contain very little bias suggest that these tests predict the academic performance of any ethnic group in the same way that they predict performance of white children and adults: high IQs predict academic success and low IQs predict low school grades (Pennock-Roman, 1992). This means that any student of any ethnic group who scores high on an IQ test is likely to have fine grades in college.

Environment and Intelligence

Compare yourself with any person in the classroom. You may find someone of the same age, height, weight, nationality, income, and even lifestyle as you are. However, we do not live in identical environments. Our diversity is determined by natural factors, such as individual, professional, educational, social, and cultural circumstances. This is a popular view in psychology—accepted by cross-cultural psychologists—that human intellectual skills can be influenced by external environmental factors (Carroll, 1983;

Sternberg, 1985). In general, these factors include the overall availability of and access to resources, variety of perceptual experiences, predominant type of family climate, educational opportunities, access to books and travel, presence or absence of cultural magical beliefs, general attitudes, and cultural practices. These and other conditions have been found to influence performance on intelligence tests (Vernon, 1969). Settings such as educational incentives, quality of teaching, and teacher–student communications may also influence test scores (Irvine, 1983; Mackie, 1983). Special training programs (Keats, 1985) and additional instructional efforts (Mishra, 1997) can determine how well a person scores on an intelligence test as well. For example, Ogbu (1994) suggested that negative attitudes about testing in general, feelings of hopelessness, and exposure to stereotypes may lower the intelligence scores of African Americans and other minority groups in the United States. Research data suggest that at least some black students do not perform well on cognitive tests because they are inhibited by a concern of being evaluated according to a negative "you are not smart" stereotype and the fear of performing poorly that would inadvertently confirm that stereotype (Steele, 1999).

There is strong evidence that training can increase scores on IQ tests (Skuy et al., 2002). Raven (2000) showed that students who were encouraged to engage in complex cognitive tasks improved substantially in self-direction, understanding, and competence.

Studies show that the acquisition of many mental functions depends on interaction with the environment (Macdonald & Rogan, 1990). Take, for instance, West African traders, who spend most of their adult life traveling and negotiating. One well-known study found that the merchants are better on cognitive tasks—including problem solving—than West African tailors, who spend most of their life in one place and do not have such diverse contacts as the merchants (Petitto & Ginsburg, 1982). In another example, Brazilian and Colombian street children who earn money by selling fruit and vegetables on the street—often at age 10 and 11—are able to conduct financial operations in their "minds" without making mistakes. Similar math operations, done in paper and pencil at the request of investigators, were not successful. The children did not receive formal schooling, and, as a result, they did not learn the algorithms of adding and subtracting on paper (Aptekar, 1989). In another study, after viewing a series of pictures, European children tended to describe the pictures as a sequence of events—as if they were a comic strip that appears in children's magazines. African children who were not exposed to comics tended to report that the pictures portrayed a single instant in time, not a sequence of events (Deregowski & Munro, 1974).

Aboriginal children obtain lower verbal scores than urban Australian children do, and one cause may be a lack of interaction. If Aboriginal children have a chance to live side by side with white children, their test scores on verbal classification tests are relatively similar (Lacey, 1971). In general, serious deprivation of stimulation may result in the disorganization of a number of cognitive processes (Sinha & Shukla, 1974).

Certain types of environmental influences determine the individual's experience with these influences. However, people's experiences determine their adaptive reactions. As a result, cognitive skills that play a crucial role in an individual's survival may develop earlier than other skills (Ferguson, 1956). For example, children in hunting and gathering societies develop spatial reasoning skills earlier than their peers in agricultural communities. However, children in agricultural cultures achieve understanding of concepts such as conservation of quantity, weight, and volume—knowledge necessary in agricultural activities—more rapidly than children from nomadic (traveling) groups (Dasen, 1975).

Environmental factors may affect higher mental operations, such as planning abilities. One such factor is stability of the environment. In a stable environment most changes are predictable. People are certain about their lives and feel that they are in control of their future. When conditions are unpredictable, people may lack planning strategies because of the assumption that it is impossible to control the outcome of whatever you plan. All in all, in societies and communities that are stable, people perhaps have better chances of developing their planning skills than people from unstable environments (Strohschneider & Guss, 1998).

Lack of systematic schooling may also contribute to the slow development of planning strategies. Certainly, the complexity of everyday life can provide conditions for the development of planning skills even if a person has little formal education. However, if there is no access to education and if environmental conditions require simple responses, the individual would tend not to develop complex planning strategies.

Socioeconomic Factors

Intelligence scores are, in general, positively correlated with the socioeconomic status of the individual (Neiser et al., 1996). The link between socioeconomic conditions and test performance may be revealed at an early age. It was found that a child's IQ and the socioeconomic status of the child's parents are positively correlated. The higher the child's IQ, the higher her parents' socioeconomic rank, and vice versa (White, 1982). Children who grow up in a privileged environment tend to show higher scores than their peers from a deprived environment (Masters, 1997). For example, Yoruba children, living in upper-class, educated families, demonstrated superior mental age scores when compared to Yoruba children from nonliterate families (Lloyd & Easton, 1977). A similar trend was found among four-year-old Maori and Pakeha Aboriginal children living in New Zealand (Brooks, 1976). Accordingly, no substantial differences were found in the cognitive abilities of disadvantaged children from both Australian Aboriginal and European decent (Taylor & deLacey, 1974).

According to the U.S. Census Bureau (2000), 20 percent of U.S. kids lived in families below the official poverty level. Poverty could contribute to these children's lower scores on tests of intelligence and lower levels of school achievement (McLoyd, 1998). Studies in the past showed links between breast-feeding, nutrition, and cognitive performance of the child. Breast-feeding reduces the infants' exposure to metal pollutants, while providing infants the long chains of proteins necessary for brain development. Mothers from low socioeconomic groups typically do not breast-feed their infants. Black mothers in the United States, for instance, in the past, were only one-third as likely to breast-feed their infants as white mothers (Jensen, 1998). A 40-year study showed that students from lower-income families making $37,000 or less are less likely to be proficient in both math and reading compared to higher income families (Strauss, 2008). The individual's socioeconomic status may have both direct and indirect impact on test performance. For instance, social environments with limited amounts of resources may stimulate the development of particular cognitive traits that are useful only for those environments. If we compare large clusters of countries—for example, Western developed and traditional societies—we will find that people in Western countries generally outscore members of traditional societies on intelligence tests (including tests that do not include culture-specific tasks, questions, and problems).

Socioeconomic factors have a more pronounced effect on intelligence test scores in developing countries than in industrialized ones. One explanation of this phenomenon is that in developed countries the gap between the rich and the poor is not as profound as it is in developing countries. The official poverty level in the United States, which is slightly more than $9,800 per person per year, exceeds the average annual income of most other countries.

Some researchers suggest that high IQ scores may predict people's high social status and income (Herrnstein & Murray, 1994). The middle-class population generally has higher IQ scores than the lower-class population. Does this mean that individual socioeconomic success is possible only when an individual has high intellectual skills? This is not necessarily true. Yes, higher IQ scores may determine the success of the individual, in particular his social status and income. Nevertheless, availability and access to resources—or the lack thereof—may also affect the person's intellectual potential, which results in higher or lower IQ scores. One should not forget that the individual's social status determines her position in the society and access to resources and power. Both middle-class and well-to-do parents establish connections and develop personal and professional relationships with people from the same social stratum, thus paving the way for their own children to reach high levels on the social ladder. In other words, psychometric intelligence alone cannot decide social outcome; there are many other variables in this equation. For example, individuals who have the same IQ scores may be quite different from one another in their income and social and professional status.

Those who believe in the crucial role of socioeconomic factors in our intellectual functioning consider them the most salient influences contributing to the difference between intelligence test scores of blacks and whites in the United States. Generally, blacks have lower incomes, occupy less prestigious positions, and receive less adequate care than other minority groups. Poverty is also linked to inconsistent parenting and persistent exposure to stress that can and does affect cognitive functioning.

The Family Factor

An affluent and educated family is likely to provide a better material environment for a child and also has more resources to develop a child's intellectual potential than a poorer family. Middle-class parents typically have enough resources to stimulate the child's learning experience at home (Gottrfried, 1984). Such parents are likely to be educated and subsequently have general understanding of the importance of education. They are able to buy developmental toys, including video games and computer software. Most of them do not have problems that would prevent them from talking to their children about various topics, exposing them to interesting events, and stimulating their imagination. On the contrary, poor families have fewer resources and fewer opportunities to stimulate a child's intellectual development (Shiraev, 1988). If the parents' prime activity is to secure food and safety for the family members, then collective survival—not necessarily the intellectual development of the child—is the prime goal of the parents' activities.

In 2003, for instance, children of parents of Indian origin, living in England and Scotland, outperformed all other students at school. Similar data were received regarding students of Chinese and mixed backgrounds. One of the factors proposed by researchers is that, in most cases, immigrant parents start their lives with low-paid jobs and see in their children's education the key to their sons' and daughters' success in life. As a result, these parents pay special attention to their children's school performance (Sonwalkar, 2004). A similar conclusion was drawn in a study involving 6,000 U.S. middle-school students. Across ethnic groups, students whose parents were concerned about their children's academic performance and who were able to boost the educational aspirations of their children showed significantly higher academic scores than other students (Hong and Ho, 2005).

It has been found in some studies that intelligence scores decline as a function of birth order. According to one theory, this trend has little to do with biological factors (Munroe & Munroe, 1983). Every immature member of a family develops intelligence linked to the intellectual level of the older family members. The firstborn in the family has the initial advantage of an immediate environment consisting of only himself and the adult parents, who have a particular set of cognitive skills. When a second child is born, she enters an environment consisting of herself, the parents, and an individual with an immature intellectual level, that is, the older sibling. Thus, in general, the intellectual environment encountered by the firstborn is "superior" to that of the second born, and so on.

These data, although controversial, found additional support in some other studies. For example, a continuous increase in IQ scores in the African American population is correlated with the increasingly smaller family size since the 1970s. Children from smaller families tend to achieve higher IQ scores than their counterparts from larger families (Vincent, 1991). However, extra caution is needed in such interpretations. First, the relationship here may be reverse: higher scores on IQ tests stand for higher cognitive abilities, which, in turn, affect individual attitudes about pregnancy and unprotected sex. Another explanation for the change in IQ scores is a more significant increase in the educational level of parents in black families in the 1980s and 1990s.

Parental influence can be one of the factors contributing to the difference in IQ scores between white and some other ethnic groups—predominantly minorities—that represent the middle class. Minority parents—especially those who arrived to the United States before the 1960s—are likely to be less educated than the white population. As it was mentioned earlier, parents' cognitive skills contribute to the development of the child's cognitive skills. Moreover, some minority parents may pay less attention to educational opportunities for their children than white families do. Overall pessimism and a lack of opportunity and success can cause such attitudes. On the contrary, Chinese and Japanese Americans tend to emphasize the importance of education for their children and see it as the only opportunity for future advancement. Partly because of family values and partly because of their academic success, Asian Americans tend to seek and get appointments in professional, managerial, or technical occupations to a greater extent that any other ethnic group (Flynn, 1991).

"Natural Selection" and IQ Scores

According to the bell curve principle, a normal distribution of IQ scores in any given population can be roughly divided into three large categories: people with low, average, and high IQ scores. This same principle can also be used in the distribution of peoples' heights. However, although a bell curve of IQ scores and a bell curve of peoples' heights may paint a similar picture, the meanings people assign to these pictures may be quite different. For instance, we find people of all different heights in various social circles, with various occupations, and of varying intelligence. An individual's location on the bell curve of height may place him next to numerous types of people that he may never interact with in everyday life.

The bell curve of IQ scores is another story. In the United States, for example, people with high IQ scores are disproportionally represented among doctors, scientists, lawyers, and business executives. Individuals with low intelligence scores are disproportionally represented among people on welfare, prison inmates, single mothers, drug abusers, and high-school dropouts (see, for example, Rushton and Jensen, 2005).

Perhaps there is nothing unusual about people with similar interests and occupations tending to communicate with one another significantly more often than with people of other occupations and interests. For example, a high IQ score indicates that you will be likely to (1) attend college, (2) gain employment in a setting conducive to meeting and making friends with people of similar educational levels, and perhaps intelligence, and (3) marry someone with an educational background similar to yours. Likewise, people with lower scores will likely seek love and friendship among people of the same cognitive level. Therefore, according Herrnstein and Murray (1994), two polls of people have been "constructed" over the years: one with relatively high and the other with relatively low intelligence scores. The former is placed in an advantageous social niche with prestigious jobs, good income, and fine living conditions. The latter group finds itself in the disadvantaged stratum of low-paying jobs, unstable social environment, and low-quality living conditions.

Unfortunately, for a variety of reasons, many representatives of ethnic minorities remain in the disadvantaged group. Low IQ scores, as was mentioned earlier, predict low academic grades and fewer opportunities for individuals to get high-income jobs. Lack of resources would contribute greatly to keeping these individuals in low-income communities. Low salaries and low cost of property produce significantly less taxes than in affluent districts. Therefore, local schools—most of which depend on local property taxes—are not able to provide high-quality education comparable to the quality of education in affluent communities. Poor schooling conditions, lack of qualified teachers, and the absence of modern educational equipment affect the developing child's cognitive skills. In addition, as we saw earlier, poverty is responsible for a variety of indirect impacts on the intellectual development of children and adults.

> He who knows others is learned; he who knows himself is wise.
>
> LAO-TSE (604–531 B.C.E.)—CHINESE PHILOSOPHER

Cultural Values of Cognition

Let us get back to Roberto's test on cognitive skills mentioned in the beginning of the chapter (remember, he designed an inventory on problem solving). According to this test, what types of problem solving are likely to be considered most efficient for a business person? There are several, a few of which are independent judgment, creativity, and speed of decision making. Will these qualities be equally valuable in all business environments and in all countries?

Judging from an ethnocentric perspective, one might suggest that the most "valuable" features for any problem-solving process are analytical, rational skills, and quick reasoning. However, such a view—though prevailing in most contemporary societies—is not universal in all cultures. Some societies may have diverse sets of cognitive values different from the ones highly regarded, for example, in Western societies (Berry, 1988). In some societies holistic—emphasizing the importance of the whole—rather than analytic decision making is valued (Dasen, 1984; Serpell, 1993). In such cases, careful reflection rather than promptness is considered the most appropriate course of action. In these primarily agricultural societies, collective discussion rather than individual consideration is generally the preferred cognitive style. Therefore, in such cultures, individuals tested with a standard Western psychological instrument—such as Roberto's test—will likely display a low level of cognitive development according to criteria that measure only independence and speed of judgment.

Nisbett (2003) proposed a view of the differences in cognitive styles between Western and East Asian students. Using experimental data, he suggested that students from China, Korea, and Japan tend to be more holistic in their perceptions than do students of Western descent. In other words, East Asian students tend to see and remember objects as being interconnected, while Western students pay attention to details and issues that clearly stand out. Studies show, for instance, that Western infants learn nouns faster than verbs, while East Asian infants tend to learn verbs (indicating connections between objects) more rapidly. Differences in reasoning styles between Chinese and European Americans were observed during a comparative study that revealed Chinese students, both bilingual and not speaking English, organized objects in pictures in a more relational and less categorical way than European Americans (Ji et al., 2004).

> Desire to have things done quickly prevents their being done thoroughly.
>
> CONFUCIUS (551–479 B.C.E.)—CHINESE PHILOSOPHER

According to another approach to the interpretation of test scores on general intelligence, the problem is in the way people across cultures value and construe intelligence. For instance, as already mentioned, the conceptualization of intelligence as quick and analytic is not shared in all cultures. If one group's concept includes being detailed and precise in responding, and the other group does not mention these features (and mentions improvisation as an element of intelligence), then precision cannot be used as a criterion according to which the two groups are compared (Berry, 1969).

In the United States, different ethnic groups may use different frames of reference regarding intelligence (Heath, 1983; Okagaki & Sternberg, 1993). For instance, in most cases, European Americans emphasize the importance of cognitive skills such as memorization, classification, and problem solving, whereas other groups tend to emphasize characteristics such as motivation, social, and practical skills. In light of this, Sternberg (1997) found that the emphasis on formal mental abilities does not give a fair chance to many individuals with high creative and practical mental abilities. For example, on measures of

Box 7.2 CRITICAL THINKING

A "Chinese Way" in Thinking? Compare Socrates and Confucius

Do you believe that there is a special, unique, Chinese way of thinking and processing information? Do you think there is a special European style? According to one view, there ought to be a special "cultural" way rooted in customs and early European and Chinese philosophical systems. Supporters of this argument use an example of the teachings of two prominent philosophers of China and Greece—Confucius and Socrates—and their impact on the general learning principles cultivated in Chinese and Western (European) cultures. It is argued that Socrates, a major contributor to the Western scholarly thought, valued critical thinking and skepticism by encouraging the questioning of common knowledge. He taught his students and, subsequently, millions of followers of other generations, to be independent thinkers and generate their own ideas. Confucius, to the contrary, is viewed as valuing the effortful, respectful, and pragmatic acquisition of essential knowledge based on respect toward educators and the constant search for patterns of useful behavior to follow (Tweed & Lehman, 2002; Yang & Sternberg, 1997). While Confucius urged his followers to respect elders, Socrates urged his followers to challenge them.

If you accept these arguments, you are likely to agree with the idea that there are culture-based patterns of learning and thinking. Thus, Socrates impacted the cultural characteristics of the "typical" European student who is primarily a critical thinker, while Confucius impacted the characteristics of the "typical" Chinese student who is an efficient follower and problem-solver.

If you disagree, you are likely to suggest that respect of authority, acceptance of teachers, and search for practical applications of knowledge are, in fact, universal features of any educational system, whether it is Greek, or Chinese, or Mexican. Therefore, to attribute them exclusively to a particular culture or any other philosophy is simply inaccurate (Li, 2003).

Which side of the argument do you find easier to support and why?

creativity, flexibility, and originality, black children and other minority groups typically do as well, and frequently better, than white children (Hayles, 1991).

We understand now that intellectual skills are judged according to a group's standards. For example, if a culture places an emphasis on hunting, a person's good vision and ability to make quick visual judgments will be considered extremely adaptive. In other cultures, the quickness of one's response will not be as essential as a critical evaluation of a task or problem at hand. In other words, the people, as representatives of a particular culture, define intelligence. If we argue for this, we inevitably move in the fields of cultural relativism. Why? Because we would challenge the existence of universal criteria for human mental activities. However, cultural relativism can also be challenged. For example, do you think that in an era of globalization of economy and informational revolution, people can, may, and probably should develop similar perceptions of what specific mental abilities are considered to be adaptive and valuable in the global community unified by the global economy?

There have been many attempts to explain the differences between Western and African cultural values and views on healthy cognitive functioning and intelligence. Boykin (1994), for example, suggested that blacks do not accept materialistic beliefs and do accept the influence of nonmaterial forces to a greater extent than other groups. They appreciate high levels of stimulation and energy and emphasize the importance of emotions and expressiveness. Furthermore, African American culture is rooted in spirituality, harmony, and affect, as well as verbal elements of communication. These features may not fit well into the Western values of rationality, calculation, discipline, individualism, and achievement, which are embodied in IQ tests. The author even suggests that the whole idea of intelligence assessment may be foreign to the African American mentality.

Most non-African theories of behavior, according to Baldwin and colleagues (1991), emphasize the critical role of the gratification of desires. The emphasis of black psychology is that the essential goal of human behavior is survival. Moreover, African theology assumes that the most direct experience of the self is one that goes through affect. Therefore IQ measures, according to Baldwin, cannot measure the psychology of individuals who grew up in African or African American cultures. Intelligence, from the perspective of African psychology, is a collective moral responsibility.

Shade (1992) suggested that African Americans value a unique **cognitive style**—a way in which individuals organize and comprehend the world. In the study of 178 ninth-grade students, sampled African Americans tended to be spontaneous, flexible, open-minded, and less structured in the perception of people, events, and ideas. European Americans in the sample appeared to be self-regulated, judgmental, and less open-minded than their counterparts. In another study, African American children generally learned in ways characterized by emotional emphasis, harmony, holistic perspectives, expressive creativity, and nonverbal communication (Wills, 1992). Some explain the below-average standardized test scores of African American children by referring to the tests' emphasis: the abstract, analytic thinking valued by Europeans—the features that are somewhat deemphasized by blacks (Whethrick & Deregowski, 1982).

It was also implied that students of non-European origin use different cognitive styles of information processing: They are more field dependent than their European counterparts in the classroom (Kush, 1996). For example, **field-dependent** learners are more attentive to external references, contexts, and instructions in their learning tasks. **Field-independent** learners tend to be autonomous in learning, solving problems, and making decisions. It was found that in U.S. academic settings, field-independent students are more successful than field-dependent students. Although an individual's cognitive style is determined by many factors, studies also show that people in predominantly individualist cultures, such as Germany and the United States, tend to be more field independent than people in collectivist cultures, such as Russia and Malaysia, as is shown in cross-cultural studies (Kuhnen et al., 2001).

Certain ideological conditions may affect what people of a certain country value most in cognitive skills. Consider this example. If authorities, whoever they are—central government or local boss—make most decisions in your life, then apparently the number of choices you have may be restricted. Given a limited amount of choices, the number of activities available to you will also be limited, which is likely to affect your creativity and problem-solving ability. For example, creative thinking and self-expression are highly regarded in Western democratic societies. The paradox is that creative thinking is not a necessary asset in authoritarian societies. Why? Because this type of thinking may put the individual "above the crowd," which is neither appreciated nor tolerated by authorities. The same logic may be applied to those societies that promote dogmatic thinking and punish individuals for free exchange of ideas (Shiraev & Sobel, 2006).

■ Exercise 7.1

Please analyze the following theory differentiating dichotomous variables and continuous variables. Jackson (1991) introduces the following assumptions about the cognitive skills of African Americans:

- Blacks in the United States tend to perceive events as the whole visual picture, whereas whites perceive reality as broken down into parts.
- African Americans tend to prefer reasoning based on contextual and interpersonal factors, whereas European Americans prefer inductive and deductive reasoning.
- African Americans prefer to approximate space, numbers, and time. European Americans tend to prefer precision based on the concert of one-dimensional time and "objective" space between individuals.
- African Americans prefer to focus on people and their activities as opposed to Europeans, who show a propensity toward things based on a Eurocentric orientation and norms.
- African Americans prefer cooperation, preservation of life, affiliation, and collective responsibility; European Americans prefer competition, conflict, control of life, ownership, and individual rights.
- African Americans are more altruistic and concerned about the "next person," while European Americans value individualism and independence.
- African Americans prefer novelty, freedom, and personal distinction to a greater degree than European Americans.

■ General Cognition: What Is "Underneath" Intelligence?

Numerous facts about cultural diversity as well as empirical evidence about universal principles of cognition (see the definition of cognition in the beginning of the chapter) have contributed to the foundations of many theories exploring the links between culture and intelligence. There are several cognitive processes—recognition, categorization, thinking, and memory—the analysis of which will perhaps shed some light on differences and similarities in intellectual functioning among various ethnic groups.

Classification

Are there any differences in how people classify their environment? Humans tend to see things in highly similar fashions. One of the most universal classifications is the cognitive distinction made between plants and animals (Berlin, 1992). However, those plants and animals that are essential for the survival of individuals become most carefully distinguished and named. In general, the importance of objects and animals as well as a person's familiarity with them are the most significant factors that influence categorization. Groups that are relatively distant from each other should have some differences in classifications (Schwanenflugel & Rey, 1986). This may become a source of a potential bias in the testing of cognitive skills.

Sorting

If you ask a seven-year-old child of any nationality to sort 100 colored cards into color categories, the child should be expected to perform this operation without difficulty. Now ask an elderly resident of a small Ethiopian village to sort 100 compact discs according to the musical genres they represent—rock, classical, and hip-hop—and this person will likely experience serious difficulties (unless he is familiar with musical genres).

We can sort various objects even though no instructions are given on how to do it. Generally, we choose a dimension of categorization, that is, concept or characteristic. Linguists suggest that many categories used in sorting are universal. We use synonyms, such as "quick" and "fast"; antonyms, such as "clean" versus "dirty"; subcategories, such as "skunk" and "animal"; and parts, such as "heart" and "body" (Raybeck & Herrmann, 1990).

Research suggests that cultural groups tend to categorize objects in terms of their specific cultural experiences associated with these objects (Okonji, 1971; Wassmann, 1993; Wassmann & Dasen, 1994). In other words, according to experience people know what the objects are used for and then base their categorization on this knowledge (Mishra, 1997). It has also been shown that the degree of familiarity with the environment influences classificatory behavior. For example, according to a well-known study, rural Liberians performed at a lower level, compared with students from New Mexico, in a card-sorting task. However, the Liberians were superior at sorting bowls of rice (Irwin et al., 1974). In several studies, Middle Eastern immigrants to North America were found to have better integrative thinking than other immigrants who performed similar object-sorting tasks in laboratory experiments. These differences were likely to reflect differences in national educational systems (Zebian & Denny, 2001). It was also found that many African Americans may have superior skills of categorizing people, but not objects (Shade, 1992).

Memory

Many comparative tests on memory contain tasks that require the subject to remember storylike information and then recall it. Are there any cultural differences in memory? Mandler and colleagues (1980) found relatively few differences in the recollection of stories between U.S. and Liberian children and adults. Similarly, common patterns in immediate recall of information were found among such distant cultural groups as English, Polish, and Shona in Zimbabwe (Whethrick & Deregowski, 1982).

Common patterns in how people recall stories do not mean there are common patterns in what people recall or how fast they process this information. Cultural, social, and educational experiences affect what we remember. Two groups of students, Australians and Asians (including Chinese, Japanese, and Korean), were asked to provide information about so-called "self-defining memories." These memories were to be autobiographical recollections of events they believed shaped them as individuals. Australians provided more elaborate self-focused memories and Asians produced more elaborate memories involving other people and relationships (Jobson & O'Kearney, 2008). Children of higher socioeconomic status receive better scores on various memorization tests compared with other students (Ciborski & Choi, 1974). Steffensen and Calker (1982) tested U.S. and Australian Aboriginal women by asking them to recall two stories about a child getting sick. The child was treated by Western medicine in one story (a situation familiar to U.S. women), and by native medicine in the other (a situation familiar to Australian women). The stories were recalled better when they were consistent with the subjects' knowledge. Similar results have been reported by other psychologists working with different cultural populations (Harris et al., 1992). Deregowski (1974) showed that urban children in Zambia recalled more test information than did rural residents. Perhaps better educational opportunities of urban boys and girls and emphasis on memorization in school activities influence children's test performance.

Formal and Mathematical Reasoning

Formal reasoning is a basic cognitive operation that is based on abstract analysis of given premises and deriving a conclusion from them. It is particularly sensitive to systematic schooling (Scribner & Cole, 1981). Formal reasoning is different from **empirical reasoning**, which is drawn from everyday experience. A person may develop skills of empirical reasoning but do poorly on a test that measures formal reasoning skills. Russian psychologist Luria (1976) demonstrated in one of his studies that illiterate peasants in Uzbekistan, a republic of the former Soviet Union, were able to understand empirical reasoning—when objects involved in reasoning were observable—but often failed to comprehend abstract formal reasoning that required assumptions and imagination.

Many cross-cultural studies have specifically focused on mathematical problems. This was the case not only because these studies provided a good test of reasoning ability, but also because math symbols appear to be culturally neutral. One of the important findings was that Eastern cultures—such as China and Japan—are often thought to be advanced in the development of numerical abilities in their members.

Indeed, Chinese participants performed significantly better on several mathematical measures than did U.S. students (Geary et al., 1992; Stevenson et al., 1990). Davis and Ginsburg (1993) compared Beninese (African), North American, and Korean children and found little difference in performance on informal life-related mathematical problems. However, on formal problems, the Korean children performed best. Why does this trend exist? The most common explanation is based on the assumption that there is a particular set of social norms developed in East Asian countries. In particular, parents and teachers spend more time and effort on the development of formal mathematical skills in children than their overseas counterparts typically do. The differences in educational norms and attitudes most likely cause the differences in test performance between American and East Asian children (van de Vijver & Willemsen, 1993). It was shown that European American and Asian American students as groups tend to be different in terms of using speech while solving reasoning problems. Talking is apparently more helpful to Europeans than it is to Asians because, as researchers suggested, Asians tend to use internal speech less than do European Americans (Kim, 2002).

Creativity

If you write a verse in English and rhyme "forever" and "together," this cannot be called creative poetry. Why? Because **creativity** typically means originality or the ability to produce valued outcomes in a novel way. The rhyme "forever–together" has already been used in hundreds of verses and songs.

Creativity is typically defined as the process of bringing into being something that is both novel and useful. Specifically, the creative cognition approach identifies two kinds of cognitive processes implicated in creative thinking—generative processes and exploratory processes. First, people actively retrieve or seek out relevant information that might have creative potential. Next, they examine these ideas to determine which ones should receive further processing, such as modification, elaboration, and transformation (Leung et al., 2008). In cross-cultural psychology, studies examining the role of culture in creativity focus mainly on social factors and socialization practices (Harrington, 1990; Stein, 1991). For example, persistent parental support and positive stimulation appear as good predictors of creativity (Simonton, 1987). In a comparative Mexican American study, children from economically advantaged families showed higher creativity scores than did disadvantaged children (Langgulung & Torrance, 1972). It was also found that Arab subjects tended to score higher on verbal creativity than on spatial creativity, which is probably due to the emphasis Islamic cultures place on achieving verbal proficiency and the religious restrictions placed on pictorial reflections of reality (Abou-Hatab, 1997; Mari & Karayanni, 1982). The same study showed that in Arab cultures males score higher than females on creativity tests. However, those subjects who were equally exposed to television, Western education, and travel showed little evidence of sex differences in their scores of creativity.

Cultural experiences may either help or hinder creativity. Our learned routines often help us to coordinate our social behaviors (Chiu & Hong, 2006). On the other hand, when an individual is immersed in and exposed to only one culture, the learned routines and conventional knowledge of that culture may limit his or her creative responses and growth. Studies show that multicultural experience is positively related to a preference for sampling ideas from unfamiliar cultures. However, foreign living, but not necessarily short-term foreign traveling, affects creative thinking. When living abroad, we encounter many opportunities for cognitive and behavioral adaptation and change. In addition, multicultural experience does not improve an individual's performance in a creativity task unless the individual is predisposed to being open to experience (Leung et al., 2008).

In the worlds of education and employment, decision makers have become overly dependent on tests of cognitive abilities, knowledge, or skills for making high-stakes decisions affecting the life opportunities of many individuals (Helms, 2007).

Box 7.3 A CASE IN POINT

Multicultural experience may foster the creative expansion of ideas. What do you think about expatriate artists and writers whose brilliant insights emerged when they left their homeland and settled in a foreign country? Explore the biographies of some writers, composers, and artists. Where did they create their major masterpieces? Gabriel G. Marquez (born in Colombia), Vladimir Nabokov and Sergei Rachmaninoff (both born in Russia), Paul Gauguin (born in France), Nâzım Hikmet (born in Turkey), Rabindranath Tagore (born in India). Could you suggest other names of people who created their masterpieces mainly abroad? Does this mean that a different culture inspires imagination or stimulates creative work? We should understand, however, that there are many other artists and writers who did not travel much and yet no one has doubts about their creativity and talent. Take, for example, Nezami, a great Persian poet. He stayed in one place for his entire life.

Box 7.4 CRITICAL THINKING

Are U.S. children behind the rest of the world in math and other academic disciplines? The notion that "we are losing" in education is now a new phenomenon in mass media. A 1957 cover story in a March issue of Life magazine read: "Crisis in Education." The article suggested that hard-working and disciplined students in the communist Soviet Union were surpassing languid and care-free Americans in educational achievement. Back in the 1980s, numerous reports about the achievements of Japanese students compared to their American counterparts implied an inevitable and rapid economic decline vis-à-vis the growing might of the Japanese economy rising on the shoulders of highly educated Japanese workers.

Today, when compared with students in the world's most industrialized countries, U.S. students are on the same level with the others in every subject. Moreover, Americans commonly outperform everyone in disciplines such as civics (studies dealing with public affairs and the rights and duties of citizens). Of course, being on the same level with others does not mean that everything is great in U.S. educational system. Educational challenges of the United States are related to institutional and cultural factors. First, with a few exceptions, U.S. public schools are locally funded and are not directed by the federal government unlike in most countries in the world including Russia, China, and India. Second, college education is widely available to a majority of U.S. students (through a huge network of state universities and two-year colleges), which does not require the highschool student to have perfect grades and highest scores. Third, the U.S. educational system has historically placed a special emphasis on individual development, freedom of choice, creativity, and unconventional problem solving. This focus subsequently diffuses attention away from test-taking preparations (Fahri, 2007).

Cognitive Skills, School Grades, and Educational Systems

It has been shown in numerous studies that IQ scores correlate with school grades. In other words, if Ali has a higher IQ than John, one can anticipate that Ali's grades in math, science, literature, and social studies will be better than John's. Can one then make a suggestion that higher intelligence scores determine higher school grades? Yes, such an assumption is correct, but it may contain a logical error. Why? Because the high grades one receives at school may also be determined by one's effort, motivation, interest in learning, and individual discipline. These characteristics, in turn, may be largely influenced by one's family. Add peers' influence, teachers' effort and commitment, and the availability of educational resources at school and home—all may determine a particular individual's grades and test scores.

We should not forget that around the globe, national school systems are organized differently. In the United States public education is primarily based on the guidelines determined by local communities. The federal government cannot dictate to the states or counties what students have to study in kindergarten, middle school, or high school. In many other countries, however, schools use standard curricula and students nationwide have similar textbooks on every subject. To illustrate, children in Japan are generally more advanced than their U.S. counterparts in math. This is not happening because of a difference in IQ—the average scores are similar—but rather because the Japanese school curriculum places a heavy emphasis on mathematics.

Studies also show a high correlation between total years of education and IQ scores. To put it simply, people with a higher IQ are likely to continue their education at college; people with a college degree are likely to have a higher IQ than individuals with a highschool diploma (Neiser et al., 1996). A higher IQ may predict higher grades; that, in turn, may increase a person's motivation to stay in school.

> The first mark of intelligence, to be sure, is not to start things; the second mark of intelligence is to pursue to the end what you have started.
>
> PANCHATANTRA—THE ANONYMOUS COLLECTION OF SANSKRIT ANIMAL FABLES

Culture, Tests, and Motivation

IQ test scores may be determined not only by one's intellectual skills, but also by the individual's motivation, anxiety, and attitudes toward testing. For example, why is there a gap in intelligence test scores between whites and African and Mexican Americans, whereas no such gap exists for other immigrant groups, such as Arabs, Chinese, or Iranians? Explaining the difference, scholars sometimes refer to the so-called **low-effort syndrome** (Ogbu, 1991). The low-effort syndrome is an example of a coping strategy: "No matter how hard I try, I will be held back."

Why does this syndrome exist? In the United States, and perhaps in some other countries, there are at least two kinds of minorities. The first is immigrant minorities, most of whom come voluntarily in search of better conditions and opportunities. These minorities make use of high academic achievement as a condition of success. Caste minorities, on the contrary, were brought to the United States through slavery or forceful colonization. They developed a different attitude that was based on an assumption that academic success does not lead to advancements because society does not want them to advance educationally.

Indeed, it is hard to disagree with the idea that people ought to see successful results for their hard work. Otherwise, pessimism may discourage many of us from studying, learning, and striving for a better future (Raspberry, 2000). Those who argue that some ethnic minorities express less motivation on intelligence tests typically suggest that such individuals do not try to excel on these tests because they believe that they will not go to college anyway, the tests are biased against them, and test results are unimportant. Perceiving themselves as minority groups and understanding that power and resources do not belong to them, some individuals believe that there is no reason for them to try to succeed because success is not achievable and their effort will not be rewarded by society just because of their minority status. Moreover, tests may be seen by some as another instrument by which the government tries to advance the discrimination of minorities (Williams & Mitchell, 1991).

Such negative attitudes may be passed on to younger generations and become part of value systems, which encourage people to seek alternative ways to survive that do not include education. Moreover, some blacks stereotypically define academic achievement as "white" behavior that is inappropriate for nonwhite individuals, especially African Americans (Ogbu, 1986).

Some scholars argue that the motivational levels of blacks and whites—those who take intelligence tests—are not substantially different (Herrnstein & Murray, 1994). The authors give as an example, the "digit span test." During this test the subject is instructed to repeat a sequence of numbers in the order read to her, for example: 11, 17, 20, 16, 9, 49. After a certain number of forward sequences or a certain number of mistakes, the tester asks the subject to repeat a sequence of numbers backward. These two parts of the test are conducted immediately, one after the other, and have identical content: the person has to repeat the same numbers presented to her.

The black–white differences on this test are about twice as great on backward digits as on forward digits. The authors argue that it is impossible to suggest that lack of motivation in black subjects is responsible for such differences: how come the differences are minimal on the "forward" sequence and substantial on the "backward" sequence?

However, if you think critically, you may find that the two halves of the test are not equal in their meaning to the participant. The first half of the test requires a relatively simple operation of memorizing and repeating. The second half of the test—when the subject is asked to repeat numbers backward—requires a substantial mental effort. This may activate psychological resistance in subjects who consider such a difficult task impossible to overcome and therefore not worth the sustained effort.

> A man of humanity is one who, in seeking to establish himself, finds a foothold for others and who, desiring attainment for himself, helps others to attain.
>
> CONFUCIUS (551–479 B.C.E.)—CHINESE PHILOSOPHER

> Justice is like a train that's nearly always late.
>
> YEUGENY YEVTUSHENKO—RUSSIAN CONTEMPORARY POET AND WRITER

IQ, Culture, and Social Justice

Is the power of the few based on their intellectual skills? Exceptions notwithstanding, in most contemporary societies the amount of education received by people should predict, in general, their social status. Indeed, the higher your educational degree, the more prestigious and well paid the profession you can apply for and eventually receive. Moreover, as indicated earlier, individuals with a higher educational degree should ultimately earn more than those with fewer years of completed education. For example, in most societies, occupations such as doctors, lawyers, dentists, college professors, and some other professions require up to 20 years of formal schooling. In other words, a high IQ score indicates higher grades in school and may eventually lead toward a higher social status—the value of which is measured by income generated and occupational prestige.

Now use your critical thinking. Can you hypothesize that there can be societies in which certain prestigious professions do not require the person to pass a series of tests or have a high academic degree? In such cases, the relationship between IQ and earning potential will not be so evident and, therefore, IQ would probably lose its discriminatory power over people's lives. Does this mean that in contemporary societies, people are divided into "upper" and "lower" social categories according to their test scores?

Some easily argue that in the contemporary democratic societies people are born to be equal and laws protect their equal rights. Therefore, it is fundamentally wrong to continue to divide people socially based on their test scores. Why does the contemporary system have to be accepted as fair if it discriminates against certain groups? For instance, some ethnic minorities, primarily blacks, Hispanics, and Native Americans, have less opportunity to go to college and fewer chances of getting better jobs than those individuals who show higher IQ scores. Looking at this situation from a slightly different perspective, one could ask a question: "How could we call this a democratic society if we have only one system, which links societal success to test scores and indicates what jobs people should pursue and eventually how much money they can make?"

Others may reply: "So what is the problem? We are all different. Some people are tall and some other people are short. We have different skills. We want to achieve different goals. We are not entitled to perform in the same way. We have to accept diversity. Diversity assumes some sort of inequality." As it was mentioned, intelligence test scores predict what profession an individual is likely to obtain. In the United States and many other countries certain occupations require an applicant to earn a particular college degree and pass special qualification tests. No doubt, these professions require individuals to use their intellectual skills. For example, imagine yourself as a physician. What do you have to do daily? Most likely, you have to examine different patients with different symptoms and problems; you have to develop your research skills and observation proficiency to come up with the correct diagnosis; you have to communicate with insurance companies and your supervisors; you have to understand how to write prescriptions; you have to know how to talk to patients and their relatives; you must read scientific and other professional journals. Should we continue? This job requires a high academic degree. People with lower degrees or without formal schooling should be expected to perform less complex activities.

Perhaps people will compete with and discriminate against one another in certain walks of life. Maybe there is no way to achieve equal performance and, therefore, equal scores on school tests. However, wherever it is possible, people living in a democratic society can reduce the impact of discrimination, whether intentional or not. For the sake of argument, suppose that two children are born in the year 2005. Should we expect that they are both entitled to have an equal opportunity to compete for a better future? Perhaps. However, in reality, from the beginning of their lives they may join the race for happiness at different "speeds." One child will have better conditions for intellectual growth, whereas the other will not live in such a favorable environment.

Will these two children have equal chances to develop equal cognitive skills, given their unequal environments, even though they had equal potential at birth? The answer is likely to be "no." However, what can one do about this situation? Should the government force everyone to give up property and resources and be equal economically and ideologically? Such attempts were made in the twentieth century by many Communist and totalitarian governments. The attempts eventually failed.

Very few of us will demand that people be totally equal and receive the same benefits regardless of their effort, skills, and moral behavior. However, we believe that a wealthy democratic society is capable of creating better conditions for its citizens by helping the disadvantaged to compete for and pursue happiness. This debate, however, brings about not only psychological, but also many moral and political questions that are beyond the scope of the present analysis.

The situation with IQ testing and scores may be changing, however. Flynn (1987, 2007) has shown an interesting tendency of a continuous and steady worldwide rise in intelligence test performance. Detected primarily in developed countries, this effect stands for a three-point increase in IQ scores every 10 years. From a broader perspective, one can suggest that every new generation is expected to be scoring higher than their parents and others and the difference will be from 6 to 9 points. Such a difference may be caused by an increase in the technological advancement of the population. As an example, in the 1980s most video games were simple and one-dimensional with two or three slow-moving objects. Today's video games—mostly three-dimensional and multicolored—require significant preparation and training before one can successfully play any of them. Increased access to television and the Internet also adds to the complexity of the surrounding world and perhaps stimulates the development of individual psychological skills. Technology and other resources make a difference in people's lives. For example, in recent years the gap in IQ scores between U.S. rural and urban populations has significantly decreased (Neiser et al., 1996), which may be explained by a changing environment. In rural areas children have greater access to various sources of information, such as television and the Internet, compared to the situation 20 or 40 years ago.

High test scores and overall academic success involve knowledge and skill acquisition, as well as motivation for learning. As many specialists imply, although academic learning is a primary goal of education, ideas about how best to achieve this goal need to be broadened to include children's participation in learning, their self-confidence as students, and their capacity to work effectively with other children and with adults (Bemak et al., 2005).

An honest heart being the first blessing, a knowing head is the second.

THOMAS JEFFERSON (1743–1826)—THIRD U.S. PRESIDENT

And in the End, Moral Values

All in all, the contemporary view supported by many psychologists is that the most essential elements of intelligence are so-called higher level abilities, namely reasoning, problem solving, and decision making. Intelligence is not just a reaction to changes in environmental conditions. It is also one's global capacity to learn about this environment. Persons with higher intelligence are more capable of noticing, understanding, and explaining surrounding phenomena—in various situations and forms of activities—than are persons with lower-level intelligence. One belief is that people who have higher IQs have a better chance of changing our environment (Sternberg, 2004).

However, a person with a high IQ score and a better potential for changing the environment may also possess little or no moral values and be lacking compassion, sympathy, or good will.

Back in the 1970s Chomsky (1976), one of the most renowned specialists in human development, criticized a very popular approach to intelligence. This approach was based on an assumption that the individual's success is based on the amount of money that person makes. In fact, income and prestige are not and should not be the only measure of social success. In many countries, social accomplishment is largely determined, not necessarily by the person's ability to score high on IQ tests, but also and most important, by her survival skills. This may include the ability to (1) carry on with a limited supply of food and resources, (2) adapt to the environment, and (3) change the environment despite the overwhelming pressure of lawlessness, violence, pollution, and disease. Moreover, many people do not base their individual happiness, reason for working, and success only on extrinsic rewards and material factors. There are also moral satisfaction, love, friendship, and many other elements of human experience that may not be related to scores on an IQ test.

Exercise 7.2

Memory and Experience

Our familiarity with a subject or topic can affect how precisely we memorize and retrieve information. Different cultural experiences, therefore, could affect the quality of our memory in particular circumstances. Consider the following sentence: ***The quarterback threw an incomplete pass and his mistake forced the team to punt the ball right before the two-minute warning.*** Select five people who are familiar with U.S. football and five people who know very little or nothing about this game. Read the sentence to people in both groups. Then ask them to write down what they remembered. What kinds of results will you expect to receive? Indeed, even though it is difficult to recall all 22 words of this sentence, people from the first group (those who know football) would correctly remember most of the words. On the contrary, those who are not familiar with football will, perhaps, make several mistakes trying to convey the meaning of the sentence. Could you test these hypotheses?

Box 7.5 A CASE IN POINT

Rational Calculations and Moral Values

What would you do in the following situation? Imagine you are captain of a space ship that landed with a crew of 10 people on a remote planet to conduct scientific research. You learn, however, that due to some catastrophic problems, the ship cannot be launched from the planet with all the crewmembers aboard: It is 170 pounds over the carrying capacity. Now the oxygen tank is almost drained. What would you do? In a famous classical series of "Star Trek," Mr. Spock, a character with superior intellectual skills—far exceeding those of other crew members—offered a very "logical" solution: To leave the least valuable crew member on the planet (where this person would die and, by this sacrifice, save the lives of the other crew members). Apparently "less intelligent" characters opposed this heartless reasoning and offered an alternative solution. Moral values in this case overcame logical calculations.

Exercise 7.3

Searching for a Possible Bias in Written Tests

Three-quarters of the nation's schoolchildren (sample of 60,000 in the fourth, eighth, and twelfth grades) were unable to compose a well-organized, coherent essay, according to results of a federally sponsored writing test. Most students were able to compose short essays they were asked to write. However, their writing had neither the sophistication nor proficiency expected by a national board of educators, state officials, and business leaders (Cooper, 1999). There was also a gap in the performance of different racial and ethnic groups. White and Asian students were writing better than African Americans, Hispanics, and Native Americans were. That gap was narrower in schools located on military bases, where minority students scored higher than their counterparts elsewhere. Perhaps minority students benefited from an equitable distribution of resources at the Defense Department schools and the attitudes, education, and financial security of the schools located on military bases.

However, did anyone examine the possibility of a cultural bias of the tests? Apparently no. Below are the sample questions used by the National Assessment Governing Board to test the writing skills of students in various grades. Could you examine them and write your suggestions about whether the assignments are biased against certain ethnic groups? Explain your arguments and try to achieve both sophistication and proficiency in your analysis.

Fourth graders. We all have favorite objects that we care about and would not want to give up. Think of one object that is important or valuable to you. For example, it could be a book, a piece of clothing, a game, or any object you care about. Write about your favorite object. Be sure to describe the object and explain why it is valuable or important to you.

Eighth graders. Imagine this situation! A noise outside awakens you one night. You look out the window and see a spaceship. The door of the spaceship opens, and out walks a space creature. What does the creature look like? What does the creature do? What do you do? Write a story about what happens next.

Twelfth graders. Your school is sponsoring a voter registration drive for 18-year-old high school students. You and three of your friends are talking about the project. Your friends say the following:

Friend 1: "I'm working on the young voters' registration drive. Are you going to come to it and register? You're all 18, so you can do it. We're trying to help increase the number of young people who vote and it shouldn't be too hard—I read that the percentage of 18- to-20-year-olds who vote increased in recent years. We want that percentage to keep going up."

Friend 2: "I'll be there. People should vote as soon as they turn 18. It's one of the responsibilities of living in a democracy."

Friend 3: "I don't know if people should even bother to register. One vote in an election isn't going to change anything."

Do you agree with friend 2 or 3? Write a response to your friends in which you explain whether you will or will not register to vote. Be sure to explain why and support your position with examples from your reading or experience. Try to convince the friend with whom you disagree that your position is the right one.

Chapter Summary

- Most definitions of intelligence include phrases such as knowing and understanding the reality around us. Intelligence is also defined as a set of mental skills that helps individuals reach a goal. Intelligence is also seen as the ability to use knowledge and skills to overcome obstacles. And finally, intelligence is defined as helping one to adapt to a changing environment.
- Intelligence is inseparable from cognition, diversified processes by which the individual acquires and applies knowledge. It usually includes processes such as recognition, categorization, thinking, and memory. Altogether, cognitive development is neither totally culturally relative nor completely uniform everywhere.
- In psychology, most attention has been given to the so-called psychometric approach to intelligence. This view is based on the assumption that our intelligence can "receive" a numerical value.
- Today various tests show differences in intelligence scores among large cultural groups. For example, in the United States, Asian Americans (of East Asian origins) score the highest, followed by European Americans, Hispanics, and lastly African Americans. Thus, on the average, African American schoolchildren score 10–15 percent lower on a standardized intelligence test than white schoolchildren.
- In an attempt to explain some group differences on intelligence test scores, Sternberg suggested

distinguishing between intelligence and intelligent behavior. Intelligence, from his standpoint, is a mental process that may or may not result in particular behavioral patterns. These patterns of intelligent behavior may vary from culture to culture. Something considered to be intelligent among members of one culture may not be viewed as such in other cultures.

- According to the nativist approach to intelligence, human cognitive phenomena are inborn. They unravel as a result of biological "programming," and environmental perception requires little active construction by the organism. There is evidence that heredity plays an important role in human intelligence. However, genetic links for individual differences and similarities do not imply that group differences—on the national level, for example—are also based on genetic factors.
- Some specialists imply that most intelligence tests benefit specific ethnic groups because of the test vocabulary—words and items used in the test questions. Tests may contain internal bias because they use words that are familiar to only some groups. As a result, members of these groups receive higher scores than those who do not belong to these groups.
- Many environmental conditions have been found to influence performance on intelligence tests. Among them are availability of and access to resources, variety of perceptual experiences, predominant type of family climate, educational opportunities, access to books and travel, presence or absence of cultural magical beliefs, general attitudes, and cultural practices.
- Intelligence scores are, in general, positively correlated with the socioeconomic status of the individual and the link between socioeconomic conditions and test performance shows at an early age. A child's IQ and the socioeconomic status of the child's parents are also positively correlated. An affluent and educated family is likely to provide a better material environment for a child and also has more resources to develop the child's intellectual potential than a poorer family. Poverty is responsible for a variety of indirect impacts on the intellectual development of children and adults.
- In the United States people with high IQ scores are disproportionally represented among doctors, scientists, lawyers, and business executives. Individuals with low intelligence scores are disproportionally represented among people on welfare, prison inmates, single mothers, drug abusers, and high school dropouts.
- There is a difference in the way people across cultures value and construe intelligence. For instance, the conceptualization of intelligence as quick and analytic is not shared in all cultures. If one group's concept includes being detailed and precise in responding, but the other group does not mention these features (and mentions improvisation as an element of intelligence) then precision cannot be used as a criterion according to which the two groups are compared.
- According to a theory, there are differences in cognitive styles revealed by Western and East Asian students: students from China, Korea, and Japan tend to be more holistic in their perceptions than do students of Western descent.
- Cognitive processes have cross-cultural similarity but may also develop in different ways according to specific cultural norms and societal demands. People develop cognitive characteristics best adapted to the needs of their lifestyle. Cross-cultural findings suggest that differences in categorization, memorization, labeling, creativity, and formal reasoning may be rooted in cultural factors. Various cultural groups categorize stimuli differently in terms of their specific cultural experiences associated with these objects. Many cognitive processes can develop either in similar or in different ways according to specific cultural norms and societal demands.
- U.S. children, generally, are allowed more freedom in choosing school activities than their overseas counterparts. The emphasis is typically placed on individual development, enjoyable activities, and respect for the child's personality. In Asian countries, on the contrary, the active promotion of the mathematical development of children is crucial. From the beginning the child learns rules of discipline, perseverance, and sacrifice for the sake of educational goals.
- Some ethnic minorities may display the so-called low-effort syndrome, or low level of motivation on intelligence tests. This typically suggests that such individuals do not try to excel on these tests because they believe that they will not go to college anyway, the tests are biased against them, and test results are unimportant.
- Overall, in developed Western societies, high IQ scores are correlated with social success. The situation with IQ testing and scores may be changing, however. There is an interesting tendency of a continuous and steady worldwide rise in intelligence test performance. Detected primarily in developed countries, this effect stands for a three-point increase in IQ scores every 10 years and may be attributed to educational efforts and technological developments.

Key Terms

Cognition A general term that stands for a series of processes by which the individual acquires and applies knowledge.

Cognitive Style An individual way in which individuals organize and comprehend the world.

Creativity Originality or the ability to produce valued outcomes in a novel way.

Empirical Reasoning Experience and cognitive operations drawn from everyday activities.

Field-Dependent Style A general cognitive ability of an individual to rely more on external visual cues and to be primarily socially oriented.

Field-Independent Style A general cognitive ability of an individual to rely primarily on bodily cues within themselves and to be less oriented toward social engagement with others.

Formal Reasoning Basic cognitive operations based on abstract analysis of given premises and deriving a conclusion from them.

Intelligence Global capacity to think rationally, act purposefully, overcome obstacles, and adapt to a changing environment.

Low-Effort Syndrome Low level of motivation on intelligence tests based on the belief that the tests are biased and test results are unimportant for success in life.

Nativist View The view that all cognitive phenomena are inborn, that they unravel as a result of biological "programming," and that environmental perception requires little active construction by the organism.

Psychometric Approach to Intelligence A view based on an assumption that our intelligence can "receive" a numerical value.

chapter

8

Social Structure and Social Interaction

"Suddenly one of the men jumped up, smashed the empty bottle against the sidewalk, and . . ."

My curiosity had gotten the better of me. When the sociology convention finished, I climbed aboard the first city bus that came along. I didn't know where the bus was going, and I didn't know where I would spend the night.

"Maybe I overdid it this time," I thought, as the bus began winding down streets I had never seen before. Actually, this was my first visit to Washington, D.C., so everything was unfamiliar to me. I had no destination, no plans, not even a map. I carried no billfold, just a driver's license shoved into my jeans for emergency identification, some pocket change, and a $10 bill tucked into my sock. My goal was simple: If I saw something interesting, I would get off the bus and check it out.

"Nothing but the usual things," I mused, as we passed row after row of apartment buildings and stores. I could see myself riding buses the entire night. Then something caught my eye. Nothing spectacular—just groups of people clustered around a large circular area where several streets intersected.

I climbed off the bus and made my way to what turned out to be Dupont Circle. I took a seat on a sidewalk bench and began to observe what was going on around me. As the scene came into focus, I noticed several streetcorner men drinking and joking with one another. One of the men broke from his companions and sat down next to me. As we talked, I mostly listened.

As night fell, the men said that they wanted to get another bottle of wine. I contributed. They counted their money and asked if I wanted to go with them.

Although I felt my stomach churning—a combination of hesitation and fear—I heard a confident "Sure!" come out of my mouth. As we left the circle, the three men began to cut through an alley. "Oh, no," I thought. "This isn't what I had in mind."

I had but a split second to make a decision. I found myself continuing to walk with the men, but holding back half a step so that none of the three was behind me. As we walked, they passed around the remnants of their bottle. When my turn came, I didn't know what to do. I shuddered to think about the diseases lurking within that bottle. I made another quick decision. In the semidarkness I faked it, letting only my thumb and forefinger touch my lips and nothing enter my mouth.

When we returned to Dupont Circle, we sat on the benches, and the men passed around their new bottle of Thunderbird. I couldn't fake it in the light, so I passed, pointing at my stomach to indicate that I was having digestive problems.

Suddenly one of the men jumped up, smashed the emptied bottle against the sidewalk, and thrust the jagged neck outward in a menacing gesture. He glared straight ahead at another bench, where he had spotted someone with whom he had some sort of unfinished business. As the other men told him to cool it, I moved slightly to one side of the group—ready to flee, just in case.

Levels of Sociological Analysis

On this sociological adventure, I almost got in over my head. Fortunately, it turned out all right. The man's "enemy" didn't look our way, the man put the broken bottle next to the bench "just in case he needed it," and my intriguing introduction to a life that up until then I had only read about continued until dawn.

Essentials of Sociology: A Down-to-Earth Approach,
Eighth Edition by James M. Henslin

Sociologists Elliot Liebow (1967/1999), Mitchell Duneier (1999), and Elijah Anderson (1978, 1990, 2006) have written fascinating accounts about men like my companions from that evening. Although streetcorner men may appear to be disorganized—simply coming and going as they please and doing whatever feels good at the moment—sociologists have analyzed how, like us, these men are influenced by the norms and beliefs of our society. This will become more apparent as we examine the two levels of analysis that sociologists use.

Macrosociology and Microsociology

The first level, **macrosociology,** focuses on broad features of society. Conflict theorists and functionalists use this approach to analyze such things as social class and how groups are related to one another. If they were to analyze streetcorner men, for example, they would stress that these men are located at the bottom of the U.S. social class system. Their low status means that many opportunities are closed to them: The men have few job skills, little education, hardly anything to offer an employer. As "able-bodied" men, however, they are not eligible for welfare—even for a two-year limit—so they hustle to survive. As a consequence, they spend their lives on the streets.

In the second level, **microsociology,** the focus is on **social interaction,** what people do when they come together. Sociologists who use this approach are likely to analyze the men's rules or "codes" for getting along; their survival strategies ("hustles"); how they divide up money, wine, or whatever other resources they have; their relationships with girlfriends, family, and friends; where they spend their time and what they do there; their language; their pecking order; and so on. Microsociology is the primary focus of symbolic interactionists.

Because each approach has a different focus, macrosociology and microsociology yield distinctive perspectives, and both are needed to gain a fuller understanding of social life. We cannot adequately understand streetcorner men, for example, without using *macrosociology.* It is essential that we place the men within the broad context of how groups in U.S. society are related to one another—for, as is true for ourselves, the social class of these men helps to shape their attitudes and behavior. Nor can we adequately understand these men without *microsociology,* for their everyday situations also form a significant part of their lives—as they do for all of us.

Let's look in more detail at how these two approaches in sociology work together to help us understand social life.

The Macrosociological Perspective: Social Structure

Why did the street people in our opening vignette act as they did, staying up all night drinking wine, prepared to use a lethal weapon? Why don't *we* act like this? Social structure helps us answer such questions.

The Sociological Significance of Social Structure

To better understand human behavior, we need to understand social structure, the framework of society that was already laid out before you were born. **Social structure** refers to the typical patterns of a group, such as its usual relationships between men and women or students and teachers. *The sociological significance of social structure is that it guides our behavior.*

Sociologists use both macro and micro levels of analysis to study social life. Those who use macrosociology to analyze the homeless—or any human behavior—focus on broad aspects of society, such as the economy and social classes. Sociologists who use the microsociological approach analyze how people interact with one another. This photo illustrates social structure—the disparities between power and powerlessness.

Because this term may seem vague, let's consider how you experience social structure in your own life. As I write this, I do not know your race–ethnicity. I do not know your religion. I do not know whether you are young or old, tall or short, male or female. I do not know whether you were reared on a farm, in the suburbs, or in the inner city. I do not know whether you went to a public high school or to an exclusive prep school. But I do know that you are in college. And this, alone, tells me a great deal about you.

From this one piece of information, I can assume that the social structure of your college is now shaping what you do. For example, let's suppose that today you felt euphoric over some great news. I can be fairly certain (not absolutely, mind you, but relatively confident) that when you entered the classroom, social structure overrode your mood. That is, instead of shouting at the top of your lungs and joyously throwing this book into the air, you entered the classroom in a fairly subdued manner and took your seat.

The same social structure influences your instructor, even if he or she, on the one hand, is facing a divorce or has a child dying of cancer or, on the other, has just been awarded a promotion or a million-dollar grant. Your instructor may feel like either retreating into seclusion or celebrating wildly, but most likely he or she will conduct class in the usual manner. In short, social structure tends to override personal feelings and desires.

Just as social structure influences you and your instructor, so it also establishes limits for street people. They, too, find themselves in a specific location in the U.S. social structure—although it is quite different from yours or your instructor's. Consequently, they are affected in different ways. Nothing about their social location leads them to take notes or to lecture. Their behaviors, however, are as logical an outcome of where they find themselves in the social structure as are your own. In their position in the social structure, it is just as "natural" to drink wine all night as it is for you to stay up studying all night for a crucial examination. It is just as "natural" for you to nod and say, "Excuse me," when you enter a crowded classroom late and have to claim a desk on which someone has already placed books as it is for them to break off the neck of a wine bottle and glare at an enemy. To better understand social structure, read the Down-to-Earth Sociology box on football on the next page.

In short, people learn their behaviors and attitudes because of their location in the social structure (whether they be privileged, deprived, or in between), and they act accordingly. This is as true of street people as it is of us. *The differences in behavior and attitudes are due not to biology (race, sex, or any other supposed genetic factors), but to people's location in the social structure.* Switch places with street people and watch your behaviors and attitudes change!

Because social structure so crucially affects who we are and what we are like, let's look more closely at its major components: culture, social class, social status, roles, groups, social institutions, and societies.

Culture

Sociologists use the term *culture* to refer to a group's language, beliefs, values, behaviors, and even gestures. Culture also includes the material objects that a group uses. Culture is the broadest framework that determines what kind of people we become. If we are reared in Chinese, Arab, or U.S. culture, we will grow up to be like most Chinese, Arabs, or Americans. On the outside, we will look and act like them; and on the inside, we will think and feel like them.

Social Class

To understand people, we must examine the social locations that they hold in life. Especially significant is *social class,* which is based on income, education, and occupational prestige.

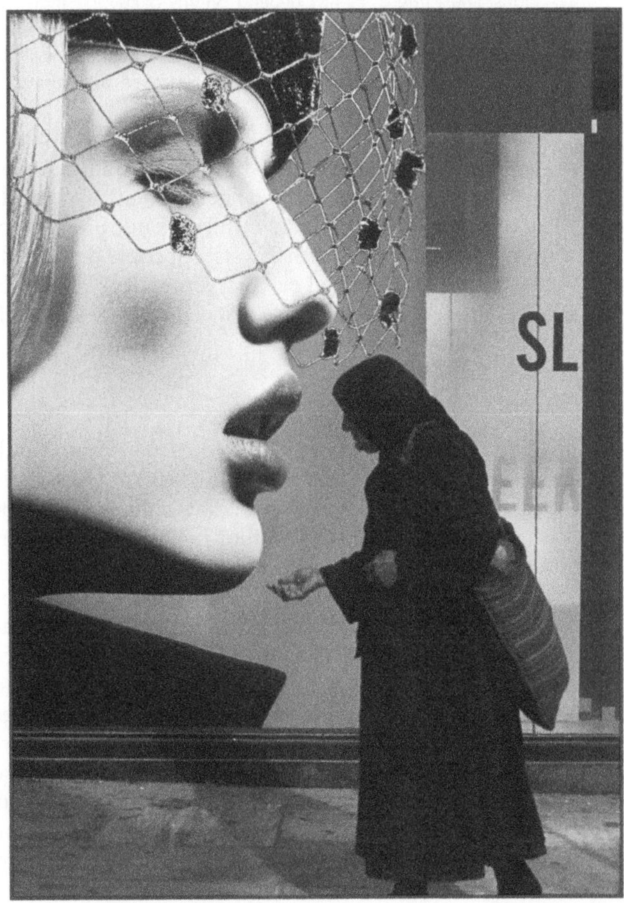

Social class is one of the most significant factors in social life. Fundamental to what we become, social class lays down our orientations to life. Can you see how this photo illustrates this point?

Box 8.1 **Down-to-Earth Sociology**

College Football as Social Structure

To gain a better idea of what social structure is, think of college football (see Dobriner 1969a). You probably know the various positions on the team: center, guards, tackles, ends, quarterback, running backs, and the like. Each is a status; that is, each is a social position. For each of the statuses shown on Figure 8.1, there is a role; that is, each of these positions has certain expectations attached to it. The center is expected to snap the ball, the quarterback to pass it, the guards to block, the tackles to tackle or block, the ends to receive passes, and so on. Those role expectations guide each player's actions; that is, the players try to do what their particular role requires.

Let's suppose that football is your favorite sport and you never miss a home game at your college. Let's also suppose that you graduate, get a great job, and move across the country. Five years later, you return to your campus for a nostalgic visit. The climax of your visit is the biggest football game of the season. When you get to the game, you might be surprised to see a different coach, but you are not surprised that each playing position is occupied by people you don't know, for all the players you knew have graduated, and their places have been filled by others.

This scenario mirrors social structure, the framework around which a group exists. In football, that framework consists of the coaching staff and the eleven playing positions. The game does not depend on any particular individual but, rather, on social statuses, the positions that the individuals occupy. When someone leaves a position, the game can go on because someone else takes over that position or status and plays the role. The game will continue even though not a single individual remains from one period of time to the next. Notre Dame's football team endures today even though Knute Rockne, the Gipper, and his teammates are long dead.

Even though you may not play football, you do live your life within a clearly established social structure. The statuses that you occupy and the roles you play were already in place before you were born. You take your particular positions in life, others do the same, and society goes about its business. Although the specifics change with time, the game—whether of life or offootball—goes on.

FIGURE 8.1 Team Positions (Statuses) in Football

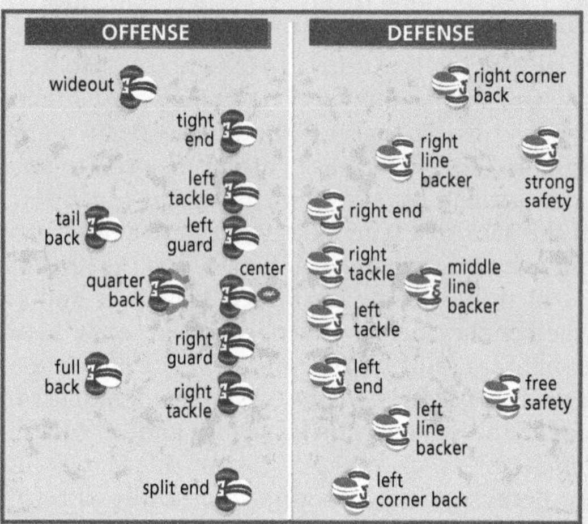

Large numbers of people who have similar amounts of income and education and who work at jobs that are roughly comparable in prestige make up a **social class.** It is hard to overemphasize this aspect of social structure, for our social class influences not only our behaviors but even our ideas and attitudes. We have this in common, then, with the street people described in the opening vignette: We both are influenced by our location in the social class structure. Theirs may be a considerably less privileged position, but it has no less influence on their lives. Social class is so significant that we shall spend an entire chapter on this topic.

Social Status

When you hear the word *status,* you are likely to think of prestige. These two words are welded together in people's minds. As you saw in the box on football, however, sociologists use **status** in a different way—to refer to the *position* that someone occupies. That position may carry a great deal of prestige, as in the case of a judge or an astronaut, or it may bring little prestige, as in the case of a convenience store clerk or a waitress at the local truck stop. The status may also be looked down on, as in the case of a streetcorner man, an ex-convict, or a thief.

All of us occupy several positions at the same time. You may simultaneously be a son or daughter, a worker, a date, and a student. Sociologists use the term **status set** to refer to all the statuses or positions that you occupy. Obviously your status set changes as your particular statuses change. For example, if you graduate from college and take a full-time job, get married, buy a home, have children, and so on, your status set changes to include the positions of worker, spouse, homeowner, and parent.

Like other aspects of social structure, statuses are part of our basic framework of living in society. The example I gave of students and teachers who come to class and do what others expect of them despite their particular circumstances and moods illustrates how statuses affect our actions—and those of the people around us. Our statuses—whether daughter or son, worker or date—serve as guides for our behavior.

Ascribed and Achieved Statuses An **ascribed status** is involuntary. You do not ask for it, nor can you choose it. At birth, you inherit ascribed statuses such as your race–ethnicity, sex, and the social class of your parents, as well as your statuses as female or male, daughter or son, niece or nephew.

Achieved statuses, in contrast, are voluntary. These you earn or accomplish. As a result of your efforts you become a student, a friend, a spouse, a lawyer, or a member of the clergy. Or, for lack of effort (or for efforts that others fail to appreciate), you become a school dropout, a former friend, an ex-spouse, a debarred lawyer, or a defrocked member of the clergy. In other words, achieved statuses can be either positive or negative; both college president and bank robber are achieved statuses.

Each status provides guidelines for how we are to act and feel. Like other aspects of social structure, statuses set limits on what we can and cannot do. Because social statuses are an essential part of the social structure, they are found in all human groups.

Status Symbols People who are pleased with their social status often want others to recognize their particular position. To elicit this recognition, they use **status symbols,** signs that identify a status. For example, people wear wedding rings to announce their marital status; uniforms, guns, and badges to proclaim that they are police officers (and not so subtly to let you know that their status gives them authority over you); and "backward" collars to declare that they are Lutheran ministers or Roman Catholic or Episcopal priests.

Some social statuses are negative and so, therefore, are their status symbols. The scarlet letter in Nathaniel Hawthorne's book by the same title is one example. Another is the CONVICTED DUI (Driving Under the Influence) bumper sticker that some U.S. courts require convicted drunk drivers to display if they wish to avoid a jail sentence.

Status symbols are part of our lives. *All* of us use them to announce our statuses to others and to help smooth our interactions in everyday life. Can you identify your own status symbols and what they communicate? For example, how does your clothing announce your statuses of sex, age, and college student?

Master Statuses A **master status** cuts across your other statuses. Some master statuses are ascribed. An example is your sex. Whatever you do, people perceive you as a male or as a female. If you are working your way through college by flipping burgers, people see you not only as a burger flipper and a student but also as a *male* or *female* burger flipper and a *male* or *female* college student. Other master statuses are race and age.

Some master statuses are achieved. If you become very, very wealthy (and it doesn't matter whether your wealth comes from a successful invention or from winning the lottery—it is still *achieved* as far as sociologists are concerned), your wealth is likely to become a master status. For example, people might say, "She is a very rich burger flipper"—or, more likely, "She's very rich, and she used to flip burgers!"

Similarly, people who become disfigured find, to their dismay, that their condition becomes a master status. For example, a person whose face is scarred from severe burns will be viewed through this unwelcome master status regardless of occupation or accomplishments. In the same way, people who are confined to wheelchairs can attest to how their handicap overrides all their other statuses and influences others' perceptions of everything they do.

Master statuses are those that overshadow our other statuses. Shown here is Stephen Hawking, who is severely disabled by Lou Gehrig's disease. For many, his *master status* is that of a person with disabilities. Because Hawking is one of the greatest physicists who has ever lived, however, his outstanding achievements have given him another *master status,* that of world-class physicist in the ranking of Einstein.

Although our statuses usually fit together fairly well, some people have a contradiction or mismatch between their statuses. This is known as **status inconsistency** (or discrepancy). A 14-year-old college student is an example. So is a 40-year-old married woman who is dating a 19-year-old college sophomore.

These examples reveal an essential aspect of social statuses: Like other components of social structure, they come with built-in *norms* (that is, expectations) that guide our behavior. When statuses mesh well, as they usually do, we know what to expect of people. This helps social interaction to unfold smoothly. Status inconsistency, however, upsets our expectations. In the preceding examples, how are you supposed to act? Are you supposed to treat the 14-year-old as you would a young teenager or as you would your college classmate? Do you react to the married woman as you would to the mother of your friend or as you would to a classmate's date?

Roles

All the world's a stage
And all the men and women merely players.
They have their exits and their entrances;
And one man in his time plays many parts . . .
(William Shakespeare, *As You Like It,* Act II, Scene 7)

Like Shakespeare, sociologists see roles as essential to social life. When you were born, **roles**—the behaviors, obligations, and privileges attached to a status—were already set up for you. Society was waiting with outstretched arms to teach you how it expected you to act as a boy or a girl. And whether you were born poor, rich, or somewhere in between, that, too, attached certain behaviors, obligations, and privileges to your statuses.

The difference between role and status is that you *occupy* a status, but you *play* a role (Linton 1936). For example, being a son or daughter is your status, but your expectations of receiving food and shelter from your parents—as well as their expectations that you show respect to them—are part of your role. Or, again, your status is student, but your role is to attend class, take notes, do homework, and take tests.

Roles are like a fence. They allow us a certain amount of freedom, but for most of us that freedom doesn't go very far. Suppose that a woman decides that she is not going to wear dresses—or a man that he will not wear suits and ties—regardless of what anyone says. In most situations, they'll stick to their decision. When a formal occasion comes along, however, such as a family wedding or a funeral, they are likely to cave in to norms that they find overwhelming. Almost all of us follow the guidelines for what is "appropriate" for our roles. Few of us are bothered by such constraints, for our socialization is so thorough that we usually want to do what our roles indicate is appropriate.

The sociological significance of roles is that they lay out what is expected of people. As individuals throughout society perform their roles, those roles mesh together to form this thing called society. As Shakespeare put it, people's roles provide "their exits and their entrances" on the stage of life. In short, roles are remarkably effective at keeping people in line—telling them when they should "enter" and when they should "exit," as well as what to do in between.

Groups

A **group** consists of people who regularly interact with one another. Ordinarily, the members of a group share similar values, norms, and expectations. Just as social class, statuses, and roles influence our actions, so, too, the groups to which we belong are powerful forces in our lives. In fact, *to belong to a group is to yield to others the right to make certain decisions about our behavior.* If we belong to a group, we assume an obligation to act according to the expectations of other members of that group.

Social Institutions

At first glance, the term *social institution* may seem cold and abstract—with little relevance to your life. In fact, however, **social institutions**—the ways that each society develops to meet its basic needs—vitally affect your life. By weaving the fabric of society, social institutions shape our behavior. They even color our thoughts. How can this be? Look at what social institutions are: the family, religion, education, economics, medicine, politics, law, science, the military, and the mass media.

In industrialized societies, social institutions tend to be more formal; in tribal societies, they are more informal. Education in industrialized societies, for example, is highly structured, while in tribal societies it usually consists of children informally learning what adults do. Figure 8.2 on the next page summarizes the basic social institutions. Note that each institution has its own groups, statuses, values, and norms. Social institutions are so significant that Part IV of this book focuses on them.

FIGURE 8.2 Social Institutions in Industrial and Postindustrial Societies

Social Institution	Basic Needs	Some Groups or Organizations	Some Statuses	Some Values	Some Norms
Family	Regulate reproduction, socialize and protect children	Relatives, kinship groups	Daughter, son, father, mother, brother, sister, aunt, uncle, grandparent	Sexual fidelity, providing for your family, keeping a clean house, respect for parents	Have only as many children as you can afford, be faithful to your spouse
Religion	Concerns about life after death, the meaning of suffering and loss; desire to connect with the Creator	Congregation, synagogue, mosque, denomination, charity; clergy associations	Priest, minister, rabbi, imam, worshipper, teacher, disciple, missionary, prophet, convert	Reading and adhering to holy texts such as the Bible, the Torah, and the Koran; honoring God	Attend worship services, contribute money, follow the teachings
Education	Transmit knowledge and skills across generations	School, college, student senate, sports team, PTA, teachers' union	Teacher, student, dean, principal, football player, cheerleader	Academic honesty, good grades, being "cool"	Do homework, prepare lectures, don't snitch on classmates
Economy	Produce and distribute goods and services	Credit unions, banks, credit card companies, buying clubs	Worker, boss, buyer, seller, creditor, debtor, advertiser	Making money, paying bills on time, producing efficiently	Maximize profits, "the customer is always right," work hard
Medicine	Heal the sick and injured, care for the dying	AMA, hospitals, pharmacies, insurance companies, HMOs	Doctor, nurse, patient, pharmacist, medical insurer	Hippocratic oath, staying in good health, following doctor's orders	Don't exploit patients, give best medical care available
Politics	Allocate power, determine authority, prevent chaos	Political party, congress, parliament, monarchy	President, senator, lobbyist, voter, candidate, spin doctor	Majority rule, the right to vote as a privilege and a sacred trust	One vote per person, be informed about candidates
Law	Maintain social order	Police, courts, prisons	Judge, police officer, lawyer, defendant, prison guard	Trial by one's peers, innocence until proven guilty	Give true testimony, follow the rules of evidence
Science	Master the environment	Local, state, regional, national, and international associations	Scientist, researcher, technician, administrator, journal editor	Unbiased research, open dissemination of research findings, originality	Follow scientific method, be objective, disclose findings, don't plagiarize
Military	Protection from enemies, support of national interests	Army, navy, air force, marines, coast guard, national guard	Soldier, recruit, enlisted person, officer, veteran, prisoner, spy	To die for one's country is an honor, obedience unto death	Follow orders, be ready to go to war, sacrifice for your buddies
Mass Media (an emerging institution)	Disseminate information, mold public opinion, report events	TV networks, radio stations, publishers, association of bloggers	Journalist, newscaster, author, editor, publisher, blogger	Timeliness, accuracy, large audiences, freedom of the press	Be accurate, fair, timely, and profitable

Societies—and Their Transformation

How did our society develop? You know that it didn't spring full-blown on the human scene. To better understand this framework that surrounds us, that sets the stage for our experiences in life, let's trace the evolution of societies. Look at Figure 8.3 on page 180, which illustrates how changes in technology brought changes to **society**—people who share a culture and a territory. As we review these sweeping changes, picture yourself as a member of each society. Consider how your life—even your thoughts and values—would be different in each society.

FIGURE 8.3 The Social Transformations of Society

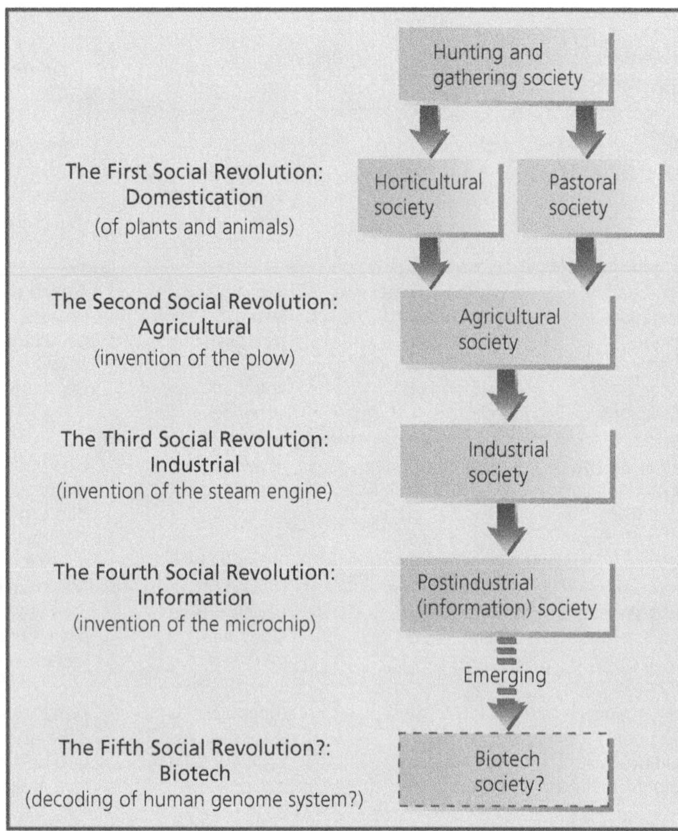

Source: By the author

Hunting and Gathering Societies

The members of **hunting and gathering societies** have few social divisions and little inequality. As the name implies, these groups depend on hunting animals and gathering plants for their survival. In some groups, the men do the hunting, and the women the gathering. In others, both men and women (and children) gather plants, the men hunt large animals, and both men and women hunt small animals. Although these groups give greater prestige to the men hunters, who supply the major source of meat, the women gatherers contribute more food to the group, perhaps even four-fifths of their total food supply (Bernard 1992).

Because a region cannot support a large number of people who hunt animals and gather plants (group members do not plant—they only gather what is already there), hunting and gathering societies are small. They usually consist of only twenty-five to forty people. These groups are nomadic. As their food supply dwindles in one area, they move to another location. Because of disease, drought, and pestilence, children have only about a fifty-fifty chance of surviving to adulthood (Lenski and Lenski 1987).

Of all societies, hunters and gatherers are the most egalitarian. Because what they hunt and gather is perishable, the people accumulate few personal possessions. Consequently, no one becomes wealthier than anyone else. There are no rulers, and most decisions are arrived at through discussion.

The simplest forms of societies are called *hunting and gathering societies*. Members of these societies have adapted well to their environments, and they have more leisure than the members of other societies. Shown here are Inuits in the tundra of Greenland.

Pastoral and Horticultural Societies About ten thousand years ago, some groups found that they could tame and breed some of the animals they hunted—primarily goats, sheep, cattle, and camels. Others discovered that they could cultivate plants. As a result, hunting and gathering societies branched into two directions, each with different means of acquiring food.

The key to understanding the first branching is the word *pasture;* **pastoral** (or herding) **societies** are based on the *pasturing of animals.* Pastoral societies developed in regions where low rainfall made it impractical to build life around growing crops. Groups that took this turn remained nomadic, for they followed their animals to fresh pasture. The key to understanding the second branching is the word *horticulture,* or plant cultivation. **Horticultural** (or gardening) **societies** are based on the *cultivation of plants by the use of hand tools.* Because they no longer had to abandon an area as the food supply gave out, these groups developed permanent settlements.

As shown in Figure 8.4, the domestication of animals and plants transformed society, ushering in the *first social revolution.* Groups grew larger because the more dependable food supply supported more people. Because it was no longer necessary for everyone to work to provide food, a *division of labor* emerged. Some people began to make jewelry, others tools, others weapons, and so on. This led to a surplus of objects, which, in turn, stimulated trade. With trading, groups began to accumulate objects they prized, such as gold, jewelry, and utensils.

These changes set the stage for *social inequality.* Some families (or clans) acquired more goods than others. With the possession of animals, pastures, croplands, jewelry, and other material goods, groups began to fight. War, in turn, opened the door to slavery, for people found it convenient to let captives do their drudge work. As individuals passed their possessions on to their descendants, wealth grew more concentrated. So did power, and for the first time, some individuals became chiefs.

Agricultural Societies When the plow was invented about five or six thousand years ago, social life once again changed forever. Compared with hoes and digging sticks, the use of animals to pull plows was immensely efficient. The larger food surplus allowed even more people to engage in activities other than farming. In this new **agricultural society,** people developed cities and what is popularly known as "culture," such as philosophy, art, music, literature, and architecture. Accompanied by the inventions of the wheel, writing, and numbers, the changes were so profound that this period is sometimes referred to as "the dawn of civilization."

The social inequality of pastoral and horticultural societies was only a forerunner of what was to come. When some people managed to gain control of the growing surplus of resources, *inequality became a fundamental feature of life in society.* To protect their expanding privileges and power, this elite surrounded itself with armed men. This small group even levied taxes on others, who now had become their "subjects." As conflict theorists point out, this concentration of resources and power—along with the oppression of people not in power—was the forerunner of the state.

Industrial Societies The *third* social invention also turned society upside down. The **Industrial Revolution** began in Great Britain in 1765 when the steam engine was first used to run machinery. Before this, a few machines (such as windmills and water wheels) had been used to harness nature, but most machines depended on human and animal power. The new form of production in the **industrial society** brought even greater surplus—and with it another leap in social inequality. Some early industrialists accumulated such wealth that their riches outran the imagination of royalty. The masses, in contrast, were thrown off the land as feudal society came to an end. Homeless, they moved to the cities, where they faced the choice of stealing, starving, or working for wages barely sufficient to sustain life (the equivalent of a loaf of bread for a day's work).

Through a bitter struggle too detailed for us to review here, workers won their fight for better working conditions, reversing the earlier pattern of growing inequality. Home ownership became common, as did the ownership of automobiles and an incredible variety of consumer goods. Today's typical worker in industrial society enjoys a high standard of living in terms of health care, longevity, material possessions, and access to libraries and education. On an even broader scale, with industrialization came the abolition of slavery, the shift from monarchies to more representative political systems, and the rights to a jury trial, to vote, and to travel. A recent extension of these equalities is the right to set up your own Internet blog, where you can bemoan life in your school or criticize the president.

FIGURE 8.4 Consequences of Animal Domestication and Plant Cultivation

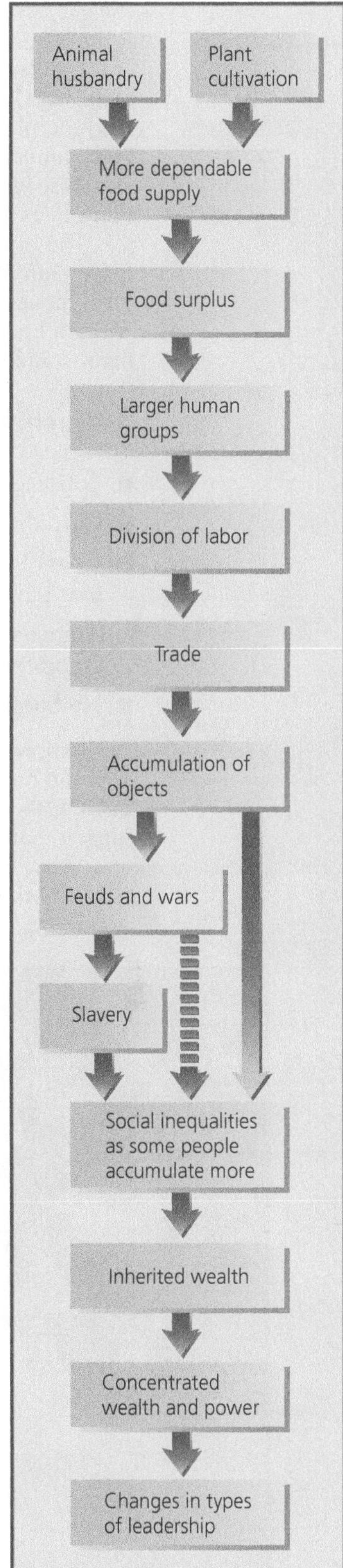

Source: By the author

Postindustrial (Information) Societies If you were to choose one word that characterizes our society, what would it be? Of the many candidates, the word *change* would have to rank high among them. The primary source of the sweeping changes that are transforming our lives is the technology centering on the microchip. The change is so vast that sociologists say that a new type of society has emerged. They call it the **postindustrial** (or **information**) **society.**

Unlike the industrial society, the hallmark of this new type of society is not raw materials and manufacturing. Rather, its basic component is *information.* Teachers pass on knowledge to students, while lawyers, physicians, bankers, pilots, and interior decorators sell their specialized knowledge of law, the body, money, aerodynamics, and color schemes to clients. Unlike the factory workers of an industrial society, these individuals don't *produce* anything. Rather, they transmit or use information to provide services that others are willing to pay for.

The United States was in the forefront of this *fourth social revolution.* It was the first country to have more than 50 percent of its workforce in service industries such as education, health, research, government, counseling, banking, investments, insurance, sales, law, and mass media. Australia, New Zealand, western Europe, and Japan soon followed. This trend away from manufacturing and toward selling information and services shows no sign of letting up.

Biotech Societies: Is a New Type of Society Emerging?

- Tobacco that fights cancer. ("Yes, smoke your way to health!")
- Corn that fights herpes and is a contraceptive. ("Corn flakes in the morning—and safe sex all day!")
- Goats whose milk contains spider silk (to make fishing lines and body armor) ("Got milk? The best bulletproofing.")
- Animals that are part human so they produce medicines for humans. ("Ah, those liver secretions. Good for what ails you.")
- No-Sneeze kitties—hypoallergenic cats at $4,000 each. (You can write your own jingle for this one.)

I know that such products sound like science fiction, but we *already* have the goats that make spider silk, and human genes have been inserted into animals so that they produce medicine (Elias 2001; Kristoff 2002; Osborne 2002). The no-sneeze cats are for sale—and there is a waiting list (Rosenthal 2006). Some suggest that the changes in which we are immersed are so extensive that we are entering another new type of society. In this new **biotech society,** the economy will center on applying and altering genetic structures—both plant and animal—to produce food, medicine, and materials.

Some social changes come without a whimper, others only violently. In this 1934 photo, a striking dock worker flees San Francisco police officers. The right to strike came with struggle—and loss of life.

If there is a new society, when did it begin? There are no firm edges to new societies, for each new one overlaps the one it is replacing. The opening to the biotech society could have been 1953, when Francis Crick and James Watson identified the double-helix structure of DNA. Or perhaps historians will trace the date to the decoding of the human genome in 2001.

Whether the changes that are swirling around us are part of a new type of society is not the main point. The larger group called society always profoundly affects people's thinking and behavior. *The sociological significance of these changes, then, is that as society is transformed, we will be swept along with it. The transformation will change even the ways we think about the self and life.*

Projecting a new type of society so soon after the arrival of the information society is risky. The wedding of genetics and economics could turn out to be simply another aspect of our information society—or we really may have just stepped into a new type of society. With cloning and bioengineering, we could even see changes in the human species. The Sociology and the New Technology box on the next page examines implications of cloning.

In Sum: Our society sets boundaries around our lives. By laying out a framework of statuses, roles, groups, and social institutions, society establishes the values and beliefs that prevail. It also determines the type and extent of social inequality. These factors, in turn, set the stage for relationships between men and women, racial–ethnic groups, the young and the elderly, the rich and the poor, and so on.

It is difficult to overstate the sociological principle that the type of society in which we live is the fundamental reason why we become who we are—why we feel about things the way we do and even why we think our particular thoughts. On the obvious level, if you lived in a hunting and gathering society, you would not be listening to your favorite music, watching TV programs, or playing video games. On a deeper level, you would not feel the same about life, have the same beliefs, or hold your particular aspirations for the future.

What Holds Society Together?

With its many, often conflicting, groups and its extensive social change, how does society manage to hold together? Let's examine two answers that sociologists have proposed.

Mechanical and Organic Solidarity Sociologist Emile Durkheim (1893/1933) found the key to **social integration**—the degree to which members of a society are united by shared values and other social bonds—in what he called **mechanical solidarity.** By this term, Durkheim meant that people who perform similar tasks develop a shared consciousness. Think of a farming community in which everyone is involved in planting, cultivating, and harvesting. Members of this group have so much in common that they know how almost everyone else in the community feels about life. Societies with mechanical solidarity tolerate little diversity in thinking and attitudes, for their unity depends on similar thinking.

As societies get larger, their **division of labor** (how they divide up work) becomes more specialized. Some people mine gold, others sell it, while still others turn it into jewelry. This division of labor makes people depend on one another—for the work of each person contributes to the well-being of the whole group.

Durkheim called this new form of solidarity based on interdependence **organic solidarity.** To see why he used this term, think about how you depend on your teacher to guide you through this introductory course in sociology. At the same time, your teacher needs you and other students in order to have a job. You and

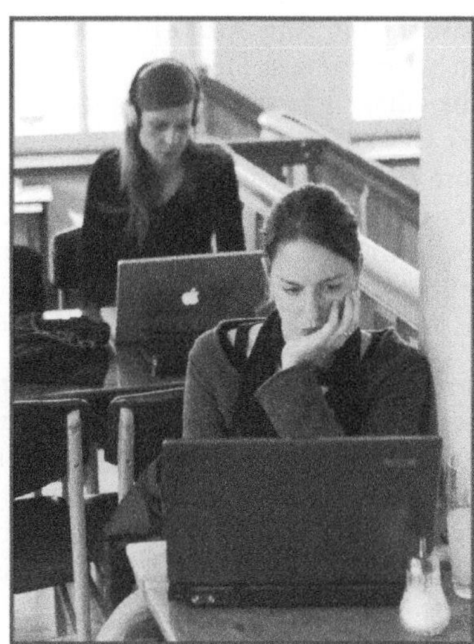

The warm, more intimate relationships of *Gemeinschaft* society are apparent in the photo taken during *Oktoberfest* in Munich, Germany. The more impersonal relationships of *Gesellschaft* society are evident in the Internet cafe, where customers are ignoring one another.

Box 8.2 Sociology and the New Technology

"So, You Want to Be Yourself?" Cloning in the Coming Biotech Society

No type of society ends abruptly. The edges are fuzzy, and the new one overlaps the old. As the information society matures, it looks as though it is being overtaken by a biotech society. Let's try to peer over the edge of our current society to glimpse the one that may be arriving. What will life be like? There are many issues we could examine, but since space is limited, let's consider just one: cloning.

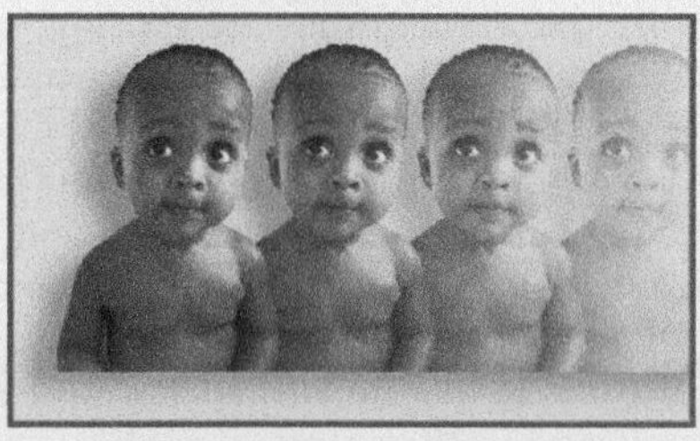

Consider this scenario:

> Your four-year-old daughter has drowned, and you can't get over your sorrow. You go to the regional cloning clinic, where you have stored DNA from all members of your family. You pay the standard fee, and the director hires a surrogate mother to bring your daughter back as a newborn.

Will cloning humans become a reality? Since human embryos already have been cloned, it seems inevitable that some group somewhere will complete the process. If cloning humans becomes routine—well, consider these scenarios:

> Suppose that a couple can't have children. Testing shows that the husband is sterile. The couple talk about their dilemma, and the wife agrees to have her husband's genetic material implanted into one of her eggs. Would this woman, in effect, be rearing her husband as a little boy?

Or suppose that you love your mother dearly, and she is dying. With her permission, you decide to clone her. Who is the clone? Would you be rearing your own mother?

What if a woman gave birth to her own clone? Would the clone be her daughter or her sister?

When genetic duplicates appear, the questions of what humans are, what their relationship to their "parents" is, and indeed what "parents" and children" are, will be brought up at every kitchen table.

For Your Consideration

As these scenarios show, the issue of cloning provokes profound questions. Perhaps the most weighty concerns the future of society. Let's suppose that mass cloning becomes possible.

Many people object that cloning is immoral, but some will argue the opposite. They will ask why we should leave human reproduction to people who have inferior traits—genetic diseases, low IQs, perhaps even the propensity for crime and violence. They will suggest that we select people with the finer characteristics—high creative ability, high intelligence, compassion, and a propensity for peace.

Let's assume that geneticists have traced the characteristics just mentioned to specific genes—along with the ability to appreciate and create beautiful poetry, music, and architecture; to excel in mathematics, science, and other intellectual pursuits; and to be successful in love. Do you think that it should be our moral obligation to populate society with people like this? To try to build a society that is better for all—one without terrorism, war, violence, and greed? Could this perhaps even be our evolutionary destiny?

Source: Based on Kaebnick 2000; McGee 2000; Bjerklie et al. 2001; Davis 2001; Weiss 2004; Regalado 2005.

your teacher are *like organs in the same body.* (The "body" in this case is the college or university.) Although each of you performs different tasks, you depend on one another. This creates a form of unity.

Gemeinschaft and Gesellschaft Ferdinand Tönnies (1887/1988) also analyzed this fundamental shift in relationships. He used the term ***Gemeinschaft*** (Guh-MINE-shoft), or "intimate community," to describe village life, the type of society in which everyone knows everyone else. He noted that in the society that was emerging, the personal ties, kinship connections, and lifelong friendships that marked village life were being crowded out by short-term relationships, individual accomplishments, and self-interest. Tönnies called this new type of society ***Gesellschaft*** (Guh-ZELL-shoft), or "impersonal association." He did not mean that we no longer have intimate ties to family and friends, but, rather, that our lives no longer center on them. Few of us take jobs in a family business, for example, and contracts replace handshakes. Much of our time is spent with strangers and short-term acquaintances.

In Sum: Whether the terms are *Gemeinschaft* and *Gesellschaft* or *mechanical solidarity* and *organic solidarity,* they indicate that as societies change, so do people's orientations to life. *The sociological point is that social structure sets the context for what we do, feel, and think and ultimately, then, for the kind of people we become.* As you read the Cultural Diversity box on the next page, which describes one of the few remaining Gemeinschaft societies in the United States, think of how fundamentally different you would be had you been reared in an Amish family.

Box 8.3 Cultural Diversity in the United States

The Amish: *Gemeinschaft* Community in a *Gesellschaft* Society

Ferdinand Tönnies' term, *Gesellschaft*, certainly applies to the United States. Impersonal associations pervade our everyday life. Local, state, and federal governments regulate many of our activities. Corporations hire and fire people not on the basis of personal relationships, but on the basis of the bottom line. And, perhaps even more significantly, millions of Americans do not even know their neighbors.

Within the United States, a handful of small communities exhibits characteristics distinct from those of the mainstream society. One such community is the Old Order Amish, followers of a sect that broke away from the Swiss-German Mennonite church in the 1600s and settled in Pennsylvania around 1727. Today, about 150,000 Old Order Amish live in the United States. About 75 percent live in just three states: Pennsylvania, Ohio, and Indiana. The largest concentration, about 22,000, resides in Lancaster County, Pennsylvania. The Amish, who believe that birth control is wrong, have doubled in population in just the past two decades.

Because Amish farmers use horses instead of tractors, most of their farms are one hundred acres or less. To the 5 million tourists who pass through Lancaster County each year, the rolling green pastures, white farmhouses, simple barns, horse-drawn buggies, and clotheslines hung with somber-colored garments convey a sense of peace and innocence reminiscent of another era. Although just sixty-five miles from Philadelphia, "Amish country" is a world away.

Amish life is based on separation from the world—an idea taken from Christ's Sermon on the Mount—and obedience to the church's teachings and leaders. This rejection of worldly concerns, writes sociologist Donald Kraybill in *The Riddle of Amish Culture* (2002), "provides the foundation of such Amish values as humility, faithfulness, thrift, tradition, communal goals, joy of work, a slow-paced life, and trust in divine providence."

The *Gemeinschaft* of village life that has been largely lost to industrialization remains a vibrant part of Amish life. The Amish make their decisions in weekly meetings, where, by consensus, they follow a set of rules, or *Ordnung*, to guide their behavior. Religion and discipline are the glue that holds the Amish together. Brotherly love and the welfare of the community are paramount values. In times of birth, sickness, and death, neighbors pitch in with the chores. In these ways, they maintain the bonds of intimate community.

The Amish are bound by other ties, including language (a dialect of German known as Pennsylvania Dutch), plain clothing—often black, whose style has remained unchanged for almost 300 years—and church-sponsored schools. Nearly all Amish marry, and divorce is forbidden. The family is a vital ingredient in Amish life; all major events take place in the home, including weddings, births, funerals, and church services. Amish children attend church schools, but only until the age of 13. (In 1972, the Supreme Court ruled that Amish parents had the right to take their children out of school after the eighth grade.) To go to school beyond the eighth grade would expose them to values and "worldly concerns" that would drive a wedge between the children and their community. The Amish believe that violence is bad, even personal self-defense, and they register as conscientious objectors during times of war. They pay no Social Security, and they receive no government benefits.

The Amish cannot resist all change, of course. Instead, they try to adapt to change in ways that will least disrupt their core values. Because urban sprawl has driven up the price of farmland, about half of Amish men work at jobs other than farming, most in farm-related businesses or in woodcrafts. They go to great lengths to avoid leaving the home. The Amish believe that when a husband works away from home, all aspects of life change, from the marital relationship to the care of the children—certainly an astute sociological insight. They also believe that if a man receives a paycheck, he will think that his work is of more value than his wife's. For the Amish, intimate, or *Gemeinschaft*, society is essential for maintaining their way of life.

Perhaps this is the most poignant illustration of how the Amish approach to life differs from that of the dominant culture: When in 2006 a non-Amish man shot several Amish girls at a one-room school, the Amish community established charitable funds not only for the families of the dead children but also for the family of the killer.

Sources: Hostetler 1980; Aeppel 1996; Kephart and Zellner 2001; Kraybill 2002; Dawley 2003; Johnson-Weiner 2007.

■ The Microsociological Perspective: Social Interaction in Everyday Life

Where macrosociology stresses the broad features of society, microsociology focuses on a narrower slice of social life. Microsociologists examine *face-to-face interaction*—what people do when they are in one another's presence. This is the primary focus of symbolic interactionists, who are especially interested in the symbols that people use. They want to know how people look at things and how this, in turn, affects their behavior and orientations to life. Of the many areas of social life they study, let's look at stereotypes, personal space, eye contact, and body language.

Stereotypes in Everyday Life

You are familiar with how strong first impressions are and the way they set the tone for interaction. When you first meet someone, you cannot help but notice certain features, especially the person's sex, race–ethnicity, age, and clothing. Despite your best intentions, your assumptions about these characteristics shape your first impressions. They also affect how you act toward that person—and, in turn, how that person acts toward you. These fascinating aspects of our social interaction are discussed in the Down-to-Earth Sociology box on the next page.

Personal Space

We all surround ourselves with a "personal bubble" that we go to great lengths to protect. We open the bubble to intimates—to our friends, children, parents, and so on—but we're careful to keep most people out of this space. In a crowded hallway between classes, we might walk with our books clasped in front of us (a strategy often chosen by females). When we stand in line, we make certain there is enough space so that we don't touch the person in front of us and aren't touched by the person behind us.

The amount of space that people prefer varies from one culture to another. South Americans, for example, like to be closer when they speak to others than do people reared in the United States. Anthropologist Edward Hall (1959; Hall and Hall 2007) recounts a conversation with a man from South America who had attended one of his lectures.

> He came to the front of the class at the end of the lecture. . . . We started out facing each other, and as he talked I became dimly aware that he was standing a little too close and that I was beginning to back up. Fortunately I was able to suppress my first impulse and remain stationary because there was nothing to communicate aggression in his behavior except the conversational distance. . . .
>
> By experimenting I was able to observe that as I moved away slightly, there was an associated shift in the pattern of interaction. He had more trouble expressing himself. If I shifted to where I felt comfortable (about twenty-one inches), he looked somewhat puzzled and hurt, almost as though he were saying, "Why is he acting that way? Here I am doing everything I can to talk to him in a friendly manner and he suddenly withdraws. Have I done anything wrong? Said something I shouldn't?" Having ascertained that distance had a direct effect on his conversation, I stood my ground, letting him set the distance.

After Hall (1969; Hall and Hall 2007) analyzed situations like this, he observed that North Americans use four different "distance zones."

1. *Intimate distance.* This is the zone that the South American unwittingly invaded. It extends to about 18 inches from our bodies. We reserve this space for comforting, protecting, hugging, intimate touching, and lovemaking.

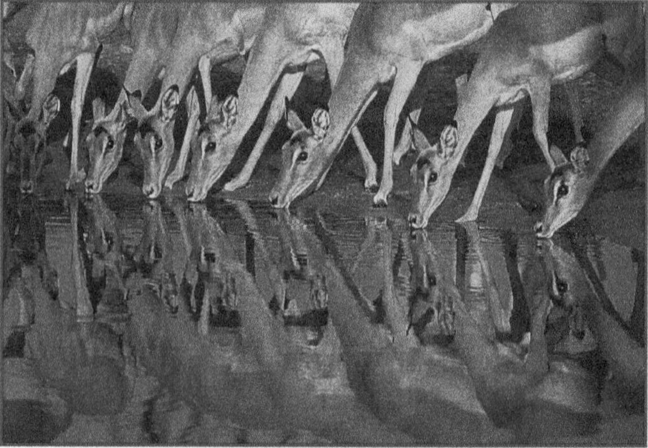

Social space is one of the many aspects of social life studied by sociologists who have a microsociological focus. What do you see in common in these two photos?

Box 8.4 Down-to-Earth Sociology

Beauty May Be Only Skin Deep, But Its Effects Go on Forever

Mark Snyder, a psychologist, wondered whether **stereotypes**—our assumptions of what people are like—might be self-fulfilling. He came up with an ingenious way to test this idea. He (1993) gave college men a Polaroid snapshot of a woman (supposedly taken just moments before) and told them that he would introduce them to her after they talked with her on the telephone. Actually, the photographs—showing either a pretty or a homely woman—had been prepared before the experiment began. The photo was not of the woman the men would talk to.

Stereotypes came into play immediately. As Snyder gave each man the photograph, he asked him what he thought the woman would be like. The men who saw the photograph of the attractive woman said that they expected to meet a poised, humorous, outgoing woman. The men who had been given a photo of the unattractive woman described her as awkward, serious, and unsociable.

The men's stereotypes influenced the way they spoke to the women on the telephone, who did not know about the photographs. The men who had seen the photograph of a pretty woman were warm, friendly, and humorous. This, in turn, affected the women they spoke to, for they responded in a warm, friendly, outgoing manner. And the men who had seen the photograph of a homely woman? On the phone, they were cold, reserved, and humorless, and the women they spoke to became cool, reserved, and humorless. Keep in mind that the women did not know that their looks had been evaluated—and that the photographs were not even of them. In short, stereotypes tend to produce behaviors that match the stereotype. This principle is illustrated in Figure 8.5.

Although beauty might be only skin deep, its consequences permeate our lives (Katz 2007). Not only does beauty bestow an advantage in everyday interaction, but people who are physically attractive are also likely to make more money. Researchers in both Holland and the United States found that advertising firms with better-looking executives have higher revenues (Bosman et al. 1997; Pfann et al. 2000). The reason? The researchers suggest that people are more willing to associate with individuals whom they perceive as good-looking.

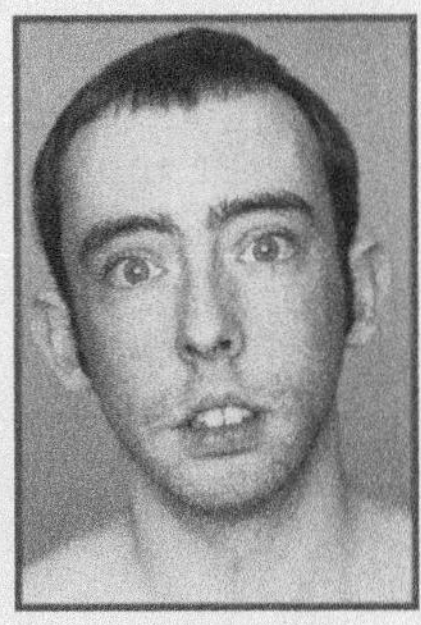

Based on the experiment summarized here, how do you think women would modify their interactions if they were to meet the two men?

For Your Consideration

Stereotypes have no single, inevitable effect, but they do affect how we react to one another.

Instead of beauty, consider gender and race–ethnicity. How do they affect those who do the stereotyping and those who are stereotyped?

FIGURE 8.5 How Self-Fulfilling Stereotypes Work

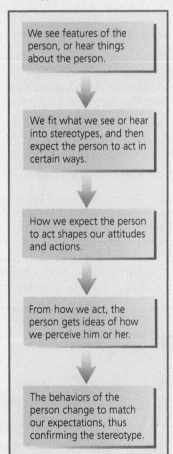

We see features of the person, or hear things about the person.

↓

We fit what we see or hear into stereotypes, and then expect the person to act in certain ways.

↓

How we expect the person to act shapes our attitudes and actions.

↓

From how we act, the person gets ideas of how we perceive him or her.

↓

The behaviors of the person change to match our expectations, thus confirming the stereotype.

2. *Personal distance.* This zone extends from 18 inches to 4 feet. We reserve it for friends and acquaintances and ordinary conversations. This is the zone in which Hall would have preferred speaking with the South American.
3. *Social distance.* This zone, extending out from us about 4 to 12 feet, marks impersonal or formal relationships. We use this zone for such things as job interviews.
4. *Public distance.* This zone, extending beyond 12 feet, marks even more formal relationships. It is used to separate dignitaries and public speakers from the general public.

Eye Contact

One way that we protect our personal bubble is by controlling eye contact. Letting someone gaze into our eyes—unless the person is our eye doctor—can be taken as a sign that we are attracted to that person and can even be taken as an invitation to intimacy. Wanting to become "the friendliest store in town," a chain of supermarkets in Illinois ordered its checkout clerks to make direct eye contact with each customer. Female clerks complained that male customers were taking their eye contact the wrong way, as an invitation to intimacy. Management said they were exaggerating. The clerks' reply was, "We know the kind of looks we're getting back from men," and they refused to make direct eye contact with them.

Applied Body Language

While we are still little children, we learn to interpret **body language**, the ways people use their bodies to give messages to others. This skill in correctly interpreting facial expressions, posture, and gestures is essential for getting us through everyday life. Without it—as is the case for people who have Asperger's syndrome—we wouldn't know how to react to other people. It would even be difficult to know whether someone were serious or joking. This common and essential skill for traversing everyday life is now becoming one of the government's tools in its fight against terrorism. Because many of our body messages lie beneath our consciousness, airport personnel and interrogators are being trained to look for telltale facial signs—from a quick downturn of the mouth to rapid blinking—that might indicate nervousness or lying (Davis et al. 2002).

This is an interesting twist for an area of sociology that had been entirely theoretical. Let's now turn to dramaturgy, a special area of symbolic interactionism.

Dramaturgy: The Presentation of Self in Everyday Life

> It was their big day, two years in the making. Jennifer Mackey wore a white wedding gown adorned with an 11-foot train and 24,000 seed pearls that she and her mother had sewn onto the dress. Next to her at the altar in Lexington, Kentucky, stood her intended, Jeffrey Degler, in black tie. They said their vows, then turned to gaze for a moment at the four hundred guests.
>
> That's when groomsman Daniel Mackey collapsed. As the shocked organist struggled to play Mendelssohn's "Wedding March," Mr. Mackey's unconscious body was dragged away, his feet striking—loudly—every step of the altar stairs.
>
> "I couldn't believe he would die at my wedding," the bride said. (Hughes 1990)

Sociologist Erving Goffman (1922–1982) added a new twist to microsociology when he recast the artistic term **dramaturgy** (or dramaturgical analysis) into a sociological term. By this term, Goffman meant that social life is like a drama or a stage play: Birth ushers us onto the stage of everyday life, and our socialization consists of learning to perform on that stage. The self that we studied in the previous chapter lies at the center of our performances. We have ideas of how we want others to think of us, and we use our roles in everyday life to communicate those ideas. Goffman called these efforts to manage the impressions that others receive of us **impression management.**

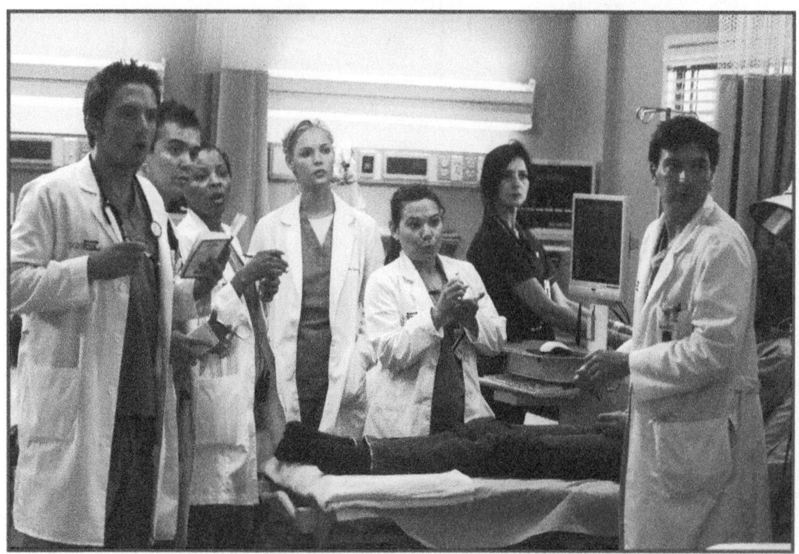

In *dramaturgy*, a specialty within sociology, social life is viewed as similar to the theater. In our everyday lives, we all are actors like those in this cast of *Grey's Anatomy*. We, too, perform roles, use props, and deliver lines to fellow actors—who, in turn, do the same.

Stages Everyday life, said Goffman, involves playing our assigned roles. We have *front stages* on which to perform them, as did Jennifer and Jeffrey. (By the way, Daniel Mackey didn't really die—he had just fainted.) But we don't have to look at weddings to find front stages. Everyday life is filled with them. Where your teacher lectures is a front stage. And if you make an announcement at a meal, you are using a front stage. In fact, you spend most of your time on front stages, for a front stage is wherever you deliver your lines. We also have *back stages,* places where we can retreat and let our hair down. When you close the bathroom or bedroom door for privacy, for example, you are entering a back stage.

Role Performance, Conflict, and Strain Everyday life brings with it many roles. As discussed earlier, the same person may be a student, a teenager, a shopper, a worker, and a date, as well as a daughter or a son. Although a role lays down the basic outline for a performance, it also allows a great deal of flexibility. The particular emphasis or interpretation that we give a role, our "style," is known as **role performance.** Consider your role as son or daughter. You may play the role of ideal daughter or son—being respectful, coming home at the hours your parents set, and so forth. Or this description may not even come close to your particular role performance.

Ordinarily, our statuses are sufficiently separated that we find minimal conflict between them. Occasionally, however, what is expected of us in one status (our role) is incompatible with what is expected of us in another status. This problem, known as **role conflict,** is illustrated in Figure 8.6, in which family, friendship, student, and work roles come crashing together. Usually, however, we manage to avoid role conflict by segregating our statuses, although doing so can require an intense juggling act.

Sometimes the *same* status contains incompatible roles, a conflict known as **role strain.** Suppose that you are exceptionally well prepared for a particular class assignment. Although the instructor asks an unusually difficult question, you find yourself knowing the answer when no one else does. If you want to raise your hand, yet don't want to make your fellow students look bad, you will experience role strain. As illustrated in Figure 8.6, the difference between role conflict and role strain is that role conflict is conflict *between roles,* while role strain is conflict *within* a role.

Teamwork Being a good role player brings positive recognition from others, something we all covet. To accomplish this, we often use **teamwork**—two or more people working together to make certain that a performance goes off as planned. When a performance doesn't come off quite right, however, it may require **face-saving behavior.** We may, for example, ignore flaws in someone's performance, which Goffman defines as *tact.*

FIGURE 8.6 Role Strain and Role Conflict

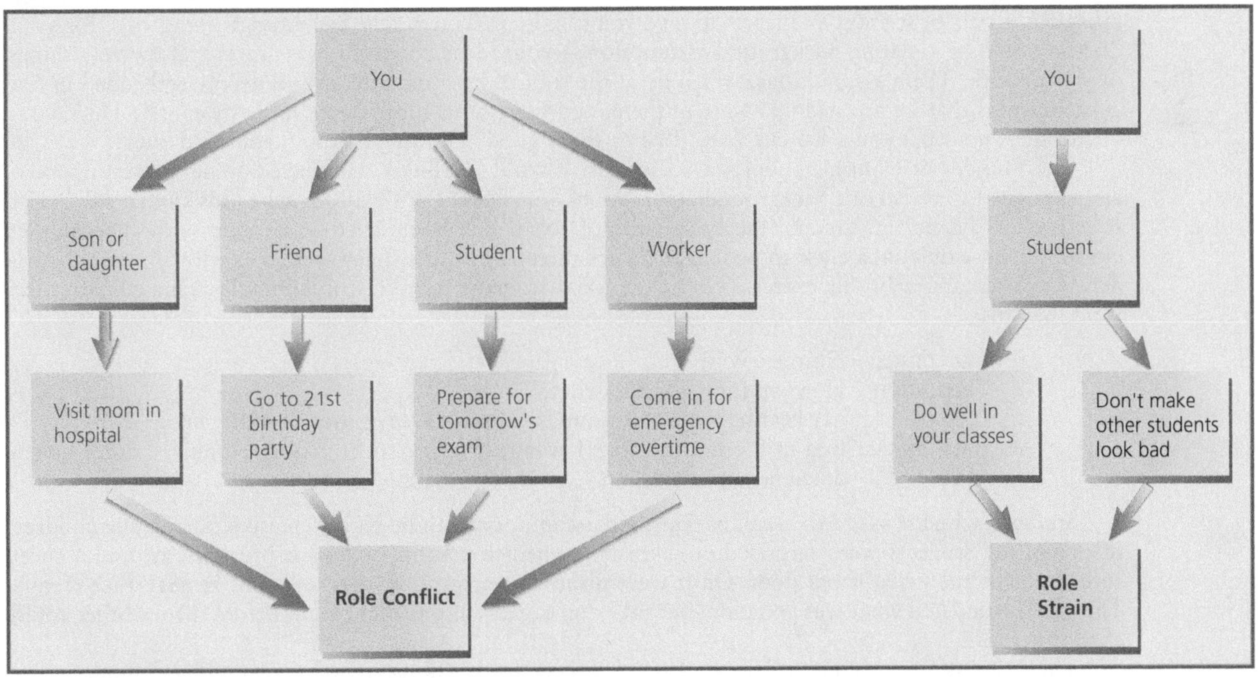

You
Son or daughter
Friend
Student
Worker
Visit mom in hospital
Go to 21st birthday party
Prepare for tomorrow's exam
Come in for emergency overtime
Role Conflict
You
Student
Do well in your classes
Don't make other students look bad
Role Strain

Source: By the author

> Suppose your teacher is about to make an important point. Suppose also that her lecturing has been outstanding and the class is hanging on every word. Just as she pauses for emphasis, her stomach lets out a loud growl. She might then use a *face-saving technique* by remarking, "I was so busy preparing for class that I didn't get breakfast this morning."

It is more likely, however, that both class and teacher will simply ignore the sound, giving the impression that no one heard a thing—a face-saving technique called *studied nonobservance.* This allows the teacher to make the point or, as Goffman would say, it allows the performance to go on.

Because our own body is identified so closely with the self, a good part of impression management centers on "body messages." The messages that are attached to various body shapes change over time, but, as explored in the Mass Media in Social Life box on pages 191 and 192, thinness currently screams "desirability."

Applying Impression Management I can just hear someone saying, "Impression management is interesting, but is it really important?" In fact, it is so significant that the right impression management can make a vital difference in your career. To be promoted, you must be perceived as someone who *should* be promoted. You must appear dominant. You certainly cannot go unnoticed. But how you manage this impression is crucial. If a female executive tries to appear dominant by wearing loud clothing, using garish makeup, and cursing, this will get her noticed—but it will not put her on the path to promotion. How, then, can she exhibit dominance in the right way? To help women walk this fine line between femininity and dominance, career counselors advise women on fine details of impression management. Here are two things they recommend—that women place their hands on the table during executive sessions, not in their lap, and that they carry a purse that looks more like a briefcase (Needham 2006).

Male or female, in your own life you will have to walk this thin line, finding the best way to manage impressions in order to further your career. Much success in the work world depends not on what you actually know but, instead, on your ability to give the impression that you know what you should know.

Ethnomethodology: Uncovering Background Assumptions

Certainly one of the strangest words in sociology is *ethnomethodology.* To better understand this term, consider the word's three basic components. *Ethno* means "folk" or "people"; method means how people do something; *ology* means "the study of." Putting them together, then, *ethno-method-ology* means "the study of how people do things." Specifically, **ethnomethodology** is the study of how people use common-sense understandings to make sense of life.

Let's suppose that during a routine office visit, your doctor remarks that your hair is rather long, then takes out a pair of scissors and starts to give you a haircut. You would feel strange about this, for your doctor would be violating **background assumptions**—your ideas about the way life is and the way things ought to work. These assumptions, which lie at the root of everyday life, are so deeply embedded in our consciousness that we are seldom aware of them, and most of us fulfill them unquestioningly. Thus, your doctor does not offer you a haircut, even if he or she is good at cutting hair and you need one!

The founder of ethnomethodology, sociologist Harold Garfinkel, conducted some interesting exercises designed to reveal our background assumptions. Garfinkel (1967, 2002) asked his students to act as though they did not understand the basic rules of social life. Some tried to bargain with supermarket clerks; others would inch close to people and stare directly at them. They were met with surprise, bewilderment, even anger. In one exercise Garfinkel asked students to take words literally. One conversation went like this:

ACQUAINTANCE: How are you?
STUDENT: How am I in regard to what?
My health, my finances, my schoolwork, my peace of mind, my . . .?
ACQUAINTANCE: (red in the face): Look! I was just trying to be polite. Frankly, I don't give a damn how you are.

Students who are asked to break background assumptions can be highly creative. The young children of one of my students were surprised one morning when they came down for breakfast to find a sheet spread across the living room floor. On it were dishes, silverware, lit candles—and bowls of ice cream. They, too, wondered what was going on, but they dug eagerly into the ice cream before their mother could change her mind.

This is a risky assignment to give students, however, for breaking some background assumptions can make people suspicious. When a colleague of mine gave this assignment, a couple of his students began to wash dollar bills at a laundromat. By the time they put the bills in the dryer, the police had arrived.

Box 8.5 Mass Media in Social Life

You Can't Be Thin Enough: Body Images and the Mass Media

An ad for Kellogg's Special K cereal shows an 18-month-old girl wearing nothing but a diaper. She has a worried look on her face. A bubble caption over her head has her asking, "Do I look fat?" (Krane et al. 2001)

When you stand before a mirror, do you like what you see? To make your body more attractive, do you watch your weight or work out? You have ideas about what you should look like. Where did you get them?

TV and magazine ads keep pounding home the message that our bodies aren't good enough, that we've got to improve them. The way to improve them, of course, is to buy the advertised products: hair extensions for women, hairpieces for men, hair transplants, padded bras, diet programs, anti-aging products, and exercise equipment. Muscular hulks show off machines that magically produce "six-pack abs" and incredible biceps—in just a few minutes a day. Female movie stars effortlessly go through their own tough workouts without even breaking into a sweat. Women and men get the feeling that attractive members of the opposite sex will flock to them if they purchase that wonder-working workout machine.

Although we try to shrug off such messages, knowing that they are designed to sell products, the messages still get our attention. They penetrate our thinking and feelings, helping to shape ideal images of how we "ought" to look. Those models so attractively clothed and coiffed as they walk down the runway, could they be any thinner? For women, the message is clear: You can't be thin enough. The men's message is also clear: You can't be muscular enough.

Woman or man, your body isn't good enough. It sags where it should be firm. It bulges where it should be smooth. It sticks out where it shouldn't, and it doesn't stick out enough where it should.

And—no matter what you weigh—it's too much. You've got to be thinner.

Exercise takes time, and getting in shape is painful. Once you do get in shape, let yourself slack off for just a few days, and your body seems to sag into its previous slothful, drab appearance. You can't let up, you can't exercise enough, and you can't diet enough.

But who can continue at such a torrid pace, striving for what are unrealistic cultural ideals? A few people, of course, but not many. So liposuction is appealing. Just lie there, put up with a little discomfort, and the doctor will vacuum the fat right out of your body. Surgeons can transform flat breasts into super breasts overnight. They can lower receding hairlines and smooth furrowed brows. They can remove lumps with their magical tummy tucks and can take off a decade with their rejuvenating skin peels, face lifts, and Botox injections.

With impossibly shaped models at Victoria's Secret and skinny models showing off the latest fashions in Vogue and Seventeen, half of U.S. adolescent girls feel fat and count calories (Hill 2006). Some teens even call the plastic surgeon. Anxious lest their child violate peer ideals and trail behind in her race for popularity, parents foot the bill. Some parents pay $25,000 just to give their daughters a flatter tummy (Gross 1998).

With peer pressure to alter the body already intense, surgeons keep stoking the fire. A sample ad: "No Ifs, Ands or Butts. You Can Change Your Bottom Line in Hours!" Some surgeons even offer gift certificates—so you can give your loved ones liposuction or Botox injections along with their greeting card (Dowd 2002).

The thinness craze has moved to the East, where glossy magazines feature skinny models. In China and India, a little extra padding was once valued as a sign of good health. Today, the obsession is thinness, and not-so-subtle ads scream that fat is bad (Prystay and Fowler 2003; Jung and Forbes 2007). In China, some teas come with a package of diet pills. Weight-loss machines, with electrodes attached to acupuncture pressure points, not only reduce fat but also build breasts—or so the advertisers claim.

All of us contrast the reality we see when we look in the mirror with our culture's ideal body types. The thinness craze, discussed in this box, encourages some people to extremes, as with Keira Knightley. It also makes it difficult for larger people to have positive self-images. Overcoming this difficulty, Jennifer Hudson is in the forefront of promoting an alternative image.

Not limited by our rules, advertisers in Japan and China push a soap that supposedly "sucks up fat through the skin's pores" (Marshall 1995). What a dream product! After all, even though our TV models smile as they go through their paces, those exercise machines do look like a lot of hard work.

Then there is the other bottom line: Attractiveness does pay off. U.S. economists studied physical attractiveness and earnings. The result? "Good-looking" men and women earn the most, "average-looking" men and women earn more than "plain" people, and the "ugly" earn the least (Hamermesh and Biddle 1994). In Europe, too, the more attractive workers earn more (Brunello and D'Hombres 2007). Then there is that potent cash advantage that "attractive" women have: They attract and marry higher-earning men (Kanazawa and Kovar 2004).

More popularity and more money? Maybe you can't be thin enough after all. Maybe those exercise machines are a good investment. If only we could catch up with the Japanese and develop a soap that would suck the fat right out of our pores. You can practically hear the jingle now.

For Your Consideration

What image do you have of your body? How do cultural expectations of "ideal" bodies underlie your image? Can you recall any advertisement or television program that has affected your body image?

What is considered ideal body size differs with historical periods and from one ethnic group to another. The women who posed for sixteenth-century European sculptors and painters, for example, were much "thicker" than the so-called "ideal" young women of today. (As I was looking at a painting in the Vatican, I heard a woman remark, "Look at those rolls of fat!") Why do you think that this difference exists?

Most advertising and television programs that focus on weight are directed at women. Women are more concerned than men about weight, more likely to have eating disorders, and more likely to be dissatisfied with their bodies (Honeycutt 1995; Hill 2006). Do you think that the targeting of women in advertising creates these attitudes and behaviors? Or do you think that these attitudes and behaviors would exist even if there were no such ads? Why?

In Sum: Ethnomethodologists explore *background assumptions,* the taken-for-granted ideas about the world that underlie our behavior. Most of these assumptions, or basic rules of social life, are unstated. We learn them as we learn our culture, and we violate them only with risk. Deeply embedded in our minds, they give us basic directions for living everyday life.

The Social Construction of Reality

Symbolic interactionists stress how our ideas help determine our reality. In what has become known as *the definition of the situation,* or the **Thomas theorem,** sociologists W. I. and Dorothy S. Thomas said, "If people define situations as real, they are real in their consequences." Consider the following incident:

> On a visit to Morocco, in northern Africa, I decided to buy a watermelon. When I indicated to the street vendor that the knife he was going to use to cut the watermelon was dirty (encrusted with filth would be more apt), he was very obliging. He immediately bent down and began to swish the knife in a puddle on the street. I shuddered as I looked at the passing burros that were urinating and defecating as they went by. Quickly, I indicated by gesture that I preferred my melon uncut after all.

For that vendor, germs did not exist. For me, they did. And each of us acted according to our definition of the situation. My perception and behavior did not come from the fact that germs are real, but, rather, from *my having grown up in a society that teaches they are real.* Microbes, of course, *objectively* exist, and whether or not germs are part of our thought world makes no difference as to whether we are infected by them. Our behavior, however, does not depend on the *objective* existence of something but, rather, on our *subjective interpretation,* on what sociologists call our *definition of reality.* In other words, it is not the reality of microbes that impresses itself on us, but society that impresses the reality of microbes on us.

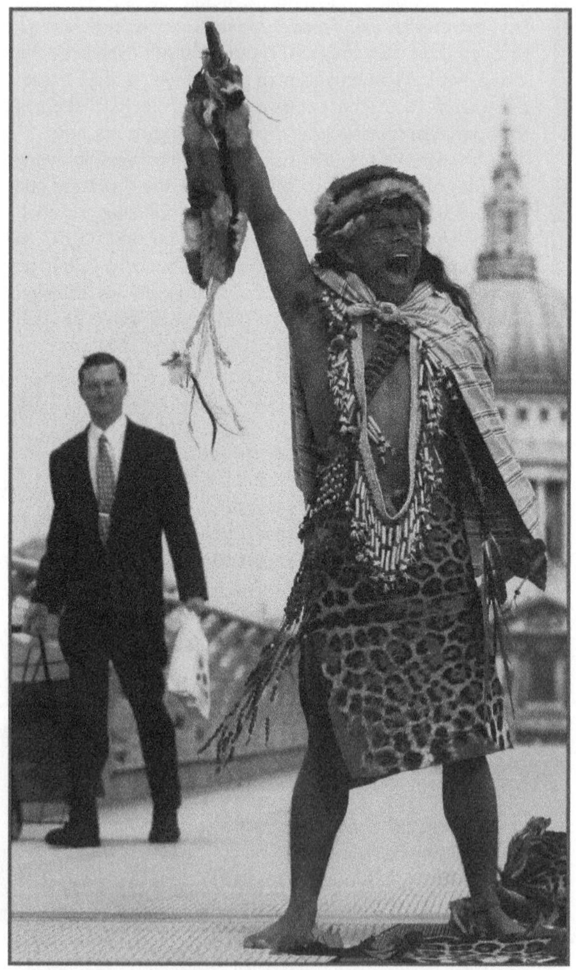

All of us have *background assumptions,* deeply ingrained assumptions of how the world operates. How do you think the background assumptions of this Londoner differ from those of this Ecuadoran shaman, who is performing a healing ceremony to rid London of its evil spirits?

This is the **social construction of reality.** Our society, or the social groups to which we belong, holds particular views of life. From our groups (the *social* part of this process), we learn ways of looking at life—whether that be our view of Hitler or Osama bin Laden (they're good, they're evil), germs (they exist, they don't exist), or *anything else in life.* In short, through our interaction with others, we *construct reality;* that is, we learn ways of interpreting our experiences in life.

Gynecological Examinations To better understand the social construction of reality, let's consider an extended example.

To do research on vaginal examinations, I interviewed a gynecological nurse who had been present at about 14,000 examinations. I focused on how doctors construct social reality in order to define this examination as nonsexual (Henslin and Biggs 1971/2007). It became apparent that the pelvic examination unfolds much as a stage play does. I will use "he" to refer to the physician because only male physicians were part of this study. Perhaps the results would be different with women gynecologists.

> **Scene 1 (the patient as person)** In this scene, the doctor maintains eye contact with his patient, calls her by name, and discusses her problems in a professional manner. If he decides that a vaginal examination is necessary, he tells a nurse, "Pelvic in room 1." By this statement, he is announcing that a major change will occur in the next scene.

> **Scene 2 (from person to pelvic)** This scene is the depersonalizing stage. In line with the doctor's announcement, the patient begins the transition from a "person" to a "pelvic." The doctor leaves the room, and a female nurse enters to help the patient make the transition. The nurse prepares the "props" for the coming examination and answers any questions the woman might have.

What occurs at this point is essential for the social construction of reality, for *the doctor's absence removes even the suggestion of sexuality.* To undress in front of him could suggest either a striptease or intimacy, thus undermining the reality so carefully being defined: that of nonsexuality.

The patient also wants to remove any hint of sexuality, and during this scene she may express concern about what to do with her panties. Some mutter to the nurse, "I don't want him to see these." Most women solve the problem by either slipping their panties under their other clothes or placing them in their purse.

> **Scene 3 (the person as pelvic)** This scene opens when the doctor enters the room. Before him is a woman lying on a table, her feet in stirrups, her knees tightly together, and her body covered by a drape sheet. The doctor seats himself on a low stool before the woman and says, "Let your knees fall apart" (rather than the sexually loaded "Spread your legs"), and begins the examination.

The drape sheet is crucial in this process of desexualization, for it *dissociates the pelvic area from the person:* Leaning forward and with the drape sheet above his head, the physician can see only the vagina, not the patient's face. Thus dissociated from the individual, the vagina is dramaturgically transformed into an object of analysis. If the doctor examines the patient's breasts, he also dissociates them from her person by examining them one at a time, with a towel covering the unexamined breast. Like the vagina, each breast becomes an isolated item dissociated from the person.

In this third scene, the patient cooperates in being an object, becoming, for all practical purposes, a pelvis to be examined. She withdraws eye contact from the doctor and usually from the nurse, is likely to stare at the wall or at the ceiling, and avoids initiating conversation.

> **Scene 4 (from pelvic to person)** In this scene, the patient becomes "repersonalized." The doctor has left the examining room; the patient dresses and fixes her hair and makeup. Her reemergence as a person is indicated by such statements to the nurse as, "My dress isn't too wrinkled, is it?" indicating a need for reassurance that the metamorphosis from "pelvic" back to "person" has been completed satisfactorily.

> **Scene 5 (the patient as person)** In this final scene, the patient is once again treated as a person rather than as an object. The doctor makes eye contact with her and addresses her by name. She, too, makes eye contact with the doctor, and the usual middle-class interaction patterns are followed. She has been fully restored.

In Sum: To an outsider to our culture, the custom of women going to a male stranger for a vaginal examination might seem bizarre. But not to us. We learn that pelvic examinations are nonsexual. To sustain this definition requires teamwork—patients, doctors, and nurses working together to *socially construct reality.*

It is not just pelvic examinations or our views of microbes that make up our definitions of reality. Rather, *our behavior depends on how we define reality.* Our definitions (or constructions) provide the basis for what we do and how we feel about life. To understand human behavior, then, we must know how people define reality.

The Need for Both Macrosociology and Microsociology

As was noted earlier, both microsociology and macrosociology make vital contributions to our understanding of human behavior. Our understanding of social life would be vastly incomplete without one or the other. The photo essay on the next two pages should help to make clear why we need *both* perspectives.

To illustrate this point, let's consider two groups of high school boys studied by sociologist William Chambliss (1973/2007). Both groups attended Hannibal High School. In one group were eight middle-class boys who came from "good" families and were perceived by the community as "going somewhere." Chambliss calls this group the "Saints." The other group consisted of six lower-class boys who were seen as headed down a dead-end road. Chambliss calls this group the "Roughnecks."

Boys in both groups skipped school, got drunk, and did a lot of fighting and vandalism. The Saints were actually somewhat more delinquent, for they were truant more often and engaged in more vandalism. Yet the Saints had a good reputation, while the Roughnecks were seen by teachers, the police, and the general community as no good and headed for trouble.

The boys' reputations set them on distinct paths. Seven of the eight Saints went on to graduate from college. Three studied for advanced degrees: One finished law school and became active in state politics, one finished medical school, and one went on to earn a Ph.D. The four other college graduates entered managerial or executive training programs with large firms. After his parents divorced, one Saint failed to graduate from high school on time and had to repeat his senior year. Although this boy tried to go to college by attending night school, he never finished. He was unemployed the last time Chambliss saw him.

In contrast, only four of the Roughnecks finished high school. Two of these boys did exceptionally well in sports and were awarded athletic scholarships to college. They both graduated from college and became high school coaches. Of the two others who graduated from high school, one became a small-time gambler and the other disappeared "up north," where he was last reported to be driving a truck. The two who did not complete high school were convicted of separate murders and sent to prison.

To understand what happened to the Saints and the Roughnecks, we need to grasp *both* social structure and social interaction. Using *macrosociology*, we can place these boys within the larger framework of the U.S. social class system. This reveals how opportunities open or close to people depending on their social class and how people learn different goals as they grow up in different groups. We can then use *microsociology* to follow their everyday lives. We can see how the Saints manipulated their "good" reputations to skip classes and how their access to automobiles allowed them to protect those reputations by spreading their troublemaking around different communities. In contrast, the Roughnecks, who did not have cars, were highly visible. Their lawbreaking, which was limited to a small area, readily came to the attention of the community. Microsociology also reveals how their respective reputations opened doors of opportunity to the first group of boys while closing them to the other.

Through the Author's Lens

When a Tornado Strikes

Social Organization Following a Natural Disaster

As I was watching television on March 20, 2003, I heard a report that a tornado had hit Camilla, Georgia. "Like a big lawn mower," the report said, it had cut a path of destruction through this little town. In its fury, the tornado had left behind six dead and about 200 injured.

From sociological studies of natural disasters, I knew that immediately after the initial shock the survivors of natural disasters work together to try to restore order to their disrupted lives. I wanted to see this restructuring process firsthand. The next morning,I took off for Georgia.

These photos, taken the day after the tornado struck, tell the story of people in the midst of trying to put their lives back together. I was impressed at how little time people spent commiserating about their misfortune and how quickly they took practical steps to restore their lives.

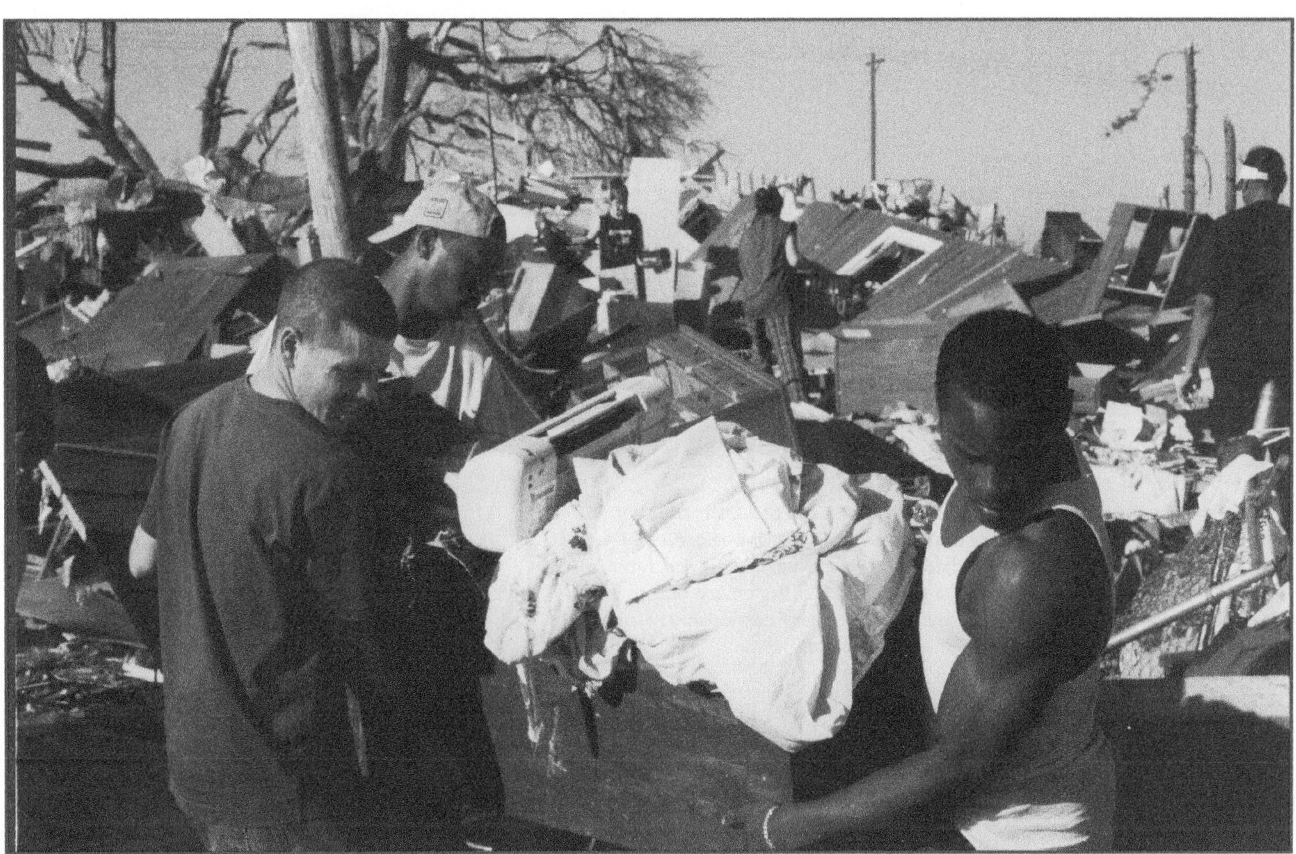

After making sure that their loved ones are safe, one of the next steps people take is to recover their possessions. The cooperation that emerges among people, as documented in the sociological literature on natural disasters, is illustrated here.

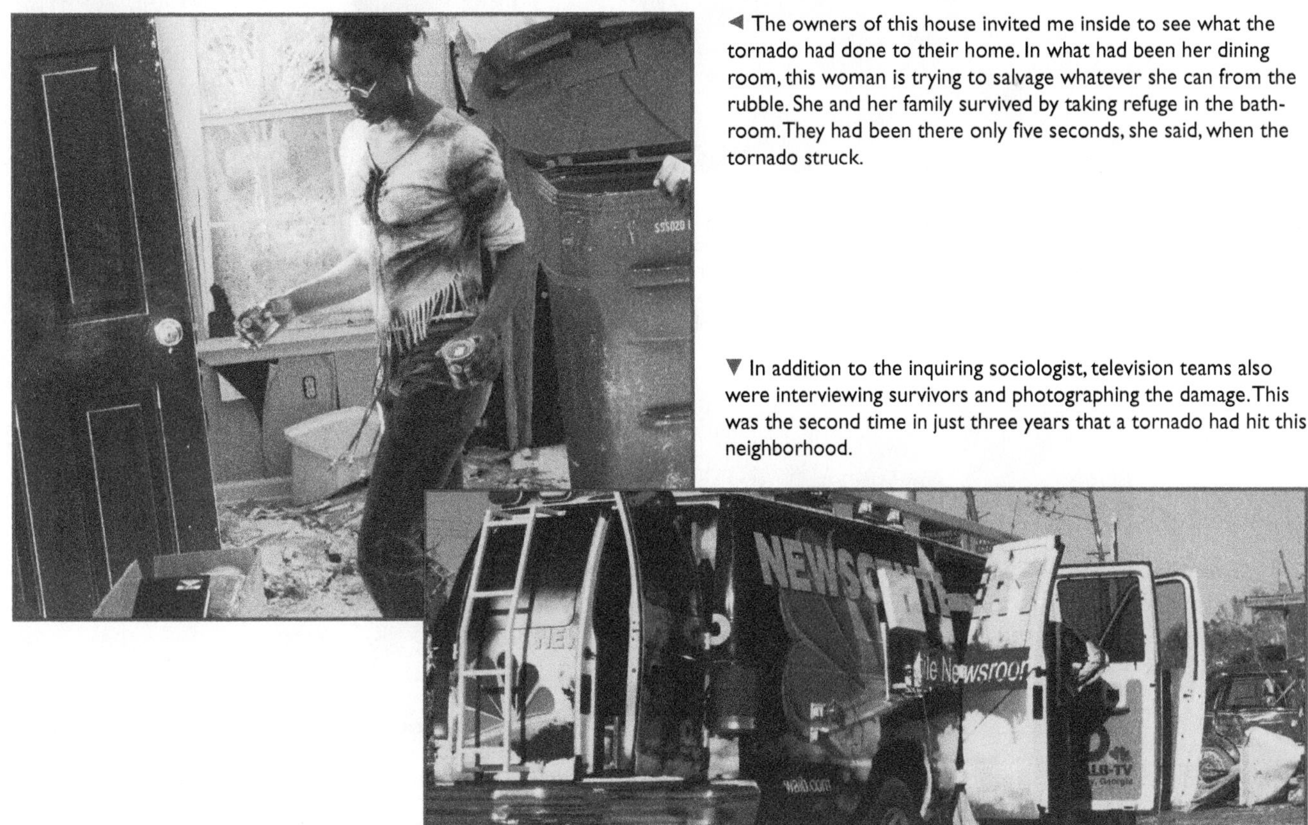

◀ The owners of this house invited me inside to see what the tornado had done to their home. In what had been her dining room, this woman is trying to salvage whatever she can from the rubble. She and her family survived by taking refuge in the bathroom. They had been there only five seconds, she said, when the tornado struck.

▼ In addition to the inquiring sociologist, television teams also were interviewing survivors and photographing the damage. This was the second time in just three years that a tornado had hit this neighborhood.

▲ No building or social institution escapes a tornado as it follows its path of destruction. Just the night before, members of this church had held evening worship service. After the tornado someone mounted a U.S. flag on top of the cross, symbolic of the church members' patriotism and religiosity—and of their enduring hope.

▲ Personsal relationships are essential in putting lives together. Consequently, reminders of these relationships are one of the main possessions that people attempt to salvage. This young man, having just recovered the family photo album, is eagerly reviewing the photos.

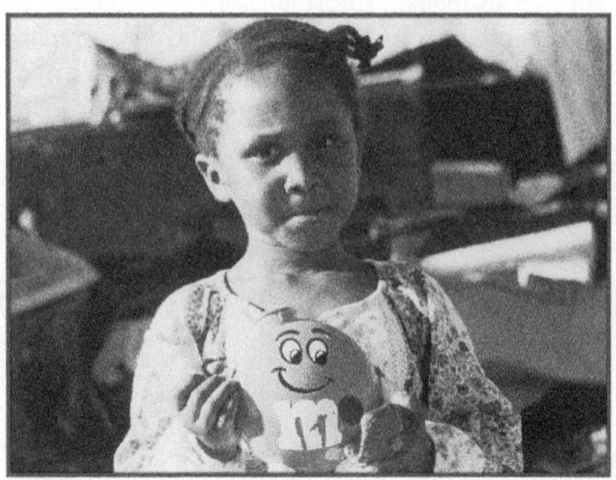

▲ For children, family photos are not as important as toys. This girl has managed to salvage a favorite toy, which will help anchor her to her previous life.

▲ A sign of the times. Like electricity and gas, cable television also has to be restored as soon as possible.

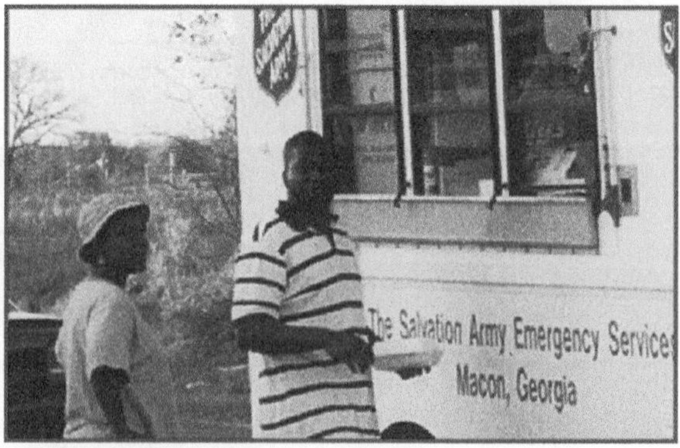

▲ Formal organizations also help the survivors of natural disasters recover. In this neighborhood, I saw representatives of insurance companies, the police, the fire department, and an electrical co-op. The Salvation Army brought meals to the neighborhood.

As you look at these photos, try to determine why you need both microsociology and macrosociology to understand what occurs after a natural disaster.

Summary and Review

Levels of Sociological Analysis

What two levels of analysis do sociologists use?
Sociologists use macrosociological and microsociological levels of analysis. In **macrosociology,** the focus is placed on large-scale features of social life, while in **microsociology,** the focus is on **social interaction.** Functionalists and conflict theorists tend to use a macrosociological approach, while symbolic interactionists are more likely to use a microsociological approach. P. 173.

The Macrosociological Perspective: Social Structure

How does social structure influence our behavior?
The term **social structure** refers to the social envelope that surrounds us and establishes limits on our behavior. Social structure consists of culture, social class, social statuses, roles, groups, and social institutions. Our location in the social structure underlies our perceptions, attitudes, and behaviors.

Culture lays the broadest framework, while **social class** divides people according to income, education, and occupational prestige. Each of us receives **ascribed statuses** at birth; later we add **achieved statuses.** Our behaviors and orientations are further influenced by the **roles** we play, the **groups** to which we belong, and our experiences with social institutions. These components of society work together to help maintain social order. Pp. 174-178.

What are social institutions?
Social institutions are the standard ways that a society develops to meet its basic needs. As summarized in Figure 8.2 (page 178), industrial and postindustrial societies have ten social institutions—the family, religion, education, economics, medicine, politics, law, science, the military, and the mass media. Pp. 178–179.

What social revolutions have transformed society?
The discovery that animals and plants could be domesticated marked the *first* social revolution. This transformed **hunting and gathering societies** into **pastoral** and **horticultural societies.** The invention of the plow brought about the *second* social revolution, as societies became **agricultural.** The invention of the steam engine, which led to **industrial societies,** marked the *third* social revolution. The *fourth* social revolution was ushered in by the invention of the microchip, leading to the **postindustrial** or **information society.** Another new type of society, the **biotech society,** may be emerging. As in the previous social revolutions, little will remain the same. Our attitudes, ideas, expectations, behaviors, relationships—all will be transformed. Pp. 179–182.

What holds society together?
According to Emile Durkheim, in agricultural societies people are united by **mechanical solidarity** (having similar views and feelings). With industrialization comes **organic solidarity** (people depend on one another to do their more specialized jobs). Ferdinand Tönnies pointed out that the informal means of control in ***Gemeinschaft*** (small, intimate) societies are replaced by formal mechanisms in ***Gesellschaft*** (larger, more impersonal) societies. Pp. 183–184.

The Microsociological Perspective: Social Interaction in Everyday Life

What is the focus of symbolic interactionism?
In contrast to functionalists and conflict theorists, who, as macrosociologists, focus on the "big picture," symbolic interactionists tend to be microsociologists, who focus on face-to-face social interaction. Symbolic interactionists analyze how people define their worlds and how their definitions, in turn, influence their behavior. Pp. 185–186.

How do stereotypes affect social interaction?
Stereotypes are assumptions of what people are like. When we first meet people, we classify them according to our perceptions of their visible characteristics. Our ideas about those characteristics guide our behavior toward them. Our behavior, in turn, may influence them to behave in ways that reinforce our stereotypes. Pp. 186-187.

Do all human groups share a similar sense of personal space?
In examining how people use physical space, symbolic interactionists stress that we surround ourselves with a "personal bubble" that we carefully protect. People from different cultures use "personal bubbles" of varying sizes, so the answer to the question is no. Americans typically use four different "distance zones": intimate, personal, social, and public. Pp. 186-187.

What is dramaturgy?
Erving Goffman developed **dramaturgy** (or dramaturgical analysis), in which everyday life is analyzed in terms of the stage. At the core of this analysis is **impression management,** our attempts to control the impressions we make on others. Our performances often call for **teamwork** and **face-saving behavior.** Pp. 188–190.

What is the social construction of reality?
The phrase **the social construction of reality** refers to how we construct our views of the world, which, in turn, underlie our actions. **Ethnomethodology** is the study of how people make sense of everyday life. Ethnomethodologists try to uncover **background assumptions,** our basic ideas about the way life is. Pp. 192–193.

The Need for Both Macrosociology and Microsociology

Why are both levels of analysis necessary?
Because each focuses on different aspects of the human experience, both microsociology and macrosociology are necessary for us to understand social life. P. 194.

Thinking Critically about Chapter 8

1. The major components of social structure are culture,social class, social status, roles, groups, and social institutions. Use social structure to explain why Native Americans have such a low rate of college graduation.
2. Dramaturgy is a form of microsociology. Use dramaturgy to analyze a situation with which you are intimately familiar (such as interaction with your family or friends, or in one of your college classes).
3. To illustrate why we need both macrosociology and microsociology to understand social life, analyze the situation of a student getting kicked out of college as an example.

Additional Resources

What can you find in MySocLab? www.mysoclab.com

- Complete Ebook
- Practice Tests and Video and Audio activities
- Mapping and Data Analysis exercises
- Sociology in the News
- Classic Readings in Sociology
- Research and Writing advice

Where Can I Read More on This Topic?

Suggested readings for this chapter are listed at the back of this book.

9 chapter

Social Groups and Formal Organizations

Kody, you got eight shots, you don't come back to the car unless they all are gone.

When Kody Scott joined the L.A. Crips, his initiation had two parts. Here's the first:

"How old is you now anyway?"

"Eleven, but I'll be twelve in November."

I never saw the blow to my head come from Huck. Bam! And I was on all fours. . . . Kicked in the stomach, I was on my back counting stars in the blackness. Grabbed by the collar, I was made to stand again. A solid blow to my chest exploded pain on the blank screen that had now become my mind. Bam! Another, then another. Blows rained on me from every direction. . . .

Up until this point not a word had been spoken. . . . Then I just started swinging, with no style or finesse, just anger and the instinct to survive. . . . (This) reflected my ability to represent the set [gang] in hand-to-hand combat. The blows stopped abruptly. . . . My ear was bleeding, and my neck and face were deep red. . . .

Scott's beating was followed immediately by the second part of his initiation. For this, he received the name *Monster,* which he carried proudly:

"Give Kody the pump." [12-gauge pump action shotgun] . . . Tray Ball spoke with the calm of a football coach. "Tonight we gonna rock they world." . . . Hand slaps were passed around the room. . . . "Kody, you got eight shots, you don't come back to the car unless they all are gone."

"Righteous," I said, eager to show my worth. . . .

Hanging close to buildings, houses, and bushes, we made our way, one after the other, to within spitting distance of the Bloods. . . . Huck and Fly stepped from the shadows simultaneously and were never noticed until it was too late. Boom! Boom! Heavy bodies hitting the ground, confusion, yells of dismay, running. . . . By my sixth shot I had advanced past the first fallen bodies and into the street in pursuit of those who had sought refuge behind cars and trees. . . .

Back in the shack we smoked more pot and drank more beer. I was the center of attention for my acts of aggression. . . .

Tray Ball said. "You got potential, 'cause you eager to learn. Bangin' [being a gang member] ain't no part-time thang, it's full-time, it's a career. It's bein' down when ain't nobody else down with you. It's gettin' caught and not tellin'. Killin' and not caring, and dyin' without fear. It's love for your set and hate for the enemy. You hear what I'm sayin'?"

Kody adds this insightful remark:

Though never verbally stated, death was looked upon as a sort of reward, a badge of honor, especially if one died in some heroic capacity for the hood. . . . The supreme sacrifice was to "take a bullet for a homie" [fellow gang member]. The set functioned as a religion. Nothing held a light to the power of the set. If you died on the trigger you surely were smiled upon by the Crip God.

Excerpts from Scott 1994:8–13, 103.

Groups Within Society

Could you shoot strangers in cold blood—just because others tell you to pull the trigger? Although none of us want to think that we could be like Kody, don't bet on it. You are going to read some surprising things about groups in this chapter.

Groups, people who think of themselves as belonging together and who interact with one another, are the essence of life in society. Groups are vital for our well-being. They provide intimate relationships and a sense of belonging, something that we all need. This chapter, then, is highly significant for your life.

Before we analyze groups, we should clarify the concept. Two terms sometimes confused with group are *aggregate* and *category.* An **aggregate** consists of people who temporarily share the same physical space but who do not see themselves as belonging together. Shoppers standing in a checkout line or drivers waiting at a red light are an aggregate. A **category** is simply a statistic. It consists of people who share similar characteristics, such as all college women who wear glasses or all men over 6 feet tall. Unlike group members, the individuals who make up a category don't think of themselves as belonging together and they don't interact with one another. These concepts are illustrated in the photos on the next page.

Groups are so influential that they determine who we are. If you think that this is an exaggeration, recall that even our minds are a product of society—or, more specifically phrased, of the groups to which we belong. To better understand the influence of groups on your own life, let's begin by looking at the types of groups that make up our society.

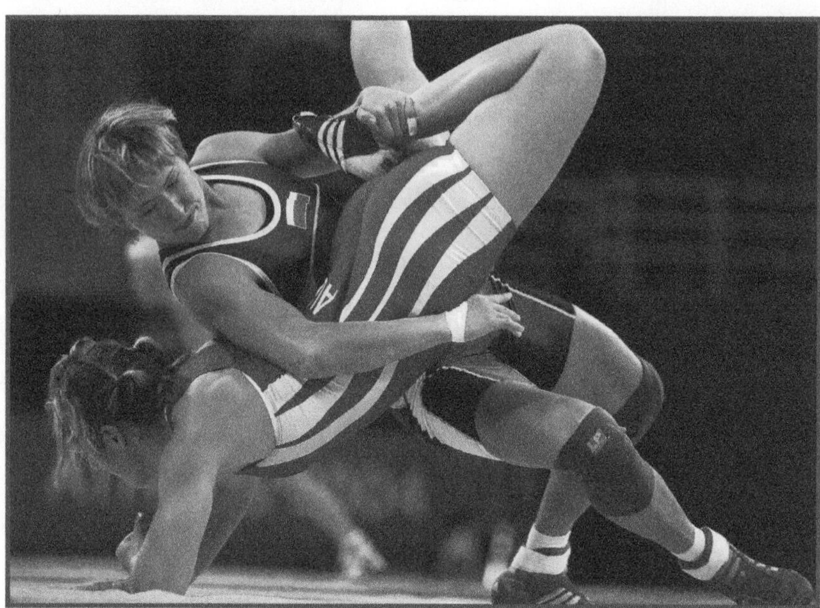

As society—the largest and most complex type of group—changes, so, too, do the groups, activities, and, ultimately, the type of people who form that society. This photo of Russian and Austrian wrestlers in the Olympics at Greece captures some of the changes occurring in Western societies. What social changes can you identify from this photo?

Categories, Aggregates, Primary and Secondary Groups

Groups have a deep impact on our views, orientations, even what we feel and think about life. Yet, as illustrated by these photos, not everthing that appears to be a group is actually a group in the sociological sense.

Aggregates are simply people who happen to be in the same place at the same time. ▶

▲ The outstanding trait that these three people have in common does not make them a group, but a **category.**

Secondary groups are larger and more anonymous, formal, and impersonal than primary groups. Why are the participants of a dog show an example of a secondary group? ▶

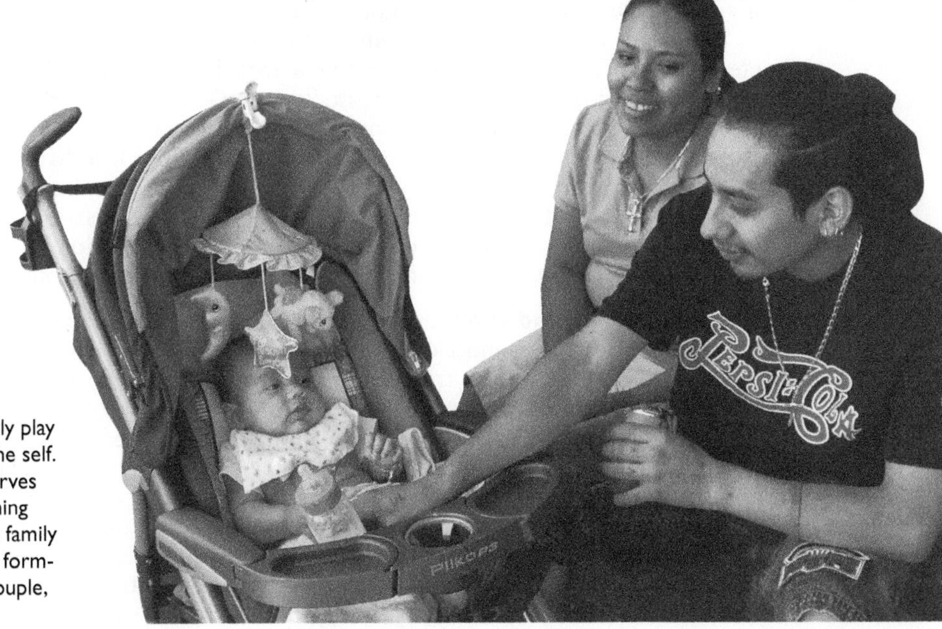

Primary groups such as the family play a key role in the development of the self. As a small group, the family also serves as a buffer from the often-threatening larger group known as society. The family has been of primary significance in forming the basic orientations of this couple, as it will be for their son. ▶

Primary Groups

Our first group, the family, gives us our basic orientations to life. Later, among friends, we find more intimacy and an expanded sense of belonging. These groups are what sociologist Charles Cooley called **primary groups.** By providing intimate, face-to-face interaction, they give us an identity, a feeling of who we are. As Cooley (1909) put it,

> By primary groups I mean those characterized by intimate face-to-face association and cooperation. They are primary in several senses, but chiefly in that they are fundamental in forming the social nature and ideals of the individual.

Producing a Mirror Within Cooley called primary groups the "springs of life." By this, he meant that primary groups, such as family and friends, are essential to our emotional well-being. As humans, we have an intense need for face-to-face interaction that generates feelings of self-esteem. By offering a sense of belonging and a feeling of being appreciated—and sometimes even loved—primary groups are uniquely equipped to meet this basic need. From our opening vignette, you can see that gangs are also primary groups.

Primary groups are also significant because their values and attitudes become fused into our identity. We internalize their views, which then become the lenses through which we view life. Even when we are adults—no matter how far we move away from our childhood roots—early primary groups remain "inside" us. There, they continue to form part of the perspective from which we look out onto the world. Ultimately, then, it is difficult, if not impossible, for us to separate the self from our primary groups, for the self and our groups merge into a "we."

Secondary Groups

Compared with primary groups, **secondary groups** are larger, more anonymous, more formal, and more impersonal. Secondary groups are based on some common interest or activity, and their members are likely to interact on the basis of specific statuses, such as president, manager, worker, or student. Examples are a college class, the American Sociological Association, and the Democratic Party. Contemporary society could not function without secondary groups. They are part of the way we get our education, make our living, spend our money, and use our leisure time.

As necessary as secondary groups are for contemporary life, they often fail to satisfy our deep needs for intimate association. Consequently, *secondary groups tend to break down into primary groups.* At school and work, we form friendships. Our interaction with our friends is so important that we sometimes feel that if it weren't for them, school or work "would drive us crazy." The primary groups that we form within secondary groups, then, serve as a buffer between ourselves and the demands that secondary groups place on us.

Voluntary Associations A special type of secondary group is a **voluntary association,** a group made up of volunteers who organize on the basis of some mutual interest. Some groups are local, consisting of only a few volunteers; others are national, with a paid professional staff.

Americans love voluntary associations and use them to express a wide variety of interests. A visitor entering one of the thousands of small towns that dot the U.S. landscape is often greeted by a highway sign proclaiming the town's voluntary associations: Girl Scouts, Boy Scouts, Kiwanis, Lions, Elks, Eagles, Knights of Columbus, Chamber of Commerce, American Legion, Veterans of Foreign Wars, and perhaps a host of others. One type of voluntary association is so prevalent that a separate sign sometimes indicates which varieties are present in the town: Roman Catholic, Baptist, Lutheran, Methodist, Episcopalian, and so on. Not listed on these signs are many other voluntary associations, such as political parties, unions, health clubs, the National Right to Life, the National Organization for Women, Alcoholics Anonymous, Gamblers Anonymous, Association of Pinto Racers, and Citizens United For or Against This and That.

The Inner Circle and the Iron Law of Oligarchy A significant aspect of a voluntary association is that its key members, its inner circle, often grow distant from the regular members. They become convinced that only they can be trusted to make the group's important decisions. To see this principle at work, let's look at the Veterans of Foreign Wars (VFW).

Sociologists Elaine Fox and George Arquitt (1985) studied three local posts of the VFW, a national organization of former U.S. soldiers who have served in foreign wars. They found that although the leaders conceal their attitudes from the other members, the inner circle views the rank and file as a bunch of ignorant boozers. Because the leaders can't stand the thought that such people might represent them in the community and at national meetings, a curious situation arises. Although the VFW constitution makes rank-and-file members eligible for top leadership positions, they never become leaders. In fact, the inner circle is so effective in controlling these top positions that even before an election they can tell you who is going to win. "You need to meet Jim," the sociologists were told. "He's the next post commander after Sam does his time."

At first, the researchers found this puzzling. The election hadn't been held yet. As they investigated further, they found that leadership is actually determined behind the scenes. The current leaders appoint their favored people to chair the key committees. This spotlights their names and accomplishments, propelling the members to elect them. By appointing its own members to highly visible positions, then, the inner circle maintains control over the entire organization.

Like the VFW, most organizations are run by only a few of their members. Building on the term *oligarchy,* a system in which many are ruled by a few, sociologist Robert Michels (1876–1936) coined the term **the iron law of oligarchy** to refer to how organizations come to be dominated by a small, self-perpetuating elite (Michels 1911/1949). Most members of voluntary associations are passive, and an elite inner circle keeps itself in power by passing the leadership positions among its members.

What many find disturbing about the iron law of oligarchy is that people are excluded from leadership because they don't represent the inner circle's values—or, in some instances, their background. This is true even of organizations that are committed to democratic principles. For example, U.S. political parties—supposedly the backbone of the nation's representative government—are run by an inner circle that passes leadership positions from one elite member to another. This principle also shows up in the U.S. Senate. With their statewide control of political machinery and access to free mailing, about 90 percent of U.S. senators who choose to run are reelected (*Statistical Abstract* 2006:Table 394).

"So long, Bill. This is my club. You can't come in."

How our participation in social groups shapes our self-concept is a focus of symbolic interactionists. In this process, knowing who we are not is as significant as knowing who we are.

In-Groups and Out-Groups

Groups toward which we feel loyalty are called **in-groups;** those toward which we feel antagonism are called **out-groups.** For Monster Kody in our opening vignette, the Crips were an in-group, while the Bloods were an out-group. That the Crips—and we—make such a fundamental division of the world has far-reaching consequences for our lives.

Implications for a Socially Diverse Society: Shaping Perception and Morality The sense of belonging that membership in a group brings often leads to positive consequences. A common example is our tendency to excuse the faults of people we love and to encourage them to do better. Unfortunately, dividing the world into a "we" and "them" also leads to discrimination, hatred, and, as we saw in our opening vignette, even murder.

At the center of it all is how in-group membership shapes our perception of the world. Let's look at two examples. The first you see regularly, prejudice and discrimination on the basis of sex. As sociologist Robert Merton (1968) said, our favoritism creates a fascinating double standard. We tend to view the traits of our in-group as virtues, while we perceive those *same* traits as vices in out-groups. Men may perceive an aggressive man as assertive but an aggressive woman as pushy. They may think that a male employee who doesn't speak up "knows when to keep his mouth shut," while they consider a quiet woman as too timid to make it in the business world.

The "we" and "they" division of the world can lead to such twisted perception that harming others comes to be viewed as right. The Nazis provide one of the most startling examples. For them, the Jews were an out-group who symbolized an evil that should be eliminated. Many ordinary, "good" Germans shared this view and defended the Holocaust as "dirty work" that someone had to do (Hughes 1962/2005).

An example from way back then, you might say—and the world has moved on since then. But our inclination to divide the world into in-groups and out-groups has not moved on—nor has the twisting of perception that follows. After the terrorist attacks of September 11, 2001, top U.S. officials came to view Arabs as sinister, bloodthirsty villains. They even said that it was OK for interrogators to be "cruel, inhuman, and degrading" to prisoners—as long as they didn't call it torture (Gonzales 2002). Alan Dershowitz, a professor at Harvard Law School, who usually takes very liberal views, went even further. He said that we should make torture legal, but, he added, judges should determine if torture is necessary and, if so, issue "torture warrants" (Schulz 2002). After 9/11, cruel interrogation and torture—justified for the sake of the in-group—became "dirty work" that someone had to do. Can you see the principle at work—and understand that in-group/out-group thinking can be so severe that even "good people" can torture and kill? And with a good conscience.

All of us have reference groups—the groups whose standards we use to evaluate ourselves. How do you think the reference groups of these members of the KKK who are demonstrating in Jaspar, Texas, differ from those of the police officer who is protecting their right of free speech? Although the KKK and this police officer use different groups to evaluate their attitudes and behaviors, the process is the same.

Economic downturns are especially perilous in this regard. The Nazis took power during a depression so severe that it was wiping out the middle classes. If such a depression were to occur in the United States, immigrants would be transformed from "nice people who for low wages will do jobs that Americans think are beneath them" to "sneaky people who steal jobs from friends and family." A national anti-immigration policy would follow, accompanied by a resurgence of hate groups such as the neo-Nazis, the Ku Klux Klan, and skinheads.

In short, to divide the world into in-groups and out-groups is a natural part of social life. But in addition to bringing functional consequences, it also brings dysfunctional ones.

Reference Groups

Suppose you have just been offered a good job. It pays double what you hope to make even after you graduate from college. You have only two days to make up your mind. If you accept it, you will have to drop out of college. As you consider the matter, thoughts like this may go through your mind: "My friends will say I'm a fool if I don't take the job . . . but Dad and Mom will practically go crazy. They've made sacrifices for me, and they'll be crushed if I don't finish college. They've always said I've got to get my education first, that good jobs will always be there. . . . But, then, I'd like to see the look on the faces of those neighbors who said I'd never amount to much!"

Evaluating Ourselves This is an example of how people use **reference groups,** the groups we refer to when we evaluate ourselves. Your reference groups may include your family, neighbors, teachers, classmates, co-workers, and the Scouts or the members of a church, synagogue, or mosque. If you were like Monster Kody in our opening vignette, the "set" would be your main reference group. Even a group you don't belong to can be a reference group. For example, if you are thinking about going to graduate school, graduate students or members of the profession you want to join may form a reference group. You would consider their standards as you evaluate your grades or writing skills.

Reference groups exert tremendous influence over our lives. For example, if you want to become a corporate executive, you might start to dress more formally, try to improve your vocabulary, read the *Wall Street Journal,* and change your major to business or law. In contrast, if you want to become a rock musician, you might wear jewelry in several places where you have pierced your body, get elaborate tattoos, dress in ways your parents and many of your peers consider extreme, read *Rolling Stone,* drop out of college, and hang around clubs and rock groups.

Exposure to Contradictory Standards in a Socially Diverse Society From these examples, you can see how we use reference groups to evaluate our behavior. When we see ourselves as measuring up to a reference group's standards, we feel no conflict. If our behavior—or even aspirations—does not match the group's standards, however, the mismatch can lead to inner turmoil. For example, wanting to become a corporate executive would create no inner turmoil for most of us. It would, however, for someone who had grown up in an Amish home. The Amish strongly disapprove of such aspirations for their children. They ban high school and college education, suits and ties, and corporate employment. Similarly, if you want to join the military and your parents are dedicated pacifists, you likely would feel deep conflict, as your parents would have quite different aspirations for you.

Two chief characteristics of our society are social diversity and social mobility. This exposes most of us to standards and orientations that are inconsistent with those we learned during childhood. The "internal recordings" that play contradictory messages from different reference groups, then, are one price we pay for our social mobility.

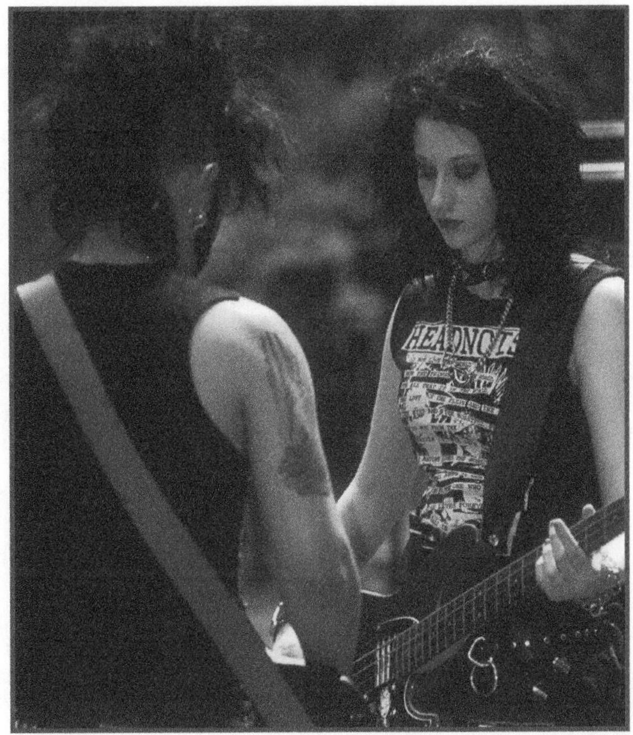

Social networks start with the people we associate with and expand outward from there. How do you think the social networks and *reference groups* of these two people differ from your own? How do you think they are similar?

Social Networks

Although we live in a huge and diverse society, we don't experience social life as a sea of nameless, strange faces. Instead, we interact within social networks. The term **social network** refers to people who are linked to one another. Your social network includes your family, friends, acquaintances, people at work and school, and even "friends of friends." Think of your social network as lines that extend outward from yourself, gradually encompassing more and more people.

If you are a member of a large group, you probably associate regularly with a few people within that group. In a sociology class I was teaching at a commuter campus, six women who didn't know one another ended up working together on a project. They got along well, and they began to sit together. Eventually they planned a Christmas party at one of their homes. This type of social network, the clusters within a group, or its internal factions, is called a **clique** (cleek).

"Network analysis" has moved from theory and laboratory study to the practical world. One of the most striking examples is how U.S. forces located Saddam Hussein. Social scientists analyzed people's relationship to Hussein. They then drew up a "people map," placing names and photos of these people closer and farther from a central photo of Hussein. This let them see who was close enough to Hussein to know where he might be but distant enough to perhaps be willing to cooperate. It worked.

The Small World Phenomenon Social scientists have wondered just how extensive the connections are between social networks. If you list everyone you know, each of those individuals lists everyone he or she knows, and you keep doing this, would almost everyone in the United States eventually be included on those lists?

It would be too cumbersome to test this hypothesis by drawing up such lists, but psychologist Stanley Milgram (1933–1984) came up with an interesting idea. In a classic study known as "the small world phenomenon," Milgram (1967) addressed a letter to "targets": the wife of a divinity student in Cambridge and a stockbroker in Boston. He sent the letter to "starters," who did not know these people. He asked them to send the letter to someone they knew on a first-name basis, someone they thought might know the "target." The recipients, in turn, were asked to mail the letter to someone they knew who might know the "target," and so on. The question was: Would the letters ever reach the "target"? If so, how long would the chain be?

Think of yourself as part of this study. What would you do if you were a "starter," but the "target" lived in a state in which you knew no one? You would send the letter to someone you know who might know someone in that state. This, Milgram reported, is just what happened. Although none of the senders knew the targets, the letters reached the designated individual in an average of just six jumps.

Milgram's study caught the public's fancy, leading to the phrase "six degrees of separation." This expression means that, on average, everyone in the United States is separated by just six individuals. Milgram's conclusions have become so popular that a game, "Six Degrees of Kevin Bacon," was built around it.

Is the Small World Phenomenon an Academic Myth? Unfortunately, things are not this simple. There is a problem with Milgram's research, as psychologist Judith Kleinfeld (2002a, 2002b) discovered when she decided to replicate Milgram's study. When she went to the archives at Yale University Library to get more details, she found that Milgram had stacked the deck in favor of finding a small world. The "starters" came from mailing lists of people who were likely to have higher incomes and therefore were not representative of average people. In addition, one of the "targets" was a stockbroker, and that person's "starters" were investors in blue-chip stocks. Kleinfeld also found another discrepancy: On average, only 30 percent of the letters reached their "target." In one of Milgram's studies, the success rate was just 5 percent.

Box 9.1 Cultural Diversity in the United States

How Our Own Social Networks Perpetuate Social Inequality

Consider some of the principles we have reviewed. People tend to form in-groups with which they identify; they use reference groups to evaluate their attitudes and behavior; and they interact in social networks. Our in-groups, reference groups, and social networks are likely to consist of people whose backgrounds are similar to our own. For most of us, this means that just as social inequality is built into society, so it is built into our own relationships. One consequence is that we tend to perpetuate social inequality.

To see why, suppose that an outstanding job—great pay, interesting work, opportunity for advancement—has just opened up where you work. Whom are you going to tell? Most likely it will be someone you know, a friend or at least someone to whom you owe a favor. And most likely your social network is made up of people who look much like you do—especially in terms of their age, social class, race–ethnicity, and probably also gender. This tends to keep good jobs moving in the direction of people whose characteristics are similar to those of the people already in an organization. You can see how our social networks both reflect the inequality that characterizes our society and help to perpetuate it.

Consider a network of white men who are established in an organization. As they learn of opportunities (jobs, investments, real estate, and so on), they share this information with their networks. Opportunities and good jobs flow to people who have characteristics similar to their own. Those who benefit from this information, in turn, reciprocate with similar information when they learn of it. This bypasses people who have different characteristics—in this example, women and minorities—while it perpetuates the "good old boy" network. No intentional discrimination need be involved.

To overcome this barrier, women and minorities do **networking.** They try to meet people who can help advance their careers. Like the "good old boys," they go to parties and join clubs, churches, synagogues, mosques, and political parties. African American leaders, for example, cultivate a network of African American leaders. As a result, the network of African American leaders is so tight that one-fifth of the people composing the entire national African American leadership are personal acquaintances. Add some "friends of a friend," and *three-fourths* of the entire leadership belong to the same network (Taylor 1992).

Similarly, women cultivate a network of women. As a result, some women who reach top positions end up in a circle so tight that the term "new girl" network is being used, especially in the field of law. Remembering those who helped them and sympathetic to those who are trying to get ahead, these women tend to steer business to other women. Like the "good old boys" who preceded them, the new insiders have a ready set of reasons to justify their exclusionary practice (Jacobs 1997).

For Your Consideration

The perpetuation of social inequality does not require intentional discrimination. Just as social inequality is built into society, so is it built into our personal relationships. How do you think your own social network helps to perpetuate social inequality? How do you think we can break this cycle? (The key must lie in creating diversity in social networks.)

Social networks, which open and close doors of opportunity, are important for careers. Despite the official program of business and professional conventions, much of the "real" business centers around renewing and extending social networks.

Since most letters did not reach their targets, even with the deck stacked in favor of success, we can draw the *opposite* conclusion from the one that Milgram reported: People who don't know one another are dramatically separated by social barriers. How great the barriers are is illustrated by another attempt to replicate Milgram's study, this one using e-mail. Only 384 of 24,000 chains reached their targets (Dodds et al. 2003).

As Kleinfeld says, "Rather than living in a small world, we may live in a world that looks a lot like a bowl of lumpy oatmeal, with many small worlds loosely connected and perhaps some small worlds not connected at all." Somehow, I don't think that the phrase "lumpy oatmeal phenomenon" will become standard, but the criticism of Milgram's research is valid.

Implications for a Socially Diverse Society Besides geography, the barriers that separate us into many small worlds are primarily those of social class, gender, and race–ethnicity. Overcoming these social barriers is difficult because even our own social networks contribute to social inequality, a topic that we explore in the Cultural Diversity box on the next page.

Implications for Science Kleinfeld's revelations of the flaws in Milgram's research reinforce the need for replication. For our knowledge of social life, we cannot depend on single studies—there may be problems of generalizability on the one hand, or those of negligence or even fraud on the other. Replication by objective researchers is essential to build and advance solid social knowledge.

A New Group: Electronic Communities

In the 1990s, a new type of human group, the **electronic community**, made its appearance. People "meet" online in chat rooms to talk about almost any conceivable topic, from donkey racing and bird watching to sociology and quantum physics. Some online encounters meet our definition of *group*, people who interact with one another and who think of themselves as belonging together. They pride themselves on the distinctive nature of their interests and knowledge—factors that give them a common identity and bind them together. Although sociologists have begun to study these groups, the results are preliminary and tentative.

Bureaucracies

About 100 years ago, sociologist Max Weber analyzed the *bureaucracy*, a group that has since become dominant in social life. To achieve more efficient results, this form of social organization shifts the emphasis from traditional relationships based on personal loyalties to the "bottom line." As we look at the characteristics of bureaucracies, we will also consider their implications for our lives.

The Characteristics of Bureaucracies

What do the Russian army and the U.S. postal service have in common? Or the government of Mexico and your college? The sociological answer is that all are *bureaucracies*. As Weber (1913/1947) pointed out, **bureaucracies** have

1. *Clear levels, with assignments flowing downward and accountability flowing upward.* Each level assigns responsibilities to the level beneath it, while each lower level is accountable to the level above it for fulfilling those assignments. Figure 9.1 below shows the bureaucratic structure of a typical university.
2. *A division of labor.* Each worker has a specific task to fulfill, and all the tasks are coordinated to accomplish the purpose of the organization. In a college, for example, a teacher does not fix the heating system, the president does not approve class schedules, and a secretary does not evaluate textbooks. These tasks are distributed among people who have been trained to do them.
3. *Written rules.* In their attempt to become efficient, bureaucracies stress written procedures. In general, the longer a bureaucracy exists and the larger it grows, the more written rules it has.
4. *Written communications and records.* Records are kept of much of what occurs in a bureaucracy ("Be sure to CC all immediate supervisors."). In some organizations, workers spend a fair amount of time sending memos and e-mail back and forth.
5. *Impersonality and replaceability.* It is the office that is important, not the individual who holds the office. You work for the organization, not for the replaceable person who heads some post in the organization.

Weber viewed bureaucracies as such a powerful form of social organization that he predicted they would come to dominate social life. He called this process the **rationalization of society**, meaning that bureaucracies, with their rules and emphasis on results, would increasingly dominate our lives. Weber was right. These five characteristics have made bureaucracies so successful that, as illustrated by the Down-to-

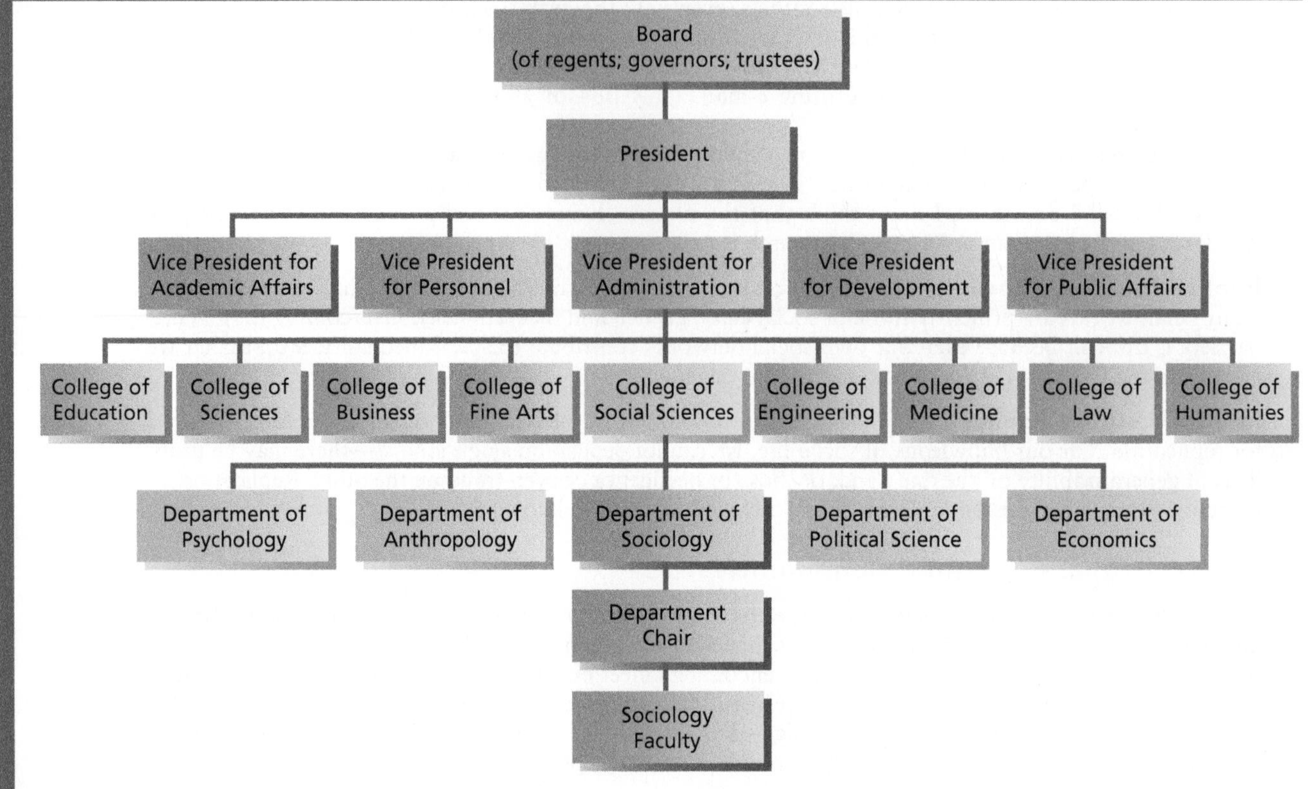

FIGURE 9.1 The Typical Bureaucratic Structure of a Medium-Sized University
This is a scaled-down ersion of a university's bureaucratic structure. The actual lines of a university are likely to be much more complicated than those depicted here. A large university may have a chancellor and several presidents under the chancellor, each president being responsible for a particular campus. Although in this figure extensions of authority are shown only for the Vice President for Administration and the College of Social Sciences, each of the other vice presidents and colleges has similar positions. If the figure were to be extended, departmental secretaries would be shown and, eventually, somewhere, even students.

Earth Sociology box on the next page, they have even begun to take over cooking, one of the most traditional areas of life.

The Perpetuation of Bureaucracies

Bureaucracies have become a standard feature of our lives because they are a powerful form of social organization. They harness people's energies to reach specific goals. Once in existence, however, bureaucracies tend to take on a life of their own. In a process called **goal displacement,** even after the organization achieves its goal and no longer has a reason to continue, continue it does.

A classic example is the March of Dimes, organized in the 1930s with the goal of fighting polio (Sills 1957). At that time, the origin of polio was a mystery. The public was alarmed and fearful, for overnight a healthy child could be stricken with this crippling disease. To raise money to find a cure, the March of Dimes placed posters of children on crutches near cash registers in almost every store in the United States. (See the photo on the next page.) The organization raised money beyond its wildest dreams. When Dr. Jonas Salk developed a vaccine for polio in the 1950s, the threat was wiped out almost overnight.

Did the staff that ran the March of Dimes quietly fold up their tents and slip away? Of course not. They had jobs to protect, so they targeted a new enemy—birth defects. But then in 2001, researchers finished mapping the human genome system. Perceiving that this information could help to eliminate birth defects—and their jobs—officials of the March of Dimes came up with a new slogan, "Breakthroughs for Babies." This latest goal should ensure the organization's existence forever: It is so vague that we are not likely to ever run out of the need for "breakthroughs."

Then there is NATO (North Atlantic Treaty Organization), founded during the Cold War to prevent Russia from invading Western Europe. When the Cold War ended, removing the organization's purpose, the Western powers tried to find a reason to continue their organization. I mean, why waste a perfectly good bureaucracy? They appear to have found one: to create "rapid response forces" to combat terrorism and "rogue nations" (Tyler 2002). To keep this bureaucracy going, they even allowed Russia to become a junior partner.

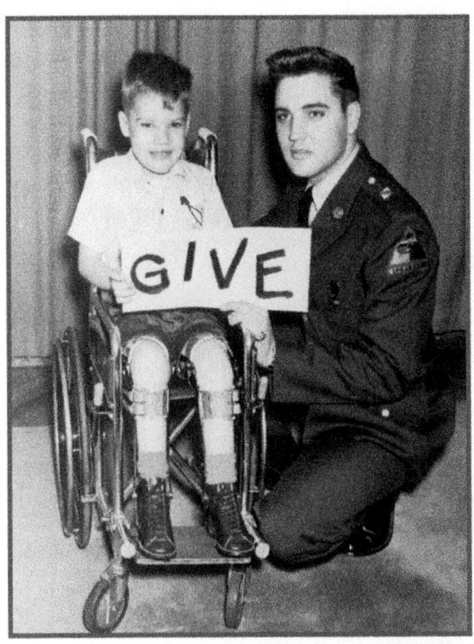

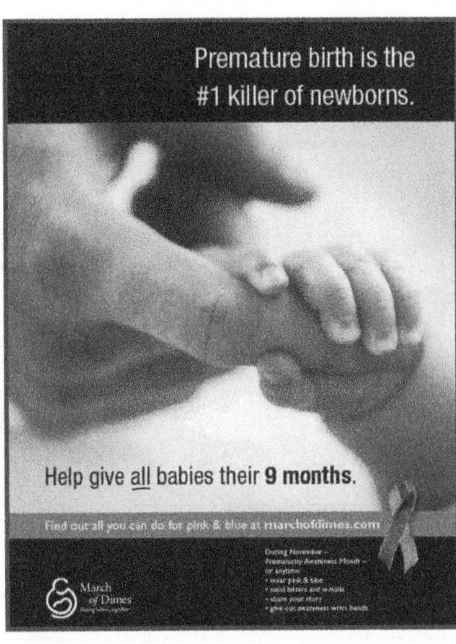

Premature birth is the
#1 killer of newborns.
Help give all babies their 9 months.
Find out all you can do for pink & blue at marchofdimes.com
March of Dimes

The March of Dimes was founded by President Franklin Roosevelt in the 1930s to fight polio. When a vaccine for polio was discovered in the 1950s, the organization did not declare victory and disband. Instead, its leaders kept the organization intact by creating new goals—fighting birth defects. Sociologists use the term *goal displacement* to refer to this process of adopting new goals.

Box 9.2 Down-to-Earth Sociology

The McDonaldization of Society

The McDonald's restaurants that seem to be all over the United States—and, increasingly, the world—have a significance that goes far beyond the convenience of quick hamburgers and milk shakes. As sociologist George Ritzer (1993, 1998, 2001) says, our everyday lives are being "McDonaldized." Let's see what he means by this.

The McDonaldization of society does not refer just to the robotlike assembly of food. This term refers to the standardization of everyday life, a process that is transforming our lives. Want to do some shopping? Shopping malls offer one-stop shopping in controlled environments. Planning a trip? Travel agencies offer "package" tours. They will transport middle-class Americans to ten European capitals in fourteen days. All visitors experience the same hotels, restaurants, and other scheduled sites—and no one need fear meeting a "real" native. Want to keep up with events? *USA Today* spews out McNews—short, bland, non-analytical pieces that can be digested between gulps of the McShake or the McBurger.

Efficiency brings dependability. You can expect your burger and fries to taste the same whether you buy them in Los Angeles or Beijing. Although efficiency also lowers prices, it does come at a cost. Predictability washes away spontaneity, changing the quality of our lives. It produces a sameness, a bland version of what used to be unique experiences. In my own travels, for example, had I taken packaged tours, I never would have had the eye-opening experiences that have added so much to my appreciation of human diversity. (Bus trips with chickens in Mexico, hitchhiking in Europe and Africa, sleeping on a granite table in a nunnery in Italy and in a cornfield in Algeria are just not part of tour agendas.)

For good or bad, our lives are being McDonaldized, and the predictability of packaged settings seems to be our social destiny. When education is rationalized, no longer will our children have to put up with real professors, who insist on discussing ideas endlessly, who never come to decisive answers, and who come saddled with idiosyncrasies. At some point, such an approach to education is going to be a bit of quaint history.

Our programmed education will eliminate the need for discussion of social issues—we will have packaged solutions to social problems, definitive answers that satisfy our need for closure. Computerized courses will teach the same answers to everyone—the approved, "politically correct" ways to think about social issues. Mass testing will ensure that students regurgitate the programmed responses.

Our coming prepackaged society will be efficient, of course. But it also means that we will be trapped in the "iron cage" of bureaucracy—just as Weber warned would happen.

McDonalds in Tokyo, Japan

This is the way that some people view bureaucracies: stilted, slow-moving, and destructive to the individual. Bureaucracies can be like this, but not all bureaucracies are alike. Some are innovative and unleash creative energy.

Dysfunctions of Bureaucracies

Although in the long run no other form of social organization is more efficient, as Weber recognized, bureaucracies also have a dark side. Let's look at some of their dysfunctions.

Red Tape: A Rule Is a Rule Bureaucracies can be so bound by red tape that when officials apply their rules, the results can defy all logic. I came across an example so ridiculous that it can make your head swim—if you don't burst from laughing first.

> In Spain, the Civil Registry of Barcelona recorded the death of a woman named Maria Antonieta Calvo in 1992. Apparently, Maria's evil brother had reported her dead so he could collect the family inheritance.
>
> When Maria learned that she was supposedly dead, she told the Registry that she was very much alive. The bureaucrats at this agency looked at their records, shook their heads, and insisted that she was dead. Maria then asked lawyers to represent her in court. They all refused—because no dead person can bring a case before a judge.
>
> When Maria's boyfriend asked her to marry him, the couple ran into a serious obstacle: No living man in Spain (or elsewhere, I presume) can marry a dead woman—so these bureaucrats said, "So sorry, but no license."
>
> After years of continuing to insist that she was alive, Maria finally got a hearing in court. When the judges looked at Maria, they believed that she really was a living person, and they ordered the Civil Registry to declare her alive.

The ending of this story gets even happier, for now that Maria was alive, she was able to marry her boyfriend. I don't know if the two lived happily ever after, but, after overcoming the bureaucrats, they at least had that chance ("Mujer 'resucita'. . ." 2006).

Bureaucratic Alienation Perceived in terms of roles, rules, and functions rather than as individuals, many workers begin to feel more like objects than people. Marx termed these reactions **alienation,** a result, he said, of workers being cut off from the finished product of their labor. He pointed out that before industrialization, workers used their own tools to produce an entire product, such as a chair or table. Now the capitalists own the tools (machinery, desks, computers) and assign each worker only a single step or two in the entire production process. Relegated to performing repetitive tasks that seem remote from the final product, workers no longer identify with what they produce. They come to feel estranged not only from the results of their labor but also from their work environment.

Resisting Alienation Because workers need to feel valued and want to have a sense of control over their work, they resist alienation. Forming primary groups at work is a major form of that resistance. Workers band together in informal settings—at lunch, around desks, or for a drink after work. There, they give one another approval for jobs well done and express sympathy for the shared need to put up with cantankerous bosses, meaningless routines, and endless rules. In these contexts, they relate to one another not just as workers, but as people who value one another. They flirt, laugh and tell jokes, and talk

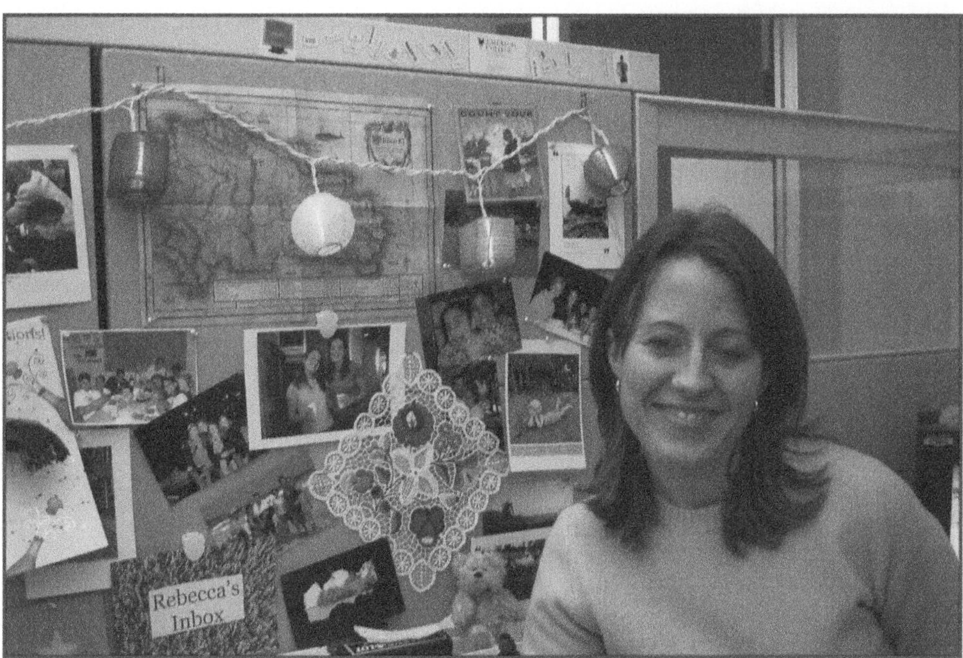

Workers develop many ways to avoid becoming a depersonalized unit in a bureaucratic-economic machine. In this photo, which I took at a major publisher, you can see how Rebecca, by personalizing her work setting, is claiming an identity that transcends that of worker. What "personalized messages" do you see in this photo?

about their families and goals. Adding this multidimensionality to their work relationships maintains their sense of being individuals rather than mere cogs in a machine.

As in the photo above, workers often decorate their work areas with personal items. The sociological implication is that of workers who are striving to resist alienation. By staking a claim to individuality, the workers are rejecting an identity as machines that exist simply to perform functions.

Bureaucratic Incompetence In a tongue-in-cheek analysis of bureaucracies, Laurence Peter proposed what has become known as the **Peter principle:** Each employee of a bureaucracy is promoted to his or her *level of incompetence* (Peter and Hull 1969). People who perform well in a bureaucracy come to the attention of those higher up the chain of command and are promoted. If they continue to perform well, they are promoted again. This process continues *until* they are promoted to a level at which they can no longer handle the responsibilities well—their level of incompetence. There they hide behind the work of others, taking credit for the accomplishments of employees under their direction.

Although the Peter principle contains a grain of truth, if it were generally true, bureaucracies would be staffed by incompetents, and these organizations would fail. In reality, bureaucracies are remarkably successful. Sociologists Peter Evans and James Rauch (1999) examined the government bureaucracies of thirty-five developing countries. They found that prosperity comes to the countries with central bureaucracies that hire workers on the basis of merit and offer them rewarding careers.

Working for the Corporation

Since you are likely to end up working in a bureaucracy, let's look at how its characteristics might affect your career.

Self-Fulfilling Stereotypes in the "Hidden" Corporate Culture

As you might recall, stereotypes can be self-fulfilling. That is, stereotypes can produce the very characteristics that they are built around.

Stereotypes also operate in corporate life—and are so powerful that they can affect *your* career. Here's how they work.

Self-Fulfilling Stereotypes and Promotions Corporate and department heads have ideas of "what it takes" to get ahead. Not surprisingly, since they themselves got ahead, they look for people who have characteristics similar to their own. They feed better information to workers with these characteristics, bring them into stronger networks, and put them in "fast track" positions. With such advantages, these workers perform better and become more committed to the company. This, of course, confirms the boss's initial expectation, or stereotype. But for workers who don't look or act like the corporate leaders, the opposite happens. Thinking of them as less capable, the bosses give them fewer opportunities and challenges. When these workers see others get ahead and realize that they are working beneath their own abilities, they lose morale, become less committed to the company, and don't perform as well. This, of course, confirms the stereotypes the bosses had of them.

In her studies of U.S. corporations, sociologist Rosabeth Moss Kanter (1977, 1983) found such self-fulfilling stereotypes to be part of a "hidden" **corporate culture.** That is, these stereotypes and their powerful effects on workers remain hidden to everyone, even the bosses. What bosses and workers see is the surface: The workers getting promoted are those who have superior performance and greater commitment to the company. To everyone, this seems to be just the way it should be. Hidden below this surface, however, as Kanter found, are these higher and lower expectations and the open and closed opportunities that produce the attitudes and accomplishments—or the lack of them.

As corporations grapple with growing diversity, the stereotypes in the hidden corporate culture are likely to give way, although slowly and grudgingly. In the following Thinking Critically section, we'll consider other aspects of diversity in the workplace.

Thinking Critically

Managing Diversity in the Workplace

Times have changed. The San Jose, California, electronic phone book lists ten times more *Nguyens* than *Joneses* (Albanese 2007). More than half of U.S. workers are minorities, immigrants, and women. Diversity in the workplace is much more than skin color. Diversity includes age, ethnicity, gender, religion, sexual orientation, and social class.

In our growing global context of life, diversity is increasing. In the past, the idea was for people to join the "melting pot," to give up their distinctive traits and become like the dominant group. Today, with the successes of the civil rights and women's movements, people are more likely to prize their distinctive traits. Realizing that assimilation (being absorbed into the dominant culture) is probably not the wave of the future, most large companies have "diversity training" (Johnson 2004; Hymowitz 2007). They hold lectures and workshops so that employees can learn to work with colleagues of diverse cultures and racial–ethnic backgrounds.

Coors Brewery is a prime example of this change. Coors went into a financial tailspin after one of the Coors brothers gave a racially charged speech in the 1980s. Today, Coors offers diversity workshops, has sponsored a gay dance, and has paid for a corporate-wide mammography program. In 2004, Coors opposed an amendment to the Colorado constitution that would ban the marriage of homosexuals. The company has even had rabbis certify its suds as kosher. Its proud new slogan: "Coors cares" (Cloud 1998). Now, that's quite a change.

What Coors cares about, of course, is the bottom line. It's the same with other corporations. Blatant racism and sexism once made no difference to profitability. Today, they do. To promote profitability, companies must promote diversity—or at least pretend to. The sincerity of corporate leaders is not what's important; diversity in the workplace is.

Diversity training has the potential to build bridges, but it can backfire. Managers who are chosen to participate can resent it, thinking that it is punishment for some unmentioned insensitivity on their part (Sanchez and Medkik 2004). Some directors of these programs are so incompetent that they create antagonisms and reinforce stereotypes. For example, the leaders of a diversity training session at the U.S. Department of Transportation had women grope men as the men ran by. They encouraged blacks and whites to insult one another and to call each other names (Reibstein 1996). The intention may have been good (understanding the other through role reversal and getting hostilities "out in the open"), but the approach was moronic. Instead of healing, such behaviors wound and leave scars.

Pepsi provides a positive example of diversity training. Managers at Pepsi are given the assignment of sponsoring a group of employees who are unlike themselves. Men sponsor women, African Americans sponsor whites, and so on. The executives are expected to try to understand work from the perspective of the people they sponsor, to identify key talent, and to personally mentor at least three people in their group. Accountability is built in—the sponsors have to give updates to executives even higher up (Terhune 2005).

For Your Consideration

Do you think that corporations and government agencies should offer diversity training? If so, how can we develop diversity training that fosters mutual respect? Can you suggest practical ways to develop workplaces that are not divided by gender and race–ethnicity?

Technology and the Control of Workers

As mentioned in the last chapter, the microchip has revolutionized society. Among the changes it has ushered in is the greater ease of keeping tabs on people. Computers make it easier for governments to operate a police state by monitoring our every move (Bradsher 2007b). The Big Brother in Orwell's classic novel *1984* may turn out to be a master computer to which we all become servants.

We'll know shortly. Already, many workers are closely monitored by computers. In some workplaces, cameras even transmit workers' facial expressions for computer analysis (Neil 2008). These cameras, called "little brothers" (as compared with Orwell's "Big Brother"), are making their appearance in shopping malls, on streetcorners, and in our homes. As some analysts suggest, we seem to be moving to a *maximum-security society* (Marx 1995).

Maximum-security society seems an apt term. As with the workers in the Sociology and the New Technology box on the next page, few of us realize how extensively our actions are being monitored.

Group Dynamics

As you know from personal experience, the lively interaction *within* groups—who does what with whom—has profound consequences for how you adjust to life. Sociologists use the term **group dynamics** to refer to how groups influence us and how we affect groups. Let's consider how the size of a group makes a difference and then examine leadership, conformity, and decision making.

Before doing so, we should see how sociologists define the term *small group*. In a **small group**, there are few enough members that each one can interact directly with all the other members. Small groups can be either primary or secondary. A wife, husband, and children make up a primary small group, as do workers who take their breaks together, while bidders at an auction and students in an introductory sociology class are secondary small groups.

Effects of Group Size on Stability and Intimacy

Writing in the early 1900s, sociologist Georg Simmel (1858–1918) noted the significance of group size. He used the term **dyad** for the smallest possible group, which consists of two people. Dyads, which include marriages, love affairs, and close friendships, show two distinct qualities. First, they are the most intense or intimate of human groups. Because only two people are involved, the interaction is focused on them. Second, because dyads require that both members participate and be committed, it takes just one member to lose interest for the dyad to collapse. In larger groups, by contrast, even if one member withdraws, the group can continue, for its existence does not depend on any single member (Simmel 1950).

A **triad** is a group of three people. As Simmel noted, the addition of a third person fundamentally changes the group. With three people, interaction between the first two decreases. This can create strain. For example, with the birth of a child, hardly any aspect of a couple's relationship goes untouched. Attention focuses on the baby, and interaction between the husband and wife diminishes. Despite this, the marriage usually becomes stronger. Although the intensity of interaction is less in triads, they are inherently stronger and give greater stability to a relationship.

Yet, as Simmel noted, triads, too, are inherently unstable. They tend to form **coalitions**—some group members aligning themselves against others. In a triad, it is not uncommon for two members to feel a stronger bond and to prefer one another. This leaves the third person feeling hurt and excluded. Another characteristic of triads is that they often produce an arbitrator or mediator, someone who tries to settle disagreements between the other two. In one-child families, you can often observe both of these characteristics of triads—coalitions and arbitration.

The general principle is this: *As a small group grows larger, it becomes more stable, but its intensity, or intimacy, decreases.* To see why, look at Figure 9.2 on page 215. As each new person comes into a group, the connections among people multiply. In a dyad, there is only 1 relationship; in a triad, there are 3; in a group of four, 6; in a group of five, 10. If we expand the group to six, we have 15 relationships, while a group of seven yields 21 relationships. If we continue adding members, we soon are unable to follow the connections: A group of eight has 28 possible relationships; a group of nine, 36 relationships; a group of ten, 45; and so on.

It is not only the number of relationships that makes larger groups more stable. As groups grow, they also tend to develop a more formal structure to accomplish their goals. For example, leaders emerge and more specialized roles come into play. This often results in such familiar offices as president, secretary, and treasurer. This structure provides a framework that helps the group survive over time.

Box 9.3 Sociology and the New Technology

Cyberloafers and Cybersleuths: Surfing at Work

Few people work constantly at their jobs. Most of us take breaks and, at least once in a while, goof off. We meet fellow workers at the coffee machine, and we talk in the hallway. Much of this interaction is good for the company, for it bonds us to fellow workers and ties us to our jobs.

Our personal lives may even cross over into our workday. Some of us make personal calls from the office. Bosses know that we need to check in with our child's preschool or make arrangements for a babysitter. They expect such calls. Some even wink as we make a date or nod as we arrange to have our car worked on. And most bosses make personal calls of their own from time to time. It's the abuse that bothers bosses, and it's not surprising that they fire anyone who talks on the phone all day for personal reasons.

Using computers at work for personal purposes is called *cyberslacking*. Many workers fritter away some of their workday online. They trade stocks, download music, gamble, and play games. They read books, shop, exchange jokes, send personal e-mail, post messages in chat rooms, and visit online red-light districts. Some cyberslackers even operate their own businesses online—when they're not battling virtual enemies during "work."

To take a day off without the boss knowing it, some use remote devices to make their computer switch screens and their printer spew out documents (Spencer 2003). It looks as though they just stepped away from their desk. Some equip their cell phones with audio recordings: Although they may be sitting on the beach when they call the office, their boss hears background sounds of a dentist's drill or of honking horns (Richtel 2004).

Some workers defend their cyberloafing. They argue, reasonably enough, that since their work invades their homes—forcing them to work evenings and weekends—employers should accommodate their personal lives. Some Web sites protect cyberloafers: They feature a panic button in case the boss pokes her head in your office. Click the button and a phony spreadsheet pops onto your screen while typing sounds emerge from your speakers.

Cyberslacking has given birth to the cybersleuth. With specialized software, cybersleuths can recover every note employees have written and every Web site they have visited (Nusbaum 2003). They can bring up every file that employees have deleted, even every word they've erased. What some workers don't know (and what some of us forget) is that "delete" does not mean erase. Hitting the delete button simply pushes the text into the background of our hard drive. With a few clicks, the cybersleuth, like magic ink, exposes our "deleted" information, opening our hidden diary for anyone to read.

For Your Consideration

Do you think that cybersleuthing is an abuse of power? An invasion of privacy? Or do employers have a right to check on what their employees are doing with company computers on company time? Can you think of a less invasive solution to cyberloafing?

Effects of Group Size on Attitudes and Behavior

Imagine that your social psychology professors have asked you to join a few students to discuss your adjustment to college life. When you arrive, they tell you that to make the discussion anonymous they want you to sit unseen in a booth. You will participate in the discussion over an intercom, talking when your microphone comes on. The professors say that they will not listen to the conversation, and they leave.

You find the format somewhat strange, to say the least, but you go along with it. You have not seen the other students in their booths, but when they talk about their experiences, you find yourself becoming wrapped up in the problems that they begin to share. One student even mentions how frightening he has found college because of his history of epileptic seizures. Later, you hear this individual breathe heavily into the microphone. Then he stammers and cries for help. A crashing noise follows, and you imagine him lying helpless on the floor.

Nothing but an eerie silence follows. What do you do?

Your professors, John Darley and Bibb Latané (1968), staged the whole thing, but you don't know this. No one had a seizure. In fact, no one was even in the other booths. Everything, except your comments, was on tape.

Some participants were told that they would be discussing the topic with just one other student, others with two, others with three, four, and five. Darley and Latané found that all students who thought they were part of a dyad rushed out to help. If they thought they were part of a triad, only 80 percent went to help—and they were slower in leaving the booth. In six-person groups, only 60 percent went to see what was wrong—and they were even slower.

This experiment demonstrates how deeply group size influences our attitudes and behavior: It even affects our willingness to help one another. Students in the dyad knew that it was up to them to help the other student. The professor was gone, and if they didn't help there was no one else. In the larger groups, including the triad, students felt *a diffusion of responsibility:* Giving help was no more their responsibility than anyone else's.

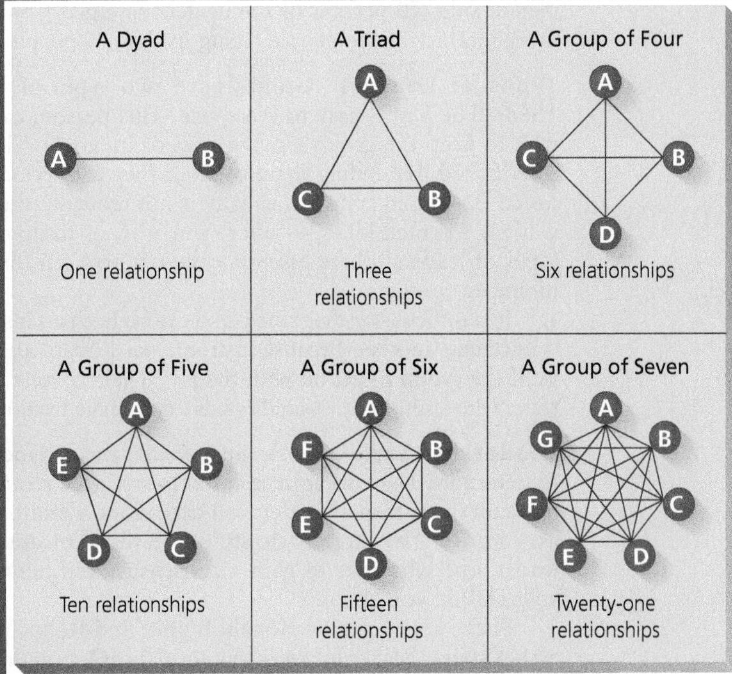

FIGURE 9.2 The Effects of Group Size on Relationships

You probably have observed the second consequence of group size firsthand. When a group is small, its members act informally, but as the group grows, the members lose their sense of intimacy and become more formal with one another. No longer can the members assume that the others are "insiders" in sympathy with what they say. Now they must take a "larger audience" into consideration, and instead of merely "talking," they begin to "address" the group. As their speech becomes more formal, their body language stiffens.

You probably have observed a third aspect of group dynamics, too. In the early stages of a party, when only a few people are present, almost everyone talks with everyone else. But as others arrive, the guests break into smaller groups. Some hosts, who want their guests to mix together, make a nuisance of themselves trying to achieve their *idea* of what a group should be like. The division into small groups is inevitable, however, for it follows the basic sociological principles that we have just reviewed. Because the addition of each person rapidly increases connections (in this case, "talk lines"), conversation becomes more difficult. The guests break into smaller groups in which they can look at each other directly and interact comfortably with one another.

Leadership

All of us are influenced by leaders, so it is important to understand leadership. Let's look at how people become leaders, the types of leaders there are, and their different styles of leadership. Before we do this, though, it is important to clarify that leaders don't necessarily hold formal positions in a group. **Leaders** are simply people who influence the behaviors, opinions, or attitudes of others. Even a group of friends has leaders.

Who Becomes a Leader? Are leaders born with characteristics that propel them to the forefront of a group? No sociologist would agree with such an idea. In general, people who become leaders are perceived by group members as strongly representing their values or as able to lead a group out of a crisis (Trice and Beyer 1991). Leaders also tend to be more talkative and to express determination and self-confidence.

These findings may not be surprising, as such traits appear to be related to leadership. Researchers, however, have also discovered traits that seem to have no bearing on the ability to lead. For example, taller people and those who are judged better looking are more likely to become leaders (Stodgill 1974; Judge and Cable 2004). The taller and more attractive are also likely to earn more, but that is another story (Deck 1968; Feldman 1972; Case and Paxson 2006).

Many other factors underlie people's choice of leaders, most of which are quite subtle. A simple experiment performed by social psychologists Lloyd Howells and Selwyn Becker (1962) uncovered one of these factors. They formed groups of five people who did not know one another, seating them at a rectangular table, three on one side and two on the other. After discussing a topic for a set period of time, each group chose a leader. The findings are startling: Although only 40 percent of the people sat on the two-person side, 70 percent of the leaders emerged from that side. The explanation is that we tend to direct more interactions to people facing us than to people to the side of us.

Types of Leaders Groups have two types of leaders (Bales 1950, 1953; Cartwright and Zander 1968). The first is easy to recognize. This person, called an **instrumental leader** (or *task-oriented leader*), tries to keep the group moving toward its goals. These leaders try to keep group members from getting sidetracked, reminding them of what they are trying to accomplish. The **expressive leader** (or *socioemotional leader*), in contrast, usually is not recognized as a leader, but he or she certainly is one. This person is likely to crack jokes, to offer sympathy, or to do other things that help to lift the group's morale. Both types of leadership are essential: the one to keep the group on track, the other to increase harmony and minimize conflicts.

It is difficult for the same person to be both an instrumental and an expressive leader, for these roles contradict one another. Because instrumental leaders are task oriented, they sometimes create friction as they prod the group to get on with the job. Their actions often cost them popularity. Expressive leaders, in contrast, who stimulate personal bonds and reduce friction, are usually more popular (Olmsted and Hare 1978).

Leadership Styles Let's suppose that the president of your college has asked you to head a task force to determine how the college can improve race relations on campus. Although this position requires you to be an instrumental leader, you can adopt a number of **leadership styles,** or ways of expressing yourself as a leader. The three basic styles are those of **authoritarian leader,** one who gives orders; **democratic leader,** one who tries to gain a consensus; and **laissez-faire leader,** one who is highly permissive. Which style should you choose?

Social psychologists Ronald Lippitt and Ralph White (1958) carried out a classic study of these leadership styles. Boys who were matched for IQ, popularity, physical energy, and leadership were assigned to "craft clubs" made up of five boys each. The experimenters trained adult men in the three leadership styles. As the researchers peered through peepholes, taking notes and making movies, each adult rotated among the clubs, playing all three styles to control possible influences of their individual personalities.

The *authoritarian* leaders assigned tasks to the boys and told them exactly what to do. They also praised or condemned the boys' work arbitrarily, giving no explanation for why they judged it good or bad. The *democratic* leaders discussed the project with the boys, outlining the steps that would help them reach their goals. They also suggested alternative approaches and let the boys work at their own pace. When they evaluated the project, they gave "facts" as the bases for their decisions. The *laissez-faire* leaders were passive. They gave the boys almost total freedom to do as they wished. They offered help when asked, but made few suggestions. They did not evaluate the boys' projects, either positively or negatively.

The results? The boys who had authoritarian leaders grew dependent on their leader and showed a high degree of internal solidarity. They also became either aggressive or apathetic, with the aggressive boys growing hostile toward their leader. In contrast, the boys who had democratic leaders were friendlier and looked to one another for mutual approval. They did less scapegoating, and when the leader left the room they continued to work at a steadier pace. The boys with laissez-faire leaders asked more questions, but they made fewer decisions. They were notable for their lack of achievement. The researchers concluded that the democratic style of leadership works best. Their conclusion, however, may have been biased, as the researchers favored a democratic style of leadership in the first place (Olmsted and Hare 1978). Apparently, this same bias in studies of leadership continues (Cassel 1999).

You may have noticed that only boys and men were involved in this experiment. It is interesting to speculate how the results might differ if we were to repeat the experiment with all-girl groups and with mixed groups of girls and boys—and if we used both men and women as leaders. Perhaps you will become the sociologist to study such variations of this classic experiment.

Leadership Styles in Changing Situations Different situations require different styles of leadership. Suppose, for example, that you are leading a dozen backpackers in the Sierra Madre mountains north of Los Angeles, and it is time to make dinner. A laissez-faire style would be appropriate if the backpackers had brought their own food, or perhaps a democratic style if everyone were supposed to pitch in. Authoritarian leadership—you telling the hikers how to prepare their meals—would create resentment. This, in turn, would likely interfere with meeting the primary goal of the group, which in this case is to have a good time while enjoying nature.

Now assume the same group but a different situation: One of your party is lost, and a blizzard is on its way. This situation calls for you to exercise authority. To simply shrug your shoulders and say "You figure it out" would invite disaster—and probably a lawsuit.

The Power of Peer Pressure: The Asch Experiment

How influential are groups in our lives? To answer this, let's look first at *conformity* in the sense of going along with our peers. Our peers have no authority over us, only the influence that we allow.

Imagine that you are taking a course in social psychology with Dr. Solomon Asch and you have agreed to participate in an experiment. As you enter his laboratory, you see seven chairs, five of them already filled by other students. You are given the sixth. Soon the seventh person arrives. Dr. Asch stands at the front of the room next to a covered easel. He explains that he will first show a large card with a vertical line on it, then another card with three vertical lines. Each of you is to tell him which of the three lines matches the line on the first card. (See Figure 9.3)

Dr. Asch then uncovers the first card with the single line and the comparison card with the three lines. The correct answer is easy, for two of the lines are obviously wrong, and one is exactly right. Each person, in order, states his or her answer aloud. You all answer correctly. The second trial is just as easy, and you begin to wonder why you are there.

Then on the third trial, something unexpected happens. Just as before, it is easy to tell which lines match. The first student, however, gives a wrong answer. The second gives the same incorrect answer. So do the third and the fourth. By now, you are wondering what is wrong. How will the person next to you answer? You can hardly believe it when he, too, gives the same wrong answer. Then it is your turn, and you give what you know is the right answer. The seventh person also gives the same wrong answer.

On the next trial, the same thing happens. You know that the choice of the other six is wrong. They are giving what to you are obviously wrong answers. You don't know what to think. Why aren't they seeing things the same way you are? Sometimes they do, but in twelve trials they don't. Something is seriously wrong, and you are no longer sure what to do.

When the eighteenth trial is finished, you heave a sigh of relief. The experiment is finally over, and you are ready to bolt for the door. Dr. Asch walks over to you with a big smile on his face, and thanks you for participating in the experiment. He explains that you were the only real subject in the experiment! "The other six were stooges. I paid them to give those answers," he says. Now you feel real relief. Your eyes weren't playing tricks on you after all.

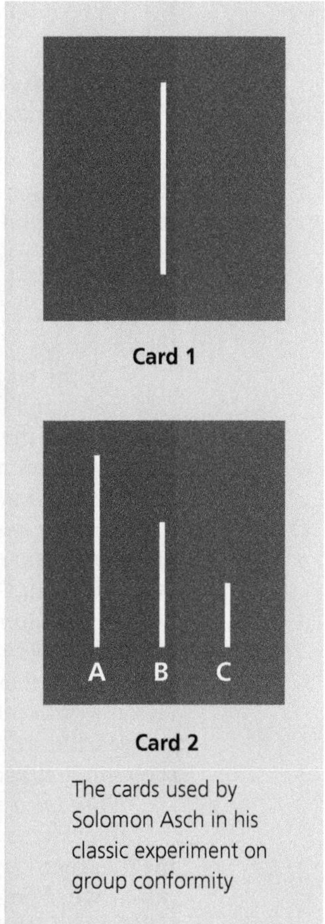

The cards used by Solomon Asch in his classic experiment on group conformity

Source: Asch 1952: 452–453

FIGURE 9.3 Asch's Cards

What were the results? Asch (1952) tested fifty people. One-third (33 percent) gave in to the group half the time, providing what they knew to be wrong answers. Another two out of five (40 percent) gave wrong answers, but not as often. One out of four (25 percent) stuck to their guns and always gave the right answer. I don't know how I would do on this test (if I knew nothing about it in advance), but I like to think that I would be part of the 25 percent. You probably feel the same way about yourself. But why should we feel that we wouldn't be like *most* people?

The results are disturbing, and researchers are still replicating Asch's experiment (Bond 2005). In our "land of individualism," the group is so powerful that most people are willing to say things that they know are not true. And this was a group of strangers! How much more conformity can we expect when our group consists of friends, people we value highly and depend on for getting along in life? Again, maybe you will become the sociologist to run that variation of Asch's experiment, perhaps using female subjects.

The Power of Authority: The Milgram Experiment

Even more disturbing are the results of the experiment described in the following Thinking Critically section.

Thinking Critically

If Hitler Asked You to Execute a Stranger, Would You? The Milgram Experiment

Imagine that you are taking a course with Dr. Stanley Milgram (1963, 1965), a former student of Dr. Asch's. Assume that you do not know about the Asch experiment and have no reason to be wary. You arrive at the laboratory to participate in a study on punishment and learning. You and a second student draw lots for the roles of "teacher" and "learner." You are to be the teacher. When you see that the learner's chair has protruding electrodes, you are glad that you are the teacher. Dr. Milgram shows you the machine you will run. You see that one side of the control panel is marked "Mild Shock, 15 volts," while the center says "Intense Shock, 350 Volts," and the far right side reads "DANGER: SEVERE SHOCK."

"As the teacher, you will read aloud a pair of words," explains Dr. Milgram. "Then you will repeat the first word, and the learner will reply with the second word. If the learner can't remember the word, you press this lever on the shock generator. The shock will serve as punishment, and we can then determine if punishment improves memory." You nod, now very relieved that you haven't been designated the learner.

"Every time the learner makes an error, increase the punishment by 15 volts," instructs Dr. Milgram. Then, seeing the look on your face, he adds, "The shocks can be extremely painful, but they won't cause any permanent tissue damage." He pauses, and then says, "I want you to see." You then follow him to the "electric chair," and Dr. Milgram gives you a shock of 45 volts. "There. That wasn't too bad, was it?" "No," you mumble.

The experiment begins. You hope for the learner's sake that he is bright, but unfortunately he turns out to be rather dull. He gets some answers right, but you have to keep turning up the dial. Each turn makes you more and more uncomfortable. You find yourself hoping that the learner won't miss another answer. But he does. When he received the first shocks, he let out some moans and groans, but now he is screaming in agony. He even protests that he suffers from a heart condition.

How far do you turn that dial?

By now, you probably have guessed that there was no electricity attached to the electrodes and that the "learner" was a stooge who only pretended to feel pain. The purpose of the experiment was to find out at what point people refuse to participate. Does anyone actually turn the lever all the way to "DANGER: SEVERE SHOCK"?

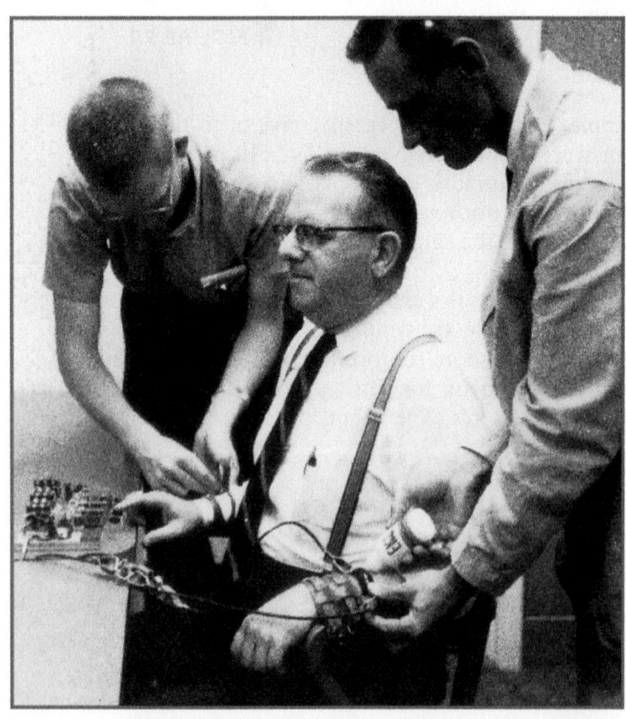

In the 1960s, U.S. social psychologists ran a series of creative but controversial experiments. From this photo of the "learner" being prepared for one of Stanley Milgram's experiments, you can get an idea of how convincing the situation would be for the "teacher."

Milgram wanted the answer because millions of ordinary people did nothing to stop the Nazi slaughter of Jews, gypsies, Slavs, homosexuals, people with disabilities, and others whom the Nazis designated as "inferior." The cooperation of so many ordinary people in the face of all this killing seemed bizarre, and Milgram wanted to see how ordinary, intelligent Americans might react in an analogous situation.

Milgram was upset by what he found. Many "teachers" broke into a sweat and protested that the experiment was inhuman and should be stopped. But when the experimenter calmly replied that the experiment must go on, this assurance from an "authority" ("scientist, white coat, university laboratory") was enough for most "teachers" to continue, even though the "learner" screamed in agony. Even "teachers" who were "reduced to twitching, stuttering wrecks" continued to follow orders.

Milgram varied the experiments (Nestar and Gregory 2005). He used both men and women. In some experiments, he put the "teachers" and "learners" in the same room, so the "teacher" could clearly see the suffering. In others, he put the "learners" in a separate room and had them pound and kick the wall during the first shocks and then go silent. The results varied. When there was no verbal feedback from the "learner," 65 percent of the "teachers" pushed the lever all the way to 450 volts. Of those who could see the "learner," 40 percent turned the lever all the way. When Milgram added a second "teacher," a stooge who refused to go along with the experiment, only 5 percent of the "teachers" turned the lever all the way, a result that bears out some of Asch's findings.

A stormy discussion about research ethics erupted. Not only were researchers surprised and disturbed by what Milgram found, but they were also alarmed at his methods. Universities began to require that subjects be informed of the nature and purpose of social research. Researchers agreed that to reduce subjects to "twitching, stuttering wrecks" was unethical, and almost all deception was banned.

For Your Consideration

What connections do you see between Milgram's experiment and the actions of Monster Kody in our opening vignette? Taking into account how significant these findings are, do you think that the scientific community overreacted to Milgram's experiments? Should we allow such research? Consider both the Asch and Milgram experiments, and use symbolic interactionism, functionalism, and conflict theory to explain why groups have such influence over us.

Global Consequences of Group Dynamics: Groupthink

> Suppose you are a member of the president's inner circle. It is midnight, and the president has just called an emergency meeting to deal with a terrorist attack. At first, several options are presented. Eventually, these are narrowed to only a couple of choices, and at some point, everyone seems to agree on what now appears to be "the only possible course of action." To express doubts at that juncture will bring you into conflict with all the other important people in the room. To criticize will mark you as not being a "team player." So you keep your mouth shut, with the result that each step commits you—and them—more and more to the "only" course of action.

From the Milgram and Asch experiments, we can see the power of authority and the influence of peers. Under some circumstances, as in this example, these factors can lead to **groupthink.** Sociologist Irving Janis (1972, 1982) coined this term to refer to the collective tunnel vision that group members sometimes develop. As they begin to think alike, they become convinced that there is only one "right" viewpoint and a single course of action to follow. They take any suggestion of alternatives as a sign of disloyalty. With their perspective narrowed and fully convinced that they are right, they may even put aside moral judgments and disregard risk (Hart 1991; Flippen 1999).

Groupthink can bring serious consequences. Consider the *Columbia* space shuttle disaster of 2003.

> Foam broke loose during launch, and engineers were concerned that it might have damaged tiles on the nose cone. Because this would make reentry dangerous, they sent e-mails to NASA officials, warning them about the risk. One engineer even suggested that the crew do a "space walk" to examine the tiles (Vartabedian and Gold 2003). The team in charge of the Columbia shuttle, however, disregarded the warnings. Convinced that a piece of foam weighing less than two pounds could not seriously harm the shuttle, they refused to even consider the possibility (Wald and Schwartz 2003). The fiery results of their closed minds were transmitted around the globe.

The consequences of groupthink can be even greater than this. In 1941, President Franklin D. Roosevelt and his chiefs of staff had evidence that the Japanese were preparing to attack Pearl Harbor. They simply refused to believe it and decided to continue naval operations as usual. The destruction of the U.S. naval fleet ushered the United States into World War II. In the war with Vietnam, U.S. officials had evidence of the strength and determination of the North Vietnamese military. They arrogantly threw such evidence aside, refusing to believe that "little, uneducated, barefoot people in pajamas" could defeat the U.S. military.

In each of these cases, options closed as officials committed themselves to a single course of action. Questioning the decisions would have indicated disloyalty and disregard for "team playing." Those in power plunged ahead, unable to see alternative perspectives. No longer did they try to objectively weigh evidence as it came in; instead, they interpreted everything as supporting their one "correct" decision.

Groupthink knows few bounds. Consider the aftermath of 9/11, when government officials defended torture as moral, "the lesser of two evils." Groupthink narrowed thought to the point that the U.S. Justice Department ruled that the United States was not bound by the Geneva Convention that prohibits torture. Facing protests, the Justice Department backed down (Lewis 2005).

The U.S. military involvement in Iraq appears to be a similar example. Top leaders, convinced that they made the right decision to go to war and that they were finding success in building a new Iraqi society, continuously interpreted even disconfirming evidence as favorable. Opinions and debate that contradicted their mind-set were written off as signs of ignorance and disloyalty. Despite mounting casualties, negative public sentiment, and even political opposition to the war, it was as though the president and his advisors had been blinded by groupthink.

Preventing Groupthink Groupthink is a danger for government leaders, who tend to surround themselves with an inner circle that closely reflects their own views. In "briefings," written summaries, and "talking points," this inner circle spoon-feeds the leaders the information it has selected. The result is that top leaders, such as the president, become cut off from information that does not support their own opinions.

Perhaps the key to preventing the mental captivity and intellectual paralysis known as groupthink is the widest possible circulation—especially among a nation's top government officials—of research that has been conducted by social scientists independent of the government and information that has been gathered freely by media reporters. If this conclusion comes across as an unabashed plug for sociological research and the free exchange of ideas, it is. Giving free rein to diverse opinions can curb groupthink, which—if not prevented—can lead to the destruction of a society and, in today's world of nuclear, chemical, and biological weapons, the obliteration of Earth's inhabitants.

Summary and Review

Groups Within Society

What is a group?

Sociologists use many definitions of groups, but, in general, **groups** consist of people who think of themselves as belonging together and who interact with one another. P. 200.

How do sociologists classify groups?

Sociologists divide groups into primary groups, secondary groups, in-groups, out-groups, reference groups, and networks. The cooperative, intimate, long-term, face-to-face relationships provided by **primary groups** are fundamental to our sense of self. **Secondary groups** are larger, relatively temporary, and more anonymous, formal, and impersonal than primary groups. **In-groups** provide members with a strong sense of identity and belonging. **Out-groups** also foster identity by showing in-group members what they are *not.* **Reference groups** are groups whose standards we refer to as we evaluate ourselves. **Social networks** consist of social ties that link people together. Developments in communications technology have given birth to a new type of group, the **electronic community.** Pp. 200–207.

What is "the iron law of oligarchy"?

Sociologist Robert Michels noted that formal organizations have a tendency to become controlled by an inner circle that limits leadership to its own members. The dominance of a formal organization by an elite that keeps itself in power is called **the iron law of oligarchy.** Pp. 202–203.

Bureaucracies

What are bureaucracies?

Bureaucracies are social groups characterized by a hierarchy, division of labor, written rules and communications, and impersonality and replaceability of positions. These characteristics make bureaucracies efficient and enduring. Pp. 207–211.

What dysfunctions are associated with bureaucracies?

The dysfunctions of bureaucracies include alienation, red tape, **goal displacement,** and incompetence (as seen in the **Peter principle**). The impersonality of bureaucracies tends to produce **alienation** among workers—the feeling that no one cares about them and that they do not really fit in. Pp. 210–211.

Working for the Corporation

How does the corporate culture affect workers?

The term **corporate culture** refers to an organization's traditions, values, and unwritten norms. Much of corporate culture, such as its hidden values and stereotypes, is not readily visible. Often, a **self-fulfilling stereotype** is at work: People who match a corporation's hidden values tend to be put on career tracks that enhance their chance of success, while those who do not match those values are set on a course that minimizes their performance. Pp. 211–212.

Technology and the Control of Workers

What is the maximum-security society?

It is the use of computers and surveillance devices to monitor people, especially in the workplace. This technology is being extended to monitoring our everyday lives. P. 213.

Group Dynamics

How does a group's size affect its dynamics?
The term **group dynamics** refers to how individuals affect groups and how groups influence individuals. In a **small group,** everyone can interact directly with everyone else. As a group grows larger, its intensity decreases but its stability increases. A **dyad,** consisting of two people, is the most unstable of human groups, but it provides the most intense of intimate relationships. The addition of a third person, forming a **triad,** fundamentally alters relationships. Triads are unstable, as **coalitions** (the alignment of some members of a group against others) tend to form. Pp. 213–215.

What characterizes a leader?
A **leader** is someone who influences others. **Instrumental leaders** try to keep a group moving toward its goals, even though this causes friction and they lose popularity. **Expressive leaders** focus on creating harmony and raising group morale. Both types are essential to the functioning of groups. Pp. 215–216.

What are the three main leadership styles?
Authoritarian leaders give orders, **democratic leaders** try to lead by consensus, and **laissez-faire leaders** are highly permissive. An authoritarian style appears to be more effective in emergency situations, a democratic style works best for most situations, and a laissez-faire style is usually ineffective. P. 216.

How do groups encourage conformity?
The Asch experiment was cited to illustrate the power of peer pressure, the Milgram experiment to illustrate the influence of authority. Both experiments demonstrate how easily we can succumb to **groupthink,** a kind of collective tunnel vision. Preventing groupthink requires the free circulation of diverse and opposing ideas. P. 217.

■ Thinking Critically about Chapter 9

1. Identify your in-groups and your out-groups. How have your in-groups influenced the way you see the world? And what influence have your out-groups had on you?
2. You are likely to work for a bureaucracy. How do you think this will affect your orientation to life? How can you make the "hidden culture" work to your advantage?
3. Milgram's and Asch's experiments illustrate the power of peer pressure. How has peer pressure operated in your life? Think about something that you did not want to do but did anyway because of peer pressure.

■ Additional Resources

What can you find in MySocLab? www.mysoclab.com

- Complete Ebook
- Practice Tests and Video and Audio activities
- Mapping and Data Analysis exercises
- Sociology in the News
- Classic Readings in Sociology
- Research and Writing advice

Where Can I Read More on This Topic?

Suggested readings for this chapter are listed at the back of this book.

chapter 10

Deviance and Crime

Sociology Now
by Michael Kimmel and Amy Aronson

There's a good chance that every person reading this book is a law-abiding citizen. We don't steal each other's cars; we don't open fire at the quarterback or point guard of opposing teams; we don't burn own dormitories, or plunder the provost's office. We pay our taxes and drive under the speed limit, at least most of the time.

Yet there is an equally good chance that each person reading this book is a criminal. We may have run a red light, had a drink while underage, or gambled on a sporting event in an unauthorized setting or while underage. We may have stolen a library book, or plagiarized a paper. (These last few might not land you in jail, but they could get you kicked out of school.)

Most of us probably shave the rules a little bit. But we're also likely to get outraged, often to the point of violence, if someone cuts into a line for tickets at the movie theater. Is it just because it's OK for us and not OK for others? Or is it because we carry inside us a common moral standard, and we are willing to cheat a little to make things come out the way we think they are supposed to but resent it when others violate that same moral contract?

> **So, is the question whether you are a law-abiding citizen or a criminal?. . . To the sociologist, you're both. . . . The more interesting questions are when and where you are one or the other,. . . .**

So, is the question whether you are a law-abiding citizen or a criminal? To the sociologist, you're both. The more interesting questions are when and where you are one or the other, under what circumstances you obey or disobey the law, and what are the social and legal consequences of your behavior. Do you get away with it or get sent to jail?

And how do we think about crime? What crimes should be punished, and how severe should those punishments be? In some respects, one might say that America is soft on crime: Most arrests are not prosecuted, most prosecutions do not result in jail time, and most prisoners are paroled before they serve their full terms. In other respects, America is hard on crime: It is the number one jailer in the world and the only industrialized nation that still has the death penalty. It seems to be a matter of working very hard to achieve very limited results. In fact, we are both soft and hard on crime; to the sociologist what is most interesting is the how and why of that "softness" and "hardness" and measuring the effectiveness of the institutions that are designed to handle deviance and crime.

What Is Deviance?

Breaking a social rule, or refusing to follow one, is called **deviance.** Deviant acts are not just illegal; they can also violate a moral or a social rule that may or may not have legal consequences. This week, many of you will do something that could be considered deviant—from the illegal behaviors we just mentioned to arriving at a party too soon or leaving too early.

More involving acts of deviance, like being a nudist or organizing a hate group, are another matter. I know full well that walking around naked or pronouncing irrational prejudices in public may get me shunned, screamed at, or beat up, so I don't bring it up in casual conversation or on the train ride to work in the morning. I might reveal this only within a group of other nudists or bigots, or very close friends or family, or not at all.

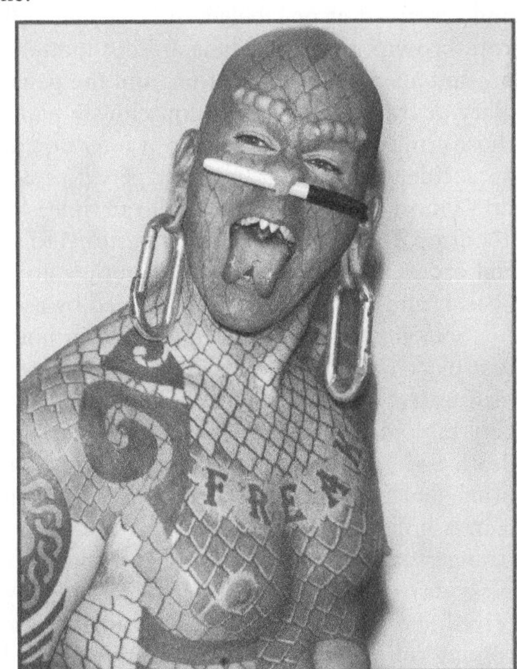

"Lizardman" is deviant because he breaks or refuses to follow social norms about appearance. Most deviance in society is not illegal.

We can also be considered deviant without doing, saying, or believing anything bad or wrong but just by belonging to a stigmatized minority group (Hispanic, gay, Jewish, for example) or by having some status that goes against what's considered "normal" (mentally ill, disabled, atheist). There is even deviance by

Sociology and our World

Crazy Laws

What we consider deviant changes over time, as people change their ideas of what is normal and what is wrong. As a result, laws prohibiting certain acts are often enforced long after most people in the society stopped considering them deviant. Men were fined for going topless on the beach as late as the 1930s. As of this writing, it is illegal for a man and a woman who are not married or relatives to share a hotel room in Florida (though the police look the other way during spring break). Some of these laws are still enforced—sometimes when the local police chief has had a bad day—but many others are unenforced and probably unenforceable. They are relics of long-vanished values, acts that some lawmakers considered deviant enough to warrant legal penalties:

- In Alabama, it is illegal to buy peanuts at night.
- In Colorado, it is illegal for a man to kiss a woman while she is asleep.
- In Florida, unmarried women are prohibited from skydiving on Sunday.
- In Boston, Massachusetts, it is illegal to take a bath unless you are under physician's orders.
- In New Mexico, it is illegal for women to appear in public with unshaven legs.
- In Tulsa, Oklahoma, heterosexual kissing is permitted, as long as it lasts less than three minutes.
- In Oregon, a man may not purchase alcohol without the written consent of his wife.

(All are from Davidson, 1998.)

association: If you have a friend who belongs to the stigmatized minority group, or a family member with a deviant status, you may be labeled as deviant just for being seen with him or her.

Most deviance is not illegal, and many illegal acts are only mildly deviant or not deviant at all. But when lawmakers consider a deviant act bad enough to warrant formal sanctions, it becomes a *crime,* and the full force of the government goes into regulating it. Some common sexual practices—like oral sex or masturbation—are illegal in a number of states because lawmakers at one time found them sufficiently deviant to be criminal and wanted anyone who committed them to "pay his or her debt to society" with fines or prison terms.

Some sociologists study minor forms of deviance, like appearing in public without your corset, but most are interested in the major forms of deviance. These are acts that can get you shunned and screamed at or labeled an "outsider" (Becker, 1966); or they are the sorts of crimes that get you thrown in prison. These are not matters of mere carelessness: The rules come from many important agents of socialization, and the penalties for breaking them are high. With some, like burglary or fraud, you have to consciously plan to commit the act, and the law distinguishes between those crimes that are the result of intention and those that could be the result of negligence or even an accident (and we adjust our penalties accordingly). So why do people break them? And why don't most of us break them all the time? What makes a deviant or a criminal? What can we do about it? These are the central questions to a sociologist because they illustrate our concern for social order and control—both when they are present, and people obey the rules and when they are absent, and people feel unconstrained by those same rules.

Sociologists are always interested in both sides of this question: How is society possible in the first place (social organization) and why does it often feel that society is "breaking down" or some institution is on the verge of collapse (social disorganization)? Recall the example of the New York City tabloid newspapers featuring screaming headlines about a person being pushed to his or her death on the subway tracks at rush hour. On the one hand, sociologists ask: What could possibly bring someone to push someone else, a stranger, in front of an oncoming subway train? Society, we fear, is breaking down right in front of our eyes. And yet, at the same time, more than one million strangers ride in those metal tubes going 75 miles an hour underneath the streets of New York City every day—crowded conditions with people you don't know, don't especially like, and all sleep deprived and buzzed on coffee. Sociologists also ask: Why aren't more people pushed in front of oncoming trains every day? We're interested in both questions: Why do most of us conform to social norms most of the time, and why do most of us decide to break some of them at other times? We want to know: What accounts for conformity? What accounts for deviance? And who decides which is which?

Conformity and Social Control

Each culture develops different types of rules that prescribe what is considered appropriate behavior in that culture. They vary by how formalized they are, how central to social life, and the types of sanctions that are threatened should you break them:

1. **Folkways** are routine, usually unspoken conventions of behavior; our culture prescribes that we do some things in a certain way, although other ways might work just as well. For example, we face forward instead of backward in an elevator, and answer the question "How are you?" with "Fine." Breaking a folkway may make others in the group uncomfortable (although they sometimes don't understand why they're uncomfortable), and violators may be laughed at, frowned on, or scolded. Folkways are rarely made into laws.
2. **Mores** are norms with a strong moral significance, viewed as essential to the proper functioning of the group: We absolutely should or should not behave this way. You might break a *mos* (the singular form of mores) by assaulting someone or speaking abusively to someone. Breaking mores makes others in the group upset, angry, or afraid, and they are likely to consider violators bad or immoral. Mores are often made into laws.
3. **Taboos** are prohibitions viewed as essential to the well-being of humanity. To break a taboo is unthinkable, beyond comprehension. For example, Sigmund Freud considered the incest taboo—one should not have sex with one's own children—to be a foundation of all societies. If parents and children had sex, then lines of inheritance, family name, and orderly intergenerational property transfer would be completely impossible. Taboos are so important that most cultures have only a few. In the United States, for instance, murder and assault break mores, not taboos. Breaking taboos causes others to feel disgusted. The violators are considered sick, evil, and monstrous. Taboos are always made into laws, unless they are so unthinkable that lawmakers cannot believe that anyone would break them.

Did you know?

Taboos vary from culture to culture and from time period to time period. For a hundred years, scholars believed that Charles Dodgson, or Lewis Carroll (1832–1898), had a romantic and probably a sexual interest in 7-year-old Alice Liddell, and that he wrote *Alice in Wonderland* and *Through the Looking-Glass* as a means of courting her. But in her 1999 book, Karoline Leach examines all of the old documents and concludes that Dodgson was really having an affair with Alice's mother. After his death, his sister was so worried about a scandal that she manipulated his papers to make it appear that he was interested in Alice instead. In 1898, pedophilia was much less taboo than an extramarital fling!

Stigma

If some part of you—your race or sexuality, for example—is considered deviant, without your actually having to do anything, you would be considered "stigmatized." The sociologist Erving Goffman (1963) used the term **stigma** to mean an attribute that changes you "from a whole and usual person to a tainted and discounted one." Deviant behavior or a deviant master status creates stigma, although not in every case. Other people might ignore our deviance, or "forgive" it as an anomaly. Goffman believed that people with stigmatized attributes are constantly practicing various strategies to ensure minimal damage. Because being stigmatized will "spoil" your identity, you are likely to adopt one of three strategies to alleviate it.

Goffman identified three strategies to neutralize stigma and save yourself from having a spoiled identity. He listed them in order of increased social power—the more power you have, the more you can try and redefine the situation. (These terms reflect the era in which he was writing, since he obviously uses the Civil Rights movement as the reference.)

1. *Minstrelization:* If you're virtually alone and have very little power, you can overconform to the stereotypes that others have about you. To act like a minstrel, Goffman says, is to exaggerate the differences between the stigmatized and the dominant group. Thus, for example, did African Americans overact as happy-go-lucky entertainers when they had no other recourse. A contemporary example might be women who act ultrafeminine—helpless and dependent—in potentially harassing situations. Note that minstrels exaggerate difference in the face of those with more power; when they are with other stigmatized people, they may laugh about the fact that the powerful "actually think we're like this!" That's often the only sort of power that they feel they have.
2. *Normification:* If you have even a small amount of power, you might try to *minimize* the differences between the stigmatized groups. "Look," you'll say, "we're the same as you are, so there is no difference to discriminate against us." Normification is the process that gays and lesbians refer to when they argue for same-sex marriage or that women use when they say they want to be engineers or physicists. Normification involves exaggerating the similarities and downplaying the differences.

Box 10.1

Censoring Perceived Deviance

What do *you* think?

All groups have tendencies toward social control. The desire to censor people or ideas we think are deviant is strong, especially when those ideas seem in opposition to widely held values. At the same time, America prides itself on being a free country, and free speech is protected by the U.S. Constitution. Let's look at how you and other Americans feel about an antireligionist, a homosexual, and a racist teaching college or having books in the library. So, what do you think?

1. Should someone who is against all church and religion be allowed to teach in a college or university, or not?
   - ❍ Allowed
   - ❍ Not allowed
2. And what about a man who admits he is a homosexual?
   - ❍ Allowed
   - ❍ Not allowed
3. Should a person who believes Blacks are genetically inferior be allowed to teach?
   - ❍ Allowed
   - ❍ Not allowed
4. Should an antireligion book be removed from the library?
   - ❍ Remove
   - ❍ Don't remove
5. What about a book written in favor of homosexuality?
   - ❍ Remove
   - ❍ Don't remove
6. What about a book that suggests Blacks are inferior?
   - ❍ Remove
   - ❍ Don't remove

See the back of the chapter to compare your answers to national survey data.

3. *Militant chauvinism:* When your group's level of power and organization is highest, you may decide to again maximize differences with the dominant group. But militant chauvinists don't just say "we're different," they say "we're also better." For example, there are groups of African Americans ("Afrocentrists" or even some of the Nation of Islam) who proclaim black superiority. Some feminist women proclaims that women's ways are better than the dominant "male" way. These trends try to turn the tables on the dominant group. (*Warning:* Do not attempt this if you are the only member of your group in a confrontation with members of the dominant group.)

These three responses to stigma depend on the size and strength of the stigmatized group. If you're all alone, minstrelizing may be a lifesaving technique. If there are many of you and you are strong, you might try to militantly turn the tables.

Deviant Subcultures

A **subculture** is a group that evolves within a dominant culture, always more or less hidden and closed to outsiders. It may be a loose association of friends who share the same interests, or it may be well organized, with its own alternative language, costumes, and media. While most subcultures are not deviant, the separation from the dominant culture allows deviant subcultures to develop their own norms and values. For a deviant subculture to develop, the activity, condition, identity, and so on must meet three characteristics:

1. It must be punished but not punished too much. If it is not punished enough, potential recruits have no motivation to seek out the subculture. If it is punished too much, the risks of membership are too great.
2. It must have enough participants but not too many. If it has too few participants, it will be hard to seek them out locally. If it has too many, it would be pointless.
3. It must be complex but not too complex. If it is not complex enough, you could engage in it by yourself. If it is too complex, it could exist only within a counterculture or dominant culture: You would need a college degree.

Notice that each of these criteria is not a simple either/or proposition, but rather the achievement of a balance or middle way between heavy punishment and leniency and between size and complexity.

Youth Gangs as Deviant Subculture. Youth gangs are a good example of a deviant subculture. Before the 1950s, we often considered youth gangs as relatively innocent. Their deviance consisted of swiping apples from fruit stands and swimming in the East River in spite of the "no trespassing" signs. Meanwhile

Deviants or Folk Heroes? Jesse James and the Black Panthers were considered criminals by law enforcement agencies, but they were folk heroes in their communities, celebrated in folk songs and tributes.

they helped out mothers and friends in distress and sometimes even cooperated with the police. They were juvenile delinquents with hearts of gold, mischievous but not bad. It was the adult gangsters who posed a threat, trying to seduce them into lives of adult, hard-core crime.

Today, though, our image of youth gangs is quite different, closer to the film *Boyz in the Hood* (1991). And they no longer swipe the occasional apple. There are some 24,000 youth gangs in the United States, with 760,000 members, a figure that doesn't even include informal ganglike cliques, crews, and posses (Snyder and Sickmund, 2006). Nearly eight in ten cities with populations of 50,000 or more now have a "gang problem." For example, nearly one-quarter of high school students surveyed in Virginia belonged to a gang and another 18 percent to a ganglike group. Minority students and those in urban schools have a higher proportion of gangs. Sometimes gangs can be distinguished from other sorts of groups by their distinctive marks of membership: symbols on clothing, dress styles and colors, or tattoos. However, many high school and junior high "wannabes" with no gang ties adopt gang symbols and styles anyway, in an attempt to be cool.

Most gangs are composed of poor or working-class adolescents, typically male (Jankowski, 1991). Members are startlingly young, often preteen when they start, and they generally retire (or go to prison or die) by their mid-twenties. Ethnic minorities are overrepresented, in part because, as numerical minorities, they often feel a stronger need to belong to a group that can provide identity and protection. The National Youth Gang Survey found that 49 percent of gang members are Hispanic, 37 percent Black, 8 percent White, 5 percent Asian, and 1 percent all others (Snyder and Sickmund, 2006). The racial composition of gangs, however, reflects the characteristics of the larger community and so varies considerably with location (Howell, Egley, and Gleason, 2002).

While females represent a small proportion of youth gang members, their numbers have been increasing in recent years (Moore and Hagedorn, 2001; National Youth Gang Center, 2007). As young teenagers, roughly one-third of all youth gang members are female (Esbensen and Winfree, 1998; Gottfredson and Gottfredson, 2001); however, females tend to leave gangs at an earlier age than males (Gottfredson and Gottfredson, 2001; Thornberry, Krohn, Lizotte, et al., 2003). Emerging research has begun to suggest that the gender composition of a gang affects its delinquency rates. In one study, females in all- or majority-female gangs had the lowest delinquency rates, whiles both males and females in majority-male gangs had the highest—including higher rates than males in all-male gangs (Peterson, Miller, and Esbensen, 2001).

Why do adolescents join gangs? Sociologists have conducted many interviews with gang members, and the reasons most commonly given are friends and relatives who already belong to the gang, a desire for excitement, a need for protection, and the availability of money, drugs, and alcohol. While earlier psychological research suggested that gang membership was "irrational"—leading to high arrest rates, likelihood of dying a violent death, chronic physical danger, instability—sociologists also stress that in some circumstances, gang membership can be a rational decision. Sociologist Martin Sanchez-Jankowski interviewed gang members in New York and Los Angeles, and he found that their motivations were similar to any underemployed job seeker: Gang membership provided economic opportunities to support a family,

Youth gangs are seen as deviant subcultures, with their own norms, values, and rules of conduct. The number of female gang members has been increasing, but most gang members are male.

opportunities of career enhancement (moving up the ladder), feelings of belonging and camaraderie in a hostile world, and status to attract girls (Sanchez-Jankowski, 1991).

Youth Gangs Today. Today youth gangs are well-armed and financed because of their involvement in drug trafficking. In some communities, offences are more violent, and they now interact with members of organized crime (National Youth Gang Center, 2007). In one nationwide study of high-crime areas, gang members reported committing large percentages of various types of youth crimes. In Rochester, gang members admitted committing 68 percent of all violent crimes by adolescents; Seattle gangs self-reported committing 85 percent of adolescent robberies; Denver gangs admitted to 79 percent of all serious violent crimes by adolescents (Howell, 2006). Prison terms, usually shorter for minors, give youth gang members the opportunity to form alliances with older criminals and learn from them (Greene and Pranis, 2007).

Gangs are a new form of organized crime—less organized but more violent than the Mafia ever was. Their agenda is usually purely financial, but some commentators worry about the implications if well-armed, highly organized gangs acquire a political agenda. For instance, the FBI is particularly worried about the Mara Salvatrucha, a gang based in northern Virginia. Its membership is drawn not only from local youth but from former paramilitary guerillas who came north from Central America. They still have ties in Central America, which facilitate a brisk traffic in guns and drugs (*The Economist,* 2005).

However, most disturbing to the FBI are reports that gang members have met with al-Qaeda members in El Salvador (*The Economist,* 2005). Potential links between American gangs and international terrorist groups fuel much of the current concern about gangs.

Most gangs are not involved in such far-ranging criminal activities. Most provide a sense of belonging and connection for members, protection against perceived hostility, and a sense of menace to those who are not in the gang. Most important to some is that they have good parties, provide easy access to alcohol and drugs, and "know how to have fun," as one gang member told me.

Deviance and Social Coherence

Because there is always deviance in society, some sociologists ask what purpose it might serve. One of the founders of modern sociology, Émile Durkheim, wrote that having some members of a society castigated as deviant actually helps the society maintain itself as a coherent entity (Durkheim, 1964a,b). Durkheim argued that deviance is useful to society in four ways:

1. *It affirms cultural norms and values.* Without defining what is wrong, we do not know what is right: There can be no good without evil, no justice without crime. Deviance is needed to define and sustain morality.
2. *It clarifies moral boundaries.* We don't really know what the rule is until we see someone breaking it. Deviance lets societies draw a clear distinction between good and bad, right and wrong. If there are no clear distinctions, the society falls victim to anomie (normlessness).
3. *It heightens group solidarity.* When someone commits an act of major deviance, other people in the society react with collective anger: They are outraged. In responding to the deviant, they reaffirm the moral ties that bind them together.
4. *It encourages social change.* Someone who breaks a social rule makes us wonder if the rule is all that important after all. Deviant people push moral boundaries, suggesting alternatives to the status quo. Today's deviance can be tomorrow's morality (Durkheim, 1964a,b).

Try It Applying Theories to Deviance in the News

Contributed by Katherine Rowell, *Sinclair Community College*

Objective: Apply what you have been learning about theoretical explanations of deviance to the real world of deviance and crime.

STEP 1: Research

Search for examples of news articles that demonstrate each of the above theoretical perspectives of deviant behavior (you will have three different articles and are not permitted to use the same article twice). There are numerous ways to find the news in our world today, and for this project you may use news sources online or your local newspaper.

STEP 2: Compile Information

After finding the three news articles, complete the following information for each one. If your news article is not available on the Internet, you will need to make a copy of it to attach to your completed information sheet.

For each news article, provide the following information:

1. Title of article
2. Author
3. Date and specific citation information
4. An explanation of why you think this particular news article demonstrates the particular theory. Please note you will have one newspaper article for each theory. Complete these four questions for each theory/newspaper article.

STEP 3: Discuss

Be prepared to share your results in class. Please note that some instructors may collect this activity for a grade.

Deviance is socially useful because it reminds "us" that we are "normal"—it's *they* who are different and deviant.

Explaining Deviance

Durkheim's explanation explains what deviance *does* for the larger society, but it doesn't explain why deviance happens, especially major acts of deviance that will result in major punishment.

Differential Association. Edwin H. Sutherland's theory of **differential association** (1940) suggests that it is a matter of rewards and punishment: Deviance occurs when an individual receives more prestige and less punishment by violating norms rather than by following them. What is deviant to one group might be something that enhances our status in another group. For example, students who behave in an irreverent, disrespectful fashion in class may be seen as deviant by the teachers and even punished for it, but they might also receive a great deal of prestige from their peers. They may calculate that the benefit (increased prestige) is better than the minor punishment they might receive. Thus, Sutherland argued, individuals become deviant by associating with people or joining groups that are already deviant and therefore are in the position to award deviant behavior (Sutherland, 1940).

Sutherland's theory helps to explain the way we sometimes have multiple moral voices in our heads—like the little devil and angel versions of ourselves often depicted on TV—and why sometimes we choose to be deviant. But the theory does not explain how the "carriers of criminality" became deviant in the first place. It also does not explain acts that occur without a community, when everyone around disapproves, or when no one is even aware of the deviance.

Control Theory. Travis Hirschi (1969; Gottfredson and Hirschi, 1995) argued that people do not obey lots of hidden forces: They are *rational,* so they decide whether or not to engage in an act by weighing the potential outcome. If you knew that there would be absolutely no punishment, no negative consequences of any sort, you would probably do a great many things that you would never dream of otherwise, like propositioning an attractive co-worker or driving like a maniac. You are constrained by the fear of punishment.

Hirschi imagined that people do a "cost-benefit analysis" during their decision-making process, to determine how much punishment is worth a degree of satisfaction or prestige. In a cost-benefit analysis, you weigh the respective costs of doing something (the likelihood or severity of punishment, for example) against the benefits of doing it (like the money you might get, the increased prestige, the thrill of doing it in the first place). People who have very little to lose are therefore mostly likely to become rule-breakers because for them the costs will almost always be less than the potential benefits.

According to **control theory,** an assembly-line worker whose job training has been significantly less, and who earns considerably less money, might make a different calculation, and get into the fight and risk losing the job, figuring that at such a low wage, one can easily get a comparable job.

Of course, we often fail to break rules even when the benefits would be great and the punishment minimal. I often arrive on campus at 6:00 a.m., before dawn, and just inside, I usually have to stop at one of those stoplights that feels as if it takes five minutes to change from red to green. I could easily run it. There would be a substantial benefit, in arriving at the office five minutes early and not wasting the gas and oil it takes to just sit there. There would be no punishment: No one is around, and I am certain that no police officers are monitoring a deserted intersection from a hidden camera. I do not even agree that the rule is just; stoplights are a good idea in general, but forcing a driver to wait five minutes to cross a deserted street is idiotic. Nevertheless, in spite of my objections, in spite of the benefits and lack of punishment, I always just sit there.

Walter Reckless (1973) would suggest that I am subject to **social controls.** If I really think that a police car is lying in wait to give me a traffic ticket, I am subject to *outer controls:* family, social institutions, and authority figures (like the police) who influence us into obeying social rules (Costello and Vowell, 1999). But even when my mother can't see me, I am subject to *inner controls:* internalized socialization, religious principles, my self-conception as a "good person" (Hirschi, 1969; Rogers and Buffalo, 1974).

Inner and outer controls do their job in four ways:

1. *Attachment.* Strong attachments encourage conformity; weak attachments encourage deviance.
2. *Commitment.* The greater our commitment to the norms and values of the group, the more advantages we derive from conforming, and the more we have to lose through deviance.
3. *Involvement.* Extensive involvement in group activities—job, school, sports—inhibits deviance.
4. *Belief.* A strong belief in conventional morality and respect for authority figures inhibits deviance.

Control theory suggests that deviants/delinquents are often individuals who have low levels of self-control as a result of inadequate socialization, especially in childhood.

Labeling Theory. We used to think that the wrongdoing in deviance resided somewhere in the wrongdoer: You break a social rule because you are "that kind of person," with faulty genes, a criminal personality, or a defective soul. But now we know that wrongdoing is not inherent in an act or an actor, but in the social context that determines whether an act is considered deviant or not and how much punishment it warrants.

Howard Becker (1966) used the term labeling theory to stress the relativity of deviance. Labeling describes a relationship between a dominant group and the actor. For something to be deviant, it has to be labeled as deviant by a powerful group—a group powerful enough to make that label stick. (If you do something wrong and your little sister declares it deviant, it doesn't have the same sort of weight as if all your friends label it deviant, or, even more, if the police and the juvenile courts call it deviant.) **Labeling theory** understands deviance to be a *process,* not a categorical difference between the deviant and the non-deviant. The label depends on the group's relative amount of power.

The same act might be deviant in some groups and not in others. It might be deviant when one person commits it but not when another person commits it. In fact, an action, belief, or condition is neutral in itself. It only becomes "deviant" when someone decides that it is wrong, bad, or immoral and labels it as deviant. For example, think of women who are sexually aggressive or enjoy pornography. Society might call them "sluts" and shun them. But if a man did any of those things, other men might call him a "stud" and perhaps hang out with him.

But deviance does not only reside in whether other people apply the label "deviant" to your acts. To become a deviant actor, you also have to believe the deviant label; you have to to agree with the labels other people ascribe to you.

Edwin Lemert (1972) theorized that most acts, which he called **primary deviance,** provoke very little reaction and therefore have little effect on your self-concept. If I decide one day to run that red light on campus at 6:00 a.m., a passing police office may label me as reckless and irresponsible, but I am unlikely to believe it. Only when I repeatedly break a norm, and people start making a big deal of it, does **secondary deviance** kick in. My rule breaking is no longer a momentary lapse in judgment, or justifiable under the circumstances, but an indication of a permanent personality trait: I have acquired a deviant identity. Finally, sociologists also have identified **tertiary deviance,** in which a group formerly labeled deviant attempts to redefine their acts, attributes, or identities as normal—even virtuous. John Kitsuse (1980) and others point to the ways some formerly deviant groups have begun to stand up for their rights, demanding equality with those considered "normals." Similar to "militant chauvinism" defined by Goffman when discussing stigma, examples might include the disability rights movement, which has attempted to redefine disabilities from deviant to "differently abled."

Deviance and Inequality

Some sociologists argue that deviance is not solely a product of "bad" people or "wrong" behaviors but also of the bad, wrong, and/or unfair social conditions of people's lives. What is labeled as deviant is applied differently to different people. The powerful and the privileged escape the label and the punishment. Therefore, deviance in itself is the product of social inequality.

In a groundbreaking article entitled "Nuts, Sluts, and Perverts: The Poverty of the Sociology of Deviance" (1972), Alexander Liazos noted that the people commonly labeled deviant are always powerless. Why? The answer is not simply that the rich and powerful make the rules to begin with or that they have the resources to avoid being labeled deviant. The answer lies in the fact that those who have the power can make us believe that the rules are "natural" and "good" to mask their political agenda. They can then label actors and acts deviant to justify inequalities in gender, sexual orientation, race, ethnicity, and social class (Daly, 1989; Daly and Chesney-Lind, 1988; Goode, 2005; Hagan and Peterson, 1995; Lang, 2002).

In a classic study of a suburban high school, there were two "gangs" of boys, what the researcher called the "Saints" and the "Roughnecks." The Roughnecks were working-class boys, who were in the vocational track and not college bound. Teachers thought of them as deviant, and they wore clothing styles like those in the movie *Grease*—black leather jackets, jeans, and white T-shirts. They were known to commit petty crimes and were called "hooligans" by the school administrators. The "Saints," by contrast, were middle-class boys, and they dressed the part—crew cuts, button-down "preppy" shirts, and penny loafers. They played sports, were popular, and were headed for college. They also spent their weekends breaking into people's homes and committing serious burglaries. But they were not considered deviant because they were "wholesome" and middle class (Chambliss, 2000).

Ironically, the relationship of inequality and deviance often leads us to see and punish the behaviors of the less fortunate and forgive the behavior of the more fortunate. From this perspective, it is more likely that a poor person who stole a few dollars from a company would end up in jail than a CEO who steals millions of dollars from millions of shareholders.

Deviance and Crime

Most theories of deviance also apply to crime, which is simply a legally regulated form of extreme deviance. **Crime** can be defined as any act that violates a formal normative code that has been enacted by a legally constituted body. Simple violation of a more or folkway may not be a crime, unless you violate a formal code. Likewise, you can commit a crime (actually break a law) and not be seen as deviant if other people see your act as acceptable. Sometimes, people commit crimes and are seen as heroes, like Robin Hood.

Some crimes are defined by being bad in and of themselves—bad because they violate formal group norms—like homicide, rape, or assault. Other crimes are not as obvious violations of group norms and are considered bad mostly because they have been prohibited. In some cultures or contexts they might not be crimes at all, but because they are illegal, they are crimes.

Religious observance, medical therapy or crime? Different cultural groups construct some behaviors differently, as these participants at a pot festival might attest. But who gets to decide if they go to jail?

For example, smoking marijuana is illegal in the United States, yet public opinion polls show many Americans don't see it as "bad" at all times and favor its legal use for medical purposes. Internationally, some countries, including Japan, Thailand, and Hondoras, maintain strict laws against pot use for any reason, while others, have more relaxed attitudes about pot use, especially for medical purposes. In the Netherlands, pharmacies have been legally obliged to stock and dispense medical marijuana since 2003.

The efforts to control and punish crime have become so extensive and the institutions that have developed—prisons, courts, police, to name a few—so large, that the study of crime, criminology, has developed into a subdiscipline separate from the sociology of deviance, with its own special theories about the causes and consequences of different kinds of crime.

What causes crime?

Strain Theory

Robert K. Merton (1957) argued that while some deviance benefits society, some deviance also puts an enormous *strain* on social life. He argued that excessive deviance is a by-product of inequality. When a society promotes certain goals but provides unequal means of acquiring them, the result is anomie, a conflict between accepted norms and social reality. This is called **strain theory.**

For instance, in the United States, and to some degree in all industrialized societies, we promote the *goal* of financial success and claim that it can be achieved through the *means* of self-discipline and hard work. But these qualities will lead to financial success only when channeled through a prestigious education or network of prestigious social contacts, advantages that many people do not have. They will therefore feel pressured to use alternative *means,* legitimate or illegitimate, to reach the goal (Merton, 1967).

According to Merton, there are five potential reactions to the tension between widely endorsed values and limited means of achieving them:

1. *Conformists* accept both the means and the values, whether they achieve the goal or not. They may not achieve financial success, but they will still believe that it is important and that self-discipline and hard work are appropriate means of achieving it. Most people are conformists.
2. *Innovators* accept the values but reject the means. They believe that financial success is an important goal but not that self-discipline and hard work are effective means of achieving it. Instead, they seek out new means to financial success. They may try to win the lottery, or they may become con artists or thieves.
3. *Ritualists* accept the means but reject the values. They follow rules for their own sake, conforming to standards even though they have lost sight of the values behind them. They will work hard but have no aspirations to financial success.
4. *Rebels* reject both the means and the values and substitute new ones. Instead of financial success, for instance, they may value the goal of spiritual fulfillment, to be achieved not through hard work but through quiet contemplation.
5. *Retreatists* reject both the means and the values and replace them with nothing. They do not accept the value of working hard, and they have not devised any alternative means. They have no aspirations to financial success, or any alternative goal, such as spiritual or artistic fulfillment.

Critics of strain theory point out that not everyone shares the same goals, even in the most homogeneous society. There are always many potential goals, conflicting and sometimes contradictory. And while strain theory may adequately explain some white-collar crime, such as juggling the books at work, and some property crimes, such as stealing a television set, it is less effective when explaining those crimes that lack an immediate financial motive.

Broken Windows Theory

Social psychologist Philip Zimbardo (1969) proposed the **broken windows theory** to explain how social controls can systematically weaken, and minor acts of deviance can spiral into severe crime and social decay. He placed cars without license plates and with their hoods up, but otherwise in good condition, in two different social settings, one in wealthy, mostly white Palo Alto, California (the home of Stanford University, where he worked), and the other in a poor, mostly black neighborhood in the Bronx, in New York City. The social class and race of passersby made no difference: In both sites, cars were quickly gutted. One person would conclude that the car was abandoned and "no one cared," and break a side window. The next person would see the side window broken and feel it was acceptable to smash the windshield.

The pattern would continue and escalate from there. Zimbardo concluded that breaking more windows, committing more serious crimes and acts of deviance, is rational response to situations of social disorder. Later, James Q. Wilson (1985) expanded this thesis to conclude that community characteristics, such as decayed housing, preexisting crime, and the like, contributed to increased crime. Crime rates go up, he argued, in blighted areas where people think no one cares and no one is watching.

The societal response has been proactive: policing directed at maintaining public order. However, the flaw is that the police are left to identify "social disorder" however they want. Without more systematic definition, police can see almost anything as a sign of social disorder and almost anyone as a threat.

Criminal Subcultures

In 1955, juvenile delinquency was getting a lot of publicity in the United States. Abert Cohen wondered why young people, mostly working-class and poor boys, were spurning the values of the dominant society and committing so many crimes. After studying working-class and poor youth gangs, he concluded that strain theory wouldn't work: As lower-class youths, they had the least opportunity to achieve economic success, but their crimes were usually not economically motivated. They were not trying to get rich (1955).

Cohen drew upon Edward Sutherland's theory of differential association (which we discussed earlier in the chapter) to propose that the gang members were not being socialized with the same norms and values as lower class non–gang members or the middle class. They were being subjected to differential association, socialized into a new set of norms and values that allowed them to succeed on their own terms. Cohen listed their five most important values as:

1. *Nonutilitarianism.* They had no economic motive, or any other sort of motive, for committing their crimes. They committed crimes "for the hell of it."
2. *Maliciousness.* They valued being just plain mean. The meaner gang members enjoyed considerable prestige, and the "nice" ones were deviant.
3. *Negativism.* They were aware of the norms of the dominant culture and valued doing the exact opposite. If the dominant culture disapproved of smoking, they smoked.
4. *Short-run hedonism.* They valued getting immediate gratification and disapproved of members who waited patiently, saved their money, and so on.
5. *Group autonomy.* They defied or ignored authority figures. Even within the gang, the leaders had little power. They resisted any attempt to control their behavior, except as imposed informally by gang members acting as a group.

Walter B. Miller (1970) agreed, but he argued that it is not just lower-class boys in gangs whose norms and values differ from those of the dominant society; it's the entire lower class. In other words, behavior that the main society might consider deviant actually reflects the social norms of the lower-class *subculture.* They have six core values that differ from those of the main society:

1. *Trouble.* The subculture has trouble, chronic and unsolvable: for men, fights; for women, pregnancy. They value ways of avoiding or getting out of it.
2. *Toughness.* People in the subculture are constantly facing the challenges of fights or physical deprivation, and they value physical prowess, bravery, stoicism.
3. *Smartness.* The subculture does not value "book smarts," intellectual knowledge about the world. But it values "street smarts," the ability to avoid being duped, outwitted, and conned and to successfully dupe, outwit, and con others.
4. *Excitement.* The subculture values looking for thrills, flirting with danger, risk taking.
5. *Fate.* In the dominant culture, people believe that they are responsible for their own destiny. In the subculture, people value the idea that most of their everyday activities are determined by forces beyond their control.
6. *Autonomy.* Although their fate is determined by forces beyond their control, the members of the lower-class subculture resist authority figures much more often and vigorously than members of the dominant culture. The police are the enemy. Social workers, case workers, and sociologists asking questions have a shady hidden agenda.

Miller implied, therefore, that lower-class culture was conducive to crime, despite the overwhelming number of lower-class people who are law-abiding, decent citizens and the many upper-class people who reverse Robin Hood's ethic and rob from the poor to give to themselves.

Cohen's and Miller's theories of crime rely on the public outcry about juvenile delinquency in the 1950s. Today, sociologists find this work less compelling in an era of organized gangs of lower-class males, whose motivations may be far more rational than malicious pleasure and group cohesion.

Opportunity Theory

Richard Cloward and Lloyd Ohlin (1960) argued that crime actually arises from opportunity to commit crime. **Opportunity theory** holds that those who have many opportunities—and good ones at that—will be more likely to commit crimes than those with few good opportunities. They agreed, with Merton, that those who don't have equal access to acceptable means to achieve material success may experience strain, but that doesn't explain why most poor people are not criminals. In fact, studies show that most are "conformists," with the same values and goals as the dominant society.

Cloward and Ohlin emphasized *learning*—people have to learn how to carry out particular forms of deviance, and they must have the opportunity to actually deviate. They revised differential association theory to propose several different types of deviant subcultures based on the opportunities to deviate:

1. In stable neighborhoods where most people know each other throughout their lives, *criminal subcultures* develop, devoted to such activities as burglary and theft. Young men can rely on social contacts with experienced older men to learn the roles of being a criminal, and the older men in turn can depend on the availability of younger protégés as they go to prison or retire.
2. In unstable neighborhoods where people are constantly moving in and out, there are few opportunities to learn about burglarly and theft, and boys who are mostly strangers to each other must find

some way to establish dominance. They develop *violence subcultures,* gaining tough reputations through fighting and assaults.

3. In neighborhoods too disorganized for either crime or violence to succeed, people withdraw from society altogether through the use of alcohol and drugs. They develop *retreatist* subcultures.

These are not necessarily exclusive groups. A gang that may start out as part of a violent subculture in an unstable neighborhood may become a criminal subculture as the members become involved in more stable criminal activities like protection rackets and drug trafficking and begin recruiting younger members.

Some aspects of opportunity theory have been confirmed by subsequent research (Allan and Steffensmeier, 1989; Uggen, 1999). But as with many typologies, the theory ignores the interrelation of types of crime: Drug dealers and users often depend on property crime to finance their drug use and violence for territorial defense; violence often occurs in tandem with property crime. Also, the theory defines deviance in a way that targets poor people—if we include white-collar crimes like stock fraud, neighborhood dynamics become much less significant.

Conflict Theory

We may condemn the unequal application of the law, but we give little thought to whether the laws themselves are inherently unfair. **Conflict theories** of crime resemble inequality theories of deviance—they rest on a larger structural analysis of inequalities based on class, or race, or gender for their explanation of crime. Richard Quinney (1977) argued that the dominant class produces deviance by making and enforcing laws that protect its own interest and oppress the subordinate class. Law becomes an instrument of oppression, designed to maintain the powerful in their privileged position (Chambliss, 1999). It's not simply that basically neutral and equal laws are applied unequally, meaning that poor people get longer and harsher sentences when they commit the same crimes as upper-class people. That's true. But it's also that the laws themselves are designed to make sure that the rich stay rich and the poor stay poor.

When I was in college, a student who lived in my dorm was arrested very early one morning for stealing some fresh-baked bread that had been delivered to a local grocery store. (The bread was baked by a local bakery, and then left on the steps of the store at around 4 a.m. to wait for the owner to arrive to open the store.) When he was arraigned, the local magistrate looked at him sternly. "I assume this is a fraternity prank," the magistrate said, "and so I'm going to let you go with a warning. If this had been a real crime, if you had really needed the bread, you'd be going to jail for 10 years for theft."

Types of Crimes

There are many different types of crimes. Some are crimes against other people; others are crimes against property. They are handled differently by the police, courts, and penal system, depending on how serious the society believes the crime to be. In the United States, crimes against people are almost always heard in criminal court, while crimes against property may be heard in criminal or civil courts.

Sociologists study all types of crimes, from crimes against other people, like homicide, assault, and rape, to crimes against property, like burglary, motor vehicle theft, and arson. **Violent crime** consists of four offenses, according to the FBI's definitions: murder and nonnegligent manslaughter, forcible rape, robbery, and aggravated assault. **Property crime** includes offenses like burglary and motor vehicle theft, where the object is the taking of money or property, but there is no force or threat of force against the victims (Figure 10.1).

Did you know?

When women commit fraud, they are most likely to cheat banks through bad credit cards or loans or the government by garnering benefits to which they aren't entitled. Crimes such as advertising fraud or insider trading are almost exclusively committed by men—because they still have far greater access to the high-level jobs that offer opportunities to commit such crimes (Daly, 1989).

Crime at Work

Theft at work, whether simply pocketing office supplies or exercising the "100% employee discount" at the department store, costs U.S. employers nearly $20 billion a year (National Retail Federation, 2007). But there are many other crimes that you can commit at work, using the authority of your position, with the direct or indirect consent of the boss. In 1940, Edwin Sutherland introduced the term **white-collar crime** for the illegal actions of a corporation or people acting on its behalf (Sutherland, 1940).

Some white-collar crimes are **consumer crimes** such as credit card fraud, in which the criminal uses a fake or stolen credit card to buy things for

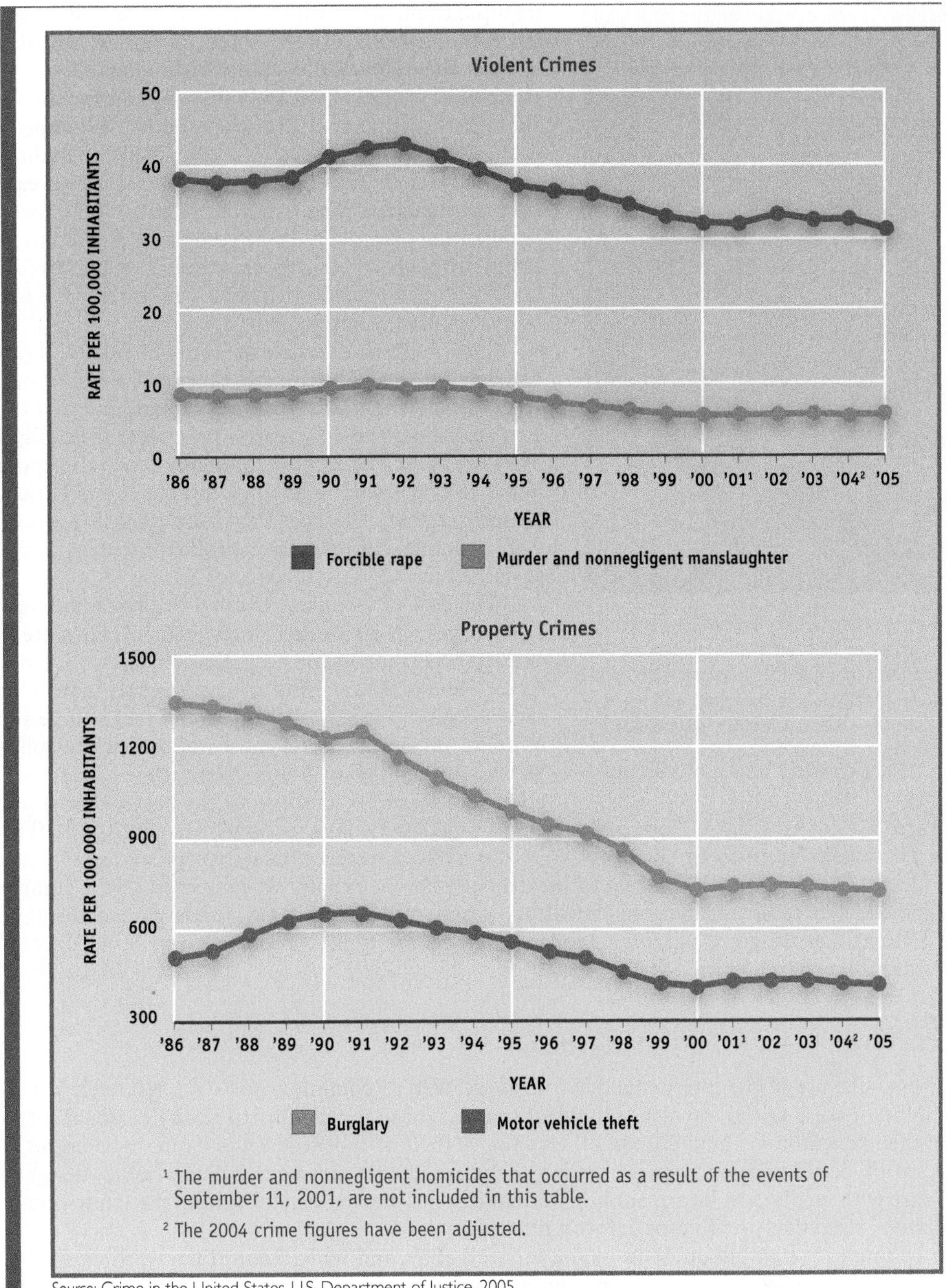

Source: Crime in the United States, U.S. Department of Justice, 2005.

FIGURE 10.1 Selected Types ofViolent Crimes, and Property Crimes, in the United States, 1986–2005.

him- or herself or for resale. Such purchases cost both retailers and, increasingly, "e-tailers" over $1 billion per year, or nearly 5 cents for every dollar spent online (Berner and Carter, 2005).

White-collar criminals might commit **occupational crime,** using their professional position to illegally secure something of value for themselves or the corporation. Some of the more common occupational crimes include income tax evasion, stock manipulation, bribery, and embezzlement. Media entrepreneur Martha Stewart went to prison for insider trading when she used her fame to find out that a company whose stock she owned was about to suffer a significant setback; she sold her stock the day before its price collapsed. (She claimed it was a coincidence.) Periodically, a famous Wall Street tycoon will be arrested for manipulating stocks or fraudulently reporting distorted earnings.

Or they might commit **organizational crime,** illegal actions committed in accordance with the operative goals of an organization. Some of the more common organizational crimes are stock

In 2006, Kenneth Lay, CEO of Enron Corporation, was found guilty of 11 counts of securities fraud in a corruption scandal that bankrupted the company, costing 20,000 people their jobs and many of them their life savings. Investors lost billions.

manipulation, antitrust violations, false advertising, and price fixing. Periodically, some corporate whistle-blower notices the remarkable coincidence that all the gasoline companies charge about the same amount for their gas, despite the fact that they are supposed to be competing with each other. In 2002, several corporations, including Enron and WorldCom, went bankrupt when they revealed they had manipulated their records to boost the stock prices. Some of the executives of the companies floated to financial safety through a "golden parachute" of hundreds of millions of dollars; their employees, who often took raises and bonuses in stock options, lost everything.

Such high-profile arrests for white-collar crime may provide the rest of us with the illusion that the system works, that criminals always get caught, and that the "little guy" can beat the corporations. In fact, these high-profile cases are rare. And it is exceptionally rare for corporate violators to ever spend a day in jail (Hagan and Parker, 1985; Sasseen, 2006). The convictions of Enron's top executives were notable because they broke precedent rather than sustained it.

The cost of white-collar crime is substantial—$400 billion per year in the United States, which is far more than the "paltry" $15 billion for "regular" street crime (Livingston, 1992; Zeune, 2001). And of course, corporate officers or their agents are breaking the law, and they can be subject to criminal prosecution. Yet most cases of white-collar crime go unpunished. Many white-collar crimes are settled out of court and never become part of the public record.

In rare cases when white-collar criminals are charged and convicted, odds are almost 50-50 that they will not go to jail. White-collar offenders are more likely to receive fines than prison sentences. Amitai Etzioni (1990) found that in 43 percent of incidents, either no penalty was imposed or the company was required merely to cease engaging in the illegal practice and return any funds gained through illegal means. Even if they do go to jail, white-collar criminals are typically sentenced to terms averaging less than 3 years (Pizzo and Muolo, 1994).

Cybercrime

Cybercrime—the use of the Internet and World Wide Web to commit crime—is a relatively new form of crime. Some of these crimes involve fraudulent maneuvers to get victims to reveal personal information that can then be used to commit crimes; others involve theft of cyber-identities. Some cybercrime is simply the adaptation of old crimes to new technology—the fraudulent messages, called *phishes,* designed to get you to part with credit card information or to make bogus purchases, are simply the latest version of an old telephone scam that preyed especially on retirees.

For example, I often bid on items online through eBay, and when I win, I pay with PayPal, a service that transfers the money directly from my checking account to the seller's. No checkbook, no stamps, no envelopes, and my item is shipped immediately. One day I received an e-mail receipt from PayPal indicating that I had paid $248 for a Myst game! I never bought a Myst game. At the bottom of the e-mail was a link to the PayPal security center.

Yeah, right. I typed in the PayPal address manually, and there was no payment for a Myst game. The e-mail was a fraud—a phish—and the perpetrator was hoping that I would be so dismayed that I would click on the link immediately, whereupon all of the personal information stored on my computer would be uploaded into the hands of some cyber-criminal. Virtually every university student and employee gets these messages. Sometimes they purport to come from the University Computer Center, or from people I know—actually they're from address books copied by Trojan horse viruses.

The rise of personal computers and the Internet have made some criminal activities, such as money laundering and fraud, easier, and it has spawned a whole new field of crime. Internet-based crime is the fastest growing category of crime in the United States. The year 2006 marked the seventh year in a row that identity theft topped the list of consumer complaints with the U.S. Federal Trade Commission, accounting for 36 percent of the total (Federal Trade Commission, 2007). An estimated 8.3 million Americans were victimized by consumer fraud and identity theft, at a cost of $1.1 billion. Much of the victimization occurs when people willingly give out the information, either believing they are about to receive a massive windfall of cash or that they've already paid that $248 for a Myst game, so they panic and "click here immediately."

But hackers are often responsible. Hackers have tapped into customer information as well as proprietary company information stored online by credit bureaus, marketing agencies, banks, credit card companies, and other financial services firms. Of the top global financial services organizations, 83 percent had some kind of hacker attack on their computer information systems in 2004, up 39 percent over a year earlier (Deloitte Global Security Survey, 2004). By 2005, the number of security breaches fell to 30 percent due to government attention and company actions (Deloitte Global Security Survey, 2005). Forty-three percent of these intrusions go unreported because private companies fear undermining the confidence of their customers and shareholders (Computer Crime and Security Survey, 2005). (Table 10.1).

TABLE 10.1 Computer Crimes, 2005

Incident	Dollar Cost
Virus	$42,787,767
Unauthorized access	$31,233,100
Theft of proprietary information	$30,933,000
Denial of service	$7,310,725
Insider Net abuse	$6,856,450
Laptop theft	$4,107,300
Financial fraud	$2,565,000
Misuse of public Web application	$2,227,500
System penetration	$841,400
Abuse of wireless network	$544,700
Sabotage	$340,600
Telecom fraud	$242,000
Web site defacement	$115,000

Source: CSI/FBI Computer Crime Security Survey, 2005.

There can be considerable variation in the types and dollar costs of computer crime from year to year. In 2003, for example, theft of proprietary information was the top hacker target, which accounted for losses of over $70 million (Computer Crime and Security Survey, 2003).

Hate Crime

A **hate crime** is a criminal act committed by an offender motivated by bias against race, ethnicity, religion, sexual orientation, or disability status. Anyone can commit a hate crime, but perpetrators usually belong to dominant groups (white, Christian, straight) and victims to disenfranchised groups (black, Jewish, Muslim, or gay). The FBI records over 7,000 hate crimes per year, but because state and local law enforcement agencies differ in their reporting procedures, and some do not report at all, this number is no doubt extremely low. Bias based on race seems to be the largest motivating factor in hate crimes (51 percent of cases), followed by religion (18 percent), sexual orientation (16.5 percent), ethnicity (14 percent), and disability (less than 1 percent).

Legislators approve of hate crime legislation sometimes and disapprove at other times. In 2001, 43 states increased their penalties for hate crimes. However, in October 2004, leadership in House of Representatives stripped language that would have expanded current federal hate crime protection from a defense bill, the Local Law Enforcement Enhancement Act, after it was approved in Congress.

Advocates of these laws argue that hate crimes affect not only the individual but the entire community, so they should be punished more harshly than ordinary crime. The lynchings in the American South were used not only to victimize an individual but to terrorize the entire Black population, and contemporary antigay hate crimes are not meant to express hatred of a single gay person but to demonstrate to all gay people that they are unwelcome and unsafe in the community.

But opponents of these laws argue that they punish attitudes, not actions. Why does the motivation of a crime matter? If I am planning to commit a robbery, I may select a gay man, believing the stereotype that he is fragile and weak and therefore unlikely to resist. My prejudice didn't motivate the crime, merely my choice of an appropriate victim.

Crime in the United States

In 2005, the violent crime rate in the United States was 21 victims per 1,000 people, and the property crime rate was 154 victims per 1,000 people, according to the Justice Department. While these statistics are considerably lower than they were 30 years ago, the United States still has higher crime rates than many other countries in the world: It ranks third in drug offenses per capita, fifth in assaults, eighth in murders with firearms, ninth in rape, eleventh in robberies, and sixteenth in burglaries.

When compared with most other advanced countries, the United States stands out for its very high homicide rates (Van Kesteren, Mayhew, and Nieuwbeerta, 2000; Kurki, 1997). With six murders for every 100,000 people, the rate of lethal violence in America is nearly five times higher than that of France,

Germany, or England (van Kesteren, Mayhew, and Nieuwbeerta, 2000; Wacquant, 2006; Zimring and Hawkins, 1997).

What social factors explain our rates of crime? And why would we feel so safe, considering that our violent crime rate is so high?

Sociologists have considered three explanations:

1. American culture emphasizes on individual economic success as *the* measure of self-worth, at the expense of family, neighborhood, artistic accomplishment, and spiritual well-being (Currie, 1985).
2. Not everyone has a high standard of living. The United States has one of the largest income differentials in the world. When the gap begins to shrink, as it did during Clinton-era prosperity, the crime rate declines (Martens, 2005).
3. Guns—that is, the easy availability of guns and the lax enforcement of loose gun control measures, coupled with an American value system that places gun ownership as a sacred right—are a contributor to the crime rate.

Despite the fact that our overall crimes rates are higher than some other advanced countries, such as Ireland and Austria, and our outsize homicide rate distinguishes the United States from all of Western Europe (Wacquant, 2006), it is also true that crime rates in the United States have been falling. The National Crime Victimization Survey (2005), which addresses victims of crime (and therefore leaves out murder), reports that the violent crime rate has dropped by 58 percent and the property crime rate has dropped by 52 percent since 1973. Violent crime dropped 14 percent in just two years, between 2001 and 2003, and stayed the same between 2004 and 2005 (U.S. Department of Justice, 2005). (Figure 10.2).

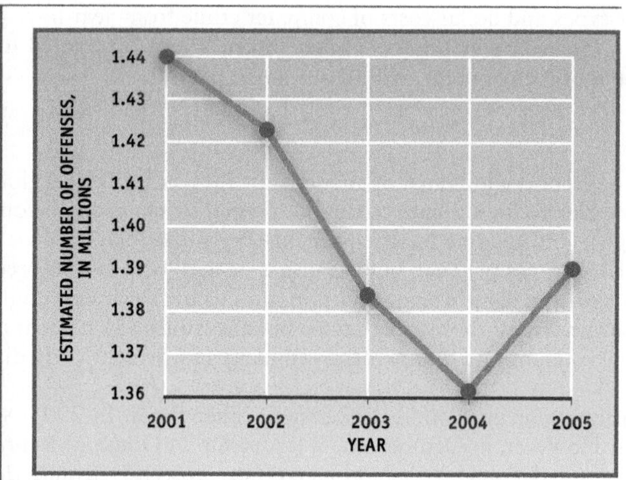

Source: Crime in the United States, U.S. Department of Justice, 2005.

FIGURE 10.2 Violent Crime Offense: A Five-Year Trend.

So sociologists have to ask two questions: Why are some of our crime rates so high? And why should the crime rate be falling? Research by sociologists and criminologists has identified a legion of factors that contributed to the drop in crime, including:

- An expanding economy (and thus more legitimate opportunities for employment)
- An aging population (more older people means crime rate goes down)
- An increase in the number of police officers
- A decrease in the number of young males in their late teens and early 20s
- Longer jail sentences for hard-core criminals
- Declining sales of crack cocaine and the violence associated with the drug trade

How do we know what we know?

Abortion and the Crime Rate

Did the legalization of abortion cause the decline of crime? In the book *Freakonomics* (2005), economist Steven Levitt and journalist Stephen Dubner suggest the controversial idea that the legalization of abortion in 1973 meant that far fewer unwanted children were born, and that these children would have had few economic opportunities and lower levels of education and employment. They would have become adults in the mid-1990s—which is exactly when the crime rate began to decline. Thus, many would-be criminals—those with the demographic "profile" of criminals—were never born. Some disagree with their calculations (Foote and Goetz, 2005).

This is a marvelous example of what sociologists call a specious correlation. Sure, the two variables may be correlated, but there are so many intervening variables, not to mention 20 years of other factors that might have influenced things, that one cannot possibly say with any certainty that this one variable caused another. For one thing, how do we know that the fetuses that were aborted were more likely to be criminals? Or that the legalization of abortion was not also connected to a larger set of social and economic reforms that reduced the crime rate? Do you think, perhaps, that all the recent efforts to make abortions more difficult will result in a dramatic increase in crime 20 years from now? I doubt it.

- An increase in immigration by females, especially from Russia and China
- The legalization of abortion
- The "little-brother syndrome" by which younger boys did not grow up to become criminals after witnessing what happened to their older mentors (Bourgois, 1995; Fox, 2000; Freeman, 2000; Greene, 1999; Jackall, 1997; Kelling and Souza, 2001; Wacquant, 2006)

The decline of these "little brothers" is pronounced. During the 1980s, a great deal of violent crime was concentrated in inner-city neighborhoods. Studies find that in some of those areas, significant numbers of young boys saw the consequences of older boys' actions and opted not to follow in their footsteps to prisons or graveyards. Crime rates came down when the younger boys reached the peak age for involvement in crimes (Blumstein and Wallman, 2000; Glassner, 1999; Wacquant, 2006).

Crime and Guns

The United States has the weakest laws on handgun ownership in the industrialized world. As a result, there are as many guns as there are people, and it shows in crime statistics. Four million Americans carry a gun on a daily basis. Half of all U.S. households have a gun at home (Wacquant, 2006). Nearly 70 percent of murders, 42 percent of robberies, and 20 percent of aggravated assaults are committed with guns (U.S. Department of Justice, 2005).

Globally, the United States ranks in the middle of all countries' rates of deaths by guns (Figure 10.3). But no other industrialized country comes close to the U.S.; indeed our rate is nearly double that of our nearest 'rival.' The United States has had difficulty passing minimal regulations to monitor the distribution of guns. Federal efforts to institute simple safeguards such as criminal background checks on prospective gun owners have met with fierce opposition from gun lobbyists. Many efforts—such as attempts to block convicted criminals from obtaining guns or to revoke the licenses of gun dealers who break the law—remain under attack by gun advocates. In fact, since approximately 2000, some of the scattered state laws that had been in effect for a decade or more have been weakened or repealed, particularly in the

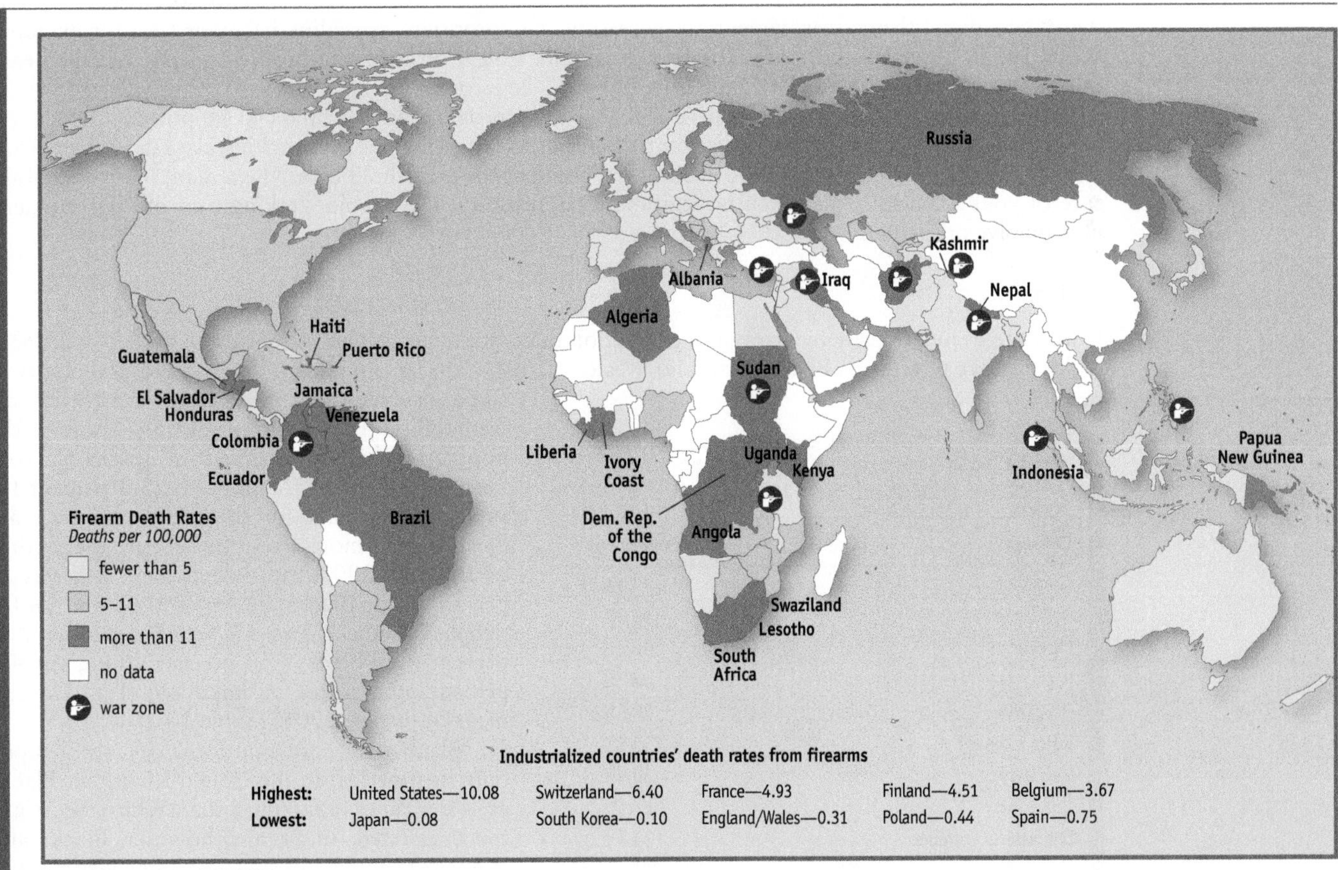

Source: Newsweek, April 30, 2007.

FIGURE 10.3 Guns: The Global Death Toll

South (Hemenway, 2005). For example, although criminologists have shown that limiting volume purchases of handguns is effective at stemming illegal gun trafficking, South Carolina abolished a one-per-month purchase rule in 2004 that had been in place for nearly 30 years. That same year, the state of Virginia weakened a similar law that had been on the books since 1993 (Wirzbicki, 2005). Despite stupendous rates of violent crime involving guns, America has seen a general relaxing of gun regulation so far in the twenty-first century (Hemenway, 2005).

Crime and Gender

When looking at crime statistics, we are often astonished by the gender gap. In the United States in 2003, only 23 percent of people arrested for all crimes were women. The gender gap narrowed only in three white-collar crimes—forgery, fraud, and embezzlement—and women outranked men in prostitution and runaways. Otherwise, women were significantly less likely to be arrested, less likely to be convicted, and less likely to serve sentences. And yet the United States has the largest female arrest and conviction rate in the world: 8.54 per 1,000, nearly double the United Kingdom and four times higher than Canada (Justice Policy Institute, 2005; Schaffner, 2006). Nonetheless, when we say *crime,* we might as well say *male.*

The gender gap may be influenced by the "chivalry effect": police, judges, and juries are likely to perceive women as less dangerous and their criminal activities less consequential, so they are more often let go with a warning (Pollak, 1978). Women who belong to stigmatized groups, who are Black, Hispanic, or lesbian, are more likely to be arrested and convicted, perhaps because they are not granted the same status as women in the mainstream. Feminists note that women receive harsher treatment when their behavior deviates from feminine stereotypes, that is, when they "act like a man" (Edwards, 1986).

But even when we take the chivalry effect into account, men still commit more violent crimes and property crimes than women. Some criminologists argue that biologically, males are a lot more aggressive and violent, and that explains the high levels of assaults and other violent crimes. However, this biological theory does not explain why crime (or at least criminal arrests) occur primarily in working-class and poor communities. Middle-class men have testosterone, too; shouldn't they be committing assault and murder? Nor can "male aggression" explain the gender gap in property crime.

A more sociological explanation is the model of working-class masculinity: In the working-class and poor subcultures where most crimes (or at least most criminal arrests) occur, men are socialized to believe that "defending" themselves, violently if necessary, is appropriate masculine behavior (see, for example, Willis 1977). On television, *Judge Joe Brown* is quite lenient on men and boys who have assaulted each other: "Part of being a man is learning how to fight," he intones.

Men are further socialized to believe that they must provide the sole financial support in a heterosexual household. Judge Joe Brown is constantly berating his litigants (mostly working class or poor) when a man allows his mother, wife, or girlfriend to pay some of the household bills: "Be a man!" he yells. "Take care of your women!" And when no legitimate opportunity is available, "taking care of your women" may involve property crime.

Crime and Race

If we were to judge solely by arrest and conviction rates, we might conclude that if the gender of crime is male, the race of crime is Black (Pettit and Western, 2004). African Americans are arrested at a rate two, three, or even five times greater than statistical probability: They comprise 12.5 percent of the population but 54.5 percent of arrests for robbery, 48.5 percent for murder, 33.3 percent for rape, 32.6 percent for drug use. And they are considerably more likely to become the victims of crime. In 2003, the violent crime rate was 29 per 1,000 for Blacks, 22 for Whites, and 16 for people of other races. Of murder victims 48.6 percent were Black, 47.3 percent White, and 4.1 percent other races or unknown (U.S. Department of Justice, 2005) (Table 10.2).

Black overrepresentation does not happen only in America. In the United Kingdom, Blacks are three times more likely than Whites or Asians to be arrested. In Britain, however, Blacks and Whites are equally likely to be crime victims, and it is Asians who face a significantly higher risk (*Home Office,* 2004).

TABLE 10.2 Percentage of Arrestees Who Were Black, 2005

Offense	Percentage
Gambling	71.1%
Robbery	56.3%
Murder	48.6%
Rape	32.7%
Burglary	28.5%
Drug offenses	33.9%
Vagrancy	38.4%
Loitering	35.5%
Disorderly conduct	33.6%

Blacks represent 12% of the U.S. population.
Source: Crime in the United States, U.S. Department of Justice, 2005.

Sociology and our World

"DWB"

The perceived connection between race and crime is often painful to those who are targeted. African Americans sometimes refer to the phenomenon of being constantly stopped by the police as "DWB"—"driving while Black." Studies of traffic stops have found that while 5 percent of the drivers on Florida highways were Black or Latino, nearly 70 percent of those stopped and 80 percent of those searched were Black or Latino. A study in Maryland found that although Blacks were 17 percent of the motorists on one freeway, they were also 73 percent of those stopped and searched. A study in Philadelphia found that 75 percent of the motorists were White and 80 percent of those stopped were minorities (Cannon, 1999; Cole, 1999). Stopping and searching minorities is a form of "racial profiling" in which members of minority groups are seen as "more likely" to be criminals and therefore stopped more often. It's more a self-fulfilling prophecy: Believing is seeing.

But it isn't just African Americans; Latinos are overrepresented in the U.S. criminal justice system as well. While Latinos make up about 13 percent of the U.S. population, they are 31 percent of those incarcerated in the federal system. Latino defendants are imprisoned three times as often as Whites and are detained before trial for first-time offenses almost twice as often as Whites, despite the fact that they are the least likely of all ethnic groups to have a criminal history (Walker, et al., 2004). They are also disproportionately charged with nonviolent drug offenses and represent the vast majority of those arrested for immigration violations (HRW, 2002; National Council of La Raza, 2004; Weich and Angulo, 2000).

What is the link between crime and race? Each of the theories we have discussed in this chapter offers a perspective on this issue:

1. *Strain theory.* It's really a matter of social class, not race. Most Blacks are poor, and poor people living amidst affluence are more likely to perceive society as unjust and turn to crime (Anderson, 1994; Blau and Blau, 1982). This theory fails to take into account the fact that even within the lower classes, Blacks are significantly more likely to be arrested and sentenced than Whites.
2. *Differential opportunity.* Black children are much more likely to be raised by single mothers than are White children. They receive less supervision, so they turn to crime. But the vast majority of children raised by single parents (mostly mothers) do not turn to crime. No significant correlation has been found between growing up in single-parent households and juvenile or adult crime.
3. *Labeling.* Being Black is a master status, automatically labeled deviant, equated with violence and criminality. So people (Black or White) tend to view Black behavior as more threatening and report on it more often, police officers (Black or White) tend to arrest Blacks more often, and juries (Black or White) tend to give them stiffer sentences.
4. *Conflict.* The crime records omit fraud, income tax evasion, embezzlement, and other crimes that are more often committed by Whites, thus producing misleading statistics.

Did *you* know?

Latinos have a one in six chance of being incarcerated in their lifetime. Black men have a one in three chance. White men have a one in 17 chance of ever serving time (Bureau of Justice Statistics, 2003).

Crime and Age

When we say *crime,* we might also say *young*. Since the rise of the first adolescent subcultures in the 1940s, minors have been committing far more than their share of crimes. In 2000 and 2001, 15- to 24-year-olds constituted 14 percent of the U.S. population but 47 percent of arrests for property crime, and 39 percent of arrests for violent crime.

In search of explanations, many sociologists point to gang activity, which has infiltrated every aspect of community life. Also, because most of the youthful offenders are male, the culture of masculinity may also be at fault: A 15 year-old boy can hardly demonstrate his "masculine" toughness, aggression, and control through academic or artistic accomplishments. He can go out for sports, but in the inner city, school sports have substandard facilities and underpaid staff, and there are few private after-school programs. He proves his masculinity by violence and crime.

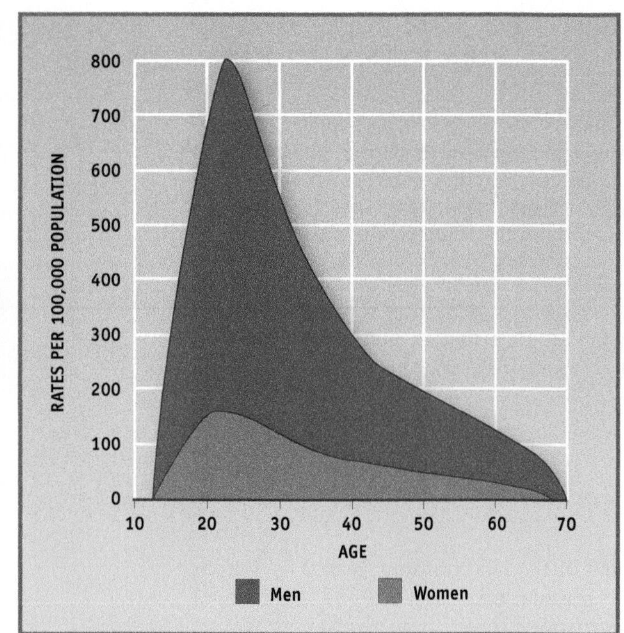

Source: Based on data from F.G. P. Neison, *Contributions to Vital Statistics . . .*, 3d ed. (London, 1857), 303–304, as plotted by Travis Hirschi and Michael Gottfredson, "Age and the Explanation of Crime," AJS 89 (1983): 556.

FIGURE 10.4 Criminal Offenders by Age and Gender, England and Wales, 1842–1844.

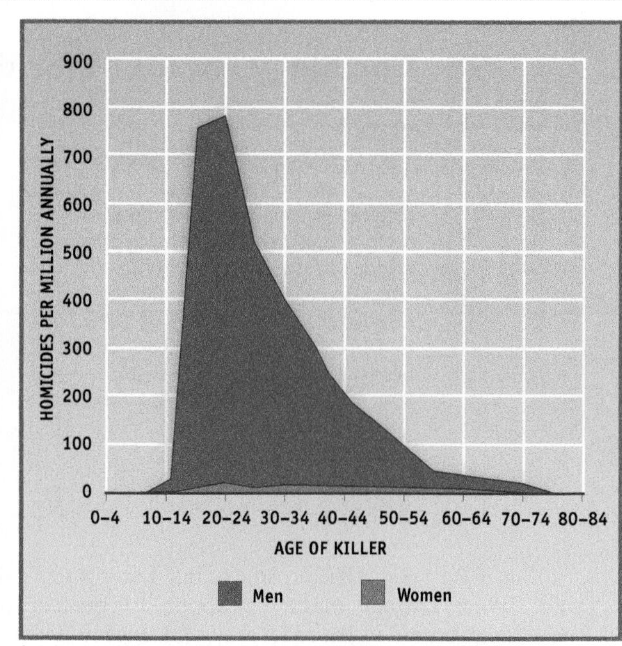

Source: From "Guns: The Global Death Toll", *Newsweek*, April 30, 2007.

FIGURE 10.5 Homicide Rates by Age and Gender, Chicago, 1965–1990.

Certainly, there are female gangs, and crimes by young females have increased in recent decades. But even the phrase "prove your femininity" is hard to translate into a provocation to crime. And the data make it clear that crime is largely an activity of young males—and it has been for some time. Figures 10.4 and 10.5 show data on age and gender of homicide rates in two different places, England and Chicago, separated by more than a century—midnineteeth century to the late twentieth century. And yet the charts look very familiar—as they would virtually anywhere.

Just because other males are the most frequent victims of violent crimes doesn't mean that girls are not also vulnerable. They are. In 2005, according to the FBI, 2,053 boys under the age of 18 were arrested on charges of rape and sexual assault (9.5 percent of the total). Over 30 percent (632) were under the age of 15. There are over 1,000 treatment programs in the United States devoted solely to treating youthful sex offenders. Psychologists believe that these boys are still developing their notions of appropriate sexual behavior, so their preference for coercive and violent sexual activity is capable of change.

But college students are old enough to have already developed their sexual "scripts"—their cognitive map about how to have sex and with whom—and they sometimes exhibit a similar interest in sexual coercion. According to a 2003 Bureau of Justice Statistics study, rape is the most common violent crime at colleges and universities in the United States; 2.8 percent of college women experience either a completed rape or an attempted rape every year, most often by a male peer, boyfriend, or classmate (90 percent of college women know their assailants) (Bureau of Justice Statistics, 2003; Cole, 2006). Another 13 percent of college women have been stalked, as compared with 8 percent of women of all ages. Aggression and control seem still integral to hegemonic masculinity in young adulthood.

Crime and Class

Historically, those with less power in society—women, minorities, young people—have been more likely to be arrested. So, too, with class. The poorer you are, the more likely that you will be arrested for a crime. While the crime rate goes up as the person's socioeconomic status goes down, this may be caused less by economic deprivation—people stealing because they are hungry or don't have enough money to pay their rent—and more because their crimes are more visible and their "profile" is more likely to fit a criminal profile. When the poor rob the rich, it makes the papers; when the rich rob the poor, it's often called "business."

Equally, the poorer you are, the more likely you are to be the victim of crime. The wealthy are more insulated in their neighborhoods, better served by the police, and more likely to press charges in assaults.

The Criminal Justice System

"In the criminal justice system, there are two separate but equally important groups: the police who investigate crimes and the district attorneys who prosecute the offenders. These are their stories." So says the narrator at the beginning of each episode of *Law and Order,* the most successful crime series in television history.

It's mostly right. The criminal justice system is a complex of institutions that includes the police and the courts, a wide range of prosecuting and defense lawyers, and also the prison system.

Police

The number of police officers in the United States has roughly doubled over past 30 years. In 2005, there were nearly 582,000 full-time law enforcement employees in the United States, or about three for every 1,000 people (Crime in the United States, 2005; U.S. Department of Justice, 2005). This is more than most countries: France has 2.06, Japan 1.81, and Canada 1.73.

But police officers actually spend only about 20 percent of their time in crime-fighting activity. A surprising amount of their daily routine involves completing departmental paperwork: arrest and accident reports, patrol activity reports, and judicial statements. Their "on time" mostly involves routine public order activity and communicating information about risk control to other institutions in society (insurance companies, public health workers, social welfare agencies, and schools). Today the police have become "knowledge workers" as much as they are "crime fighters" (Ericson and Haggerty, 1997): They offer tips and techniques, such as "stay in well-lighted areas," but in the end you are responsible for your own safety.

Did *you* know?

Americans say they feel safer than almost anyone in the world: 82 percent report that they feel safe walking after dark, second only to Sweden. Seventy-eight percent feel that they are not at risk or only slightly at risk for burglary, compared to 58 percent in the United Kingdom and 43 percent in France (U.N. International Crime Victim Survey, 2001).

The police have a split image. To some people, seeing a police officer on the street makes them feel safe and secure, as if no harm will come to them. To others, seeing that same police officer is a terrible threat, and they might feel that they are in danger of being arrested or killed simply for being there. Some people see the police as protection, others see them as an occupying army.

The police understand this dichotomy. In many cities, like Los Angeles, their motto is "to protect and to serve"—they want people to feel safe, and they want to be of service to those who feel threatened. The

"You look like this sketch of someone who's thinking about committing a crime."

Source: © The New Yorker Collection 2000. David Sipress from cartoonbank.com. All Rights Reserved. Reprinted by permission.

most important trends in police forces across the country have been to embed the police within the communities they serve; to encourage more minority police, especially in minority areas; and also to train new groups of female officers, especially to respond to complaints about domestic violence. Since the 1990s, the number of female and minority police officers has increased. Minority representation among local police officers increased from 14.6 percent in 1987 to 23.6 percent in 2003. Women's representation increased from 9 percent in 1990 to 11.6 percent in 2005 (National Center for Women and Policing, 2002; U.S. Department of Justice, 2005).

Courts

The court system is an important arena of the criminal justice system. In criminal court, the district attorney's office prosecutes those arrested by the police for criminal offenses; the accused are defended in adversarial proceedings by a defense attorney. Thus, criminal proceedings pit the government (its agents, the police, lawyers, and the like) against a defendant, unlike civil courts in which the court is an arbiter of arguments between two individuals or groups. While the criminal courtroom drama is a staple of American movies and television, over 90 percent of criminal cases never go to trial. Instead, most are resolved by plea bargaining or pleading guilty to a lesser crime.

In the early 1990s, mandatory sentencing rules were enacted across the United States. These laws applied to about 64,000 defendants a year and required certain sentences for certain crimes, allowing no room for discretion. The laws were supposed to be tough on crime and eliminate bias in prosecutions and sentencing. However, the main result has been an explosion in the prison population. Bias remains in both arrests and prosecutions. Only under mandatory sentencing judges couldn't take circumstances—which could help the poor, minorities, mentally unstable, the sick or addicted—into account. In early 2005, the Supreme Court ruled that federal judges no longer must abide by the guidelines, saying they violated a defendant's right to a fair trial.

Punishment and Corrections

Today the United States has 2.2 million people in jail or prison, 7.1 per 1,000 people, many more than any country in the world (Figure 10.6). Russia is in second place, with 5.8. The United States has four times more prisoners than the world average, four to seven times more than other Western nations such as France, Germany, Italy, and the United Kingdom, and up to 32 times more than nations with the lowest rates, Nepal, Nigeria, and India (National Council on Crime and Delinquency, 2006). We imprison three times more people per capita than Iran, five times more than Tanzania, and seven times more than Germany. We also imprison at least three times more women than any other nation in the world (Hartney, 2006). And it's not because the United States has higher crime rates; with the single exception of incarceration rates in Russia for robbery, we lock up more people per incident than any other country in the world (National Council on Crime and Delinquency, 2006).

When we add the 4.8 million people on probation or parole, we come up with an amazing statistic: 3.2 percent of the adult American population is currently immersed somewhere in the criminal justice system. And the numbers are increasing dramatically (Figure 10.7). Since 1995, the number of people in jail has increased by an average of 4 percent per year, in prison 3.4 percent per year, and on probation 2.9 percent per year (Bureau of Justice Statistics; *New York Times,* 2004). The American prison system now employs well over half a million people and costs $57 billion a year to maintain (Bureau of Justice Statistics, 2003).

Prisons. People convicted of crimes may be asked to pay fines and restitution to victims or to engage in community service, but for most offenses, the main penalty is incarceration: jail or prison terms of up to 84 months for violent crimes, 48 months for drug crimes, and 41 months for property crimes (not including those rare instances when life in prison or the death penalty is imposed). But criminologists, lawgivers, and private individuals have often wondered *why:* What are the goals of incarceration, and are they being achieved? Four goals have been proposed (Goode, 2004; Siegel, 2000):

1. *Retribution.* People who break rules must be punished; they "owe a debt to society." Children who break their parents' rules are often grounded, temporarily losing their liberty and some of their privileges (the freedom to watch television or play video games, for instance). In the same way, adults who break laws can be effectively punished through the loss of their liberty and some of their citizenship privileges (the freedom to vote, sign contracts, take gainful employment, and so on).

   A problem with the retribution goal is that we believe that the punishment should fit the crime: The greater the degree of social harm, The worse the punishment. However, incarceration can only be extended, not worsened. Also, justice is not blind: Prison terms are longer for minorities than Whites, and for men than for women, even when both have been convicted of the same offense (Mustard, 2001).

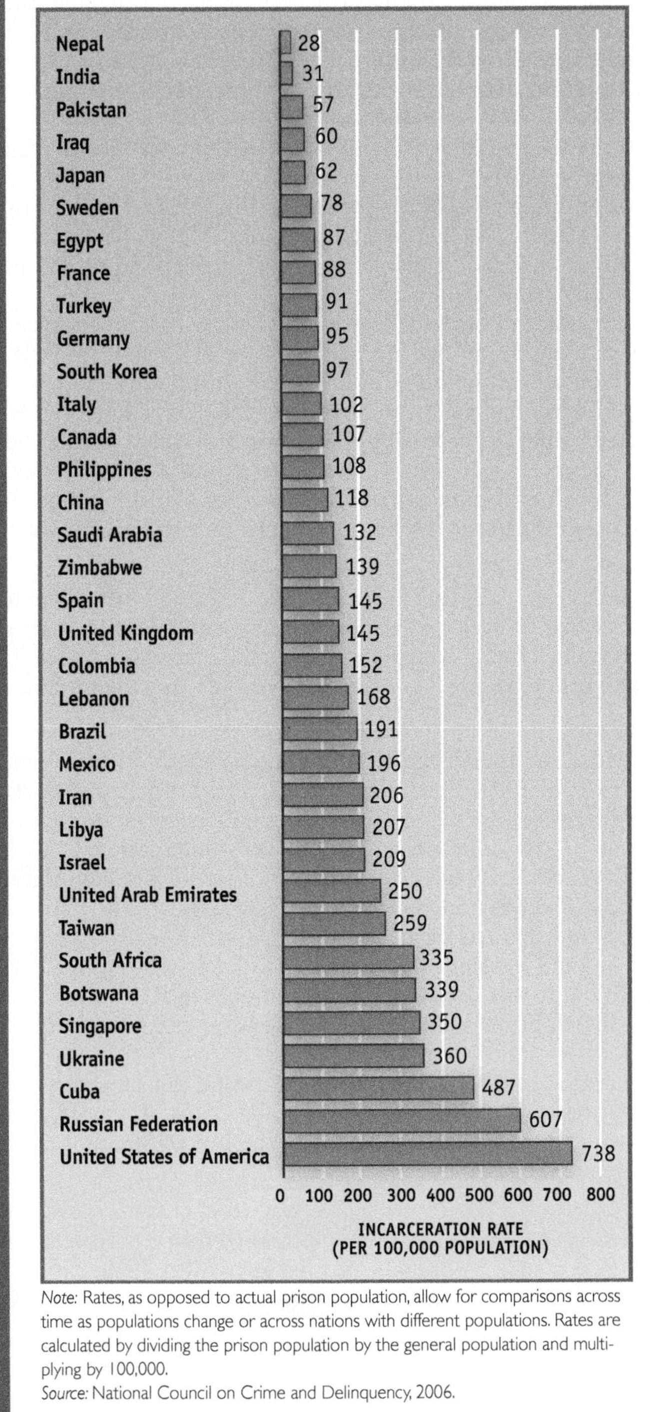

Note: Rates, as opposed to actual prison population, allow for comparisons across time as populations change or across nations with different populations. Rates are calculated by dividing the prison population by the general population and multiplying by 100,000.
Source: National Council on Crime and Delinquency, 2006.

FIGURE 10.6 Selected Comparative International Incarceration Rates, 2006.

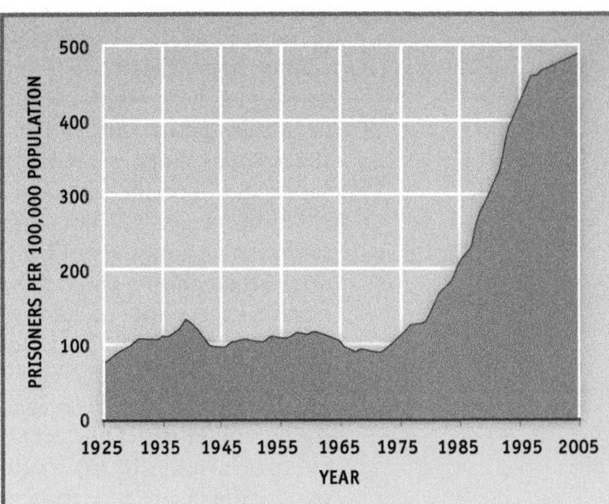

Source: From "NCCD Fact Sheet, U.S. Rates of incarceration: A Global Perspective" by Christopher Hartney, November 2006. Data from International Centre for Prison Studies, 2006. *World Prison Brief Online* version. London: University of London, Kings College London, International Centre for Prison Studies. Used by permission of National Council on Crime and Delinquency.

FIGURE 10.7 Incarceration Rates for Men in Federal and State Prisons, 1925–2005.

Did *you* know?

The American prison system has become partially privatized. That means that prisons are run like a business, with an eye toward profits. The more prisoners, the more profit. And the cheaper it is to house them—food, computers and television, libraries—the higher the profit. A large number of people now have a vested interest in making the prison system even bigger and perhaps also less "hospitable."

2. *Deterrence.* Children may not understand or agree with the reasoning behind their parents' rules, but threat of grounding deters them from most rule breaking in the first place, and the memory of punishment is sufficient to hinder future rule breaking. In the same way, the threat of prison decreases the likelihood of a first offense, and the memory of prison is assumed to deter people from future crimes.

   But does it? Between 30 and 50 percent of people released from prison commit new crimes, often of the same sort that got them the prison sentence in the first place. Criminologists have found that fear of prison itself plays virtually no role in the decision-making process of either first-time or repeat offenders, although quality of life in prison can affect criminal behavior (Katz, Levitt, and Shustorovich, 2003). To people who belong to subcultures, prison is seen as an occupational hazard. Inside or out makes little difference in their social network, their norms and values, their goals, their problem-solving techniques, their social world. In some ways, inside is even preferable, offering regular meals and free medical care.

3. *Protection.* When we "take criminals off the streets," they will not be able to commit further crimes (at least, not on the streets), and society is protected.

   However, only a few of the most violent criminals stay off the streets forever. The average time served in a county jail is 7 months, and in a state prison 2 years and 3 months. Many social scientists argue that during those months the criminals are in "crime school," with seasoned professionals teaching them how to commit more and better crimes (Califano, 1998).
4. *Rehabilitation.* Criminals lack the skills necessary to succeed (or even survive) in mainstream society. The National Literacy Survey of 16,000 inmates found that 63 percent were at the lowest levels of functional illiteracy. Less than half have high school diplomas or GEDs. So prison time can be used for rehabilitation. They can get drug and alcohol therapy, learn a trade, get their GED, and even take college classes. A four-year study conducted by the Department of Education found that inmates who participate in any education program are 23 percent less likely to be reincarcerated. A CUNY study at Bedford Hills Correctional Facility, New York's only maximum-security women's prison, found that prisoners who took college courses were over 60 percent less likely to return than those who did not (Clark, 1991).

But prisons actually offer few rehab programs, and those available are seriously understaffed and underfunded. Most prisoners do not receive counseling or drug and alcohol therapy, and budget cuts terminated almost all of the prison education programs in 1994. Those prisoners who do take classes often find that they have not acquired the skills for real-world jobs, nor have they received any training on how to find work.

The Death Penalty. In 1998, Estonia, Canada, and the United Kingdom abolished their death penalties. Malta followed in 2000 and Cyprus in 2002. In 2004, Bhutan, Samoa, Greece, Senegal, and Turkey joined the 99 countries worldwide that ban executions for all crimes (128 countries are abolitionist in practice, having not carried out an execution in 10 years or more) (Amnesty International, 2005). Fewer than half of the countries in the world (69) currently have death penalties—countries like Algeria, Benin, China, Mongolia, Thailand, and Uganda. There is none in the industrialized West. The European Union will not accept as a new member any country that has the death penalty.

This means the United States could not become a member of the EU. As of this writing, the death penalty exists in all but 12 of the states. In 2004, it was declared unconstitutional in Kansas and New York. That same year, the United States was fourth in the number of executions, after China, Iran, and Vietnam (Amnesty International, 2005).

What crimes are heinous enough deserve death? Most countries that have capital punishment invoke it only for extraordinary crimes (murder or war-related crimes), while others, like China, Malaysia, Saudi Arabia, and Singapore, use it for some business and drug-related offenses. In the United States, it is usually invoked only in cases of murder and treason.

Box 10.2

What do *you* think?

Death Penalty for Murder

The death penalty is one of the most controversial and extreme forms of social control for deviance. As of 2006, 38 states have provisions for the death penalty on their books. Lately, DNA testing has led to a number of death sentences being overturned, raising questions about wrongfully convicted people facing capital punishment. The disproportionate number of minorities who are executed makes it an even more contentious issue. There are many valid arguments both in favor of and in opposition to the death penalty. So, what do you think?

Do you favor or oppose the death penalty for persons convicted of murder?

- ❍ Favor
- ❍ Oppose

See the back of the chapter to compare your answers to national survey data.

Who can be executed? In 1989, the Supreme Court decided that it was constitutional to execute John Paul Penry, a 44-year-old man who had the reasoning ability of a 6-year-old. However, in 2002, the Supreme Court reversed its earlier ruling and held that the death penalty constituted "cruel and unusual punishment" for mentally retarded persons.

What about kids? It was once commonplace to execute children as young as 12 or 13 for everyday sorts of crimes; in 1944, George Junius Stinney, age 14, was electrocuted in South Carolina. In 1988, the Supreme Court determined that it was unconstitutional to administer the death penalty to persons aged 15 or younger at the time of the crime, but, the court ruled, 16 and 17 were acceptable. In 2005, the Supreme Court outlawed the death penalty for crimes committed by persons under the age of 18, leaving only two countries in the world where juvenile executions are still legal (Iran and Congo).

The American public generally favors the death penalty for adult offenders—by about two to one, with more support among men than women, and more among Whites than among minorities. They typically cite the death penalty's value in deterring crime. However, as we have seen, few, if any, offenders actually stop to consider the prospect of being executed before committing the crime. Many violent crimes are committed in the heat of passion, when rational calculation is largely or entirely blocked by emotion (Bouffard, 2002). Besides, for deterrence to work, the punishment must be swift and certain. Neither is the case in the U.S. criminal justice system.

Many scholars have noted that the death penalty is unjustly applied. Race plays a major factor: Blacks convicted of murdering Whites are most likely to get the death penalty, and Whites convicted of murdering Blacks are the least likely (Baldus and Woodworth, 1998; General Accounting Office, 1990). Location also plays a factor. Some states, such as Illinois and New York, have strong public defender offices with sufficient financial resources to attract the top lawyers. Cases can then be assured of vigorous defense through several appeals. Other states, such as Texas and Alabama, do not coordinate public defense or fund it at the state level—the judge appoints a lawyer, who is paid on a fixed scale that does not cover federal appeals.

Cases there are represented by inexperienced lawyers who often lack the resources to mount a vigorous defense and the incentive to stick through the appeals process. As a result, a crime committed in Texas is much more likely to get a conviction than the same type of crime committed in Illinois, where two-thirds of capital cases are overturned (Liebman, Fagan, and West, 2000).

Finally, the death penalty, once applied, is irreversible, leading to worries that innocent people might be wrongly executed. In the twentieth century, at least 18 executed offenders were later found innocent (Radelet and Bedau, 1992), and today new techniques of DNA analysis are thinning the ranks of death row.

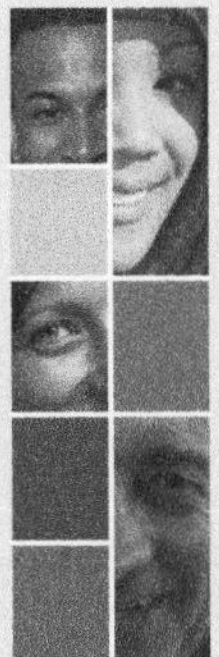

Sociology and our World

After Prison: Parolee and Ex-Con Disenfranchisement

If you have been incarcerated and are released after completing your sentence, your punishment may still not be over. Virtually all released prisoners are released before their complete sentence is served, often for "good behavior," and they are placed on parole, which means they are still under the surveillance of the penal system. Parolees are subject to regular screenings, must find specific types of jobs, and may have travel restrictions placed on them. They are also often prohibited from socializing with their old "criminal" friends. Rarely do parolees get state support or counseling to help them; more often they are simply punished if they violate their parole. Violations of parole may mean being sent back to prison to complete their sentence.

But even if you are released from prison and have completed parole, you still may not have all your citizenship rights restored—even if you have "paid your debt to society." "Felon disenfranchisement" is the denial of the right to vote because of having been convicted of a felony. There are 5.4 million Americans—that's one out of every 40 voting age adults—who are denied the right to participate in democratic elections because of a past or present felony conviction. The vast majority of these disenfranchised Americans are not in prison (Manza and Uggen, 2006). More than half of these disenfranchised Americans are African American; in several states, one in four Black men cannot vote due to a felony conviction. The United States is the only nation that disenfranchises nonincarcerated felons (Manza and Uggen, 2006).

Is felon disenfranchisement "politically" motivated? Sociologists Jeff Manza and Christopher Uggen examined the data in the 2000 presidential election, an election that was decided by a tiny margin in the state of Florida. Manza and Uggen used voter registration and election data to calculate that 35 percent of these disenfranchised felons would vote in any given presidential election and, given national and state trends, 74 percent of them would vote Democratic. (That's a conservative estimate: Nationwide, in 2000, the Democratic candidate, Al Gore, received more than 90 percent of the African American vote.) In Florida, there would have been a net Democratic gain of 63,079 votes and a Gore margin of victory of 62,542. Al Gore would have been elected president had the disenfranchised felons been able to vote (Uggen and Manza, 2002).

Globalization and Crime

Every day I receive an e-mail message informing me that I've won a national lottery in England, giving me a hot stock tip, or saying that the wife of a dearly departed African dictator would like my help in spiriting away several million dollars (for which I will be handsomely compensated). These are phishes, and they originate in many different crime cells all over the world.

While the Internet may have expanded the global networks of crime, crime as a global enterprise has a long history, from ancient slave traders (who kidnapped their "cargo") to criminal networks operating in many different countries. There were pirates on the seven seas, hoisting their proverbial black flags beyond territorial waters; and there are contemporary pirates who operate in countries where it is legal to steal and duplicate material from the Internet or to ransack corporate funds into offshore bank accounts.

Today, global criminal networks operate in every arena, from the fake Gucci handbags for sale on street corners to the young girls who are daily kidnapped in Thailand and other countries to serve as sex slaves in brothels around the world; from street gangs and various ethnic and national organized crime networks (the "Russian Mafia," the Italian Mafia) to the equally well-organized and equally illegal offshore bankers and shady corporate entities that incorporate in countries that have no regulations on toxic dumping, environmental devastation, or fleecing stockholders.

And yet much crime also remains decidedly "local"—an individual is assaulted or robbed, raped or murdered in his or her own neighborhood. Despite the massive networks of organized global crime, it is still true that the place where you are most likely to be the victim of a violent crime is your own home (Bureau of Justice, 2005; National Crime Victimization Survey).

How do we know what we know?

Does the Death Penalty Act as a Deterrent to Crime?

When we ask that question, we are really concerned with causality: Does knowing about the possibility of going to the gas chamber or electric chair *cause* people to reconsider their murder plans?

The best way to determine causality is through experiment: Introduce variable *A* into a situation and determine if variable *B* results. If *B* only happens after *A* is introduced, and never before *A* or without *A*, then can we state with some certainty that *A* caused *B*.

But sociologists obviously can't turn the death penalty on and off to look at the results. Instead, we turn to the somewhat riskier business of correlation. We look at places where the death penalty has ended, or where it has been instated, to see what happens to the serious crime rate.

Imagine a country that has no death penalty and a murder rate of 0.10 per 1,000 people, significantly higher than that of the United States (0.04). The country decides to institute the death penalty, and within 5 years the death penalty drops 10 percent, to 0.09. Sociologists all over the world would stare at the statistics in amazement: The death penalty (variable *A*) is correlated with a decrease in the murder rate (variable *B*)! Is it possible that someone stops to consider the consequences before he sets out to shoot his nuisance of a brother-in-law?

Maybe. Correlation cannot prove causality. Maybe the country is enjoying a period of remarkable economic prosperity, so there is less crime in general. Maybe it has instituted strict gun control laws, so there is no way for anyone to shoot his brother-in-law. Maybe the population is aging, and murder is mostly a young person's activity. We can never know for sure that the death penalty, and not other intervening variables, caused the drop in the murder rate.

Even though a positive correlation is not always a good indication of a causal relationship, the *lack* of correlation is a pretty good indicator of a *lack* of causality. If *B* happens sometimes before *A*, sometimes after *A*, and sometimes without A, we can be reasonably sure that the two variables are not causally linked. When real-life countries and states put in a death penalty, or revoke one, the rate of murder and other serious crime does not go up or down in any systematic fashion. There is no significant correlation.

In fact, it might actually seem to go the other way. Florida and Texas, the two states with the highest numbers of executions, actually have a higher murder rate than states with no death penalty or death penalties on the books but few or no executions. Is there another variable behind both the executions and the murder rate?

Of course, no one would seriously make the argument that the death penalty *causes* murders! But neither can anyone make a convincing argument that the death penalty deters murder either.

Therefore, despite what "everybody knows" sociologists conclude that the death penalty has no significant effect on serious crime. What "everybody knows" in this case turns out to be wrong.

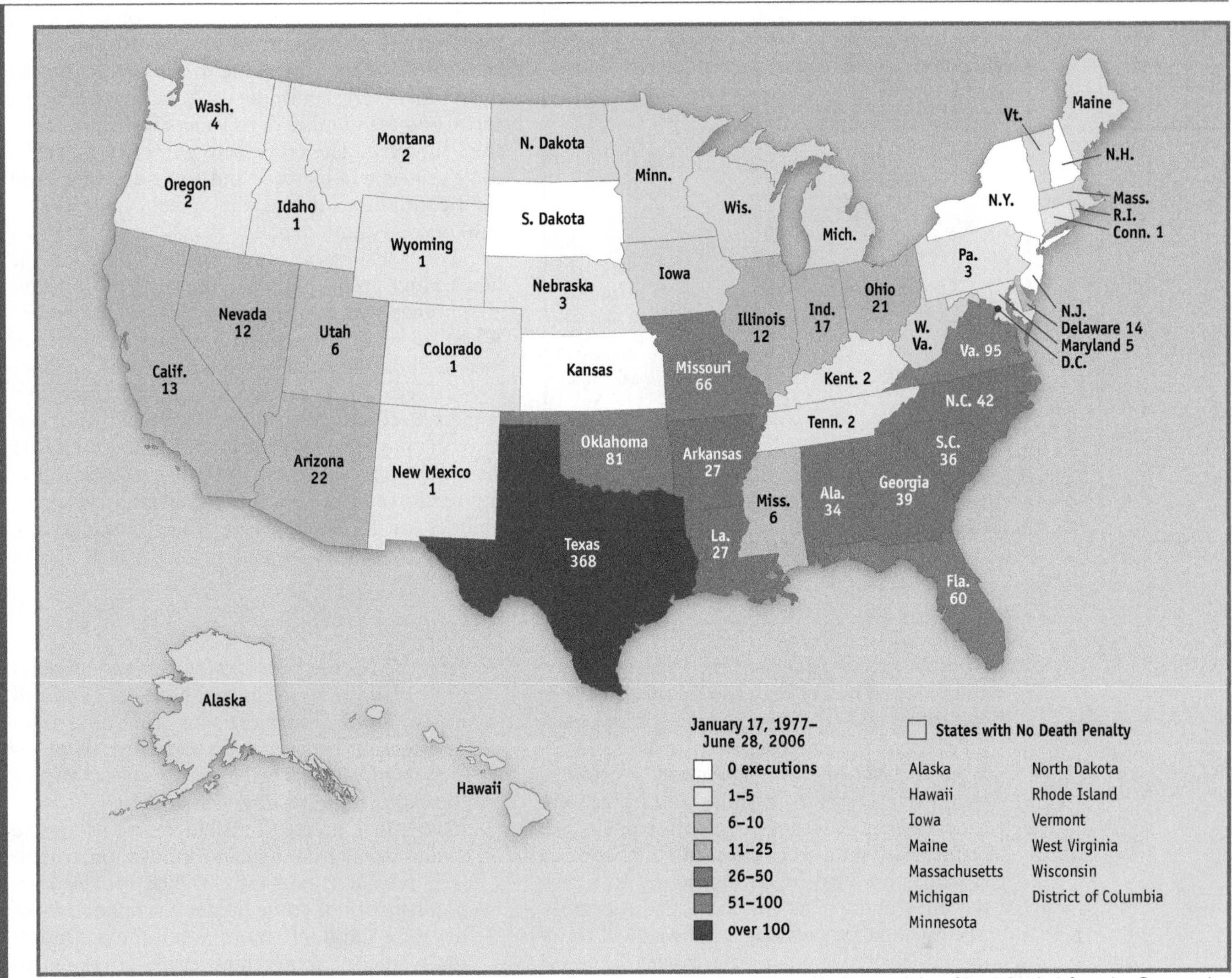

Source: From the Death Penality Information Center website, www.deathpenaltyinfo.org. Cartography by James Woods. Used by permission of Death Penalty Information Center and James Woods.

FIGURE 10.8 Death Penalty Executions in the United States.

Deviance and Crime in the 21st Century

I still wait each morning at 6:00 a.m. for that red light on campus to change to green. I stare at my watch. One minute. Two minutes. Today I'm going to run it. There are no police cars around. There are no cars around at all. Three minutes. I'm going to run it. I'm really going to run it. I'm a rebel—I make my own rules! Four minutes. There are no hidden cameras. There will be no punishment. I'm going to run it. Just watch me!

Five minutes. The light turns green. I say a bad word under my breath and drive through the intersection.

The main question in deviance and crime is not why so many people break the rules. It's also why so many people don't. The question of order is the flip side of the question of deviance—and both are of significant interest. We may all be deviants, but we're also, most of the time, law-abiding citizens. And we obey the law not only because we are afraid to get caught but because, deep down, we believe that the system of laws is legitimate and that we all will benefit somehow from everyone obeying them.

Global crime occurs in every arena, from fake Harry Potter books made in China, to cybercrime rings that steal identities or financial information, to young girls kidnapped to serve as sex slaves around the world.

In the future, we'll continue to obey most of the rules and also decide which ones we can break and legitimate their breaking to ourselves. Our society will likely continue its anticrime spending spree, and the number of prisoners will continue to spiral upward. The crime rate will shift unevenly; some crimes will increase and some decrease. And we'll continue to debate the age-old questions of guns and the death penalty.

The sociological questions will remain the same: How do people make the sorts of decisions about what laws to obey and which ones to break? Who decides what laws are, how they are to be enforced, and how equally the law is to be applied? How does our understanding of deviance and crime reflect and reinforce the inequalities of our society even as the institutions that administer them—the police, courts, and prisons—also reflect and reinforce those inequalities? What are the possibilities of more equitable understandings and policies?

Chapter Review

1. *How do we define deviance?* Deviance is any failure to follow a norm, or social rule. Deviance sometimes takes the form of behavior and other times is as simple as group membership.
2. *What is social control?* Following or breaking norms often leads to reactions called sanctions. Sanctions can be positive or negative and formal or informal. As a mechanism of social control, sanctions are used to get individuals to follow the rules, and like norms, they exist in degrees. The sanction for breaking a folkway will be informal (such as a smile or a frown) while the sanction for breaking a law will be formal (such as jail or a fine). Because social control contributes to smooth social functioning, all groups and societies have some form of it.
3. *How do sociologists explain deviance? Differential association* explains deviance as an excess of definitions. When an individual sees that there is a reward for deviance, the deviance is defined as rewarding. *Control theory* assumes that individuals are rational actors and weigh the costs and benefits of any action. If benefit outweighs cost, an individual is more likely to be deviant. The more connected individuals are with others and with institutions, the less likely they are to engage in deviance. Inner and outer controls work through attachment, commitment, involvement, and belief. According to labeling theory, something or someone has to be labeled as deviant before it is considered deviant. Once a person is labeled as a criminal, he or she will always be viewed as one. *Conflict theory* explains reactions to deviance in terms of inequality, as those with more power are less likely to suffer negative consequences.
4. *How do sociologists explain crime?* Crimes are violations of norms that have been codified in law. *Strain theory* explains crime as a result of a tension between the accepted goals of society and the accepted means of obtaining those goals, means to which everyone does not have equal access. Possible reactions to the strain include conformity, innovation, ritualism, rebellion, and retreat. The *broken windows theory* of crime holds that minor acts of deviance spiral into more serious ones. Opportunity theory shows how crime is related to specific opportunities and availability. *Conflict theory* says that crime is a result of inequality.
5. *How is deviance related to gender, race, and age?* Most people arrested for crimes are male, especially those who are arrested for blue-collar crimes. Women are less likely to be arrested, to be convicted, and to serve time. At the same time, the United States arrests and convicts more women proportionally than the rest of the world. Most arrests, however, are among working-class and poor men. The difference in arrest rates between Whites and minorities is huge. African Americans and Hispanics are far more likely to be arrested for crime and also more likely to be the victims of crime. Individuals who are arrested are also more likely to be young than old.
6. *What types of crimes are there?* Crimes occur against people or against property. The FBI categorizes crimes as violent crimes or as property offenses; the difference is force or threat of force. Some crimes are workplace crimes, including white-collar, consumer, and occupational crimes, which benefit the individual. Organizational crimes benefit an organization

as a whole. Cybercrimes use the Internet, either for personal gain or to cause trouble, as with viruses. Crimes are classified as hate crimes when the act was motivated by bias based on one's social group membership.

7. *What role does the criminal justice system play?* Police are responsible for fighting crime, protecting citizens, and serving their communities. The court system is responsible for prosecuting crimes. Jails and prisons are responsible for punishment and correction. The United States has a higher incarceration rate than the rest of the world. Incarceration is used for restitution, deterrence, protection of potential victims, and rehabilitation. The criminal justice system is the main mechanism for social control in any society.

KeyTerms

Broken windows theory (p. 232)
Conflict theory (p. 234)
Consumer crime (p. 234)
Control theory (p. 229)
Crime (p. 231)
Cybercrime (p. 236)
Deviance (p. 223)
Differential association (p. 229)
Folkways (p. 225)
Hate crime (p. 237)
Labeling theory (p. 230)
Mores (p. 225)
Occupational crime (p. 235)
Opportunity theory (p. 233)
Organizational crime (p. 235)
Primary deviance (p. 230)
Property crime (p. 234)
Secondary deviance (p. 230)
Social controls (p. 230)
Stigma (p. 225)
Strain theory (p. 232)
Subculture (p. 226)
Taboos (p. 225)
Tertiary deviance (p. 230)
Violent crime (p. 234)
White-collar crime (p. 232)

What does *America* think?

10.1 Censoring Perceived Deviance

This is actual survey data from the General Social Survey, 1972–2004.

1. **There are always some people whose ideas are considered bad or dangerous by other people. For instance, somebody who is against all churches and religion . . . Should such a person be allowed to teach in a college or university?** Data from 2004 show the following: 65.1 percent said yes, 34.9 percent said no. The percentage of people saying yes has steadily increased from 1972, when data showed 41.9 percent of respondents saying yes and 58.1 percent saying no. The current percentage of 65.1 is the highest it has been since the survey started in 1972.
2. **What about a man who admits that he is a homosexual? Should such a person be allowed to teach in a college or university?** Data from 2004 show the following: 80.1 percent said yes, 19.9 percent said no. The percentage of people who agree that a homosexual should be allowed to teach has been steadily increasing from 1973, when 49.4 percent of the respondents said yes, and 50.6 percent said no.
3. **Should a person who believes that Blacks are genetically inferior be allowed to teach in a college or university?** Data from 2004 show the following: 47.8 percent said yes, 52.2 percent said no. There has been very little variation in responses since the question was first asked in the 1976 survey.
4. **If some people in your community suggested that a book written against churches and religion should be taken out of your public library, would you favor removing this book?** In 2004, the responses were 25.3 percent to remove the book and 74.7 percent to not remove it. Attitudes have changed somewhat since 1982, when 40.2 percent said to remove the book.
5. **If some people in your community suggested that a book written in favor of homosexuality should be taken out of your public library, would you favor removing this book?** In 2004, 26.4 percent of respondents said remove the book and 73.6 percent said don't. The percentage of people advocating removing the book has been in a steady decline since 45 percent said remove in 1973.
6. **If some people in your community suggested that a book that said Blacks are inferior should be taken out of your public library, would you favor removing this book, or not?** In 2004, 32.9 percent of respondents said they would be in favor of removing the book, while 67.1 percent said they would not. Although those numbers have remained pretty steady since the 1970s, the percentage of people wanting to remove the book peaked in 1982 at 40.4 percent.

CRITICAL THINKING | DISCUSSION QUESTIONS

1. It appears that American's attitudes toward censoring unpopular ideas have changed significantly in the past 30 years. How does this change reflect changes in American society and in American values?
2. Why do more Americans seem to be tolerant of books in the library having perceived deviant views than they are of college teachers having perceived deviant views?
3. What does it say about American values that more Americans would censor an antireligion point of view than a prohomosexual view?

10.2 Death Penalty for Murder

This is actual survey data from the General Social Survey, 2004.

Do you favor or oppose the death penalty for persons convicted of murder? In 2004, almost 70 percent of respondents were in favor of the death penalty. When we look at the responses by race, though, we see a very large and significant difference. Seventy-two percent of White respondents favor the death penalty for murder, while only 40 percent of Black respondents do so.

CRITICAL THINKING | DISCUSSION QUESTIONS

1. How can we explain the difference in White and Black responses to the survey question?

▶ Go to this website to look further at the data. You can run your own statistics and crosstabs here: **http://sda.berkeley.edu/cgi-bin/hsda?harcsda+gss04**

REFERENCES: Davis, James A., Tom W. Smith, and Peter V. Marsden. General Social Surveys 1972–2004: [Cumulative file] [Computer file]. 2nd ICPSR version. Chicago, IL: National Opinion Research Center [producer], 2005; Storrs, CT: Roper Center for Public Opinion Research, University of Connecticut; Ann Arbor, MI: Inter-University Consortium for Political and Social Research; Berkeley, CA: Computer-Assisted Survey Methods Program, University of California [distributors], 2005.

chapter

Psychological Disorders

The madman thinks the rest of the world is crazy.

PUBLILIUS SYRUS (FIRST CENTURY B.C.E.)—
ROMAN WRITER

Human salvation lies in the hands of the creatively maladjusted.

MARTIN LUTHER KING, JR. (1929–1968)—
U.S. CIVIL RIGHTS LEADER

The names and particular details in this story were changed in order to protect the identities of the people involved. Melissa N. was finishing her master's degree in education at one of the southern universities in the United States. Brian W., her fiancée—they had dated since their high school graduation—decided to go back to college after several years of working and saving money. Neither had anticipated that their problems would begin at school. At the beginning of the spring semester, Brian unexpectedly received a 12-page letter handed to him by one of his classmates, a woman who appeared to be a bit older than most of the other students in the group. In the letter, filled with bizarre innuendo and a number of religious references, the woman confessed that she was in love with Brian. Moreover, she admitted that she was ready to divorce her husband and abandon her teenage children for Brian, the love of her life. Brian was shocked by this totally inexplicable confession and showed the letter to Melissa. She suggested that Brian should talk to the woman and ask her to stop pursuing him. However, things got worse after Brian had this conversation with the woman. She started to call him on the phone. She was frequently seen waiting near the townhouse that Brian and his fiancée were renting. The story became more complicated when the woman explained in a new letter that her soul and Brian's soul had met 300 years ago. According to the woman's religion (she was a Hindu Indian brought to the United States by her parents in the 1960s), a long time ago she and Brian were married and now she wanted to restore the union of the two souls that naturally belonged together. Brian and Melissa got scared. Assuming that the woman was delusional, they abruptly dropped out of school and moved to another state, thousands of miles away from their former university. Did they talk to school officials, hire a lawyer, or complain to the police? They didn't. Melissa later explained their decision: "That woman was sick. Period. She could have killed us. Thank God we escaped quickly. Neither the school nor police could have helped us. That woman was evil. That woman was ill."

Or was she? How can one judge another human being without a careful assessment of all available facts and circumstances surrounding the person? Some people familiar with this story, including psychologists, suggest to us that the woman could be absolutely "normal." The reason she was misunderstood is that people are afraid of behaviors that do not look familiar. Some argue that eccentric or odd behaviors are not psychopathological. Behavior we do not like is not necessarily abnormal either. Maybe the woman was dangerously eccentric? One can raise serious doubts about this too. Hinduism values the idea of reincarnation and it is a "normal" belief for people who practice this religion. Besides, no one should say what beliefs we should have, right?

"Wrong," say other commentators and imply that if someone displays personal, religious, or any other type of belief, he should understand the cultural context in which he lives. The woman in this story failed to understand and adjust to the cultural realities of U.S. society: you can have your beliefs but do not impose them on other people without their consent. Therefore, her behavior, being intrusive and harmful in the eyes of Brian and Melissa—and presumably in the eyes of millions of Americans—could be called bizarre and even abnormal. But wait a minute. Does the previous sentence indicate that if one dislikes the ideas of another person, it is a solid foundation for labeling that person as mentally ill? What about freedom of speech, a fundamental human right? Besides, the woman in the story apparently did not do anything illegal. So, was the woman's behavior abnormal? Are the specialists able, in principle, to clearly separate psychiatric symptom or psychopathological syndrome from a cultural norm without confusing the two? We will try to answer these and many other questions related to culture and psychological disorders.

American Background: *DSM-IV*

According to the American Psychiatric Association's *Diagnostic and Statistical Manual of Mental Disorders*, fourth edition, text revision, or *DSM-IV-TR*, a **mental disorder** is "a clinically significant behavioral and psychological syndrome or pattern that occurs in an individual and that is associated with present distress (a painful syndrome) or disability (impairment in one or more important areas of functioning) or with a significantly increased risk of suffering death, pain, disability, or an important loss of freedom" (*DSM-IV*, p. xxi). U.S. clinicians usually assess the information that they have available to them about an individual from the standpoint of five axes, each of which helps professionals to examine the situation from five different viewpoints or domains of information (see Table 11.1). Today the *DSM-IV* has become the main system of classification of psychological disorders in the United States. It is used by the vast majority of mental health professionals, including psychiatrists, psychologists, social workers, and counselors working in both private and government agencies (Mirin, 2002).

The *International Statistical Classification of Diseases and Related Health Problems* (*ICD*) is a detailed description of known diseases and injuries and is published by the World Health Organization, a branch of the United Nations. It is revised periodically and is currently in its tenth edition, known as the *ICD-10*. It also contains descriptions of mental disorders. Because of the help and cooperation from U.S. clinicians, the mental disorders section of *ICD-10-CM* is very close to the *DSM-IV* and its latest version in terms of terminology and structure.

> What is madness? To have erroneous perceptions and to reason correctly from them.
>
> VOLTAIRE (1694–1778)—FRENCH PHILOSOPHER

Two Views on Culture and Psychopathology

Culture can affect psychological disorders in at least five areas. The first area is the individual's culture-based *subjective experience*, including knowledge about psychological problems. The second area is culture-based *idioms of distress*, that is, the ways individuals explain and express their symptoms according to culture-based display rules. The third area is culture-based diagnoses for various forms of psychological

TABLE 11.1 Multiaxial Diagnostic System

Axis I indicates clinical syndromes and other important conditions that could be a focus of clinical attention. Axis II is for reporting personality disorders or mental retardation. Axis III is for reporting the individual's current medical conditions that are potentially relevant to the understanding or management of the individual's mental disorder. Axis IV is for reporting psychosocial and environmental problems that may affect the diagnosis, treatment, and prognosis of mental disorders. Among these problems are ones related to social environment and primary support group, educational and occupational problems, housing and economic problems, problems related to access to health-care services, and legal and other social problems. Axis V is for reporting the clinician's judgment of the individual's overall level of functioning. Those professionals who prefer not to use the multiaxial system list the appropriate diagnoses for the individual.

disorders, including professional and nonprofessional judgments. The fourth area is culture-based *treatment*, the way people, including professionals, attempt to overcome psychopathological symptoms. The fifth area is culture-based *outcome*, or principles, according to which the results of treatment are evaluated (Castillo, 1997).

Subjective experience, idioms of distress, and outcomes of treatment necessary for diagnosis of psychopathological symptoms can be assessed by judgments about at least three types of symptoms: physical, behavioral, and psychological. People tend to experience and explain their symptoms, largely, according to accepted cultural standards and their individual knowledge. The professional who evaluates the reported symptoms also places her judgment on the platform of a particular experience. Having these discourses in mind, we could propose two alternative hypotheses.

First: Human beings develop ideas, establish behavioral norms, and learn emotional responses according to a set of cultural prescriptions. Therefore, people from different cultural settings should understand psychological disorders differently, and the differences should be significant. This view is called the **relativist perspective** on psychopathology because it puts psychological phenomena in a relative perspective.

Second: Despite cultural differences, people share a great number of similar features, including attitudes, values, and behavioral responses. Therefore, the overall understanding of mental disorders ought to be universal. This view is called the **universalist perspective** on psychopathology because it suggests the existence of absolute, invariable symptoms of psychopathology across cultures.

Let us argue in defense of the relativist view first and assume that psychopathology is unique for each culture and cannot be understood beyond the context in which it develops. According to this view, psychopathology is culture-specific and should have different meanings in different societies. Religious, social, and political norms of each country should therefore determine the way various psychological symptoms are displayed, understood, and treated. If we accept this view, we may no longer apply views on psychopathology formed in one cultural environment to other cultures' circumstances. Thus, it may be futile to study major depressive disorder in Japan using North American diagnostic methods because people in this Asian country may interpret and describe feelings and bodily reactions differently, as compared to most Americans, Germans, or Canadians.

According to the relativist view, what is considered psychopathological in one culture could be regarded as normal in another cultural setting and vice versa. Spirit-possession syndromes are common and considered natural for some indigenous cultures in Africa and South America. When one claims that the alien spirits possess his body, this symptom, often marked by overwhelming anxiety, is likely to be diagnosed as schizophrenia in any Western country. Similar to most U.S. citizens worrying about the possibility of contracting a contagious disease, people in some African societies experience fear of bewitchment.

Dissociative fugue, a disorder marked by sudden travel away from home or work, is known only in few countries (*DSM-IV*, pp. 482, 485). Its prevalence could be caused by such conditions as a natural disaster or violence that targets particular ethnic or religious groups. In the United States, up until the 1960s, and in the former Soviet Union, until the late 1980s, homosexual behavior was considered criminal and pathological. An admission of homosexuality could carry a serious punishment, such as a prison term or

Box 11.1 A CASE IN POINT

Idioms of Distress

Have you heard expressions such as "I have a gut feeling" or "I am sick to the stomach"? The English language is rich in its range of terms for psychological distress, even by contrast with other European languages. Thus, an African's complaint of "pain in the heart" may have to cover a range of symptoms for which we would use different names. Culture-based idioms of distress—the expressions in which the individual describes his or her symptoms—are very important channels through which the culture affects the subjective experience, clinical picture, and public expression of a disorder. This could include emotional expressions, cognitive emphasis on certain symptoms while ignoring others, as well as mannerisms; physical actions, including seeking out clinical care; and the culture-based explanations of mental disorders. For example, it is very common in many parts of the world to use both scientific and spiritual explanations for mental illness (Hinton & Kleinman, 1993). In Eastern Europe, in particular the Ukraine, Belarus, and Russia, an "average" patient may have a belief that his headaches are a direct consequence of fluctuations of atmospheric pressure; in this case, the patient will be looking for medicine that would make him invulnerable to that atmospheric disturbance (even newspapers publish medical recommendations for those people who suffer from such headaches). For the "average" U.S. citizen these atmosphere–headache connections do not fit into the repertoire of idioms of distress. Cultural relativists are highly skeptical about applicability of Western diagnostic criteria in other cultures. They believe that indigenous views, concepts, and expressions of distress are considered fundamental to understanding the cultural context of illness (Tanaka-Matsumi, 1995).

mandatory psychiatric detention. Moreover, at the end of the 1990s a sizable portion of Russians believed that homosexuals are ill and should be physically exterminated (Shiraev & Sobel, 2006). In the 2000s, homosexuality is still considered pathological or even criminal in many countries such as Iran, Angola, Cameroon, most Arabic and Islamic countries.

Defenders of the relativist view particularly target and criticize ethnocentrism, or judgment of one cultural reality from the position of the other. The most salient type of ethnocentrism, in the eyes of critics, is one promoted by cultural majorities. Values and norms accepted by any cultural majority—such as ethnic, religious, or racial—have great power because of the sheer size of the majority and because of the fact that its members hold most of positions of power (Lewis-Fernández & Kleinman, 1994).

While defending the universalist view, many experts prefer not to overemphasize the extent of cultural impact on the diagnosis and treatment of mental disorders (Beardsley & Pedersen, 1997). Moreover, some specialists maintain an opposite view on the nature of psychopathology. According to this position, psychopathological phenomena across countries are universal in terms of their origin and expression. There are many examples that suggest such cross-cultural similarities. For instance, many disorders are characterized by almost identical symptoms across cultures. Among these symptoms are those of the Alzheimer's dementia, Parkinson's disease, schizophrenia, mental retardation, and autism. There are no reports of different incidences of bipolar disorder based on race or ethnicity (*DSM-IV*, p. 352). In a study of Japanese and U.S. women, both samples, despite many cultural dissimilarities between them, did not report and display significant differences in their symptoms of postpartum depression, a mood disorder occurring in some women after birth of a child (Shimizi & Kaplan, 1987).

Central and Peripheral Symptoms: An Outcome of the Debate between Universalists and Relativists

Which view, absolutist or relativist, describes psychological reality with a greater accuracy? While understanding both the relative cultural uniqueness and the universal nature of psychopathology, it is useful to implement an inclusive approach to psychopathology that combines the two previously described viewpoints. That is, major features of psychopathology—abnormality, maladaptiveness, and distress—should be considered universal. However, these features manifest by individuals in specific environmental, social, and cultural contexts. Each disorder, therefore, can manifest as:

- A set of **central symptoms** that can be observed in practically all world populations, and
- A set of **peripheral symptoms** that are culture-specific.

For example, central symptoms for a case of major depressive episode, such as dysphoria, loss of energy, tension, and ideas of insufficiency, could be seen cross-culturally as

1. caused by biochemical factors;
2. a bodily syndrome manifested in the form of fatigue, lack of concentration, and various pains; or
3. psychological complaints such the inability to take pleasure in previously enjoyable activities.

Peripheral (culture-specific) signs of this illness vary. Thus, many Canadian patients may display guilty feelings. Some of them would report preoccupations with suicidal thoughts. Most patients from Taiwan will be unlikely to report guilty feelings. Guilt, shame, bodily pain, or behavioral disturbance may

Box 11.2 A CASE IN POINT

Neurasthenia across the Globe

Neurasthenia can be a diagnostic category. At the same time, it is a social construct with a variety of cultural connotations. Historically, the use of that diagnosis stemmed from the difficulty experienced by clinicians to explain the etiology of several symptoms including various forms of anxiety and depression. Clinicians attributed these symptoms to the weakness of the nervous system, assuming—mostly implicitly—that in the future the science will further progress and specific neurological causes of that disorder will be discovered. In addition, until the recent past, neurasthenia has been a popular diagnosis because it was very general and vague enough to be used with numerous patients who otherwise would be diagnosed with a more severe disorder. Neurasthenia was one of the most widely used diagnoses worldwide because, as a diagnosis, it almost never caused serious social limitations in the patient's life. Still, there is no cross-national consensus on what the "core" characteristics of neurasthenia are; however, this did not prevent clinicians all over the world from using this diagnostic label (Starcevic, 1999).

be the dominant presentation, depending on one's learned expectation of what is relevant to his or her particular illness (Turner, 1997). In the section on schizophrenia, we will learn that hallucinations and delusions can be considered central symptoms of this disorder. However, the images and thoughts conveyed through these symptoms are profoundly affected by historic and cultural circumstances in which the patient lives.

Culture-Bound Syndromes

Culture-bound syndromes comprise a set of psychological phenomena of particular interest to psychologists. The eclectic nature of the category makes it hard to define precisely. It has even invited much dispute over the best definition for it. *DSM-IV* defines a culture-bound syndrome as recurrent, locality-specific patterns of aberrant behavior, and troubling experience that may or may not be linked to a particular *DSM-IV* diagnostic category. Many of these patterns are indigenously viewed as "illnesses," or at least afflictions, and most have local names.

Culture-bound syndromes do not have a one-to-one correspondence with a disorder recognized by "mainstream" systems. Most of these syndromes were initially reported as confined to a particular culture or set of related or geographically proximal cultures. At least seven broad categories can be differentiated among phenomena often described as culture-bound syndromes:

1. An apparent set of psychopathological symptoms, not attributable to an identifiable organic cause, which is recognized as an illness in a particular cultural group, but does not fall into the illness category in the West. *Amok*, a sudden explosion of rage, recognizable in Malaysia, is an example. In London or New York, a person with these symptoms is likely to be described as "having anger-control problem."
2. An apparent set of psychopathological symptoms, not attributable to an identifiable organic cause, which is locally recognized as an illness and which resembles a Western disease category, but which has (1) locally salient features different from the Western disease and (2) is lacking some symptoms recognizable in the West. One example is *shenjing shaijo* or neurasthenia in China, which resembles major depressive disorder but has more salient somatic features and often lacks the depressed mood that defines depression in the West.
3. A discrete disease entity not yet recognized by Western professionals. A fine example of this is *kuru*, a progressive psychosis and dementia indigenous to cannibalistic tribes in New Guinea. *Kuru* is now believed to result from an aberrant protein or "prion" that is capable of replicating itself by deforming other proteins in the brain. (A 1997 Nobel Prize was awarded for the elucidation of prions.) *Kuru* has also been compared to a form of Creuzfeldt–Jakob disease and may be equivalent or related to *scrapie*, a disease of sheep, and a form of *encephalopathy* labeled "mad cow disease."
4. An illness, the symptoms of which occur in many cultural settings; however, it is only elaborated as an illness in one or a few cultural settings. An example is *koro*, the fear of retracting genitalia, which may sometimes have a physiological–anatomical reality, and which appears to occur as a delusion or phobia in several cultural groups.
5. Culturally accepted explanatory mechanisms or idioms of illness, which do not match Western idioms of distress, and which, in a Western setting, might indicate culturally inappropriate thinking and perhaps delusions or hallucinations. Examples of this include witchcraft, *rootwork* (in Caribbean), or the *evil eye* (common in Mediterranean and Latin American traditions).
6. A state or set of behaviors, often including trance or possession states: hearing, seeing, and/or communicating with the dead or spirits or feeling that one has "lost one's soul" from grief or fright. These may or may not be seen as pathological within their native cultural framework, but if not recognized as culturally appropriate could indicate psychosis, delusions, or hallucinations in a Western setting.
7. A syndrome allegedly occurring in a given cultural setting which does not in fact exist but which may be reported to the professional. A possible example is *windigo* (in Algonkian Indians), a syndrome of cannibal obsessions, the existence of which is questionable (Marano, 1985); this allegation, however, may be used to justify the expulsion or execution of a tribal outcast in a manner similar to the use of witchcraft allegations (see Table 11.2).

Debates over culture-bound syndromes often revolve around confusions or conflations among these different categories. Many so-called culture-bound syndromes actually occur in many unrelated cultures, or they appear to be merely locally flavored varieties of illnesses found elsewhere. This fact is especially interesting because it shows that culture-bound syndromes could be viewed as an accentuation of the universal trends. Specific cultures construe certain behaviors as syndromes of psychopathology, name them disorders, and treat them as illnesses. Some are not so much actual illnesses as explanatory mechanisms, such as beliefs in witchcraft or humoral imbalances (a shift in the balance of some "bodily liquids"). These beliefs can lead to behaviors that seem to indicate disordered thought processes or emotional instability. The concept of culture-bound syndromes is therefore useful insofar as it brings culture (religion and ethnic identity in particular) to the attention of psychiatrists and psychologists trained in a different cultural tradition (Simons & Hughes, 1985).

TABLE 11.2 Specific Culture-Bound Syndromes

These are recurrent, locally specific patterns of atypical behavior and troubling experiences that may or may not be linked to a particular *DSM-IV* diagnostic category (*DSM-IV*, p. 844). Culture-bound syndromes are generally limited to specific societies or areas and indicate repetitive and troubling sets of experiences and observations. Consider examples of some culture-bound disorders. Try to find both central and peripheral symptoms in each syndrome.

Amok. Known in Malaysia; similar patterns may occur elsewhere. Amok is a sudden rage in which an otherwise normal person goes berserk, sometimes hurting those in his path. Brooding is followed by a violent outburst; it is often precipitated by a slight or insult. The symptoms seem to be prevalent among men. It was well known to the British colonial rulers of Malaysia and has therefore passed into the English language: "running amok." To this day, cases of amok are reported in Malaysian newspapers (Osborne, 2001).

Ataque de nervios. Also known as "attack of nerves." Common in Latin America and Mediterranean groups. Symptoms include uncontrollable shouting, attacks of crying, trembling, heat in the chest rising to the head, and verbal or physical aggression. Ataque de nervios frequently occurs as a result of a stressful family event, especially the death of a relative, but also a divorce or fight with a family member. Studies of *ataque de nervios* revealed that 26 percent of people who suffer from this condition had a strong risk factor for other psychiatric disorders. More than 80 percent of these people have symptoms associated with anxiety, mood, suicidal, psychotic, or substance use dysfunctions (Tolin et al., 2007).

Bilis, colera, or muina. Part of a general Latin American idiom of distress and explanation of physical or mental illness as a result of extreme emotion that upsets the humors (described in terms of hot and cold). Other symptoms include tension, headache, trembling, screaming, and so on. Bilis and colera specifically implicate anger in the cause of illness. In Korea, similar symptoms are labeled *Hwa-byung* or *wool-hwa-bung*, or the "anger syndrome." Symptoms are attributed to suppression of anger and include insomnia, fatigue, panic, fear of impending death, indigestion, anorexia, palpitations, generalized aches and pains, and a feeling of a mass in the epigastrium.

Brain fag. Known in West Africa. Sometimes labeled "brain tiredness," this is a mental and physical reaction to the challenges of schooling, a condition experienced primarily by male highschool or university students. Symptoms include difficulties in concentrating, remembering, and thinking. Students often state that their brains are "fatigued." Additional symptoms center around the head and neck and include pain, pressure, tightness, blurring of vision, heat, or burning. "Brain tiredness" or fatigue from "too much thinking" is an idiom of distress in many cultures. The symptoms resemble anxiety, depressive, or somatoform disorders in *DSM-IV*.

Dhat. Occurs in India; similar conditions are described in Sri Lanka and China too. This syndrome is characterized by excessive concern about loss of semen through excessive sexual activity or in the urine. Dhat syndrome presents with weakness, depression, and sexual problems and symptoms, such as palpitations, in a rather nonspecific form; similar to *jiryan* (also in India), *sukra prameha* (in Sri Lanka), and *shenkui* (in China). Symptoms are attributed to excessive semen loss from frequent intercourse, masturbation, nocturnal emission, or urine. Excessive semen loss is feared because it represents the loss of one's vital essence and can thereby be life-threatening.

Falling out. Recognized in Southern United States, and "blacking out," as known in the Caribbean. Symptoms: sudden collapse; loss of sight even though eyes remain open. The person usually hears and understands what is occurring around him but feels powerless to move. These symptoms are labeled obmorok in Russian culture. May correspond to conversion disorder or dissociative disorder (*DSM-IV*).

Frigophobia. There is a condition that the Chinese call wei han zheng, or "fear of being cold." Patients bundle up in the steamy heat, wearing wool hats and gloves. Frigophobia seems to stem from Chinese cultural beliefs about the spiritual qualities of heat and cold; these symptoms are described primarily in the Chinese population of Singapore.

(Continued)

TABLE 11.2 (*Continued*)

Ghost sickness. Reported in people from Native American Indian. Symptoms include preoccupations with death and the dead, bad dreams, fainting, appetite loss, fear, witchcraft, hallucinations, a sense of suffocation, confusion, and so on.

Koro. Is known to people of Chinese ethnicity in Malaysia; related conditions are described in some other parts of East Asia. Main symptom: people experience sudden and intense anxiety that sexual organs will recede into body and cause death.

Latah. Occurs in Malaysia, Indonesia, Thailand, and Japan. Symptoms include hypersensitivity to sudden fright, often with nonsense mimicking of others, and trancelike behavior. Over time, the person with these symptoms becomes so sensitive that trances can be triggered by a falling coconut. *Latahs* (people who display the symptoms of latah) tend to blurt out offensive phrases, much like sufferers of Tourette's syndrome. (Indeed, Georges Gilles de la Tourette, the French discoverer of the syndrome in the 1880s, explicitly compared it to latah.) *Latahs* also often mimic the actions of people around them or obey commands, including requests to take off their clothes. Afterward, people often claim to have no memory of what they said or did.

Locura. Incidents are known in the United States and Latin America. Symptoms include incoherence, agitation, auditory and visual hallucinations, inability to follow rules of social interaction, unpredictability, and possible violence.

Mal de ojo ("evil eye"). Known in people from the Mediterranean and elsewhere. Sufferers, mostly children, are believed to be under the influence of an "evil eye," causing fitful sleep, crying, sickness, and fever.

Pibloktoq. Known in people from the Arctic and sub–Arctic Inuit communities, such as Greenland Eskimos. The syndrome is found throughout the Arctic with local names. Symptoms include extreme excitement, physical violence, verbal abuse, convulsions, and short coma. During the attack, the individual may tear off his clothing, break furniture, shout obscenities, eat feces, flee from protective shelters, or perform other irrational or dangerous acts. The individual may be withdrawn or mildly irritable for a period of hours or days before the attack and will typically report complete amnesia of the attack.

Qi-gong. Known in China. A short episode of symptoms, such as auditory and visual hallucinations, occurs after engaging in Chinese folk practice of qi-gong, or "exercise of vital energy," which resembles meditation (Lim & Lin, 1996). In the United States, reports about persistent hallucinations are likely to suggest schizophrenia or schizophreniform disorder.

Rootwork. Symptoms are known in the Southern United States and the Caribbean. They include anxiety, such as fear of poisoning or death, ascribed to those individuals who put "roots," "spells," or "hexes" on others.

Sin-byung. Known in Korea. This is the syndrome of anxiety and bodily complaints followed by dissociation and possession by ancestral spirits. The syndrome is characterized by general weakness, dizziness, fear, loss of appetite, insomnia, and gastrointestinal problems.

The sore-neck syndrome. This is a syndrome observed in Khmer refugees. The main feature involves a fear that blood and wind pressures will cause vessels in the neck area to burst. Additional symptoms include palpitations, shortness of breath, panicking, headache, blurry vision, a buzzing in the ear, dizziness, and trembling.

Spell. Symptoms are described by some individuals in the Southern United States and elsewhere in the world. This is a trance in which individuals communicate with deceased relatives or spirits. At times this trance is associated with brief periods of personality change. This is not considered psychopathological in the folk tradition; however, this phenomenon is often labeled "psychotic episodes" in Western clinical settings.

Susto. Found in Latin American groups in the United States and labeled "fright" or "soul loss" among some people from the Caribbean. Symptoms are tied to a frightening event that makes the soul leave the body, causing unhappiness and sickness.

Taijin kyofusho. In Japan, it is an intense fear that one's body, body parts, or bodily functions are displeasing, embarrassing, or offensive to other people in appearance, odor, facial expressions, or movements. This malady is included in the official Japanese classification of mental disorders. The symptoms are perhaps similar, in some respect, to social phobia (*DSM-IV*).

Zar. Known in Ethiopia, Somalia, Egypt, Sudan, Iran, and elsewhere in North Africa and the Middle East. This is the belief in possession by a spirit, causing shouting, laughing, head banging, singing, or weeping. Individuals may show apathy and withdrawal, refusing to eat or carry out daily tasks, or may develop a long-term relationship with the possessing spirit. Such behavior is not necessarily considered pathological in local settings.

> Our health is our sound relation with external objects.
>
> RALPH WALDO EMERSON (1803–1882)—U.S. POET AND PHILOSOPHER

Now we will explore some specific mental disorders identified in the United States from a broader cross-cultural context.

Anxiety Disorders

The definition of an **anxiety disorder** is subject to interpretations that are rooted in value judgments that may vary across cultures (Satcher, 2000). However, no matter where the person lives, each anxiety disorder can manifest itself as a set of central symptoms that can be observed in practically every culture as well as a set of peripheral symptoms that are culture-specific. For example, symptoms of an anxiety disorder can be universally reported as a persistent worry, fear, or a constant state of apprehensive anticipation—the conditions are maladaptive and cause significant distress in the individual. Although one person may experience overwhelming fear of scorpions, and another person may develop a devastating fear of college examinations, they both report the existence of an emotion labeled "fear" that disrupts their daily functioning. For example, central symptoms for a case of generalized anxiety disorder could be seen cross-culturally as: (1) a bodily syndrome manifested in the form of fatigue, lack of concentration, and muscle tension; and (2) a psychological syndrome manifested as the individual's persistent worry about particular social performance or activity. Peripheral (culture-specific) signs of this specific anxiety disorder can vary. In most Western and some industrialized countries, individual anxiety is often related to the way the person views her success. Financial failures and slow pace of promotion may be named as the sources of persistent concerns for thousands of U.S., Canadian, or Japanese professionals. Such concerns may appear absolutely unessential for people in many other countries in which achievement motivation in the "material" field has not become a major life beacon (Tanaka-Matsumi & Draguns, 1997).

Each national, religious, or ethnic group may develop conditions for the development of particular peripheral symptoms of various anxiety disorders. In Japan and Korea, for example, individuals with social phobia may express persistent fear of being offensive to others. Some cultural conditions may cause the development of "normal" concerns, which may be viewed differently from the standpoint of other cultures. Some Middle Eastern countries, for instance, restrict the participation of women in public life, and strict rules are applied to women's clothes and behavior in public places. Therefore, a woman's reluctance to appear in public should not be automatically considered by a U.S. professional as agoraphobia (*DSM-IV*, pp. 399, 413). The environment in which the individual lives often determines the type of fear he experiences. Fear of magic spirits, perhaps, should not be diagnosed as a phobia in a culture where this type of fear is culturally appropriate. However, if this fear becomes excessive, so that it disrupts the individual's everyday activities and causes extraordinary suffering, this condition can be labeled a phobia (*DSM-IV*, p. 407).

Take for example obsessive-compulsive disorder (OCD), which is manifested as recurrent and persistent thoughts and impulses. Should every type of compulsive behavior or obsessive thought be diagnosed as OCD? Not necessarily. Specific repetitive behavior—praying, for example—should be judged in accordance with the norms of the individual's culture and should clearly interfere with social role functioning to be diagnosed as OCD (*DSM-IV*, p. 420).

Despite the variety of culture-specific, peripheral symptoms of anxiety disorders, there are also significant similarities. For instance, various traumatic events have direct and indirect impact on the development of anxiety problems across countries. Cheryl Koopman (1997), a psychologist from Stanford University, conducted a cross-national examination of emotional symptoms caused by various traumatic events different in scope and intensity. She found that traumatic events such as the Holocaust, terrorism, captivity, torture, rape, political assassinations, and political asylum could produce similar behavioral responses in individuals of different national, cultural, and religious backgrounds. These reactions could be described as post-traumatic stress disorder, acute stress disorder, or acute stress reaction (*ICD-10*). Individuals who were exposed to such traumatic events—for example, political refugees, asylum seekers, and victims of ethnic "cleansing"—typically have highly elevated rates of post-traumatic stress disorder compared to the general population.

Similarities in symptoms do not necessarily suggest that the severity of the condition is the same across various cultural groups. In case of agoraphobia, for instance, it was established that this disorder is more prevalent among African Americans than among whites. Moreover, African Americans are less likely than other groups to seek treatment for agoraphobia (Chambless & Williams, 1995; Eaton et al., 1991).

Depressive Disorders

In the past, **melancholy** (often **melancholia**) was the most common label for symptoms known today as **depressive disorders**. The word *melancholy* originates from the Greek *melas* (black) and *khole* (bile, the liver-generated bitter liquid stored in the gallbladder). Used throughout centuries, this term was replaced by the term *affective disorder*, with *depressive disorders* being a subtype. Various written accounts and detailed descriptions of mood-related maladies, depression in particular, are found in the texts of ancient civilizations including China, Babylon, Egypt, India, and Greece. According to the Old Testament, Saul, the ruler of Israel, was deprived of his favors with God and was doomed to suffer from long-term distress and sorrow. He finally committed suicide. In *Ramayana*, the classical Indian epic, the King Dasaratha goes through three episodes of deep sorrow caused by tragic family events. Depression figures prominently in another sacred Indian epic, *Mahabharata*. In this tale a young man named Arjuna becomes afflicted with the symptoms of a serious depressive illness. These symptoms are later relieved by Lord Krishna. It is believed that Prince Gautama Siddhartha, the future Buddha, displayed symptoms of depression early in his life. To cheer him up, his worried father and foster mother built three palaces, one for cold weather, one for hot weather, and one for the rainy season. Various descriptions of manic and depressive states are found in the Homeric epics, the earliest known works of Greek literature.

The first scientific accounts of depressive disorders are associated with the works of Greek scholars, physicians, and philosophers. Despite noticeable differences in their interpretations, Greek philosophers overall shared several common views on human emotions (Simon, 1978; Tellenbach, 1980). These views were largely supported by Roman and Middle Eastern scholars and physicians. The most remarkable observations and assumptions included the following:

- There are physical or somatic causes of depressive symptoms.
- The balance of bodily functions (either surplus or deficiency) is associated with certain problems manifested through emotions.
- Life events and experiences of the individual can predispose him to develop particular mood maladies.

The first English text entirely devoted to affective illness was Robert Burton's *Anatomy of Melancholy*, published in 1621 (later editions of the book are available today). Burton suggested that mood disorders have a wide variety of indicators, including many of those that are today considered symptoms of dissociative and anxiety disorders. He included environmental factors such as diet, alcohol, biological rhythms, and intense love as contributing forces to melancholy. During the period when Burton lived, melancholia was commonly considered a condition to which noblemen, artists, thinkers, and other intellectuals were predisposed because of their exceptional compassion. It was frequently labeled as "love sickness" (Gilman, 1988). In addition to this type, Burton also describes "religious" melancholia. Overall, the author not only discussed causes and symptoms of melancholy, but also introduced principles of their treatment. In the eighteenth century, more physicians began systematically observing psychiatric patients in clinical settings. Detailed considerations were given to less "extraordinary" cases, involving nonviolent patients, who did not express bizarre acts and ideas. The differentiation of the psychological knowledge resulted in very detailed descriptions of mood disorders.

Several cross-cultural studies of mood disorders showed that people tend to report a broad range of common symptoms. An earlier World Health Organization study (1983) found that more than three-quarters of individuals diagnosed with depression reported similar symptoms, such as sadness, tension, lack of energy, loss of interest, ideas of insufficiency, and an inability to concentrate. Earlier comparative research of affective disorders also showed qualitative similarities among national samples. According to the results of a 1972 study, symptoms were similar in patients living in countries with communist repressive governments and in those living under democratic governments such as Sweden, Germany, Spain, England, and the United States (Zung, 1972).

In a comprehensive cross-cultural analysis of depressive symptoms, Tanaka-Matsumi and Draguns suggested that *universal core symptoms* of depression include dysphoria, anxiety, tension, lack of energy, and ideas of insufficiency. Beyond these core symptoms, cultural variations in the expressions of depression are found. For example, more patients from Western countries express guilt feelings than do non-Western patients. Diagnostic practices may also partly explain the low-reported prevalence of depression, particularly in some Asian cultures (Tanaka-Matsumi & Draguns, 1997). *DSM-IV* refers to several peripheral symptoms of depression. The headaches reported by the patients in Latino and Mediterranean countries, weakness, imbalance, and tiredness in Chinese and Asian countries, and problems of the "heart" reported in Middle Eastern countries could all be interpreted as depressive. The combination of Asian cultures' belief in the unity of the mind and body with the Asian tendency not to express feelings openly may lead to the presentation of somatic complaints and the underreporting of psychological symptoms (Goldston et al., 2008).

Do ethnic or national groups differ in prevalence of affective disorders? Quantitative studies in the United States produced mixed results. Some epidemiological surveys conducted in the past 30 years indicated equal frequencies of occurrence of major depressive episodes in African American, Hispanic, and European American groups (Garrison et al., 1990; Tanaka-Matsumi & Marsella, 1976). Other studies reported differences, in most of which minority individuals reported greater levels of depressive symptoms (Emslie et al., 1990). Explanations for these mixed results refer to stress-related factors and coping strategies: On the one hand, some disadvantaged minority groups experience greater distress than other groups. On the other hand, coping mechanisms supported by in-group norms help individuals overcome stress and burden of daily hassles.

At least three factors—(1) diagnostic practices, (2) understanding of the symptoms by the individual, and (3) disclosure of the symptoms—together influence the content of the clinical picture of mood disorders around the world.

Research in this field yielded results suggestive of particular cultural differences in diagnostic practices and reporting of affective symptoms. Ian Neary from University of Essex undertook a three-year-long study of diagnostic practices in Japan. He suggested that some medical professionals avoid giving the "depression" diagnosis, especially to young women, because such a verdict in the eyes of relatives and friends would automatically place the woman's condition in the category of "incurable" mental illness. As a result, the woman (or the man) could face serious problems finding a husband (or a wife) and starting a family: Many men (and women too) avoid any engagement with mentally ill individuals. Being aware of stigmatization of depression, clinicians try to avoid it by giving their patients different diagnoses, such as neurasthenia or any other dysfunction, which is seen as a bodily problem treatable by conventional means (Neary, 2000).

Health professionals in some countries—due to historic tendencies in their medical systems—are often trained not to recognize illness, in particular psychological symptoms. As an illustration, health-care providers in African countries, chiefly in rural areas, tend to view mental illness predominantly as marked behavior with strong psychotic features, such as hallucinations and delusions. Affective disturbances are not overlooked, though. Instead, they are commonly explained by situational factors. A physician who spent two years working in Zimbabwe reported a case in which health-care providers were given a case summary for evaluation. In this description, a 40-year-old woman expressed sadness, decreased motivation, lack of energy, loss of interest, and persistent ideas of personal ineptness. She reportedly said that life was not worth living and even said she once attempted suicide. What was the most common diagnosis? The most common interpretations of the woman's problem referred to her excessive thinking, preoccupation with her husband's infidelity, her neighbors' jealousy, and possible witchcraft conducted "against" her. A mood disorder was not mentioned in the evaluations (Patel, 1996). Besides identifiable cultural factors, diagnostic practice in any given country depends on the guidelines specified by the official national classification system.

Symptoms, if they are not directly observable by the clinician during an interview, are typically recorded according to the patient's own accounts. Could it be that some individuals have particular symptoms suggestive of an affective disorder, but do not report them? There is evidence in support of this assumption. It was found in one study that many Chinese patients do not acknowledge several of their own psychological symptoms, such as lack of joy, hopelessness, and loss of self-esteem. With further questioning, these symptoms were eventually revealed (Kleinman, 1986). Similarly, Yap (1965) initially noted that Chinese depressed patients had a low incidence of guilty feelings. However, additional observations and questions revealed the presence of affective experiences related to guilt. These examples suggest that affective and cognitive dimensions of depression were not necessarily "absent" in some Chinese patients. These symptoms were underreported, compared to other, primarily bodily, symptoms (Yen et al., 2000).

One of the most interesting cross-cultural findings is a difference in displaying somatic versus psychological symptoms of affective illness. Some groups tend to "psychologize," whereas others tend to "somaticize" their distressful experiences (Marsella, 1980; Tanaka-Matsumi & Draguns, 1997). A study of word associations to the word "depression" in Japan and the United States found that the Japanese subjects preferred to use more external referent terms, such as "rain" and "cloud," and somatic-referent terms, such as "headache" and "fatigue." In contrast, both Japanese Americans and European Americans associated predominantly mood-state terms, such as "sad" and "lonely" (Tanaka-Matsumi & Marsella, 1976). Studies conducted with Chinese and Chinese American populations in the United States supported other reporting of an emphasis on the expression of somatic symptoms among Chinese groups (Yen et al., 2000). Similar observations about cultural differences were established in a study by Ulusahin and colleagues (1994): among British patients (representing a Western country) with depressive symptoms, there were high scores on psychological complaints such as sadness, guilt, and pessimism; the participating Turkish patients (representing a non-Western country) showed higher scores on somatic complaints such as sleep disturbances, pains, and aches.

Why do such differences in the reporting of bodily and psychological symptoms occur? Most authors refer to cultural rules of emotional display; others analyze the differences between Chinese on one hand, and other ethnic groups on the other. Chinese interpersonal connectedness tends to dominate their attitudes and consequent behavior. In this context, duty, obligation, conformity, reciprocity, and avoidance of conflict, disapproval, and shame are highly valued. For the individual raised in Chinese culture, for instance, affective expression of depression is often perceived as self-centered, asocial, distancing, and threatening to interpersonal relationships. However, the expression of physical sufferings and bodily pain, which are amenable to treatment and do not threaten social ties, are more acceptable in the Chinese culture (Ying et al., 2000). Other experts theorize about a greater separation of psychological and bodily phenomena in Western countries compared to Chinese society. In Chinese culture and medicine, according to these observers, the mind and body are integrated with each other, as well as with the social context (Wu, 1982). Furthermore, aspects such as stigmatization of mental illness and inadequate mental health care resources, both of which exist in Communist China, may serve as mediating variables. In contrast, the reporting of somatic symptoms would facilitate the patient receiving support from family and friends. As a result, neurasthenia as a "medical" verdict became a preferred diagnosis over the psychological diagnosis of major depression in Chinese society (Cheung, 1995).

Even though cultural differences can have a significant impact on depressive symptoms, try not to rush to judgment when you analyze reported symptoms. Somatic complaints are not a unique set of characteristics typically found only in non-Western patients. Somatic symptoms can be frequently identified among "mainstream" Western patients. When carefully made by a practicing specialist, the diagnosis usually reads: "masked depression."

> To be conscious is an illness—a real thorough-going illness.
>
> FYODOR DOSTOYEVSKY (1821–1881)—RUSSIAN NOVELIST

■ Schizophrenia

Schizophrenia is a disorder characterized by the presence of delusions, hallucinations, disorganized speech, and disorganized or catatonic behavior. Approximately 1 percent of the world's population is affected by schizophrenia, the symptoms of which appear to be universal. As an example, in a multicultural survey conducted in nine countries more than 12,000 schizophrenic patients were carefully studied. It was found that more than three-quarters of the patients were diagnosed as schizophrenic based on the results of a standard diagnostic instrument used in the survey (Berry et al., 1992). (However, it is important to notice that almost 25 percent of the examined patients could not be diagnosed with schizophrenia based on the diagnostic procedure used.)

Despite general similar occurrence rates, there are some cultural variations. For example, there is a relatively high admission rate with this diagnosis in the Republic of Ireland. In the United States, blacks have relatively higher rates of schizophrenia than whites (Levinson & Simmons, 1992). Acute and catatonic cases of schizophrenia were more prevalent in developing countries compared with developed nations (Sartorius, 1992). Delusional ideas in one culture may be nondelusional in others. Visual and auditory hallucinations could have different interpretations in various places, and speech could be mistakenly diagnosed as disorganized due to different forms of verbal presentation.

Despite the assumed biological causes, social conditions can and do affect the course of schizophrenia. Higher educational statuses of patients, for instance, were predictive of whether the illness would remain chronic, but this trend was confirmed for only non-Western countries. People may internalize their environmental influences differently, such as peer pressure, requirements, and expectations from others. Warner (1994) explained this fact by suggesting that in the Third World countries, the better educated experience higher work-related stress. However, national differences in schizophrenia rates could also be explained by differences in access to hospitals. As far as this assumption goes, if access to medical services and facilities is limited, a more severe case is more likely to get attention than less severe cases of illness.

Schizophrenia is more common in men than in women in most parts of the world. However, a recent study conducted by Phillips and colleagues in China (2004) showed that this trend is reversed in China. Their results suggested that for every three Chinese men diagnosed with schizophrenia five cases of schizophrenia are established in females. The researchers used census data and information from the Ministry of Health and other sources to estimate that 4.25 million people in China have symptoms of schizophrenia. This research challenges the assumption that schizophrenia has a uniform prevalence worldwide with only minor variations. As researchers of this study suggested, cultural, social, and economic characteristics of communities may influence the onset and course of schizophrenia. The study raises further questions about diagnostic procedures, stigma associated with schizophrenia, and government control of the health statistics reported. Because of the substantial gender gap related to behaviors considered appropriate for men and women, doctors may be more reluctant to diagnose men with schizophrenia. However, this reluctance is not as likely to affect the diagnosis of women. In addition, the Communist authorities in China (as they did in the former Soviet Union) may for political reasons lower the number of cases reported. The researchers of this study also detected a link between schizophrenia and suicide. Their data suggested that nearly 10 percent of the 285,000 deaths from suicide in China each year are committed by people suffering from schizophrenia. Additionally, those who commit suicide are also more likely to be women than men.

In developed countries today, schizophrenia is treated primarily by neuroleptic drugs, which aims at reducing the most profound symptoms of this illness. Later a variety of psychological methods can be used to reduce relapses. Therefore, the role of the caring family and community becomes extremely important in the life of the patient.

Culture and Suicide

Approximately every 15 minutes somebody in the United States takes his or her life. In high-pressure cultures, such as Germany, Taiwan, and the United States, suicide rates are much higher than in less achievement-oriented cultures: the ratio, for instance, between the United States and India is approximately 2:1. Japan has even higher rates of suicide than the United States, especially among the elderly.

Countries such as Syria, Egypt, Jordan, and Kuwait have low suicide rates. Many countries in Central and South America have low rates also, with the exception of Surinam, El Salvador, and Cuba. Scandinavian countries, as well as Central and East European states, have higher suicidal rates compared with other countries studied. Some Asian countries, such as Japan, Singapore, and Sri Lanka, have relatively higher rates. Elsewhere in the world, higher suicide rates are reported for males, with the exception of Cuba, Paraguay, and Thailand. The world's highest suicide rates are reported in Sri Lanka (47 per 100,000) and Hungary (39 per 100,000). Some hypothesize that ethnic violence is a cause of the high suicide rate in Sri Lanka. As to Hungary, its high suicide rates are explained by the confusion caused by rapid social developments and the country's transition from communism. However, this explanation is not correct. There are other formerly communist countries, as well as countries torn by ethnic wars, that have significantly lower suicide rates. In addition, there is no certainty about whether some national data are accurate. Some argue, for example, that in countries such as Iran, North Korea, China, and the former Soviet Union, the "official" numbers of suicides did not and do not reflect the real course of events. Suicide rates tend to be higher in those nations that rank high on subjective well-being (Inglehart, 1997). In other

Box 11.3 A CASE IN POINT

Suicide in Finland: From a Conversation with a Finnish Doctor

Do you know that Finnish men are killing themselves at the highest rate among Western nations? The suicide rates in this prosperous Scandinavian country are about 30 suicides per 100,000 population (the rate for the United States is about 12 per 100,000). The numbers for Finnish men are five times higher than they are for women. Remarkably, ethnic Swedes who live in Finland have lower suicide rates and ethnic Finns who live abroad still have higher suicide rates than those of native groups. How can we explain such high rates of suicide? Some would choose explanations that are easily accessible: "It's climate! It is too cold in Finland!" However, we know that people in Iceland live in a colder climate, and the suicide rates are much lower there. One may guess: "Is it alcoholism?" Indeed, Finland has high alcohol consumption rates and specialists suggest that suicides occur more frequently among the inebriated. However, there are countries with high alcohol consumption rates, such as Korea, but with lower suicide rates. "Is it societal violence? Could suicide be self-directed aggression?" The murder rates in Finland are among the highest in Europe. There are other countries that have higher rates of violence (the United States, for example) but lower rates of suicide, compared to Finland. "It is social and economic problems!" In fact, suicide rates jumped about 25 percent during the 1980s, the years of economic prosperity for Finland. However, rapid economic development is not linked to higher suicide rates in other countries. Finally, the most knowledgeable could suggest: "Is it the linguistic factor? Finns, Hungarians, and Estonians all have high suicide rates and their languages belong to the Finno-Ugric linguistic family."

Questions: Could the language alone be a cause of high suicide rates? Or maybe we should consider all of these factors together?

words, nations in which people tend to be happier than people in other nations have higher suicide rates. Perhaps being deeply unhappy in a society where everybody is expected to be happy is even more difficult than it would be in a society where most people believe that their lives are tough and full of misery.

Suicide rates have always been high in Japan, where there are about the same number each year as in the United States (31,655 deaths in 2002), which has more than double the population. In the 2000s, Japan reported about 30,000 cases of suicide per year. No religious prohibitions exist in Japan against suicide and it has long been seen as a way to escape failure or to save loved ones from embarrassment. Moreover, in Japan, where honor is an ultimate virtue, many people have long regarded suicide as an "honorable" death, rather than an act of shame and cowardice. Suicide remains almost a taboo subject in Japan. The public awareness about the problem remains low and individuals experiencing suicidal ideation are unlikely to seek help from psychology professionals.

Although the overall suicide rate among African Americans ages 10–19 years declined from 4.5 to 3.0 per 100,000 in the United States from 1995 to 2004, suicide remains the third leading cause of death among African Americans aged 15–19 years old (CDC, 2007). Depressive illness remains the most serious contributor to suicide. Unfortunately, African American youths are underrepresented in outpatient mental health services and many, as a result, do not receive preventive care. Lack of preventive care is one of the risk factors of suicide. Latino youths may be less likely than some other groups to die by suicide. However, studies show that newly immigrated Latinos lack familiarity with the service system and are often apprehensive of it because of fear of being reported as being undocumented.

Suicide rates are generally lower in cultures in which religion strongly opposes "self-murder." There are relatively low levels of suicide in predominantly Catholic and Muslim countries compared with many Western and Protestant nations, where suicide is considered by some as a legitimate way of escaping physical pain, personal loss, and other misfortunes of life. However, along with religious prescriptions, there are other cultural factors that might affect people's attitudes toward suicide. As an example, suicide rates in Puerto Rico are higher than those in Mexico, both of which are Catholic countries. The difference may be explained by the coexistence among Puerto Ricans of both Catholic doctrines and Indian folk beliefs (i.e., assumptions of communications between the dead and those who are alive). However, there are also suicides inspired by religious and ideological beliefs including the acts of terrorism. Several factors contribute to suicide. One is a major depressive disorder. Another risk factor is substance abuse. Severe or progressed alcohol and substance use is strongly associated with increased risk of suicidal behavior in most ethnic groups. In the United States, serious problems related to drinking affect suicidal rates among Native American and Mexican American youths (Goldston et al., 2008).

Another factor contributing to suicide is group pressure. In some groups, particularly Americans of Asian origin (primarily Chinese and Japanese), one of the most serious psychological problems is associated with shame or "loss of face" due to an individual's inappropriate behavior. Loss of face can serve as a precipitant for suicidal behavior if shame is perceived as intolerable or if the group views suicide as an

Box 11.4 CROSS–CULTURAL SENSITIVITY

When Jeff, an exchange student from Oregon, was invited to a birthday party, he was thrilled. This was the first party he would attend in Russia and he knew how well Russians mastered the art of celebration. The day of the birthday, he dug out a nice souvenir from his suitcase, then caught a taxicab, and decided to stop by a flower market to buy a nice bouquet—he was invited by a female student and he thought flowers would be a nice addition to the souvenir he brought from Portland. He could not anticipate that the flowers would cause so much anxiety and frustration an hour later. He bought a dozen roses—a very nice gesture according to U.S. standards. But when he presented flowers to the host, he noticed how visibly upset she became when she put the flowers into a vase. He even saw her crying in the kitchen. A couple of friends were trying to comfort her. Jeff began to wonder if his behavior had been the cause of the young woman's crying. What he learned, as he later said, was one of the strangest experiences in his life. He said that the young woman was extremely upset because he brought an even number of flowers. Coincidentally, she had recently survived a deadly illness and was extremely sensitive to the issue of death and dying. Apparently, Russians bring an even number of flowers to funerals, memorial services in church, and cemeteries. An odd number of flowers is designed for dates, weddings, and other happy celebrations. Apparently, the flowers—the number of them, in fact—that Jeff brought to the party became a disturbing signal that brought the woman's traumatic experience back to her memory. In general, Russians will not react in the same dramatic way if you bring an even number of flowers to their celebration. However, you will notice that one flower—out of the dozen or half-a-dozen you bring—disappears from the vase. Fears, phobias, and superstitions are at times rooted in folk customs and practices.

honorable way of dealing with difficulties. On the other hand, if the group views suicide as a detestable act, the adolescent may be less likely to attempt suicide, even in the presence of loss of face (Goldston et al., 2008).

Studies also show that suicidal youths were more likely than nonsuicidal youths to have been born outside of the United States. English language proficiency, a present rather than past time orientation, and social support from families and ethnic communities protect against depression among Southeast Asians (Hsu et al., 2004).

Some theories of suicide suggest that there may be a relationship between societal complexity and frequency of suicide (Durkheim, 1897). A cross-cultural sample of 58 societies was selected to test this hypothesis formulated more than 100 years ago. Each selected society was rated on a scale of social development, and the number of cases of suicide in the literature for each society was recorded. There emerged a significant relationship between societal complexity (for example, urbanization, organizational ramification, and craft specialization) and rate of suicide (Krauss, 1970).

Personality Disorders

Personality disorders are viewed as enduring patterns of behavior and inner experience that deviate markedly from the expectations of the individual's culture. It is not just a single act. It is a persistent behavioral pattern that leads to the individual's distress and impairment in one or several important areas of functioning (Akhtar, 2002). Professionals in many nations recognize personality disorders as a special diagnostic category. There is growing consistency in the way these disorders are diagnosed today. However, it is also important to consider which symptoms of personality disorders are relatively consistent across cultures and which symptoms are culturally bound.

The *DSM-IV* suggests that judgments about appropriate and inappropriate traits vary across cultures. Psychologists are expected to make a determination of whether the diagnosis is applicable to the individual given the cultural context in which the patient lives. Someone's flashy, unusual clothes may get attention from people on the street; in the same way, personality traits may be seen as unusual and ambiguous when compared to a social standard. **Tolerance threshold** is a term that stands for a measure of tolerance or intolerance toward specific personality traits in a cultural environment. Low thresholds stand for relative societal intolerance against specific behaviors and underlying personality traits, while high thresholds stand for relative tolerance. If a society accepts the diversity of behaviors, then tolerance thresholds should be relatively high. In Table 11.3 you will find a description of the impact of specific cultural constructs on manifestation and evaluation of personality disorders. Overall, personality disorders represent a deviation from what is considered "standard" personality in a specific social and cultural environment.

In a unique comparative study sponsored by the World Health Organization, Loranger and associates (1994) employed the help of 58 psychiatrists who interviewed 716 patients in 11 countries in North America, Europe, Africa, and Asia. A specially designed semistructured clinical interview was used (called International Personality Disorder Examination), which was compatible with evaluations used in the United States and in the *ICD-10*. The main result of the study was that personality disorders have relatively similar features that can be assessed with a reasonably high degree of reliability across different nations, languages, and cultures. Additional studies reveal similar outcomes, suggesting that certain symptoms can be diagnosed with a degree of consistency across different racial and national groups (Fountoulakis et al., 2002). Unfortunately, reliable comparative empirical evidence has been accumulated only for antisocial personality disorder (Murphy, 1976). Symptoms of this *personality* disorder can be recognized in all social and cultural groups (Robins et al., 1991). In particular, in the United States, individuals with symptoms of antisocial personality disorder are charged with a greater number and variety of criminal offenses than people without these symptoms, regardless of race (Cooke & Michie, 1999; Hare, 1991). However, at least at this stage of psychological research, there are many reasons to believe that personality disorders represent categories and symptoms which vary in a range of cultures.

Psychologists focus largely on two basic sets of assumptions related to the manifestation and diagnoses of these disorders. The first set includes hypothesis about specific culture-bound personality traits that are prevalent in some cultural groups and less prevalent in others. According to this view, similarities in coping strategies cause the development of similar traits in many individuals belonging to the same cultural group. As an example, conscientiousness and deeply seated habits of self-discipline, as some may argue, have been cultivated in the German culture for many years. Therefore, there should be many individuals raised in Germany who developed personality traits consistent with self-discipline and conscientiousness. Additionally, if a person is born outside Germany but raised there, this individual is likely to develop such traits. If this hypothesis is correct, there should be a higher statistical probability of the occurrence of the symptoms of obsessive-compulsive personality disorder. In other words, these symptoms should be found with a greater frequency in Germans than in people of other nations whose cultural conditions cultivate a set of different personality traits.

TABLE 11.3 Assumptions about the Links Between Cultural Variables and Manifestation and Evaluation of Symptoms

Cultural Variables	Manifestations and Evaluations of Symptoms
Collectivism	Collectivist norms allow very limited deviance from what is considered appropriate behavior. Therefore, there should be less tolerance to and more social sanctions against any exhibition of histrionic or antisocial traits. Personality traits that disengage individuals from the group are also among the least tolerated; these include narcissistic, borderline, and schizoid features. Dependent and avoidant personality traits should be tolerated, in general. Obsessive-compulsive traits can be useful in cases that they help an individual to follow strict requirements and rules. Paranoid tendencies may not be seen as pronounced if most people share similar fears and concerns.
Individualism	Tolerance thresholds are relatively high. Individualist norms cultivate tolerance to independent behavior and a range of deviations from the norm. Many symptoms of personality disorders in their mild form could be accepted as signs of a person's unique individuality or the person's right to choose his own behavioral scripts. However, due to expectations that individualism is based on self-regulation and self-discipline, antisocial and borderline features may stand out and be rejected.
High-power distance	Tolerance thresholds are relatively high toward behavior that is in accordance with the power hierarchy. Narcissistic personality tendencies are tolerated in individuals of higher status. Antisocial traits are particularly resisted because they challenge the established order in relationships between older and younger family members, authority figures and lay people. Obsessive-compulsive traits can contribute to coping in interpersonal relationships because the person maintains the rules of subordination. Dependent personality traits are tolerated. Avoidant personality traits are likely to be tolerated. Schizoid personality traits are required for some social roles.
Low-power distance	Personality characteristics that are viewed anti-egalitarian are not likely to be tolerated. Among these characteristics are narcissistic and dependent features for their association with the idea of personal subordination.
Traditionalism	Personality traits that are viewed as challenging the established order and tradition will likely be rejected. Therefore, there are very low tolerance thresholds toward histrionic and antisocial features. Other personality traits are evaluated based on the criterion of whether these traits help to maintain the existing traditional establishment.
Modernity	Traits that are not in line with the customs of openness, exchange of ideas, flexibility of customs, and individual freedom are likely to be resisted.

(Continued)

TABLE 11.3 (Continued)

Cultural Variables	Manifestations and Evaluations of Symptoms
Specific social and cultural circumstances	Obsessive-compulsive and dependent personality traits are likely to be more appropriate in the context of social stability and less appropriate if a society is in transition. Antisocial personality traits can be useful as a means of self-preservation in especially difficult social conditions, such as rampant violence and lawlessness. Borderline personality traits can develop in extreme social circumstances. Narcissistic personality traits can develop within conditions of extreme social mobility, where individuals are able to achieve enormous success and wealth. Histrionic personality traits may be common in younger individuals from nontraditional settings. Paranoid personality traits are useful in dangerous situations, such as instances of social turmoil.

The second set embraces assumptions about the existence of specific social and cultural circumstances that determine our views serving as "filters" for evaluations of personality traits and personality disorders. Some traits can be seen as common and "standard" from a particular national or cultural standpoint, while they can be seen as excessive and even abnormal (if they fit specific criteria) from another cultural point of view. For instance, if a woman from a traditional culture does not go in public places often, prefers solitary activities at home, does not have close relationships with anyone outside her family, and appears "cold" or unemotional in conversations with a researcher, these characteristics should not be considered indicative of schizoid personality disorder. Her behavior should be judged from a broader cultural context, which contains specific gender scripts, or rules of behavior for men and women. Therefore, some symptoms of *DSM-IV* personality disorders could be valued as nonexcessive, nonpathological, and even normal in certain cultural settings. Thus, cultural sensitivity is essential when attempting to apply DSM-based diagnoses to individuals from different cultural environments.

The idea about the existence of culture-bound or specific "national" or "ethnic" personality traits was explored by many intellectuals of the past and present. From the times of the Greek philosopher Aristotle (fifth century b.c.e.) who claimed that the Greeks had a particular inclination to philosophy, while people of other nations develop skills, there were numerous written statements or even scientific theories about personality traits developed on entire peoples and cultural groups (Cooper, 2003). Little empirical evidence, of course, was produced to back up the theories espousing the existence of a distinct "Greek," "Babylonian," or any other collective personality. Even in more recent times, at the dawn of scientific psychology, there has been no shortage of such stereotypical theories about prevalence of specific personality traits in national or cultural groups. Most popular assumptions were established about the differences between European and Asian cultures. Karl Jung, for instance, believed in substantial differences between the Eastern and the Western types of individuals. The Western type is rooted in reason but little in intuition and emotion, which is more common in the Eastern type. The Western type is an extravert. To the contrary, the Eastern type is an introvert (Kleinman & Kleinman, 1991). While evaluating Chinese and European personality types, other authors focused their attention on the peasant roots of the Chinese civilization associated with pragmatism and down-to-earth considerations on one hand, and mercantilism of Europeans with their love of numbers and abstract theories on the other (Fung, 1948). Generalizations about personality traits appear in contemporary publications. Authors continue to make sweeping assumptions about fundamental cultural differences shaping different types of behavior in individuals who are brought up in different countries (Li, 2003; Mahbubani, 1999). Most of these assumptions—although intriguing—are not accompanied by strong empirical evidence or support. (See Box 11.5.) It is very difficult to validate theories about the existence of "national" personality types and personality disorders for a host of reasons. The most substantial is that there is a tremendous diversity of personality traits within an ethnic or national group. Furthermore, studies show with consistency that the variation of characteristics within national samples is typically greater than the differences between any two national samples (Barrett & Eysenck, 1984; Zuckerman, 1990).

Box 11.5 CRITICAL THINKING

Stereotype–Based Anticipations Related to Personality Disorders

Researchers try to avoid stereotypical and other non-scientific judgments in assessments of the cultural impact on personality disorders (Widiger & Spitzer, 1991). Nevertheless, even educated individuals are not free from making stereotypical assumptions about the psychological symptoms of other individuals (Funtowitz & Widiger, 1999). In one study, psychology students were asked to sort diagnostic characteristics of personality disorders by racial groups, according to the most common classification in the United States: white, black, Hispanic, and Native American. The results were quite surprising because psychology students were not expected to make judgments based on popular stereotypes. However, many students did in fact demonstrate such stereotypical judgments. Specifically, criteria for antisocial and paranoid personality disorders were assigned mostly to African Americans, criteria for schizoid personality disorders were mostly applied to Asian Americans, and criteria for schizotypal personality disorders were mostly applied to Native Americans. The study also revealed that five of the DSM-IV personality disorders were attributed mostly to whites and practically none to Hispanics. You can see a sort of two-step-stereotyping: some personality features are assigned to the racial groups and thus corresponding personality disorders are associated with the same racial groups (in the absence of empirical evidence to prove these assessments). The authors of this study used the term pathologization, which stands for assigning pathological characteristics to ordinary, nonpathological psychological phenomena (Iwamasa et al., 2000).

Could you find out about other personality traits ("labels") that are stereotypically assigned in folk theories (popular knowledge) to certain national or ethnic groups? To begin, think about your own cultural group. What kind of stereotypical judgments do you know exist about this group? Why do you think these stereotypical judgments exist?

Certain personality traits may "flourish" in particular circumstances and be "suppressed" in others. Certain personality types can contribute to successful coping in a set of cultural conditions, while other personality types may interfere with an individual's successful coping. Take, for example, avoidant traits. In China, interpersonal relationships are largely based on a deep cultural tradition of exchange of favors, or, in Western terms, reciprocal relationships guided by moral norms. If a person believes that, under specific circumstances, she is not capable of exchanging favor with others, this could be an embarrassing blow to her reputation. Therefore, to save face, it is generally appropriate for such individuals to develop avoidant tendencies, because avoidance is perceived as less embarrassing than the inability to exercise appropriate social acts. Individuals from outside this social context may be inclined to perceive these behaviors as symptoms of avoidant personality disorder. Similarly, it is not uncommon for young adults from Greece to seek support (both emotional and financial) from their parents until the age of 30. However, a foreign observer may construe this as a form of dependent personality disorder (Fountoulakis et al., 2002).

Assumptions of the similar kind exist about obsessive-compulsive personality traits in Japan. As one Japanese expert in education put it, in Japanese society, many people are brought up to model themselves faithfully on "role models" or general behavioral standards. This environment creates conditions that stimulate people's preoccupation with discipline, formal rules, and procedures (Esaki, 2001). If these behavioral traits are taken out of cultural context, there could be a temptation to view them as symptoms of obsessive-compulsive personality disorder. However, within the Japanese context, to a certain degree, these personality traits are considered normal and mainstream.

Is Substance Abuse Culturally Bound?

There are cultural and national standards for substance use and abuse. There are also wide cultural variations in attitudes toward substance consumption, patterns of substance use, accessibility of substances, and prevalence of disorders related to substance (*DSM-IV*, p. 188) (Table 11.4). Marijuana is outlawed in the United States, but is legal under certain conditions in Holland. The legal drinking age in the United States is 21. In contemporary Russia, however, it is 18, and the laws against selling alcohol to minors are not heavily enforced. You can buy a bottle of wine in a student cafeteria in France, but this is impossible to do at UCLA or George Mason University. Smoking opium was legal in some Asian American communities at the turn of the century.

There is no universal criterion that would distinguish normal from abnormal drinking. Muslims and Mormons prohibit any alcohol consumption. In contrast, Spanish and Greek respondents indicate that drinking alcohol is an essential part of their culture (Bennet et al., 1993). Europeans, although only 15 percent of the world population, consume about 50 percent of the alcohol on earth. The top consumers

TABLE 11.4 *DSM-IV* on Cultural Variations of Substance Abuse

Caffeine consumption varies across cultures with males drinking coffee more often than females. In European and other developed countries the rates are 400 mg/day or more, whereas in the developing world the rate is approximately 50 mg/day. The cost of coffee may also be a factor contributing to consumption rates (p. 214). Cannabis (usually marijuana) is among the first drug of experimentation for all cultural groups in the United States (p. 219). Cocaine use affects all races, ethnic groups, and both sexes in the United States but is most commonly found in 18–30-year-olds (p. 228). Hallucinogens may be used as part of established religious practices. Inhalants are more commonly abused by the young from economically depressed areas (p. 241). The prevalence of smoking is decreasing among industrial nations, but increasing among developing countries. Prevalence of smoking is decreasing more rapidly among males than females (p. 246). Opioid dependence historically is more common in members of minority groups living in economically deprived areas in the United States. However, at the beginning of the twentieth century, opioid dependence has been seen more often among middle-class individuals (p. 254). Prescription drug abuse is more common in women, but the prevalence has many cultural variations, partly caused by different prescription practices around the world (p. 268).

are Portugal and France. Their residents consume seven times as much as the lowest consumer, Israel (countries in which alcohol is outlawed, such as Saudi Arabia, were not included in the analysis). The United States is in the middle of the list. In most Asian countries (except Korea), the overall prevalence of alcohol-related disorders is relatively low, and the male–female ratio is very high. Various East Asian populations have a sort of "protective mechanism" against alcohol abuse. It was found that approximately 50 percent of Korean, Japanese, and Chinese individuals lack a particular chemical in their blood, *aldehyde dehydrogenase*, that eliminates the first breakdown product of alcohol. When such individuals consume alcohol, they experience a flushed face and palpitations. Therefore, they are not as likely to consume large amounts of the substance. Cultural norms and peer pressure could change behavioral patterns, though. When Asian youth immigrate to the United States, they tend to drink more than their peers who live in their home countries (Halonen & Santrock, 1995).

Some researchers refer to biological factors that cause differences in addictive behavior in certain cultural groups. For example, the *Journal of the American Medical Association* reported that cells of blacks who smoke absorb more nicotine than do cells of white or Hispanic smokers. This difference, as experts suggest, could explain why blacks tend to suffer more from tobacco-related diseases—lung cancer, for example—and have more trouble quitting the habit (Schwartz, 1998).

Alcohol-related disorders are associated with lower educational levels, lower socioeconomic status, and higher rates of unemployment. However, it is difficult to say what is cause and what is effect. For example, people who drop out from either high school or college have particularly high rates of alcohol-re-

Box 11.6 A CASE IN POINT

Hikikomori is a complex form of withdrawal behavior, observed in Japan, that resembles the symptoms of schizoid personality disorder. This behavioral pattern has become the subject of worldwide attention and the topic of numerous television documentaries and newspaper and magazine articles (Rees, 2002). According to a government survey, approximately 1 million people in Japan choose to live for a long time in relative isolation (Tolbert, 2002). These individuals, typically male, shut themselves in the homes of their parents, seldom go out, and have very limited face-to-face contact with other people. They spend their days browsing the Web or chatting online and only occasionally see their parents, who continue to support their adult children financially. Economic and social conditions of contemporary Japan may contribute to this form of self-isolation. Young individuals lose the incentive for hard work and abandon ambitions, partly because the society in which they live guarantees a certain level of well-being. In addition, electronic communication and computer games give these shut-ins a chance to interact with others without face-to-face contact. Studies suggest that this phenomenon is growing in other countries, too (Sax, 2007). But do these people display symptoms of schizoid personality disorder? Again, you analyze the symptoms within the cultural context in which they appear. For a professional, who tends to base his or her evaluations on the existing culture-bound model of a "normal" personality (someone who is outgoing, balanced, and ambitious), many cases of the shut-ins would likely be linked to schizoid personality traits. However, if the standard for normality were to change, a different type of evaluation ought to follow. One important observation: the Japanese survey mentioned earlier did not find any evidence that the shut-ins displayed a higher prevalence of any psychological disorders compared to the general population.

Box 11.7 A CASE IN POINT

Some Smoking Patterns

Worldwide, approximately 1.3 billion people (1 billion of them men) currently smoke cigarettes or other tobacco products. Globally, the prevalence of tobacco use is substantially higher in men (47 percent) than in women (12 percent), but significantly increasing smoking rates among women were noted in Cambodia, Malaysia, and Bangladesh. Female smoking prevalence is actually higher than male smoking prevalence in the Cook Islands, Nauru, Norway, Papua New Guinea, and Sweden, thanks largely to aggressive tobacco industry marketing of cigarettes to women. In the 2000s, more smokers lived in low- and middle-income countries (933 million) than in high-income countries (209 million). About 35 percent of men in developed countries smoke, compared to almost 50 percent of men in developing nations and almost two-thirds of men in China. Currently, more than 600,000 annual smoking-attributable deaths occur in China alone. If current smoking patterns continue, deaths from smoking in Asia—home to one-third of the world's population—are expected to increase to 4.9 million per year by 2020 (Shafey et al., 2003).

lated disorders (*DSM-IV*, p. 201). Does the individual develop a substance-related problem because he dropped out of school or did this person drop out from school because of the substance-related problem?

Nearly 33 percent of U.S. youth have used some type of illegal drug at some point in their lives. Reported rates are generally similar among males and females. White and Hispanic males have reported higher rates of illegal drug use than black males. White females reported higher rates than both Hispanic and black females. Thirty percent of white males and females have used marijuana compared to less than 25 percent of black males and females. Use of cocaine was found to be highest among Mexican American males. White youths use drugs such as LSD, heroine, and amphetamines five times more often than black youths, with use among Hispanics somewhere in the middle (Russell, 1995).

Psychodiagnostic Biases

The cultural background of the professional can influence his perception of different behaviors. Psychologists are likely to have their own perceptions and attributions about the links among culture, ethnicity, and mental illness (Lopez, 1989). It is also known that doctors can misdiagnose particular diseases due to cross-cultural differences in the perception, attribution, and expression of signs of disease.

Mental health specialists should notice, for example, the importance of social distance between their patients and themselves across different cultural groupings. Even the way we observe abnormality may be affected by our own social status, and this phenomenon was noticed a long time ago. For instance, it was suggested that substantial differences in psychiatric symptoms between low- and high-status groups in the Austro-Hungarian Army in 1914 were influenced by the fact that most psychiatric observers belonged to high-status nationalities (Murphy, 1982).

As another illustration of the diagnostic bias in the clinical setting, consider how therapist's beliefs and expectations may predispose them to "see" psychopathology wherever they look. Suppose you were to ask a therapist to explain the meaning of behaviors that clients might exhibit on arriving for their scheduled therapy session. Let us imagine further that this therapist happens to view the world through a densely filtered cultural schema of psychopathology. The therapist thus calmly and confidently offers you the following interpretations:

> *If the patient arrives early for his appointment, then he's anxious. If he arrives late, then he's hostile. And if he's on time, then he's compulsive.*

This witticism about psychoanalysis dates back to the 1930s. Although originally intended as a joke, it was far more prophetic than most people at that time could have anticipated. It is not just a humorous illustration of "noncritical" thinking; it is also a revealing and sobering parable that alerts us to the dangers inherent in maintaining schemas that allow—and even encourage—virtually any human behavior to be subsumed under one or another of pathological categories.

As we suggested earlier, some specialists are skeptical about the applicability of Western diagnostic criteria in other cultures and vice versa. They insist that distress is experienced and manifested in many culture-specific ways. Different cultures may either encourage or discourage the reporting of psychological or physiological components of the stress response (Draguns, 1996). In addition, in some cultures persistent nightmares are viewed as a spiritual and supernatural phenomenon, whereas others observe nightmares as indicators of mental or physical disturbance (*DSM-IV*, p. 581).

Some existing culture-specific disorders are difficult to interpret in terms of other national classifications. A neurological weakness, typically diagnosed in China, includes symptoms of weakness, fatigue, tiredness, headaches, and gastrointestinal complaints (Tung, 1994). The Western diagnostic assessments of patients with this disorder varied with different diagnostic procedures employed. It could be anxiety disorder, depressive disorder, or bipolar disorder (Kleinman, 1986).

Some symptoms can be consistent across different national samples. A study in Russia conducted by V. Ruchkin, D. Sukhodolsky, and colleagues (2007) showed that prevalence rates of attention deficit/hyperactivity disorder were similar to those of many other countries. Recent studies on culture-specific disorders suggest that different cultures have specific labels for behavioral disorders. Culture-bound syndromes challenge any universal categorization because of the culturally specific content of the disorders (Tanaka-Matsumi & Draguns, 1997). But no matter how you describe a problem, it would manifest as a maladaptive and distressful symptom, as inability to cope with stressful situations. The key to success in diagnostic practices is to identify distress and maladaptive symptoms correctly and in their cultural context.

Much unhappiness has come into the world because of bewilderment and things left unsaid.

The greatest happiness is to know the source of unhappiness.

FYODOR DOSTOYEVSKY (1821–1881)—RUSSIAN NOVELIST

Psychotherapy

The twenty-first century brought rapid changes to many countries' attitudes toward mental illness and psychotherapy. In China, for example, rising wealth and growing complexity of life have produced a stressful environment of competition, which many people have difficulty adjusting to. Twenty years ago, the government would provide for almost everything including salaries, health care, and pensions. Today, individuals must pay more attention to their own well-being. Therefore, people in China will inevitably face more emotional and stress-related problems than those faced two or three decades ago. In addition, the stigma attached with mental illness and psychotherapy is gradually disappearing and more people see psychological problems as special conditions that they should not be ashamed of. Over this decade, Chinese psychologists will be facing an important question: Which forms of psychotherapy should they adopt? Should they be Western behavioral or cognitive therapy adapted to Chinese culture or should these methods be uniquely Chinese?

If different cultural settings can affect diagnostic practices, one can assume that culture may also play a significant role in **psychotherapy**, which is the treatment of psychological disorders through psychological means, generally involving verbal interaction with a professional therapist. Research cases show, for example, that many drug rehabilitation and prevention programs designed for one particular ethnic and social category (white middle-class subjects) are applicable to other ethnic and social categories. In tolerant and supportive cultures (as well as in supportive communities and families), individuals with mental disorders may function better than those in less-tolerant surroundings. In Japan, depressed patients could rely on other people to make decisions for them. In U.S. culture, depressed patients rely more on individual decision making and therefore are more avoidant and show lower self-esteem than Japanese patients (Radford et al., 1991). It was also shown in a World Health Organization study (1979) that patients from collectivist cultures had a better prognosis for schizophrenia, whereas patients from individualist cultures showed fewer signs of improvement (Tanaka-Matsumi & Draguns, 1997).

Different ethnic groups could have various attitudes about mental health services. Some studies imply that Mexican Americans are significantly less likely to use outpatient mental help than other ethnic groups. Only 50 percent of Hispanics with a recent diagnosis of a mental disorder actually seek mental health treatment, compared with 70 percent of non-Hispanic whites. Asian Americans also seek disproportionately fewer treatment services. African Americans and Native Americans appear to use outpatient mental health services at higher rates than whites. Some studies have found that ethnic minority patients have a tendency to drop out of treatment before it can be effective more frequently than whites. Many factors can contribute to the above tendency, for example, whether those providing mental health services are themselves members of an ethnic minority group, fluent in the language of their patients, or aware of culturally specific therapeutic procedures. However, the differences in the dropout rates among various ethnic groups do not appear to be statistically significant.

Many psychologists today argue that professionals could use religion as a factor facilitating psychotherapy. A person turning to God for strength and hope is, in fact, looking for inner resources that help at times of adversity and pain. Therapeutic interventions involving spiritual healing are gaining popularity. Studies show, for example, that for African Americans, the sense of spiritual connectedness and wholeness helps to improve quality of life by influencing the way that individuals cope with adversity. In-

Box 11.8 A CASE IN POINT

Cross–cultural

Some psychiatrists point out that many Asian and Asian American patients undergoing psychotherapy tend to observe the social etiquette of formal hierarchical expectations of age and gender in which they are supposed to show deference, respect, and agreement with the superior and keep most disagreements and negative feelings to themselves (Roland, 2006). Although this observation is an interesting one, it is lacking a serious empirical investigation. How many clients do express this attitude toward therapists? What are the specific circumstances under which such observations were made? Without reliable empirical facts, even the most prolific observations about a client's behavior may feed ethnic stereotypes and misconceptions. Stereotypical expectations about client's behavior could easily influence the effectiveness of therapy. Besides showing cultural competence, psychologists should turn to evidence-based practice and use the methods that are proven to be effective within specific cultural contexts (Whaley and Davis, 2007).

dividuals higher in spirituality have greater inner resources that facilitate adaptive coping and positive health outcomes. Overall, the current findings are consistent with the extensive literature indicating that spirituality has historically been an important mechanism by which African Americans manage adverse life circumstances (Utsey et al., 2007). Native Americans, compared to other groups, have stronger beliefs in the healing nature of traditional practices (frequently based on folk beliefs) even when they seek professional health services. For example, one study has found that about 40 percent of American Indian adolescents and adults with a lifetime history of depressive or anxiety disorders sought services from a mental health professional, but almost 50 percent also sought help from a traditional healer (Beals et al., 2005).

Shame of mental illness may facilitate the development of so-called repressive adaptive style rooted in an individual's desire to hide the symptoms (for example, elevated anxiety or depressive symptoms that are actually present) and prove that he or she is fine and healthy. Several studies (Steele et al., 2003) reported a higher prevalence of repressors among children with a serious illness than among healthy children. Psychologists also report that people in collectivist cultures are more likely to display repressive adaptive style than people from other groups. This was shown, for example, in an interesting study of European American, Mexican American, and Mexican children (Varela et al., 2007). Probably, because collectivism rewards behavior that brings positive outcomes to a group or community, individuals learn to hide some of their distressful symptoms so that they will not attract unnecessary attention to themselves. In fact, this assumption is probably consistent with the fact that Latin American children tend to manifest many of their emotional problems through somatic symptoms such as pains, aches, and other forms of physical discomfort (Canino, 2004). Complaining about abdominal pain looks more appropriate than acknowledging one's own panic attacks. However, these assumptions need further studies. It is also probable that cultural traditionalism is a serious factor preventing millions of people around the world from acknowledging their abnormal psychological symptoms without fear of being considered "sick" or "crazy."

Culture Match?

Many factors can affect therapists' diagnostic judgments. Among these factors is the cultural background of both the therapist and the client. We should always keep in mind that every therapist is not destined to make erroneous decisions about her client of a different cultural background. However, the mistakes are made and there are at least two reasons for possible misjudgments. First, some clinicians may not understand the cultural backgrounds of their clients and therefore may misinterpret their responses. Moreover, some clients express their thoughts and emotions according to the common rules in their culture. Second, knowledge of certain cultural trends may be lacking critical thinking emphasis and thus distort diagnosis. Stereotypes and schemas create expectations about the "typical" symptoms of particular ethnic groups.

Scores of research studies have concluded that schemas greatly influence what we perceive and the manner in which we perceive it (see, for example, Bruner & Potter, 1964; Kelley, 1950; Reason & Mycielska, 1982; Vokey & Read, 1985). For instance, Li-Repac (1980) investigated the effect of sociocultural differences between therapists and clients on clinical impressions, perceptions, and judgments. In her study, a sample consisting of white therapists and Chinese American therapists assessed a series of videotaped clinical interviews. The therapists were told that they would be evaluating both white and Chinese clients. They were not, however, informed of the experiment's true purpose, namely, to compare therapists' clinical perceptions as a function of their own ethnicity.

Results showed that although both groups of therapists agreed in their general conceptions of psychological "normality," they differed significantly in their actual assessments of the same clients. Specifically, in comparison to the Chinese American therapists, the white therapists viewed the Chinese clients as more depressed

Box 11.9 CRITICAL THINKING

Imagine a psychotherapist tells you that "Most every ethnic minority patient I've treated has dropped out of therapy prematurely." What are some possible explanations for this correlation? Can you propose that ethnicity is the factor affecting the patients' commitment? Remember that correlation does not necessarily prove causation. Could you suggest some other factors?

1. ____________________
2. ____________________
3. ____________________

Suppose you read an article reporting an inverse correlation between religiosity and depression (i.e., the less religious, the more depressed). What factors could account for this relationship?

1. ____________________
2. ____________________
3. ____________________

and inhibited and as possessing less social poise and interpersonal capacity. Conversely, Chinese American therapists judged the white clients to be more severely disturbed than did the white therapists. These findings, notes Li-Repac, demonstrate that "cultural stereotyping is a two-way street" (p. 339).

As evidenced in this experiment, the impact of culture on diagnosis of mental disorders can be profound. In essence, each group of therapists had filtered (i.e., assimilated) the clients' behavior through their respective sociocultural schemas, and, as a consequence, arrived at strikingly different judgments. The underlying principle here again becomes manifest: More than believing what we see, we tend to see what we believe.

Ethnic match, that is, a situation where the psychotherapist and his client belong to the same ethnic group, may determine several developments. For instance, if the therapist and the client are "matched," it is a meaningful predictor of the duration of psychotherapy (Sue et al., 1991). African Americans with depressive symptoms tend to be misdiagnosed with schizophrenia if they are evaluated by non-black professionals. In general, matched therapists judge clients to have higher psychological functioning than do mismatched therapists. This means that ethnically matched therapists see less pathology in their clients than therapists from a different culture. Overall, although there is a common view that "matching" counselors or psychotherapists are more culturally competent in working with ethnic groups than their white American counterparts, recent studies suggest that such a view does not have strong empirical support (Karlsson, 2005). More studies will be necessary.

These results can be interpreted in several ways. It appears that an ethnic match between a patient and a therapist reduces diagnostic mistakes. So far, so good, but should we then always match patients and therapists? Not until we first consider the finding that ethnically matched professionals may not see some significant symptoms in their clients, thus underdiagnosing them (Russell et al., 1996).

Another potential factor that may affect therapy is the counselor's accent. If she speaks English (or French, German, Spanish, etc.) with an accent, it is not clear yet if it is helpful or not in terms of the therapy's effectiveness (Fuertes et al., 2002). Some clients may develop a sense of "solidarity" with the therapist because he will be seen as a member of the same group (particular ethnic or general immigrant group), whereas others may devaluate this therapist's status and competence.

Components of cognitive and behavioral therapies frequently require some linguistic adaptations so that

Box 11.10 A CASE IN POINT

Arab–Americans and Treatment of Psychological Disorders

Some Arab Americans resist seeking psychological treatment, in part because of a general skepticism about therapists and in part because they hold negative attitudes about mental illness in general. Clients may have strong fears about being branded *majnun*, or crazy. Another factor contributing to Arab Americans' reluctance to seek mental health services is a lack of experience with or exposure to contemporary counseling approaches. When an Arab person develops a psychological problem, he seeks out the help of a family member of the same gender. Talking about family or personal problems with a professional may be seen as a threat to group honor or as being disloyal to the family. Many patients (and especially immigrants of the Arab descent) with significant needs for psychotherapeutic services often resist referrals to mental health counselors or therapists. Encouragement about a client's mental stability and the confidential nature of the counseling relationship should help clients feel more comfortable in making the most of mental health services.

Sources: Abudabbeh (1996); Jackson (1997); Erickson & Al-Timimi (2001).

instructions and explanations provided by therapists become more relevant to people's experiences. For example, Muñoz and Mendelson (2005) gave the culturally relevant example from Latino culture of using the saying *la gota de agua labra la piedra* (which means, a drop of water carves a rock) to illustrate how an individual's thoughts can gradually influence one's view of life and contribute to depression.

Different countries have different laws and rules regarding the hospitalization of mental patients. In most totalitarian societies (such as Nazi Germany in the 1930s and the Soviet Union prior to 1991) it was the state's prerogative to decide whether a person should be hospitalized. In the history of the twentieth century, psychiatry has been used countless times for political and ideological purposes. In U.S. society today only those who show signs of imminent danger to themselves or others may be held in mental facilities against their will. In many other countries the rules required for hospitalization are not as strict as in the United States. But in general, studies indicate that mental health specialists show substantial agreement among themselves as to which patients should be considered dangerous, suicidal, or unable to testify or take care of themselves (Swenson, 1993).

All in all, the context of therapy should be consistent with the client's culture (Bemak & Chung, 2004; Tanaka-Matsumi, 1989). For example, Kleinman (1978) offered a framework for successful patient–therapist interactions. At the beginning, the therapist asks clients to give their interpretation of the existing problem. Then the therapist offers her explanation of the problem. Then both types of explanations are compared. Finally, both therapist and clients come up with a joint explanatory concept, so that they communicate in the same language and can discuss therapy and its potential outcome.

Snacken (1991) described three desirable types of therapy between the specialist and the patient who represent different cultures. *Intercultural* therapy includes a professional who knows the language and culture of the client (he could belong to this cultural group). *Bicultural* therapy includes two types of healers: both the Western and the native who work together. *Polycultural* therapy involves the patient's meetings with several therapists who represent different cultures.

Exercise 11.1

Here is a list of some culture-bound mental problems. Using *DSM-IV*, please find analogies in the U.S. classification of mental disorders to each of the syndromes below. Write your answers.

- Possession (in some African countries) is a belief that one's body has been taken over by a spirit, which leads to unusual and unexpected emotional and behavioral changes.
- *Koro* (in China) is a severe anxiety based on the assumption that the penis is retracting; this fear leads to another belief of inevitable death.
- *Latah* is a syndrome known in some Asian and African countries that is marked by altered states of consciousness, including exaggerated obedience and impulsivity.
- *Malgri* is a severe abdominal pain that is believed to be caused by entering forbidden territory without purification rituals.
- Nuptial psychosis occurs among very young women in India whose lives are disrupted by arranged marriages. Sexual trauma, separation from the family, and stress contribute to symptoms of confusion, hysteria, and suicidal intentions.
- Kayak angst is an extreme anxiety, known among the Eskimos of Western Greenland. This anxiety strikes after hours of solitary hunting in unfavorable environments.

Chapter Summary

- Two perspectives on psychological disorders and culture—relativist and universalist—have been developed in cross-cultural psychology. The relativist perspective on psychopathology puts psychological phenomena in a relative perspective and pays attention to unique cultural context of psychological disorders. According to the universalist perspective on psychopathology, there are absolute, invariable symptoms of psychopathology across cultures.
- Attempting to diagnose and treat an individual, the professional should know the client's reference groups and the ways in which cultural context is relevant to clinical care, including psychotherapy. In particular, the specialist should pay attention to the following: (1) the cultural identity of the individual, that is, his or her ethnic, religious, and other cultural reference groups; (2) the cultural explanations of the individual's illness; (3) the cultural interpretations of social stressors and social supports, such as religion, level of functioning, and disability; and (4) the cultural elements of the relationship between the individual and the clinician.
- American clinicians use a special diagnostic manual (*DSM-IV*) to diagnose mental disorders. Clinicians usually assess information available to them about the individual from the standpoint of five axes, each of which helps professionals to examine the situation from five different view-

points or domains of information. There are disorders that may or may not be linked to a particular *DSM-IV* diagnostic category. These are recurrent, locally specific patterns of aberrant behavior and troubling experiences that are called culture-bound syndromes. They are generally limited to specific societies or areas and indicate repetitive and troubling sets of experiences and observations.

- Cultural norms, availability of resources, national standards on health, access to technology, social inequality, and many other environmental factors could affect the individual's health and general well being.
- Despite general similar occurrence rates, there are some cultural variations in how schizophrenia is viewed, diagnosed, and treated. There are some substantial ethnic variations in the expression of depression, which are also based on various individual differences, socialization experiences, cultural definitions of disorders, and stress. There is empirical evidence concerning the links between suicide and religiosity, age, sex, nationality, substance use, and various cultural traditions. There are substantial cultural variations in the expression of anxiety that range from somatic to cognitive to behavioral symptoms. Differences in diagnostic practices account in some way for cross-cultural differences in reported symptoms and could explain great cross-cultural variability for anxiety disorders. It is suggested that personality disorders should be viewed, diagnosed, and treated in the context of each culture's norms and thresholds of tolerance for a particular behavior. There are cultural and national standards for substance use and substance abuse. There are also wide cultural variations in attitudes toward substance consumption, patterns of substance use, accessibility of substances, and prevalence of disorders related to substance use.
- The cultural background of the professional can influence his or her perception of different behaviors. Psychologists are likely to have their own perceptions and attributions about the links of culture, ethnicity, and mental illness. It is also known that doctors can misdiagnose particular diseases due to cross-cultural differences in the perception, attribution, and expression of signs of disease. Psychotherapy across countries has different historical and cultural roots and varied cultural expressions. Different countries have different laws and rules regarding the hospitalization of mental patients. General psychological and cultural factors may affect the cross-cultural relationship between the professional and his client. Different ethnic groups could have various attitude patterns about mental health services. In general, the context of therapy should be consistent with the client's culture to achieve the goal of cultural accommodation.

Key Terms

Anxiety Disorders A category of mental disorders characterized by persistent anxiety or fears.

Central Symptoms Symptoms of mental disorders observable in practically all cultures.

Culture-Bound Syndromes Recurrent, locally specific patterns of aberrant behavior and troubling experience that may or may not be linked to a particular *DSM-IV* diagnostic category. Culture-bound syndromes are generally limited to specific societies or areas and indicate repetitive and troubling sets of experiences and observations.

Depressive Disorder A category of psychological disorders characterized by a profound and persistent feeling of sadness or despair, guilt, loss of interest in things that were once pleasurable, and disturbance in sleep and appetite.

Melancholy The most common label used in many countries in the past for symptoms known today as depression (often spelled *melancholia*).

Mental Disorder A clinically significant behavioral and psychological syndrome or pattern that occurs in an individual and that is associated with present distress (a painful syndrome) or disability (impairment in one or more important areas of functioning) or with a significantly increased risk of suffering death, pain, disability, or an important loss of freedom.

Peripheral Symptoms Symptoms of mental disorders that are culture-specific.

Personality Disorders Enduring patterns of behavior and inner experience that deviate markedly from the expectations of the individual's culture.

Psychotherapy The treatment of psychological disorders through psychological means, generally involving verbal interaction with a professional therapist.

Relativist Perspective A view of psychological disorders, according to which human beings develop ideas, establish behavioral norms, and learn emotional responses according to a set of cultural prescriptions. Therefore, people from different cultural settings should understand psychological disorders differently, and the differences should be significant.

Schizophrenia A disorder characterized by the presence of delusions, hallucinations, disorganized speech, and disorganized or catatonic behavior.

Tolerance Threshold A measure of tolerance or intolerance toward specific personality traits in a specific cultural environment.

Universalist Perspective A view of psychological disorders, according to which people, despite cultural differences, share a great number of similar features, including attitudes, values, and behavioral responses. Therefore, the overall understanding of psychological disorders ought to be universal.

12 chapter

Power and Social Class

Power Relations and Social Stratification

stratification classifying people and ranking the classifications on a superiority-inferiority scale

All known societies have some method of classifying their members using some system of rankings. Although many societies claim to grant "equality" to their members, in no society have people in fact been considered equal. The **stratification** of society involves the classification of individuals and the ranking of classifications on a superiority-inferiority scale. This system of classification and ranking is itself a source of prestige, wealth, income, authority, and power. In some societies, there is greater mobility of individuals between different strata; in other societies, individuals remain in the strata to which they were born.

Individuals can be classified on a wide variety of characteristics—physical strength, fighting prowess, family lineage, ethnicity or race, age, gender, religion, birth order, and so on. *But the most important bases of stratification in a modern industrial society are the various roles that individuals play in the economic system.*

Individuals are ranked according to how they make their living and how much control they exercise over the livelihood of others. Ranking by occupation and control of economic resources occurs in not only the United States but also most other modern nations.[1]

stratification results in inequality deference

The evaluation of individuals along a superiority-inferiority scale means a differential distribution of prestige. Thus, the top strata will receive the *deference* of individuals who are ranked below them. Deference may take many forms: acquiescence in the material advantages or privileges of the elite (the use of titles and symbols of rank, distinctive clothing, housing, and automobiles), accordance of influence and respect, acceptance of leadership in decision making, and so on.

lifestyles wealth and income

The stratification system also involves *different* lifestyles: foods eaten, magazines and books read, places of residence, favorite sports, schools attended, pronunciation and accent, recreational activities, and so forth. The stratification system is also associated with the *uneven distribution of wealth and income:* In every society, higher-ranking persons enjoy better housing, clothing, food, automobiles, and other material goods and services than persons ranked lower on the scale.

power

Finally, the stratification system involves the *unequal distribution of power*—the ability to control the acts of others. Sociologists agree that power and stratification are closely related, but they disagree on the specific value of this relationship. Some theorize that power is a *product* of economic well-being, prestige, or status. Others believe that power *determines* the distribution of wealth, prestige, and status.[2] Some sociologists see the merits of both arguments and contend that while power does determine the distribution of wealth, power and status, it also is self-perpetuating in that these attributes also create power.

social class a category and ranking in the stratification system

The stratification system creates social classes. The term **social class** simply refers to all individuals who occupy a broadly similar category and ranking in the stratification system. Members of the same social class may or may not interact or even realize that they have much in common. Because all societies have stratification systems, all societies have social classes.

Stratification in American Society

methods of identifying and measuring stratification

Social classes are of interest to sociologists, with their concern for the relationships among individuals and groups. Sociologists have devised several methods of identifying and measuring social stratification. These include (1) the subjective method, in which individuals are asked how they see themselves in the class system; (2) the reputational method, in which individuals are asked to rank positions in the class system; and (3) the objective method, in which social scientists observe characteristics that discriminate among patterns of life that they associate with social class.

Subjective Self-Classification

subjective identification individuals identify their own social class

The American ideology encompasses the notion that status should be based on personal qualities and achievements. Individuals in a free society should have the opportunity to achieve the social rankings that they can earn by ability, effort, and moral worth. These individuals are supposed to rise or fall according to their merits. In view of this ideology, it is not surprising that most Americans think of themselves as middle class. Nearly nine out of ten will describe themselves as middle class when they are forced to choose between this term and either upper or lower class. Even when the choices are broadened, more people identify themselves as middle class than any other (Table 12.1), and more people consider themselves working class than upper middle class. It is apparent that characterizing oneself as upper class is regarded as "snobbish" (only 1.3 percent identified themselves as upper class) and that a stigma is attached to viewing oneself as lower class (with only 9 percent identifying themselves as such). Even people who admit to being poor consider it an insult to be called lower class.[3]

Table 12.1 Social Class Self-Identification

"If You Were Asked to Use One of Five Names for Your Social Class, Which Would You Say You Belong In?"

Social Class	Percent
Upper	1.3
Upper Middle	13.9
Middle	47.2
Working	28.3
Lower	9.0

Source: Gallup Poll, April 4–7, 2005, http://brain.gallup.com/documents/question.aspx?question=15274 (accessed November 6, 2006)

Reputational Prestige

reputational prestige individuals ranking the prestige of occupations

Occupations differ in their **reputational prestige.** The prestige rankings of occupations are often used as a measure of the stratification system of modern societies. It is not polite to ask people how much money they make or how much money they have accumulated, but it is socially acceptable to ask what they do for a living. Often people ask others this question in order to identify social ranking.

Occupational prestige scores obtained from national surveys are fairly consistent (Table 12.2). Note that prestige is not exactly the equivalent of income although occupations near the top generally pay more than those at the bottom. ("College professor" is a notable exception.) Prestigious occupations, addition to paying well, also tend to involve substantial authority; in contrast, close supervision and taking orders lower the prestige of occupations. Moreover, most highly ranked occupations require extensive education; indeed, some sociologists believe that education is the most important single factor influencing occupational prestige ranking.[4] Finally, it is interesting to note that most prestigious jobs are white-collar occupations that involve mental activity rather than blue-collar occupations that require physical labor. These rankings have remained stable for several decades.

Objective Classifications

The principal **objective criteria** of social class are income, occupation, and education. If sociologists are correct in assuming that occupation and control of economic resources are the source of stratification in society, then these indexes are the best available measure of class. Certainly, income, jobs, and education are unequally distributed in American society as they are in all other societies.

objective criteria determining social class by ranking income, occupation, or education

College graduates comprise a little over 25 percent of the adults in the United States (Figure 12.1). Over 84 percent are high school graduates, and about 16 percent dropped out of formal education without a high school diploma. This is a dramatic increase in formal education over previous generations.

Income is closely related to education. Generally, individuals who have acquired higher educations tend to enjoy higher annual incomes. However, Table 12.3 also shows that there is disparity in income distribution based on sex, race, and ethnicity. Women, blacks, and Hispanics with equivalent educations tend to earn less than men and whites.

Race and Ethnicity

Ethnic and racial stratification is visible on virtually all measures of social class—income, education, and occupation. For example, in Figure 12.1, showing adult educational attainment levels since 1960, while all groups have gained in education, African-American and especially Hispanic high school and college completion percentages remain below those of whites. (On the other hand, the educational attainment of Asian-Americans and Pacific Islanders surpasses other races, particularly in the percentage of completion of four years of college or more.) The educational gap between blacks and whites has narrowed somewhat over the years, but not the gap between Hispanics and whites. Of course, given the previously noted importance of education's impact on income and occupational prestige, we can see that unequal levels of educational attainment create continued inequality in American society.

Table 12.2 Occupational Prestige Rankings

Separate National Surveys Indicate That Americans Are Quite Consistent in Their Ranking of Various Occupations.

Occupation	Ranking	Occupation	Ranking
Physician	82	Physician	95.8
College/university professor	78	Lawyer	90.1
Lawyer	76	College professor	90.1
Bank officer	72	Architect	88.8
Architect	71	Stockbroker	81.7
Airplane pilot	70	Electrical engineer	79.5
Clergy	69	Registered nurse	75.0
Secondary school teacher	63	Accountant	71.2
Registered nurse	62	High school teacher	70.2
Pharmacist	61	Grade school teacher	65.4
Elementary school teacher	60	Social worker	63.2
Electrician	49	Electrician	62.5
Machinist	48	Insurance agent	62.5
Police officer	48	Private secretary	60.9
Bookkeeper	48	Plumber	58.7
Insurance agent	47	Police officer	58.3
Secretary	46	Carpenter	53.5
Firefighter	44	Office secretary	51.3
Mail carrier	42	Auto mechanic	44.9
Farmer	41	Postal clerk	42.3
Welder	40	Beautician	42.1
Auto-body repairperson	37	Truck driver	40.1

(continued)

Occupation	Ranking	Occupation	Ranking
TV repairperson	35	Hairdresser	39.4
Hairdresser	33	Cashier	35.6
Bulldozer operator	33	Hospital aide	29.5
Truck driver	32	Assembly-line worker	28.3
Cashier	31	Delivery truck driver	26.9
File clerk	30	Housekeeper	25.3
Taxi driver	22	Coal miner	24.0
Bartender	20	Server in a restaurant	22.1
Waiter/waitress	20	Short-order cook	21.5
Farm laborer	18	Baby-sitter	18.3
Car washer	17	Garbage collector	16.3
		Janitor	12.5

Source: (a) Adapted from *General Social Surveys, 1972–1996: Cumulative Codebook* (Chicago: National Opinion Research Center, 1999); (b) Adapted from C. E. Bose and Peter H. Rossi, "Gender and Jobs," *American Sociological Review* 48 (1983): 316–330.

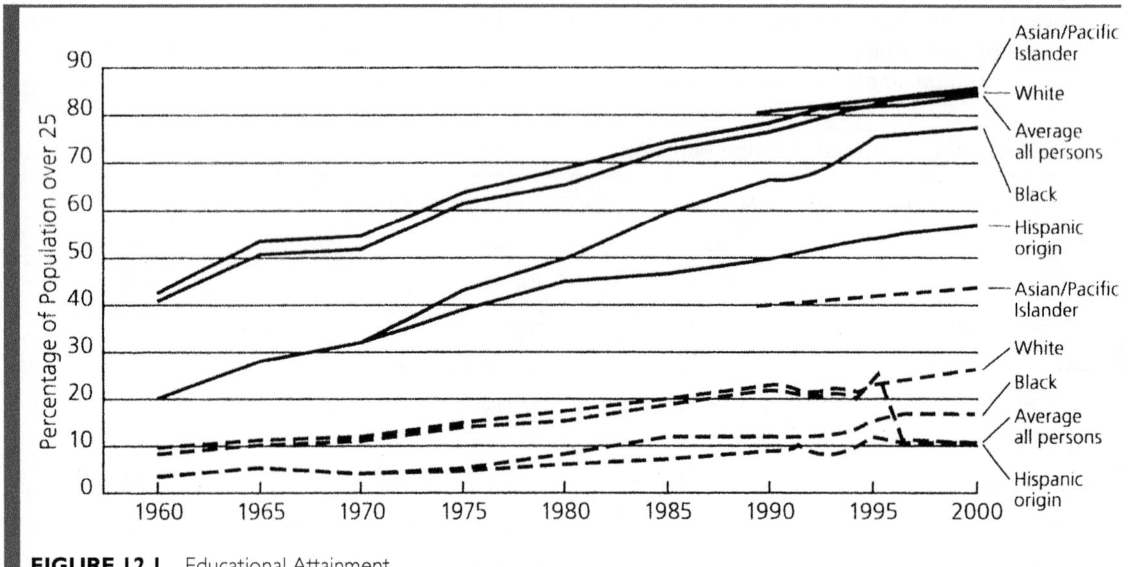

FIGURE 12.1 Educational Attainment

Source: U.S. Bureau of the Census, *Statistical Abstract of the United States 2002* (Washington, DC: Government Printing Office, 2003), 208.

Table 12.3 Education and Earnings

	Mean Earnings ($)					
	All persons	**Men**	**Women**	**White**	**Blacks**	**Hispanics**
Not a high school graduate	16,121	18,855	12,145	16,623	13,569	16,106
High school graduate only	24,572	30,414	18,092	25,270	20,991	20,704
College Associate Degree	32,152	40,047	25,079	32,686	28,772	29, 329
College Bachelor's Degree	45,678	57,706	32,546	46,894	37,422	36,212
Master's Degree	55,641	68,367	42,378	55,622	48,777	50,576
Professional Degree	100,987	120,352	59,792	103,450	75,509	64,029
Doctorate	86,833	97,357	61,136	87,746	B	B

Source: U.S. Bureau of the Census, *Statistical Abstract of the United States 2002* (Washington, DC: Government Printing Office, 2003), 210.
B = Base figure too small to meet statistical standards for reliability of derived figure.

Sociology and the Study of Social Classes

Sociologists disagree on why societies distribute wealth, power, and prestige unequally. On one side are the functional theorists, who argue that stratification is necessary and perhaps inevitable for maintaining society. On the other side are the conflict theorists, who argue that stratification results from the selfish interests of groups trying to preserve their advantages over others.[5] Still yet another perspective, the symbolic interactionists, argue that social stratification is the result of interactions between individuals. And postmodernists cite the inability of the three previous perspectives to adequately address social stratification in a postindustrial society.

Functional Theory

The functional argument assumes that society is stable and orderly and that a stable society requires inequality within it. Functionalism might be summarized as follows:

- Certain positions are more important to a society's survival than other positions and require special skills. For example, in most societies, occupations such as governor, physician, teacher, and priest are considered vital.
- Only a few persons in society have the ability (intelligence, energy, and personality) to perform well in these positions.
- These positions require persons who have ability to undergo extensive training and education before they occupy these positions.
- To motivate able people to endure the training and to sacrifice their time and energy for education, society must provide them with additional rewards.
- The result is social inequality with some classes of people receiving more rewards than others. Inequality is inevitable and essential to ensure "that the most important positions are conscientiously filled by the most qualified persons."[6]

In other words, an expectation of inequality is essential in getting people to work harder in more difficult jobs that require longer training and greater skill.[7]

Sociologists who advocated functionalist theory included Talcott Parsons and Robert Merton. Parsons stressed the need for a **division of labor** (when individuals perform distinct, assigned functions) within families and within society. If individuals and institutions perform their tasks, society can remain stable. Merton described various aspects of function within society, including **manifest functions** (the acknowledged and expected functions of societal relations or an institution), **latent functions** (unrecognized or unanticipated functions of societal relations or an institution), and **dysfunctions** (the undesirable by-products of relations or institutions). For example, the media is a social institution whose manifest function is to inform and entertain. Its latent function may be to socialize young Americans and immigrants to a common culture. But its dysfunctional impact may be that it discourages social and civic interaction by providing a "too convenient" form of entertainment.

Conflict Theory

In contrast, **conflict theory** focuses on the struggle among competing groups in society over scarce resources. Conflict theorists have argued as follows:

- People who possess property, income, power, or prestige—the upper classes—simply wish to protect their position in society. Thus, the stratification system is perpetuated.
- There are many "functionally important" positions in society that are not highly rewarded. It might be argued that a garbage collector, electrician, an auto mechanic, or a plumber is just as important to the survival of society as is a physician or a lawyer.
- Many people in the lower classes have the ability to perform in high-status occupations, but because of unequal educational opportunities, they never get the chance to do so.
- Wealth is not the only way of motivating people. Conceivably, societies might reward people merely by recognizing their services. Cooperation could then replace competition as a motivating force.
- Stratification negatively affects the thinking of members of the lower class. Stratification may even be "dysfunctional" to society if it fosters feelings of suspicion, hostility, and disloyalty to society among those in the lower classes.

functional theory inequality is neccessary to get people to work harder in more demanding jobs that require longer training and greater skills

functionalist theorists Talcott Parsons

Robert Merton

division of labor individuals perfrom distinct, assigned functions

manifest funtion the acknowledged and expected function of societal relations or an institution

latent function the unrecognized or unanticipated function of societal relations or an institution

dysfunction the undesirable by-product of relations or institutions

conflict theory inequality is imposed on society by those who want to retain their wealth and power

conflict theorists Max Weber

C. Wright Mills

power elite Mills's term for a ruling class who dominates decision making

feminist theory a form of conflict theory, a theory of social stratification that uses a gendered prism and emphasizes the struggle for equality of women with men

subjective reality one individual's idea of what occurred in a social interation; that individual's interpretation of events

symbolic interaction theorists George Herbert Mead

Herbert Bloomer

Chicago School the first Sociology Department in the United States at the University of Chicago

In short, the stratification system is imposed on society by those at the top. It allows them to use their power and prestige to keep what they have.

Sociologists who used the conflict perspective in their research include Max Weber (pronounced VAY-ber) and C. Wright Mills. Weber argued that power is the ability of an individual in a social relationship to carry out his or her will despite resistance from others in the social relationship. Mills saw society as competition between groups in society, and he argued that in the United States a ruling class exists. That is, the power structure is composed of a small **power elite** that includes top business executives, media moguls, and military and government leaders who dominate decision making in this country. Later in this chapter, we examine the ideas of Karl Marx, who argued that the struggle between classes was the driving force in history and politics.

Feminist theory, which regards society through a gendered prism and emphasizes the patriarchical nature of society, is considered a form of conflict theory. Feminist theory emphasizes the struggle for equality of women with men and the transformative nature a change in relations between the sexes could have on society.

Symbolic Interaction Theory

Symbolic interaction theory differs from both the functionalist and conflict theories in that it focuses on a microlevel of analysis. That is, whereas functionalism and conflict theory analyze large groups and institutions within societies, symbolic interaction theory focuses on individuals and small groups in society. Specifically, symbolic interaction theory examines the role that symbols play in creating meaning for communication between individuals (interaction). There are a few key tenets of symbolic interaction theory:

- Symbols include not only written language but also facial expressions, gestures, signs, and common meanings.
- Symbols help people assign meanings to social situations. For example, a couple flirting might engage in behaviors like increased eye contact, smiling, tilting of the head, and close physical contact. Flirting can occur with spoken language.
- The assessment of social interaction is through a **subjective reality.** That is, one individual's idea of what occurred in a social interaction is just that—an individual's interpretation of events.
- Our assessment of social interaction prescribes our behavior.
- Our identities and concept of self are shaped by social interactions and our perceptions of these interactions.

Symbolic interactionists view social class as the result of individuals' actions. That is, social structures, classes, and institutions come from the interaction between individuals and the use of symbols in their everyday communications. Symbolic interactionists concede that these interactions can be structured and defined by larger political and economic structures, but they argue that interaction between individuals and the meaning ascribed to that interaction is constantly changing. For example, even in a brief encounter, one individual can discern a great deal about another. We often evaluate individuals and subjectively compare them to ourselves by using such symbols as

- Possessions: What kind of car does the person drive? What kind of clothing does she wear? Is it neatly pressed or rumpled? Are her nails manicured? What kind of shoes and sunglasses does she wear, handbag does she carry?
- Language: Does she sound educated? Have a large vocabulary? Have an accent associated with rich or poor areas?
- Facial expression and demeanor: Is she commanding or reticent, proud, or meek?

Oftentimes our interaction is impacted by our subjective perception of who we are interacting with. We might respond to someone in a higher social class with deference and might respond to someone in a lower social class with a lack of respect.

Theorists using the symbolic interaction theory include George Herbert Mead and Herbert Bloomer. Both Mead and Bloomer, who coined the term *symbolic interaction,* were part of the Chicago School. The **Chicago School** refers to the Sociology Department at the University of Chicago—the first Sociology Department in the United States. The faculty at the Chicago School were instrumental in nurturing the new discipline and also formed the professional sociological organization now called the American Sociological Society.

Postmodernism

Postmodernism asserts that the functionalist theory, conflict theory, and symbolic interaction theory have proven inadequate in analyzing societies in a postindustrial world. Postmodernism rejects these theories as unsuccessful and asserts that discipline—specific borders within the social sciences (for example, psychology, political science, and economics)—undermine the ability of the social sciences to effectively analyze postmodern societies. Postmodern societies typically have certain characteristic traits including

- An information explosion facilitated by the print and electronic media.
- An economy with high levels of information and service related job.
- An emphasis on consumerism.
- Increased globalization.

Postmodernism is an emerging theory in sociology and the rest of the social sciences. While rejecting older theories, it also calls into question key assumptions on which those theories are based. Critics of postmodernism contend that, although the theory succeeds in forcing a reevaluation of old assumptions, it ignores some object realities within society, including inequality in power relationship within and between societies.

Inequality in America

Income is a key component of stratification, and income is unequally distributed in all societies. As long as societies reward skills talents, knowledge, hard work, innovation, initiative, and risk taking, there will be inequalities of income. But the question remains: How much inequality is required to provide adequate rewards and incentives for education, training, work, enterprise, and risk?

Income Distributions

measuring inequality percentage of total national income received by each fifth of income earners

Let's try to systematically examine income inequality in America. Table 12.4 divides all American families into five groups—from the lowest one-fifth in income to the highest one-fifth – and shows the percentage of total family income received by each group over the years. (If perfect income equality existed, each fifth would receive 20 percent of all family income, and it would not even be possible to rank fifths from highest to lowest.) The poorest one-fifth received 3.5 percent of all family personal income in 1929; by 1970 this group had increased its share of all family personal income to 5.4 percent. (Most of the increase occurred during World War II.) The highest one-fifth received 54.5 percent of all family personal income in 1929; by 1970 this percentage had declined to 40.9. The income share received by the top 5 percent of families declined from 30 percent in 1929 to 15.6 percent in 1970.

Table 12.4 Income Inequality

Percentage Distribution of Family Income, by Quintiles, and Top 5 Percent

Quintiles	1929	1970	1980	1990	2000
Lowest	3.5	5.4	5.2	4.5	4.3
Second	9.0	12.2	11.6	10.7	9.8
Third	13.8	17.6	17.5	16.6	15.5
Fourth	19.3	23.9	24.1	24.1	22.8
Highest	54.4	40.9	41.5	44.2	47.4
Top 5 percent	30.0	15.6	15.6	17.1	20.8

Source: U.S. Bureau of the Census, *Statistical Abstract of the United States 2002* (Washington, DC: Government Printing Office, 2003), 659.

Rising Income Inequality

increased inequality since 1970

Note, however, an increase in inequality in the United States since 1970. The income share of the lowest group of families has declined from 5.4 in 1970 to 4.3 percent in 2000, while the income share of the highest group has risen from 40.9 in 1970 to 47.4 in 2000. Finally, the income share of the top 5 percent of American families has risen from 15.6 in 1970 to 20.8 percent in 2000.

Social scientists, policy makers, and advocates for the poor have voiced concern over this reversal of the historical trend toward greater income equality. This recent increase in inequality appears to be a product of several social and economic trends: (1) the relative decline of the manufacturing sector of the economy, with its middle-income blue-collar jobs, and the ascendancy of the information and service sectors, with a combination of high-paying and low-paying jobs; (2) an increase in the number of two-wage families, making single-wage households relatively less affluent; (3) demographic trends that include larger proportions of aged and larger proportions of female-headed families; and (4) global competition, which lowers wages in unskilled and semiskilled jobs while rewarding people in high-technology, high-productivity occupations.

Inequality of Wealth

Inequalities of wealth in the United States are even greater than inequalities of income. Wealth is the total value of a family's assets—bank accounts, stocks, bonds, mutual funds, business equity, houses, cars, and major appliances—minus outstanding debts such as credit card balances, mortgages, and other loans. The top 1 percent of families in the United States own almost 40 percent of all family wealth (Table 12.5). Inequality of wealth appeared to be diminishing until the mid-1970s, but in recent years it has surged sharply. (Like income, if wealth was evenly distributed, each fifth would hold 20 percent of the wealth and could not be rank-ordered.) Not surprisingly, age is the key determinant of family wealth; persons 55 to 64 years old are by far the wealthiest, with persons 65 to 74 years old close behind; young families generally have less than one-fourth of the assets of older retirees. From Table 12.5, we also can see that those in the bottom fifth have a negative family net worth. This means that their family debt on bank loans, mortgages, credit cards, automobile loans, and other debts exceeded the value of their assets.

Table 12.5 Changes in the Distribution of Family Wealth

	1962	1983	1992	1998
Top 1%*	33.4	33.8	37.2	38.1
Top fifth	81.0	81.3	83.8	83.4
Second fifth	13.4	12.6	11.5	11.9
Third fifth	5.4	5.2	4.4	4.5
Fourth fifth	1.0	1.2	0.9	0.8
Bottom fifth	-0.7	-0.3	-0.5	-0.5

Source: Authors' calculations based on U.S. Bureau of the Census, *Statistical Abstract of the United States 2002* (Washington, DC: Government Printing Office, 2003), 659; and U.S. Department of Commerce, http://www.sipp.census.gov/sipp/sb94_02.pdf
* The top 1% also is included in the top-fifth data because it contains a portion of that quintile.

Equality of Opportunity

equality of opportunity equal chances for success based on ability, work initiative, and luck.

Most Americans are concerned more with **equality of opportunity** than with equality of results (see "International Perspective: Beliefs about Equality and Opportunity"). Equality of opportunity refers to the ability to make of oneself what one can, to develop talents and abilities, and to be rewarded for work, initiative, and achievement. Equality of opportunity means that everyone comes to the same starting line in life with the same chance of success and that whatever differences develop over time do so as a result of abilities, talents, initiative, hard work, and perhaps good luck. Americans do not generally resent the fact that physicians, engineers, airline pilots, or others who have spent time and energy acquiring particular skills make more money than those whose jobs require fewer skills and less training. Nor do most Americans resent the fact that people who risk their own time and money to build a business, bring new or better products to market, and create jobs for others make more money than their employees. Nor do many Americans begrudge multimillion-dollar incomes to sports figures, rock singers, or movie stars, whose talents entertain the public. Indeed, few Americans object when someone wins a million-dollar lottery, as long as everyone had an equal chance at winning.

Equality of Results

equality of results equal incomes regardless of ability, work, or initiative

Equality of results refers to the equal sharing of income and material rewards regardless of one's condition in life. Equality of results means that everyone starts and finishes the race together, regardless of ability, talent, initiative, or work. Most Americans support a "floor" on income and material well-being – a level below which no one, regardless of their condition, should be permitted to fall. But very few Americans want to place a "ceiling" on income or wealth, though Table 12.6 indicates that Americans' opinions on the distribution of wealth is a divisive issue, with nearly 60 percent of all poll respondents saying that wealth should be more evenly distributed. Nonetheless, unwillingness to limit top income extends to nearly all groups in America, the poor as well as the rich. Generally, Americans want people who cannot provide for themselves to be well cared for, especially children, the elderly, the ill, and the disabled. However most Americans believe that a "fair" economic system rewards people for ability and hard work.

Beliefs about Equality and Opportunity

American social culture emphasizes equality of opportunity over equality of results. The Western European democracies also foster a belief in equality of opportunity but are much more inclined toward equality of results—reducing income differences between people—than Americans. Americans generally believe that government should provide a floor, or safety net, to protect people against true hardship; but they are generally less willing to place a ceiling on incomes or to give government the power to equalize income differences among people. Europeans are more likely than Americans to perceive obstacles to equality of opportunity in their countries. Thus, for example, Europeans are more likely than Americans to think that "coming from a wealthy family" or "having political connections" is very important for getting ahead in life. The three tables in the list that follows demonstrate the various international beliefs about equality and opportunity.

Table 1 "It is the government's responsibility to reduce income differences between people."

Country	Agree (%)
Italy	81
Hungary	77
Netherlands	64
Great Britain	62
Germany	56
Australia	42
United States	29

Source: Table 1: Gallup International Research Institute as reported in *U.S. News & World Report,* August 7, 1989, 25; Tables 2 and 3: International Social Survey Program, 1987, as reported in Rodney Stark, *Sociology,* 5th ed. (Belmont, CA: Wadsworth, 1994), 273.

Table 2 "Differences in income in my country are too large."

Country	Strongly Agree (%)
Austria	47
Italy	44
Hungary	41
Great Britain	27
Germany	25
Netherlands	19
Switzerland	19
Australia	14
United States	12

Table 3 "For getting ahead in life, how important is . . ."

	"Coming from a Wealthy Family?" Very Important (%)	"Having Political Connections?" Very Important (%)
Italy	40	55
Hungary	34	30
Austria	30	43
Germany	25	23
Great Britain	22	7
Australia	18	15
Switzerland	15	25
United States	14	9
Netherlands	11	7

Table 12.6 American Opinion on Wealth Accumulation [In Percent]

Do You Feel That the Distribution of Money and Wealth in This Country Today Is Fair, or Do You Feel That the Money and Wealth in This Country Should Be More Evenly Distributed among a Larger Percentage of the People?	
Distribution is fair	34
Should be more evenly distributed	59.4
Don't know	5.6

Source: Gallup Poll, January 10–12, 2003, http://brain.gallup.com/documents/questions.aspx?question=142268 (Accessed November 6, 2006).

Social Mobility: The Ups and Downs

social mobility the movement of people upward or downward in social class

Although all societies are stratified, societies differ greatly in **social mobility**—that is, in the opportunity people have to move from one class to another. The social mobility of individuals may be upward, when they achieve a status higher than that of their parents, or downward, when their status is lower. In the United States, there is a great deal of social mobility, both upward and downward.

The United States describes itself as the land of opportunity. The really important political question may be how much real opportunity exists for individual Americans to improve their conditions in life relative to others. The impression given earlier by Table 12.4 is one of a static distribution system, with families permanently placed in upper or lower fifths of income earners.

But there is considerable evidence of both upward and downward movement by people among income groups. Children do not always end up in the same income category as their parents.

Traditional Upward Mobility

Throughout most of the twentieth century, Americans experienced more upward mobility than downward mobility. As the economy grew and changed, most Americans were able to improve their conditions in life or, at least, see their children do better than themselves. Early in the century, higher-paid factory jobs replaced farm work. With the growth of the American organized labor movement in the 1940s, many factory jobs paid a living wage. Later, the ranks of professional, managerial, sales, and other white-collar workers grew. By 1970 white-collar workers outnumbered blue-collar workers—machine operators, mechanics, trade and craft workers, and laborers. Many sons and daughters of working-class parents were able to go to college and prepare themselves for careers in white-collar occupations.

The Shrinking Middle Class

In recent years, however, this general movement of upward social mobility has been replaced by a pattern of both upward and downward mobility. Today's young people can no longer assume that they will be better off than their parents. America may be experiencing a "shrinking middle class."

The American economy is undergoing **deindustrialization**—a decline in its manufacturing sector accompanied by increases in its financial, technical, information, and service sectors. Deindustrialization had resulted in the loss of millions of well-paying, mostly unionized, blue-collar jobs in manufacturing, including the once-dominant American steel and auto industries. In the 1950s and 1960s, these jobs allowed noncollege-educated workers to own their own homes in the suburbs and send their children to college. But the new information age economy replaced many of these jobs with two very different categories of jobs. The first category consists of such highly skilled, highly paid technical jobs as computer engineer, systems analyst, information specialist, financial and investment adviser, accountant, and science technician. The second category consists of such unskilled and semiskilled, low-paying service jobs as data processor, health-care aide, food server, and packager. This division of the occupational structure into high-paying and low-paying jobs adds to both inequality in society and to a pattern of upward and downward mobility.

deindustrialization
a decline in the manufacturing sector of the economy

Deindustrialization has been accompanied by economic **globalization**—increasing exchanges of goods and services by firms in different countries. Today, about one-quarter of the world's total economic output is sold in a country other than the one in which it was produced. Global competition heavily impacts the American economy and social structure. The opening of world markets benefits America's most productive workers—its highly skilled, well-educated, high-tech workers who are capable of competing and winning in the global marketplace. But at the same time, America's unskilled and semiskilled workers are placed at a serious disadvantage in competition with workers in less-developed countries. It is difficult to maintain the wage levels of American manufacturing jobs in the face of competition from huge numbers of extremely low-paid workers in economies such as Mexico, China, and India. Thus, the benefits of globalization flow unequally: Upper middle-class Americans benefit, while lower middle-class Americans suffer.

globalization
increasing exchanges of goods and services by firms in different countries

Mobility and Education

Education is the most common path to social mobility. As indicated earlier, education is closely related to earnings (see Table 12.3). It is not surprising, then, that leaders in business and government in the United States argue that the "solution" to worsening inequality in downward social mobility is for American workers to improve their productivity through better education and increased training. And it is not surprising that many middle-class American families emphasize education as a means of upward mobility.

Class as a Determinant of Lifestyle

Life in each social class is different. Differences in ways of life mean differences in culture or (because the lifestyle in each class is really a variant of one common culture in American society) a division of the culture into subcultures. Many sociologists have described class subcultures. Class differences exist in almost every aspect of life: health, vocabulary, table manners, recreation and entertainment, religion, family and child-rearing practices, political beliefs and attitudes, club memberships, dress, birthrates, attitudes toward education, reading habits, and so on. It is impossible to provide a complete description of all the class differences that have been reported by sociologists. Moreover, class lifestyles overlap, and in America there are no rigid boundaries between classes. Class subcultures should be thought of as being on a continuous scale with styles of life that blend; thus there are many in-between positions. Finally, it should be remembered that any generalizations about broad classes in the United States do not necessarily describe the lifestyle of any particular individuals; the following paragraphs are merely a general summary of the subcultures.

The Upper Class

The typical upper-class individual is future oriented and cosmopolitan. Persons of this class expect a long life, look forward to their future and the future of their children and grandchildren, and are concerned about what lies ahead for the community, the nation, and humanity. They are self-confident, believing that within limits they can shape their own destiny and that of the community. They are willing to invest in the future—that is, to sacrifice some present satisfaction in the expectation of enjoying greater satisfaction in time to come. They are self-respecting; they place great value on independence and creativity and on developing their potential to the fullest. The goals of life include individuality, self-expression, and personal happiness. Wealth permits a wide variety of entertainment and recreation: theater, concerts, art, yachting, tennis, skiing, travel abroad, and so on. Upper-class individuals generally take a tolerant attitude toward unconventional behavior in sex, the arts, fashions, lifestyles, and so forth. They feel they have a responsibility to "serve" the community and to "do good." They are active in public service and contribute time, money, and effort to worthy causes. This "public-regardingness" inclines them toward liberal politics; the upper classes provide the leadership for the liberal wings of both the Republican and Democratic parties.

The upper class relies on publications like the *New York Times,* the *Wall Street Journal,* and the *New Yorker* magazine for news and information. They also are more likely to listen to National Public Radio (NPR) shows like *All Things Considered* and *Marketplace* and watch public television (PBS).

Although the presence of an American upper class is obvious, political scientists and sociologists question whether the upper class actually constitutes a ruling class. As stated previously in this chapter (see page 281), conflict theorist C. Wright Mills argued that a power elite exists in America and that this ruling class with its disproportionate share of wealth and connections is hereditary. (See "Masters of Social Thought: C. Wright Mills and the Power Elite.")

pluralist
a theorist who argues that groups are the dominant influence in public policy making

Other scholars argue that an American upper class exists but little evidence points to a power elite. These theorists, called **pluralists,** emphasize the role that groups play in influencing public policy. They point to policies that do not benefit the upper class as evidence of a lack of a power elite. Political scientist Nelson Polsby argued that competition, even within the upper class, results in a lack of unity that means there can be no cohesive, unified power elite.[8]

Box 12.1 Masters of Social Thought

C. Wright Mills and the Power Elite

The most popular and controversial analysis of power in the United States is *The Power Elite,* by sociologist C. Wright Mills. Since its appearance in 1956, most writers have been unable to discuss national power without reference to this important study.

According to Mills, power in the United States is concentrated at the top of the nation's corporate, government, and military organizations, which closely interlock to form a single structure of power: a power elite. Power rests in these three domains: "the corporation chieftains, the political directorate, and the warlords." Occasionally there is tension among them, but they share a broad consensus about the general direction of public policy. Other institutions (the family, churches, schools, and so forth) are subordinate to the three major institutions of power.

The power elite holds power because of its position at the top of the institutional structures of society. These people are powerful not because of any individual qualities—wealth, prestige, skill, or cunning—but because of the institutional positions that they occupy. As society has concentrated more and more power in a few giant institutions, the people in command of these institutions have acquired enormous power over all of us.

As Mills explains it,

> *The history of modern society may readily be understood as the story of the enlargement and the centralization of the means of power—in economic, in political, and in military institutions.**

Mills is aware that his description of power in the United States conflicts with the "pluralist" interpretation (see discussion of the upper class on page 287-288). However, he believes that notions of powerholders who balance and compromise interests or who engage in competition between parties and groups apply to middle-level powerholders in America and not to the top power elite.

The *unity* of the top elite rests on several factors. First of all, these people are recruited from the same upper social classes; they have similar education, wealth, and upbringing.

Moreover, they continue to associate with each other, reinforcing their common feelings. They belong to the same clubs, attend the same parties, meet at the same resorts, and serve on the same civic, cultural, and philanthropic committees. Factions exist and individual ambitions clash, but their community of interest is far greater than any divisions among them. Perhaps what accounts for their consensus more than anything else is their experience in command positions in giant institutions. "As the requirements of the top places in each of the major hierarchies become similar, the types of men occupying these roles at the top—by selection and by training in the jobs—become similar."†

Mills and his work are frequently cited by radical critics of American society. According to Mills, the power elite is guilty of "a higher immorality"—that is, not necessarily personal corruption or even mistaken policies and deeds, but rather the moral insensitivity of institutional bureaucracy. More important, it is the failure of the power elite to be responsive and responsible to "knowledgeable publics." Mills implies that true democracy is possible only where persons in power are truly responsible to "men of Knowledge." He is not very specific about who the "men of Knowledge" are, but the reader is left with the impression that he means intellectuals like himself.

* C. Wright Mills, "The Structure of Power in American Society," in *Power, Politics and People: The Collected Writings of C. Wright Mills,* ed. Irving L. Horowitz (New York: Oxford University Press, 1963), 24.

† Ibid., 273.

The Middle Class

Middle-class individuals are also future oriented; they plan ahead for themselves and their children. They are not likely to be as cosmopolitan as the upper-class person, however, because they are more concerned with their immediate families than with "humanity" in the abstract. They are confident about their ability to influence their own futures and those of their children, but they do not really expect to have an effect on community, state, or national events. Investing time, energy, and effort in self-improvement and getting ahead are principal themes of life. Middle-class people strongly want their children to go to college and acquire the kind of formal training that will help them get ahead. Recreation and entertainment often includes golf, swimming, movies, sports events, and travel usually within the United States. Middle-class individuals tend to be middle-of-the-road or conservative in politics. Though they join voluntary organizations, many of which are formally committed to community service, they give less of their money and effort to public causes than do those in the upper class.

This said, it would be untrue to paint a picture of a unified American middle class. Although many of the above characteristics are true for most members of the middle class, we actually can refer to multiple middle classes in America. The upper middle class—composed largely of professionals employed in stable occupations like medicine, architecture, advanced education, the law, and engineering—often have incomes well over $100,000 and often more than double the income of others who consider themselves "middle class." This group enjoys a good deal of economic stability, and their leisure activities may include some "upper-class" activities.

At the other end of the middle class spectrum are those that are struggling to maintain a middle-class existence in the face of economic uncertainty. Often, these are single-income families (either because one person is staying at home or because the income earner is not part of a couple). Sometimes, the presence of two income earners means the difference between a working-class and a middle-class lifestyle.

Politically, the middle class is probably the most important social class because it is the largest class in American society, therefore a large (though not unified) voting bloc. Political scientist Stanley Greenberg analyzed the impact of the middle class on electoral politics in his book *Middle Class Dreams*. This book shows the importance of the middle class in electoral politics to the two dominant political parties in America.

The Working Class

Working-class people are obliged to concern themselves more with the present than the future. They expect their children to make their own way in life. They are self-respecting and self-confident, but these feelings extend over a narrower range of matters than they do in middle-class individuals. The horizon of the working class is limited by job, family, immediate friends, and neighborhood. Working-class individuals work to maintain themselves and their families; they do not look at their jobs as a means of getting ahead or as a means of self-expression. Their deepest attachment is to family; most visiting is done with relatives rather than friends. Working-class persons usually do not belong to many organizations other than union and church. In their views toward others in the community, they are "private regarding"; they believe that they work hard for a living and feel others should do the same. They tend to look down on people who accept welfare unless those people are forced to do so by circumstances over which they have no control. When they vote, they generally vote Democratic, but they are often apathetic about politics and are less likely to vote than members of the other classes. The working-class position in politics is motivated not by political ideology but by ethnic and party loyalties, by the appeal of personalities, or by occasional favors. For recreation the working-class individual turns to bowling, stock-car racing, circuses, fairs, and carnivals.

The Lower Class

Lower-class individuals must live from day to day. They have little confidence in their ability to influence what happens to them. Things happen to them; they do not make them happen. When they work, it is often from payday to payday, and they frequently drift from one unskilled job to another. Their self-confidence is low, they feel little attachment to community, and they tend to resent authority (for example, that of police officers, social workers, teachers, landlords, and employers). (For a look at the lower class in other countries, see "International Perspective: Global Inequalities.")

The lower-class family is frequently headed by a woman. For the male off-spring of a lower-class matriarchal family, the future is often depressing, with defeat and frustration repeating themselves throughout his life. He may drop out of school in the eighth or ninth grade because of lack of success. Without parental supervision and having little to do, he may get into trouble with the police. The police record will further hurt his chances of getting a job. With limited job skills, little self-discipline, and low aspiration levels, the lower-class male is not likely to find a steady job that will pay enough to support a family. Yet he yearns for the material standard of living of higher classes—a car, a television set, and other conve-

Box 12.2 International Perspective: Global Inequalities

Three of every four persons in the world today live in less-developed countries (LDCs).* Traditionally, these countries encompass most of the globe: South and Central America; Africa; the Middle East, with the exception of Israel; and Asia, with the exception of Japan and the rapidly developing "Four Dragons"—Hong Kong, South Korea, Taiwan, and Singapore.

While this broad category of LDCs is commonly used by social scientists and others, it is important to remember that it encompasses societies with different languages, diverse people, and distinct cultures. Nonetheless, there are common characteristics of LDCs that can be observed by visitors as well as by social scientists. Americans can better appreciate their own society by knowing how the majority of the world's population lives.

Poverty

Poverty in LDCs is widespread and severe. The vast majority of the world's population lives well below the standard of living of America's poorest families. Hunger and ill health are common. It is estimated that one out of every five persons in the world today does not eat enough to enable him or her to work; one child in four dies before reaching 5 years old. Life expectancy is short (see the accompanying table).

Inequality

The limited resources of most LDCs are unequally distributed, with small elites controlling large proportions of land and wealth. In some societies, a caste system determines one's social position at birth with no opportunity for upward social mobility. The subordination of women in these societies is very pronounced; women are commonly denied education, land ownership, and a voice in public affairs.

Traditionalism

The cultures of LDCs generally place great value on traditional ways of life passed down, virtually unchanged, from generation to generation. Traditionalism also means the acceptance of one's life and one's fate, however poor. It also means resisting innovation and change.

High Fertility

Birthrates are generally very high in LDCs. Family reliance on human labor, high infant mortality rates, the low status of women, and the absence of birth control information or technology all contribute to high birthrates. Because of its enormous population and fears that the government would be unable to feed and support unfettered population growth, China has attempted to force families to have only one child; sterilization and abortion are common, as are abortions of female fetuses and the abandonment of female babies.

Primitive Technology

Most energy in these societies is directly supplied by human and animal muscle power. A lifetime of hard manual labor, just to meet minimum needs, confronts most of the people of the world. Animal labor is more common than farm machinery.

* A note on terminology: Less-developed countries were once referred to as the "third world." This term was used during the Cold War to distinguish between industrialized Western democracies ("First World"); the stagnating communist economies of Eastern Europe ("Second World"); and poorer, nonindustrialized societies in Asia, Africa, and Latin America ("Third World").

Life in the Less-Developed World

	GNP per capita ($U.S.)	Birthrate*	Life expectancy (years)	Infant Mortality Rate†
U.S.	34,000	14.1	77.3	6.8
Mexico	5,070	22.8	71.8	25.4
Colombia	2,020	22.4	70.6	24
Venezuela	4,310	20.7	73.3	25.4
Egypt	1,490	24.9	63.7	60.5
Nigeria	260	39.7	51.1	73.3
Vietnam	390	21.2	69.6	30.2
Sri Lanka	850	16.6	72.1	16.1
China	840	16	71.6	28.1
India	450	24.3	62.9	63.2
Pakistan	440	31.2	61.5	80.5
Bangladesh	370	25.3	60.5	69.9

Source: U.S. Bureau of the Census, *Statistical Abstract of the United States 2002* (Washington, DC: Government Printing Office, 2003), 833, 829.
* Live births per one thousand population per year.
† Number of deaths of children under 1 year age per one thousand live births per year.

niences. Frequently, to compensate for defeat and frustration, the lower-class male will resort to risk taking, conquest, and fighting to assert his masculinity. Entertainment may be limited to drinking and gambling. Many aspects of lower-class culture are unattractive to women. Sociologist Herbert Gans wrote, "The woman tries to develop a stable routine in the midst of poverty and deprivation; the action-seeking man upsets it."[9]

Social Classes: Conflict and Conciliation

An awareness of class membership is not the same as class consciousness. **Class consciousness** is the belief that all members of one's social class have similar economic and political interests that are adverse to the interests of other classes and ought to be promoted through common action. As we have already seen, Americans are aware of class membership, but members of the same class do not always share political interests, feel that collective class action is necessary, or see themselves as locked in a struggle against opposing classes. Few Americans believe in the militant ideology of class struggle. Americans do not have a strong sense of class consciousness.

class consciousness believing that all members of one's class have similar political and economic interests, adverse to those of other classes

Nonetheless, there is some evidence of awareness of class interest in voting behavior. Although Democratic and Republican candidates draw their support from all social classes in America, social-class bases of the Democratic and Republican parties are slightly different. Professional and managerial groups and other white-collar employees give greater support to the Republican Party than do skilled, semiskilled, and unskilled workers. Likewise, people with some college education tend to vote Republican more often than persons with a high school or grade school education do. Of course, not all the upper-class vote goes to the Republican Party, and not all the lower-class vote goes to the Democratic Party. In fact, the differences in voter support are not very great. But there is some indication that class has an impact on voting behavior.

Box 12.3 Masters of Social Thought

Karl Marx and the Class Struggle

Conflict between social classes is a central feature of communist ideology. In the opening of his famous Communist Manifesto, Karl Marx wrote:

> The history of all hitherto existing society is the history of class struggles. Freeman and slave, patrician and plebeian, lord and serf, guild-master and journeyman, in a word, oppressor and oppressed....*

Karl Marx was born in Prussia in 1818. His parents were Jews who converted to Christianity when Marx was a child. He studied history, law, and philosophy at Bonn, Berlin, and Jena and received his doctor of philosophy degree in 1841. Soon after, he entered revolutionary socialist politics as a journalist and pamphleteer; he was expelled from Prussia and engaged in conspiratorial activities in France and Belgium from 1843 to 1849. The *Communist Manifesto,* written with Friedrich Engels, appeared in 1848 as a revolutionary pamphlet. In 1849 Marx fled to London where he spent the remainder of his life writing occasional pamphlets on socialism, advising socialist leaders, and setting forth his views in a lengthy work, *Das Kapital ("Capital").*

According to Marx, social classes develop on the basis of the different positions that individuals fulfill in the prevailing "mode of production" – that is, the economy. In an agricultural economy, the principal classes are landowner and tenant, serf, or slave; and in an industrial economy, the capitalist or "bourgeois" (pronounced bore-jwah) (owner of the factory) and the nonproperty-owning worker, or "proletarian." The bourgeoisie have an interest in maximizing profit and seek to keep for themselves the surplus of profit that has been created by the worker. Workers are exploited in that they produce more than they receive in wages; this "surplus value" is stolen from the workers by the capitalists.

Marx viewed class consciousness as an important prerequisite to successful proletarian revolution. Class consciousness would increase as the proletariat grew in numbers, as workers communicated among themselves and achieved solidarity in unions and political organization, and as conflict between workers and owners intensified. The bourgeoisie would not relinquish their control over the means of production without a fight, and therefore violent revolution was necessary and inevitable. Marx said little about the details of revolution; this aspect of communist ideology was developed later by Lenin. But after the successful proletarian revolution, Marx envisioned a society without social classes.

This classless society would be a "dictatorship of the proletariat" with all other social classes eliminated. The state would control the means of production, and everyone would be in the same relationship to the state as everyone else. Eventually, the state, which functions in bourgeois society to help the bourgeoisie oppress the masses, would gradually "wither away" in a communist society. The truth is of course that neither capitalist societies nor communist societies conform to Marx's analysis. Yet much of the history of the twentieth century centered on the rise and fall of communism in the world.

* Karl Marx, *The Communist Manifesto,* ed. A. J. P. Taylor (New York: Penguin, 1967), p. 79.

Absence of Class Conflict

class conflict conflict between upper and lower social classes over wealth and power

Why is there no militant class consciousness or **class conflict** in America? This is a difficult question to answer precisely, but we can summarize some factors that appear to help stabilize the existing class system in America and reduce class conflict:

factors in American life reducing class conflict

- A relatively high standard of living of Americans of all social classes
- A great deal of upward mobility in the American system, which diverts lower-class attention away from collective class action and focuses it toward individual efforts at "getting ahead"
- The existence of a large middle-income, middle-prestige class
- Widespread belief in the legitimacy of the class structure and the resulting acceptance of it
- Many cross-cutting allegiances of individuals to churches, races, unions, professional associations, voluntary organizations, and so forth, which interfere with class solidarity

In stabilizing the class system, these factors also stabilize the existing distribution of power in America.

high standard of living

The American system has produced a high level of material comfort for the great majority of the population. The real possibilities of acquiring greater income and prestige have reinforced efforts to strive within the system rather than to challenge it. Even individuals who realize that their own social mobility is limited can transfer their hope and ambition to their children. A large middle class, diverse in occupation and ambiguous in political orientation, helps blur potential lines of class identification and conflict. This class stands as a symbol and an embodiment of the reality of opportunity. Finally, cross-pressuring cleavages caused by religious affiliations, ethnic backgrounds, and racial categories, as well as by other types of diversity (for example, region, skill level, and occupation group), have all worked against the development of unified class movements.

upward mobility

large middle class

widespread belief in the system

many cross-cutting allegiences

Social Class and Political Power

Government leadership is recruited mainly from the upper and upper-middle social classes. For example, although millionaires comprise less than 1 percent of all Americans, about one-third of the members of Congress are millionaires. Most government officials, particularly at the national level (cabinet officers, presidential advisers, congressional representatives, Supreme Court judges, and so on), are well-educated, prestigiously employed, successful, and affluent—part of the upper or upper-middle classes. With few exceptions, they are the children of professionals, business owners and managers, or successful farmers and landowners. Only a small minority are the children of hourly wage earners.

The occupational characteristics of representatives also show that they are generally of higher social standing than their constituents; professional and business occupations dominate the halls of Congress. One reason is that congressional candidates are more likely to win the election if their occupations are socially "respectable" and provide opportunities for extensive public contacts. The lawyer, insurance agent, and real estate agent establish in their businesses the wide circle of friends necessary for political success. Another subtler reason is that candidates and elected legislators must come from occupational groups with flexible work responsibilities. Lawyers, landowners, and business owners can adjust their work to the campaign and legislative schedules, whereas office and factory workers cannot.

Lawyers in Politics

The overrepresentation of lawyers as an occupational group in Congress and other public offices is particularly marked. (Lawyers constitute no more than two-tenths of 1 percent of the labor force.) Lawyers have always played a prominent role in the American political system. Twenty-five of the fifty-two signers of the Declaration of Independence and thirty-one of the fifty-five members of the Continental Congress were lawyers. The legal profession has also provided 70 percent of the presidents, vice presidents, and cabinet officers of the United States and one-third to one-half of all U.S. senators and members of the House of Representatives (see Table 12.7). Lawyers are in a reasonably high-prestige occupation, but so are physicians, businesspeople, and scientists. Why, then, do lawyers, rather than members of those other high-prestige groups, dominate the halls of Congress?

It is sometimes argued that lawyers bring a special kind of skill to Congress. Because their occupation is the representation of clients, they make no great change in occupation when they move from representing clients in private practice to representing constituents in Congress. Also, they are trained to deal with public policy as it is reflected in the statute books, so they may be reasonably familiar with public policy before entering Congress. But professional skills alone cannot explain the dominance of lawyers in public office. Another answer is that of all those in high-prestige occupations only lawyers can really afford to neglect their careers for political activities. For the physician, the corporate businessperson, and the scientist, such slighting of their vocations is very costly. However, for the lawyer, political activity can be a positive advantage in terms of occupational advancement; free public advertising and opportunities to make contacts with potential clients are two important benefits. Yet another answer is that lawyers naturally have a monopoly on public offices in the legal and judicial system, and the office of judge or prosecuting attorney often provides a steppingstone to higher public office, including Congress. Finally, inasmuch as the tradition of lawyers in public office is well known, many politically ambitious young people enter law school, not so much with the expectation of practicing law in the future, but rather with the notion of using their law school experience as a springboard to a career in politics.

Table 12.7 Occupational Backgrounds of Congress Members

	House	Senate	Congress Total
Actor/Entertainer	3		3
Aeronautics	2		2
Agriculture	28	5	33
Artistic/Creative	2*		2*
Business/Banking	163	30	193
Clergy	3		3
Education	86*	12	96*
Engineering	4	1	5
Health Care	6		6
Homemaker/Domestic	4		4
Journalism	10*	7	17*
Labor	8	3	11
Law	160	58†	218†
Law Enforcement	9		9
Medicine	16	4	20
Military	3	1	4
Professional Sports	1	1	2
Public Service/Politics	164	32	196
Real Estate	38	3	41
Secretarial/Clerical	4		4
Technical/Trade	3		3

Source: Congressional Quarterly, 109th Congress (2005–2007), "Statistically Speaking," http://oncongress.cq.com/corp/flatfiles/editorialFiles/temporaryItems/mon20041103-3demographics.pdf (accessed November 6, 2006).

* Includes Rep. Bernard Sanders, I-Vt.

† Includes Sen. James M. Jeffords, I-Vt.

Note: Because some members have more than one occupation, totals are higher than total memberships.

Social Class and Executive Power

Power in the executive branch, which most analysts now see as more important than Congress in policy formulation, is also exercised by individuals from the upper and upper-middle classes. Cabinet secretaries, undersecretaries, and top civil servants tend to come disproportionately from Ivy League schools; most are lawyers or businesspeople at the time of their appointment; many accept lower salaries out of a sense of obligation to perform public service.[10]

Upper-Class Rule?

We know that political power is largely exercised by individuals from upper social classes, but what does this really mean for the great majority of Americans? We might infer that people drawn from upper social classes share values and interest different from those of the majority of people. On the other hand, several factors may modify the impact of upper social classes in politics.

upper-class power

First, there may be considerable conflict among members of upper social classes about the basic directions of public policy; that is, despite similarity in social backgrounds, individuals may not share a consensus about public affairs. Competition rather than consensus may characterize their relationships.

modified by competition

Second, the elite may be very "public regarding" in their exercise of power; they may take the welfare of the masses into account as an aspect of their own sense of well-being. Indeed, there is a great deal of evidence that America's upper classes are liberal and reformist and that "do-goodism" is a widespread impulse. Many public leaders from very wealthy families of the highest social states (for instance, Franklin D. Roosevelt, Adlai Stevenson, and John F. Kennedy) have championed the interests of the poor and the downtrodden. Thus upper-class values may foster public service rather than political exploitation.

public regarding values

electoral accountability

Third, upper-class leaders, whatever their values, can be held accountable for their exercise of power by the majority in elections. Our system of parties and elections forces public officials to compete for mass support to acquire public office and the political power that goes with it. This competition requires them to modify their public statements and actions to fit popular preferences. Hence, in a democracy, the fact that the upper social classes tend to hold public office does not necessarily mean that the masses are oppressed, exploited, or powerless.

About This Chapter

After traveling to the new American nation in 1835, the French social commentator Alexis de Tocqueville wrote, "When it is birth alone, independent of wealth, which classes men in society, every one knows exactly what his own position is upon the social scale; he does not seek to rise, he does not fear to sink. . . . [But in America] as the social importance of men is no longer ostensibly and permanently fixed by blood, and is infinitely varied by wealth, ranks still exist, but it is not easy clearly to distinguish at a glance those who respectively belong to them."* Thus, Tocqueville acknowledged that there were social classes in America, but unlike Europe at the time, class membership was based on wealth and achievement, not birth, and individuals could rise or fall in social position.

In this chapter, we looked at how Americans "stratify" themselves into social classes, how sociologists measure this stratification, and the relationship between social class and lifestyle and power. Now that you have read this chapter, you should be able to

- Describe the stratification system and the methods that sociologists use to identify and measure stratification.
- Describe functional and conflict explanations of social classes.
- Define class consciousness and identify the factors that help stabilize the existing class system in America.
- Discuss the basic notions set forth by Karl Marx about social classes and describe what some of the problems are in Marxist analysis.
- Discuss the relationships between social class and lifestyle and between social class and political power.

* Alexis de Tocqueville, *Democracy in America* (New York: New American Library, 1956), 40.

For Discussion

1. Discuss the social stratification system. Include in your discussion a description of the bases used for stratification, as well as the characteristics associated with the stratification system.
2. Explain each of the perspectives used by sociologists: functionalism, symbolic interactionism, conflict theory, and postmodernism.
3. If you were studying social class, what methods might you use to identify and measure social stratification?
4. If in the course of your study you were to ask average Americans how they see themselves in the class system, what class would they choose, and why? How might the respondents' subjective evaluations differ from the results you as a social scientist obtained? What are the objective criteria you would use to identify social class?
5. Choose two of the American social classes and contrast them according to orientation toward life, individual self-confidence, women's roles, activities and interests, and political participation and party identification.
6. Contrast class consciousness with class awareness. Discuss the factors that appear to stabilize the existing class system in the United States and reduce class conflict.

7. Distinguish between inequality and social mobility. How is inequality usually measured? How can we measure mobility?
8. Discuss Karl Marx's views of economic roles and class consciousness in the struggle for power among social classes.
9. Define the power elite that was identified by C. Wright Mills and describe the factors that contribute to the emergence of such an elite. What is its actual base of power, and on what factors does its unity rest? How does Mills's interpretation of power in the United States conflict with the pluralist interpretation?

On the Web

The website for this textbook (academic.cengage.now/login) offers resources for exploring power and social class on the Internet. Sociology covers a very broad range of subject matter—social life, social change, and the social causes and consequences of human behavior. This chapter has focused on power and social class, but the subject matter of social class ranges from the intimate family to the hostile mob, from organized crime to religious cults, and from the sociology of work to the sociology of sports.

- **American Sociological Association/Society for Applied Sociology** For a better understanding of the full range of sociology, begin by visiting the websites maintained by the American Sociological Association (ASA, www.asanet.org) and the Society for Applied Sociology (SAS, www.appliedsoc.org). The ASA site is oriented toward academic sociology, primarily teachers of sociology in colleges and universities, but it also provides student career information including "Job Prospects for the BA Graduate." The SAS site is oriented toward practicing sociologists in government, health care, law enforcement, and human resources. It includes information on "Becoming a Sociologist' and "Sociology Job Listings."
- **U.S. Census Bureau** Current information on income, education, and occupation of Americans, as well as information on poverty and inequality can be found in U.S. Census Bureau date (www.census.gov). An "A to Z" index includes direct links to data on "income," "poverty," "inequality," and so on.

chapter 13

Race and Ethnicity: Some Basic Concepts

Our species has existed for approximately 90,000 years. In those years, people have wandered to every piece of real estate available, searching for new food sources and responding to climactic changes. But the geographical separation among those wanderers has not really been all that long in biological time. The fact that all people are members of the same species attests to that, since separation does produce biological differences. Although biological differences among people do exist, we will see that they are relatively minor and we only pay attention to some of them.

Geographical separation also has produced differences in the way people live. Technology, beliefs, and patterns of behavior have moved in as many different directions as the people themselves. The longer the separation, the greater those differences grow. Our main concern in this book is what happens when such different people become reunited.

How can we begin to make sense of these differences? How are these differences related to one another? I could make several predictions about you just from knowing what you are doing right now. This text is written in English, so you must know how to read English. You might have acquired this skill in a wide variety of circumstances—in non-English speaking countries or perhaps as an adult—but the odds are that you learned the language as an infant (when we learn languages quickly and easily) and were later taught to read. If you fall into the latter category, you were probably born in an area where English is a common language. And inhabitants of the areas where English is spoken also share many other habits, skills, and beliefs along with language. I might guess, for example, that you prefer not to eat insects in your diet—very few English speakers do.

There are things about you I do not know. I do not know for example whether you are male or female. Whatever your gender, however, I know it has been a critical factor in making you who you are today. Gender gives people different life experiences in every human society, whether they want those experiences or not. I also do not know whether or not you have wisdom teeth and, if you do not, whether you had them pulled or were born without them. But whichever the case, I can guess that the presence or absence of wisdom teeth has not had a major impact on your life (except, possibly, the day you had them removed). In American society, gender is an important social category, whereas possession of wisdom teeth is not.

Social categories occur whenever a collection of individuals shares some socially important characteristic in common. Which characteristics are important? The people with whom we share our lives dictate just which characteristics deserve our attention and which do not. American society does not attach any special significance to wisdom teeth, so we generally ignore them. We are not, however, invited to ignore our gender. Nor are we invited to ignore how we speak, how we worship (or if we do), the color of our skin, or how we earn our living. Other people will judge us on these characteristics and, as a result, we will probably come to judge ourselves. In short, social categories happen whenever differences become meaningful, and they become meaningful only when social agreement occurs. If that agreement changes, categories lose their importance and assume the significance of wisdom teeth; the differences may remain, but we choose to ignore them.

Assuming you already know something about racial groups and ethnic groups, you may well be wondering why you are reading about teeth. As with so many topics we try to understand, race and ethnic relations are often better grasped if we do not get too close to them. If you grew up in American society, you probably cannot imagine a society in which skin color would be totally ignored. But the importance

Reprinted from *Race and Ethnicity in the United States: Our Differences and Our Roots* (2002), by permission of Cengage Learning.

people in American society give to skin color could just as easily be taken away. An important question facing us is how human differences are made important in our thinking about social relations. An even more important question is *why* we choose to make them important. As we will see, race and ethnicity together account for a great many of those characteristics that thrust different life experiences upon us.

This chapter provides a foundation as we focus on these questions in a journey toward an understanding of the concepts of *race* and *ethnicity.* When members of either group gain power in a society, or are denied access to it, they become *dominant groups* and *minority groups,* respectively. Finally, we explore some of the ongoing relationships that racial and ethnic groups develop as they interact over time. As we will see, a separatist minority wanting its own state might successfully assimilate into a dominant group over time; they also might become the victims of genocide if the dominant group should find their mass deaths convenient.

Ethnic and Racial Groups

Culture is the most basic concept used by social scientists. It refers to everything that people create, share with one another, and pass along to the next generation. This includes creations you can touch, such as clothes, buildings, or this book; these objects are part of **material culture.** Cultural creations also can be part of **nonmaterial culture**, which includes knowledge, language, beliefs, expectations, hopes, and dreams. We learn all of these things as we grow up in our societies, ultimately becoming much like the older members who teach us unless something or someone interferes with the process.

The more we learn about our culture, the more it becomes part of us. By the time you were a teenager, you not only *knew* about your culture, but you also *cared* about it. Cultural beliefs became your personal beliefs and cultural norms (or rules for behavior) became patterns you chose to follow. As you acquired all these beliefs, you also received the ultimate belief of every culture—the belief that your culture is the best of all possible cultures. This means that your food is the best food, your religion is the only true religion, your music is the most entertaining, and so on. When you reached this point, you had acquired **ethnocentricism**—the belief that your culture is superior to all others

One curious aspect of culture is that we take so much of it for granted. If everyone you know wears clothes when they leave the house, you will not consciously notice the presence of clothing on people around you. Likewise, when you wake in the morning, you consciously decide *what* you should wear but do not consider whether you should leave the house clothed or nude. We notice different types of clothing because they vary; we do not notice clothing per se because everyone is wearing something. In short, the only parts of culture that receive our conscious attention are those that vary, confronting us with alternatives. This observation is extremely important as we follow the movements of people from many different cultures and note the outcomes when cultures collide. Meeting someone from a different culture allows us to contrast our way of life because now we have a means of comparison. More often than not, these confrontations bring out the ethnocentrism in which we have been steeped.

The Changing Boundaries of Ethnicity

The term *ethnic group* is both fundamental to our study and also elusive because social scientists define it in so many ways. These definitions, however, are derived from the many ways that real people think of themselves. We can incorporate that variation, however, with the following definition: An **ethnic group** is a group of people who

1. share a common culture and/or ancestry, or
2. are defined by themselves or others as sharing a common culture and/or ancestry.

In each case, boundaries exist among groups of people, and these boundaries are subject to change over time (see Barth, 1969). Although such boundaries are linked to culture and/or ancestry, the connection may be loose indeed. Ethnic groups can exist even when the "common ancestry" is totally imagined. It really does not matter. If people believe themselves (or are believed by others) to share such commonalities, that sharing becomes real in its consequences for all involved.

A personal example illustrates this point. When I was about nine years old, I was playing baseball with my best friend in the park one afternoon when a classmate rode by on his bicycle and shouted, "Hey, kike!" I had not heard the term before, but my friend explained that *kike* was an insulting term for a Jew, much like the term *nigger* was insulting to black people. I asked him why it had been shouted at us. My friend said it was because he was a Jew.

I was confused. I knew my friend's family quite well, and I knew his father's parents attended a place called a temple on Saturday because they were Jews, and I knew that Judaism was a religion. But I also knew my friend's parents attended neither temples nor churches, having no religious preference in particular. In addition, I knew no one was Jewish on his mother's side. It seemed to me that being Jewish should stop when one left the religion. To others, at least to non-Jews, my friend was Jewish no matter what he thought, said, or did. To many Jews, you have to have a Jewish mother to be considered Jewish, and my friend's mother was not Jewish in any sense of the word. As he tells me to this day, he is the opposite of whatever you are.

I received an early lesson in ethnic boundaries from that experience. Ethnic groups are similar to all human groups in that they have boundaries. There is a clear line, for example, between your relatives and nonrelatives. We keep track of such boundary lines because we want to know who is in our group and who is not. If we want to keep our definition of *ethnic group* in line with the real world, we have to pay attention to those boundaries, *regardless of who believes them to exist.* As with brick walls, ethnic group boundaries can be built to keep your people in or other people out. Ethnicity, in short, can be imposed upon us from the outside as long as those outside people have enough power to make their boundaries strong. Culture may have nothing to do with it.

That same power can be used to create one ethnic group from many. Consider the case of Native Americans. In North and South America in 1491, many different ethnic groups existed, many of them clearly fitting our first definition (i.e., sharing a common culture and/or ancestry). But the coming of Europeans changed all that because they had far more power than the native peoples and they tended not to distinguish among the different groups, lumping them all together as "Indians." Today, Native Americans identify themselves with their tribe as they would have centuries ago, but most have acquired a second, more general, self-identity as Native Americans. They have, in short, come to agree with the early Europeans that *all* the native people have something more in common with each other than any one group has with Europeans, even though they reached that conclusion by very different means.

This same process of merging ethnic groups can occur in a completely voluntary manner. A classic example in the United States is "white people" or, as referred to in this book, European Americans. In the nineteenth century, most Americans clearly drew lines to distinguish German Americans from English or Italian Americans. Today, their descendants barely notice such distinctions.

What about boundaries created from within? We can look to Jews once again for an illustration. A few thousand years ago, this group fit our first definition of an ethnic group; however, Jews have since scattered all around the world, acquiring different cultures. Some have even changed their religion or given it up completely. Yet many of these people prefer to identify themselves as Jews, basing their ethnic boundaries on their common ancestry and little else. Are they encouraged to do this through experiences such as the one my friend had on the playground? No doubt they are. But they might wish to maintain their identity anyway. And ethnic identity may arise from a complex selection process based on which ethnic backgrounds are perceived to be the most significant; the case of Afro-Amerasians such as Tiger Woods provides such complexity, as most Americans emphasize his African ancestry over his Asian ancestry (Williams and Thornton, 1998).

If any single defining characteristic can be derived from all these examples, it is this: Ethnic groups exist wherever and whenever people believe ethnic boundaries exist and act on those beliefs. Those boundaries may be based on cultural differences or differences in ancestral heritage, both either real or imagined. This definition allows us to include racial groups as ethnic groups.

Does Race Exist?

A racial group is generally thought to be collection of people who share a common genetic heritage that distinguishes them biologically from other racial groups. Are racial groups so different? Although the concept of biological differences among races is questionable and its definition is rooted in the biological sciences, the social scientist has to deal with this concept. In this text, we use the term **racial group** to refer to ethnic groups *that have been labeled as* biologically different from other ethnic groups. Almost always, the group developing the label attaches biological superiority to itself. Groups so labeled receive different treatment. Keep in mind, however, that groups labeled as racially different always begin ethnically different. They also usually stay that way because racial group boundaries are always more solid than ethnic group boundaries. This is why we can fit racial groups within the definition of ethnic group offered earlier.

Race first appeared on the scientific scene with works such as *Systema Naturae* by Carolus Linnaeus published in 1758 and the 1775 *De Generis Humani Varietate Nativa* by Johann Friedrich Blumenbach (Gould, 1994). The latter suggested that humans belong to five races: Caucasians (whites), Mongolians (Asians), Ethiopians (blacks), Americans (Native Americans), and the Malays (Polynesians, Melanesians, and Australian aborigines). Scientists who give credence to the concept of race use pretty much the same groupings today. The fact that we have seen little change in this area of science for over two centuries should perhaps make us a little suspicious; high quality scientific inquiry is typically marked by regular theoretical change.

We noted earlier that people have a history of wandering. Because most large groups of people in different corners of the globe did not search far for mates for so many centuries, different kinds of biological change occurred in different areas. If one travels on foot, the changes appear gradual. Travel by ship or plane, however, allows us to cover vast distances, magnifying the biological differences among geographical areas, and notions of race seem to make more sense. But even given such biological differences, we would still need to be able to compile long lists of genetic traits present in one race but absent from another for the concept to be of much scientific use (see Cartmill, 1998).

Jared Diamond (1994) offers some alternative views of race. He notes that racial characteristics are both genetically fairly trivial and not interconnected. For example, the grandchildren of a European American and African American couple could range from curly haired and light skinned to straight haired and darker skinned. This is not a roll with one set of dice, but rather many rolls with many sets in each generation. You can observe the same "mix and match" with any family's physical traits. But more important, argues Diamond, are the biological traits we ignore in categorizing races. For example, we would categorize on the basis of fingerprints, separating those with mostly loops from those with mostly whorls. This would place most Europeans and Africans in one race, Jews and some Indonesians in a second, and aboriginal Australians would occupy the third. Grouping by lactose tolerance, sickle-cell traits, or tooth shape would create three more (and totally different) sets of races. The traits we have picked out as significant for race may be more important for social reasons than biological.

In the coming chapters, we find racial categories used in all sorts of ways. But we generally find an interesting similarity in the social circumstances in which racial distinctions arise. Almost always with race classifications, a relatively powerless ethnic group (or groups) faces terrible abuse from a much more powerful ethnic group (or groups). Why race? Imagine biological differences between yourself and someone else that allow you to label the other person (and their descendants) as permanently inferior to you. If the differences were only cultural, they would be capable of becoming your equal, given the time to learn. If the abuse is bad enough—consider slavery, for example—your behavior is much easier to rationalize if your victim is thought of as biologically (thus permanently) different. Just as we have different rules for the treatment of human babies and kittens based on biology, *race* allows us the same flexibility with people. You cannot enslave your equal any more than you can drown a bag full of babies.

■ Minority and Dominant Groups

When Bill Clinton ran for President of the United States in 1992, his main campaign advisor was a seasoned professional name James Carville. A campaign advisor serves many purposes, but among the most important is to identify political issues that will attract the attention of voters and win their support. The best issue is the one that works. His candidate was running against George Bush, and a sitting president can be hard to beat. Carville began with a huge array of issues that appeared in various Clinton speeches. Finally, Carville woke up one morning and banged the palm of his hand against his forehead, having realized the obvious. The United States economy was in a recession and that was the only issue Clinton needed. Economic survival tops almost everyone's list of needs. Carville created a sign to hang over his desk that constantly reminded him, "It's the economy, stupid," lest he once again forget the obvious (Wayne, 1996).

We might want to borrow Carville's sign both for this chapter section and the rest of this text as a reminder to us all that economic factors are integral to understanding ethnic and racial differences. Although it would seem that we should focus only on human culture—language, religion, political systems, child rearing and so on—in our search for understanding, cultural variations comprise only part of the picture. Because cultural differences between groups of people have motivated some of the most horrendous atrocities imaginable, they are a focus of this text. Such atrocities create intense motivations for victims to relocate, far from their tormentors, only to encounter yet more cultural differences among the people with whom they finally settle.

But Carville's advice to himself should be kept in mind here. Undoubtedly the oldest human motivation for moving is economic. This is no less true for people who came to North and South America during the early days of European expansion than it was for early nomadic humans thousands of years ago. As we now turn to examine how different ethnic groups relate to one another when they meet, we need to keep in mind that their cultural interactions will have much to do with their varying economic positions. People who move because of poverty typically have few choices, either before or after they move. When they arrive at their destinations, they often find themselves powerless and unable to prevent yet further economic disadvantage.

Size versus Power

A **minority group** is an ethnic or racial group that occupies a subordinate position in a society, unable to gain equal access to wealth or influence. Their subordinate status is maintained through limitations placed on them by the structure of their society. Those limitations either are enforced at the level of national government or, at least, allowed to exist by that government. By contrast, a **dominant group** is an ethnic or racial group that occupies the dominant positions in a society, monopolizing positions of power and wealth. They are the creators of the limitations minority groups face, and they benefit from the lack of options available to minority group members.

The critical distinction between dominant and minority groups is power, not size. The term *minority* can be misleading because it suggests a group small in number rather than a powerless group. Minority groups often are small—lack of numbers can be one of the factors that limits power—but power alone is the key. For years, the Republic of South Africa was run by white South Africans with nineteenth century ties to England and Holland. Together, they represented a tiny minority of South Africa's population, but for over a century they controlled all the power and wealth of that country. It is easier to maintain dominance if the dominant group is large, but size is not the most critical factor.

Linking Power with Ethnicity

Imagine the following scene: A farmer is standing on a country road looking fondly at his most prized possession—several hundred acres of good farmland. A stranger comes walking down the road and strikes up a conversation.

"That's a mighty nice piece of land there," says the stranger.
"Yup," replies the farmer.
"Belongs to you?" asks the stranger.
"Yup," replies the farmer.
"How did you come by it?" asks the stranger.
"Well," replies the farmer, "I got it from my father, who worked it all his life and left it to me."
"Well, how did he get it?"
"From my grandfather."
"But how did he get it?"
"From his father before him."
"But how did he get it?"
"Well," replies the farmer, "he fought for it."
"That's fine," counters the stranger, "I'll fight you for it."

Why does the stranger not have a right to fight for the land? No piece of land on the face of the earth is occupied by its original owner or even the descendants of the original owner. All ownership is initially or subsequently fought for. At some point following a fight, a political state takes over to maintain the status quo. In our story, the farmer's great-grandfather took the land by force, but he subsequently received a legal deed to the property from the state. That deed means that the next person who wants to fight for the land will have to fight both the state and the farmer.

As this example suggests, the study of racial and ethnic groups in any society also will be the study of power and its centralization in a government. In most societies, the central government can be viewed as a stand-in for the dominant group, legislating its wishes and enforcing them. It is easy to think of dominant groups as those who make their way to the top, but the trick is to stay there. The backing of a government makes staying there much easier than the initial climb. The connection between dominant ethnic groups and governments is therefore critical if that ethnic group is to maintain its dominance. When we later examine some American history followed by contemporary American race and ethnic relations, we will pay close attention to the role of the central (or federal) government (Enloe, 1973).

Ethnic Group Encounters: From Genocide to Separatism

When ethnic groups migrate and encounter one another, their subsequent relationships vary widely. They may dislike each other immediately; if one of the groups is significantly less powerful than the other, it will undoubtedly suffer greatly. Economics also may play a major role in such outcomes. Weaker ethnic groups may be quite welcome if they are willing to work for lower wages than the current labor force. And immigrants may well arrive with their own agenda, determined to avoid all other ethnic groups in their adopted country in hopes of maintaining their ethnic distinctiveness. Although the reality of such ethnic group encounters covers a wide range of relationships, social scientists have created a basic typology of encounters that attempts to categorize those relationships into the most common occurrences.

Genocide and Expulsion

Genocide occurs when the dominant group deliberately acts to cause the deaths of many or all members of a minority group. In some cases, genocide is clear cut, as in Hitler's efforts to exterminate Jews from

Europe—an intended mass murder that, for the most part, succeeded. In other cases, genocide is less obvious. Massive deaths among Native Americans after the arrival of Europeans occurred mainly through the spread of European diseases to which Native Americans had little immunity. This was not intentional. On the other hand, most Europeans were generally happy with the outcome and found numerous ways to cause Native American deaths over the years when nature did not succeed. All in all, was this genocide? Although the killing may not have been as evidently systematic as in the Holocaust, Native Americans were targeted for genocide.

Expulsion refers to the forcible removal of minority group members beyond the borders of a country. You might want to think about this as mass deportation. American history offers us several examples of this process. The first, dating back to the early 1800s, was the forcible removal of eastern Native American peoples by the federal government. They were relocated in Indian Territory in what is now the state of Oklahoma. Although land west of the Mississippi belonged to the United States, it was not then viewed as valuable, or the government would not have foolishly signed so many land treaties that would later come back to haunt it. Although the minorities in question did not exactly wind up outside the borders, the intent to remove ethnic groups from a society was clearly present.

Kosovo refugees endured crowded evacuation routes to escape genocide during the 1999 Serbian invasion.

Perhaps a better example of expulsions comes from the twentieth century in the United States. Since 1900, Mexican Americans had been welcomed in the United States when their labor was needed. During recessions or depressions, however, they would be out of work and potential cost to social welfare systems. During the 1930s and again during the 1950s, Mexican Americans were rounded up and transported across the border to Mexico. Both times, some American citizens found themselves deposited outside the borders of their country.

Many historical events combine genocide and expulsion. For example, in the 1999 Serbian invasion of Kosovo, the initial actions of the Serbs appeared to be genocide. Many Kosovars were simply lined up and shot. But such events also greatly affected survivors, many of whom became immediate refugees as they made their way out of Kosovo and into neighboring Macedonia and Albania. Because Serbian troops interfered relatively little with the refugees, one can only conclude that their expulsion from Kosovo was an equally acceptable outcome. Indeed, genocide appears to have created the expulsion.

These two terms are discussed together because the motives behind their use are identical as are the outcomes for the dominant group. In either case, the dominant group cannot gain wealth from the presence of minority group members. As we will see, one of the main uses of minority groups for the dominant group is to supply inexpensive labor. If the minority cannot or will not work (or if no work currently needs doing), it is generally beneficial to the dominant group if they are removed. Genocide solves the problem neatly, but public opinion may make it a poor alternative. In addition, as was the case with Mexican labor, the minority may be wanted later. When considering long-standing cultural hatreds between Serbs and Kosovars, however, economic concerns may well be of little consequence to a strong ethnic group with a centuries-old vendetta motivating them.

A quick glance at American history shows us that the normal state of affairs involved neither genocide nor expulsion. Centuries of open door immigration coupled with slavery (forced immigration) suggests that minorities were very welcome indeed. When the need for labor decreased in the early twentieth century, the solution was to turn off the faucet of immigration rather than killing or expelling those already here. Nevertheless, both of these "solutions" have occurred around the world far more often than anyone would like, and continue to take place to the present day.

Assimilation vs. the "Melting Pot"

What happens over time to minority groups whose members are neither killed nor expelled? For many years, the experience of immigrants to the United States was described as their joining a melting pot. Popularized by the playwright Israel Zangwill in his play of the same name, the **melting pot** refers to a multicultural society in which members of different groups intermarry and, in so doing, blend their respective cultures into a new culture that had never before existed. Just as a cooked dish receives its taste from the blend of its many ingredients, so too might a society take on a totally new character that would arise from the blend of its members. The melting pot is an appealing and romantic ideal, but it just does not happen.

Families who immigrate often become more acculturated with each new generation.

The melting pot rarely occurs because it is almost never in the interests of dominant group members. As we saw earlier, dominant groups use their power to impose their culture on the societies they control. They do this not only out of ethnocentrism but also for very practical reasons. Consider language. Every society contains more than one version of its primary language (termed dialects), but there is almost always just one prestige version. Mastery of the prestige version opens doors and leads to opportunities. How and when do we learn language? From our parents, as infants. It will be many generations before any immigrant group will produce many parents with this mastery; by contrast, infants in the dominant group learn this prestige version automatically. It is therefore in the dominant group's interests, even looking ahead to descendants, to maintain control over a society's culture, so that it continues to reflect their own. Giving into anything like the melting pot would be giving up these privileges. Since, by definition, a dominant group is in a position to keep the melting pot from occurring, the melting pot will not occur.

What will take place is some form of assimilation. **Assimilation** is the process by which minority group members come to acquire the dominant group's culture and receive acceptance to higher social status within that society. The first half of the definition—the acquisition of the dominant group's culture—is often termed **acculturation.** The second part of the definition calls our attention to the limitations that minority group members face and suggests that the reward for acculturation is either a partial or total removal of those limitations by the dominant group. If all limitations are lifted, the minority group in question ceases to be a minority and can be described as completely assimilated as, for the most part, are German Americans. Many millions immigrated to the United States, but you will not find much evidence of German culture. The people (or their descendants) are still in the United States, but the *group* is gone. All those immigrants ultimately learned to speak English and were rewarded with both social and economic acceptance.

In his study of assimilation, Milton Gordon (1964) renames acculturation—the first stage—**behavioral assimilation.** The second stage, which focuses on dominant group acceptance of the newly acculturated immigrant, he terms **structural assimilation.** He describes behavioral assimilation as being under the control of the minority group; its members have to (1) want to acquire the dominant group's culture and (2) be willing to put in the work necessary to do so. Much of this work can be accomplished by simply having the second generation come along—the first generation born in the host country. These children acquire language and other cultural elements more naturally and more effectively. But some minorities do not want this to happen. Some—the Amish, for example—care very deeply about not assimilating and have gone to great pains to keep their children away from the dominant culture. More often, however, the strength of the dominant culture practically kidnaps minority children. For groups whose members wish to maintain an immigrant culture, both physical and social isolation is necessary.

Gordon describes structural assimilation as being under the control of the dominant group. Because they control the centers of politics, education, and employment in any society, they can choose whether or not to open those doors to any given minority. Behavioral assimilation is prerequisite. A minority group member will not get far in education, for example, unless he or she has acquired at least the basics of the dominant group's language and knowledge. But behavioral assimilation guarantees nothing. If the dominant group dislikes a given minority for any reason whatsoever, all the behavioral assimilation in the world will not result in the integration of that group into the main structures of society.

Gordon (1978) further elaborates on the structural assimilation process by dividing it into two steps. The first step he terms structural assimilation at the level of secondary relationships. Secondary relationships refer to those social relationships we maintain that are more casual and/or businesslike than emotion filled. For example, the people with whom you work, attend PTA meetings, or meet in university classrooms are largely secondary relationships. You may enjoy their company, but it would not be the end of the world if you never saw them again. Gordon describes this first level of structural assimilation as easier for the dominant group to tolerate. Dominant group members may not think highly of a given minority, but they may well be able to work in the same factory with them. We should also note that this level of structural assimilation is probably the most important goal for a minority. Giving up one's culture of assimilation is a painful loss; at the very least, one would expect civil rights and occupational advancement in return.

The second level of structural assimilation is the level of primary relationships. Primary relationships are those social relationships characterized by strong emotional ties and the involvement of one's whole self. In general, these relationships are limited to family relationships and close friends. At this level of acceptance, minority group members will find themselves welcome in country clubs, at private parties, and ultimately as marriage partners. At this final and complete level of assimilation, the minority group may safely be said to have disappeared. We should also note that the members of many minority groups may have no desire for this acceptance. Having achieved political and economic rights at the preceding level, they may prefer to socialize within their own group so as to maintain some cultural distinctiveness, however quietly.

Before leaving Gordon's typology, a word of caution is in order. Real life never fits typologies neatly. In particular, Gordon's levels suggest that minority group members first finish the job of behavioral assimilation before structural assimilation begins. In the real world, some degree of structural assimilation is necessary before behavioral assimilation can get very far. You will not learn English well if you are confined on a reservation, for example. We should also keep in mind that some behavioral assimilation is expensive to acquire and/or requires social acceptance from the dominant group. Consider the following list of cultural skills and knowledge in the United States and consider the difficulties facing a poor immigrant group member in his or her efforts to acquire each item:

1. Knowledge of how to act at a formal dinner party.
2. Skill in playing the game of polo.
3. Computer skills.
4. Knowledge of how to write a formal research paper for a university course requirement.

When you begin thinking in these ways, you will understand why immigrant children who work hard in American schools excel much more rapidly in mathematics than in language arts: far less background knowledge is necessary.

Forms of Pluralism

As with assimilation, pluralism is a term developed to describe what people were already doing. In the coming chapters, you will see examples of it with early German immigrants who wanted to keep to themselves and retain their culture. You will also see it in the distinctive Chinatowns created by Chinese immigrants of "Little Havana" in Miami where many Cuban immigrants live. The idea of immigrant groups retaining both their group boundaries and their cultures while living inside a country dominated by a very different culture is what Horace Kallen had in mind when he wrote about pluralism in early twentieth century America.

Kallen's concern was the future of Jewish Americans. He wanted them to be in America but not of it. The important goal was for Jews to retain a clear sense of their own distinctiveness yet not be penalized for it. **Pluralism,** for Kallen (1915, 1924), meant that cultural minorities could retain their distinctive cultures, but also acquire the dominant group's culture and receive both respect and acceptance from the dominant group. This respect and acceptance often takes the form of special group recognition of the minority. For example, the government might be called upon to protect the group should they face persecution, or perhaps provide special services to that group if their cultural distinctiveness required it. Kallen's conclusion was that pluralism would produce both a more interesting and a more humane society.

The political battleground in pluralism arises over the special group recognition. Invariably, someone or some group will lose while another gains. A classic version of this battle involves the United States Constitution, which created a representative government. The argument revolved around how representation should occur. One solution was to have each state send a set number of representatives to Congress. This would provide equality for states but not for individuals; those people living in populous states would wind up having less clout. Another solution was to have one representative in Congress for every so many people back in a home district. This, of course, would be fair to individuals but would penalize states with small populations. The compromise, of course, was to do both. Think of the United States Senate as pluralism in action where groups (states) get special treatment. And what is so special about states? Nothing, except that we have decided they are. Kallen would have us decide that ethnic *groups* are also important and deserve this recognition.

In action, you can see the political battles that pluralism produces. The French in the Canadian province of Quebec, for example, saw their culture disappearing as English speakers grew in power and numbers in the province. The pluralistic solution from French-Canadians was to eliminate most English language schools in the province and require a knowledge of French for almost all employment. This special group recognition of one group simultaneously damages other groups. In this case, English speakers find that they are no longer qualified for most occupations in Quebec. To the extent that groups do not play the assimilation game but demand rights for their distinctive culture, the dominant group loses. Much of its power, you will recall, comes from its control of culture.

Yet another example of the battleground between pluralism and assimilation is provided by author Timothy Fong in the article that follows this chapter. Fong traces the racial and ethnic history of Monterey Park, California, showing interrelationships among white, Latinos, African Americans, and Asians. An earlier period of general assimilation produced relative harmony; more recent immigration by pluralistically minded Chinese has produced some interesting conflicts and still more interesting group alliances.

Ethnic Nationalism and the Road to Separatism

The previously mentioned dispute between Quebec and the rest of Canada may eventually result in a political separation between the two. Much as the American South attempted to leave the Union in 1861, Quebec may well declare itself an independent state, albeit a civil war in Canada over this issue is extremely unlikely. Nevertheless, nationalism and separatism create major and serious changes in ethnic relations. They are included here because they are best thought of as extreme versions of pluralism (or where pluralism might lead once you head down that road).

Nationalism is the political goal of achieving a state to represent the interests of a particular ethnic group. **Separatism** refers to the actual political process through which such a state is constructed. They are probably the ultimate solutions to ethnic or racial strife. If you return to the definitions of dominant and minority groups, you will note that the entire problem stems from having two ethnic groups but only one government. If one of those ethnic groups, controls that government, the rulings it makes will undoubtedly reflect its interests; the remaining group is therefore a minority. But if you create two governments, each with jurisdiction over two pieces of real estate (one for ethnic group A and the other for ethnic group B), any further disputes between them fall under the realm of international relations and are not in the scope of this book. Still, we have to study the processes by which such changes come about.

As a political movement, ethnic nationalism is always characterized by a glorification of the minority ethnic group's culture coupled with constant reference to the many injustices suffered at the hands of the dominant group. Both of these factors must be present for cultural nationalism to succeed. Members of the minority must acquire enough pride in and recognition of their distinctiveness to draw those ethnic boundaries a little more distinctly in their minds. They also have to be involved in the cause emotionally, because separatism is extremely disruptive and is not a move to be taken lightly.

Separatism can occur in only two ways: either people move or political boundaries move. Israel is probably the best modern example of the former. Jews from all over the world congregated at their ancestral home of Palestine and created a new state to be run by Jews. This was the only assurance, many felt, for Jews avoiding minority status in the future. The problem with this form of separatism is that unoccupied real estate is dwindling. When you move to form a new state, you will have to displace the people currently living there. It should come as no great surprise that Israel has been in a state of war or near war for the full half century of its existence.

The second method of achieving separatism is generally much more agreeable unless you have someone like Abraham Lincoln in the way. Moving political boundaries means that you take what had been one country and slice it up as one would a pie, setting aside this sector for that group and another sector for another group. Modern India and Pakistan were created this way out of the newly independent India following World War II. India at that time was composed of both modern India and Pakistan, but ethnic strife convinced all concerned that the formation of two separate countries was the only solution. This method of separatism can be bloodless, but it is a move never taken lightly. Very few governments look fondly on giving up large sectors of the land they control.

■ Summary

In terms of their species, people are all the same; if we view them as individuals, no two are alike. Between those extremes, certain characteristics of people are often selected to create subgroups. People can be separated according to gender, language, religion, skin color, or virtually any characteristic that varies. When these characteristics are treated as significant in any society, they are social categories.

Many such categories are culturally based. Cultural differences among groups of people elicit attention because the differences are usually numerous and varied, including language, religious beliefs, clothing styles, child-rearing practices, and food preferences. Although all of these are subject to change (and often do change from one generation to the next), they are impossible to ignore when they are present. When such differences create dislike or hostility between groups, those groups may be described as ethnocentric.

Cultural differences are typically described as ethnicity. By most definitions, *ethnicity* includes both cultural distinctiveness and an awareness by group members of that distinctiveness. That awareness is often coupled with an emphasis on ancestral distinctiveness. Boundaries between ethnic groups are in a state of constant change as both cultures and attitudes about group membership change over generations. Ethnic groups can both merge and separate over time. Whichever occurs, the roots of such changes are in the particular social contexts within which people live.

Racial groups are social categories based on presumed biological differences among people. Of the many biological differences that have developed over the years due to the physical separation of different peoples, only certain observable traits are usually selected to define racial differences. Ancestry also creates racial differences, even if the physical traits are not present. From a social standpoint, racial distinctions serve efficient rationalizations or justifications for the mistreatment and subordination of others.

When racial and/or ethnic groups share a society (that is, one government), they often develop unequal power relationships. More powerful groups are dominant groups while the less powerful groups are minority (or subordinate) groups. Dominant groups typically use their power to force the minority to behave in ways beneficial to the dominant group. Depending upon circumstances, very different behaviors may be thrust upon (or opened to) the minority.

When minority groups are "in the way" from the dominant group's perspective, genocide or expulsion may occur. Genocide represents the systematic killing of minority group members; expulsion refers to the forced removal of minority group members from that society's boundaries, either returning them to the country of their original ancestry or anywhere else convenient. Both solutions remove the minority group from the society.

Some level of assimilation is a more common outcome for minorities because their continued presence in society is often useful to the dominant group. Assimilation refers to various degrees of the dominant group's acceptance of the minority, coupled with equally various degrees of inclusion into the society. Behavioral assimilation (or acculturation) refers to attempts by minority group members to acquire the dominant group's culture; structural assimilation measures the degree to which minority members are included in the mainstream society. This inclusion may range from complete inclusion (which generally makes future generations of the minority largely invisible with their culture jettisoned) to only partial inclusion.

Minorities may respond to their circumstances by seeking either pluralism or separatism. Pluralism represents minorities' attempts to maintain their cultural distinctiveness while simultaneously achieving dominant group acceptance of that distinctiveness. Separatism refers to the minority group's efforts to separate politically from the dominant group, either by partitioning the current state into two states or by leaving voluntarily to form a new country elsewhere.

Chapter 13 Reading
The First Suburban Chinatown: The Remaking of Monterey Park, California

Timothy P. Fong

Many immigrants to the United Sates in the past assimilated into American culture. The choice was often made for them, however, by the necessity to make a living. Opportunity typically carried the price of acquiring the host culture. By contrast, some recent immigrants to the United States appear to be following a path of pluralism, finding economic opportunities in strong ethnic communities. Timothy Fong invites us to visit Monterey Park, California—a community near Los Angeles with a complex ethnic history. As you will see, new immigrants from China have created ethnic tension and generated complaints from whites, Latinos, African Americans and Asian Americans whose ancestors long ago assimilated.

A New and Dynamic Community

On an early morning walk to Barnes Memorial Park, one can see dozens of elderly Chinese performing their daily movement exercises under the guidance of an experienced leader. Other seniors stroll around the perimeter of the park; still others sit on benches watching the activity around them or reading a Chinese-language newspaper.

By now children are making their way to school, their backpacks bulging with books. They talk to each other in both English and Chinese, but mostly English. Many are going to Ynez Elementary, the oldest school in town.

When a nearby coin laundry opens its doors for business, all three television sets are turned on: one is tuned to a Spanish novella, another to a cable channel's Chinese newscast, and the third to Bryan Gumbel and the Today show.

Up the street from the park a home with a small stone carved Buddha and several stone pagodas in the well-tended front yard is an attractive sight. The large tree that provides afternoon shade for the house has a yellow ribbon tied around its trunk, a symbol of support for American troops fighting in the Persian Gulf. On the porch an American flag is tied to a crudely constructed flagpole. Next to it, taped to the front door, Chinese characters read "Happiness" and "Long Life" to greet visitors.

These sights and sounds are of interest not because they represent the routine of life in an ethnic neighborhood but because they signal the transformation of an entire city. Monterey Park, California, a rapidly growing, rapidly changing community of 60,000 residents, is located just eight miles east of downtown Los Angeles. An influx of immigrants primarily from Taiwan, Hong Kong, and the People's Republic of China has made Monterey Park the only city in the continental United States the majority of whose residents are of Asian background. According to the 1990 census, Asians make up 56 percent of the city's population, followed by Hispanics with 31 percent, and whites with 12 percent.[1]

In the early 1980s Monterey Park was nationally recognized for its liberal attitude toward newcomers. In fact, on June 13, 1983, *Time* magazine featured a photograph of the city council as representative of a successful suburban melting pot. The caption read, "Middle-class Monterey Park's multiethnic city council: two Hispanics, a Filipino, a Chinese, and, in the rear, an Anglo."[2] Another national public relations coup came in 1985 when the National Municipal League and the newspaper *USA Today* named Monterey Park an "All-America City" for its programs to welcome immigrants to the community. Nicknamed "City with a Heart," it took great pride in being a diverse and harmonious community.[3] But despite these accolades, there were signs that the melting pot was about to boil over.

Tensions had begun to simmer with the arrival in the late 1970s of Chinese immigrants, many of whom were affluent and well educated. New ethnic-oriented businesses sprang up to accommodate them: nearly all the business signs on Atlantic Boulevard, the city's main commercial thoroughfare, conspicuously displayed Chinese characters with only token English translations. In 1985, the same year Monterey Park received its "All-America" award, some three thousand residents signed a petition attempting to get an "Official English" initiative on the municipal ballot; a local newspaper printed an article accusing the Chinese of being bad drivers; and cars displayed bumper stickers asking, "Will the Last American to Leave Monterey Park Please Bring the Flag?"[4]

In April 1986 the two Latinos and the Chinese American on the city council were defeated in their bids for reelection. Voted into office were three white candidates, one a proponent of controlled growth, the other two closely identified with the official-English movement in Monterey Park and the state. In June the new council passed Resolution 9004, which, among other things, called for English to be the official language of the United States of America.[5] Though the resolution was purely symbolic and carried no legal weight, it was immediately branded as a deliberate slap at the city's Chinese and Latino population. Undaunted, the council continued to take controversial actions that critics labeled "anti-Chinese," among them adopting a broad moratorium on new construction and firing the city planning commission that had approved many Chinese-financed developments. But it was rejection of the plans proposed by a Taiwanese group to build a senior housing project that prompted a rare display of public protest by the usually apolitical Chinese community. Four hundred people, mostly elderly Chinese, marched to City Hall carrying American flags and signs reading, "Stop Racism," "We Are Americans Too," and "End Monterey Park Apartheid."[6]

These high-profile controversies, lasting throughout the 1980s were not isolated or incidental cases of cultural conflict. Indeed, events in this community have received publicity in local, national, and even international media; recently, scholars too have become interested in Monterey Park, focusing primarily on ethnic politics and race relations.[7] Close study of the community is important for several reasons. To begin with, Monterey Park's Chinese residents reflect the changing pattern of Chinese immigration nationwide. Chinese newcomers to Monterey Park and elsewhere are not analogous to the historically persecuted and oppressed male laborers who came to this country in the mid-nineteenth century; they are men and women generally much better educated and more affluent than either their Chinese predecessors or their white counterparts.[8] Further, similar demographic and economic changes are occurring not just in Monterey Park but throughout southern California's San Gabriel Valley and Orange County, and in the northern California cities of San Francisco, Mountain View, and San Jose. Increasing Chinese influence is felt in New York's boroughs of Manhattan and Queens (particularly Flushing), in Houston, Texas, and Orlando, Florida. Outside the United States, recent examples of a rapid influx of Chinese people and capital are found in Sydney, Australia, and in Vancouver and Toronto, Canada.[9]

Next, because demographic change and economic development issues have created a complex controversy in Monterey Park, the intersection of ethnic, racial and class conflict shows up quite clearly there. One prominent aspect of the social, economic, and political dynamics in Monterey Park is the popular call for controlled growth combined with a narrow nativist, anti-Chinese anti-immigrant tone in debates that crossed ethnic lines throughout the community. And again, these developments too are relevant nationwide, occurring as they did at a time of increasing concern over immigration: over statistics showing that almost 90 percent of all legal immigrants coming to the United States since 1981 have been from non-European countries,[10] and over the numbers of undocumented immigrants crossing the southern U.S. borders. Documented and undocumented immigrants are rapidly changing the face of many urban centers.

Finally, the conflicts in Monterey Park took place in a period of increased anti-Asian sentiment and violence. Debate occasioned by the large trade deficit between the United States and Japan, suspicion raised by large Asian investments throughout the nation, and envy generated by repeated headlines about Asian superachievers in education all fueled the fires of resentment throughout the 1980s. The 1982 killing of Vincent Chin in Detroit, a widely cited act of anti-Asian violence, prompted a U.S. Commission on Civil Rights investigation.[11] The commission concluded that the upswing in animosity toward Asians reflected a perception that all Asian Americans, immigrants, and refugees are "foreigners" and as such are responsible for the economic woes of this country.[12]

This study of Monterey Park examines the evolution of conflict in the city and locates the beginnings of its recovery from internal strife and unwanted negative media attention. I argue that what was generally seen by the media and outsiders as a "racial" conflict was in fact a class conflict. At the same time, I demonstrate the highly charged saliency of ethnicity and race in the political arena and show how they were used to obscure class interests and to further political interests.

■ Effects of Chinese Immigration

As the influx of Chinese to Monterey Park began, most community leaders and residents compared the newcomers with the American-born Japanese *nisei* who had moved to the community twenty years earlier and quickly assimilated. Together they welcomed the Chinese as yet another group of hardworking people who would naturally be more happy to settle into the established wholesome life of the community.

But because these Chinese were new immigrants, expectations for their immediate assimilation proved unrealistic, and several areas of friction developed—involving business and social organizations, schools, and even supermarkets.

Divided Organizations

When it became obvious that no one could stop the influx of Chinese immigrants to the community, Eli Isenberg wrote a conciliatory column in December 1977 titled, "A Call for Open Arms," which was later translated into Chinese and republished in the [Monterey Park] *Progress:*

> Twenty years ago, Monterey Park became a prestige community for Japanese. At first they settled in Monterey Hills. Today they live throughout and are active in the community. They were invited and accepted invitations to become involved. Today George Ige is our mayor, Keiji Higashi, a past president of chamber of commerce, is president-elect of Rotary. Fifty other Japanese men and women served on advisory boards and in other leadership roles.
>
> Today we must offer the same hand of friendship to our new Chinese neighbors. They should be invited to join service clubs, serve on advisory boards, become involved in little theater and PTA .... To become and stay a good community, there must be a structured effort to assimilate all those who want to become a part of Monterey Park. The city itself should coordinate this effort through the community relations commission and call on all organizations in Monterey Park to play their part in offering a hand of friendship to our new neighbors.[13]

Isenberg may have written partly in response to the formation of an independent Monterey Park Chinese Chamber of Commerce in September 1977—much to the chagrin of the original chamber. A great deal of animosity and criticism were leveled at this separate group for their reluctance to cooperate with established merchants. Shortly after Isenberg's column appeared, a series of meetings between the two groups resulted in the admission of the Chinese organization to the regular city Chamber of Commerce and the formation of a new Chinese American committee. "Helping keep the doors open was Fred Hsieh," recalls Isenberg. "Fred played an important role in maintaining an integrated Monterey Park Chamber of Commerce."[14]

After the proposed "Chinatown theme" was rejected in 1978, however, some dissatisfied Chinese business people resurrected the idea of a separate Chinese business organization, and grumbled about other aspects of their chamber membership. For one thing, few of the Chinese businessmen spoke much English and could understand little of what was being said during meetings. Chinese merchants also resented having to seek chamber approval for business decisions; they wanted more autonomy. Furthermore, unlike Frederic Hsieh, most of the Chinese saw little to be gained by interacting with established merchants who, they felt, were antagonistic. Though they remained in the chamber, the tension was not resolved, and flare-ups periodically occurred.

The Lions Club was even less successful at amalgamating with the newcomers. In the early 1980s an ad hoc group of Chinese asked Lions Club International to charter the Little Taipei Lions Club in Monterey Park. Given the historical prestige of the Lions Club in Monterey Park, its aging and dwindling membership was embarrassed by the formation of a separate club. Although they formally voted to sponsor the Chinese Lions organization in 1985, there was a great deal of reluctance. "The effort to recreate Little Taipei in Southern California," says Joseph Graves, was "unfortunate": "We would infinitely rather they had joined the existing, strong, long-time club with traditions." Graves spoke with pride of the original club's accomplishments, such as "screening all the children's eyes in Monterey Park.... [And] it looks like about 50 percent to 60 percent are Oriental."[15]

The projects of the little Taipei Lions Club have been admirable, as well. Twice a year, during Chinese New Year's Day and on Thanksgiving, it sponsors a free lunch for senior citizens in Monterey Park's Langley Center, and it has raised considerable money for various non-profit organizations in the community—for example, making major donations to the city's public library to purchase Chinese-language books. But Graves objects that the Little Taipei Lions Club just gives out money rather than organizing work projects: "The Lions Club believed in the idea of going down and pouring cement to build a Memorial Bowl, or hammering nails to the roof of the pavilion at the park," he insists. "As older members, we look down our noses at any organization that doesn't get their hands dirty."[16]

In the mid-1980s the Monterey Park Kiwanis Club refused to sponsor a separate Chinese chapter, but one was formed anyway. To persistent rumors that a Chinese Rotary Club would soon be organized as well, long-time rotary member Eli Isenberg responded in 1985: "Apartheid, whether in South Africa or in service clubs in Monterey Park, is a giant step back." In a tone quite different from that of his 1977 "Call for Open Arms," he continued: "Asians do not have a Constitutional right to form service clubs where they will be comfortable with members of their kind. All service clubs, from their international, should ban this happening. Provided, of course, that the Anglo clubs are willing to accept Asians as is the case in Monterey Park."[17]

Little Taipei Lions Club members interviewed during their Thanksgiving day luncheon in 1990, however, denied that they are separatist. While passing out plates of turkey and trimmings to senior citizens, many said they meant no disrespect toward the established Lions Club and had no intention of competing with it in service to the community. As a master of ceremonies in the background called out winning door prize numbers in both English and Chinese, one member asserted that there was plenty of room for both clubs. Another member found nothing surprising about preferring to be with people his own age who spoke his language: "What is wrong with a service club that happens to be sensitive and in touch with the Chinese community?" Angered by any perception that the Little Taipei Lions Club serves only the Chinese, he added: "Look around you. There are lots of different people here. We happily serve them [all].... But we do things for the Chinese in this city that no one else would."[18]

Bilingual Education

The impact of the newcomers on the local schools also generated a great deal of tension. Brightwood Elementary School is located in the heart of one of the most heavily concentrated Asian sections in Monterey Park (census tract 4820.02), and surrounded by well maintained middle-class homes built in the 1950s. In early 1978 a Chinese bilingual education plan initiated at Brightwood School opened what the PTA president called "a bucket of worms."[19]

On January 21, 1974, the United States Supreme Court had ruled in the landmark *Lau v. Nichols* case that the San Francisco Unified School District had failed to provide necessary assistance to nearly 2,000 Chinese American students who did not speak English. The district was ordered to implement "appropriate relief," subject to approval by the court. This precedent-setting case established bilingual education in public schools for students who speak limited or no English.[20]

In 1976 the school district of which Brightwood was a part was cited by the Department of Health, Education and Welfare's Office of Civil Rights for having an inadequate English-as-a-second language (ESL) program. The department ruled that affirmative steps should be taken to correct the language deficiency of many minority children, in order to give them equal educational opportunity. The district complied the following year with a Spanish bilingual program in elementary and secondary school and planned to phase in a Chinese bilingual program in 1978.

The proposal divided the Brightwood School—which was 70 percent Asian at the time—along English- and non-English-speaking lines. The plan called for all students from kindergarten to third grade to be taught in Chinese *and* English. Opposition to the program was led by American-born parents of Japanese and Chinese ancestry who were fearful that implementation would impede their children's educational progress in the future. Some threatened to take their children out of Brightwood and place them in private schools, or move them out of the district entirely. Supporters of the plan, mostly immigrant parents, welcomed bilingual education because they believed it would help their children maintain their native language and provide them with emotional and psychological support and the acceptance they needed within a new environment. A small third group of more moderate parents supported bilingual education but wanted the district to consider a "transitional" program that would instruct children in their native language but at the same time teach them enough English to allow their eventual transfer to a regular classroom.

During meetings to discuss the plan, the debate became intense. "Let them talk English," cried out one angry mother. "Why don't they leave the whole damn school as it is?"[21] Eventually, even supporters of the program asked the school board to delay implementation until the district could provide parents with more information and options. The delay was granted, and the bilingual program at Brightwood School did not start until early the following year. The result of months of meetings by the Brightwood Bilingual Committee turned out to be a much weaker variation of the original plan. Only one second grade class offered Chinese bilingual instruction; other Chinese students were taught English by "traveling teachers" at the parents' request.

Asian Markets

The prominence of Chinese-owned and –operated businesses in town became an even greater source of resentment. Non-Asians in Monterey Park commonly complain that Chinese merchants quickly replaced many established businesses and catered almost exclusively to an Asian and Chinese-speaking clientele. The best examples are food stores and eateries. Chinese have taken over all but two of the town's major chain supermarkets. Bok choy is more common than lettuce in produce departments, and dim sum and tea more readily available than a hamburger and coffee in the restaurants.

The first Asian grocery in Monterey Park was opened in 1978 by Wu Jin Shen, a former stockbroker from Taiwan. Wu's Diho Market proved to be an immediate success because the owner hired workers who spoke both Cantonese and Mandarin, and sold such popular items as preserved eggs and Taiwan's leading brand of cigarettes. Wu built the Diho Market into a chain of stores with 400 employees and $30 million in sales.[22] Likewise, the Hong Kong Supermarket and the Ai Hoa, started in Monterey Park, were so successful that today they operate satellite stores throughout the San Gabriel Valley.

In Monterey Park there are now half a dozen large Asian supermarkets and about a dozen medium-sized stores. Their proprietors also lease out small space to immigrant entrepreneurs who offer videos, newspapers, baked goods, tea, ginseng, and herbs. Together, these enterprises attract Chinese and other Asian residents in large numbers to shop for the kinds of groceries unavailable or overpriced in "American" chain stores: fifty-pound sacks of rice, "exotic" fruits and vegetables, pig parts (arranged in piles of ears, snouts, feet, tails, and innards, as well as buckets of fresh pork blood), live fish, black-skinned pigeon, and imported canned products used in Chinese, Vietnamese, Indonesian, Thai, Philippine, and Japanese menus. In these markets, Chinese is the dominant language of commerce, and much of the merchandise is unfamiliar to non-Asian shoppers.

Growth and Resentment

For many residents, the redevelopment and replacement of businesses in the Garvey-Garfield district, along Atlantic Boulevard, and throughout other areas in the city seemed sudden and dramatic. In January 1979, under the headline "Monterey Park Is Due for Big Facelift," the *Monterey Park Progress* reported that a northern portion of Atlantic Boulevard was set to "be transformed so it's unrecognizable." Construction there was to include the completion of a shopping center, office, and theater complex developed by the Kowin Development Company; ground breaking for a new office building at the northeast corner of Atlantic and Newmark Avenue; and a hillside condominium project on the west side of Atlantic Boulevard. The article went on to state with great anticipation that "a large international concern" planned to "locate its international service center in Monterey Park," that substantial construction in anticipation of new tenants was to be done at McCaslin Industrial Park in the eastern section of town, and that several street and park improvement projects were in the works. In addition, a major city-sponsored Community Redevelopment Agency (CRA) project would erect a new civic center complex and make necessary improvements on a senior center, a school cafetorium, a community center, and the municipal library.[23]

Between the influx of new Chinese immigrants, the infusion of large amounts of capital, the rapid introduction of Chinese-owned and –operated businesses, and the disruptions caused by construction crews tearing up the city and starting new projects, rumblings of discontent among long-time established residents became quite audible.

"I Don't Feel at Home Anymore!"

At first the new Chinese-owned businesses seemed novel, innocuous, even humorous. "The gag was that if it wasn't a bank, it was going to be a real estate office, or another Chinese restaurant," says Lloyd de Llamas.[24] But as these and other Chinese businesses proliferated rapidly from 1978 on—taking over previously established merchants, displaying large Chinese-language signs, and seeming to cater only to a Chinese-speaking clientele—residents became increasingly hostile.

The famous Laura Scudder potato chip factory, converted into a Safeway store in the 1960s, became a bustling Chinese supermarket. Frederic Hsieh bought the Edwards Theater and began showing Chinese-language movies; when people complained he added such English-language films as *Gone with the Wind, Doctor Zhivago,* and *Ryan's Daughter* to the afternoon repertoire. Even the locally revered Garvey Hardware Store was sold to new Chinese owners who divided the premises into mini-shops, relegating the much-reduced hardware department to the back of the building. Kretz Motorcycle, Paris' Restaurant, and the Midtown Pharmacy were similarly redeveloped, engendering resentment among many residents, particularly older whites. For "old-timers" the loss of a familiar business could be akin to the loss of an old friend. "Just a few years before they sold Paris' Restaurant I walked in there for lunch alone," remembers Ed Rodman, "and . . . there wasn't a single person in there that I knew by name! That describes the changes in Monterey Park."[25]

Such losses were compounded when many long-time residents felt they were not welcomed by new businesses because they were not Chinese. Avanelle Fiebelkorn told the *Los Angeles Times:* "I go to the market and over 65 percent of the people there are Chinese. I feel like I'm in another country. I don't feel at home anymore," Emma Fry agreed: "I feel like a stranger in my own town. You can't talk to the newcomers because many of them don't speak English, and their experiences and viewpoints are so different. I don't feel like I belong anymore. I feel like I'm sort of intruding."[26]

Joseph Graves particularly remembers an incident that occurred in the late 1970s when he was a member of the Monterey Park Chamber of Commerce. A group of visiting dignitaries from Taiwan asked the chamber whether a statue of Confucius could be built in one of the parks to remind young Chinese to respect and honor his teachings. Graves had no objection but told them that "the people coming over here ought to be building Statues of Liberty all over town." Graves, who was born in Monterey Park the year the city was incorporated, continues to live there and says he harbors no resentment toward the Chinese. "I ride my bike everywhere and I see all these Chinese people out there taking their walks. They are so warm and friendly. How can you end up with anger? And yet, [if] I look at something they're doing that forces me to change, then I can be temporarily angry. I reserve the right to be temporarily angry as long as I don't nurse grievances."[27]

Others, however, have nursed grievances, and white flight has been the most obvious reaction to the changes in the community. While the Asian population in Monterey Park has grown and the Latino population has remained relatively stable, the white population has plummeted. In 1960 the 32,306 white residents made up 85 percent of the population; by 1990 the number of white had dropped to 16,245, or just 12 percent. When former Monterey Park resident Frank Rizzo moved out, he cited the large condominium complexes on either side of his house and the people in them as reasons he could no longer stay. Prior to the influx of Chinese, Rizzo said, his neighborhood had been a quiet and friendly block of mostly single-family homes with expansive yards. But his new neighbors lived in large extended families in cramped quarters, spoke little English, and seemed unwilling to give up their traditions and settle into an American way of life. Rizzo, who sold his home to a Chinese developer, was emphatic about leaving Monterey Park: "What I might do is hang a little American flag on my truck and drive through town on my way out and wave goodbye to all my old friends.... I'm moving far away from here."[28]

Latinos in Monterey Park too were concerned that they were losing the integrated community they thought they'd moved into. David Barron has lived in the city since 1964 and raised his family there. Previously, he attended nearby East Los Angeles Community College and California State University, Los Angeles. He still remembers when Monterey Park was referred to as the "Mexican Beverly Hills." Fluent in Spanish and proud of his heritage, Barron thought he had found the ideal integrated community. He is still involved in many of the city's social and civic activities and has no immediate plans to move, but he misses the diversity he initially found in the town. "I would like to see a balance maintained," he explains. "I cannot live in a mono-ethnic community. I wouldn't want to live in an all-Hispanic . . . or all-Chinese . . . or all-white community. I want to live in a mixed community."[29]

Similar sentiments were expressed by Fernando Zabala, a hair stylist who grew up in East Los Angeles and also found Monterey Park a stepping-stone out of the barrio. "It was very important that my children grow up in a racially diverse community," Zabala said. "When we moved to Monterey Park, we had a little bit of everybody: whites, blacks, Latinos, and some Chinese and Japanese. But we lost that mix. In my neighborhood alone, it went from twenty-five Latino families to three."[30] Unlike Barron, Zabala sold his house and moved out.

One woman, who asked not to be identified, said that she was one of the first Mexican Americans to move into a new hillside housing tract in Monterey Park in the late 1950s and that she had worked very hard to integrate into the community. Like many whites, she expressed anxiety about the rapid change in the commercial areas in town: "It wasn't like one business changing at a time, it was like two or three at a time. When they put in the Diho [supermarket], that right away changed the appearance of Atlantic Boulevard." She recalled with particular sadness a Mexican restaurant she and her mother used to frequent. This small restaurant, greatly appreciated for its home-style cooking and family atmosphere, was forced to close when new owners bought the property. "The owner was very upset, and she put [up] a big sign.... 'I'm not leaving my friends because I want to, but the mall has been bought and my rent has been raised and I cannot afford it.' Things like that you would get upset about."[31]

Like the Latinos who had settled in Monterey Park, long-time Asian American residents had lived their entire lives believing in the "American Dream" that proclaimed just rewards for hard work and initiative. It was an affront to their sensibilities to see so many newcomers acquire the fruits of a material society seemingly without having to struggle. The newcomer Chinese were simply not playing by the rules of assimilation: they bought property, started businesses and banks, and built shopping malls as soon as they arrived—and many of them didn't even speak English! John Yee—whose great-great-grandfather had come to California during the gold rush, whose great-grandfather died building the transcontinental railroad, and whose grandfather and father owned a Chinese laundry business that served steel factory workers in Midland, Pennsylvania—is particularly articulate in this regard. "When I first came to L.A., I lived in Chinatown, went into the service, came out, worked in a lot of jobs, and step by step I moved to Monterey Park. It took how many years? Thirty, forty years? It seems like these immigrants . . . want to live in Monterey Park as soon as they get off the boat. Not the boat, now they come by airplane. Give them another forty years, they'll be in Beverly Hills. I won't ever get to that point.... Maybe I'm jealous like everybody else."[32]

The resentment of the older Latinos and Asian Americans who had experienced racial segregation and witnessed the civil rights struggles of the 1960s also stemmed from a feeling that Monterey Park's new Chinese immigrants were taking for granted the equality won by the struggles of others. Yee says: "I don't mind the people too much, don't get me wrong; I am of Chinese descent. But the thing is, you get these people with this attitude.... they think [everything] was like this all the time. It wasn't. I hear people say, 'China got strong and now the United States and the rest of the world has more respect for us.' Maybe so, but . . . if it wasn't for some of these guys [people of color born in the United States] who squawked about it, went into the service, these changes wouldn't happen. You got the blacks and Mexicans, they all helped change the government.... That attitude [among new Chinese immigrants] just burns me up."[33]

Particularly for Asian Americans born in the United States, the appearance of Chinese immigrants raised questions about their assumed assimilation and acceptance into American society. "When there were just Japanese people in Monterey Park, it was no problem because we were just like them [whites]," explains long-time resident Kei Higashi. "But now all of a sudden [with the arrival of the new immigrant Chinese] when we walk into a place and start talking perfect English, they [non-Asians] look at us like we're some foreign creature," he laughs. "That's what happened in Monterey Park."[34]

In the middle of all this are many of the Chinese immigrant professionals, who found themselves lumped together with the development- and business-oriented newcomers. Many express appreciation for the large Chinese population that makes them feel welcome, but at the same time, they say, had they wanted to live in a crowded, exclusively Chinese environment, they never would have left home. This is the case for Dr. Frances Su, who moved to Monterey Park in 1971, after she was accepted in the doctoral program at the University of Southern California. Born and educated in China, Wu lived in Taiwan for four years following the Communist takeover; in 1953 she went to Canada to earn a master's degree from McGill University, then spent fifteen years in New York working in the Child Welfare Department.

When Wu came to southern California, she changed her social work specialty to gerontology, and shortly after earning her Ph.D. she started the Golden Age Village, a retirement center located in Monterey Park. Although the project is open to all elderly people who qualify, Wu told the *Monterey Park Progress,* "My motivation was to develop a social program for elderly Chinese and we selected Monterey Park because of its growing Chinese population," as well as its uncongested, small-town atmosphere.[35] The overall design of the Golden Age Village is obviously Asian, with its curved roofs and a courtyard that features a babbling brook surrounded by a decorative Oriental-style garden. The majority of residents are retired Chinese, many of whom speak little or no English, and the communal food garden grows bok choy and Chinese parsley among other vegetables. But the serene environment that Wu found in Monterey Park and recreated at the Golden Age Village is threatened by what she considers too much growth too fast. "I would rather keep this community a bedroom community," she says. "For retired people, we like a quiet environment.... People describe Monterey Park as 'Little Taipei,' but Taipei is horrible. I don't want Monterey Park to be like that."[36]

Notes

[1]U.S. Bureau of the Census, "Monterey Park, City, California," 1990 Census of Population and Housing Summary Tape File 1, May 13, 1991.

[2]Kurt Anderson, "The New Ellis Island: Immigrants from all Over Change the Beat, Bop and Character of Los Angeles," *Time,* June 13, 1983, p. 21.

[3]Several newspapers have incorrectly cited this honor as the "All-American" award. According to the official entry form, the term is "All-America."

[4]Mike Ward, "Language Rift in 'All-American City,'" *Los Angeles Times,* November 13, 1965; Gordon Dillow, "Why Many Drivers Tremble on the Streets of Monterey Park," *Los Angeles Herald,* July 8, 1985; "English Spoken Here, OK?" *Time,* August 25, 1981.

[5]Monterey Park City Council Minutes, June 2, 1986.

[6]Mike Ward, "Racism Charged over Monterey Park Vote," *Los Angeles Times,* July 15, 1986; Ray Babcock, "'Sanctuary' Resolution Stays," *Monterey Park Progress,* July 16, 1986; Evelyn Hsu, "Influx of Asians Stirs Up L.A. Area's 'Little Taipei,'" *San Francisco Chronicle,* August 1, 1986.

[7]See Jose Calderon, "Latinos and Ethnic Conflict in Suburbia: The Case of Monterey," *Latino Studies Journal* 1 (May 1990): 23-32; John Horton, "The Politics of Ethnic Change: Grass-Roots Response to Economic and Demographic Restructuring in Monterey Park, California," *Urban Geography* 10 (1989): 578-592; Don Nakanishi, "The Next Swing Vote? Asian Pacific Americans and California Politics," in *Racial and Ethnic Politics in California,* ed. Bryan O. Jackson and Michael D. Preston (Berkeley: University of California, Institute of Governmental Studies, 1991), pp. 25–54; Mary Pardo, "Identity and Resistance: Latinas and Grass-Roots Activism in Two Los Angeles Communities" (Ph.D. diss., University of California, Los Angeles, 1990); Leland Saito, "Politics in a New Demographic Era: Asian Americans in Monterey Park, California" (Ph.D. diss., University of California, Los Angeles, 1992); Charles Choy Wong, "Monterey Park: A Community in Transition" in *Frontier of Asian*

American Studies, ed. Gail M. Nomura, Russel Endo, Stephen H. Sumida, and Russell Leong (Pullman: Washington State University Press, 1989), pp. 113–126; Charles Choy Wong, "Ethnicity, Work, and Community: The Case of Chinese in Los Angeles" (Ph.D. diss., University of California, Los Angeles, 1979).

[8]U.S. Commission on Civil Rights, *The Economic Status of Americans of Asian Descent: An Exploratory Investigation,* Publication no.95 (Washington, D.C.: Clearinghouse, 1988), p. 109.

[9]See Marshall Kilduff, "A Move to Ease Racial Tensions in S.F. Neighborhood," *San Francisco Chronicle,* August 11, 1986; Tim Fong, "The Success Stereotype Haunts Asian-Americans," *Sacramento Bee,* July 4, 1987; David Reyes, "'Asiantown' Plan Taking Shape in Westminster," *Los Angeles Times,* March 22, 1987; "Chinese Enclaves Abound in New York," *Asian Week,* October 3, 1986; Kevin P. Helliker, 'Chinatown Sprouts in and near Houston with Texas Flavor," *Wall Street Journal,* February 18, 1983; "$50 Million 'Orlando Chinatown' Features Hotel-Retail Complex and 30 Restaurants," *AmeriAsian News,* March-April 1987; Russell Spurr, "Why Asians Are Going Down Under," *San Francisco Chronicle,* December 7, 1988; Howard Witt, "British Columbia's Anti-Asian Feelings Suddenly Surface," *Chicago Tribune,* February 5, 1989.

[10]U.S. Immigration and Naturalization Service, 1989 *Statistical Yearbook of the Immigration and Naturalization Service* (Washington D.C.: Government Printing Office, 1990), p. xiv.

[11]In June 1982 Vincent Chen, a Chinese American draftsman, was beaten to death by a Chrysler Motors supervisor and his stepson. One of the assailants was alleged to have yelled, "It's because of you motherfuckers we're out of work." The two men later confessed to the crime, were fined $3,780 each, and placed on three years' probation. Neither spent a day in jail. See Ronald Takaki, *Strangers from a Different Shore* (Boston, Little, Brown, 1989), p.481.

[12]U.S. Commission on Civil Rights, *Recent Activities against Citizens and Residents of Asian Descent:* Publication no. 88 (Washington, D.C.: Clearinghouse, 1986), p. 3.

[13]Eli Isenberg, "A Call for Open Arms," *Monterey Park Progress,* December 7, 1977.

[14]Interview with Eli Isenberg.

[15]Interview with Joseph Graves.

[16]Ibid.

[17]Eli Isenberg, "It Seems to Me," *Monterey Park Progress,* February 27, 1985.

[18]Fieldnotes from November 20, 1990.

[19]Art Wong, "Bilingual Plan Opens Up 'Buckets of Worms,'" *Monterey Park Progress,* June 7, 1978.

[20]L. Ling-chi Wang, "Lau v. Nichols: History of a Struggle for Equal and Quality Education," *Amerasia Journal* 2 (1974): 16-46.

[21]Wong, "Bilingual Plan."

[22]See Andrew Tanzer, "Little Taipei," *Forbes,* May 6, 1985, pp. 68–71; Mike Ward, "Cities Report Growth—and Some Losses—from Asian Business," *Los Angeles Times,* April 19, 1987; and Randye Hoder, "A Passion For Asian Foods," *Los Angeles Times,* June 5, 1991.

[23]Malcolm Schwartz, "Monterey Park is Due for Big Facelift in 1979," *Monterey Park Progress,* January 3, 1979.

[24]Interview with Lloyd de Llamas by Tim Fong, for the Monterey Park Oral History Project, sponsored by the Monterey Park Historical Heritage Commission, March 29, April 13, and May 11, 1990.

[25]Interview with Ed Rodman by Tim Fong, for the Monterey Park Oral History Project, sponsored by the Monterey Park Historical Heritage Commission, October 17 and 24, 1990.

[26]Mark Arax, "Selling Out, Moving On," *Los Angeles Times,* April 12, 1987.

[27]Interview with Joseph Graves.

[28]Arax, "Selling Out, Moving On."

[29]Interview with David Barron by Tim Fong, for the Monterey Park Oral History Project, sponsored by the Monterey Park Historical Heritage Commission, October 9, 1990.

[30]Mark Arax, "Nation's 1st Suburban Chinatown," *Los Angeles Times,* April 6, 1987.

[31]Fieldnotes from August 17, 1990.

[32]Interview with John Yee by Tim Fong, for the Monterey Park Oral History Project, sponsored by the Monterey Park Historical Heritage Commission, May 31 and June 4, 1990.

[33]Ibid.

[34]Interview with Kei Higashi by Tim Fong, for the Monterey Park Oral History Project, sponsored by the Monterey Park Historical Heritage Commission, May 7 and 30, 1990.

[35]Second Housing Project for Seniors on Horizon," Monterey Park Progress, Sept. 13, 1978.

[36]Interview with Dr. Frances Wu by Tim Fong, for the Monterey Park Oral History Project, sponsored by the Monterey Park Historical Heritage Commission, June 22, and July 6, 1990.

References

Anderson, Kurt, "The New Ellis Island: Immigrants from All Over Change the Beat, Bop and Character of Los Angeles." *Time,* June 13, 1983.

Calderon, Jose. "Latinos and Ethnic Conflict in Suburbia: The Case of Monterey Park" *Latino Studies Journal* 1 (May 1990): 23–32.

Horton, John. "The Politics of Ethnic Change: Grass-Roots Responses to Economic and Demographic Restructuring in Monterey Park, California." *Urban Geography* 10 (1989): 578–592.

Monterey Park, City of. City Council *Minutes,* June 2, 1986.

Nakanishi, Don. "The Next Swing Vote? Asian Pacific Americans and California Politics." In *Racial and Ethnic Politics in California,* ed. Bryan O. Jackson and Michael D. Preston, pp. 25–54. Berkeley: University of California, Institute of Governmental Studies, 1991.

Pardo, Mary. "Identity and Resistance: Latinas and Grass-Roots Activism in Two Los Angeles Communities." Ph.D. diss., University of California, Los Angeles, 1990.

Saito, Leland. "Politics in a New Demographic Era: Asian Americans in Monterey Park, California," Ph.D. diss., University of California, Los Angeles, 1992.

Takaki, Ronald. *Strangers from a Different Shore. A History of Asian Americans.* Boston: Little, Brown, 1989.

Tanzer, Andrew. "Little Taipei." *Forbes,* May 6, 1985.

U.S. Bureau of the Census. *Census of Population and Housing Summary Tape File 1* (STF1): Monterey Park City, California, 1990.

U.S. Commission on Civil Rights. *The Economic Status of Americans of Asian Descent.* Publication no. 95. Washington, D.C.: Clearinghouse, 1988.

_________. *Recent Activities against Citizens and Residents of Asian Descent.* Publication no. 88. Washington, D.C. Clearinghouse, 1986.

U.S. Immigration and Naturalization Service. *1989 Statistical Yearbook of the Immigration and Naturalization Service.* Washington, D.C.: Government Printing Office, 1990.

Wang, L. Ling-chi. "Lau v. Nichols: History of a Struggle for Equal and Quality Education." *Amerasia Journal* 2 (1974): 16–46.

Wong, Charles Choy. "Ethnicity, Work, and Community: The Case of Chinese in Los Angeles." Ph.D. diss., University of California, Los Angeles, 1979.

_________. "Monterey Park: A Community in Transition:" In *Frontiers of Asian American Studies,* ed. Gail M. Nomura, Russell Endo, Stephen H. Sumida, and Russell Leong, pp. 113–126. Pullman: Washington State University Press, 1989.

Newspapers

AmerAsian News, March-April 1987.
Asian Week, October 3, 1986.
Chicago Tribune, February 5, 1989.
Los Angeles Herald, July 8, 1985.
Los Angeles Times, November 13, 1985-June 5, 1991.
Monterey Park Progress, December 7, 1977-July 16, 1986.
Sacramento Bee, July 4, 1987.
San Francisco Chronicle, August 11, 1986-December 7, 1988.
Wall Street Journal, February 18, 1983.

14 chapter

Minority Status: Age, Gender, and Sexuality

IN THIS CHAPTER, YOU WILL LEARN

- *that people are also treated unequally on the basis of such ascribed characteristics as age, gender, and sexuality;*
- *that the United States is becoming a society with an increasing proportion of elderly people;*
- *of the existence and meaning of ageism;*
- *that women are treated unequally;*
- *how we acquire gender roles;*
- *why sexism is an ideology that is detrimental to both men and women;*
- *that sexual orientation is also subject to differential treatment.*

Societies differentiate among their members not only according to wealth, power, and status, not only according to race, ethnicity, and religion but also according to age, gender, and sexual orientation. In every society, each age group and each gender is assigned different duties, responsibilities, privileges, and roles. Some of this differentiation is a result of common sense. In the United States, young people cannot drive before they are 16, they cannot vote before they are 18, and they cannot run for the Senate before they are 30. These age restrictions have been set by law on the basis of the belief that people are too immature to engage in these activities at younger ages. On a more informal basis, a person in his seventies would hardly be expected to work on the construction of a 30-story office building, nor has it been thought fit, throughout human history, to have women in charge of protecting societies by going to war. Women's biological role in reproduction made them too precious to be allowed to be killed in war. Similarly, prohibitions against homosexuality can also be thought of as based on a societal fear that not enough new members will be produced if sex is not strictly heterosexual. In other words, to a certain degree, age, gender, and sexuality differentiation is based on what works best for individuals and society. Still, differentiation and the consequent stratification always imply inequality, and it is this factor that this chapter examines.

The Aging Society

The elderly—people aged 65 and older—constituted about 12.3 percent of the American population in the year 2003. This figure—35.9 million—is expected to rise to 72 million by 2030, when one in five people will be age 65 or older. The "old old" segment of the population—people 85 years and over—is growing at an even faster rate. In 2003, they accounted for 4.7 percent of all Americans, but projections show this percentage increasing rapidly by 2030 when the baby boomers begin to move into this age group. The Census Bureau projects that this population could grow to nearly 21 million by 2050 (Figure 14.1). Finally, in 2003 there were about 50,000 persons age 100 or older, and their number is also projected to grow quickly, provided that the dramatic gains in longevity continue. The problems of the elderly, then, are everyone's concern. On the other hand, because of advances in medicine, health care, and nutrition, the elderly are really becoming "younger" in the sense not only that they can expect to live much longer than previous generations but also that they can do so in reasonably good health.

Age is an ascribed characteristic according to which we are assigned a status. Unlike gender, however, which is a permanent status, age is transitional: we are constantly getting older, thus our chronological age and the consequent statuses change. At each stage of the transition, we must be socialized to age-appropriate behavior, and our relationship relative to the dimensions of stratification (how we fit into the stratification system) continually shifts.

We view aging and the elderly as problematic because our society is unable or unwilling to provide some of its members with satisfactory roles at certain ages. The reason is that industrial and postindustrial societies have tended to devalue the roles of the elderly, whereas the agrarian and other preindustrial societies assign honorable and prestigious roles to them. (Not all of them, however. The Tiwi of North Australia used to treat their old quite brutally, going so far as to bury alive—with only their heads uncovered—old women who could not care for themselves and leaving them to starve to death.)

Theoretical Framework

Social gerontologists—scientists who study the aging process as it affects the individual and society—examine aging from the perspective of a number of theoretical frameworks. Among the best known, **disengagement theory** posits that there is a reciprocal process of withdrawal occurring between an aging individual and society. An elderly person willingly withdraws from society because of awareness of his or her diminished capacities and impending death. And society withdraws from the aging person to allow a younger person to occupy his or her former statuses. The society's stability is thus maintained, and social roles are passed peacefully from one generation to the next. **Modernization theory** assumes that the status of older people declines as the society of which they are a part becomes more modern. Industrial and

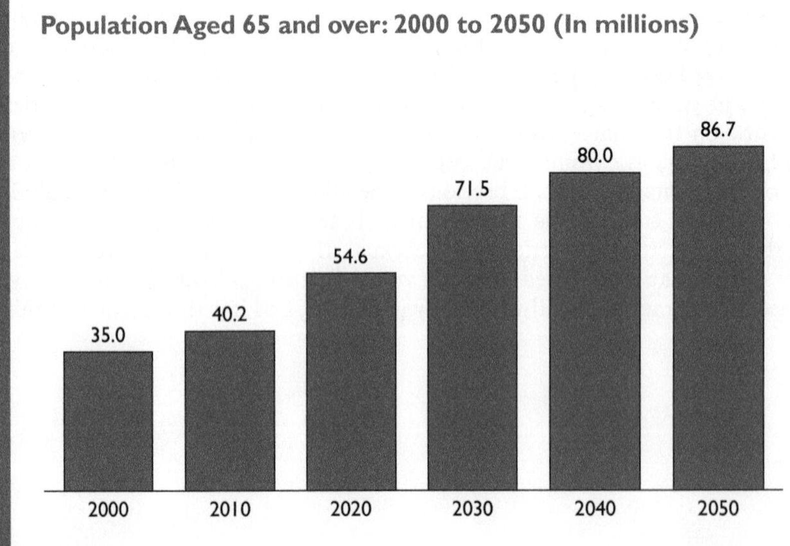

FIGURE 14.1

Note: The reference population for these data is the resident population.

Sources: 2000, U.S. Census Bureau, 2001, Table PCT 12; 2010 to 2050, U.S. Census Bureau, 2004.

postindustrial societies like the United States stress youth and the importance of highly skilled occupations for which the elderly are not prepared. Hence, the elderly lose status.

Activity theory, the direct opposite of disengagement theory, maintains that the elderly person who remains active, replacing old roles with new ones that also require interaction with others, is best adjusted and most ready to accept the physical changes that lead eventually to death.

Disagreeing with both disengagement and activity theories, the **conflict perspective** focuses on the disadvantaged elderly and stresses political and economic factors that impinge on them and force them into a condition of dependence. An extension of the conflict view is **exchange theory**, in which the elderly are seen as being in a subservient position in American society. They lack the social and material resources that would make them valuable to others; therefore, they lose status (Dowd, 1980a, 1980b).

A Growing Minority. Social scientists also look at the elderly as a minority group because they have unequal access to the rewards of society and experience prejudice and discrimination. Moreover, a definite ideology directed against them, ageism, is easily discerned in the society. Specialists in gerontology use all these elements to examine the conditions of the elderly in society.

Ageism

The ideology of **ageism**, whose existence can be readily picked up in even casual conversation, asserts, essentially, that the young are superior to the old. It provides the justification for prejudice and discrimination against the elderly in economic, political, and social areas.

One need not go far to uncover evidence of prejudice and discrimination against the elderly in society. First, the elderly are highly visible: they are wrinkled, their hair is white or they are bald, and many walk haltingly with canes or stooped over. Like most minorities, they are stereotyped: as senile, unproductive, poor, lonely, living in nursing homes and institutions, having no interest in or capacity for sex, being set in their ways and unable to change, and feeling miserable (Palmore, 1977). Although these stereotypes have some basis in fact, they can be proved to be mostly false.

Health. *Senescence*, or the process of growing old, consists of *primary aging*, a biological process that starts early in life and affects all body systems, and *secondary aging*, which results not from natural aging alone but from disease, abuse, and/or disuse (Horn & Meer, 1987, 81). Primary aging affects all persons, and speed, strength, endurance, perception, and sensation eventually decline. However, these difficulties develop gradually and usually do not affect functioning until the eighties. In fact, in 2003 around 73 percent of older persons assessed their health as excellent or very good, compared to only 66.6 percent of persons aged 18 to 64. Nonetheless, most older persons have at least one chronic condition, and many have multiple conditions. Compared to the young, the elderly are less likely to suffer from acute or short-term diseases, such as the common cold and infectious diseases, but are more likely to suffer from chronic or long-term diseases, such as hypertension, heart disease, arthritis, cancer, or emphysema. The latter pose serious problems principally to those in their eighties. In addition, more than half of the older population report having at least one disability. Disabilities may be physical or nonphysical, and many are minor, but they increase in severity with age. About 80 percent of the elderly report at least one chronic health condition, and about one-half of people 80 and over have more than one disability and need assistance. Curiously, health care costs decrease as a person ages, because the oldest of old—those 85 and over—are fittest and tend to die rapidly of pneumonia or multiple-organ failure (Angier, 1995, B5).

Senility, involving serious memory loss, confusion, and loss of the ability to reason, is not a natural consequence of aging. In fact, such disorders occur in at most 20 percent of 80-year-olds, while only 10 percent of elderly Americans show mild loss of memory. The symptoms of senility may derive from other causes, including a reaction to drugs. However, about 2.5 million Americans do suffer from neurological diseases, particularly Alzheimer's, an incurable disease of the brain.

TABLE 14.1 Labor Force Participation Rates (percent) of Men Age 55 and over, by Age Group, Annual Averages, 2004–2005

	Men			
Year	**55–61**	**62–64**	**65–69**	**70 and over**
2004	74.4	50.8	32.6	12.8
2005	74.7	52.5	33.6	13.5

Few of the elderly are incapacitated to the point of being relegated to nursing homes. As of 2002, 53.6 percent of older persons lived with a spouse. Many more men than women live with their spouses: approximately 74 percent of older men and 54 percent of older women aged 65 to 74. Moreover, the proportion living with their spouse decreases with age, especially for women. Of women 75 and older, only about 29 percent lived with a spouse in a family setting in 2002. About 30 percent of the elderly, 7.9 million women and 2.6 million men, lived alone. With advanced age, the frequency of living alone increases: among women 75 and over, half lived alone in 2002. At the same time, almost 400,000 grandparents 65 years old and older had primary responsibility for their grandchildren (Department of Health and Human Services, Administration on Aging. A Profile of Older Americans: 2006).

As noted, only a minority of the elderly live in nursing homes: in 2000, only 1.56 million, representing 4.5 percent of the over 65-year-old population did. Again, however, this proportion increases with age: for those 85 and over the percentage rises to 18.2. An additional 5 percent of the elderly live in some type of senior housing with supportive services available.

Work and Retirement. Although in the past the elderly continued to be employed, sometimes until they died, in 2007 approximately 25,000 Americans 55 years and older were in the labor force (Table 14.1). Interestingly, although labor force participation of men 65 and older has decreased steadily, the participation rate for women of this age group has been rising slightly, to 11 percent since 1988. In addition, 21 percent of workers over 65 were self-employed in 1999, compared to only 7 percent of younger workers (Bureau of Labor Statistics web site, **http://stats.bls.gov/news/release/empsit.t06.htm**).

One reason for the decline in employment for men is that industrial and postindustrial economies need highly skilled and educated workers, which places the elderly at a disadvantage with respect to younger workers—their skills tend to be obsolete. Ageism also promotes the idea that older workers are not as productive as younger ones. In reality, although the elderly experience a decline in perception and reaction speed, they perform as well as if not better than younger workers. The elderly tend to be consistent in their output, change jobs less frequently, have fewer accidents, and have a lower absenteeism rate than younger workers (Giniger, Dispenzieri, & Eisenberg, 1983). The Age Discrimination Act of 1967 protects elderly workers to a certain extent, especially the amendment prohibiting forced retirement before the age of 70. Individuals are not all alike in their readiness to retire. For some, retirement may indeed be welcome; for others, it may cause feelings of uselessness and of being dispensable, leading to depression, and in acute cases, to a wish for early death. The higher the social status of the worker, the higher the job satisfaction and the less likelihood of early retirement (Atchley, 1982). After retirement, the higher-status workers also tend to continue to be involved in their professions. The bottom line, however, is the amount of income during retirement: if that is adequate, most persons choose to retire.

Finances. Although many elderly people—particularly women and minorities—find themselves living in straitened circumstances, the majority do not live in poverty. In 2003, the median household income of persons 65 and over was $36,006. However, it was only $17,359 for male householders living alone and

The elderly do not have to stop being productive. This woman, helping children learn to read, feels much happier being useful, while the children are less likely to accept the stereotype of the elderly as useless.

only $13,775 for female householders living alone. Of course, wealth is apportioned very unequally in this age group. For instance, for households containing families headed by persons 65 and over, the median income was $35,219 for whites, $26,599 for African Americans, and $22,512 for Hispanics (U.S. Bureau of the Census, *Current Population Reports* 2003). Still, some 3.5 million of the elderly 65 and over lived in poverty, with a poverty rate of 10.1 percent (Figures 14.2– 14.3).

Not only in the United States but also in other wealthy countries, the elderly live quite well, according to a study of pensioners that showed that their disposable income is 80 percent of the income of working people in their later years of work. In some countries, retirees have even more disposable income than younger working people: in Germany, for instance, the overall income of persons over 60 is 25 percent higher than that of younger Germans (*The Economist*, 2004, 6).

Median Household Money Income for Older Households by Household Type and Age of Householder: 2003

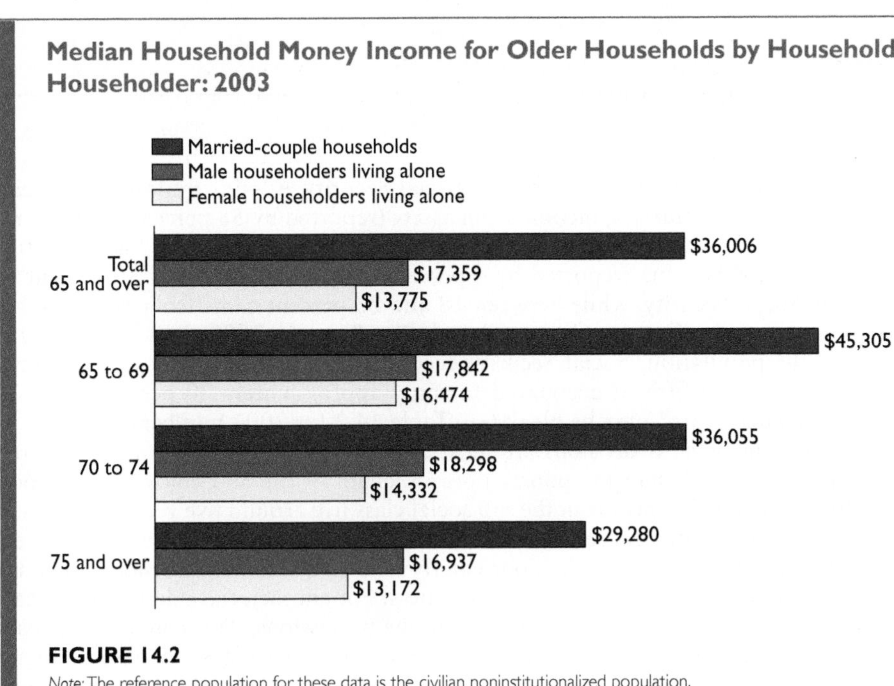

FIGURE 14.2

Note: The reference population for these data is the civilian noninstitutionalized population.
Source: U.S. Census Bureau, 2004, Table HINC-02.

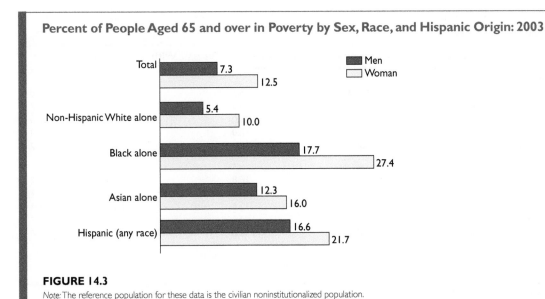

Percent of People Aged 65 and over in Poverty by Sex, Race, and Hispanic Origin: 2003

Men
Woman

Total 7.3 12.5

Non-Hispanic White alone 5.4 10.0

Black alone 17.7 27.4

Asian alone 12.3 16.0

Hispanic (any race) 16.6 21.7

FIGURE 14.3

Note: The reference population for these data is the civilian noninstitutionalized population.
Source: U.S. Census Bureau, 2004, Table POV01.

TABLE 14.2 Aggregate Income for the Population Age 65 and over, by Source and Income Quintile (percent), 2004

Income Source	Lowest Fifth	Second Fifth	Third Fifth	Fourth Fifth	Highest Fifth
Total	100.0	100.0	100.0	100.0	100.0
Social security	82.6	83.4	66.6	47.5	18.9
Asset income	2.3	3.8	6.0	8.4	17.8
Pensions	3.5	7.0	16.6	25.7	21.2
Earnings	1.2	2.8	7.1	15.7	40.1
Public assistance	8.4	1.6	0.9	0.2	0.1
Other	2.0	1.5	2.7	2.6	1.9

Reference population: These data refer to the civilian noninstitutionalized population.

Source: U.S. Census Bureau, Current Population Survey, Annual Social and Economic Supplement.

In 2002, the major sources of income reported by the Social Security Administration were Social Security (reported by 91 percent of the elderly); income from assets (reported by 58 percent), public and private pensions (reported by 40 percent), and earnings (reported by 22 percent), public assistance (reported by 5 percent), and veterans' benefits (reported by 4 percent). The elderly derived 38 percent of their aggregate income from Social Security, while between 18 and 23 percent came from pensions, assets, and earnings (U.S. Bureau of the Census, *Current Population Reports*, 2002, P60-221). But for those in the lowest fifth of the population, Social Security accounted for most of their total income, while for those in the highest income fifth, it accounted for only approximately 20 percent. For too many Americans, then, the "golden years" may be bleak (see Table 14.2 for 2004 numbers).

Interestingly, but not surprisingly, class divisions are most distinct in old age, in the sense that the wealthier elderly are so much better off than the poorer ones in length of life and enjoyment of good health and the good life. In most countries, people in the top social class live around five years longer than those in the bottom class (in Britain, the difference is 15 years). There are differences in life expectancy, especially in healthy life expectancy. For one thing, the poor elderly tend to live in neighborhoods that are crime-ridden and unfriendly, leading to their isolation and loneliness. For another, the elderly poor generally lack much education and did not spend their working life in the professions. This condition appears to lower their ability to remember things and solve puzzles: people with university degrees at 75 do better at those activities than people with little education in their 50s. Mortality rates for white American men with the highest levels of education were about 10 percent lower than for white men with the least education, and the difference in the period 1990–1997 rose to 70 percent (*The Economist*, 2004, 7). Those with little education also tend to live unhealthier lives: they smoke, are overweight, and do not exercise. Finally,

TABLE 14.3 Living Arrangements of the Population Age 65 and over, by Sex and Race and Hispanic Origin (percent), 2004

Selected Characteristic	With Spouse	With Other Relatives	With Nonrelatives	Alone
Men				
Total	72.4	6.1	2.7	18.8
Non-Hispanic white alone	74.3	4.5	2.4	18.7
Black alone	55.6	13.0	4.9	26.6
Asian alone	77.0	12.0	1.1	9.9
Hispanic (of any race)	64.4	16.3	3.6	15.7
Women				
Total	41.6	16.8	1.9	39.7
Non-Hispanic white alone	43.7	13.3	1.9	41.1
Black alone	23.9	32.6	2.2	41.4
Asian alone	47.1	24.8	1.7	26.7
Hispanic (of any race)	37.1	36.0	2.1	24.8

Reference population: These data refer to the civilian noninstitutionalized population.

Source: U.S. Census Bureau, Current Population Survey, Annual Social and Economic Supplement.

the perception of where one is in the pecking order (the stratification system of the society) is also important. Those who rank themselves as being low in status and not in control of their lives suffer worse health than those who rank themselves higher and in control of their lives.

Widowhood. Loneliness and other negative consequences follow the death of a spouse, particularly of a husband, for it seems that men adjust to widowhood a little better than women (however, there are five times more widows than widowers; see Table 14.3 on page 320 for living arrangements). Men tend to remarry more often, are members of more organizations, know more people from their preretirement years, are more likely to own and drive a car, and have higher incomes than women. However, elderly widowers fare worse than women: they are much more likely to die from a number of causes, from heart attacks to suicide, than elderly women.

Death and Dying. Historically, death has been accepted as a normal part of human existence. Lack of knowledge regarding hygiene and disease prevention coupled with subsistence economies resulted in very high death rates in both hunting–gathering and agricultural societies. It was not until the industrial societies were well established that death rates plummeted. With the ability of societies to control death—to a certain extent, of course—came a change in attitude toward it. When death was common and was within the experience of everyone, it was considered an ordinary event. As it became rarer, it tended to become associated with old age, because, barring wars and accidents, it was mostly the old who died. Today, death is considered an out-of-the-ordinary event if it occurs at any time in the life cycle except in old age. As a result, it has acquired an aura of unnaturalness. And because religious beliefs that explained life and death as part of a divine plan have declined in importance in modern societies, the acceptance with which former generations greeted death has given way to the expectation that the miracles of modern medicine will bring us immortality. Death is no longer the natural capping of life; it is to be avoided at all costs and is considered separate, an antithesis to life.

Box 14.1 The Silver Century

Within a year or two, and for the first time in history, there will be more people over 60 than toddlers under 5 in the world. Throughout recorded history, people aged 65 and over have made up, at most, 2 to 3 percent of most societies. Today, this age group makes up 15 percent of the inhabitants of wealthy nations. The defining demographic trend of this century, then, will be the increase in the proportion of the world's elderly persons.

What will this trend mean? Three situations are already visible. First, by the 2020s, there will be a bulge in retirement when the last baby boomers leave the work force. This will mean that a large number of elderly and very elderly (65+ and 85+) will need to be supported by a smaller and smaller proportion of the young still in the work force. The smaller proportion of young workers is a result of the widespread fall in fertility rates in industrial countries in which women are not having enough children to replace those who die. This is especially true in continental Europe and Japan, but even in the United States births only just equal deaths (in Japan, the number of persons 100 years and over doubled in five years, setting a record for the 33rd straight year as the world's longest-living nation). Therefore, when the baby boomers retire, the size of the labor force will plummet. Finally, with life expectancy rising, people are spending much more time in retirement (again, Japan's life expectancy as of 2002 is the longest in the world: 85.2 years for women and 78.3 for men). In the United States, 16 percent of men are still in the work force at 65, while in Europe only 4 percent are. Consequently, the large number of older people will have to be supported for a longer period of time by fewer younger workers. The welfare state system in Europe and America's Social Security system provide near-universal coverage for the retired, paid for by the current workers—who, as we saw, are a diminishing number.

Even some of the developing nations face similar problems. China, Iran, Brazil, and Turkey will be below replacement rate within 15 years. In China, thanks to the one-child policy, the fertility rate has decreased from six or seven children per woman in the 1960s, to below replacement rate. When the Red Guard generation reaches retirement age in around 2015, the working-age population will be too small to allow the continuous growth of China's economy.

Economists believe that there is a decade-long window of opportunity in which governments can forestall the collapse of systems that support the elderly. The negative impact of the retiring baby boomers will not be felt for another 10 years. At this time, governments will have to convince their citizens to postpone their retirements. This will not be easy. The idea of retirement is fairly recent—for most of history, people worked almost until they died—but it is a very popular idea. Workers began to retire as soon as they could afford to do so, even before social benefits were available, and they like retirement even more now that they live longer and more leisure activities are open to them. Governments will have to change the structure of pensions and benefits to make it more attractive to continue working longer. One thing is certain: a workplace revolution is coming. In the 1970s and 1980s, a large number of women entered the labor force. The next 25 years will bring in a large number of "older" workers, perhaps on a part-time basis. Such a future holds many positives: staying in the labor force can provide elderly workers with a more stimulating environment, companionship, and a bit of extra money (Cairncross, 2004, 3, 4)

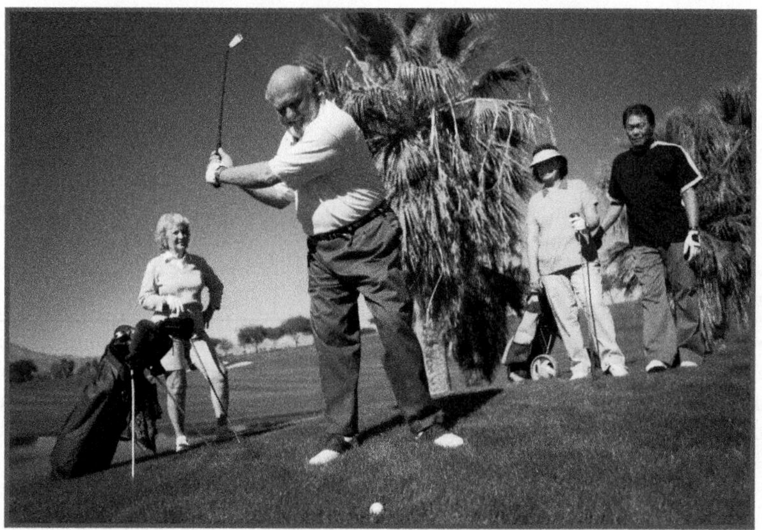

Not all the elderly are able to retire to play golf in fancy resorts, but for most elderly, the rocking chair on the porch is an idea from the past.

This attitude toward death is reinforced by the fact that death has been removed from public life. People typically no longer die at home, in full view of family and friends; instead, they die in hospitals and nursing homes, and even there, dying patients are isolated from those expected to recuperate. Coupled with the fact that many elderly people are isolated from the rest of society to begin with, the result is that the population at large has seldom faced death, in the sense of seeing a person die.

Box 14.2 The Eight Americas

Location, race, and income play such an important role in disparities in life spans that some scientists have said that there are really eight Americas, not just one. The healthiest Americans, and the longest lived, live about 30 years longer than the least healthy. Asian American women living in Bergen County, New Jersey, have an average life expectancy of 91 years. On the other hand, Native Americans in South Dakota have an average life expectancy of 58 years. Such a short life expectancy is comparable to that of some of the developing nations of Southeast Asia and sub-Saharan Africa. The gaps and disparities, moreover, have not closed over the last two decades in spite of the fact that about $5,000 a year per person is spent for health care in the United States.

These differences in mortality and longevity are not due solely to disparities in income, the availability of health insurance, violence, or the presence of AIDS, although these factors certainly contribute to them. According to a study conducted by Harvard University and partly funded by the National Institute on Aging, the principal contributors to increased mortality are smoking, alcohol, obesity, high blood pressure, high cholesterol, diet, and physical inactivity. In other words, much of the disparity is dependent on cultural patterns and lifestyles. As one researcher stated, "It's not just low income. It's what people eat, it's how they behave, or simply what's available in supermarkets" (Neergard, 2006). As an example, Native Americans who live in cities, away from the reservations in the West, have life expectancies similar to whites. Disparities were most pronounced in Americans aged 15 to 59 because according to the researchers, this age group is the most neglected by health policy initiatives, which focus mainly on children and the elderly. Thus, a 15-year-old black urban male is 3.8 times as likely to die before the age of 60 as an Asian American.

The eight Americas consist of:

1. 10.4 million Asians, with a per capita income of $21,566 and life expectancy of 84.9 years
2. 3.6 million low-income whites, average income $17,758, life expectancy 79 years
3. 214 million middle Americans scattered across the country, average income $24,640, life expectancy 77.9 years
4. 16.6 million low-income whites in rural counties in Appalachia and the Mississippi Valley, average income $16,390, life expectancy 75 years
5. 1 million western Native Americans, average income $10,029, life expectancy 72.7 years
6. 23.4 million black middle Americans, average income $15,412, life expectancy 72.9 years
7. 5.8 million southern low-income blacks in rural counties, average income $10,463, life expectancy 71.2 years
8. 7.5 million high-risk urban blacks in thirteen urban counties, average income $14,800, life expectancy 71.1 years.

Finally, the healthiest state in which to live is Hawaii, with an average life span for both men and women of 80 years. The least healthy place to live is the District of Columbia, with a life expectancy of only 72 years. The researchers conclude that because socioeconomic inequalities are not being addressed in the United States, public health strategies must be established that would attempt to reduce risk factors for chronic diseases and injuries (Murray et al., 2006).

In spite of this strong avoidance of death, the elderly seem less afraid of it than younger people, particularly if their health is such that they see little chance of a normal lifestyle in their future. The elderly are socialized into accepting death because they are more likely to see it in their spouses and peers. As an increasing number of Americans join the ranks of the elderly, the idea of death is likely to lose some of its sting. It is already more acceptable to speak about death, and many of the elderly make it clear that they do not want to have their lives prolonged artificially if it means suffering or isolation rather than improvement in quality of life. During the past two decades, institutions called hospices—which do not attempt to cure but rather care for the dying—have sprung up to attempt to help the dying in the difficult period preceding death.

Women: Differentiation According to Gender

It is clear to all that the human race comes in two genders, male and female, and that both are needed if that race is to continue to exist. Yet it seems that a state of war is being waged between men and women all over the globe, producing neither winners nor losers, but much conflict. In developed countries, a high incidence of rape, various varieties of sexual harassment, domestic violence directed at women, and many other types of discrimination are the order of the day. In developing nations, especially where political conflicts are raging, women are the victims of virtual horror stories: they are denied education and the simplest human rights, rape on massive levels is used against them as a weapon of war, and they are still considered chattel or property of men. To what do we owe this enmity between the sexes?

As we saw in the previous two chapters, societies assign unequal statuses to various segments of their population. Women (and children) have usually had an inferior status in most societies of the world, and particularly where the family form has remained stubbornly patriarchal. One can understand why children should be somewhat subordinate to adults: they are physically weak and lack life experience and knowledge. But why women? What really differentiates men and women? Is it true that "Women are from Venus, Men are from Mars," as a best-selling book would have it? Why is rape so prevalent a crime even in our society when sexual mores are so relaxed that there is no stigma attached to having sex among consenting adults?

Biological Facts

One is born either male or female; maleness and femaleness, then, are *biological* terms, descriptive of biological facts. Masculine and feminine, on the other hand, are adjectives reflecting *social* conditions, that is, descriptive of how males and females are expected to behave in a given society, and how they come to feel about themselves and each other. The first is a **sex status**, ascribed and not subject to change except in extraordinary circumstances; the second is a **gender role**, achieved and, thus, subject to change according to place and time. The first lies within the realm of biology, the second within that of culture, but both are subject to social interpretations and influences and can be detached from one another only for the sake of analysis. In reality, biology and culture are deeply intertwined.

The biological differences between men and women may be roughly divided into those that are of an anatomical nature, those that are of a genetic nature, and those that are of a hormonal nature. **Anatomical differences** are the most obvious, for they consist of the physical structure and appearance of the two sexes. These differences include height, weight, distribution of body fat and hair, and musculature. Such traits are called the **secondary sex characteristics**, and they may be measured on a continuum: that is, not every woman is shorter, lighter, more rounded, less hairy, and less muscular than a man, just as not every man is taller, heavier, more angular, more hairy, and more muscular than a woman. In fact, the most important anatomical difference lies in the distinct reproductive systems of males and females. The reproductive system of women allows them to become pregnant and give birth. The reproductive system of men allows them to impregnate women.

Pregnancy and nursing force women to be unable periodically to perform certain economic and social functions, whereas the role of men in reproduction ends with impregnation. These facts have profound social consequences.

Genetic differences become apparent when analyzing the sex chromosomes, which contain the genes that determine heredity in all living creatures. All humans inherit two sex chromosomes, one from the mother and one from the father. Females inherit two X-chromosomes (XX), while males inherit one X chromosome and one Y chromosome (XY). A male is born when an ovum (egg) bearing the X-chromosome is fertilized by a sperm bearing a Y-chromosome (each month a female produces one ovum throughout her fertile years, which contains an X-chromosome; a male produces sperm, half of which is made up of X-chromosomes inherited from his mother and the other half of Y-chromosomes inherited from his father). Whether chromosomal differences influence the personalities, abilities, and behaviors of males and females has not yet been scientifically established.

Hormonal differences begin to be felt at about three months after fertilization and are responsible for the differentiation into the two genders. Up to this time, the fetus is sexually undifferentiated: it may become either a male or a female. Hormones are chemicals that are secreted into the bloodstream by glands located in the body. The function of hormones is to stimulate some chemical processes and inhibit others. The hormones involved in the development of sex characteristics are estrogen and progesterone, produced by the ovaries in females, and testosterone and androgens produced by the testes in males. Both males and females produce male and female sex hormones, but the proportion in which they are produced varies by gender. The fetus with the XY chromosomal formation begins to secrete testosterone, which has the function of inhibiting the development of female characteristics; hence, the fetus will be born a male. At puberty, it is again the sex hormones that determine the development of secondary sex characteristics—they induce the growth of beards in males and breasts in females. Hormones, then, are influential in physical development. They also affect human behavior. Animal experiments have shown that an increase of testosterone, even in females, produces an increase in aggressive behavior and sex drive. Research into the hormone oxytocin, present in humans and other mammals, shows that it is responsible for feelings of satisfaction and good will toward others. It also stimulates the sensations of sexual arousal and climax, ensures that new mothers nurture their young, and that the uterus contracts during childbirth. Researchers are going so far as to say that the hormone is an excellent candidate for involvement in the formation of social bonds, and they liken it to a bridge between anatomy and behavior (Angier, 1991).

Other researchers also attribute the differences between men and women to hormonal causes, especially to the infusion of hormones at the proper moment—before birth, and especially at puberty—which influences the brain to behave in a gender-specific way: males with more aggression, females with more nurturance. These conclusions are based on animal experiments that show that females injected with the equivalent of the hormone testosterone—or even female siblings who develop beside a male fetus in the womb—invariably exhibit more aggressiveness, acting more like males. Nonetheless, there is no conclusive evidence that hormonal differences explain differences in the behavior of the two sexes. Even where correlations between the level of testosterone and aggressive behavior exist, it is impossible to show a cause-and-effect relationship. At most, it may be said that there is an association between the two (Hoyenga & Hoyenga, 1979, 139).

Studies in medicine also point to evidence that male and female brains function differently. Researchers have discovered, for instance, that in women such functions as language are more evenly divided between the left and right halves of the brain, whereas in men they are much more localized in the left half.

Cultural Differences

The differences in behavior between the two sexes are obviously not due strictly to biological influences. Culture plays a significant part, although less so than was at first believed by social scientists and feminists. For instance, a well-known study by researchers Money and Erhardt (1972) involved a pair of identical twin males, one of whom, in a tragic accident, was totally castrated during circumcision. The parents of the twins were subsequently convinced to raise this twin as a female. Other than surgically constructing a vagina, nothing was done to the twin until puberty except that the parents treated "her" as a little girl: the mother let her hair grow long, adorned her with hair ribbons, and dressed her in frilly clothes. According to the researchers, soon the little girl was behaving as little girls are expected to behave in our society: she was neater than her brother, she was more willing to help with housework, and she requested dolls and a dollhouse as Christmas presents. Even though the twin was, biologically, a male, "she" acted as a female does in American society. However, it was observed that she tended to be a leader in games with peers and was rather a tomboy.

The story, however, does not end with ". . . and she lived happily ever after." In fact, a follow-up study paints a totally different picture. New research shows that, far from being satisfied with her assigned gender, the girl/boy rejected the female identity and at 14 years of age chose to live as a man, undergoing extensive reconstructive surgery to attempt to attain a semblance of the male genitals he had lost. "Despite everyone telling him constantly that he was a girl, and despite his being treated with female hormones, his brain knew he was a male. It refused to take on what it was being told" (Angier, 1997, A10). The recollections of the adult girl/boy (identified only as "John") and his parents were that he had never accepted a feminine identity. On the contrary, he had torn off the dresses in which his parents had dressed him, had refused dolls, had sought out male friends, had imitated his father shaving rather than his mother putting on makeup, and had even tried to urinate standing up. His -attempts to engage in feminine behavior were made only to obtain parental approval. He became especially unhappy when, at age 12, he was given female hormones and began growing breasts. At age 14 he threatened suicide, being friendless and thoroughly unhappy. When told by his father what had happened to him as an infant, "John" was relieved to hear it: "For the first time everything made sense, and I understood who and what I was" (Angier, 1997, A10). In short, what had been considered a classic case illustrating the importance of nurture and socialization on gender identification was turned on its head.

Nonetheless, the impact of culture cannot be discounted. If the behavior of the two sexes differed strictly on the basis of biology, then in all societies of the world, and in all instances, men and women would behave distinctly in the same ways. But they do not. Cross-cultural evidence indicates how deeply nurture can affect behavior. A classic study by anthropologist Margaret Mead (1935), who based her findings on an analysis of three preliterate tribes of New Guinea, revealed that men can act the way people think women do and vice versa. For instance, in one of the societies Mead studied, both men and women were gentle, emotionally responsive, noncompetitive, and lacking in aggression. In addition, both men and women were responsible for the care of children. In another tribe, however, both men and women had personality types that could be characterized as masculine; that is, both men and women were aggressive and violent. Women disliked anything connected with motherhood, such as pregnancy, nursing, and caring for their children. They were especially obnoxious to their daughters. Finally, in the third tribe, Mead found profound differences in the behavior of men and women. Contrary to expectations, however, each sex behaved in a manner that Americans would consider the opposite of how men and women "ought" to behave: women were domineering and aggressive and were the economic providers in the household. Men were passive, took care of the children, engaged in gossip, and liked to adorn themselves. Mead concluded from her analysis that sex roles vary in different societies; that is, a person born either a male or a female does not necessarily and always act in ways determined by his or her biological makeup. However, Mead never proclaimed the reversibility of sex roles and, in fact, tried to correct the mistaken assumptions—that females can be made to act exactly like males and vice versa—that a number of commentators made about her conclusions. She also found, and reported in her book, *Male and Female* (1949), that the seven cultures she studied exhibited homicidal violence, headhunting, plotting, and fighting, all on the part of males. In short, to conclude that culture is solely responsible for gender roles is equally shortsighted.

Another cross-cultural comparison of six societies also showed that in all of them boys were more aggressive and violent than girls, and girls were more nurturing and emotionally responsive, especially to children (Whiting, 1963). Findings such as this substantiate long-standing conclusions that fighting and leadership are associated predominantly with males and that males are more prone to aggressiveness, sexual attack, promiscuity, homosexuality, voyeurism, and other forms of aggressive sexual activity (Ford & Beach, 1951; Murdock, 1957). The conclusions regarding the greater aggressiveness of males seem to be so overwhelming that a well-known anthropologist was moved to state categorically: "In every known society, homicidal violence, whether spontaneous and outlawed or organized and sanctioned for military purposes, is committed overwhelmingly by men" (Konner, 1988, 34). This view is supported by the work of

We are born male or female, but we are made men or women. It is culture that directs our behavior according to sex roles, some of which are anachronistic. These little girls are learning to play traditional gender roles in American society, but there are other gender scripts for women.

sociologist Steven Goldberg in *The Inevitability of Patriarchy* (1977), in which he maintains that according to his research: (a) patriarchy is a universal characteristic of societies; (b) roles performed by males are given higher status than those performed by females; and (c) men are dominant in male–female relationships (Goldberg, 1989, 16–18).

What conclusions can be drawn from these conflicting facts? Do men and women behave differently because they are biologically different? Or is it rather that they are socialized to accept different roles? In short, what makes us men or women? Nature or nurture? As usual, the issue cannot be answered simplistically. Biological differences between the sexes surely exist, in some areas to a significant extent. The concern, however, is the social significance that these differences acquire in human societies.

Sex and Gender Differentiated

Although *sex* and *gender* are used interchangeably in common parlance, in the social sciences the two terms need to be differentiated. *Sex* refers to a person's biological identity, whereas *gender* refers to the socially learned behaviors and cultural expectations that attach to males and females. Sex merely marks us as male or female and determines whether we have a reproductive system that enables us to bear children or one that provides some of the material necessary to conceive them. As we have seen, this biological fact is not sufficient to ensure that we become men and women. Femininity—being a woman—and masculinity—being a man—are cultural concepts. Therefore, they differ from society to society, they are associated with specific historical eras and geographical settings, and they are learned and interpreted differently even by members of the same society. That is why some women and men, having acquired a sexual identity that does not correspond to their physical sex, attempt to change the latter by surgical and medical means.

■ The Cultural Construction of Gender

We saw earlier that culture provides us with a script according to which we essentially organize our lives. We learn this script so well that we—at least, most of us—become absolutely convinced that the way we do things in our society is the right and only way to do them. We accept a set of assumptions that we seldom bother to examine, and we come to believe that they are the "truth" that should guide and direct our lives. We, therefore, often cringe at the way things are done in other societies.

Traditional Gender Roles

We live out our lives by fulfilling a variety of roles. Among the most important of such roles are **gender roles**. The traditional gender roles assigned to males and females in our society, as well as in most others, are the **instrumental role** for males and the **expressive role** for females. The instrumental role stresses rationality, competitiveness, aggression, and goal-orientation. The expressive role emphasizes nurturing, emotion, and peace-making. Such traditional divisions of roles assume that there is a polarity between

Women have entered previously male-only fields, including such sports as boxing.

male and female roles, with behavior divided in two, as it were, and between opposite poles: emotion and nurturance at one end, reason and aggressiveness at the other. In reality, of course, there is a great deal of variety within each gender, and there are countless similarities in the roles of men and women (and the same roles may be filled by either men or women when the need arises or is perceived as arising).

Because they give birth to the young who depend for their survival on them, women have developed emotions and skills consonant with nurturing and care-giving. These have extended to other family members in need of care, such as the elderly or disabled. When societies were predominantly agricultural, women did a share of work outside the house alongside the men, in addition to tasks inside the house. But when economies began to depend on industry, men became the chief breadwinners outside the home. This occurred mostly in the middle classes, in which women were able to stay at home, expanding the expressive role. The notion then emerged that women were expected to sacrifice their personal goals and desires in favor of those of others. Working-class women incorporated all of these roles—they had to work outside the home, at menial or industrial jobs, and fulfill the caretaker functions at home. This traditional division of roles crystallized during the industrial age, when men began to perform their instrumental role through their work outside the home.

In general terms, traditional roles, both masculine and feminine, have been upheld as the expected cultural models throughout the societies of the world, becoming stereotyped in the process. In our society, when people refer to the "typical" roles of men and women, they mean those that, in the past, were characteristic of a white, middle-class family. The stereotypes for other groups vary somewhat.

Gender Scripts

Gender roles, like all roles, are based on cultural scripts. The masculine script in our society has several variations. The traditional script includes distancing oneself from anything feminine ("sissy"), and being occupationally and financially successful. Those who cannot achieve success through legitimate means may embrace some subcultural ways, including violence and physical aggression, and/or adopting a "cool" pose consisting of a manner of dress and posture that bespeaks fearlessness and emotional detachment. This pose is used as a survival mechanism in a society perceived as hostile and discriminatory. Another masculine script is one in which the expectation is for the man to be self-reliant and confident to the point of being "tough" (a John Wayne type of person). A fairly popular script focuses on adventure, sometimes accompanied by violence and a need to humiliate an opponent. This script expects men to excel in contact sports, never to walk away from a fight, and to kill and maim the enemy (do what must be done) in war. Finally, an optional script that has been emerging of late is one in which the "new" male is emotionally sensitive and expressive and values an egalitarian relationship with women.

Feminine scripts are based on the expectation that a woman, in addition to being nurturant, will be attractive in looks, not overly competitive, a listener rather than a talker, and one capable of adapting to various circumstances. The script provides that a woman not show her intelligence but rather support, facilitate, and cheer on from the sidelines her husband's (or man's) accomplishments. She is considered lucky to have a man in her life, and his care as well as any needs of their children are to come before her own needs. Again, the script may differ somewhat for women in other ethnic groups, but it always includes primary responsibility for child care.

Box 14.3 Women and Science

In spite of the pervasive scripts and the traditional roles women are expected to play in most societies of the world, many of them, today and throughout history, have overcome these obstacles. In addition to rulers known for their wisdom or shrewdness (Cleopatra, the female pharaoh Hatshepsut, Queen Elizabeth I, in addition to more modern prime ministers, such as Indira Gandhi and Golda Meir), many women have excelled in fields in which men predominate. Today, a substantial number of women are earning doctoral degrees in science and engineering and are working in such professions as architecture and construction, not to mention medical research. A number have even received Nobel prizes in science:

Marie S. Curie, Nobel Prize Winner in Physics, 1903, and in Chemistry, 1911
Irene Curie (Marie's daughter), Chemistry, 1935
Grety Radnitz Cori, Biochemistry, 1947
Maria Goeppert Mayer, Physics, 1963
Dorothy Crowfoot Hodgkin, Chemistry, 1964
Rosalyn Sussman Yalow, Medicine, 1977
Barbara McClintock, Medicine, 1983
Rita Levi-Montalcini, Medicine, 1986
Gertrude Elion, Medicine, 1988
Christiane Nüsslein-Volhard, Medicine, 1995

("Women Nobel Prize Winners," **http://www.factmonster.com/ipka/A0801697.html**. Accessed September 6, 2004).

In recent years the traditional feminine script has been pushed to the back, while the script of "professional" or "working woman" has emerged (see Table 14.4). Often, women try to combine the traditional script with the working woman script, producing the "superwoman" script. This script is very difficult to achieve and maintain, and it causes much role strain. A lesser number of women appear to follow a "contented single" script, in which a working woman seems satisfied with a lifestyle that does not include a relationship with a man, although it may involve the creation of a family (perhaps in a lesbian relationship). Finally, we should mention a theme that is woven through all the cultural scripts for women, and that is the division of women into "good girl/slut." Even elementary school children are aware of this distinction attributed to females who are either sexually conservative or sexually active.

As is obvious, gender scripts are perceived as being opposite and mutually exclusive: women are one thing, men something else. In reality, as was already noted, men and women differ only slightly in the traits they display. A good portion of these traits overlap, and this is true of both physical traits (such as height, for instance) and behavioral traits (such as aggressiveness). Moreover, there are more differences within each gender group than between the two genders. The only exception to this pattern of overlapping traits seems to be dominance.

Male Dominance

Male dominance is a fact of life in the majority of the world's societies. In our own case, in spite of our belief that we are an egalitarian society, a group of little boys will invariably take over playground equipment in a situation of mixed-gender play, unless prohibited to do so by an adult (Franklin, 1988, 30). The many sexual harassment situations on jobs and in the military are another indication of such dominance. On an institutional level, a realistic look is sufficient to illustrate the clear prevalence of men in the political, economic, social, and even religious arenas. There has never been a female President of the United States, and strong personality and interest in politics of a first lady have generally brought her nothing but criticism.

In the 110th Congress, there are 16 women in the Senate (out of 100 senators), and 71 women in the House of Representatives (out of 435 representatives). In administrative and managerial positions, women's share increased from 38 percent in the mid-1980s to 50 percent in 2005, the highest proportion in Western Europe and other developed nations (Women's Bureau, 2005). As for wage parity, it has never been achieved. In 2005, women earned approximately 81.0 percent as much as men. Median weekly earnings of female full-time wage and salary workers were $585 in 2005 compared to $722 for their male counterparts. (see Figure 14.4). African American and Hispanic women earned 63 cents and 53 cents, respectively, for every dollar that a white male earned. Women and men under 25 had fairly similar earnings,

TABLE 14.4 Women in the Labor Force in 2005

- Women made up 46% of the labor force and are projected to account for 47% in 2014.
- Women will likely account for 51% of the increase in total labor force growth between 2004 and 2014.
- 66 million women were employed in the United States in 2005, more than ever before.
- Half of all workers in high-paying management and professional jobs are women. They outnumber men in many occupations, including financial manager, human resource manager, accountant, budget analyst, teacher, and nurse.
- The median weekly earnings of women working full-time are 81% of the median weekly earnings of men working full-time.

Unemployment rates

By Gender	
Men	5.1%
Women	5.1%
By Race	
Asian women	3.9%
White women	4.4%
Hispanic women	6.9%
Black women	9.5%
By Education (Women Only)	
No high school diploma	9.7%
High school diploma	4.8%
Some college, no degree	4.5%
Bachelor's degree or higher	2.4%

Female-to-Male Earnings Ratio and Median Earnings of Full-Time, Year-Round Workers 15 Years and Older by Sex: 1960 to 2006

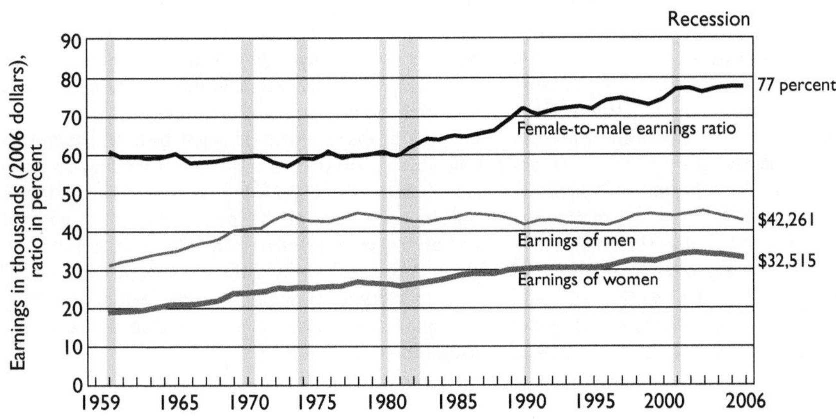

FIGURE 14.4

Note: The data points are placed at the midpoints of the respective years. Data on earnings of full-time, year-round workers are not readily available before 1960.

Source: U.S. Census Bureau, *Current Population Survey*, 1961 to 2007 Annual Social and Economic Supplements.

but women's earnings were much lower than men's in older age groups: women 25 and over made less than 80 percent of what men in the same age group earned (U.S. Department of Labor, Bureau of Labor Statistics, 2006).

In addition, many subtle gender expectations show male dominance expressed in the course of social interaction: men interrupt women more often than the other way around, women smile more often than men do, and men stare at women more often than the opposite (Mehrabian, 1971; Frieze & Ramsey, 1976; Frieze et al., 1978). And women seldom win arguments with men even though they may be good at reasoning things through and expressing themselves. This conclusion was reached by a 10-year study of the way in which men and women argue by British psychologist Elizabeth Mapstone (Kozma, 1997, 4E).

> What I expected to be able to show was that really there were no differences between men and women. What I discovered was that it mattered terribly who the other person was in the argument, and most especially it mattered what gender the other person was. . . .It's not true that all men are cool, rational beings and it's not true that all women are gentle, warm, nurturing creatures.

Theories of Gender Role Development

Why and how do gender roles emerge in a society? How do they become so deeply embedded in the culture that they are eventually incorporated into our very personalities and behavior? Such questions cannot be answered with any degree of certainty. We can only speculate by referring to a number of theories that have been used in an attempt to answer them.

Structural Functionalist Theory. This theory is one of the most dominant ones in sociology. It assumes that those elements are retained in a social system that aid in the survival of that system. The development of the instrumental and expressive roles in the family institution is a kind of specialization that occurs within all small groups. Such specialization is *functional* because it meets social needs as well as institutional needs. A strong family needs someone to make important decisions and someone to foster the emotional well-being of members. Because of the close bond between mother and child, the expressive role is more consonant with a woman's nature; the male acquires the instrumental role by default.

The critique that may be made of this theory is that it assumes that male dominance and female subordination are natural and inevitable, based on biological makeup. We have seen, however, that research does not prove the absolute truth of this assumption.

Conflict Theory. Conflict theory is the other of the two most popular sociological theories. This theory assumes that power and privilege are based on the resources that an individual possesses. In turn,

Box 14.4 God Should Not Give Daughters to the Poor

Women in the United States have achieved an almost egalitarian status with men, certainly as pertains to their political and civil rights. We have seen, however, that there still are differences in wages between the sexes, and women certainly suffer other discriminatory conditions in the United States. One such condition relates to their sexuality. Many men divide women either into saints—their mothers or sisters—or women of easy virtue. Such an attitude is prevalent in many societies around the world. A number of societies keep women in conditions of subjugation that may as well be considered slavery. Women are often the targets of vicious assaults by warring factions—this was the case when the former Yugoslavia was in the process of breaking up and one ethnic group was attempting to cleanse its territory of another ethnic group. One of its methods was by brutal sexual attacks on women. Currently, the same actions are occurring in Darfur, a region of Sudan, in which women are continually raped and killed. In many developing countries, girls and women are sold by impoverished parents into brothels, or they are held like slaves by husbands and in-laws who abuse them and often kill them. They are also exploited and abused—and often killed—by feudal-like wealthy landowners who control the police and other government authorities, so that the women have no recourse and must suffer in silence. Poverty and being a woman are heavy burdens to carry in many places in the world. This condition prompted one mother to say that God should never give daughters to the poor.

power is the ability to influence or control the lives of others, and it also derives from the economic resources that an individual can muster. Frederick Engels, Karl Marx's co-author, maintained in his book, *The Origins of the Family, Private Property and the State* (1884), that male dominance in the family was the result of his control over the family's economic resources. He also insisted that the concept of patriarchy developed in tandem with that of property, because if property were to be inherited, it became important for a man to know that the children born to his wife were indeed his own. In this sense, simple societies were much more egalitarian because there was no need to worry about who was going to inherit what—there was precious little surplus to leave anyone. A more recent interpretation of the theory holds that those individuals who have a higher income, educational attainment, and occupational status have the greater power even in a relationship such as marriage. And because most men tend to marry women who are younger, less well educated, and who earn less money, they naturally become the more powerful partner.

Conflict theory has its shortcomings, also. There seems to be too much emphasis on economics, and too little concern over other facets of relationships, such as sex, love, and companionship, as well as traditional societal expectations that would force women into a more submissive stance vis-a-vis men. In particular, gender roles and stereotypes, which have a tremendous impact on behavior, are ignored.

Feminist Theory. Feminist theory has borrowed much of the framework of conflict theory, especially the fact that women are underrepresented in positions of power in the society at large, a reflection of the lack of power women have within the family. Feminists also point out the existence of the wage differential between men and women, of prevalent gender discrimination in hiring and promotion, of sexual harassment in the workplace, of the frequency of divorce and out-of-wedlock births, which have led to the phenomenon of the "feminization of poverty" and of violence as a means of controlling the behavior of family members.

As is true of conflict theory, feminist theory is also criticized for its emphasis on the negative side of male–female relationships, while paying scant attention to the positives of such relationships: companionship, affection and love, sexual satisfaction, and intimacy. Feminism as a social movement has also been accused of not doing enough for certain groups of women: minorities, the poor, those in traditional women's jobs, stay-at-home mothers, rural residents, and single welfare mothers. They are seen as representing mainly white, highly educated women, interested in such issues as abortion, gay rights, and political equality, while the average woman must contend with child care and economic survival.

Theories of Gender Socialization

Another group of theories focuses on the way cultural ideas about gender become part of an individual's personality and behavior patterns. Among the most influential theories are the social learning theory, the cognitive developmental theory, and the identification theory.

The Social Learning Theory. The social learning theory is based on the behaviorist notion that learning consists of observation, imitation, and reinforcement. In this view, children observe all kinds of behavior on the part of parents, peers, and others. They imitate some of this behavior: if they receive positive reinforcement for it—if parents seem delighted, or their friends approve, or teachers give them good grades—they continue this behavior. If the reinforcement is negative—parents scold them, friends laugh at them, teachers discipline them—they discontinue the behavior. Gender roles are learned in the same way.

If a little girl puts on her mother's dress and primps in front of a mirror, and her mother smiles and says she looks pretty, the little girl assumes that females are supposed to dress up and look pretty. If a little boy does the same, and his father scowls and tells him that boys do not wear dresses unless they are sissies, then the boy realizes that his behavior is not proper for his gender.

Socialization into gender roles begins early. Parents respond to male and female infants differently, speaking more often to their daughters, whom they also touch more frequently and treat more delicately. The kinds of toys and games parents choose, the kinds of clothing they select for their children, the way they themselves behave and what they say directly about gender, even the jobs they hold—whether they are traditional for each gender or not, all offer subtle messages to their children regarding what is appropriate behavior for each gender.

Indeed, children observe and imitate the behavior of their parents, their siblings and peers, and characters encountered in the mass media. And they continue behavior that is rewarded. But not always, and not entirely. First, they do not imitate the same-sexed parent alone but both. Second, they are not merely passive entities but react to the messages they receive.

Cognitive Development Theory. According to the cognitive development theory, children learn gender roles according to which stage of cognitive development they have reached at any point. Cognitive development, in turn, is the way information is processed by individuals at different stages of physical maturation (Piaget, 1950, 1954; Kohlberg, 1969). For instance, even though children at two years of age may have noticed that there are two genders, they are not sure to which one they belong, nor whether it is a permanent or a temporary condition (they may think that it depends on wearing dresses or having long hair). It is not until children are six or seven years old that they realize the reality of gender and its permanent nature. At this point, they proceed to select behavior befitting their gender, preferring to play with same-sexed playmates and sex-typed toys. They see gender as being rigidly defined; it is not until they are more mature that they perceive gender as more flexible, and gender roles as somewhat overlapping (Vogel et al., 1991, 605).

Children do not reach their ideas about gender roles without much input from the culture. With help from the numerous agents of socialization—parents, siblings, peers, teachers, the media—they construct what sociologists call *gender schema*, or a set of traits that are perceived as being central to a particular gender (Bem, 1981, 1983, 1985). These vary according to age: at first, they are quite concrete—only girls wear barrettes in their hair, only boys play hockey, for instance. With maturity, the schema grow more abstract: men do not display emotions, women do not make the important decisions. Whether these perceptions are correct or incorrect, they contribute to the individual's gender identity.

Identification Theory. Building on Freudian ideas, sociologist Nancy Chodorow maintains that children of both genders initially identify and develop strong attachments to their primary caretaker, who is generally the mother (Chodorow, 1978). For girls, the problem later is the issue of separation from the mother, which may lead, during the teenage years, to hostility and feelings of competition with her. For boys, the issue is to make a dramatic identification shift from identification with the mother to identification with the father. This shift usually occurs by the age of six or seven. In fact, in both agricultural and traditional, craft-based societies, at this age boys begin to leave the mother, going out with the father to farm or learn a skill. To detach successfully from identifying with the mother, boys must reject activities associated with women. Hence, in traditional societies there are *rites of passage* designed specifically to mark a young man's passage from childhood to adulthood and from boyhood to manhood. These changes are then reinforced by membership in exclusively male organizations. In our own society, although the change in identification does not occur so dramatically, there is a general turning away from the feminine role on the part of young boys: they organize "boys-only clubs," as well as enjoying camping and fishing trips in male-only company. Moreover, in contemporary societies it is more difficult to make this switch in identity, because fathers are often absent for most of the day and do not offer a ready model. As a result, the young male often accepts a stereotypical gender role, one offered by peers and the media and often not corresponding to reality. This leads the young male to be anxious about whether he is fulfilling his role adequately and to overcompensate by trying to fill a rigid mold of the masculine role. This is one explanation for the "macho" image that some young males, particularly those whose status on the cultural totem pole is low, attempt to present to the world, as for instance, by joining gangs.

Agents of Gender Socialization

It should be clear that those most directly involved in creating gender identities for individuals are those closest to them. Therefore, parents, siblings, extended family members, peers, teachers, and, today especially, the mass media play the most significant roles in this activity. These are the same agents who socialize each new generation.

The Media. The media have probably become more influential than any of the other socializing agents in maintaining gender stereotypes. In particular, it is television that has the impact, because children spend more time watching it than they do interacting with parents, siblings and other family members, teachers, and friends. In fact, the average child will have watched more hours of television by high school graduation than she will have spent in class! Television has tremendous educational value—children can be exposed to a great variety of skills, speech patterns and vocabulary, factual information, and emotions. At the same time, the medium is perceived as being authoritative, and children are not sophisticated enough to distinguish reality from fantasy. Fictional accounts of life, as represented in many of the situation comedies, are taken at face value by children, which is unfortunate because they hardly ever reflect reality. Women, especially, are almost universally presented in highly professional occupations—doctors, lawyers, newspaper reporters—although they are seldom shown actually working. Moreover, they are always beautiful and thin, seldom lose their tempers, and never lose their jobs, even when they are assertive with bosses. In spite of documentaries and news items focusing on gender inequality, family violence, and sexual assaults, most prime-time shows still show men more frequently than women and in more authoritative positions, thus persevering in the traditional gender role stereotype.

Even when factual news stories are reported, they tend to be more frequently about men, and when they deal with women they include such information as the woman's marital status, her age, her physical attributes, and often what she is wearing—information that would never appear with regard to a man.

In Sum. Newspapers and magazines also repeat the gender stereotypes. In the past, every daily paper had a section dedicated to women, which dealt with issues thought to be important to women—new recipes for feeding the family thriftily and cosmetics to keep the wife and mother looking spiffy. Today, they no longer call the section "for women," but they present the same material in the guise of "food" or "fashion." Some magazines are clearly addressed to either men or women; *Playboy, Penthouse, Sports Illustrated, Gentlemen's Quarterly*, and others, are directed at men. *Vogue* and a myriad of other fashion magazines and *Good Housekeeping* and tens of other magazines dedicated to food preparation and other facets of housekeeping are intended strictly for female consumption.

We have been making the point that gender stereotypes are alive and well. Because we do acknowledge the very real differences between men and women, however, we might wonder whether it matters that gender roles are stereotyped. Unfortunately, there are consequences for individuals, families, and the society at large, a fact supported by polls showing that many people feel men in the United States enjoy a better quality of life than women. Although gender roles have undergone a dramatic change—from a hierarchical arrangement in which one sex was subordinated to the other to an androgynous arrangement in which both sexes fill both the instrumental and the expressive roles—gender expectations still limit a woman's lifestyle choices. Although about 60 percent of women of working age are in the workforce, it is still expected that a woman's most important role is that of wife and mother. Women who choose a single lifestyle, or who want to combine marriage, motherhood, and a career—or simply have a job—are subject to criticism as radicals who are undermining "family values."

Indeed, combining outside work and the care of children and family is a difficult enterprise. Even where spouses are willing to take on a fair share of tasks, it is hard to divide one's time in such a way that everything and everybody are satisfied. Although research shows that men are spending more time in child-care and nurturing activities, in most cases housework is still the woman's responsibility, with men taking on automobile maintenance and lawn-mowing duties. In short, in spite of a greater flexibility in gender roles, gender stereotypes continue to constrain both men and women. For women, the constraints—in addition to the sheer difficulty of managing several roles at once—take the form of low self-esteem and a high incidence of mental illness. One of every four women experiences clinical depression at some time during her life (McGrath et al., 1990), a ratio of about 2 to 1. The high ratio may be an indication that women are more likely to seek help for this condition than men, but it may also be an indication that the unequal power in marital relationships and inequalities in other areas of their life—as well as the subtle and obvious humiliations and harassment to which most women are subjected at some points in their lives—seriously impact on women's mental health.

Another example of women's feelings of inadequacy is the efforts a large majority of them expend to constantly improve their appearance. In spite of the advances women have made in aiming for and achieving careers, delaying marriage and motherhood, and having more egalitarian marriages, they seem to have internalized conformist cultural expectations of beauty and femininity. Every woman's magazine (including those written for teenage girls) has article after article about perfecting the size of her thighs, abs, and glutes, and beyond diet and exercise, when to undergo plastic surgery. Cosmetic surgery, once the province of the rich and the old, is now suggested to women at the appearance of their first wrinkle—that is, in their 30s. Some women have even been known to undergo toe-shortening or pinky-toe removal for the sake of fitting into high-heeled, pointy shoes. Collagen, botox, and implants into various parts of the anatomy are the order of the day, and the so-called reality TV shows are reinforcing women's preoccupa-

Women in our society are expected to look forever young, thin, and glamorous. This societal ideal has begun to worry health professionals who have declared that models who look like the one here are unacceptably thin.

tion with looks, subjecting contestants to extensive surgery in a relentless pursuit of physical perfection. This attitude is hardly what the feminists of the 1960s meant when they complained about the narrow roles prescribed for women and decried in Betty Friedan's book *The Feminine Mystique*. Nor is it strictly the fault of men, although women undertake these procedures mainly to please or to appeal to men.

In fact, men, too, experience difficulty with gender stereotyping. Not all men are comfortable fulfilling the instrumental role, especially where that role requires assertiveness or even aggressiveness. Moreover, the role of breadwinner is not easy, particularly in times of economic downturn or for individuals who lack marketable skills. Partly as a result of this difficulty, we see many men walking away from their families or being delinquent in supporting their children. Or they substitute the role of breadwinner for one of "macho man," fathering a number of children for whom they do not care and behaving in a deviant manner that eventually leads to prison.

Box 14.5 Adam's Curse

Perhaps we need not worry about changing stereotypical sex roles at all. A well-known and world-acclaimed geneticist, Dr. Bryan Sykes, has published a book based on his research of the Y chromosome, the chromosome that differentiates men from women. His research has led him to a startling conclusion: in about 5,000 generations, or in approximately 125,000 years, male fertility will be roughly 1 percent of what it is now. Eventually, then, males will be unable to breed, and reproduction will have to take place some other way. One of the ways in which it could take place has already been tried: Japanese researchers have created a mouse from the fusion of two eggs, that is, without the involvement of a male. As Dr. Sykes says: "I feel sure that humans will one day be able to reproduce by the fusion of two eggs. The children will always be girls . . . This is very feasible, and I think will happen in my lifetime. Importantly: This is not reproductive cloning because you are not making a genetic copy of a person. Here you are creating an entirely new individual with a mixture of genes from two parents, though both of them are female" (Dreifus, 2004, D2).

The name of the book is *Adam's Curse*, and it is based on the notion that the Y chromosome is flawed and doomed. The reason is that the chromosome is passed on from father to son without the ability to mix or exchange DNA with any other chromosomes. Thus, it cannot repair mutations through genetic recombination, even though it is subject to a higher mutation rate than other chromosomes. It is this process that will eventually lead to its total disappearance, according to Dr. Sykes.

Another interesting fact the author describes is the history of the Y chromosome. Dr. Sykes is one of the scholars who discovered ways to extract DNA from fossilized bones, and he has done so extensively. Tracing the distribution of the Y chromosome, he and other researchers have been able to discover a common ancestor of many contemporary people; for instance, people named Sykes or Macdonald. They also traced the extent of Viking settlement and intermarriage in the British Isles and northern Europe. Another finding was that the Y chromosome of Genghis Khan is now present in a million men in Central Asia. How did it happen that so many men carry the chromosome of one man who lived in the twelfth century? Apparently, when Genghis Khan conquered a territory, he killed all the men and impregnated as many of the women as possible, thus spreading his genes far and wide, and through time. Sykes's conclusion from this example and others is that there may be a genetic cause for male greed, aggression, and promiscuity. He maintains, in fact, that whenever geneticists look at evolutionary diagrams, they see some frequently occurring Y chromosomes that are not closely related to others. "These genetic 'explosions' are the legacy of a relatively few very successful men who have supplanted the Y chromosomes of their contemporaries, as Genghis Khan did. My guess is that the Y chromosome of every living man has spent at least one generation in the testis of a warlord" (Dreifus, 2004, D2). Research of this type shows that the social sciences and the exact sciences sometimes produce results that each type of scientific endeavor alone could not.

How Can We Change?

Because of these reasons, it seems logical to attempt to change the stereotypes surrounding gender roles. Such changes, however, appear impossibly difficult to attain. Students of gender have suggested that *androgynous* roles, combining the expressive and instrumental roles in the same individual, would be ideal. An androgynous individual could pick and choose among feminine and masculine traits (or emotions or behaviors); he or she could be more flexible in a relationship; and could feel more "complete" and satisfied, in the sense of not being obligated to behave one way or another because of limitations superimposed by one's gender. Some researchers, however, have denied that androgyny leads to greater self-confidence and satisfaction. Rather, they believe that assuming the instrumental role on the part of both men and women leads to higher rates of self-esteem, flexibility, and mental health. Masculine-oriented persons appear to experience a lesser incidence of stress, anxiety, depression, neuroticism, conflicts in work and achievement, and general dissatisfaction with their lives than do feminine-oriented individuals (Basow, 1992). Obviously, the problem of changing stereotypes, or changing the gender roles based on them, will not be solved easily or rapidly, if indeed a solution exists.

■ Sexuality

While we agree that we are all sexual beings because of the biological imperative to reproduce the species, we are less in agreement with the statement that there are many ways of being sexual. These ways are elements of our cultural learning. In other words, it is our particular culture that tells us how, with whom, under what circumstances, and where it is proper to have sex. In most Western societies, a heterosexual, patriarchal pattern has been the most common cultural script.

Homosexual Behavior

Although homosexuality has been known to exist throughout history, it had been forced to live underground. Only recently has our society, and many others, accepted homosexuality as a right and prohibited discrimination against individuals who practice it. Homosexuals have transformed their status rapidly and dramatically. When World War II began, gay people in America had no legal rights, no organizations, a handful of private thinkers, and no public advocates. Today, the situation is much different. Homosexuals are out in the open and have a number of organizations that work to secure their rights and prevent discrimination. Before World War II, the societal attitude was that heterosexual sex (that between men and women) was the only "normal" form of sexual expression. Homosexual expression was stigmatized, and the majority of Americans practiced homophobia, meaning that they feared and dreaded being associated with homosexuality, and often acted on their hatred of homosexuals with violence. This attitude still exists, but homosexuals, who prefer to be referred to as "gays" when male and as "lesbians" when female, have become advocates for their rights as a minority group. As such, they have become not only visible but also politically active and have succeeded in convincing a large portion of Americans that heterosexuality need not be the only form of sexual expression (Kaiser, 1997).

There is no agreement among scholars as to why some people are heterosexual, others are homosexual, and still others are bisexual. The general consensus is that we are born with a sexual orientation that impels us to search out the opposite sex, the same sex, or both sexes. This orientation, however, may be culturally changed or suppressed. In the past, homosexuality was considered deviant behavior, even mental illness. In 1974, however, the American Psychiatric Association officially took it off the mental illness list.

What proportion of the population is homosexual has remained questionable. First, not everyone admits to it in surveys. Second, some

Gay weddings, once unheard of, are becoming fairly common, as an increasing number of states are allowing them.

homosexual behavior is only episodic in nature—perhaps in the form of teenage experimentation. Kinsey et al. (1948) had reported that about 10 percent of the population was homosexual, but a group of contemporary social scientists has developed more accurate samples, and they conclude that about 2.8 percent of men think of themselves as homosexual, and only 1.4 percent of women do (Laumann et al., 1994).

Although greater tolerance toward this lifestyle currently exists among the public at large, instances of "gay bashing" still occur and homophobia is a prevalent attitude among many Americans. In fact, in a book in which he interviewed in depth suburban residents of Tulsa, Atlanta, San Diego, and Boston, sociologist Alan Wolfe found that although middle-class Americans live by the precepts of nonjudgmentalism and are willing to accept almost anything, they are not prepared to accept homosexuality (Wolfe, 1998, 46–47). The majority still refers to homosexuality as abnormal, immoral, sinful, sick, and wrong. Nonetheless, as a result of the active engagement of gay and lesbian groups who invoked the civil rights legislation to maintain that they have the right to marry, a number of states have granted such couples some legal rights. Massachusetts is the only state that actually allows gays and lesbians to marry, but New Jersey, Vermont, Connecticut, and California offer a variety of civil unions or domestic partnerships that afford the same privileges as married couples have as far as taxes, health care, and inheritance are concerned.

Explanatory Theories of Homosexuality

No theory has successfully explained the causes of homosexuality. Psychoanalytic theories suggest that homosexuality is caused by a specific family configuration, namely, a dominating mother and a weak father or a rejecting mother and an absent father. However, these theories fail to explain why many in such families do not become homosexual and, vice versa, why children in some closely knit and loving families do.

Learning theories maintain that homosexuality, like other elements of socialization, is learned through such processes as imitation or rewards and punishments. These theories, too, do not take into account that homosexuals embrace this lifestyle in spite of punishment, and that heterosexual parents may produce homosexual children and homosexual parents may produce heterosexual children.

Biological theories attribute homosexuality either to inherited genes or to sex hormones. Geneticists have found higher rates of homosexuality among identical twins as compared to fraternal twins, thus leading them to believe that a shared recessive gene may be a causal factor. Scientists have also suggested that hormones affect future sexual orientation prenatally, inasmuch as they found that rates of homosexuality and bisexuality were "clumped" in specific families (Pillard & Weinrich, 1986). One neuroscientist examined the brain tissue of a number of homosexual men and heterosexual men and women. The tissue came from the hypothalamus—a zone in the center of the brain that regulates a number of essential body functions, including the sex drive. The finding emerged that, in heterosexual men, the specific area is three times as large as in homosexual men and heterosexual women. However, the scientist did not conclude that homosexuality depends on this cause, and his sample was very small (Suplee, 1991).

Nonetheless, it does appear that homosexuality is heritable, that is, that there is a genetic component to it, in spite of the difficulty of supplying cause and effect. In fact, because gay men have only one-fifth as many children as heterosexual men, a gene for homosexuality should soon disappear, according to evolutionary theory. Inasmuch as it has not disappeared, researchers have set forth a number of speculations. One is that homosexuality may be a by-product of a gene that persists because it enhances fertility in other family members. Studies have found that gay men have more relatives than heterosexual men, especially on their mother's side (Wade, 2007, D6). Another clue to the origin of homosexuality is birth order. According to another study, it appears that having older brothers increases the chances that a man will be gay. This theory is based on the speculation that some event in the womb produces some type of antibodies to successive male pregnancies. According to this study, approximately 15 percent of gay men can attribute their homosexuality to the birth order, and with each older brother, the odds of same-sex attraction increases by 33 percent (Wade, 2007, D6).

The conclusion of other researchers in this area suggests that sexual orientation is probably arrived at through a combination of factors. There may be biological causes—for instance, sex hormones that could be influencing the brain in the prenatal and early neonatal phases of development. There may also be cultural factors that strengthen hormonal predispositions. Some women, for example, may be attracted to a lesbian lifestyle because they are drawn to the more emotional and expressive way women love.

Bisexuality

Another form of sexual expression is bisexuality, or a person's attraction to both men and women (some researchers prefer the term *ambisexuality*). The percentages of people who define themselves as bisexuals have remained small; Kinsey's surveys (1953) indicated that 16 percent of single men and 9 percent of single

Box 14.6 Acquiring a Homosexual Identity

During the socialization process, children assume that they will play the roles consonant with their gender. By adolescence, however, some individuals begin to see that their fantasies and actual behavior do not agree with the heterosexual model. They note their disinterest in persons of the opposite sex or in activities that are perceived as characteristic of their biological gender. The result is that they experience feelings of confusion and turmoil.

At some point during or after late adolescence, most homosexuals accept their identity and begin to present themselves to others with that label. However, they are selective in their presentation. They may, for instance, be known to friends and relatives, or in the local homosexual community, but keep their sexual identity hidden on the job. This situation used to be almost universal but has changed in the past decade, as even persons in government and the church have "come out." One researcher summarized these stages in a model that includes sensitization (before puberty, when future homosexuals begin to be aware of feeling "different"); identity confusion (in adolescence); identity assumption (accepting and "coming out"); and commitment (the decision to accept homosexuality as a way of life) (Troiden, 1988).

Gays and lesbians appear to differ in their sexual behavior in the same way that men and women do. Differences appear to be due to gender more than to sexual orientation. Lesbians tend to have monogamous relationships just as heterosexual women do; they tend to equate love and sex; they are less sexually aroused by visual stimuli; they are not likely to objectify sex as a commodity; they are not very interested in sex with strangers or in public places; they look for long-term relationships; and they are less interested in sexual experimentation. All these characteristics are true of heterosexual women as well. Gays, on the other hand, are more promiscuous, just as heterosexual males are; they tend to separate love and emotional intimacy and sex; they are interested in pornography and are excited by visual stimuli; they are likely to objectify sex as a consumer product; they are not opposed to sex with strangers or in public places, often cruising for sexual partners in such locations; they like sexual variety and experimentation. Finally, such industries as prostitution, pornography, topless bars, escort services, and adult bookstores tend to be supported by both heterosexual and homosexual males, rather than by women of either sexual orientation (Goode, 1990).

women in their thirties could be termed bisexual. Later surveys (Knudson, 1990; Hite, 1981) both showed that approximately 6 percent of adults defined themselves as being bisexual, although Hite's survey concerned only male respondents.

Again, perspectives on bisexuality differ. On the one hand, some scientists maintain, as Kinsey did, that sexuality exists on a continuum and is not an either/or behavior. In this view, bisexuality represents a combination of heterosexuality and homosexuality. Other scientists have insisted that heterosexuals, homosexuals, and bisexuals form separate categories, basing their arguments on the facts that sex drive, production of testosterone, and certain psychological and social traits differ among the categories.

As to the causes of bisexuality, no specific or general theory has been proposed. In the largest study of bisexuality attempted, the findings were inconclusive: most men and women had no homosexual experiences before adulthood and seemed to drift into relationships with both men and women, almost casually. However, the reasons for entering into various relationships with either same-sexed or other-sexed individuals differed according to gender. Women who defined themselves as bisexual noted that their emotional needs are sometimes filled by men and at other times by women, while bisexual men sometimes rationalize their bisexuality as a need for variety in their sex lives (Blumstein & Schwartz, 1977).

Sexually Transmitted Diseases

An unfortunate consequence of all types of sex, but particularly of unprotected, promiscuous sex, is sexually transmitted diseases (STDs). STDs are defined as diseases transmitted from one person to another through sexual contact, including oral–genital contact, anal intercourse, and oral–anal contact. STDs include chlamydia, gonorrhea, syphilis, AIDS, and about 30 others. These communicable diseases are very common because the viruses and bacteria that cause them have become increasingly resistant to drugs and because looser sexual mores have led people to engage in sex at earlier ages and with multiple partners. STDs affect people of all ages and all social classes. Untreated, they are very dangerous, leading to infertility and, in the worst cases, death. However, most may be cured if caught early enough, and all are preventable when proper information is available and care and responsibility for one's actions is taken. Unfortunately, it seems that many people do not take such responsibility: the Centers for Disease Control (CDC) report that while approximately 700,000 cases of gonorrhea occur every year in the United States, the disease is becoming resistant to the antibiotics with which it has been traditionally treated. Should the bacterium become resistant to the new type of antibiotics as well, it would lead to a severe crisis.

Twenty years ago the nation became conscious of a scourge that afflicted homosexual males (and later drug addicts who shared needles): the emergence of the human immunodeficiency virus (HIV), the

TABLE 14.5 Estimated Numbers of Cases and Rates (per 100,000 population) of AIDS, by Race, Category, and Sex, 2005—50 States and the District of Columbia

	Adults or Adolescents							
	Males		Females		Total[a]		Children (<13 yrs)	
Race/ethnicity	No.	Rate	No.	Rate	No.	Rate	No.	Rate
White, not Hispanic	10,852	13.1	1,830	2.1	12,681	7.5	8	0.0
Black, not Hispanic	14,216	103.6	7,776	49.9	21,992	75.0	39	0.5
Hispanic	6,558	39.7	1,865	12.2	8,423	26.4	9	0.1
Asian/Pacific Islander	444	8.2	104	1.8	547	4.9	1	0.1
American Indian/Alaska Native	152	15.9	44	4.4	196	10.0	0	0.0
Total[b]	**32,430**	**27.2**	**11,710**	**9.4**	**41,140[c]**	**18.1**	**58**	**0.1**

Note: These numbers do not represent reported case counts. Rather, these numbers are point estimates, which result from adjustments of reported case counts. The reported case counts have been adjusted for reporting delays, but not for incomplete reporting. Data exclude cases in persons whose state or area of residence is unknown, as well as cases from U.S. dependent areas, for which census information about race and age categories is lacking.

[a]Because row totals were calculated independently of values for the subpopulations, the values in each row may not sum to the row total.

[b]Includes person of unknown race or multiple races. Because column totals were calculated independently of the values for the subpopulations, the values in each column may not sum to the column total.

[c]Includes 302 persons of unknown race or multiple races.

Source: **http://www.cdc.gov/hiv/topics/surveillance/resources/reports/2005report/table5a.htm**.

virus that causes autoimmunodeficiency syndrome (AIDS). Since then, AIDS has become a leading cause of death for some populations and is the fifth leading cause of death among all Americans between the ages of 25 and 44. More than 501,000 Americans with AIDS have died in the United States, including adolescents and children under 15, and the disease has become a major killer in many other societies, especially those in Africa. The number of people living with AIDS in the United States as of 2005 is estimated at more than 437,982, of whom 77 percent are males (**http://www.avert.org/statsum.htm**).

When it became clear how HIV was spread, the government and a number of health organizations initiated a strongly worded campaign among homosexuals and drug addicts with the aim of prevention and protection. For gays, it urged the absolute necessity of having safe sex, that is, sex protected by condoms.

For a while, the fear of becoming HIV infected had the desired effect: as horror stories emerged of young gay men dying horrible deaths as a result of AIDS, more and more of them abandoned unprotected sex with men they had in the past picked up in bars, in adult bookstores, or in spas catering to gays. As a result, and because of new treatments and education efforts, AIDS-related deaths had declined in recent years, by 42 percent between 1996 and 1997 and by another 20 percent between 1997 and 1998. Unfortunately, while the trend was slowing for the gay male population, it was increasing among women whose partners were bisexuals or drug abusers and for minorities (See AIDS statistics in Tables 14.5 and 14.6).

TABLE 14.6 Cases by Exposure Category: the distribution of the estimated number of diagnoses of AIDS among adults and adolescents by exposure category. A breakdown by sex is provided where appropriate.

Exposure Category	Male	Female	Total
Male-to-male sexual contact	420,790	—	420,790
Injection Drug Use	172,351	67,917	240,268
Male-to-male sexual contact and injection drug use	59,719	—	59,719
Heterosexual contact	50,793	84,835	135,628
Other*	14,350	6,519	20,869

*Includes hemophilia, blood transfusion, perinatal, and risk not reported or not identified.

Source: CDC, Division of HIV/AIDS Prevention; **http://www.cdc.gov/hiv/stats.htm**.

New treatments can prolong the lives of AIDS victims and keep at bay the emergence of AIDS among the HIV infected. However, they have also had a negative effect. Some gay men, in fact, have acquired a false sense of security and are increasingly becoming careless, again engaging in high-risk sexual behavior. In particular, it is the generation of younger gays, who have not personally seen the devastation of disease and death that AIDS causes who are the most reckless.

Internationally, about 39.5 million people are estimated to be living with HIV/AIDS, of whom almost half are women and approximately 2.3 million are children (2003). In 2006, AIDS had caused the deaths of approximately 3 million people, including 2.6 million adults and 380,000 children. In some nations, the disease is leaving millions of children orphans and is causing major catastrophes for new generations (http://**www.avert.org/worldstats.htm**).

The Chapter in Brief

The elderly in the United States suffer from loss of status, income, and prestige, even though they are an ever-increasing proportion of the population. Because of the speed of technological change in modern industrial societies, many young persons are better informed and have more skills than the old, at least in certain areas. As a result, the old are devalued. In addition, the elderly suffer from declining health and vigor and so deviate from the ideal norms that prevail in a society that extols youth, beauty, and fitness. Many of the elderly have financial difficulties in addition to health problems; this is especially true of elderly women and members of minority groups. Discrimination against the elderly has been obvious in the area of employment, where the cards are stacked against anyone over age 40. In addition, many employers enforce the retirement age of 70, which forces some employees to disengage before they are ready. Disengagement is supposed to be a mutual process by which the elderly give up social and occupational roles voluntarily so that these roles may be filled by younger persons. Other theoretical frameworks within which the elderly are studied include the modernization, interactionist, subculture, activity, exchange, and age stratification theories.

Many of the myths about the elderly are patently untrue. Not all are senile or miserable or lonely; only a minority have serious health problems; they are not all poor, nor do they all hate retirement. Most live independent lives. Many do face widowhood and the consequent loneliness of bereavement, and when their physical and mental health wane, they may face institutionalization. None of these are pleasant conclusions to life; however, inasmuch as the elderly are a growing segment of society, it is likely that the negative attitudes toward them will be somewhat reversed.

The fact that humanity exists in two sexes has brought it much conflict. In the war between the sexes, women appear to be the losers. From a biological point of view, the two sexes are needed for the species to reproduce: the function of males is to deposit sperm in the reproductive organs of females; the function of females is to carry the resulting embryo—and then the fetus—until it emerges as a fully formed human infant. Both parents can then nurture it until it can exist independently. Throughout history, these different biological functions have resulted in societies treating the two sexes differentially and unequally.

Differences between men and women are of an anatomical, genetic, and hormonal nature. These differences certainly have effects on the behavior of men and women. Some of these differences seem to indicate that females are more social, more suggestible, have lower self-esteem—at least beginning with adolescence—and are less achievement-oriented than males, who are judged to be more aggressive, assertive, and to have more analytical minds. There is also evidence that females are superior in verbal ability and seem inclined to nurture infants and children (the expressive role), while males excel in spatial and quantitative abilities, facilitating the instrumental role. What remains unclear is whether these traits are inborn or a result of differences in socialization experiences.

Even though we are born either male or female, we must become socialized into sex roles. Such socialization begins in the cradle: girl and boy babies are treated differently. Researchers theorize that socialization into sex roles occurs in the context of the functionalist and conflict theories through such processes as social learning, the cognitive developmental model, and identification. As to the agents of gender socialization, they are the family, the peer group, the school, and the mass media.

The fact that women have been treated unequally in most societies has had consequences on their lives. Traditional gender roles have been permeated by a sexist ideology that justifies the inequality between the sexes. The obvious effect of sexism is that many options have been closed to women, who have been relegated for centuries to the roles of wives and mothers and little else. Sociocultural changes in contemporary postindustrial societies have opened more avenues for women. However, the entrance of so many women into the workforce and the consequent displacement of marriage and family have left many women puzzled and confused. It remains difficult for many women to reconcile their aspirations for personal achievement with their desire for a traditional family life. As a result, both men's and women's gender roles still remain far from clear-cut.

In acquiring a sexual personality, not everyone is drawn to heterosexuality. Some individuals are drawn to members of their own gender, becoming homosexuals. Still others are attracted to both sexes, sometimes establishing a paired relationship with one gender after some experimentation, or otherwise remaining bisexual throughout their lives. Scientists have not established a definite cause for these behaviors.

A negative effect of unprotected or promiscuous sex is sexually transmitted diseases (STDs), the most dangerous of which is AIDS. This disease has killed many gay men and intravenous drug users and, increasingly, many women and children. It is also a scourge in developing nations, particularly in Africa.

Terms to Remember

activity theory In the study of the elderly, the theory that the key to successful aging is to replace former roles with new ones.

ageism An ideology that asserts the superiority of the young over the old. Used to justify discrimination against the elderly in political, economic, and social areas.

anatomical differences The differences in physical structure and appearance between the two sexes. The most important anatomical difference lies in the distinct reproductive systems of males and females.

cognitive development theory A theory that includes the idea that children learn gender roles according to which stage of cognitive development they have reached. Cognitive development is the way information is processed by individuals at different stages of physical maturation.

conflict theory A theory that assumes that power and privilege are based on the resources an individual possesses.

disengagement theory A theory of aging that posits that the elderly withdraw from their former social and occupational roles so that these may be filled by the young. This should occur by mutual consent.

exchange theory In the study of the elderly, the theory that the disadvantaged position of the elderly in American society is due to their lack of the social and material resources that would make them valuable in interactions with the young.

expressive role Emphasizes nurturing, emotion, and peacemaking.

feminist theory A theory that has borrowed much of the framework of conflict theory, especially the fact that women are underrepresented in positions of power in the society at large, a reflection of the lack of power women have within the family.

gender roles Traditionally, the **instrumental** role is assigned to males and the **expressive** role is assigned to females.

hormones Chemicals that are secreted into the bloodstream by glands located in the body, whose functions are to stimulate some chemical processes and inhibit others.

instrumental role Stresses rationality, competitiveness, aggression, and goal-orientation.

interactionist theory In the study of the elderly, a theory that focuses on the shared meanings that the elderly hold in common.

male or female Biological terms, descriptive of biological facts. They refer to a **sex status**, ascribed and not subject to change except in extraordinary circumstances.

masculine and feminine Reflect **social** conditions, describing how males and females are expected to behave in a given society and how they come to feel about themselves. They are **gender roles**, achieved and, thus, subject to change according to place and time.

modernization theory In the study of the elderly, the theory that the status of older people declines as the society in which they live becomes more modern and industrial.

secondary sex characteristics Include height, weight, distribution of body fat and hair, and musculature.

sex chromosomes Contain the genes that determine heredity in all living creatures.

social learning theory A theory based on the behaviorist notion that learning consists of observation, imitation, and reinforcement.

structural functionalist theory One of the most dominant theories in sociology, which assumes that those elements are retained in a social system that aid in the survival of that system.

Suggested Readings

Epstein, Cynthia Fuchs, Carroll Seron, Bonnie Oglensky, and Robert Saute. 1999. *The Part-Time Paradox: Time Norms, Professional Life, Family and Gender*. New York: Routledge. A discussion of the conflicts inherent in the lives of women who work, the tension between the demands of career and family, and suggestions as to how to solve some of these conflicts with part-time work.

Faludi, Susan. 1999. *Stiffed: The Betrayal of the American Man*. New York: William Morrow. A feminist author maintains that even though American men remain the dominant sex, they feel increasingly misunderstood and unappreciated.

Dychtwald, Ken. 1999. *Age Power: How the 21st Century Will Be Ruled by the New Old*. New York: Putnam. A gerontologist takes a look at the elderly and speculates about their future social patterns.

Quadagno, Jill. 1999. *Aging and the Life Course: An Introduction to Social Gerontology*. New York: McGraw-Hill. An overview of the aged and of the process of aging from the point of view of sociology.

Stoller, Eleanor Palo, and Rose Campbell Gibson. 2000. *Worlds of Difference: Inequality in the Aging Experience.* 2nd ed. Thousand Oaks, CA: Pine Forge Press. The experience of growing old according to a diverse number of people differing in race, class, and gender. An anthology written from a sociological perspective, showing a variety of norms and social structures on the road to aging.

Westheimer, Ruth K., and Sanford Lopater. 2002. *Human Sexuality.* Baltimore: Lippincott Williams & Wilkins. As the title suggests, this is a textbook on human sexuality and deals with the entire spectrum of this subject in clear and understandable language. The well-known Dr. Westheimer answers letters and queries on a variety of sexual issues.

Web Sites of Interest

http://www.nih.gov/nia
The site of the U.S. government agency the National Institute of Aging. It provides links to other sites related to the subject of aging, as well as information on research and funding.

http://www.iwpr.org
The site of a public policy research organization whose purpose is to inform women and families on issues important to them. Deals with issues of poverty, employment, and aspects of health care, among many others.

http://www.4women.gov/owh
Another agency, part of the U.S. Department of Health and Human Services, that also specializes in women's issues, particularly those related to health.

http://www.vix.com/men/index.html
This site is a source for statistics, studies, and publications relating to men's issues.

http://www.indiana.edu/~kinsey
Web site of the Kinsey Institute where research on human sexuality continues.

http://www.who.int/hiv/strategic/en
The World Health Organization, an agency of the United Nations, provides the latest facts and figures on HIV/AIDS.

15

chapter

The Family

IN THIS CHAPTER, YOU WILL LEARN

- ***The Family Tree***
  - *Families as Kinship Systems*
  - *Culture and Forms of the Family*
  - *The Family Unit*
  - *The Development of the Family*
  - *The Origins of the Nuclear Family*
- ***Family and Ethnicity***
  - *The European American Family*
  - *The Native American Family*
  - *The African American Family*
  - *The Asian American Family*
  - *The Hispanic Family*
- ***Forming Families***
  - *Courtship and Dating*
  - *Marriage*
  - *Biracial Marriage*
  - *Same-Sex Marriage*
- ***Parenting***
  - *Gender and Parenting*
  - *Single-Parent Families*
  - *Grandparenting*
  - *Adoptive Parents*
  - *Not Parenting*
- ***Family Transitions***
  - *The Consequences of Divorce*
  - *Blended Families*
- ***Violence in Families***
  - *Intimate Partner Violence*
  - *Intergenerational and Intragenerational Violence*
- ***The Family in the 21st Century: "The Same as It Ever Was"***

Almost daily, we hear some political pundit prophesy the end of the family. The crisis of the family is so severe that in 2000, the U.S. Congress passed a Family Protection Act, as if the family were an endangered species, like the spotted owl. Divorce and remarriage have never been more common. Millions of children are growing up with single parents or in blended households. Millions of young adults are putting off marriage until their 30s, or cohabiting instead of getting married, or opting to stay single. People are selecting household arrangements today that would mystify our ancestors. Even the conservative U.S. Bureau of the Census has given in and added the category "cohabiting partners" to the old litany of single, married, widowed, or divorced.

On the other hand, the family has never been more popular. Suddenly, everyone seems to want one: single people, gay men and lesbians, even the elderly and widowed. Prime-time TV, which used to make fun of the nuclear family with shows like Married . . . with Children, is overloaded with moms, dads, and kids. And the wedding industry generates sales of about $50 billion every single year.

The family is in crisis. The family has never been more popular.

The gay marriage debate is a good example of both sides of the argument. Opponents say it would wreak "a potentially fatal blow to the traditional family," leading "inexorably to polygamy and other alternatives to one man/one woman unions" (Dobson, 2004). At the same time, gay couples across the country have been eager to pledge their love and commitment by getting married. And millions of supporters believe matrimony should not be limited to only some couples but open to everyone who wants to enter into it. How much more popular can the idea of marriage get?

The great novelist Thomas Wolfe said "you can't go home again." A few years earlier, the poet Robert Frost wrote that "Home is the place where, when you have to go there, they have to take you in." We believe both statements—in part, sociologists understand, because both are true. The family has never been more popular in part because it is in crisis—and all the cultural media, from TV to movies to pop songs, are trying to reassert its predominance in an increasingly individualized and global world. And the family is in crisis in part because of those institutional forces, like the global marketplace and its ideology of individualism, which constitute the dominant ideology around the world.

One thing is certain: The family is hardly a separate realm from the rest of society. It is a political football, tossed around by both liberals and conservatives, who appeal to it abstractly and develop policies that shape and mold it concretely. It is the foundation of the economy. And it is the basic building block of society. Always has been. Probably always will be.

What is the family? Where did it come from? Is it still necessary? How do sociologists understand the forces the hold it together and the forces that pull it apart?

Is the family in crisis—or has it never been more popular, or more supported? We believe both—in part, sociologists understand, because both are true.

The Family Tree

Unlike most animals, human beings are born helpless. For the first few years of their lives, they require round-the-clock care, and for the first decade, they require nearly constant supervision, or they won't survive to adulthood. But even after they learn basic survival skills, humans are still not qualified to make their own way in the world—an adult has to provide for all of their needs for 10 or 15 years or more. You are born into a group—and your survival depends on it. This is, of course, the family.

Families as Kinship Systems

Every human society has divided the adults into cooperative groups who take charge of the care and feeding of the children. This is the origin of the **family,** defined as "the basic unit in society traditionally consisting of two parents rearing their children" but also "any of various social units differing from but regarded as equivalent to the traditional family"—such as single parents with children, spouses without children, and several generations living together. Families also refer to those related to you through blood or marriage, extended back through generations.

Families are kinship systems that anchor our identities in shared history and culture.

Families provide us with a sense of history, both as individuals and as members of a particular culture. Families themselves are part of **kinship systems,** cultural forms that locate individuals in the culture by reference to their families. Kinship systems are groupings that include all your relatives, mapped as a network from closest (mother, father, siblings) to a little more distant (cousins, aunts, uncles) to increasingly distant (your great-uncle twice removed). Your kinship system can be imagined as a "family tree." Tracing your family tree is especially popular these days because it provides a sense of history.

Family trees can be organized in several ways to ground you in that history, depending on how you trace your descent, where you live, and whom you marry. These different ways of constructing a family tree give you a different cognitive map of the world and your place in it. Your line of descent can be:

- **Matrilineal:** through your mother's side of the family
- **Patrilineal:** through your father's side of the family
- **Bilineal:** through both your parents' sides

In many cases, your surname (last name) provides a minihistory of your ancestry. In some languages, it is literally in your name, like Johnson or Stevenson in English, Jonasdottir in Icelandic, Petrov in Russian. These names suggest different ways of tracing your family tree and lineage.

Culture and Forms of the Family

Families are not simply an expression of love between people who want to have children. They are fundamental cultural institutions that have as much to do with economics, politics, and sex as they do with raising children. As the fundamental unit of society, the social functions of the family and the regulation of sexuality have always been of interest to sociologists.

For one thing, families ensure the regular transfer of property and establish lines of succession. For another, families restrict the number of people you can have sex with. In prehistoric times, a mighty hunter might spend three weeks tracking down and killing a single mastodon. He didn't want to go through all of that time and expense to feed a child that his next-door neighbor had produced. But how could he be sure that his next-door neighbor *wasn't* the father of the children his best girlfriend had given birth to? To solve this problem, almost every society has established a type of marriage—a relationship that regulates sexual activity to ensure **legitimacy,** that is, to ensure that men know what children they have produced (women have an obvious way to know). Families then bear the economic and emotional burden of raising only the children that belong to them (Malinowski, [1927] 1974).

No society allows its members to marry or have sex with anyone they might take an interest in, but the specifics of who can marry whom vary from place to place and over time. The most common arrangement is **monogamy,** marriage between two people. Most monogamous societies allow men and women to marry each other because it takes one of each to make a baby, but same-sex monogamy is surprisingly common. Historian John Boswell found evidence of same-sex marriages existing alongside male-female marriages even in early Christian Europe (1995).

Many societies have instituted some form of **polygamy,** or marriage between three or more people, although most of those allow monogamy as well. The most common form of polygamy is **polygyny,** one man with two or more women, because a man can have children with several women at the same time. Among the Yoruba of northern Nigeria, women can have only one husband, but *they* can have as many wives as they want, so they practice a type of same-sex polygyny: One woman marries two or more women (Roscoe, 2001). **Polyandry,** one woman marrying two or more men, is rare, but it has been documented in Tibet and a few other places where men are absent for several months of the year.

Only a few societies practice **group marriage,** two or more men marrying two or more women, with children born to anyone in the union "belonging" to all of the partners equally. Group marriages appeared from time to time in the 1960s counterculture, but they rarely lasted long (Hollenbach, 2004).

Marriage does more than ensure that the proper people are responsible for the upbringing of the child; it ensures that when the child grows up, he or she will know who is off limits as a marriage partner. Almost every human society enforces **exogamy:** Marriage to (or sex with) members of your family unit is forbidden. This is the incest taboo, which Sigmund Freud argued was the one single cultural universal. (Without it, lines of succession and inheritance of property would be impossible!)

Of course, who counts as family varies from culture to culture and over time. Mom, Dad, brother, sister, son, or daughter are always off limits, except in a few cases of ritual marriage (the ancient Egyptian pharaohs married their sisters). But uncles and nieces commonly married each other through the nineteenth century, and first cousins are still allowed to marry in most countries in Europe and twenty-six of the U.S. states. In the Hebrew Bible, God struck Onan dead because he refused to have sex with his widowed sister-in-law and thereby produce an heir for his brother. But nowadays an affair with one's sister-in-law would be thought of as creepy at best. *The Brady Bunch Movie* (1995) plays with the idea that Greg and Marcia Brady are brother and sister by adoption, not by blood, so they could legally become interested in each other, date, and marry. But they won't; again, creepy.

> **Did you know?**
> The family form mentioned most often in the Bible is polygymy (multiple female partners). In fact, all of the patriarchs—Abraham, Isaac, Jacob, and Joseph—had numerous wives and concubines (sexual partners to whom they were not married to). Solomon was reputed to have had 1,000 wives, products of his many political alliances.

At the other end of the spectrum, sometimes your entire clan, totem, or kinship group is often off limits. For this reason, groups of friends usually refrain from dating within the group. Until recently, Koreans were legally forbidden from marrying anyone with their same last name. Unfortunately, nearly a quarter of the population has the last name *Kim* (Yong-Shik, 2001).

The Family Unit

Family units come in an enormously varied number of types, from the father-mother-kids model that we see on evening sitcoms to longhouses where everyone in the tribe lives together in a gigantic mass. However, individual families are usually differentiated from others with a separate dwelling, their own house, apartment, cabin, or tent. Even when the entire tribe lives together in a single longhouse, each family gets its own cooking fire and personal space to differentiate it from the other families and signify that they belong together.

Chances are that you will occupy at least two different family units during your lifetime. While you are a child, you belong to a **family of origin**—the family you are born into—with your biological parents or others who are responsible for your upbringing. When you grow up, if you marry or cohabit with a romantic partner, you now also belong to a **family of procreation,** which is the family you choose to belong to in order to reproduce. Often we consider any adults you are living with as a family of procreation, even if none of them is actually doing any procreating. In modern societies, it is customary to change residences to signify that you have moved to a new family unit, but most premodern societies didn't differentiate: Either new wives moved in with their husbands' family, or new husbands moved in with their wives' family, or everyone kept right on living together (Fox, 1984; Stone, 2000).

Families usually have some rationale, real or imaginary, for being together. They, and everyone else in the community, assume that they "belong" together because of a common biological ancestry, legal marriage or adoption, some other bond of kinship, or the connection to others by blood, marriage, or adoption. Sometimes they can't prove biological ancestry, but they still insist on a common ancestor in the distant past, human, god, or animal. When all else fails, they create symbolic kinship, blood brothers, aunties, and "friends of the family."

The Development of the Family

When our son was 5 years old, we were wandering through the ethnological exhibits at the Museum of Natural History. There were lifelike dioramas of other cultures—Eskimo, Polynesian, Amazonian—and also displays that portrayed the evolution of modern society through the Neolithic, Paleolithic, and Pleistocene ages. In each case, the diorama had exactly the same form: In the front, a single male, poised as a hunter or fisherman. Behind him, by a fire toward the back of the tableau, sat a single woman, cooking or preparing food, surrounded by several small children.

It wasn't until we passed into the hall of the animals, however, that anything seemed amiss. The dioramas kept to form: A single male—lion, gorilla, whatever—standing proudly in front, a single female and offspring lounging in the back waiting for him to bring home fresh meat.

"Look, Dad," Zachary said. "They have families just like we do."

I started to simply say "uh huh," the way parents do, half listening to their children. But something made me stop short. "Uh, actually, they don't," I said. "Most of these animals actually live in larger groupings, extended families and cooperative bands. And lionesses do most of the hunting (and caring for the young) while the males lounge about lazily most of the day."

Nor was every family throughout human history a nuclear family. Indeed, the nuclear family emerged only recently, within the past few thousand years. For most of human existence, our family forms have been quite varied and significantly larger, including several generations and all the siblings all living together.

Until my son pointed it out, though, I had never noticed that these exhibits in the museum were not historically accurate reflections of human (or animal) history, but normative efforts to make the contemporary nuclear family appear to have been eternal and universal, to read it back into history and across species—in a sense, to rewrite history so that the family didn't have a history but instead to pretend it had always been the way it is.

Nothing could be further from the truth. Families have developed and changed enormously over the course of human history.

Families evolved to socialize children, transmit property, ensure legitimacy, and regulate sexuality. They also evolved as economic units. Because children went to work alongside the adults, they contributed to the economic prosperity of the family; in fact, the family became a unit of economic production. Property and other possessions were passed down from the adults of the family to the children. Occupation, religion, language, social standing, and wealth were all dependent on kinship ties.

In all agrarian societies, including Europe and America as late as the nineteenth century, the household has been the basic economic unit. Production—and consumption—occurred within the household. Everyone participated in growing and eating the crops, and the excess might be taken to market for trade.

There was no distinction between family and society: Family life *was* social life. Families performed a whole range of functions later performed by social institutions. The family was not only a site of economic production and consumption. It was:

- *A school.* Any reading and writing you learned was at your parents' knee.
- *A church.* The head of the household led the family prayers; you might see the inside of a "real" church or temple once or twice a year.
- *A hospital.* Family members knew as much as there was to know about setting broken bones and healing diseases
- *A day care center.* There were no businesses to take care of children, so someone in the family had to do it.
- *A police station.* There were no police to call when someone wronged you, so you called on your family to take care of the situation.
- *A retirement home.* If you had no family to take care of you in your old age, you would end up in debtor's prison or begging on the streets.

Obviously, all these functions cannot be met by the nuclear family model. (That model includes the biological parents and their children, although it can also include their children from other marriages.) The most common model in the premodern era was the **extended family,** in which two or three generations lived under the same roof or at least in the same compound. No one left the household except to marry into another family, until the group got too big for the space available and had to split up. And even then, they would build a new house nearby, until eventually everyone in the village was related to everyone else.

The Origins of the Nuclear Family

Just as families are no longer concerned exclusively with socializing children, marriage developed far more functions than simple sexual regulation, ensuring that parents and children know who each other is. Marriage could also validate a gentleman's claim to nobility and establish that a boy had become a man. It could form a social tie between two families or bring peace to warring tribes. In the Middle Ages, European monarchs often required their children to marry the child of a monarch next door, on the theory that you are unlikely to go to war with the country that your son or daughter has married into (it didn't work—by the seventeenth century, all of the European monarchs were second or third cousins, and they were always invading each other).

Marriage has also come to represent a distinctive emotional bond between two people. In fact, the idea that people should select their own marriage partner is actually a very recent phenomenon. For thousands of years, parents selected partners to fulfill their own economic and political needs or those of the broader kinship group. Arranged marriages are still the norm in a number of countries. People still fall in love—romantic love is practically universal across human societies—but not necessarily with the people they intended to marry. The tradition of courtly love, praised by the troubadours of medieval France, was expressly about adultery, falling in love with someone else's spouse (De Rougemont, 1983).

Only about 200 years ago did men and women in Western countries begin to look at marriage as an individual affair, to be decided by the people involved rather than parents, church, and state.

Like the **companionate marriage,** in which individuals choose their marriage partners based on emotional ties and love, the nuclear family is a relatively recent phenomenon. It emerged in Europe and the United States in the late eighteenth century. Its emergence depended on certain factors, such as the ability of a single breadwinner to earn enough in the marketplace to support the family and sufficient hygiene and health so that most babies would survive with only one adult taking care of them.

Romantic love is virtually universal, found in all cultures. Hindu couple in South Asia.

Historians like Carl Degler (1980) trace the new nuclear family, as it emerged in the White middle class between 1776 and 1830,

Did you know?
In the American colonies, single people were penalized if they remained single too long. Maryland imposed a tax on bachelors (Lauer and Lauer, 2003). Even today, federal and state income tax laws offer substantial cuts for married people, in the hopes that single people will get the message and head for the altar.

and Christopher Lasch (1975) suggests the theory of "progressive nucleation" to explain how it gradually superseded the extended family and became the norm. During the nineteenth century, industrialization and modernization meant that social and economic needs could no longer be met by kin. It became customary for children to move far from their parents to go to school or look for work. With no parents around, they had to be responsible for their own spouse selection, and when they married, they would have to find their own home. Eventually adult children were expected to start their own households away from their parents, even if they were staying in the same town. When they had children of their own, they were solely responsible for the child rearing; the grandparents had only small and informal roles to play.

The change was not always beneficial: In every generation, husbands and wives had to reinvent child-rearing techniques, starting over from scratch, with many possibilities for mistakes. As Margaret Mead stated (1978), "Nobody has ever before asked the nuclear family to live all by itself in a box the way we do. With no relatives, no support, we've put it in an impossible situation."

The nuclear family is also a more highly "gendered" family—roles and activities are allocated increasingly along gender lines. On the one hand, because the nuclear family was by definition much smaller than the extended family, the wife experienced greater autonomy. On the other hand, in her idealized role, she was increasingly restricted to the home, with her primary role envisioned as child care and household maintenance. She became a "housewife."

Women were seen as morally superior to men (though physically and intellectually inferior), and the homes they made as nurturing and supportive, as opposed to the "cold, cruel world" of the workplace, the home was supposed to be, as de Tocqueville put it, a "haven in a heartless world." The home was a space for feelings, the workplace a space of unemotional, sometimes brutal logic. The sentimental connotations of "home" and "mother" began during this period (cited in Janara, 2001, p. 551).

Because the home was seen as the "women's sphere," middle-class women's activities outside the home began to shrink. The husband became the "breadwinner," the only one in the family who was supposed to go to work and provide economic support for the household. (Of course, families of lesser means could not always survive on the salary of a single earner, so wives often continued to work outside the home.) But the middle-class wife, now called "the little woman," was supposedly so sweet, fragile, and innocent that only her husband was supposedly tough enough to handle the sordid world of business (Welter, 1966).

As the attention of the household, and especially the mother, became increasingly centered on children, they were seen as needing more than food, clothing, education, and maybe a spanking now and then. They were no longer seen as "little savages," barbarians who needed civilizing, or corrupt sinners who would go to Hell unless they were baptized immediately. Instead, they were "little angels," pure and innocent, born "trailing clouds of glory" as they descended from heaven (instead of trailing fire and brimstone as they ascended from that other place). Therefore they had to be kept innocent of the more graphic aspects of life, like sex and death, and they needed love, nurturing, and constant care and attention. The number of children per family declined, both because they would no longer be providing economic support for the family and because each child now required a greater investment of time and emotional energy.

In modern societies, children don't often work alongside their parents, and the family has become a unit of consumption rather than production; its economic security is tied to the workplace and the national economy. Instead, the major functions of the family are to provide lifelong psychological support and emotional security. The family has been so closely associated with love and belonging that friends and even groups of co-workers express their emotional intimacy by saying they are "a family."

The nuclear family, with its strict division of household labor, is a relatively recent historical invention—and does not apply to all cultures, even in the United States. In the Chicano family, everyone cooks, so everyone eats.

Family and Ethnicity

The contemporary American nuclear family—the breadwinning husband, his homemaker wife, and their 2.2 children, who live in a detached single-family house in a suburb we call Anytown, USA—developed historically. But even today, it is only one of several family forms. Families vary not only from culture to culture but also within our society—by race and ethnicity. As each racial and ethnic group has a different history, their family units developed in different ways, in response to different conditions. For example, how can we understand the modern African American family outside the deliberate policies of slavery whereby families were broken up, and husbands, wives, and children deliberately sold to different slave owners, so as to dilute the power of family as a tie of loyalty to something other than the master?

Sociologists are interested in the diversity of family forms by race and ethnicity. Some of these differences are now so well documented that to enumerate them sounds almost like a stereotype. And, to be sure, each ethnic group exhibits wide variation in their families (not all Catholic families have nine kids, but most American families with nine kids are Catholic). Sociologists are also interested in the process by which one family form became the standard against which all other family forms were measured—and found wanting. In addition, although these family adaptations are seen largely among ethnic minorities, they are also seen among the White working class, which suggests that they are less "ethnic" adaptations to a White family norm and more "class" adaptations to a middle- and upper-class family norm. As each ethnic group develops a stable middle class, their families come to resemble the companionate-marriage nuclear family of the White middle class. It may be the case not that the nuclear family is inevitable, but that it is *expensive*—and that without significant governmental support, it does not flourish.

The European American Family

This family form that became the dominant model was itself the product of a variety of social factors that are unlikely to return. Based initially on the Anglo-Irish family of the seventeenth century, the European American family has also taken on characteristics from each of the large immigrant groups, especially those that arrived in the late nineteenth century. Many of these immigrant families were Catholic and did not use birth control, so their families tended to be larger than those of the Protestant immigrants, who did practice birth control.

But the contemporary family is also the result of deliberate social policies beginning in the first decades of the twentieth century. These policies held up a specific model as normal and natural and then endeavored to fulfill that vision by prohibitions on women's entry into the workplace or pushing them out once they found their way there, ideologies of motherhood and birth control to limit family size, a "eugenics" movement that demanded that all new immigrants conform to a specific standard of marriage and family, and a new educational and child-rearing ideology that specified how parents should raise their children. American families have always been subject to deliberate policies to encourage certain types of families and discourage others, a process that continues today.

The end of World War II saw the largest infusion of government funding toward the promotion of this new nuclear family—the interstate highway system that promoted flight to the suburban tract homes, the massive spending on public schools in those suburbs, and policy initiatives coupled with ideologies that pushed women out of manufacturing work and back into the home, while their veteran husbands were reabsorbed into the labor force or went to college on the GI Bill.

The family form that finally emerged in the 1950s—idealized in classic situation comedies of the 1950s and early 1960s like *Father Knows Best* and *Leave It to Beaver* on that newly emergent and culturally unifying medium, television—was far less a naturally emergent evolutionary adaptation and far more the anomalous result of deliberate social planning.

The Native American Family

Prior to the arrival of the Europeans, most Native Americans lived in small villages where extended families dominated; you could trace a blood relationship with almost everyone you knew, and most social interaction—from food distribution to village government—depended on kinship ties and obligations. Strangers were considered enemies unless they could be somehow included in the kinship network (Wilkinson, 1999). One of the primary means of creating kinship alliances was exogamy, the requirement that people marry outside of their clan. Marriages created allies, which were useful in any disputes with other clans in the tribe.

Native American families are, themselves, quite diverse. Most marriages are monogamous, but some tribes permitted polygyny, and a few permitted men to sleep with other women when their wives were pregnant or lactating. Many tribes, such as the Zuni and Hopi in the Southwest and the Iroquois in the Northeast, were matrilineal. Hopi children were raised by their mothers and uncles (and, to an extent, their fathers). Girls continued to live with their mothers throughout their lives. When they married, they brought their husbands home with them. When boys entered puberty, they moved into the men's ceremonial house. Eventually most of them married women of other clans and moved in with their wives' family.

The father had limited authority in the family: He was considered a guest in his wife's home, and her brothers or cousins made all of the major economic and child-rearing decisions. Children went to their uncle, not their father, for approval of their life choices.

Still, children—especially boys—learned a lot from their fathers. Although uncles had the greatest authority over their life decisions, their biological fathers taught them their occupational skills, hunting, herding animals, or growing crops.

Native American family and kinship systems were developed to provide for people's fundamental needs, such as producing enough food and defending against outsiders. Although kin often shared strong emotional bonds, families did not develop primarily out of people's desire for love, intimacy, and personal fulfillment but out of the desire to survive.

Native Americans are often torn between the social norms of their traditional culture and those of the dominant society. This grandfather shows his grandson how to mend fishing nets.

Native Americans are often torn between the social norms of their traditional culture and those of the dominant society (Garrett, 1999; Yellowbird and Snipp, 1994). One-third marry outside their ethnicity, and the extended family model of the tribal society is common only on the reservations. In the cities, most Native Americans live in nuclear families (Sandefur and Sakamoto, 1988).

As with other minority groups, social problems such as poverty put significant strains on both extended and nuclear families (Harjo, 1999; Strong, 2004).

The African American Family

Before slavery was abolished, most slaves in the United States and elsewhere were prohibited from legal marriages. It was common practice to separate husbands and wives, and children and parents, on arrival and to make sure they were sold to different plantations, which, slave owners reasoned, would keep them more obedient and less likely to maintain any attachments other than to the plantation. As a result, slaves created their own permanent marital bonds, developing strong kinship ties similar to those in the extended family models of West Africa. Mutual aid and emotional support remained centered in kinship long after slavery (Strong, 2004).

Since the early 1970s, economic changes have resulted in a massive loss of blue-collar jobs (disproportionately held by minorities), and as a result the nuclear family model has become even less common. African Americans have lower marriage rates and higher divorce rates than other ethnic groups (Clarkwest, 2006) and a greater percentage of single mothers. Over half of African American families consist of only one parent, usually the mother.

The completely self-sufficient nuclear family model is difficult enough with two parents, but only one parent, trying to provide full-time emotional and financial support, is often severely overextended. As a survival mechanism, many African American communities have adopted the convention of "fictive kinship"—that is, stretching the boundaries of kinship to include nonblood relations, friends, neighbors, and co-workers, who are obligated to help out in hard times and whom one is obligated to help out in turn (Stack, 1974).

Fictive kinship can also extend to women who have children with the same man. Far from considering each other competition or "home wreckers," they often consider each other kin, with the same bonds of obligation and emotional support due to sisters or sisters-in-law. When a woman has children with several different men, each of whom has children with several different women, the bonds of fictive kinship can extend across a community.

The Asian American Family

Asian Americans trace their ancestry to many different cultural groups in more than twenty languages, so they brought many different family systems to the United States with them. The more recent the immigration, the more closely their family system reflects that of their original culture. But even third- and fourth-generation families, who are demographically almost identical to White middle-class nuclear families (same percentage of married couples, two-parent families, and male heads of household), show some differences in orientation and family style.

Suzuki (1985) studied Chinese American and Japanese American families and found that the roles and responsibilities of various family members are based on the Confucian principles that have informed Chinese society for 2,000 years. They are more collectively based than Euro-American families, emphasizing the family as a unit rather than a group of individuals. Grown-up Euro-American children may reject their parents' wishes, saying "I have to live my own life," but Chinese and Japanese American children are more concerned about not bringing shame or dishonor to the family. If Mom and Pop say that they should go to medical school, they're going to medical school, regardless of how much they might long to audition for *American Idol.*

Euro-American families tend to be democratic, with every member having a voice in such decisions as what to have for dinner or where to go on vacation. In contrast, Chinese and Japanese American families are more hierarchical. Parents and older siblings exert full authority over children and younger siblings and require respect and obedience from them. The only exceptions are made for gender—in some situations, boys may have authority over their mothers and older sisters.

The Hispanic Family

Like Asian Americans, Hispanic Americans trace their ancestry to many different cultures with different languages, religions, and different family systems: Cuban families are very different from Puerto Rican families, which are very different from Chicano families, and so on (Baca Zinn, 1995; Carrasquillo 1994). Also like Asian Americans, the more recently Hispanic Americans have arrived in the United States, the more closely their family system resembles that of their original culture.

Demographically, Hispanic families fall somewhat between Euro-American and African American families. Most are nuclear families, but they do have characteristics of extended families, with grandparents, aunts, uncles, and more distant relatives living close together, visiting each other frequently, and bearing some of the responsibilities for child rearing and emotional support.

They tend to be hierarchical by age and gender, like Asian American families, but here, too, Hispanic families exhibit significant variation. Chicano and Puerto Rican families are more egalitarian than Dominican and Cuban families; and those from South America are somewhat more likely to be middle class, smaller, and more egalitarian than those from the Caribbean.

Gender equality also increases with length of residence in the United States. The longer the family has been in the United States, the more egalitarian it will tend to be. The families of second- and third-generation immigrants tend to be more egalitarian than families of older generations (Chilman, 1999; Wilkinson, 1999). This is probably the result of social mobility rather than ethnicity—the longer the residence in the United States, the more likely is the family to belong to the middle class.

Forming Families

Sociologists study the variations in the family form and also the processes by which we form families. To most of us, it probably seems pretty straightforward: After a few years of dating, you become increasingly serious with one special someone, you fall in love, you gradually realize that this one is "it," and you decide to marry. Historically, this has been a process known as courtship, the intensification and institutionalization of an intimate relationship from meeting to mating to marrying. And it is so common, so casually assumed, we often have no idea just how unusual and recent this process is.

Courtship and Dating

In the famous musical *Fiddler on the Roof,* a drama that centers on the breakdown of a traditional Jewish family in a small Russian village in the late nineteenth century, as each of the three daughters chooses to marry an increasingly troublesome man, the girls' parents reminisce about their courtship. "The first time I met you was on our wedding day," Golde tells her husband, Tevye. That was not uncommon. So he asks if she loves him. "Do I what?!?" she answers.

Courtship was largely unknown in ancient society, despite the efforts of Hollywood movies to show true, but unrequited love, in Rome, Greece, or Egypt. Marriages were arranged, and children often were betrothed (promised, engaged) as toddlers. But even in the days when marriages were arranged by parents, children often had a voice in the selection process, and they found ways to meet and evaluate potential partners so they could make their preferences known. By the turn of the twentieth century, they were classmates at coed high schools, and they formed romantic bonds with people that their parents didn't even know.

The custom of dating, engaging in recreational activities in pairs rather than groups and with the goal of establishing or strengthening a romantic commitment, did not arise until the 1920s. Children of working-class immigrants in major American cities were trying to distance themselves from the old-fashioned supervised visits that their parents insisted on, and fortunately they enjoyed both a great deal of personal freedom and a wide range of brand-new entertainment venues (Bailey, 1989).

By the 1930s, the custom had spread to the middle class. College-aged men and women participated in a process called "rating and dating," whereby they were rated on their desirability as a date and would ask or accept dates only with people of similar ratings. Dating was based on physical attractiveness, social desirability, and other qualities—not family name and position. Most importantly, dating was supervised and scrutinized by one's peer group, not one's parents (Nock, 2003).

College and high school became the time of unparalleled freedom for American youth and were increasingly taken up by dating and courtship. Campus wits joked that girls were attending college just to get their "Mrs." degree. By the 1950s, parents were eagerly awaiting their son or daughter's first date as a sign of their entry into adulthood. There were many stages: casual dating, going steady (dating only one person), being pinned (wearing a class ring or pin as a sign of commitment), and finally becoming engaged. Boys and girls were supposed to begin dating early in high school and date many people over the period of years, perhaps going steady several times, until they found "the one" to marry. But not for too many years: "Still dating" in the late 20s was considered sad and slightly unwholesome. In the 1970s, the increased incidence of divorce sent many people in their middle years into the world of dating again, until there was little stigma about dating at the age of 30, 40, or 50.

Today it seems that everyone is dating. Kindergarteners go on "play dates," married couples go on dates, and the recently widowed or divorced are encouraged to date again almost immediately. Internet dating sites are among the Web's most popular, and your potential dates are neatly categorized by age, gender, race, and sexual orientation. And yet it also seems that no one is dating. On campuses, the preferred mode of social and sexual interaction is "hooking up," which is so loose and indiscriminate that its connection to dating and mating has been lost.

On campuses, the preferred mode of social and sexual interaction is "hooking up," which usually consists of some form of sexual activity with someone you know who is connected to your social network, and is not expected to lead to a relationship.

Box 15.1 Dating in Japan

In 1955, parents arranged 63 percent of all marriages in Japan. In 1998, the percentage had dropped to 7 percent (Retherford, Ogawa, and Matsukura, 2001). Yet, relative to the United States, Japan has not developed a strong dating culture. You're not expected to bring a date to every recreational activity, and if you're not dating anyone at the moment, your friends don't feel sorry for you and try to fix you up. The expectation that dating leads to marriage is also absent. Japanese television and other mass media don't glorify marriage and ridicule or pity single people, as American television often does (Ornstein, 2001).

Outside of high school and college, there are few places where single men and women meet and interact. Forty-five percent of heterosexual women over the age of 16 say that they have no male friends at all. However, practically all of the heterosexual women with one or more male friends have engaged in premarital sex (probably with the male friends) (Retherford et al., 2001).

With no societal push to marriage and premarital sex available, it is no wonder that they don't feel pressured into getting married right away, or at all. In 2001, schoolgirls around the world were asked whether they agreed with the statement that "everyone should be married." Three-quarters of American schoolgirls agreed. But 88 percent of Japanese schoolgirls disagreed (Coontz, 2007).

FIGURE 15.1 Households by Type, 1970–2003

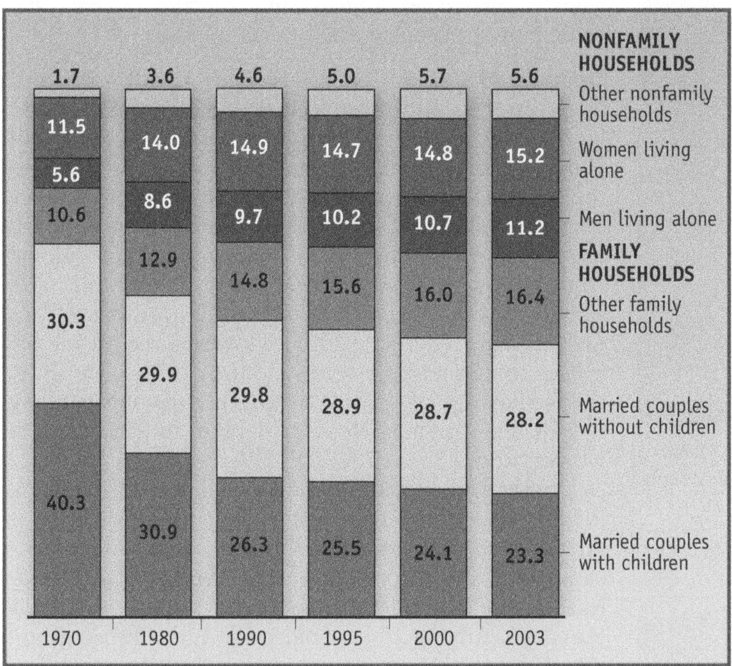

Source: Current Population Survey, U.S. Census Bureau, 2004.

Marriage

Marriage is the most common foundation for family formation in the world. The marriage of two people—a woman and a man—is universal in developed countries, although there are significant variations among different cultures.

Marriage is not identical to a nuclear family, although the two tend to go together. One can imagine, for example, marriage as a relationship between two people who are, themselves, embedded in an extended family or a communal child-rearing arrangement (such as the kibbutz). Sociologically, its universality suggests that marriage forms a stable, long-lasting, and secure foundation for the family's functions—child socialization, property transfer, legitimacy, sexual regulation—to be securely served.

Marriage is also a legal arrangement, conferring various social, economic, and political benefits on the married couple. This is because the state regards marriage—that is, stable families—as so important that it is willing to provide economic and social incentives to married couples. As a result, people who have been legally excluded from marrying—the mentally ill, gays and lesbians—have sought to obtain that right as well.

Did you know?
American men are more eager to marry than American women. From 1970 to the late 1990s, men's attitudes toward marriage became more favorable, while women's became less so. By the end of the century, more men than women said that marriage was their ideal lifestyle (Coontz, 2005).

Marriage is certainly not the only living arrangement for people in society. In America between 1900 and 2000, the number of adults living alone increased by 21 percent, single parents and children by 11 percent, unmarried partners by 63 percent, and unmarried partners with their children by 89 percent. In several developing countries, marriage is also occurring later and bringing with it numerous positive social outcomes. In industrialized countries like the United States, the implications of the shift toward later marriage and less marriage are a source of extensive sociological research and social debate.

Multigenerational households (adults of more than one generation sharing domestic space) increased by 38 percent between 1990 and 2000, until today they comprise about 3 percent of all households. In about two-thirds, the grandparents are in charge of the family, sharing their home with their grown children and grandchildren (or only their grandchildren), while in about one-third, the grown children are in charge of the family, sharing their home with both their parents and their children (Figure 15.1).

Marriage varies widely by race, ethnicity, education, and income. Nearly two-thirds (63 percent) of White women over 18 who make more than $100,000 a year are married, while only 25 percent of Black women over 18 who earn less than $20,000 per year are married (Center for Changing Families, 2007).

Marriage, itself, has changed. It no longer signifies adulthood or conveys the responsibilities and commitment that it once did. In a society where pop stars marry and divorce within a day but couples who have been together for 30 years are forbidden from marrying, it is, in some people's eyes, discredited and corrupt. People are putting off marriage, cohabiting, or opting for singlehood. On the other hand, marriage has become more desirable than ever before, bringing together couples from varying backgrounds and repeat performers and inspiring many who've been excluded to fight for the right to marry. Some of these changes are temporary, like delayed mar-

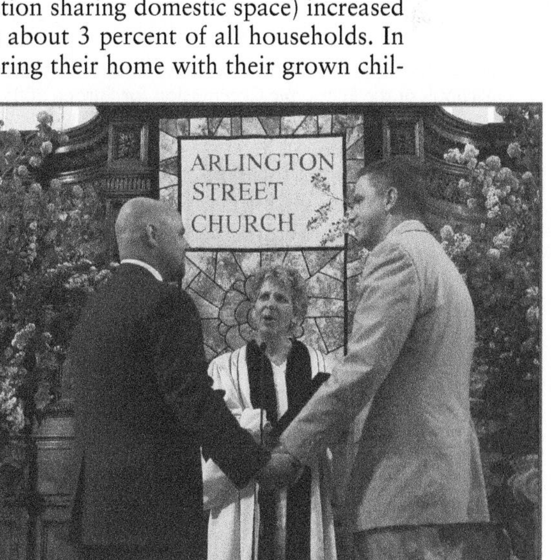

To some, gay marriage is an indication that the family is falling apart; to others, that it has never been stronger and more desirable. A very "traditional" church wedding—in a gay and lesbian church.

While the age of marriage is increasing worldwide, child marriages are still common in many countries. This Kurdish couple appears to be about 10.

Table 15.1 Age at First Marriage

	Men	Women
Poland	26.9	23.7
United States	27.4	25.8
France	29.7	27.7
Austria	30.5	28.1
Netherlands	31.0	29.1
Sweden	32.4	30.1
Denmark	32.8	30.3
Switzerland	35.0	31.3

Source: Trends in Europe and North America: The Statistical Yearbook of the Economic Commission for Europe 2003.

riage and, in most cases, cohabitation (which usually leads to marriage). Others, like singlehood, have become more permanent and less transitory.

Delayed Marriage. Early marriage—usually arranged by parents—is still the rule in Sub-Saharan Africa and South and Central Asia. In Southern Asia, 48 percent of young women—nearly 10 million—are married before the age of 18. In Africa, it's 42 percent; in Latin America and the Caribbean, 29 percent. More than half of all girls under 18 are married in some countries, including Afghanistan, Bangladesh, and India. In Ethiopia and some areas of West Africa, some girls are married as early as age 7 (UNFPA, 2005). However, the prevalence is decreasing significantly around the world. Since 1970, the median age of first marriage has risen substantially worldwide—for men from 25.4 years to 27.2 and for women from 21.5 to 23.2 (UNFPA, 2005).

In the United States, young people are experiencing longer periods of independent living while working or attending school before marriage. A 25-year-old American man today is far more likely to be single and childless than he would have been 50 years ago—or even 25 years ago. Among 25-year-old women, the fastest-growing demographic status is single, working, childless, head of household (Fussell and Furstenberg, 2004). The United States still has one of the industrial world's lowest age for first marriage (Table 15.1).

Differences among Black, White, and foreign-born populations in education and labor market opportunities have narrowed since the 1960s, creating more similarities in the lives of people of color and their White peers (Fussell and Furstenberg, 2004). However, significant educational and economic inequalities, in addition to cultural differences, mean that different groups will continue to vary in the ages of first marriage (Guzzo, 2003; Martin, 2004).

Staying Single. Not long ago, people who were "still not married" by their late 20s were considered deviant. Men were considered "big babies," who "refused to grow up" and "settle down." Women were "old maids," thought to be too unattractive or socially inept to attract a husband.

But singlehood has become commonplace, if not exactly respectable. Just over half of all Americans aged 15 (50.3 percent) and over are not married or cohabiting (U.S. Census Bureau, 2006). Sixty-three percent of all unmarried Americans have never been married. Although the percentage of single people is rising for all Americans, those rates vary considerably by race and ethnicity. Between 1970 and 2000, the proportion of White adults who had never married rose from 16 percent to 20 percent, 19 percent to 28 percent among Hispanics, and 21 percent to 39 percent among African Americans (U.S. Census Bureau, 2006).

In Europe, the proportion of women who have never married ranges from 7 percent in Bulgaria to 36 percent in Iceland. The proportion of men is substantially higher.

Women are more likely to be single than men. In fact, the majority of American women (51 percent) is living without a spouse (U.S. Census Bureau, 2006). Single women are better educated, are better employed, and have better mental health than single men (Fowlkes, 1994; Marks, 1996). But for both men and women, being single is an ambivalent experience. Sometimes singles are autonomous and free; sometimes they are lonely and disconnected. Often, they are both (Gordon, 1994). Singles may have financial independence, but they also have sole financial responsibility for their lives and futures. And singles are still living in a society of couples, so they are often the "third wheel" at social events. Friends and family may assume that they are unhappy and expend all of their efforts on trying to hook them up, but as they get older, it may become increasingly difficult to locate uncoupled people at all. It is no wonder that singleness comes with some adjustment problems.

Cohabiting. **Cohabitation** refers to unmarried people in a romantic relationship living in the same residence. A few decades ago, when nonmarital sex was illegal in most states, cohabitation was virtually impossible—landlords wouldn't rent to people unless they were related by blood or marriage. Hotel managers could lose their license if they rented rooms to unrelated people. Today, cohabitation has become commonplace, largely lacking in social disapproval (Smock, 2000). Except among the very conservative, it is no longer considered "living in sin" or even "shacking up." Almost half of people 25 to 40 years of age in the United States have cohabited, and 60 percent of all marriages formed in the 1990s began with cohabitation (Teachman, 2003).

Globally, cohabitation is common in liberal countries—in Sweden, it is four times as prevalent as in the United States. That is largely because those countries provide universal health care and education to everyone, so you don't need to get married to be covered by your spouse's health plan or to ensure your children can go to university. However, it is rare in more conservative countries and remains illegal in some countries.

We don't know exactly how many cohabiting couples there are in the United States because the U.S. Census doesn't ask about emotional bonds or sexual activities and therefore can't distinguish between romantic partners and nonromantic roommates (Babe and Allen, 1992; U.S. Census Bureau, 2004). However, in 2003, there were 4.6 million households consisting of two adults who were not related by blood or marriage (U.S. Census Bureau, 2004). Four out of ten opposite-sex unmarried partner households included at least one minor child (U.S. Census Bureau, 2006).

Is cohabitation a stage of courtship, somewhere between dating and marriage, sort of the equivalent of "going steady" among high school students? Many scholars and cohabiters think so—in the 1980s, it was even called "trial marriage." Women cohabiters are more likely to desire marriage than men (Blumstein and Schwartz, 1983), but about 25 percent do not expect to marry the man they are currently living with. Their biggest inhibiting factor is not his willingness but his socioeconomic status: They want to marry someone with greater economic potential. Some look at it as a "trial marriage," some as an experience that might or might not lead to marriage with their current partner (like dating), and others as a stable, nonmarital alternative that they could happily pursue for the rest of their lives (Fowlkes, 1994; Seltzer, 2001).

But for some cohabiters, their living situation has nothing to do with marriage. More than one million elderly Americans cohabit—for a significant financial reason. While the government strongly encourages marriage among the young and middle-aged with tax cuts and other benefits, elderly men and women receiving Social Security cannot marry without losing a significant percentage of their combined individual incomes (Brown, Lee, and Bulanda, 2006; Chevan, 1996).

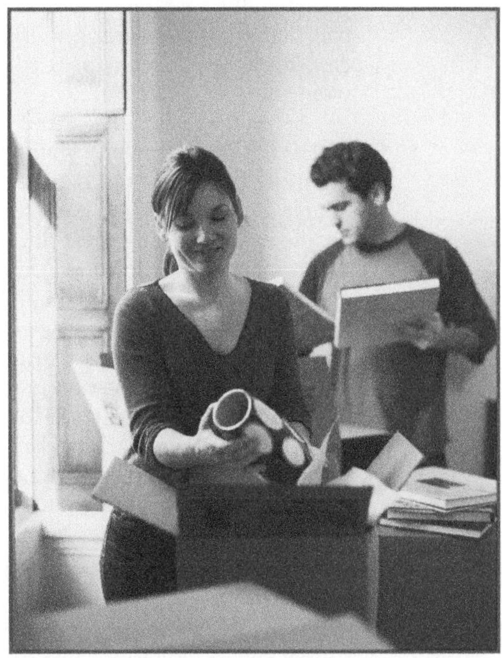
Almost half of people 25–40 in the United States have cohabited, and 60 percent of all marriages formed in the 1990s began with cohabitation.

Younger people benefit financially from being married, but marriage comes with legal restrictions, such as sexual fidelity or child support, that they may not want, at least until they decide that they are "meant for each other" (Spain and Bianchi, 1996). They may also believe in postponing marriage until they have a significant amount of money in the bank, enough to buy a house or at least finance a big wedding (Seltzer, 2000).

Race and social class have an impact on who will cohabit and who will marry. Despite the popular assumption that cohabitation is a lifestyle of the rich and famous—or at least the affluent and educated—it is actually more common among working-class and poor people with less education and financial resources (Bumpass and Lu, 2000; Casper and Bianchi, 2002). One in ten adult Hispanic women currently cohabit, and 9 percent of White women, but only 6 percent of African American women (Fields and Casper, 2001; Figure 15.2).

A lot of research has been conducted on the emotional stability of cohabiting couples. Some research finds that cohabiting women are more prone to depression than married women, especially if there are children involved. Maybe they are more prone to stress because they know that their unions can dissolve more easily than marriages; if they dissolve, there will be no legal means of distributing household resources equitably, and no spousal support after the "divorce."

FIGURE 15.2 Married Couple and Unmarried Partner Households

	Same-sex partners	Opposite-sex partners	
White alone	0.9	7.3	8.2
Black or African American alone	1.4	15.5	16.9
American Indian and Alaska Native alone	1.3	16.0	17.4
Asian alone	0.7	4.0	4.7
Native Hawaiian and Other Pacific Islander alone	1.4	10.8	12.3
Some other race alone	1.2	12.4	13.6
Two or more races	1.6	12.1	13.7
Hispanic or Latino (of any race)	1.3	10.9	12.2
White alone, not Hispanic or Latino	0.9	7.2	8.1

0 5 10 15 20

Source: U.S. Census Bureau, 2003.

Explanations of Nonmarital Choices. Sociologists offer numerous explanations for the increases in delayed marriage, singlehood, and cohabitation. First, these changes are partially explained by new practices, such as courtship and dating. After all, arranged marriages usually take place when the children are younger. But courtship and dating are linked to the worldwide increase in the status of women. While it's true that arranged marriages affected both boys and girls, increased individual choice of marriage partners enables more women to seek educational and economic advancement and rests on increasing choices for women.

Second, these changes tend to be associated with higher levels of education—for both males and females. For decades, many young people, especially in industrialized countries, have been seeking and gaining more education to compete in the global marketplace. The higher the level of education, the later people get married. In China, for example, which currently accounts for more than 20 percent of young people in the developing world, schooling has increased, and adolescent labor has decreased. The average age at marriage began to rise, and the vast majority of males and females now marries after age 20 ("Age at First Marriage and Divorce," 2007).

Third, these changes are partially explained by changing sexual behaviors and attitudes, especially increased acceptance of "premarital sex." For a long time, sexual activity before marriage was referred to as "premarital" because it was assumed that the couple involved would be in a serious, committed relationship and intend to marry. However, some people engage in sexual relations during a casual dating relationship, when marriage has not yet become a topic of discussion. Some view sex as an appropriate conclusion to a first date. Still others "hook up" and don't even go as far as dating. Others never intend to marry, or they lack the right to marry, but they still have sex, sometimes in committed relationships, sometimes not. Therefore, a more precise term might be **nonmarital sex**—sex that is not related to marriage.

In wealthy countries, especially in northern Europe, nonmarital sex has become increasingly acceptable, even during the teen years. These countries provide sex education and health care services aimed at equipping young people to avoid negative consequences of sex by encouraging contraceptive use. In the United States, public attitudes toward nonmarital sex have changed significantly over the past 20 years. In a national survey in the early 1970s, 37 percent of respondents said that nonmarital sex is always wrong. By 1990 this number had fallen to 20 percent (Michael et al., 1994). However, social and political institutions have changed more slowly. As a result, rates of teen pregnancy and sexually transmitted diseases are

Box 15.2 Understanding Trends in Marriage Behavior in the United States

Modified from an activity by Amy Guptill,* SUNY-Brockport, *and available on the Social Science Data Analysis Network

OBJECTIVE: Use census data to explore marriage trends in the United States.

Step 1: Access WebChip.
Your instructor will give you specific directions in class on how to gain access to WebChip (you can go to www.ssdan.net/datacounts/howto). This is a research tool developed by the Social Science Data Analysis Network at the University of Michigan. There is a tutorial that you may be instructed to do before attempting this assignment.

Step 2: Print the module.
Go to the module on trends in marriage behavior developed by Amy Guptill at SUNY-Brockport and print out the module for your use.

Step 3: Write your responses.
After printing out the module, follow the step-by-step directions provided to complete this assignment. Write your responses directly on the sheets you print out. (Please note that some instructors may have already copied this module for you.)

Step 4: Think about the census data.
After looking at 2000 census data, take a moment to answer the following question: What do you think 2010 census data will indicate about marriage trends? What changes do you expect to find and why?

Step 5: Share with the class.
Please plan on turning in the completed module to your instructor and to share your thoughts on Step 4 in class.

much lower in Europe than in the United States, although their rates of sexual activity are no higher. Teen abortions are also low, even though abortion services are widely available (Guttmacher Institute, 1999).

Biracial Marriage

Through most of the history of the United States, marriage or sexual relations between men and women of different races were illegal. At a time when "race science" taught that races differed dramatically in their intelligence and morality, scholars feared that interracial marriage, or **miscegenation,** would lead to children inferior to both mother and father. The evil "half-breed" was a standard fictional type up to the twentieth century. Not until the Supreme Court's *Loving v. State of Virginia* decision of 1967 were men and women of different races permitted to marry in all U.S. states.

FIGURE 15.3 Acceptance of Interracial Dating

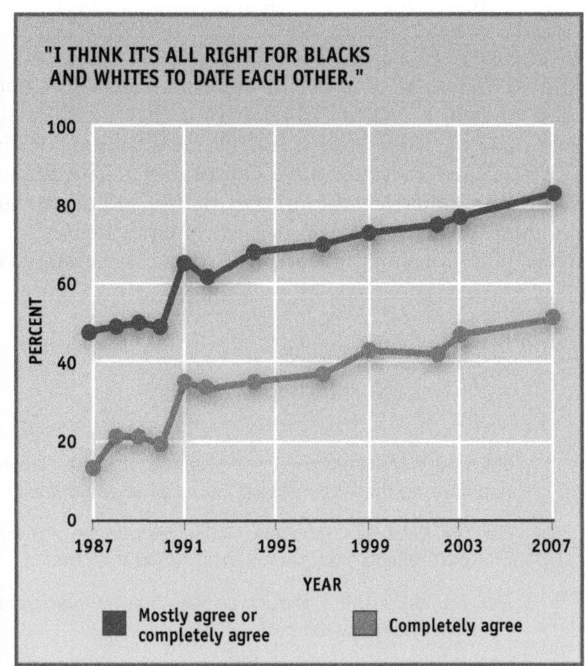

Source: From "Trends in Political Values and Core Attitudes: 1987–2007: Political Landscape More Favorable to Democrats," released March 22, 2007. Reprinted by permission of Pew Research Center for the People and the Press.

Social barriers still place dating, courtship, and marriage within clear racial categories. However, interracial marriage is evolving from virtually nonexistent to merely atypical. Today, 5 percent of the population of the United States claims ancestry in two or more races, and 22 percent of Americans have a relative in a mixed-race marriage (Pew Research Center, 2007). Blacks are twice as likely as Whites to have an immediate family member in an interracial marriage, while Hispanics fall in the middle of those two groups. The most common interracial couple in the United States is a White husband married to an Asian wife (14 percent of all interracial couples).

Euro-Americans are least likely to intermarry: Only 3.5 percent of White, non-Hispanic individuals are married to someone of another race. And non-Hispanic Whites, along with people over 65, are less accepting of interracial dating than are African Americans, Hispanics, and younger people of all races (Pew Research Center, 2003; Figure 15.3).

For Black–White couples, the most common pattern (73 percent) is a White woman and an African American man. Among cohabiting couples, there is even a sharper gap: Five times as many Black men live with White women as White men with Black women. Oddly, in the mass media, Black man–White women couples are almost nonexistent. Instead, we see a proliferation of White men and Black women, from Joey and Chandler dating a famous paleontologist (who happens to be a young Black woman) on *Friends* to Rose and her husband on *Lost*.

For Asian–White couples, the most common pattern (over 75 percent) is White men and Asian women. The difference is less severe in cohabitation: Twice as many White men are living with Asian women as Asian women living with White men. Asian–Black pairings are rare, but they are even more unbalanced than interracial pairings involving Whites. Black husband–Asian wife patterns outnumber Asian husband–Black wife by 6 to 1.

There is little imbalance among Hispanics. Just under 18 percent of married Hispanic women have non-Hispanic husbands, and just over 15 percent of married Hispanic men have non-Hispanic wives.

Same-Sex Marriage

Same-sex couples have been cohabiting for hundreds of years, although sometimes societal pressures forced them to pretend that they were not couples at all. In the seventeenth and eighteenth centuries, for example, middle-class men often "hired" their working-class partners as valets or servants, so they could live together without question. Sometimes they pretended to be brothers or cousins. In the eighteenth and nineteenth century, it was so common for women to spend their lives together that there was a special name for their bonds, "Boston marriages."

Did you know? Latin Americans are more tolerant of gay and lesbian families than North Americans are. No Latin American country has explicit prohibitions against gay and lesbian adoptions such as those in many European countries and parts of the United States. Many judges in Latin America have already granted adoptions to lesbian and gay citizens. Clinics and doctors in many Latin American countries have been providing access to assisted reproduction to lesbians since the 1990s (Sarda, 2000).

Recent research allows us to paint a portrait of the typical lesbian or gay couple, at least the ones who are open (all following data are from Ambert, 2005; Bianchi and Casper, 2000; Black et al., 2000):

1. *They're urban.* More than half of lesbian or gay male couples live in just 20 U.S. cities, including "gay meccas" like Los Angeles, San Francisco, Washington, D.C., New York, and Atlanta.
2. *They're well educated.* They tend to have higher educational attainments than men and women in heterosexual marriages.
3. *They are less likely to have children.* Fifty-nine percent of married couples versus 22 percent of lesbian couples and 5 percent of gay male couples are living with children of their own. Most are the products of previous heterosexual marriages, although artificial insemination and adoption are increasingly common.
4. *They are less likely to own their own homes than married couples.*
5. *They tend to be more egalitarian.* They are more likely to share decision making and allot housework more equally than married couples and have less conflict as a result (Allen and Demo, 1995; Carrington, 2002).

And they are not permitted to marry in the United States. As of 2006, 26 states had a constitutional amendment restricting marriage to one man and one women, 19 states had a law (not affecting their constitution) restricting marriage to a man and a woman, and the United States is debating a federal constitutional amendment to ban gay marriage (HRC, 2007). Nineteen states have constitutional amendments that bar gay or lesbian couples from emergency health care, inheritance, and more than 1,000 other rights that heterosexual couples enjoy (HRC, 2007). As of mid-2007, five states provided the equivalent of state-level spousal rights to gay couples and three states plus Washington, D.C., provided some statewide spousal rights (Figure 15.4).

Box 15.3 What do you think?

Racial and Ethnic Family Diversity

Interracial marriage was illegal in the United States until relatively recently. In 1967, the Supreme Court decided that marriage was legal between any consenting unmarried man and unmarried woman, regardless of race. Still, the general population is often uncomfortable with the idea. Interracial couples are still frequently the targets of hate crimes and discrimination. Although there are more and more interracial children in the United States, they are mostly White–Asian, White–Hispanic, or some combination other than White–Black. So, what do you think?

For the following statement, please choose the answer that best reflects your personal opinion at this time.

Do you think there should be laws against marriages between Blacks and Whites?

❍ Yes

❍ No

FIGURE 15.4 State Prohibitions of Marriage for Same-Sex Couples

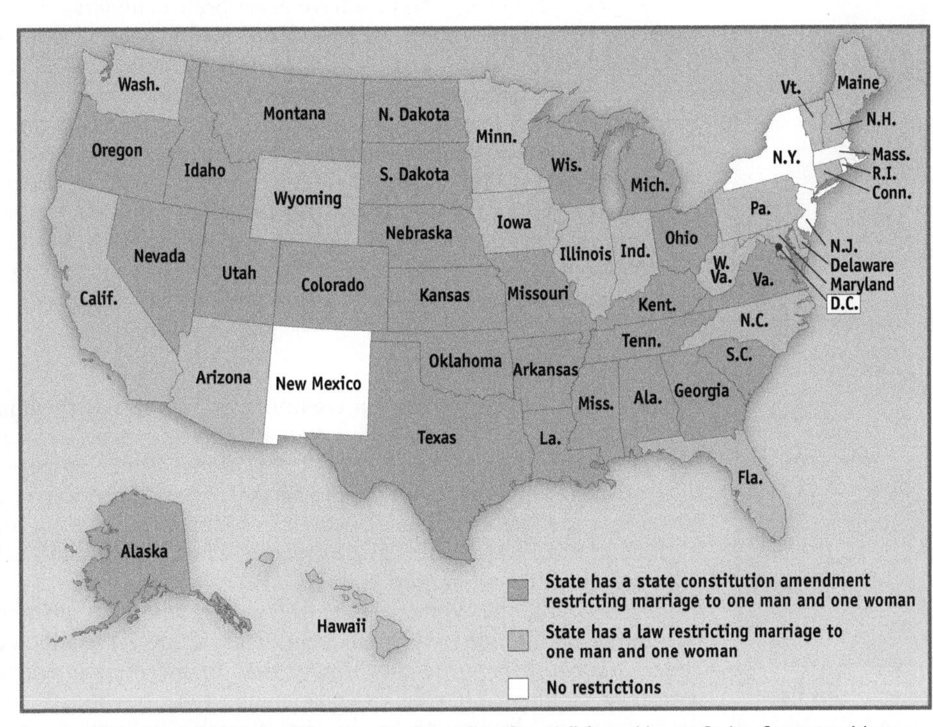

Source: "State Prohibitions on Marriage for Same-Sex Couple" from *Human Rights Campaign,* November, 2006. © Human Rights Campaign. Reprinted with permission.

However, reserving marriage and domestic partnerships to men and women applies only in the United States. As of this writing, same-sex couples can marry or enter into civil partnerships with the same rights as heterosexual couples in most European countries and can enter into civil partnerships with most of the same rights as heterosexual couples in nine others, including Brazil, France, Israel, South Africa, and Switzerland.

Parenting

In the movie *The Day the Earth Stood Still* (1951), a mysterious stranger rents a room at a boardinghouse. When one of his fellow boarders finds that she has no one to look after her son for the afternoon, the stranger volunteers. Mom hesitates; she doesn't want to inconvenience him. He insists that it would be a pleasure—he loves little boys. Mom happily agrees.

Imagine a remake of that movie today. Mom would insist on fingerprints, an FBI profile, a letter from the local police chief, and a state child care license. During the past 50 years, the answer to the question, "Who should watch the children?" has become more and more narrow, from any handy teenager or adult to licensed childcare professionals to Mom and Dad, or maybe just Mom. Today, 40 percent of all children 5 and under are cared for by a relative and 11 percent by a combination of relatives and nonrelatives. Almost 25 percent of all preschoolers are in organized child care facilities—13 percent at day care centers and 6 percent in preschools (*Who's Minding the Kids?,* 2005).

Just as children have never been so important in our cultural values, parents have never been considered so important in the lives of their children. Many people believe that biological reproduction gives you a sudden proficiency in child care, and anyone other than the biological parent will do a shoddy job at best. More people have wanted to become parents than ever before, including some who would rarely have considered parenting just 20 or 30 years ago: teenagers, 50-year-olds, gay and lesbian couples, infertile heterosexual couples. Ironically, even though parents are thought to be so utterly decisive in the outcomes of their children's lives, we also seem to believe that it's all hereditary, and socialization plays a very minor role in how our children turn out. Of course, to a sociologist, both sides are true: Parental socialization of children is enormously important, and parents also overvalue their role. The questions, as you've learned in this book, are not whether or not parents are important or biology trumps socialization, but in which arenas and under what circumstances does parental influence make a decisive difference, and does it do this in all groups, around the world?

More people are able to become parents today than ever before, including fifty-year-olds, gay and lesbian couples, and infertile heterosexual couples. In 2006, Lauren Cohen, 59, of New Jersey, became the oldest woman in the United States to give birth to twins.

And while it's true that children have never been so valued and desired, it's equally true that they have never been so undervalued and neglected. Children around the world are facing poor health care, compromised education, and the lack of basic services. In the United States, families get virtually no financial assistance to raise their children, although they receive a lot of advice about having them.

The core relationship of the family has always been between parents and children. Yet today that bond has been both loosened by other forces pulling families apart (like technology and overscheduling) and tightened by ideas that only parents know what is best for their children. It may be the case that the less time parents spend with their children, the more we insist that they spend time together.

Gender and Parenting

Although the majority of women are now working outside the home, numerous studies have confirmed that domestic work remains women's work (Gerstel and Gross, 1995). Most people agree with the statement that housework should be shared equally between both partners, and more men in male–female households are sharing some of the housework and child care, especially when the woman's earnings are essential to family stability (Perry-Jenkins and Crouter, 1990). But still, the women in male–female households do about two-thirds of the housework (Bianchi et al., 2000). That includes child care: Mothers spend much more time than fathers interacting with their children. They do twice as much of the "custodial" care, the feeding and cleaning of the children (Bianchi, 2000; Pleck, 1997; Sayer, 2001). A survey of American secondary students revealed that 75 percent of girls but only 14 percent of boys who planned to have children thought that they would stop working for awhile, and 28 percent of girls but 73 percent of boys expected their partner to stop working or cut down on work hours (Bagamery, 2004).

Over 5 million women are stay-at-home mothers, staying out of the workforce to care for their children (under the age of 15). However, there are only about 143,000 stay-at-home fathers (U.S. Census Bureau, 2006).

On the other hand, American fathers are more active and involved parents than ever before. Today's new fathers (those between 20 and 35 years old) do far more child care than their own fathers did and are willing to decline job opportunities if they include too much travel or overtime (Pleck and Masciadrelli, 2004).

Single-Parent Families

During the first half of the twentieth century, the primary cause of single-parent families was parental death. By the end of the century, most parents were living, but living elsewhere. Currently 12.2 million people in the United States, 10 million women and 2.2 million men, are single parents, raising children while unmarried. Single-parent families have become more common in all demographic groups, but the greatest increases have been among less-educated women and among African American families (Sidel, 2006). In 2002, 16 percent of White, non-Hispanic children were living in mother-only families, as were 25 percent of Hispanic children and 48 percent of Black children. Sometimes the parents are cohabiting, but most often one parent lives elsewhere and does not contribute to the day-to-day emotional and economic support of the child. Sometimes the other parent is not in the picture at all.

Most people are not single parents by choice. The pregnancy may have been an unexpected surprise that prompted the father to leave, or the relationship ended, leaving one parent with custody. Young, unprepared mothers predominate: In 2002, 89 percent of teenage mothers were unmarried but only 12 percent of mothers aged 30 to 44 (U.S. Census Bureau, 2000). And yet an increasing number of women are choosing single motherhood, either through fertility clinics and sperm banks or through adoption. In 1990 alone, 170,000 single women over 30 gave birth. White, college-educated women led this trend. The number who became mothers without marrying doubled during the 1980s; for those in professional and managerial jobs, it nearly tripled (Bock, 2000; DeParle, 1993; Hertz, 2006; Mattes, 1994).

Single mothers predominate both because it is easier for a father to become absent during the pregnancy and because mothers are typically granted custody in court cases. Although mothers predominate, the gender disparity varies from country to country. Among the countries for which data are available, Belgium has the smallest proportion of women who are the single parent ("only" 75 percent—that is, 25 percent of single parents are the fathers) with Norway, Sweden, and Finland close behind. Estonia has the

Box 15.4 How do we know what we know?

The Opt-Out Revolution

The popular view that children require round-the-clock care from Mom, not Dad or day care, has led millions of women to quit their jobs or take time off to raise their children—an "Opt-Out Revolution."

But is such a revolution really taking place? How do we know? Sociologist Kathleen Gerson and her colleagues examined the evidence that women were "opting out" of the workforce to be full-time mothers. What they found was that while it was true that between 1998 and 2002, the proportion of employed women with children under the age of one declined 4 percent from 59 percent to 55 percent, it was also true that 72 percent of mothers with children over the age of one are either working or looking for work.

One would expect that highly educated women with high-paying jobs would be the most likely to opt out, because they can afford to, but in fact they are less likely. Among mothers with children under the age of six, 75 percent of those with postgraduate degrees are working, as opposed to 65 percent of those with high school diplomas only. It turns out that one can see "opting out" only if one freezes time—at any one moment, there are, indeed, women who are leaving the labor force to raise their children. But they don't stay out; they go back to work soon after. And many would go back to work even sooner—if their husbands did a little more child care.

(*Source:* Kathleen Gerson, New York University, PR Newswire.)

largest (95 percent). Those countries in which women's status is higher would tend to have lower percentages of women who are single parents.

Grandparenting

Your kids grow up and go off to college, and your parenting is done. When they have kids of their own, you are not involved except for birthday cards and occasional visits at Thanksgiving. For good or bad, that's the nuclear family model. For good or bad, it is increasingly inaccurate. The number of grandparents raising their grandchildren has grown from 2.2 million in 1970 to nearly 4 million today.

Of this last group, grandparents raising their grandchildren alone, they tend to be African American, living in urban centers, and poor. Twenty-seven percent of children being raised by grandparents (and 63 percent being raised by grandmothers alone) are living in poverty. They tend to be working full time: 72 percent of grandfathers and 56 percent of grandmothers, as opposed to 33 percent and 24 percent, respectively, who aren't raising their grandchildren.

What happened to the parents? Often the father has abandoned the child, and the mother is incompetent, in prison, or on drugs. Courts are much more likely to grant custody of a child to a blood relative than to a legal stranger. Grandparents can even legally adopt their grandchildren, in effect becoming their parents.

Adoptive Parents

When Angelina Jolie and Madonna each adopted babies from orphanages in Africa, they were ridiculed for trying to save the world one baby at a time. These Hollywood celebrities were not an elite vanguard but latecomers to a well-worn trend in the industrial world. In the United States alone there are 1.5 million adopted children—over 2 percent of all children (Fields, 2001).

Historically, adoption was considered an option to resolve an unwanted pregnancy—that is, it was about the biological mother. For centuries, all over Europe, foundling hospitals (hospitals that received unwanted newborn babies) enabled mothers to anonymously leave babies at a back door or on the steps, and nuns would find willing families to raise the children as their own. Today, however, the interest has shifted to the adoptive families, as more and more people who want to have children use various services to adopt babies. Adoption has shifted from being about helping "a girl in trouble" to "enabling a loving family to have a child."

There are many different types of adoptions, including:

- *Foster care adoption:* adoption of children in state care for whom reunification with their birth parents is not feasible for safety or other reasons.
- *Private adoption:* adoption either through an agency or independent networks.
- *Inter-country adoption (ICA):* adoption of children from other countries by U.S. citizens. The top three countries for international adoption in 2006 were China (6,500 adoptions), Guatemala (4,135), and Russia (3,706) (U.S. Department of State, 2007).
- *Transracial adoption:* adoption of a child of a different race from the adopting parents; this involves about 10 to 15 percent of all domestic adoptions and the vast majority of ICA.

In the United States, there are 1.5 million adopted children—over 2 percent of all children. Movie star Angelina Jolie has adopted three, including daughter, Zahara, and son, Maddox (here with Jolie's partner, Brad Pitt).

Motivations for adoption vary. The couple may be incapable of conceiving a child themselves; they may be infertile or gay. Some single women adopt, while others use assisted reproductive technologies to become pregnant. In some cases, fertile couples adopt because they choose to adopt.

Adoption seems to have largely beneficial effects for all concerned (birth parents, adoptive parents, and adoptees). However, a sizeable minority of birth parents characterize their adoption experiences as traumatic, and many birth parents and adoptees spend significant time trying to locate each other and experience some reunions or closure in their relationships.

The number of adoptions by nonrelatives has declined sharply since 1970. The availability of birth control and legal abortion has meant that fewer women are having unwanted children, and adoption is still stigmatized in the United States; it is seen, as one sociologist put it, as "not quite as good as having your own" (Fisher, 2003).

Not Parenting

In the United States, the media are constantly telling us that children are the meaning of life. No woman can be truly happy or fulfilled unless she has given birth, and no man can be secure in his masculinity unless he is a father. When we see a childless couple, we think that something has gone wrong—obviously they are physically unable to conceive. However, childlessness is becoming increasingly common. In 1976, about 10 percent of women aged 40 to 44 (near the end of their childbearing years) had never conceived a child. By 2000, the percentage had grown to 18 percent (U.S. Census Bureau, 2007).

Education is an important predictor of childlessness: The more education a woman has, the more likely she is to bear no children. Race is also significant: Hispanic women are much less likely to expect no children than White and Black women. The longer they put off children, the more likely they are to opt out of having children altogether, perhaps because they become accustomed to a child-free lifestyle.

However, people have many reasons for remaining "child-free by choice," from concern about overpopulation to a desire to concentrate on their career to just not liking children. In one study, women said they enjoyed the freedom and spontaneity in their lives, while some others gave financial considerations,

Box 15.5 What do you think?

Attitudes toward Abortion

A central function of the institution of the family is to produce new members of society. Hence, family planning is a key element of the institution. Whether, and when, to have children is a personal or family decision, yet this decision is informed by societal norms and laws. Let's look at how you and other Americans view abortion and at how attitudes toward abortion have changed or not over time. So, what do you think?

Do you think it should be possible for a pregnant woman to obtain a legal abortion if:

1. The woman's own health is seriously endangered by the pregnancy?
   - ❍ Yes
   - ❍ No
2. She is married and does not want any more children?
   - ❍ Yes
   - ❍ No
3. The family has a low income and cannot afford any more children?
   - ❍ Yes
   - ❍ No
4. She became pregnant as a result of rape?
   - ❍ Yes
   - ❍ No

See the back of the chapter to compare your answers to national survey data.

worries about stress, marriages too fragile to withstand children, being housebound, and diminished career opportunities (Gerson, 1985). Men usually cite more practical considerations, including commitment to career and concern about the financial burden (Lunneborg, 1999).

Family Transitions

Through most of European and American history, marriage was a lifelong commitment, period. Divorce and remarriage were impossible. Though couples could live separately and find legal loopholes to avoid inheritance laws, they could never marry anyone else. In the sixteenth century, the English King Henry VIII had to behead two wives, divorce two others, found a new Church (the Anglican Church), and close all the monasteries in England in order to get out of marriages he didn't like. Today, it's a little bit easier.

Divorce is the legal dissolution of a marriage. Grounds for divorce may vary from "no-fault" divorces in which one party files for divorce or those divorces that require some "fault" on the part of one spouse or the other (adultery, alienation of affection, or some other reason). Divorces are decrees that dissolve a marriage; they do not dissolve the family. Parents must still work out custody arrangements of children, alimony payments, child support. Just because they are no longer husband and wife does not mean they are no longer Mommy and Daddy.

In the United States, the divorce rate rose steadily from the 1890s through the 1970s (with a dip in the Depression and a spike after World War II). During the past 25 years, it has fallen significantly, along with marriage rates overall. The annual national divorce rate is at its lowest since 1970, while marriage is down 30 percent and the number of unmarried couples living together is up tenfold since 1960 (Time, 2007, p. 6).

These trends are led by the middle class. At the lower end of the scale, however, the picture is reversed, leading some sociologists to describe a "divorce divide" based on class and race (Martin, 2006). Among college-educated women who first married between 1975 and 1979, 29 percent were divorced within 10 years; for those first married between 1990 and 1994, only 16.5 percent were. Yet for high school dropouts, 38 percent of those first married between 1975 and 1979 were divorced within a decade—and 46 percent were between 1990 and 1994. For those with a high school diploma, divorce rates for those years rose from 35 to 38 percent (Martin, 2006; Figure 15.5). And the figures mask the fact that a larger percentage of poorer women avoid divorce by never marrying in the first place.

Did you know?
Aside from a huge spike in divorce immediately after World War II, divorce rates in the 1950s were higher than in any previous decade except the Depression. Almost one in three marriages formed in the 1950s eventually ended in divorce (Coontz, 2005).

Whatever these different sociological dimensions, some commentators broadly blame divorce for nearly every social ill, from prostitution (where else are divorced men to turn?) to serial murder (evidently watching their parents break up has kids reaching for the nearest pickax). More moderate voices worry that quick-and-easy divorce undermines the institution of the family, forcing the divorced adults to start courting again when they should be engaged in child rearing and teaching children that dysfunction is the norm.

FIGURE 15.5 More Education, Less Divorce

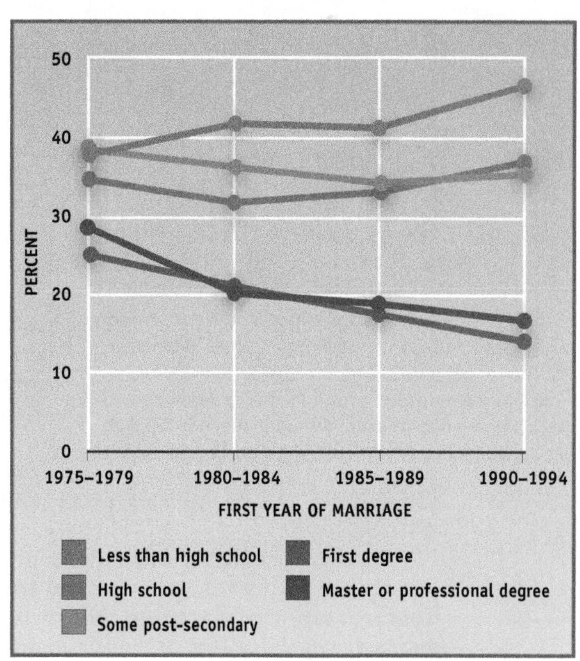

Source: Adapted from "Trends in Marital Dissolution by Women's Education in teh United States" by Steven P. Martin, *Demographic Research,* December 13, 2006, Vol. 15, #20, pp. 537–560, © 2006 Steven P. Martin. Reprinted by permission.

Sociologists understand that both statements are, at least, partially true. Some people believe that the easy availability of divorce weakens our belief in the institution of marriage. On the other hand, sociologists often counter that divorce makes families stronger by allowing an escape from damaging environments and enabling both parents and children to adapt to new types of relationships.

Who usually wants the divorce? On the average, men become more content with their marriages over time, while women become less content; the wife is usually the one who wants out. A study of divorces that occurred after age 40 found that wives initiated two-thirds of them (Coontz, 2005).

The Consequences of Divorce

Married couples opt for divorce for all sorts of reasons, and the divorce itself can be easy or hard, so it is understandable that research on the impact of divorce on the husband and wife is mixed. Some studies find that people are happier after their divorce than before (Wilson and Oswald, 2005). Others find psychological scars that never heal unless the divorcees remarry (Johnson and Wu, 2002). Still others find that individual attitudes make the difference in well-being after a divorce (Amato and Sobolewski, 2001; Wood, Goesting and Avellar, 2007).

Economically, there is clearer evidence about losses and gains. In a large majority of divorces, women's standards of living decline, while men's go up. Those men who are used to being the primary breadwinner may suddenly find that they are supporting one (plus a small amount for child support) on a salary that used to support the whole family. Those women who are more accustomed to being in charge of the household, with a secondary, part-time, or even no job, may suddenly find that their income must stretch from being a helpful supplement to supplying most of the family's necessities.

It is crucial to remember that the breadwinning husband with an income-supplementing or stay-at-home wife has rarely been an option for many minority families. Black women, for example, have a longer history of workforce participation than women of other races (Page and Stevens, 2005). Divorce plays an even bigger economic role for Black households than for Whites in the United States, partly because of this difference. While family income for Whites falls about 30 percent during the first 2 years of divorce, it falls by 53 percent for Blacks (Page and Stevens, 2005). Three or more years after divorce, White households recoup about one-third of the lost income, but the income of Black families barely improves. This may have to do with the fact that when divorce occurs, the probability of Black mothers working does not change, while recently divorced White women have an 18 percent greater probability of working (Page and Stevens, 2005).

After a divorce, children are still more likely to live with the mother, while the father visits on specified days or weeks. Not only do the children have to handle this new living situation, but many will soon move to a new home, enroll in a new school, and face the stress and depression of a mother who has suddenly entered or reentered the workforce as the primary breadwinner. And that's when the divorce is amicable. At times there is open hostility between the mother and father, with each telling the children how horrible the other is or even trying to acquire full custody, with many potential negative outcomes (Coontz, 1988).

Psychologist Judith Wallerstein (2000) studied 131 children of 60 couples from affluent Marin County, California, who divorced in 1971. She followed these children through adolescence and into adulthood, when many married and became parents of their own. She found a sleeper effect: Years later, their parents' divorce is affecting the children's relationships. They fear that their relationships will fail, fear betrayal, and, most significantly, fear any change at all. Divorce, she argued, was bad for children—both immediately and later in their lives. Couples, politicians argued, should, indeed, stay together, "for the sake of the children."

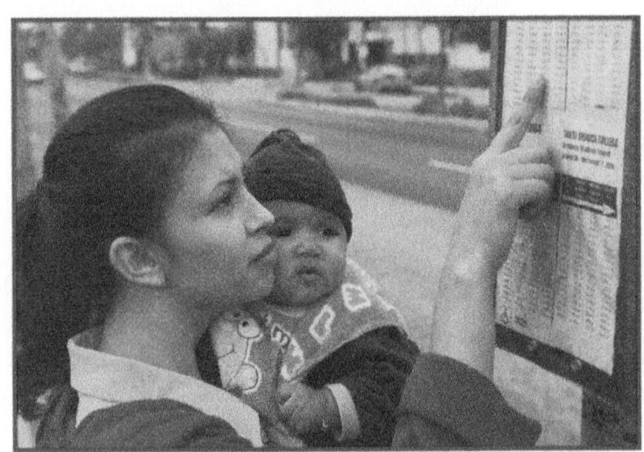

Divorce is rarely a "pleasant" experience, but its impact varies significantly by race, gender, and class. Women's standard of living declines more sharply than men's (which may even rise). Poor and minority women's standards of living decline even more, and they recoup that lost income more slowly than white women do—if at all.

However, Wallerstein's findings have been quite controversial—and, in fact, her findings have been disconfirmed by most sociological studies. After all, Wallerstein studied only children who came to see her as a therapist—that is, she based her findings on those children who were already having difficulties *before their parents divorced*. And she studied children only in wealthy ultra-liberal Marin County, California—the suburban county just north of San Francisco where the Grateful Dead live. She attributed their subsequent problems in relationships to their parents' divorce, when it is just as plausible that it was the conflict between the parents that led to both the divorce and the children's problems. Staying together might have been the worst imaginable outcome.

Sociological research consistently finds that children are more resilient and adapt successfully to their parents' divorces. Mavis Hetherington (2002), for example, studied more than 2,500 children from 1,400 families over a period of 30 years and found that the fear of a devastating effect of divorce on children is exaggerated, with 75 to 80 percent of children coping reasonably well. Other scholars agree that, although parental divorce increases the risk of psychological distress and relationship problems in adulthood, the risks are not great (Amato, 2003; see also Ahrons, 2004).

Perhaps the outcome of divorce depends less on whether one gets a divorce and more on how civilly the parents behave toward each other and how much ongoing investment they maintain in their children's lives. That is to say, what's better for children is explained less well by whether the parents are married or divorced and better by the quality of the relationships the parents have with their children—and with each other.

Box 15.6 Sociology and our World

The Social Value of Sons?

Gordon Dahl and Enrico Moretti (2004) found families with only male children are significantly more durable than those with only female children. In Vietnam, parents of a girl are 25 percent more likely to divorce than parents of a boy. The Asian preference for male children is well known, but the trend also appears in the United States: Parents of one girl are 4.4 percent more likely to divorce than parents of one boy. Parents with three girls are nearly 9 percent more likely to divorce than parents with three boys.

Even in the matter of courtship, when men discover that the woman they are dating is pregnant, they are more likely to stay with her if she is carrying a boy. When they begin dating women who are already mothers, they are more likely to marry women with sons than women with daughters.

Evidently the preference for sons is not limited to Asia. Many American men feel that their lives are incomplete or that they are insufficiently masculine unless they have sons, so much so that their decision to marry or stay in an unhappy marriage is often based less on the wife than on the offspring.

Blended Families

In the first episode of the popular teen sitcom *Drake and Josh,* two high school boys with opposing personalities find that Josh's father intends to marry Drake's mother, so they will become brothers. They accept their new arrangement with no stress or conflict. Their other parents are never mentioned. Drake calls his new Dad "Dad" and defers to his authority. Josh's new Mom never lets on that she has been parenting him for only a few months. In fact, there is only one clue that they were once separate: They have decided to keep their original last names.

Of course, this twenty-first-century revision of *The Brady Bunch* is a highly idealized view of blended families. When a divorced person remarries, the other parents are usually in the picture, and their partner's teenage children do not easily refer to them as "Mom" or "Dad." There are often considerable tensions about the blended partner's parenting rights and obligations. Sooner or later, a child is bound to yell, "I don't have to listen to you! You're not my real father (or mother)!"

At least half of all children will have a divorced and remarried parent before they turn 18 (Ahrons, 2004). They face different issues, depending on how old they are, the role that their biological parents have, whether it's Mom or Dad who remarries, and whether it's the custodial parent. Usually they must adjust to a new residence and a new school and share space with new siblings. In many families, finances become a divisive issue, placing significant strains on the closeness and stability of blended families (Korn, 2001; Martinez, 2005). Several studies have found that children in blended families—both stepchildren and their half-siblings who are the joint product of both parents—do worse in school than children raised in traditional two-parent families (see Ginther, 2004).

While the dynamics of blended families tend to be similar across class and race, the likelihood of blending families tends to be far more common among the middle classes, where parents have sufficient resources to support these suddenly larger families. Lower-class families may be "blended" in all but name: They may cohabit with other people's children but not formalize it by marrying.

Violence in Families

The famous French sociologist Alexis de Tocqueville spoke of the family as a "haven in a heartless world," but for some the family is a violent nightmare. In many families, the person who promised to love and honor you is the most likely to physically assault you; the one who promised to "forsake all others" is also the most likely to rape you; and the one who is supposed to protect you from harm is the one most likely to cause that harm.

Intimate Partner Violence

Intimate partner violence (**IPV**) represents violence, lethal or nonlethal, experienced by a spouse, ex-spouse, or cohabiting partner; boyfriend or girlfriend; or ex-boyfriend or -girlfriend. It is commonly called "domestic violence," but because some does not occur in the home, IPV is the preferred term. IPV is the

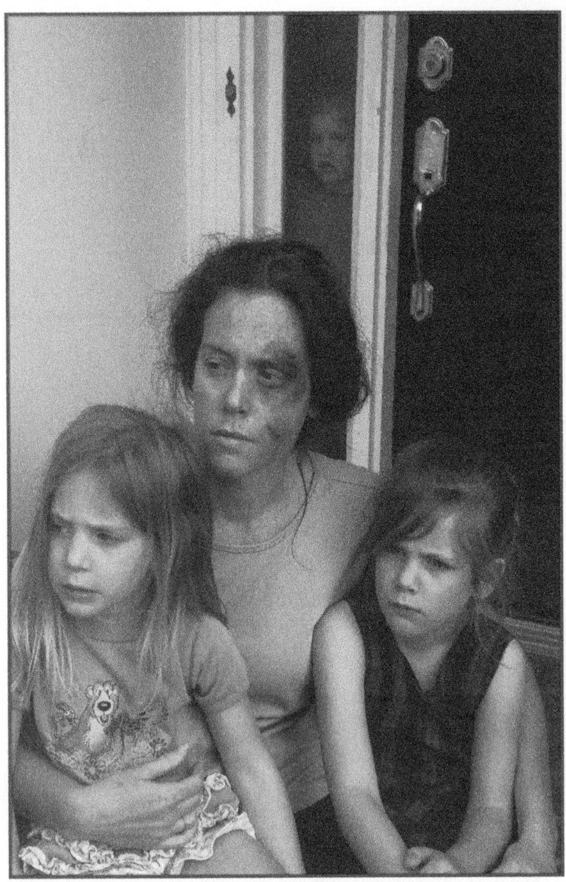

Intimate partner violence (IPV) is the single major cause of injury to women in the United States. More than 2 million women—of all races and classes—are beaten by their partners every year. Some scars may never completely heal.

single major cause of injury to women in the United States. More than 2 million women are beaten by their partners every year. Nearly one in five victims of violence treated in hospital emergency rooms was injured by a spouse, a former spouse, or a current or former boyfriend or girlfriend (Bachman and Salzman, 1994; Kellerman and Marcy 1992; Rhode, 1997; Straus and Gelles, 1990).

Globally, the problem of family violence is widespread. A study released in 2006 by the World Health Organization found that rates of IPV ranged from a low of 15 percent of women in Japan to a high of 71 percent of women in rural Ethiopia. (Rates in the European Union and United States were between 20 and 25 percent.) In 6 of the 15 sites of study, at least 50 percent of the women had been subjected to moderate or severe violence in the home at some point. Perhaps more telling, the majority of the 25,000 women interviewed in the study said that it was the first time they had ever spoken of the abuse to anyone (García-Moreno et al., 2006).

In the United States, IPV knows no class, racial, or ethnic bounds. Yet there are some differences by class, race, ethnicity, and age. For example, poor women experience significantly more violence than higher-income women, and younger women, aged 16 to 24, are far more likely to experience violence than older women. And one of the best predictors of the onset of domestic violence is unemployment.

A few studies have found rates of domestic violence to be higher in African American families than in White families (Hampton, 1987; Hampton and Gelles, 1994). Black females experienced domestic violence at a rate 35 percent higher than that of White females, and Black males experienced domestic violence at a rate about 62 percent higher than that of White males (Rennison and Welchans, 2000; Figure 15.6).

Among Latinos the evidence is contradictory: One study found significantly less violence in Latino families than in Anglo families, while another found a slightly higher rate. Rates were directly related to two factors, the strains of immigrant status and the variations in ideologies of male dominance (Klevens, 2007).

In many cases, however, these racial and ethnic differences disappear when social class is taken into account. Sociologist Noel Cazenave examined the same National Family Violence Survey and found that Blacks had *lower* rates of wife abuse than Whites in three of four income categories—the two highest and the lowest.

FIGURE 15.6 Nonfatal Intimate Partner Victimized Rate by Gender and Race, 1993–2004

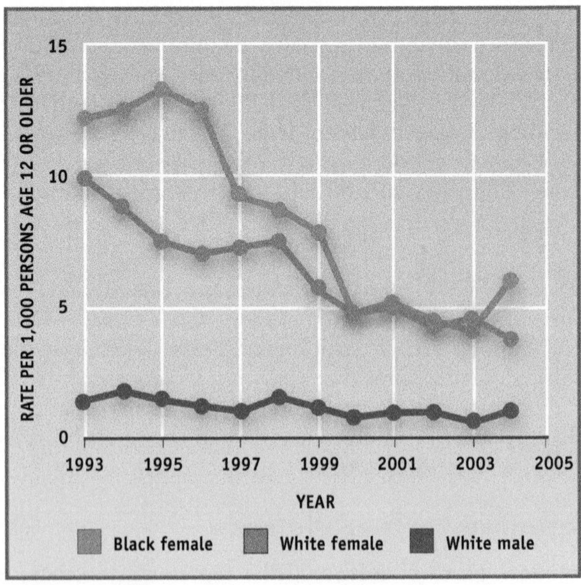

Source: U.S. Department of Justice, Bureau of Justice Statistics, 2000.

Higher rates among Blacks were reported only by those respondents in the $6,000 to $11,999 income range (which included 40 percent of all Blacks surveyed). Income and residence (urban) were also the variables that explained virtually all the ethnic differences between Latinos and Anglos. The same racial differences in spousal murder can be explained by class: Two-thirds of all spousal murders in New York City took place in the poorest sections of the Bronx and Brooklyn (Straus and Cazenare, 1990).

Gay men and lesbians can engage in IPV as well. A recent informal survey of gay victims of violence in six major cities found that gay men and lesbians were more likely to be victims of domestic violence than of antigay hate crimes.

The single greatest difference in rates of IPV is by gender. According to the Bureau of Justice Statistics, 85 percent of all victims of domestic violence are women (see Kimmel, 2002). The gender imbalance of intimate violence is staggering. Of those victims of violence who were injured by spouses or ex-spouses, women outnumber men by about 9 to 1. Eight times as many women were injured by their boyfriends as men injured by girlfriends.

Intergenerational and Intragenerational Violence

In addition to violence between domestic partners, there is also a significant amount of intergenerational and intragenerational violence in families. Intergenerational violence refers to violence between generations, such as parents to children and children to parents. Intragenerational violence refers to violence within the same generation—that is, sibling violence.

Sibling violence goes beyond routine sibling rivalry. Earlier reports found that as many as 80 percent of American children had engaged in an act of physical violence toward a sibling (Straus and Gelles, 1990). In a recent sociological study, David Finkelhor and his colleagues (2006) found that 35 percent of all children had been attacked by a sibling in the previous year. Of these, more than a third were serious attacks (Figure 15.7).

The consequences of sibling violence can be severe. Children who were repeatedly attacked were twice as likely to show symptoms of trauma, anxiety, and depression, including sleeplessness, crying spells, thoughts of suicide, and fear of the dark (Butler, 2006). Finkelhor and his colleagues found that at-

Box 15.7 How do we know what we know?

Gender Symmetry in IPV

Despite dramatic gender differences, there are some researchers and political pundits who claim that there is "gender symmetry" in domestic violence—that rates of domestic violence are roughly equal by gender (see, for example, Brott, 1994). One reason this symmetry is underreported is because men who are victims of domestic violence are so ashamed they are unlikely to come forward—a psychological problem that one researcher calls "the battered husband syndrome" (Steinmetz, 1978).

But a close look at the data suggests why these findings are so discordant with the official studies by the Department of Justice and the FBI. Those studies that find gender symmetry rely on the "conflict tactics scale" (CTS) developed by family violence researcher and sociologist Murray Straus and his colleagues over 30 years. The CTS asked couples if they had ever, during the course of their relationship, hit their partner. An equal number of women and men answered "yes." The number changed dramatically, though, when they were asked who initiated the violence (was it offensive, or defensive), how severe it was (did she push him before or after he'd broken her jaw?), and how often the violence occurred. When these three questions were posed, the results shifted back: The amount, frequency, severity, and consistency of violence against women are far greater than anything done by women to men.

There were several other problems with the CTS as a measure (see Kimmel, 2002). These problems included:

1. *Whom did they ask?* Studies that found comparable rates of domestic violence asked only one partner about the incident. But studies in which both partners were interviewed separately found large discrepancies between reports from women and from men.
2. *What was the time frame?* Studies that found symmetry asked about incidents that occurred in a single year, thus equating a single slap with a reign of domestic terror that may have lasted decades.
3. *Was the couple together?* Studies that found gender symmetry excluded couples that were separated or divorced, although violence against women increases dramatically after separation.
4. *What was the reason for the violence?* Studies that find symmetry do not distinguish between offensive and defensive violence, equating a vicious assault with a woman hitting her husband to get him to stop hitting the children.
5. *Was "sex" involved?* Studies that find symmetry omit marital rape and sexual aggression; because a significant amount of IPV occurs when one partner doesn't want to have sex, this would dramatically change the data.

Of course, women can be—and are—violent toward their husbands and partners. Criminologist Martin Schwartz estimates that women commit as much as 3 to 4 percent of all spousal violence. But research such as this requires that we look more deeply at the questions asked. Sometimes, the answers are contained in the questions.

FIGURE 15.7 Leave Your Bother Alone! Sibling Violence

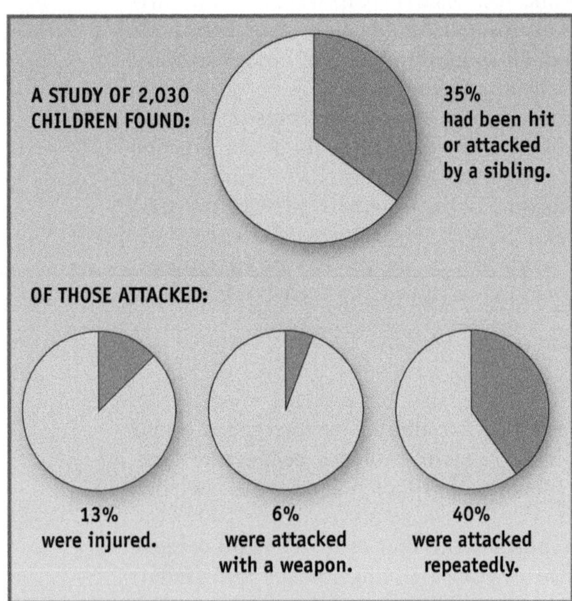
A STUDY OF 2,030
CHILDREN FOUND:
35%
had been hit
or attacked
by a sibling.
OF THOSE ATTACKED:
13%
were injured.
6%
were attacked
with a weapon.
40%
were attacked
repeatedly.

Source: From "Beyond Rivalry, a Hidden World of Sibling Violence" by Katy Butler, *The New York Times*, February 28, 2006. Reprinted with permission.

tacks did not differ by class or race, or even by gender, although boys were slightly more likely to be victims than girls. They occurred most frequently on siblings aged 6 to 12 and gradually tapered off as the child entered adolescence.

Sometime, children use violence against their parents. About 18 percent of children used violence against their parents in the past year—about half of which was considered "nontrivial," serious enough to cause pain or injury (Agnew and Huguley, 1989; Cornell and Gelles, 1982; Straus, Gelles, and Steinmetz, 1980). Rates of child-to-parent violence decrease as the child ages; it is more often younger children who hit their parents. Injuries to parents are rare, but they do happen. If the parent reacts to a child's violence with violence, the child has learned a lesson that could last a lifetime.

The rates of parental violence against children are significantly more serious. In recent years, American society has also been vitally concerned about the problem of child abuse (violence against children) and child sexual abuse (the sexual exploitation of children). The Keeping Children and Families Safe Act of 2003 defines child abuse and neglect as, at minimum: (1) Any recent act or failure to act on the part of a parent or caretaker which results in death, serious physical or emotional harm, sexual abuse or exploitation; or (2) an act or failure to act which presents an imminent risk of serious harm. This definition of child abuse and neglect refers specifically to parents and other caregivers. A "child" under this definition generally means a person who is under the age of 18 or who is not an emancipated minor.

According to the Department of Health and Human Services, rates of victimization and the number of victims have been decreasing in the first decade of the twenty-first century. An estimated 872,000 children were determined to be victims of child abuse or neglect for 2004 (the last year for which there are data). More than 60 percent of child victims were neglected by their parents or other caregivers. About 18 percent were physically abused, 10 percent were sexually abused, and 7 percent were emotionally maltreated. (A child could be a victim of more than one type of maltreatment.) The United States has rates that are significantly higher than rates in other English-speaking countries such as Australia, Canada, and Great Britain, partly, but not entirely, due to the higher rates of child poverty in the United States (poverty is a significant risk factor).

Rates of child abuse and child sexual abuse vary significantly by class but less by race or ethnicity. According to some research (Daly and Wilson, 1981), living with a stepparent significantly increases the risk of both abuse and sexual abuse. Yet other research, using the conflict tactics scale, found little difference—in generally very high rates overall. In one study, 63 percent of children who lived with both genetic parents and 47 percent of those who lived with a stepparent and 60 percent of those who lived with a foster parent were subject to violence, and about 10 percent were subjected to severe violence in all three categories (Gelles and Harrop, 1991).

Globally, the problem of child abuse and neglect is equally serious—and includes forms of abuse that are not found in the economic north. In 2006, the United Nations commissioned the first global investigation into child abuse. They found that between 80 and 98 percent of children suffer physical punishment in their homes, with a third or more experiencing severe physical punishment resulting from the use of implements.

Despite these global differences, it is equally true that Americans are far more accepting of violence against children than they may realize. Over half of all American parents (55 percent) believe that corporal punishment, including spanking, is acceptable; and one-third of parents have used corporal punishment against their adolescents (Straus, 2005). These numbers are significantly less than the 94 percent who supported the use of corporal punishment in 1968 and the two-thirds who used it with adolescents in 1975 (Straus, 2005). But it is still the case that nearly all parents—94 percent—used corporal punishment with toddlers, and they did so, on average, three times a week.

There is actually little empirical evidence that spanking serves any developmental purpose, but there is a wealth of evidence that spanking is developmentally harmful. The American Academy of Pediatrics recommends that parents avoid spanking (2007). In fact, 94 percent of all studies of the effects of corporal punishment on children showed a relationship between such forms of punishment and aggression, delinquency in childhood, crime and antisocial behavior as an adult, low levels of empathy or conscience, poor parent–child relations, and mental health problems such as depression (Gershoff, 2002).

Family violence is often difficult to remedy through policy initiatives. Globally, fewer than 10 percent of all countries even have laws against certain forms of child abuse, let alone programs to offer aid and support to victims and to prosecute perpetrators (*Rights of the Child,* 2006). In the United States, policymakers have long taken the approach that what happens "behind closed doors" is a private matter, not a social problem that can be remedied only through public policy. Rates of all forms of family violence are dramatically underreported; fear of retaliation, shame, and a general cultural acceptance of violence all greatly reduce the likelihood of reporting. And the continuum of violence, from spanking a child to murdering a spouse, is part of a culture that does not universally condemn violence but sees some instances of violence as legitimate and even appropriate and sees perpetrators as entitled to use violence.

The Family in the 21st Century: "The Same as It Ever Was"

In the first line of his novel *Anna Karenina,* the great Russian novelist Leo Tolstoy wrote, "Happy families are all alike; every unhappy family is unhappy in its own way." How unsociological! Families, happy or unhappy, are as varied as snowflakes when viewed close up and as similar around the world as all the sand in the desert.

Families are as old as the human species. We've always had them; indeed we couldn't live without them. And families have always been changing, adapting to new political, social, economic, and environmental situations. Some expectations of family may be timeless, yet families have always been different, and new relationships, arrangements, and patterns are emerging all over the world today, just as they always have been. As the musician David Byrne sang in the 1980s, the family is "the same as it ever was."

Yes, it's probably true that family is still the place where, when we go there, they have to take us in. But even if we can go home again, it's never the same.

Chapter Review

1. *How do sociologists define family?* A family is a basic unit of society. Family is also a cultural institution; the functions of the family include socializing new members and regulation of sexual activity, property ownership, and marriage. The definition of family changes over time; the nuclear family is a relatively new phenomenon. Agrarian families were extended, and the household formed the basic economic unit of society, performing all societal functions that are now handled by other institutions. The nuclear family developed in Europe and the United States in the late eighteenth century as a result of industrialization and modernization. The nuclear family model was very gendered, and the home became the women's sphere and work men's.
2. *How do families develop?* Dating emerged in the United States in the 1920s when children of immigrants shed old customs and teens had unprecedented freedom. Dating sometimes leads to marriage, the most common family formation. Marriage in the United States varies by race; White women are more likely to marry than others. Not everyone marries; increasingly people are choosing to postpone marriage, to cohabit, or to remain single. Choices are influenced by education, changing sexual mores, and the women's movement. Attitudes toward interracial marriage are also changing, which is reflected in increased rates of such marriages. Also, same-sex couples cannot marry in most states but do form partnerships and cohabit.
3. *How important is parenting?* Parenting is becoming more desirable in the United States, and more importance is being placed on parents and parenting. At the same time, children are more undervalued and neglected than before. Parenting is gendered; although most women work outside the home, they still do most of the housework and particularly the housework having to do with caring for the children. Fathers are becoming more active parents. Also, there has been an increase in single-parent families, mostly headed by mothers. Grandparents are also raising grandchildren; this is most likely for African American grandmothers. Not everyone chooses to have children; more highly educated individuals are less likely to parent than those in other groups.

4. *What transitions do families go through?* Although marriage used to mean a lifelong commitment, today divorce is common and easy to get. The effects of divorce on children are widely debated. While parental divorce increases the risk of distress and later relationship problems, most children are found to be resilient. After a divorce, the woman's standard of living typically decreases; this is even more striking among African American women. As people remarry, blended families are becoming more common, especially among those in the middle class, although unofficial blended families are prevalent in all groups.
5. *What forms does family violence take?* Family violence takes many forms. One is intimate partner violence (IPV). IPV affects people from all groups but is more likely to occur among the poorer socioeconomic strata. Eighty-five percent of IPV victims are women. Violence also occurs between and within generations. In sibling violence, which tends to taper off after age 12, boys are more likely than girls to be victims. Children do abuse parents, but parental abuse of children is a far greater social problem. In the United States, views on corporal punishment as abuse vary, but negative attitudes toward it have strengthened over time. Globally, child abuse is prevalent and includes things such as genital mutilation and sexual slavery.

Key Terms

Cohabitation (p. 353)
Companionate marriage (p. 345)
Exogamy (p. 343)
Extended family (p. 345)
Family (p. 342)
Family of origin (p. 344)
Family of procreation (p. 344)
Group marriage (p. 343)
Intimate partner violence (IPV) (p. 363)
Kinship systems (p. 342)
Legitimacy (p. 343)
Miscegenation (p. 355)
Monogamy (p. 343)
Multigenerational households (p. 352)
Nonmarital sex (p. 354)
Polyandry (p. 343)
Polygamy (p. 343)
Polygyny (p. 343)

What does *America* think?

15.1 Racial and Ethnic Family Diversity

These are actual survey data from the General Social Survey.

Do you think there should be laws against marriages between Blacks and Whites? The overwhelming majority of respondents said "no" to this question in the 2002 survey. More Black (95.1 percent) than White (89.6 percent) respondents said "no." The numbers were very different when the question was asked 30 years earlier in 1972, when about 60 percent of respondents said "no." In the 1972 survey, the race categories were limited to "White" (of whom 60.7 percent said "no") and "other" (of whom 66.7 percent said "no"). Most respondents were White.

CRITICAL THINKING | DISCUSSION QUESTIONS

1. Why do you think almost 10 percent of the population still thinks interracial marriage should be illegal, including 9 percent of black respondents?
2. Part of doing sociology is placing things in historical context. What historical changes have taken place in the past 30 years that might explain how views toward interracial marriage have changed?

15.2 Attitudes toward Abortion

These are actual survey data from the General Social Survey, 2004.

1. Do you think it should be possible for a pregnant woman to obtain a legal abortion if the woman's own health is seriously endangered by the pregnancy? In 2004, 86 percent of respondents said "yes," and 14 percent said "no." These results are almost identical to 1972 responses. The percentage of respondents saying "yes" peaked in 1991 at 91.5 percent.
2. Do you think it should be possible for a pregnant woman to obtain a legal abortion if she is married and does not want any more children? In 2004, 41.8 percent of respondents said "yes," and 58.2 percent said "no." The percentage of people saying "yes" peaked 1994 at 48 percent, but otherwise, the data were almost identical to 1972, and attitudes have remained pretty steady since then.
3. Do you think it should be possible for a pregnant woman to obtain a legal abortion if the family has a very low income and cannot afford any more children? The responses from 2004 showed 41 percent of respondents saying "yes" and 59 percent saying "no." The response for those saying "yes" was rather lower than 1972 and again peaked in 1994.
4. Do you think it should be possible for a pregnant woman to obtain a legal abortion if she became pregnant as a result of rape? In 2004, 76.2 percent of respondents said "yes," and 23.8 percent said "no." The response for those saying "yes" was lower than it was in 1972 and peaked in 1991.

CRITICAL THINKING | DISCUSSION QUESTIONS

1. What do you think lies behind the variation of responses in approval toward abortion based on the reason for abortion? The highest approval was for the pregnant woman's health, next for rape victims, lower for married women who do not want children, and lowest for women who want to abort because they are poor. What societal values does this ranking reflect?
2. Why do you think the results break down by gender the way they do?

▶ Go to this website to look further at the data. You can run your own statistics and crosstabs here: **http://sda.berkeley.edu/cgi-bin/hsda?harcsda+gss04.**

REFERENCES: Davis, James A., Tom W. Smith, and Peter V. Marsden. General Social Surveys 1972–2004: [Cumulative file] [Computer file]. 2nd ICPSR version. Chicago, IL: National Opinion Research Center [producer], 2005; Storrs, CT: Roper Center for Public Opinion Research, University of Connecticut; Ann Arbor, MI: Inter-University Consortium for Political and Social Research; Berkeley, CA: Computer-Assisted Survey Methods Program, University of California [distributors], 2005.

chapter 16

From the Plow to the Computer: Change, Collective Behavior, and Social Movements

IN THIS CHAPTER, YOU WILL LEARN

- *that change is a constant feature of life, but the speed of change has become more rapid in the modern world;*
- *that change may be viewed from several perspectives;*
- *some of the sources of change;*
- *the processes of social and cultural change;*
- *the relationship of technology to change;*
- *the meaning of collective behavior, and where and why it occurs;*
- *the definition and kinds of crowds, panics, mobs, riots, and mass hysteria;*
- *the nature of publics and public opinion;*
- *about social movements, their traits and characteristics;*
- *about some of the causes of social movements.*

A new century began a few years ago. More importantly, not only a century, but a millennium has come to an end, a dramatically large segment of time in human terms. What changes can we expect to experience in the new century? We can only conjecture about the future, though we know something of the past. Because generations that came before us left a written record, we have some insights as to what life was like. When the first thousand years of the Christian Era were ending in Europe (in 999, that is) life for the majority was a grim struggle. Men considered themselves lucky to survive past 30 years, and 50 was considered a ripe old age (although, of course, some lived into their eighties). Women, too, barely made it to their thirtieth birthday, and many died regularly at childbirth. The years we know as childhood were unknown: children in every social class had to grow up as fast as possible and become useful members of society. This meant that emperors were leading armies while still in their teens, and many popes began their tenure while still in their twenties. At the eve of that first millennium in Europe, transportation meant an oxcart, and rapid transportation consisted of a horse and rider. Housing was mud-and-thatch huts for the serfs and timber castles for the feudal lords. Disease was rampant: tuberculosis regularly decimated populations, and leper colonies flourished outside many city walls. Vitamin deficiencies produced blindness, goiter, paralysis, and bone malformations, and those so affected made up the hunchbacks and beggars living at the mercy of the healthy and wealthy. The social order was rigidly divided into clearly defined strata: the nobility, who spent their time battling enemies to preserve their privileged status; the clergy, whose chief task it was to pray for the salvation of souls (because the end of the world was thought to be imminent, this was an important function!); and the serfs, who did all the back-breaking work in the

Contemporary Society: An Introduction to Social Science, Twelfth Edition
by John A. Perry and Erna K. Perry

It has been a long way from hieroglyphics (like the one above, from a tomb in the Valley of the Kings in Egypt) to computers. Social change increases rapidly once a way is invented of communicating with many people at once, rather than one at a time.

society to feed and clothe the others. The dark nights, illuminated only by burning logs and the occasional candle, held terror for all, and each passing season was much like the one before.

In the thousand years between 999 and 1999 the world has changed dramatically. Human lives have been extended, many diseases have been tamed, transportation is rapid and efficient, communication—which did not exist except in embryonic form a millennium ago—overwhelms us. In the developed world, food and housing have become sophisticated and plentiful—though not for all individuals. Electricity enables us to work at night, and the industrial system creates millions of objects to fulfill our needs, real and imagined. But what used to be called, optimistically, progress has not been fairly distributed around the globe nor in individual societies. Nor has it eradicated totally the ancient scourges of disease, famine, war, pain, and suffering.

With all our new capabilities, can we predict what the twenty-first century holds in store? We no longer fear the end of the world, but most of us look to the future with some trepidation. The increase in global temperature, predicted by scientific entities, will lead to changes that are still unknown. Experts in the social sciences tell us that the twenty-first century will be one in which economics will play a dominant role. In the centuries ahead, the world will contain more democracies, which will mean a more peaceful coexistence among nations. The imperialism of the past, in fact, was based on the need to acquire new territory to exploit its raw materials. Increasingly, raw materials will be less important to manufacturing, as even oil is replaced by alternative fuels, solar power, and controlled nuclear fusion. The end of the petroleum age will also lead to a rearrangement in the status of nations and will force them to collaborate more fully with the United Nations to solve overarching problems that face the entire world. Europe and the United States will probably remain in the forefront as superpowers as long as they can manage to solve some of their internal problems.

Today, change is dramatic and fast. It was not always so. Human societies remained practically unchanged for many thousands of years. What has happened to cause such profound transformations? What makes change occur so rapidly now? What is change, anyway? Where does it originate? Can it be stopped or bent to our wishes? Can it be slowed or accelerated? Do we control it, or does it control us?

Society and Change

For most of human history, as we said, people born in one generation lived very much like their parents and could count on their children living very much as they had. Whatever change occurred was almost imperceptible because it was so slow. For the past 250 years, and especially for the past 50 years, such vast changes have taken place from one generation to the next that people separated by 20 or 30 years may be said to live in an altogether different society and be strangers to one another. Futurologist Alvin Toffler has called this concept "future shock," a condition akin to the culture shock that would be experienced by a person confronting a totally alien culture for the first time.

Box 16.1 The United States: A Century of Change

Among the sociocultural changes that have occurred in the United States in the last century, which have radically transformed the society, the following can be gathered from the information collected by the Census Bureau.

	1900	2000
Total Population	76 million	293 million (2004) (300+million 2007)
Women	37 million	152 million (2006)
Men	39 million	148 million (2006)
Minorities	9 million	(approx 98 million 2006)
Black	8.8 million	(38 million 2006)
American Indian	267,000	2.8 million (2005)
Chinese	119,000	Asian; Chinese, Japanese, and others approx. 14.5 million (2005)
Hispanic or Latino		42.5 million (2005)
Largest Cities	New York (3.4 million) Chicago (1.7 million) Philadelphia (1.3 million) St. Louis (575,000) Boston (561,000)	New York (8+ million) Los Angeles (3.8 million) Chicago (2.9+ million) Houston (2+ million) Philadelphia (1.5 million)
Largest States	New York (7.3 million) Pennsylvania (6.3 million) Illinois (4.8 million) Ohio (4.2 million) Missouri (3.1 million)	California (36+ million) Texas (23+ million) New York (19+ million) Florida (17.5 million) Illinois (12.5 million)
Size of Average Household	4.76 persons	2.60 persons
Births per Woman	4	2.05
Infant Mortality Rate (Deaths in the first year per 1,000 births)	165	6.8 (2005)
Number of Divorced	Men: 84,000 Women: 114,000	Men: 8.3 million Women: 11.1 million
Life Expectancy	Men: 46 years Women: 48 years	Men: 74.7 years (2001) Women: 80 years (2001)
Persons Living Alone	1%	25.5% (2000)
Persons Living in Households of 5 or More People	50%	10% (2000)
Households Headed by a Married Couple	80% (1910)	53% (2000)
Urban Residents	40%	80%
Average Yearly Income	$8.360 (adjusted for inflation)	46,242 (2005)
Percent of Income Spent on Food	43% (1901)	2.4% (2005)
Suburban Residents	12% (1910)	52%
Number of Automobiles	8,000	241 million (2005)
Percent of Housing Units with Electricity	2%	99% (1997)
High School Graduates	13% (1910)	85.2% (2005)
College Graduates	3%	27.6% (2005)
Married Women in Labor Force	6%	59% (2005)
Men Over 65 in Labor Force	63%	18.5% (2004)
Hourly Wage of Factory Workers (adjusted for inflation)	$3.80 (1909)	$13.90 (1999)
Percentage of Unionized Civilian Labor Force	3%	12% (2006)
Family Farms	5.7 million	1.9 million (1997)

Source: U.S. Bureau of the Census, 2006 "Statistics in Brief."

At the same time that dramatic changes constantly take place, a thread of stability is also apparent. The factor of stability holds societies together and binds each generation to the next.

The subject of change holds special fascination for social scientists because if the sources of change could be determined scientifically, and the course of change predicted, then the possibility of guiding change in the direction of attaining the highest common good could become a reality. Unfortunately, the subject of change is not so easily harnessed. Change is constantly analyzed, however, because it is apparent that it is the pivot around which much of contemporary life revolves.

Although change represents flux, or motion, analysis requires that social phenomena be viewed as if they were frozen in time and space (static). But they must also be observed from the perspective of dynamics, or the study of the sources of change. *Statics* and *dynamics* are two dimensions of the same phenomenon. They are coexisting entities, and the need to employ both in the study of change makes the project so much more complex. Complexity also results from the fact that change affects every aspect of individual and social life. The issues to be analyzed concerning change, then, are endless and multiform.

Levels of Change

Change may be experienced on a micro level, on a middle level, and on a macro level. On a *micro* level, change is felt through new patterns of individual and small group interaction. The family, for instance, is a much changed institution, as will become apparent in a later chapter. The chief result of these changes is that the individual is faced with a large number of options: new norms of behavior, new values, new manners. Choice, while opening some horizons, also creates anxiety and confusion. In turn, anxiety and confusion can lead to feelings of normlessness, or anomie, which are harmful to the individual and to society.

At the *middle* level of social life, change is experienced in communities as a result of alterations in the economy and in the political system. As industry became the underlying force of economies in Western societies, people began moving in large numbers to cities. Urbanization, which is what we call this trend, is perceived as having lessened communal ties. At the same time, the urban setting presents many more opportunities to individuals. Similarly, groups or classes of people that were formerly excluded from the political process or from upward mobility have been increasingly gaining inclusion as a result of trends toward greater democratization of the political system and the greater opportunities that a capitalistic economic system offers.

Finally, on the *macrosocial* level, change is generated by social forces that are large-scale and revolutionary, affecting entire societies and regions of the world. Individuals and communities, where these changes are experienced, seem to be swept away by these social forces in the sense that they must adapt to them or perish. Urbanization, industrialization, and the advent of the information society are some of these macro-level changes, and they have a domino effect, transforming the social structures and institutions of societies.

Box 16.2 Sweeping Changes in the Political Game

The widespread use of the Internet is changing the way American politics is conducted. Both Republicans and Democrats maintain that the use of e-mail, interactive web sites, candidate and party blogs, and text messaging is much superior and far less costly than the previous instruments, namely, knocking on doors and using banks of telephones manned by volunteers. The new tools politicians use in campaigning makes it possible for them to raise money, organize get-out-the-vote efforts, and assemble crowds for rallies. Even advertising on television is taking a step back and diminishing in influence because the new technology allows campaigns to address themselves personally to more specific audiences. For instance, podcasts may be used with a daily downloaded message from a candidate, e-mail chain messages with peer-to-peer distribution may be sent, and messages may be addressed to networks of persons with similar political views.

The Internet has already affected the music industry, newspapers, and retailing, so it is to be expected that it is going to impact politics. Already in the 2004 elections it was very successful in fundraising, particularly in the campaign of democratic presidential candidate Howard Dean, who was one of the early users of the Internet. In 2006, about 50 million people in the United States got their news every day from the Internet, which is available to 70 percent of Americans. With such figures, it becomes clear that the Internet will become a major tool for candidates of every stripe. In fact, its success in campaigning prompted the national chairman of the Republican Party to say that "the effect of the Internet on politics will be every bit as transformational as television was" (Nagourney, 2006, 17).

Despite its transformative power and the manner in which the Internet will in all probability change the way politics, and not only campaigning, is run, there are shortcomings with this medium. For one thing, the message will reach only those people who are interested in politics: those who are not, will not even have to hear the "bites" audiences are subjected to on television. For another, Internet use declines among persons 65 and over, yet that age group is the most faithful of voters and followers of political events. As a means of persuasion for political campaigns, therefore, the Internet is still in its infancy. There is no doubt, however, that it will become a new way of interacting with our representatives in government. Whether it will be a better or worse way, only the future will tell (Nagourney, 2006, 1 and 17).

Processes of Social and Cultural Change

Change may be willed or planned, borrowed or imitated from other societies; or phenomena may be discovered and technologies invented. And we know the processes through which change occurs.

Change occurs on both a societal and a cultural level. When change happens in society, it does so in the guise of a change in the patterns of interaction. That is, as a result of change, some members of society assume new statuses and fill new roles. For instance, the abolition of slavery was a social change because it gave former slaves a new status—that of free persons—in which they could assume new roles as the equals of other free persons. This kind of change, *social change*, occurs through planning, reform, or revolution.

On the other hand, change in culture, or *cultural change*, occurs as a result of scientific discoveries, technological inventions, new achievements in the arts, shifts in religious doctrines, and so on. In Western civilization there have been dramatic cultural changes: the belief that slavery was justified has given way to the belief that it is reprehensible; the assumption that the earth is flat has given way to the discovery that it is round; the invention of the automobile has transformed the way of life, affecting sexual mores, family traditions, and people's perceptions of the world.

Of course, society and culture do not exist one without the other. Social and cultural changes do not occur separately and distinctly. Changes in society cause changes in culture and vice versa. Social and cultural changes overlap and are viewed separately only for purposes of analysis. Social scientists use the term *sociocultural change*, or simply change, to mean both social and cultural change.

Social Change: Planning, Reform, Revolution

Planning is a self-explanatory process in which people are constantly engaged. Planning by governments at all levels results in continuous, though often slow, social change.

Reform involves efforts by either citizens or governmental agencies to correct laws or institutions. During the Great Depression, laws were reformed to provide citizens with jobs, to furnish them with the wherewithal to survive when they were unemployed, to help them with health care, and so on. In 1954, the law that allowed segregation of the races was reformed. Abortion and divorce laws have also undergone reform.

The train was an invention that put together elements already present in the society—the steam engine and wheels—when it became apparent that speed and comfort would be superior to that provided by a horse and carriage. This was especially true in the United States, where the tremendous distances made travel by the old method long, uncomfortable, and dangerous.

Revolution is change obtained through violent means by the people of a nation when their government ceases to be responsive to them or when they are occupied by another country. Revolution is analyzed in the context of social movements later in the chapter.

Cultural Change: Innovation and Diffusion

Because people are creatures of habit, they are conservative and resist giving up beliefs, values, and customs—aspects of nonmaterial culture—in favor of new ones. Nonetheless, some cultural changes necessitate giving up, or exchanging, the old for the new. The processes of cultural change include innovation and diffusion.

Innovation. Innovation produces new elements, or new combinations of old elements, for absorption into the culture. Innovation is also always cumulative. Whether we speak of music, painting, or the latest space technology, they are all built upon foundations erected earlier. Innovation can take the form of a *discovery* or of an *invention.*

A *discovery* is a new perception of an already existing fact or relationship. Principles of physics and chemistry, the organization of the solar system, the existence of viruses and bacteria, are examples of discoveries. These phenomena existed all along, but humans were not aware of them. For a discovery to effect change, it must be put to use. There must be other technological inventions to support it, and a need for the discovery must be present. The principle of the steam engine was known by the Greeks some 2000 years ago, but they saw no need for such a machine, nor did they have the necessary technology to build one.

An *invention* is a way of putting existing knowledge to new use. Ideas or objects already present in the culture are combined in a new way to produce something more important than the sum of their parts. When the steam engine was combined with a boat to produce the steamboat, the new product became a more effective mode of transportation than boats powered by rowing or sails had been previously.

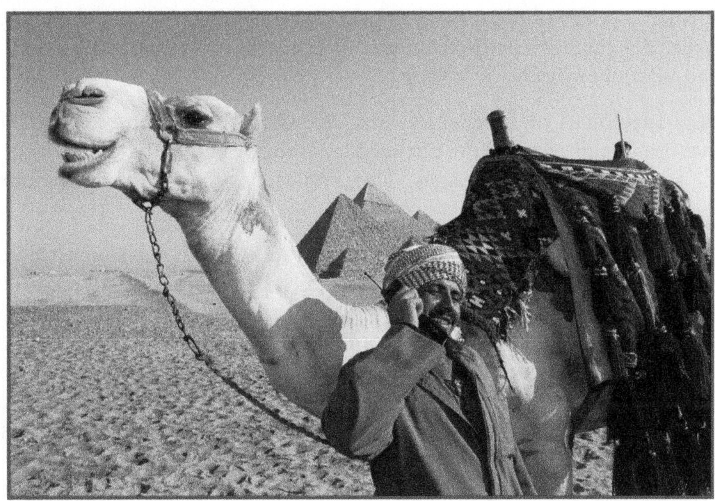

Societies do not change at the same rate, and the process of diffusion works in such a way that some, but not all, products of one society are willingly accepted by another. This desert dweller still uses camels as his mode of transportation but communicates via a cell phone.

Inventions can also occur in nonmaterial culture. The Constitution of the United States may be thought of as a cultural invention resulting from the philosophical traditions of Western Europe and the experience of the colonists in the New World.

Diffusion. Diffusion is a process in which cultural traits are spread from one society to another, or from one group within society to another. Diffusion is an important factor in cultural change. For instance, spaghetti was brought to the United States by Italian immigrants. The Italians had adopted noodles that had been brought from China, and today pasta is considered as American as apple pie (and it has become popular in many other countries, as well). Anthropologists claim that most of the content of a complex culture is the product of diffusion.

Diffusion tends to be reciprocal; that is, each culture in contact with another gives something to the other, although not always in the same proportion. A simple culture, as a rule, borrows more elements from a complex culture than the other way around, and a borrowing culture is usually selective. Asian societies have generally accepted Western technology (and fashion and music and food) but are only slowly accepting the West's system of values. Americans borrowed the idea of representative government from England but did not give it a parliamentary form. The traits that a society borrows tend to be modified rather than accepted wholesale.

The Sources of Change

What triggers change? Tracing the sources of change has been problematic for social scientists who have developed a number of theories and models to explain it. There are also more obvious sources of change, however.

The Physical Environment. The physical environment, over which people have little control, directs the cultural development of a society and the erection of social structures. It also promotes some and limits other changes. Earthquakes, volcanic eruptions, repeated flooding, severe droughts, and similar phenomena may effectively change the lives of the people in the area, sometimes wiping them out altogether.

Geography. In the past, geography played a crucial role, because change occurred more rapidly and more consistently in societies that were geographically at the crossroads, where each society was exposed to the culture of another. Conversely, little change occurred in societies that were geographically isolated from others because there were so few opportunities for cultural diffusion.

Population. Population movements, as well as increases and decreases in population size, are also sources of change. The baby boom that followed World War II required the building of many schools and the development of youth-directed industries. This same generation is today making special demands on jobs and housing and in the future will make the society top-heavy with older people. This will have consequences for the entire society.

Ideas or Belief Systems. Another source of social change originates in ideas or belief systems, also called ideologies. The American Revolution was a triggering mechanism for social change: it was fought because the idea that Americans ought to be independent of England took hold, and the idea emerged because dependence on England was an economic hardship.

Social Movements. Ideologies and belief systems are often incorporated into social movements, a form of collective behavior. Social movements attract a number of people who join together to either bring about or resist specific social or cultural changes. They represent an attempt on the part of members of a society to affect the social order through direct action.

War and Conquest. Throughout the history of the human race, much social change has occurred as a result of wars, which yielded either the conquest of territory or its loss. War casualties can have a deep impact on population. Considering that in World War II alone, about 17 million military personnel and some 34 million civilians died, it becomes clear that a society can suffer a decline in population that will unbalance it for generations. There are almost certain to be changes in the economic system, for fewer men in the labor force may mean labor shortages. In turn, shortages may bring women into the labor force, with a consequent realignment of traditions and values. Wars also necessitate the manufacture of specific products—arms, means of transportation, and so on, so that new plants tend to be built, again accelerating economic growth. The losers in war face other changes—the imposition of foreign rule and a foreign language, forced movement to other areas, economic subjugation imposed through taxation and slave labor, and in the worst but by no means unique event, death.

In addition to leaving a traumatic and sometimes indelible mark on the survivors, wars may change a nation's values and norms through the forced contacts with other cultures. The best example is provided by Japan, a formerly closed society that, initially because of its military occupation by American forces, began to absorb American norms.

Finally, war can have drastic consequences on a society's social structure, particularly institutions. The growth of large research universities in the United States followed the fact that the USSR—then our Cold War enemy—was the first nation to launch a space satellite. The growth of the central government at the expense of local governments is also related to the fact that providing for national defense and security requires a large bureaucracy and wide-ranging taxing powers.

Random Events. Random events and the acts of individual human beings can also lead to change, although there is no way to subject such phenomena to scientific inquiry. The assassination of a president, causing a vice president to take over the helm of a nation, can have dramatic consequences, as can the judgment of a general who loses a significant battle. Individuals, too, can have profound influences on the course of events in a society, although it is difficult to evaluate the effect of a single individual on social change.

Technology

The most obvious and revolutionary source of change throughout history has been technology. *Technology* includes all the methods, devices, and artifacts made by humans that help people to manage and control their environment. For prehistoric humans, technology consisted of the use of sharpened sticks and stones. For contemporary people, it includes everything from a simple shovel to a sophisticated computer.

Some technological discoveries or inventions have been so significant in terms of the sociocultural changes they have produced that they have been called technological revolutions. One such revolution occurred during the Neolithic, or New Stone Age (between 5000 and 3000 B.C.). In this period, for the first time in history, people changed their condition from food gatherers to *food producers*. They domesticated some animals and put them to use. They invented the plow. They began using four-wheeled vehicles. Later, they added the solar calendar, writing, and numbers, and they began to use bronze. Finally, they added irrigation, sailboats, looms, the making of bricks, the process of glazing, and a great architectural invention, the arch.

Results of the First Technological Revolution

Tilling the soil and keeping flocks provided people with a fairly dependable food supply and even an occasional surplus. Because the rate of starvation was drastically reduced, populations boomed. No longer needing to move in constant search of food, people settled permanently in one spot. A settled existence promoted the development of institutions—customs and traditions solidified into the family, religion, education, government, and the economy. In time, these pivotal institutions all grew in complexity. Temporary settlements became permanent villages and towns. Work that had to be done in these villages and towns was divided for the sake of greater efficiency. Goods and services began to be exchanged between a number of villages and towns, and new ways to control the environment accumulated. Villages grew into towns and then cities and eventually became city-states and nation-states. Religions progressed from beliefs in magic to more sophisticated forms, including monotheism. The family also underwent a number of changes and took on different forms in different societies.

The Industrial Revolution

By about the middle of the eighteenth century, a new technological revolution began yet another cycle of change, although the Industrial Revolution actually had its roots in much earlier events.

Inventions and Discoveries of the Industrial Revolution

The Industrial Revolution may be said to have begun with (1) the invention of a small number of basic machines, (2) the invention and discovery of some new materials, and (3) the discovery of new sources of power. The wide-ranging effects of these discoveries and inventions included the mechanization of agriculture and manufacturing, the application of power to manufacturing, the development of a factory system, a tremendous increase in the speed of transportation and communication, and dramatic changes in economic systems.

The Industrial Revolution brought us images such as this and an increased production of goods and services that much improved our life style. Now, however, a new technological revolution threatens to make ghost towns of once prosperous industrial cities such as Pittsburgh, shown here.

Among the most important machines invented during the first phase of the Industrial Revolution were the pendulum clock, the spinning jenny, the power loom, the blast furnace, and the steam engine. During the second phase, which is thought to have begun about 1860, the most important invention was the combustion engine, which enabled steam power to be applied to transportation and factory machine production. Steel was substituted for iron as the basic material of industry, and coal was replaced by gas and oil as principal sources of power (we are currently attempting to harness atomic and solar energy as well as other alternatives as sources of power). Electricity became a major form of industrial energy. The spread of electricity enabled messages to be sent over wires, telegraph, and telephones; gave people more time to work by providing light during the night hours; and supplied power for turbines and elevators so that skyscrapers could be constructed. Chemistry also flourished in this period, allowing people to manufacture products that were not originally found in nature, such as petrochemicals, synthetics, and plastics. Automatic machinery was developed, and labor became highly specialized. A third phase—which according to some is actually the beginning of a new technological revolution—began with *automation*, which was developed around the 1930s. Basically, this is a process in which machines control other machines, as contrasted with *mechanization*, which is the substitution of machines for human and animal muscle power. Automation effectively began following World War II, when the first computers were produced. Computers have been responsible for an information explosion that has practically doubled the ability to store and access knowledge in the last 30 years.

The third technological revolution is in its infancy and should mature by about the middle of the twenty-first century. This revolution consists of the joining of computers and telecommunications (image television, voice telephone, data information, text facsimile) into a single system, which will transform us into a true world society.

Industrialism

The system of production that came to be called industrialism (or industry) represented a radical departure from previous methods of manufacturing goods. In the Middle Ages, artisans or craftsmen organized in guilds (types of unions) produced an entire article and sold it directly to a buyer. As commerce expanded, some craftsmen relied on merchants to dispose of their merchandise rather than waiting for customers to come to their shops. Eventually, craftsmen began to depend on merchants to supply the raw material and to sell the finished product. Needing more workers, merchants began to employ entire families to produce a finished object out of raw or unfinished material and paid them by the piece. This system was alternately called the piece, domestic, or putting-out system. The piece system became the foundation of the English woolen industry. Farm families supplemented their small earnings by spinning the wool that merchants brought to their cottages (hence the name "cottage industry"). Eventually, the piece system became increasingly specialized as more and more articles were produced. The production of an article was divided into several steps that different members of the family or apprentices could easily perform. Specialization and division of labor are especially efficient ways of organizing production.

The Factory. With the invention and growing use of machinery in manufacturing, it became more convenient to house both the workers and the bulky machinery under one roof. This step introduced the *factory system* as the basis of industrialism. The former merchants—now called entrepreneurs and employers—had much more control over their workers when all the stages of production were housed in one location. They could pace the work of their employees—decide how many pieces had to be finished per hour or per day. And they could use their capital much more effectively when everything needed for production was at their disposal.

The Industrial Revolution came to the United States from Britain in the early part of the nineteenth century. It spread to Western Europe in the middle of that century and to Japan at the end of the century. After the Russian Revolution in 1917, Russia began a serious effort at industrialization, and in succession, so did China, India, and South America.

Technology and Social Change

Technology may also be defined as the practical application of knowledge because it builds upon existing knowledge and previous technology. Therefore, the more technologically advanced a society is, the more rapid is its technological progress. Needless to say, technological progress leads to change, and the faster the progress, the faster the pace of change. Technology is what supports the economic system of a society. The more advanced the technology, the more efficient it is as a system for creating wealth. The industrial system created wealth by mass producing millions of identical products. This production method enabled manufacturers to produce articles cheaply and make a profit by selling them to the largest market possible. Today the so-called smokestack era is coming to a close. Computer-driven technologies are reversing the previous industrial system of production in that they are making it possible to produce small runs of more customized goods and services aimed at more specific markets. In addition, constant innovation shortens the life cycles of products immensely, especially those of the technologies themselves. The approximate life of an innovative feature in the computer industry is approximately six months. As fast and as powerful as today's computers are, we will shortly see the appearance of a supercomputer that will be able to calculate more than a trillion mathematical operations each second. This phenomenal technology reached its present point very rapidly: the first mainframe computer, which took up a whole room, was built by the Univac division of Sperry Rand Corporation in 1951; by the late 1970s, the size of computers was drastically reduced so that the personal computer could make its appearance; and by 1989, a chip the size of a thumbnail, like the Intel 486, installed in desktop computers, which cost around $1,000, had the power of the million-dollar machines of the 1970s. Today, personal computers are everywhere, they are fairly inexpensive, and they have spawned a whole new lifestyle: doing research, reading news, and shopping on the Internet, listening to music on an iPod, communicating via e-mail and instant messaging, and joining employees in international networks.

Modernization

The revolutionary changes that have ushered in modern times in the West and that are continuing to push new nations and former colonial powers into a similar mold consist of a number of processes collectively called modernization. *Modernization*, an all-encompassing process of economic, social, and cultural change, originated in the technology that transformed Western societies from a preindustrial to an industrial mode of production, and went on to affect all areas of human life. Some social theorists see modernization as a movement in which all the nations of the world are converging and will eventually become modern industrialized societies. However, while the nations of the West began to modernize some 250 years ago, many poorer nations are still in the process of doing so. Consequently, the uneven rates of modernization have produced the division between the have and the have-not nations, but diffusion will eventually enable the laggard nations to catch up.

Logic suggests that an increase in the rate of technological progress triggered the chain of events leading to modernization. Of course, as was noted earlier, change is never wholesale or total. It occurs against a backdrop of stability—people still live in families, profess religious beliefs, celebrate major events in their lives, and so on, just as they did before modernization took place.

Learning to Be Modern

The process of modernization is strewn with difficulties in all societies. In the passage from agriculture to industry, modernizing has meant superimposing a totally new system of production on a relatively isolated society whose members had lived at a subsistence level (by hunting and gathering, by horticulture or pastoralism, or by agriculture). While industrialism produced wealth for some and allowed all to live somewhat better, it also destroyed a number of traditions and an entrenched way of life. In short, the social organization of societies undergoing modernization was altered, and a new type of organization and structure superseded it.

In Britain, for instance, the earliest industrialized nation in Europe, farmers and serfs had to learn to become industrial workers. They moved to urban centers, where industrial work was located. They learned to work in exchange for wages. They learned to accept a secondary relationship with their employers. And they learned to exist without the moral support of an extended family behind them. None of these learning experiences were easy or occurred rapidly. In fact, because they happened rather slowly, the new patterns had an opportunity to crystallize. New values—for instance, the value of profit, the work ethic, the desire for achievement, the deferment of gratification—new political and economic systems, and even new types of personality resulting from different methods of socialization had an opportunity to become entrenched in the society. Individuals eventually adjusted to the new social order, even though such adjustment was never perfect in any society.

In societies where modernization occurred late, rapidly, and through diffusion instead of evolution, things have been going much less smoothly. The dislocations and strains have been evidencing themselves in feelings of rootlessness, anomie, and often violence. One modern example is provided by former colonies. After gaining independence, these nations have attempted to modernize their economies as rapidly as they could, frequently creating conflicts when the forces of tradition clashed with those of modernization (Iran is one illustration of such a society). In most of them, there is still great political instability, which some groups periodically try to remedy by coups d'etat and violent overthrow of present governments to install military dictatorships. In others, various social movements are common. Some aim at a return to a previous national greatness; others stress millenarian religions promising a future paradise; still others work toward revolutions with the goal of establishing new social and economic systems or use nationalism as a motif to unite the people.

As a result, there has been an increasingly strong feeling among social scientists that the modernization model does not work for all societies. Some, in fact, suggest that it is possible that the development of technologically advanced nations actually inhibits the progress of developing nations.

Box 16.3 One Cost of Modernization: Car Wrecks

For most of the twentieth century, China was a society wracked by war, oppression by a brutal totalitarian government, and through it all, pervasive poverty. The last couple of decades, however, have seen dramatic changes occurring in this populous country. Although the communist party is still the purported ruling entity, the economic principles characteristic of communism—namely, a planned economy—have gradually given way to a system resembling capitalism in everything but name. This system has resulted in a booming economy, as better than a billion people have suddenly become voracious consumers.

The rise in consumption is evident everywhere in the country, from the well-dressed pedestrians, so unlike those in the plain and drab uniform of communist times, to the numerous cranes signaling feverish construction in many of China's cities, and especially in the increase in the number of cars.

Previously a country in which bicycles (and horses and buggies in the countryside) were a dominant feature, today the booming economy has made China the world's fastest growing car market. In the capital, Beijing, alone, the number of cars has increased by 25 percent from 2002 to 2003. This fact has created millions of new drivers who, combined with old and ineffective traffic laws, manage to contribute to a horrendous increase in road deaths. In 2002, more than 104,000 people were killed in traffic accidents, which is about two and a half times more deaths than in the United States. Of course, in the United States, cars have been a way of life for many decades, so that not only laws but also customs and traditions have evolved surrounding driving. In China, on the other hand, "the one rule is: no one stops for anyone else. Pedestrians don't stop for cars, and cars don't stop for pedestrians" (Yardley, 2004, A4). With the paucity of good roads, especially in rural areas, it is easy to see the kind of anarchy that exists. The inadequate transportation infrastructure, combined with a culture unacquainted with the demands of driving in traffic, makes current driving conditions nightmarish. Changing the prevailing culture and especially enforcing sociocultural changes for a population of 1.3 billion will be a challenge facing Chinese authorities for a long time.

(Jim Yardley. 2004. "Chinese Take Recklessly to Cars [Just Count the Wrecks]." *New York Times*. March 12, A4).

Collective Behavior

Every day, scenes of mass behavior stare at us from television screens: men and women with upraised fists, carrying signs, chanting slogans. In the past few decades, we have seen Chinese students clamoring for democracy, Eastern Europeans unhappy with their new governments, Russians lamenting the plight of their economy, Palestinians throwing rocks from the rooftops or blowing themselves up in suicide bombings. In the United States, too, on more than one occasion, we have seen the streets of our major cities erupt in violence that took many lives and destroyed whole neighborhoods. Sometimes, when a sports team wins an important victory, opposing groups of fans clash, and fights break out that may end in some persons' deaths. Traditional holidays, such as Halloween, have become occasions for mob violence in some locations.

Such events are disruptive, instances of civil disorder, and destabilizing to society. Of course, not all group gatherings are of that kind. There are happy crowds at concerts or football games; there are responsive crowds at religious services; there are worried crowds when a bank is rumored to be in financial difficulties. Even when people are not gathered personally in groups, they can fall prey to a specific kind of behavior. This is the case when fashions in clothing change.

What all these actions and events—and many other kinds of similar occurrences—have in common is that large numbers of people participate in them, and they either cause change or change brings them on. Urban, industrial and postindustrial societies with strong tendencies toward the mass society model are much more likely to exhibit this type of behavior than are traditional preindustrial or agrarian societies. Social scientists call this type of behavior **collective behavior.**

Collective behavior covers a whole range of behaviors that may be termed nonroutine and in which a large number of people engage. In essence, collective behavior differs from the interactive behavior that normally goes on in social groups, even though it may involve numbers of people reacting to the same situation. Most human behavior follows quite a regular pattern, so that it is predictable to a great degree. When people interact in the context of their statuses and roles, and within the framework of a normative system that is more or less shared, the resulting regularity is what makes life in society possible. But when people are suddenly thrust into an unusual situation for which there is no precedent in their experience, they find themselves without societal norms or guidelines to follow, without a social structure on which to fall back. They are then likely to imitate others who find themselves in the same situation. For instance, if a person is shopping in a department store and suddenly hears another customer yelling "Fire!," that person will be unsure of what to do. Such a person will likely act spontaneously, perhaps somewhat illogically or irrationally, and follow the actions of others who happen to be nearby at the time. This is the type of behavior termed collective, and it tends to occur in crowds, in mobs (riots, lynchings), at certain kinds of sports events or musical concerts, and at religious revival meetings.

We also call their behavior collective when people follow fashions, fads, or give in to a craze, when they make up a public or an audience, when they act on public opinion, propaganda, and rumors, and when they work to attain certain goals through social movements.

In spite of its lack of pattern, rarely is there a complete lack of structure in people's behavior. Only when an individual's life is threatened is he or she likely to act with complete absence of awareness of others. In most situations, even when collective behavior prevails, that behavior is partly structured and partly unstructured. Some situations of collective behavior start out being fairly structured and end up being completely disorganized. Audiences at rock concerts have been known to surge forward, jump on the stage, and destroy musical instruments. Other situations may start out disorganized and end by being structured. Many social movements—the labor movement, for one—begin by being nothing more than disorganized protests. Later they develop definite goals and apply ranked roles to their members; they evolve norms and techniques for social control such as characterize any organized group.

Many social movements, a large number of religious denominations, and several governments have originated in some form of collective behavior. An example close to Americans is that of the United States, which originated when a large number of settlers became dissatisfied with British rule and sought to change it through revolution.

Crowds

As mentioned, collective behavior occurs most often in crowd situations. A crowd is a temporary collection of people who respond to the same stimulus. There are different kinds of crowds: **casual crowds** consist of people who come together by accident, such as those waiting at a red light to cross the street; **organized crowds** come together for specific events, such as concerts or football games; **expressive crowds** gather to express feelings, as in a protest rally or religious revival meeting; and **acting crowds** come together to act out feelings, usually of a hostile nature, as exemplified by mobs, riots, and violent protest meetings.

Any crowd, even a casual one, may evolve into a panic crowd, a mob, or a riot if the right stimulus is present. Organized crowds are more receptive to mob behavior. People in crowds tend to develop a common mood. Emotions reach a high pitch, and a shared conception of what constitutes proper behav-

Box 16.4 Other Forms of Collective Behavior: Mobs and Riots, Rumors, Fashions and Crazes, Panics and Mass Hysteria

Acting crowds that get out of hand and erupt into violence are termed mobs. *Mobs* are highly emotional and are motivated by the goal of doing harm to someone or to perpetrate some form of destruction. They are usually of short duration, although their leaders can whip emotions to a frenzy. Mob behavior is best exemplified in the United States by lynching, the hanging or burning of an individual by a group not legally authorized to mete out punishment. Today lynching is seldom used, but mobs have been known to drag people who are tied to a vehicle or beating someone to death. The individuals selected for this type of punishment are perceived as representing a threat to the group making up the mob. It is a method of social control by which low-status individuals attempt to maintain their dominance over other groups.

When an out-of-control crowd has no particular goal in mind, it becomes a *riot*. Violence and destruction are the hallmarks of riots, but the high emotional pitch of the crowd has no immediate direction. Riots may be triggered by even minor events, however, when some underlying anger or grievance exists. This long-suppressed anger boils over in random violence against persons and property, and the rioters come under control only when their anger has run its course (or when the police prevail). Consequently, riots have periodically occurred in our major cities where a segment of minority populations is confined without much hope of a brighter future. Riots have also occurred among prison populations when inmates believed they were receiving unfair treatment or were subjected to substandard living conditions. And sometimes, the actions are not the result of anger but a release from stress, as happens when a crowd of students, happy to be on a spring break and fueled by alcohol, engage in high-jinks of a kind that can escalate into destroying property and harming people.

Rumors

Rumors are unsupported reports of events or projected events that often begin riots, panics, or mobs. These reports are not backed up by facts but continue to spread by word of mouth or through the mass media. Rumors may be helpful in situations of stress, when accurate information is not readily available. They may also prove disastrous because they are usually at least partially false. In accepting a rumor, rationalize their participation in some form of crowd behavior, or it may only clarify a confused situation.

Fashions, Fads, and Crazes

These kinds of collective behavior are different from the preceding ones in that they are not quite as temporary and action directed. *Fashions* refer to manners of dress, architecture, or house decor and reflect the interests, values, and motives of a society at a given point in time. They are social patterns that find favor among a large number of people for a short period of time. Fashions differ from the more established social norms in that they are transitory. But fashions have a profound hold on people in urban industrial societies in which, with the proliferation of the mass media, they are immediately transmitted to millions of people around the world, so that what is designed in New York, Paris, and Milan is sold a few weeks later in Tokyo. In traditional societies, on the other hand, fashions change very little over the years.

The intent of clothing has also changed. Clothing in the past was used to distinguish different categories of people: males from females, members of high social classes from lower social classes, and one occupational group from another (Lofland, 1973). In modern industrial societies, there is no concern with maintaining tradition because people are more future oriented and because a person from a lower social class can rise and become a member of a higher social class. It then becomes necessary to judge people according to what they can buy, not according to what they traditionally wear. New fashions, especially in clothes, tend to emerge at the top of the social scale, acquire mass popularity through the media, are copied until they can be found in discount stores, and are then abandoned. Fashion is one facet of conspicuous consumption or the practice of spending money, to display one's wealth (Veblen, 1953). However, in leisure societies ever on the lookout for novelties, fashions can also follow the opposite road; that is, they may emerge from the lower classes and be copied by the affluent. In the case of blue jeans, for instance, idealistic college students wanted to look like disadvantaged Americans and so donned the uniform of the farmer and factory worker. Soon, however, "designer jeans" costing hundreds of dollars became the rage among the wealthy, and now jeans are the uniform of the young throughout the world.

Fads, also transitory social patterns that a large number of people undertake for short periods of time, refer more to leisure-time activities or the objects one would use while engaging in leisure activities. Within the past several decades, for instance, we have had the Pet Rock, the Mood Ring, Beanie Babies, Pokémon, and activities such as streaking, or running naked in a public place. Fads tend to disappear without leaving a trace, unlike fashions, which are often recycled. Fads sometimes evolve into *crazes* and are often ploys of business for profit making. Both are minor fashions that are more irrational and short-lived than true fashions, but crazes have a slightly more obsessive character than fads.

Panics and Mass Hysteria

Panics and mass hysteria are two forms of collective behavior that are similar in that they may occur among people who are dispersed over a wide area and they are both characterized by a high emotional charge. In a *panic*, people react to a stimulus, most often a threat, with irrational, violent, and sometimes self-destructive behavior. As was mentioned, the shout of "Fire!" may provoke a panic in which people trample on each other and block off exits to the point of causing themselves harm or death. *Mass hysteria* is the ultimate kind of fad or craze, in that it is compulsive and irrational. It is also a form of dispersed collective behavior because people are not necessarily together in a crowd; in fact, more often they have no direct contact with one another. It also tends to be an exaggerated response to a perceived threat, real or imaginary.

ior emerges. This behavior is often unpredictable and antisocial. The reason, as was noted, is that a crowd lacks definite norms and is removed temporarily from most kinds of social control; one individual in a crowd does not personally know his or her neighbor. Therefore, it is easy for people to shed their identities and act as members of the anonymous crowd. In this way, no person needs feel guilty for antisocial actions.

Even though a crowd is more than the sum of the individuals who make it up (which is why there is in every society a long history of crowd violence, lynchings, and massacres), there are limits on how far a crowd will go in antisocial behavior. A crowd seldom does anything that individual members do not want to do. Crowd violence is rarely random, but rather is directed against a person or institution that is perceived as unjust or oppressive. Even then, a destructive crowd only temporarily commits acts that are strongly forbidden by societal norms.

Masses

Another form of collective behavior occurs among people who are not in close proximity, as in crowds, but who are connected to one another in more indirect ways. Contrasted to crowds, masses are more diffuse and do not necessarily find themselves in the same physical setting. Rather, masses are large numbers of people responding to the same set of shared symbols; for instance, the audience for a particular television program constitutes a mass (Lofland, 1981). Collective behavior can occur in masses, just as it does in crowds (or in both at the same time). Fear, hostility, and joy are the basic emotions that can motivate the behavior of both crowds and masses.

Publics and Public Opinion

Collective behavior is at work in publics and public opinion as well. A *public* is defined as a scattered collection of people who share a common interest or concern about an issue or who are affected by a common occurrence. The readers of the *New York Times*, for instance, university students, moviegoers, voters, and members of a fan club are all examples of publics.

The bond that holds a crowd together is emotion, whereas the bond that holds a public together is intellect. A crowd is gathered at one place, but a public is dispersed, and each member is able to communicate directly only with a small number of other members—or with none at all, as in the case of the television public. The mass media help to create and hold publics together. In fact, in industrial, technologically advanced societies, publics are really mass publics, meaning that they are large regional or national populations who can be-

Box 16.5 The Theory of Mass Society

Social thinkers have long speculated about the causes of change. They have wanted to know the reasons why change occurs at different rates in different societies; whether change is a random, haphazard process or a recurrent, patterned one; why some civilizations rise and fall whereas others never rise at all; and whether a common destiny awaits all societies or each is fated to exist in its own individual pattern. To this end, they have offered a large number of theories. None of the theories, however, answers their questions completely. One of the more interesting ones is the theory of mass society.

As noted, the process of modernization has been problematic for most societies. The United States has not escaped this fate. According to Robert Bellah, the most rapid and profound transformation in the history of the United States occurred in the years between the Civil War and the entry of the United States into World War II (Bellah et al., 1985, 42). At that time, a new national society came into being with new technologies, particularly transportation, communication, and manufacturing. This transformation of old economic and social patterns caused political conflicts and complex cultural changes. It created the figure of the entrepreneur and the "self-made" person as models of individuals to be imitated. It strengthened the importance of individualism. It also introduced the division of life into a number of separate functional sectors such as "work" and "leisure," "white collar" and "blue collar," "public" and "private." This division was well suited to the needs of the corporate form of organization that had come into being, but was in total contrast to the patterns of the preceding century in which the individual had been closely integrated in the life of family and community. In short, modernity has entailed a process of separation and individuation as opposed to the ties of kinship and community.

Modernity conditions our consciousness, and the sense of fragmentariness without any overall patterns begins to characterize the entire culture, which is thus named the "culture of separation." The fragmentary nature of culture, apparent in both intellectual pursuits and in popular culture, particularly in the mass media, has the effect of disconnecting the individual from feeling integrated into the society, a part of the whole. The danger in individuals who feel themselves to be only parts of a "mass of interchangeable fragments within an aggregate" (Bellah et al., 1985, 281) rather than members of a society in which they are well integrated, is the establishment of an authoritarian state to provide the coherence that the culture no longer provides.

The United States is not in imminent danger of such a situation, mainly because there still exist traditions, deriving from religion, from strong beliefs in republican and democratic ideals, and from families and schools, that provide the individual with the sense of "growing up in a morally and intellectually intelligible world" (Bellah et al., 1985, 282). So our culture is, despite perceptions to the contrary, still one of *cohesion*; but the danger of the erosion of meaning and coherence in our lives is ever present, and only the desire of the people, their yearning for what has been lost, keeps it at bay.

The description of the perils that face individuals who feel disconnected from their society is similar to the mass society model which social commentators developed in the 1950s. In essence, the *mass society* model described a society composed of masses of people who are widely distributed and anonymous rather than being well integrated into a social system. As a consequence, the social system is loosely organized and somewhat disorganized. The masses may react to the same stimuli—they may watch the same news on television, for instance—but they do so separately, without reference to one another. Masses, in contrast to individuals or groups, are not part of any broad social groupings, not even social classes. "The mass merely consists of individuals who are separate, detached, anonymous, and thus homogeneous as far as mass behavior is concerned" (Blumer, 1969, 86–87).

The theory of mass society helps explain why societies in which change is constant and in which people experience *anomie* (a state of normlessness) are often an easy prey for totalitarianism. The speculation is that in their confusion, anomic individuals are easily drawn into participation in mob hysteria, panics, or radical social movements. The latter, all forms of collective behavior, may indeed lead to an erosion of democratic institutions and the establishment of authoritarian institutions.

In spite of the trends pointing to an increase in the number of people who live alone, or who marry late, or who divorce, a more optimistic interpretation of mass theory was presented by social theorist Edward Shils (1961). While admitting that "a part of the population in mass society lives in a nearly vegetative torpor, reacting dully or aggressively to its environment" (Shils, 1961, 3), Shils pointed to the positive aspects of such a society, in which larger elements of the population are able to make choices more freely and have learned to value pleasures that were previously limited to a small elite. Shils concluded that even though all types of social movements tend to flourish in mass society, totalitarian regimes are bound to fail in the long run because of increasing demands for equality and political participation, also resulting from social change.

come potentially either spectators or participants in a variety of collective behaviors. Some mass publics are temporary, their composition changing quickly: the public watching a television program at 7:30 on Saturday night will dissolve at 8:00 when the program ends. The definition of a mass public may be qualified as an unstructured collectivity in which some members are constantly losing interest in the event that made them members in the first place and are constantly being replaced by others.

An organized crowd may evolve into a panic crowd, a mob, or a riot if the right stimulus is present. Such a crowd may engage in unpredictable behavior because a common mood develops and emotions reach a high pitch.

Publics are more characteristic of complex societies than of simple ones. The reason is that complex societies are heterogeneous and members have innumerable and varying interests. They are constantly confronted with a large number of issues of both a local and a national nature. These issues may be at odds with one another. One group may want to preserve our national forests, whereas another may want to be able to hunt game or to log the timber in them. In a less complex society, such issues are not likely to arise: norms and values are shared to a greater extent by all, and very few individuals question the traditional way of doing things.

Publics exert an important influence on society, particularly because mass communication is so instantaneous and pervasive. At the same time, the lifestyles of mass publics have been greatly changed by the postindustrial society in which there is time and leisure to pursue sports and hobbies, in which automobiles have long been produced for the masses, and in which the media of communication are used not only to inform but also to induce consumerism. Mass publics have changed the outward appearance of the country: highways and freeways and roads of all sorts crisscross it, while stadiums and golf courses, shopping malls, and amusement parks stretch out from coast to coast. Mass publics have also created new industries: fast food, popular music, the movies, and so on.

Public Opinion

The large number of publics, each concerned with its own issue or activity, attitude, and beliefs, give rise to public opinion. Public opinion is a generic term that refers to the attitude or judgment of a large number of people on a specific issue. It may be thought of as the dominant opinion on that issue among a specific population. It is particularly important in the political sphere.

Public opinion has a special meaning in a society characterized by mass publics, because here public opinion is diffused through the mass media. In traditional societies, governments and economies are run according to the will of ruling authorities. The leaders do not care what individual societal members think about specific issues. In industrial societies, most of which are democratic and consumption-oriented, the leaders and industrialists must take into consideration what the public thinks about their style of leadership (or they will not be reelected) or their products (or they will not be bought).

Public opinion in contemporary societies is diffused through the mass media. In an election year, much of that opinion is shaped by candidates for office who are not bashful in using censorship and propaganda in their messages.

Public Opinion and the Mass Media

It would seem logical that public opinion reflects the values and attitudes of a society, but values and attitudes internalized in childhood remain fairly continuous throughout an individual's lifetime, whereas public opinion fluctuates, sometimes very rapidly. Although there may be consensus in the society about certain values, public opinion is usually divided at any given time about a variety of issues. For instance, while there is a consensus on the value of world peace and democracy, public opinion was divided between those who saw the necessity of the United States invading Iraq and removing its dictator and those who believed peace should be maintained at any cost. How to conduct the war on terrorism is causing a similar division in public opinion, even though acts of terrorism are universally dreaded.

The strongest influence on public opinion is exerted by the mass media—newspapers, television, films, the Internet, etc. That is one reason why candidates for political office attempt to create an "image" that they can "sell" to the public. Some commentators even feel that the mass media create public opinion. Newspapers sometimes prompt public action by exposés of corruption in city government or some other local social problem. At the same time, newspapers often support certain issues or the election of specific candidates in vain. Motion pictures, but especially television, have often been accused of creating public opinion. There is little question that in fact movies and television influence the public in a variety of ways. Movies and situation comedies show how different classes of people, in different social settings, behave. Television, in addition, with its constant barrage of commercials, also influences the consumption habits of the viewing public. Advertising is not only a multibillion-dollar industry, it has become somewhat of a science, able to reduce a message to an image and a fraction-of-a-second "bite." Consumers, in this way, buy not only toothpaste or hamburgers but also political candidates, including candidates for the highest office in the land, the presidency. There are obvious dangers lurking in such methods, because such selling techniques can overcome the influences of primary, reference, occupational, and status groups.

Public opinion is also shaped by the constant repetition in the media. Both the pessimism following the Vietnam War and the optimism during the Reagan administration were equally promulgated by the media. Individuals and groups who have prestige and power in local communities or in the nation also affect public opinion. Many well-funded special-interest groups are able to alter public opinion: for instance, the American Medical Association, which represents only 2 percent of Americans, has an enormous influence on health care. Political leaders, labor leaders, religious organizations, and business all attempt to use public relations to affect public opinion. Members of a variety of groups reflect the views of the group to which they owe the highest allegiance. And people create public opinion through interaction and mold it according to their own social background and group memberships. When they are unsure of how to react with regard to a particular event, or what stance to take on a particular issue, people tend to debate, discuss, and exchange information with others.

Social movements exert one of the strongest effects on public opinion. For instance, the 1960s and 1970s saw the emergence of the civil rights and feminist movements, as well as the pro-abortion and gay rights movements. Public opinion swung from one extreme of the political pendulum—the conservatism of the 1950s—to the other. The 1980s and 1990s, as well as the first years of the twenty-first century, saw a return to political conservatism and a stress on "values."

Propaganda and Censorship

Being able to manipulate public opinion is of great benefit to some individuals and groups in society. Car manufacturers want the public to buy their products. Political candidates want to be elected. Teachers want their salaries increased. The administration in office wants to have the citizens' support. Religious organizations want their members to follow the precepts of their faith. All these groups, and countless more, exert influence on public opinion through propaganda and censorship.

Propaganda is a deliberate attempt to persuade a person to accept a particular belief uncritically or to make a certain choice rather than another. Advertising, sales promotions, public relations, political campaigns, fund-raising drives, billboards, and even Sunday school lessons use propaganda. Propaganda is a manipulative device that depends on emotional appeal, often playing on the fears and anxieties of people. Advertisements for cosmetics, deodorants, and tooth whiteners promise to make people attractive and young looking, which is what people want to be and are afraid they are not. Propaganda also relies on the "good old values" of the past (the "one-room schoolhouse," "Grandma's apple pie") and on the desire of people to belong or be popular ("Everybody's doing it").

Propaganda is quite successful when it does not attempt to change the opinion of people too drastically. However, in democratic societies, those involved in propaganda for a specific person or product have a lot of competition. The education and sophistication of the public further limit the effectiveness of propaganda. Finally, although strong trends may be temporarily thwarted by propaganda, ultimately they are not affected by it.

Because propaganda gives a one-sided interpretation of an issue or shows only the good side of a product, it distorts the information available to the public. **Censorship,** on the other hand, deletes all or parts of the information. Many of our important institutional organizations use censorship. Certain groups with their own agenda would have us pull specific books off library shelves because they do not approve of, or agree with, their contents (book censorship, as well as censorship in all forms of art, is extensive in totalitarian regimes). The government and the military institutions withhold information in the name of national security and defense. Families and religious organizations tend to censor some information regarding sex. Political candidates tell us only what they want us to know about themselves and their intentions once in office. Manufacturers choose not to tell us that the car or the refrigerator they are selling us is built so that it must be replaced every few years. The mass media report some and fail to report other news. In and of themselves, propaganda and censorship are neither good nor bad, but both may be put to uses that are either beneficial or detrimental to people.

Social Movements

Approximately 100 years ago, the autocratic empire of the all-powerful Czar Nicholas of Russia was swept away by a tide so strong that it was able to overcome an entrenched government that had wielded absolute power over the people for centuries. In the process, a backward, agricultural society was transformed into one of the two world super-powers. In the fall of 1991, a second quake shook the same society, and soon the world watched in wonder as crowds began to pull down the huge statues of the heroes of the preceding regime. As falling idols came crashing to the ground, one could not help but speculate about the forces that impelled such dramatic changes. What are these forces, how do they come into being, and why and how do they eventually decline?

One of the principal ways in which change is effected is by social movements. Social movements are a type of collective behavior that leaves the greatest impact on societies. **Social movements** are defined as "collective enterprises to establish a new order of life" (Blumer, 1951, 200), as well as collective efforts either to change the sociocultural order or to resist such change (Killian, 1964, 430). This type of collective action represents the personal involvement of individuals and their intervention in directing, redirecting, furthering, or resisting change.

A collective action may be considered a social movement when the following factors are present: (1) it has a specific ideology; (2) it awakens a strong sense of idealism and solidarity, involving dedication and loyalty in followers; (3) there is an orientation toward action; and (4) a significant number of people are involved.

Although some social movements are almost entirely unorganized, most are pursued in voluntary groups or associations. These are secondary groups organized for attaining a definite goal. Both social movements and voluntary groups are characteristic of urban industrial societies that are experiencing rapid social change. In some nations, social movements develop into political parties, pursuing their goals by attaining political power. Marxism is an example of an ideology that has prompted social movements in a number of societies, and in some has attained—and lost—political power. In other nations—such as the United States—the goals of this ideology have been pursued in voluntary associations that never acquired political power. In still other countries—France, Italy, Portugal—it has become a political party represented in Parliament. Finally, in the former Soviet Union, as well as in the People's Republic of China, the movement had become the party in power (although with alterations of the ideology), whereas in Chile, it came to power but was subsequently overthrown.

Revolutionary social movements have a profound impact on societies. The Russian Revolution, which turned out one ruling class—a monarchy—and substituted it with another—the Communist Party—transformed a backward, agricultural nation into a world power. Unfortunately, the lives of its citizens were not much improved because the new government became a dictatorship. Here, one of the leaders of the revolution, Lenin (1879–1924), making a speech in Moscow in 1919.

Types of Social Movements

According to how one views social movements, they can be classified into four types: alternative, redemptive, reformist, and revolutionary. An example of an **alternative** social movement is an organization such as Planned Parenthood, whose concern is population growth and whose goal it is to influence people of child-bearing age to practice birth control and take responsibility for their sexual conduct. **Redemptive** movements also affect selected segments of the society and not the whole society, but here the attempt is at a radical transformation. Fundamentalist Christianity is such a movement, and converts perceive themselves as having been born again. Somewhat related to the redemptive type are **expressive** movements, which are directed at individuals who are expected to change in such a way that they will work toward changes in society or adapt better to society as it is. Expressive movements are often religious in nature, but they can also turn quite revolutionary, as in the case of the Islamic revolution in Iran. On the other hand, they may be secular, as exemplified by the numerous human potential movements that were popular in the 1970s. These movements were designed to achieve self-fulfillment for the individual.

Reformist Movements

The two social movements that have had the most influence on societies and their governments have been the **revolutionary** and the **reformist** or reformative movements. Reform movements attempt to change some feature of an existing social order without changing the entire order. They want to change the society, but in a limited way. Such movements are most successful in democratic societies, where there is relative freedom to criticize institutions and channels exist through which reforms can be put into effect. Reform movements may be progressive, in the sense of wanting to promote new social patterns, or they may be reactionary, in the sense of wanting to preserve the status quo or return to past patterns. Recent reform movements in the United States have included the women's movement, the civil rights movement, and the movement to remove the social stigma of homosexuality (see Table 16.1).

Revolutionary Movements

If we were to put all forms of collective behavior on a continuum that ranked them as to the extent of their effect on societies, revolutions would be at one extreme, and fads and crazes would be at the other. In the twentieth century, for instance, there were the Russian and Chinese revolutions, which have brought in communist regimes and radically altered the societies in which they occurred, and a fascist movement, which had revolutionary consequences in European societies. On the other hand, in spite of the fact that some people become deeply involved in a fad or craze, none of the latter can be said to have left an indelible mark on a society.

Revolutionary movements consider the present social order so inadequate, corrupt, unjust, and beyond salvation that they seek its total removal and substitution. In effecting such absolute change, revolutionary movements must often resort to violence. In **nationalistic** revolutionary movements, a predominantly foreign government is overthrown and replaced with a native one. **Class** revolutionary movements substitute one ruling class for another in the same society. The American revolution was nationalistic, whereas the French, Russian, Chinese, and Cuban were all class revolutions. Revolutionary movements should not be confused with revolts, or coups d'état, which merely replace individual members of the ruling class. Revolutions change the structure of the major social institutions.

TABLE 16.1 The Most Important American Social Movements

Name	Description
Abolitionist	In the northern states during the three decades preceding the Civil War; seeking the abolition of slavery in all of the states and territories.
Populist	Disaffected farmers in the South and the West in the 1880s and 1890s sought public control over railroads, banks, grain elevators, and the provision of cheap money.
Labor	The effort of workers to protect jobs, to ensure adequate wages and benefits, and to guarantee a healthy work environment. Union building was particularly prominent during the 1880s, 1890s, and 1930s.
Women's Suffrage	This movement emerged to win voting rights for women. Active in the late nineteenth and early twentieth centuries.
Civil Rights	The purpose of this movement was to win civil and political rights for African Americans. It was especially effective during the 1960s.
Anti–Vietnam War	During the late 1960s and early 1970s, this movement was directed against the continued involvement of the United States in the Vietnam War.
Women's Liberation or Feminist Movement	A movement attempting to gain equality for women in all aspects of American life during the 1970s and 1980s and currently.
Antinuclear	A world movement, periodically active during the 1970s and 1980s, to end the nuclear arms race (e.g., "The Freeze" campaign) and the construction of nuclear power plants.
Environmental	Came to prominence in the 1970s and is growing in momentum; its goals range from control of pollution to protection of wilderness areas, and especially to counter global warming.
Religious Fundamentalist	The latest of many examples of religious fundamentalism to take political form in American history; became part of the conservative platforms of the 1970s and 1980s, as well as 2000 and 2004, aiding the electoral victories of Ronald Reagan, George Bush, and George W. Bush who used campaign slogans promising to protect family and Christian morality values.

Factors Encouraging Revolutionary Movements

The predisposing factors to joining revolutionary movements are similar to those predisposing people to join less radical social movements, but the conditions that prompt a person to join a revolutionary movement may be perceived as being extreme. Revolutionary movements are more characteristic of totalitarian societies than they are of democratic ones, because in democracies, public opinion and reformist movements exert pressure on the government, so that eventually changes desired by a majority of the people occur. In totalitarian regimes, public opinion is often ignored and social movements are not tolerated. People feel the only way they can effect change is by overthrowing the government. In this attempt, success is never certain.

The most important condition for revolution is the widespread realization that the legitimate government has failed and it is necessary to bring about change at any cost. This condition is called a **crisis of legitimacy**. Sometimes revolution is aided by a breakdown of discipline and efficiency in the ruling body. Some members of this body, especially the intellectuals, become disillusioned and may even join the revolutionary movement. Others abandon the role of rulers. Therefore, in many cases, very little violence is actually needed to wrest the government from the hands of the rulers. Many revolutions have been relatively bloodless compared to wars and genocidal programs such as those carried out in Hitler's Germany.

As to the results of revolutions, they are seldom as drastic or as ideal as they promise to be. Customs and institutions, though certainly subject to change, are difficult to uproot. Sometimes precisely the unpleasant features of the old social order survive the revolution. Nonetheless, a number of revolutions—the American, the Russian, and the Chinese, to cite the most obvious examples—have brought about changes of tremendous importance for the people of their societies.

Revolutionary movements receive considerable notoriety because they reflect the discontent of people who believe that change is occurring too slowly. However, there are movements that reflect the belief of some groups that change occurs too rapidly. These movements are called **change-resistant,** and their purpose is to stop or eradicate certain changes in society. The Ku Klux Klan is an example of a change-resistant movement, and there are many others.

The effectiveness of social movements depends on the type of organization they are able to form and maintain and how deep their influence is on the society. Although each movement is unique, it seems that all move through four definite stages (Blumer, 1969; Mauss, 1975). In the first stage, **emergence**, dissatisfaction in a segment of the society with regard to a specific issue is pinpointed by a group or an individual who brings it to public attention. In the second stage, **coalescence**, leaders must plan a strategy, determine policies, make alliances with other groups, solicit new members—in other words, they must build interest and spread their vision to the society at large. In the third stage, **bureaucratization,** it becomes necessary to establish a formal organization so that the everyday work of the movement can proceed in an orderly fashion. While adding stability and longevity to a movement, bureaucratization sometimes holds it back, because building an organization does not require the same skills as keeping the enthusiasm of the members (Piven & Cloward, 1995). In the fourth and last stage, social movements **decline** (Figure 16.1). This can happen in a positive way for the movement, that is, through institutionalization. Or, if a movement reaches its goal, it has no further need to exist, and so it breaks apart (but this seldom happens, because most movements are not single-issue oriented). Sometimes poor leadership, repression by the government, loss of interest on the part of members, or fragmentation due to a multiplicity of unresolved views are the death toll of a movement. Finally, the leaders of a movement may be diverted from their efforts by enticements offered by the established power structure. This process is called **co-optation.** And the movement itself may become a part of the power structure, as is true of the labor movement.

Social movements originate mainly as a result of **relative deprivation** and **rising expectations.** People feel relatively deprived when they compare themselves with others and find themselves to be suffering in the comparison. The failure of rising expectations is also related to dissatisfaction based on relative deprivation. **Rising expectations** are experienced when the standard of living goes up in a society, but not for all segments of the population. As life gets better, in other words, people begin to take all the improvements for granted and continue to expect more.

Social movements flourish in societies that are undergoing rapid social change, as people become subject to feelings of anomie and alienation. **Anomie** is a feeling of normlessness, of not knowing which behavioral guidelines to follow when several sets of norms coexist. **Alienation** is a feeling of separateness from society, of powerlessness and isolation, which convinces individuals that they are unable to influence

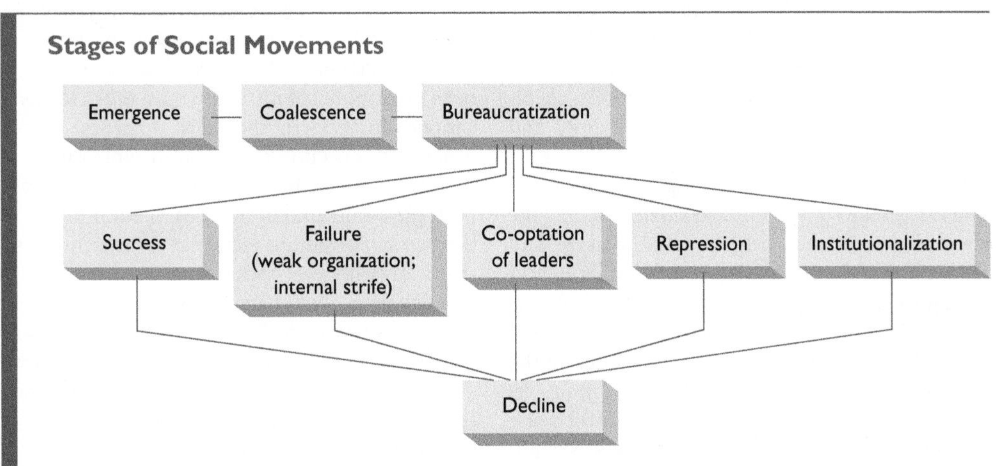

FIGURE 16.1 Although each social movement is unique, all appear to pass through a definite number of stages.

their own fate. People who have feelings of anomie and alienation are attracted to social movements, as well as those who are dissatisfied on a variety of grounds, who are restless and confused, and who need some focus in their lives.

Contemporary social movements tend to have global concerns: the environment, the danger of nuclear proliferation, women's rights, gay rights, animal rights, and similar issues. Because power to legislate is centralized in the government, most of the new social movements are national and international in scope. Additionally, the new social movements have a tendency to focus on issues regarding the quality of life, rather than on issues of economic well-being, such as the labor movement of old did. As a result, these movements attract the interest and support of middle-class people instead of workers and the dispossessed.

Terrorism

One type of social movement that is difficult to define but that has become a threat to many countries is terrorism. According to United States law, "the term 'terrorism' means premeditated, politically motivated violence perpetrated against noncombatant targets by subnational groups or clandestine agents, usually intended to influence an audience." Terrorism is not new, but whereas in the past it had been limited to individual countries—the IRA in Northern Ireland, the ETA in Spain, the Tupac Amaru (Shining Path) in Peru, the Red Brigades in Italy—with definite ideologies and goals, today terrorism has become a transnational movement of ill-defined groups with ill-defined ideologies and ill-defined goals. The difficulty in defining terrorism lies in the fact that so many different groups engage in terrorist acts. Some of these groups may be thought of as attempting to begin nationalistic revolutions, efforts to bring in new forms of government, or to gain independence from governments perceived as colonial or occupying. Other groups may be considered reactionary social movements, in that they reject changes associated with modernization and try to bring back older forms of rule, mostly ancient theocracies. The latter seems to be the intent of the terrorist group that threatens the West and especially the United States, Al Quaeda, which perpetrated the horrific destruction of September 11, 2001, and continues to plot other events around the world. It has often been said that "one man's terrorist is another man's freedom fighter," meaning that, to those who agree with the terrorists' goals, their actions appear justified. However, those actions result in the death of innumerable numbers of innocent people who have nothing to do with whatever grievance the terrorists have. Such is the case of the many victims of suicide bombers who merely wait for a bus or are doing their shopping. No ethical system can find justification for such acts.

The Chapter in Brief

Change is an integral part of nature and of all living things, although a degree of stability is equally characteristic of individuals, societies, and cultures. The mechanisms of sociocultural change are easier to determine than its causes. The principal processes of cultural change are discovery, invention, and diffusion. On the other hand, change in the structure of society—or social change—occurs through planning, reform, and revolution. Sources of change include the physical environment, the size and structure of populations, ideology, events and individuals, social movements, and technology.

Sociocultural change has been triggered chiefly by technological progress. Technology includes all the methods and devices that help humans manage and control their environment. The first technological breakthrough was the invention of agriculture. A second was the advent of the machine era, or the Industrial Revolution. Although this movement accelerated in the middle of the eighteenth century in Great Britain, its roots go back several centuries. Its effects are still being felt by the world. The most significant changes brought about by the Industrial Revolution are a surge in the growth of population; industrialization, or the dependence of the economy on industry; and urbanization, or the growth of cities at the expense of rural life.

Modernization is the kind of change that occurred in modern industrial societies. It has meant the transition from an agricultural and preindustrial to an industrial mode of production and has been a difficult process in all societies. Where it occurred slowly, over a number of generations, it was eventually integrated into the existing social order. Where it occurred rapidly, there has been great political instability and other forms of dislocations. In modern industrial societies, technological progress has occurred at the most rapid rate in history.

Technology has radically altered people's lives both physically and in the area of cultural values. It has been so important, in fact, that some thinkers speculate that it determines a society's culture, structure, and history. There is always a cultural lag when the nonmaterial aspects try to catch up with the material ones. This lag also produces problems and disorganization.

Technologically advanced societies are more often subject to various forms of collective behavior than are traditional societies. Collective behavior occurs in situations that are highly charged with emotion and in which the usual norms do not apply. Such situations include crowds (riots, mobs, panics), rumors, fashions, fads, crazes, publics and audiences, public opinion, propaganda and censorship, and social movements. Collective behavior is relatively unpatterned and unstructured.

Crowds are assemblies of people who respond to a common stimulus. Crowds may be casual or organized, expressive or acting. People in them develop a common mood and a shared concept of how to behave at the moment. Crowds are temporary and their members remain anonymous and impersonal. Therefore, crowds can commit atrocities without their members feeling guilty.

Publics—scattered collections of people who temporarily share a common interest or concern about an issue—are also a form of collective behavior. The large number of publics in advanced societies generates public opinion, which is the attitude or judgment of a majority of people on a specific issue. Public opinion is especially important in democratic societies and is greatly influenced by the mass media. The latter sometimes use propaganda and/or censorship to manipulate public opinion. Propaganda is a deliberate attempt to persuade people to accept a belief uncritically or to make a specific choice. Censorship distorts information by suppressing or deleting parts or all of it.

Social movements are collective attempts to establish a new order of life—either to change the social order or to resist change. Important factors in social movements are changing perspectives and ideologies. Social movements are rooted in discontent and flourish when a society experiences anomie, alienation, relative deprivation, and rising expectations, but their goals are long-range solutions. The ultimate aim is to effect change to the point that it becomes institutionalized. Social movements may attempt reforms by trying to change only some features of an existing social order, or they may be revolutionary, seeking the removal of a present order and substitution with a new one. The stages in social movements include emergence, coalescence, bureaucratization, institutionalization, and/or decline.

A type of social movement that is very difficult to define is terrorism. It refers to premeditated, politically motivated violence perpetrated against noncombatant targets. It may be considered nationalistic and revolutionary, but also reactionary; whatever its goals, it is impossible to justify it because of the number of innocent victims it takes.

Terms to Remember

alienation A feeling of powerlessness and insecurity, of not belonging in society, producing boredom and meaninglessness. Alienation provides a fertile ground for social movements and is characteristic of people in mass society.

censorship A method of control used to limit the information available to the public.

change-resistant movement A social movement reflecting the discontent of people who believe that change is occurring too rapidly and want to stop it or reverse it.

class revolutionary movement A revolutionary social movement in which one ruling class is replaced with another in the same society.

collective behavior Type of behavior that tends to occur in crowds, mobs, fashions, fads, crazes, rumors, panics, and in publics, public opinion, and social movements. It is characteristic of a collectivity of people who are responding to a common stimulus under conditions that are usually temporary, unstable, unstructured, and unpredictable, so that existing norms do not apply.

crowd An aggregate of people gathered in the same place, at the same time, either casually or for a predetermined reason, responding to a common stimulus. Crowds may be expressive or acting. An acting crowd may develop into a panic, mob, or riot.

cultural change Change in values, beliefs, and norms that may be brought about by scientific discoveries, technological inventions, new achievements in the arts, or shifts in religious doctrine.

diffusion A process of cultural change in which cultural traits are spread from one society to another (or from one group to another).

discovery A process of cultural change in which an already existing fact or relationship is newly perceived.

fads and crazes Minor fashions, short-lived and often irrational.

fashions A kind of collective behavior that represents a transient social pattern followed for a time by a large segment of people. Fashions affect the entire spectrum of social life.

invention A process of cultural change in which old cultural ideas or existing objects are combined in new ways to produce ideas or objects more important than the previous ones had been separately.

mass communication The relatively simultaneous exposure of large heterogeneous audiences to symbols transmitted by impersonal means from organized sources to whom audience members are anonymous.

mass society The model (theoretical construct) of a society toward which societies are ultimately drifting. It consists of an undifferentiated mass of people and an elite capable of dominating and manipulating it. It is highly urbanized and industrialized and displays secondary relationships, lack of traditional values, alienation, anomie, pressure to conform, and subjection to manipulation through the mass media.

modernization A model of sociocultural change that describes the transformation of small preindustrial societies into large industrial ones.

nationalistic revolutionary movement A revolutionary social movement in which a predominantly foreign government is overthrown and replaced with a native one.

propaganda A deliberate attempt to persuade people to uncritically accept a particular belief or to make a certain choice.

public Persons in society who are geographically dispersed but who share a common interest, who express that interest, and who know that others are aware of their interest.

public opinion The totality of opinions, attitudes, and judgments expressed by publics.

rumor An unsupported report of an event or a projected event. Important in bringing about manifestations of more active types of collective behavior.

social change Change in the patterns of social interaction in which a substantial number of society's members assume new statuses and play new roles. Takes place through planning, reform, or revolution.

technology All the methods and devices that help humans manage and control their environment.

terrorism A kind of transnational social movement that uses premeditated, politically motivated violence against noncombatant targets.

Suggested Readings

Branch, Taylor. 1988. *Parting the Waters: America in the King Years, 1954–1963*. New York: Simon & Schuster. A detailed examination of the civil rights movement with an emphasis on its charismatic leader, Martin Luther King.

Etzioni, Amitai. 1991. *A Responsive Society: Collected Essays on Guiding Deliberate Social Change*. San Francisco: Jossey-Bass. As the title implies, the author, a respected sociologist, makes suggestions as to how change may be directed to yield specific goals.

Gates, Bill. 1995. *The Road Ahead*. New York: Viking. What the chairman of Microsoft sees down the Information Highway.

Rifkin, Jeremy. 1998. *The Biotech Century: Harnessing the Gene and Remaking the World*. New York: Jeremy P. Tarcher/Putnam. A new revolution is in the making in the area of biotechnology, and the author looks at some of the changes such a revolution will produce in our lives.

Turkle, Sherry. 1995. *Life on the Screen: Identity in the Age of the Internet*. New York: Simon and Schuster. The long-term implications of millions of people interacting on the Internet are analyzed from a sociological viewpoint.

Web Sites of Interest

http://www.wfs.org/index.htm
For people concerned with how social change will shape our future, the web site of the World Future Society, a nonprofit educational and scientific organization, provides interesting information.

http://gsociology.icaap.org/report/summary2.htm
A sociological analysis of the many theories and research relating to social change.

http://www.ropercenter.uconn.edu/pom/pom_list.html
A nonprofit, nonpartisan organization that provides polling data and public opinion research on a number of topics.

http://www.interweb-tech.com/nsmnet/resources/default.asp
This web site provides links to a number of activist organizations, some of which may be social movements in the making.

http://www.fashion.net/sites/onlinefashion/websites/index.html
Inasmuch as fashion is part of collective behavior, it may prove interesting to check out some of the sites relating to fashion.

http://www.hoaxbusters.ciac.org
The Internet has become a peculiarly efficient instrument of rumor mongering. This web site attempts to stop the spread of unsubstantiated rumors.

http://people-press.org
This is the web site of the Pew Research Center for the People and the Press. It is an excellent source of surveys, polls, articles of commentary about items in the news—in short, everything that relates to public opinion.

http://www.ict.org.il
This is the web site of the International Policy Institute for Counterterrorism. It deals with all issues of terrorism and offers a wealth of resources about the subject.

Readings

Fieldwork Biography

Gilbert Herdt

© Gilbert Herdt

Between 1974 and 1993 Gil Herdt worked among the Sambia in the remote Eastern Highlands of Papua New Guinea for a total of 13 field trips and four years in all, initially as a Fulbright scholar, then as assistant professor at Stanford University, and finally as professor at the University of Chicago. Herdt focused on sexuality, gender, and identity change in his fieldwork, collecting individual life stories in the mode of what Herdt and Stoller (1990) called "clinical ethnography," the application of clinical concepts and techniques to fieldwork. He observed more than 16 male initiation ceremonies, and conducted in-depth studies of the dreams, feelings, and beliefs of individual informants. A witness to tremendous cultural change, Herdt went on to study patterns of institutional and gender role change. This led to his role as consultant on the British Broadcasting Corporation (BBC) film, *Guardians of the Flutes,* which is also the title of his first book (1981).

Fieldwork Biography

Birgitta Stolpe, PhD

© Gilbert Herdt

Birgitta Stolpe's research with the Sambia of Papua New Guinea involves the physical, psychological, social, and cultural transformation of girls into women. She worked with Sambia women in 1999 and 2000 for her dissertation research at the University of Chicago. Pioneering a new field that she calls "cultural endocrinology," Stolpe examined the manner in which cultural norms and institutions guide intimate social interactions, and how these in turn influence hormonal functioning. Among the Sambia using menarche as a marker, she compared the development of girls who more strongly adhered to traditional life with those who were less traditional. She speculated that profound cultural change is radically reorganizing social interactions, which helps to explain at least in part the remarkable significant epidemiological changes in the rates of Sambia physical development.

1/ Sambia Gender, Sexuality, and Social Change

Several decades have passed since Herdt began fieldwork with the Sambia of Papua New Guinea in the autumn of 1974. A young Fulbright scholar, Herdt was an American working from Australia on research to charter men's secret society and ritual practices (Herdt 1981). At the time of Herdt's initial fieldwork, warfare had been halted only six years earlier (in 1968), at about the time that missionaries entered the Sambia region and French anthropologist Maurice Godelier started his path-breaking studies of the Baruya people, a neighboring tribe. As Herdt recounted in his case study, *The Sambia: Culture and Gender in New Guinea* (1987), five years prior to that, Australian colonial officers and police had effectively ended Sambia tribal autonomy in 1964 when they rounded up a large number of Sambia men and youths, chained them together as a gang, and marched them two days over the mountains to the Patrol Post. There they were incarcerated, and eventually released. Over the next 30 years of dramatic cultural change, Herdt continued to conduct fieldwork.[1] Birgitta Stolpe began her fieldwork in 1999 as a graduate student at the University of Chicago. Stolpe focuses on female sexuality and adolescent maturation. In their chapter, Herdt and Stolpe document the rise of new narratives and practices of Sambia masculinity and seek to explain some of these changes by contrasting the traditional forms and means of becoming a man with newly emergent ones. This chapter thus records the resilience and continuation of Sambia society, while at the same time describing the remarkable changes that have occurred in gender and sexuality over the last three decades.

Precolonial Sambia Society

The Sambia are a mountain-dwelling people who inhabit extremely rugged high forest ranges of the Eastern Highlands of Papua New Guinea. Although their territory is vast, their numbers (around 2,300) are

Reprinted from *Globalization and Change in Fifteen Minutes* (2007), Cengage Learning.

small, with population density ranging between five and ten people per square mile. Warfare dominated their precolonial existence. Traditionally hunters and shifting agriculturists, the Sambia were sedentary at the time of colonization by Australia in the 1960s.

The world of men in precolonial society can be summed up in three domains; warfare and hunting, arranged marriage, and the rituals of initiation that socialized men into the absolute secrecy of the men's house (Herdt 1981). The world of women was restricted to the lower status domains of food production and child care.

The Sambia men's secret society was best characterized as a military-type dominance hierarchy that centered around the men's house, its nerve center. Male initiation was the basis for socialization into the men's house, male solidarity, and collective masculinity. The men employed the practice of inseminating boys through oral intercourse, a practice once referred to as "ritualized homosexuality" but now better known as boy-inseminating rites (Herdt 1984; 1993; 1999). As we have known since the critical work of Kenneth E. Read (1954) who pioneered study of the men's house in the highlands of Papua New Guinea, this was the dominant institution of these societies. Indeed the strategic place of tabooed masculinity dominated the landscape of each Sambia hamlet. Virtually everywhere across the New Guinea Highlands, men and boys lived as a body apart from women and children (Langness 1974), creating the conditions for making reality and secret reality (Barth 1975), both of which were vital to these "great men societies" (Godelier 1986). Moreover, men's living-and-sleeping arrangements in the men's house was the basis for a special kind of utopian worldview; within the men's house, men sought to perfect the imperfect, messy arrangements of the secular world (Herdt 2003).

Hamlet social organization was centered around gender and gender segregation in men's and women's areas (Herdt 1987). The hamlet was symbolically divided between male and female spaces, including separate paths for walking. At the top of each hamlet, one or more male clubhouses offered a defensive surveillance of surrounding mountains and hamlets. The clubhouses also served as living quarters for male initiates until marriage. Elders and adult men also spent much of their time there, laying strategies for ritual, defense, and warfare. Women were forbidden to enter the clubhouses or, in general, the forests above them. Men and male initiates similarly avoided the women's menstrual huts and the areas surrounding them. Men and women and all initiates were restricted by the spatial segregation of the sexes, which was reproduced within the small enclosure of the family hut, where a man lived with his wife or co-wives, his unmarried daughters, and his uninitiated sons. The interior of the hut was divided into separate male and female sleeping areas. Women were forbidden to enter their husbands' area, or to step over the central hearth where meals were prepared. By observing these restrictions, women reduced the possibility of transferring to men what the Sambia view as female polluting fluids. These restrictions least affected children, and young children of both sexes slept in their mother's area.

Gender dominated all socialization. Though very young children mixed in early childhood, later play was based on gender distinctions reinforced through the role models of parents. Implicit and explicit communication of cultural rules and norms also redundantly emphasized the divergence of the sexes and their differential cultural goals. Following weaning, children were encouraged to play in same-sex groups. Sexual segregation remained informal, however, until late childhood (ages 7-10), when boys were initiated

Sambia first-stage initation, 1975.

into an age-graded ritual society focused on secret male knowledge. In all, this male society performed six initiations collectively for hamlet clusters, taking the boys into adulthood and fatherhood, with final initiation in their early to mid-twenties (Herdt 1982a; 1982b).

A hamlet depended upon its youth as a power base and labor corvée. The bond created between mothers and their children was intense, and it is difficult to imagine more extreme attachments (Herdt 1981). This developmental condition was undoubtedly very singular in its effects on the inhibition of male agency and sexual subjectivity in boys. Boys were prevented from becoming separate agents empowered by the men's society, just at the moment—around age 10—that they were coming into an awareness of their prepubertal sexuality.

Such changes in the boy could only be achieved through gender segregation and secrecy, on the condition that the boys would be treated first as sexual objects, before they got the chance to be sexual subjects. These are separable elements of subjective development that are conflated as "sexual orientation" in the Western world, where they are also treated as part of the same "biological package." In particular, the ability to locate desire in the person – to be acted upon first as an object and then as a subject—regardless of the same-gender context of Sambia, suggests that these desires and their expression are being acquired in the microcontexts of the men's house and erotically expressed in action more often than previously believed. It is a bit too simple to say that these attractions are learned, nor must we think that they can be "unlearned" in any simple manner without doing violence either to the integrity or mental health of the person. Ultimately, such subjectivities, when they are lived realities, must be anchored in the social traditions of the community.

Traditional Gender Roles and Initiation

Countervailing theories of male and female development underlie the differences in the structure and timing of initiations for both boys and girls. Feminine behavior and female reproductive capabilities were thought to be natural outcomes of women's anatomy and early socialization. Female initiations merely affirmed girls' natural and inevitable attainment of biological and social maturity. Male development, however, was regarded as problematic in two respects. First, unlike girls, boys were thought to be biologically incomplete. Their slower physical maturation was attributed to their inability to produce semen, the biological essence of maleness. Collective male initiations, and the insemination of boys that were central to them, were performed in part to correct this perceived biological deficiency and to aid their progress toward reproductive competence. Second, boys were believed to be at greater risk than girls, because their early and prolonged contact with women exposed them to dangers of what the Sambia perceived as pollution and contamination that ultimately could kill them. Through forcible separation of boys from their mothers, dramatic nosebleeding, and other purificatory rites, men sought to eradicate the harmful effects of women's early physical and psychological presence, and instill the discipline and knowledge needed to transform weak and undisciplined boys into aggressive hunters and warriors Here, as Margaret Mead (1935) once noted, this was a difficult outcome to achieve, and it created large contradictions in masculinity (Herdt and Stoller 1990; Stoller and Herdt 1982).

Every three of four years neighboring hamlets created a truce to initiate a cohort of age-graded boys, ranging in age from 7 to 10. The boys were separated dramatically from their mothers and placed in the men's house. For months afterward they experienced a series of ritual ordeals and events that gradually removed all traces of women and the profane world from their bodies—and, the Sambia men hoped, from their psyches, too. This first ritual was secret, hidden from the women. Five additional years of initiations followed, leading up their young adulthood. The first initiation, however, had two key rituals of rebirth: first, boys underwent nosebleeding rituals that were thought to remove the pollution of their mother's menstrual blood; and second, older bachelors inseminated the young initiates through oral intercourse, a ritual they themselves had undergone at an earlier ritual stage. The physical ordeal was accompanied by many powerful ritual moods and emotions, and the separation from mother and the secular world was absolute and complete for years to come. According to Sambia belief, this ritual culminated in the third-stage initiation, when the boy's body became biologically mature, at which time he showed all the secondary sex traits, including a mature glans penis.

Female initiations were performed at menarche (between ages 17 and 19). This initiation also often made allies of neighboring warring villages. During these ceremonies women became allies and men became the enemies. This may have been an easier end for the women to achieve than for the men because women often performed these rituals with matrilineal relatives (kin on the mother's side of the family) who had been separated from them through marriage.

These rituals were intended to transform girls into women. Although the Sambia believed that female physical development was natural and occurred spontaneously, intellectual and psychological development required ritual instruction. Girl and woman were distinct categories, and it was the "knowledge" of womanhood that was instilled during these initiations.

The rituals traditionally took place over several nights and included the older women as well as the recently initiated young women who had not yet given birth to their first or sometimes even second or third child. Men were prohibited from viewing or even listening to the ceremony because secrecy was as important to the initiation of girls as it was to the initiation of boys. Cloaked in the darkness of night their mother and several of the older women prepared the female initiates for their ceremonies, painting the girls with bright yellow mud and dressing them in traditional garb of grass skirts and bark capes. The women prepared a fire in the middle of the ceremonial arena where they bathed the initiates in smoke, "cooked" them over the fire, and then ritually beat them with pieces of wood. After their preparation, the teachings began.

In an apparent paradox, the Samia regarded female development as "natural" but still requiring ritual learning. The ritual teaching instilled knowledge that was critical in how women experienced their bodies, and this "body knowledge" was created without censure or intellectual reflection. To this end, the skin was perforated to allow the knowledge to enter the body directly. The natural world was the source of "natural" knowledge, hence indigenous plants were applied to the body after it was "prepared." Of the 10 or 12 plants used, each contained specific knowledge that was to teach the girls to be industrious gardeners and obedient wives. The physical force with which natural objects were applied to their bodies was not only the means by which these objects transmitted their knowledge, but also served to prepare the young women for the pain of childbirth and the painful beatings from their future husbands (Stolpe 2003).

Social Hierarchies Among the Sambia

Male hegemony and warriorhood were the forms of political and social economy, although descent through the father's line and residence in the locale of one's father or father's people (patrilocal residential arrangements) privileged the male descent line. Thus it is not surprising that the Sambia and similar sexual cultures were constitutive of objectified boys and women and in turn regarded men as the primary icons of beauty and sex appeal. Moreover, the phallic preoccupation of these mythological traditions, in which the culture hero might sport a gigantic penis that was the cause of fertility, great power, and endless trouble, was iconic of their masculine imagery and folk psychology. The Sambia have said, for example, that a woman could not help but admire a man who achieved the ideal of prowess in war, hunting, and sexual conquest, especially if he was a good supporter of family and dutiful in his sexual obligations to his wife. She did not have to like him, for to admire and to like are different things, and Sambia marriage was a political, not a romantic, union. Sons were expected, however, both to like and admire their fathers, and to eventually enter into the secret world their fathers shared with other men and youth. Also they expected to become comrades in a warriorhood dedicated to the removal of all signs of womanliness (for example, by nosebleedng rites and other dietetics of masculine performativity). The Sambia, and many similar cultures, asserted the need to implant external signifiers of manliness, such as boy insemination. Ultimately puberty and *jerungdu*, or strength in the sense of virility, provided for successful masculine careers.

Age was a fundamental marker of social rank and status in these societies—extending beyond to the South Seas and Australian Aboriginal groups. Melanesia shared the importance of age as a means of social organization with such culturally diverse world areas as West Africa and insular Southeast Asia. Kinship and marriage systems were marked by age-graded principles of social hierarchy in which age accorded respect and was treated as a sign of accumulated ritual knowledge, social experience, and power. Age also defined a critical aspect of the relationship between the genders in virtually all sexual and reproductive matters, including arranged marriage, but also in religious practice, body rituals, and substance beliefs. As K. E. Read recognized long ago, "egalitarian" ideas and practices—such as being a leader in a war or hunt, or having a striking personality in politics were also valued by the Sambia and attained the status of social principles for men. For women, skillful gardening techniques and high fertility were sources of status. Nevertheless, age was the more consistent and powerful social classifier in these societies.

Marriage and the Traffic In Women

The ritual complex of boy insemination was part of a larger social and cultural system that included assigned marriages and the creation of enormous barriers to sexual intercourse between the genders prior to the arrangement and consummation of political marriages. Marriage and the trafficking in or exchange of women were practices based upon notions of male descent, strongly marked at all levels of social grouping. Hamlets were composed of one or two great patri-clans founded on relationships traced on the father's side of the family. Separate, constituent clans could also claim membership in these great patri-clans. Secrecy and ritual knowledge characterized the internal organization of clan ritual. Another organization, the confederacy, linked nearby hamlets together as participatory units involved in the men's secret society. These localized confederacies sometimes cut across kinship groups, uniting otherwise enemy clans and hamlets—as in the Sambia Valley—and creating wider and somewhat more tenuous political alliances. Before pacification, the stylized bow fights between hamlets sometimes got out of hand, escalating into full-scale war after casualties had been inflicted on either side—a pattern that has been well described previously. These neighboring hamlets were united as a confederacy, however, by their shared fear of attack by true enemies from other tribes.

Sambia exchanged women in marriage through three traditional customs: sister exchange (direct exchange), infant betrothal (delayed exchange), and bride service. For the purposes of this text, however, we may exclude bride service, because it accounted for less than 2 percent of all Sambia marriages. In simple terms, delayed exchange of women between clans created temporary imbalances with expectations and demands for future exchanges, offset with gifts and promises. The Sambia configured marriage as a means by which one clan–hamlet took a woman as womb, or "garden," from another hamlet; the female offspring of the new union was returned to the donor hamlet as brides in the following generation, thus achieving over time a balance in the exchange of women between different hamlets. The residents of Sambia Valley hamlets inter-married in this way, creating shifting, unstable alliances that provoked mistrust at all levels of social arrangements, interjecting suspicion and often paranoia into the marital relationship, living arrangement, child care, and other related daily interests.

Symbolically these arranged marriage resulted in transfers of blood and semen in which blood and semen flowed in opposite directions across generations. Blood was the arranged marriage of a woman from her brother's group to her husband's, and semen was the fluid inserted into her brother to make him grow big and strong, and hence, able to consummate his own marriage when an adult. Thus, blood went one way and semen the other in marriage and boy-insemination practices.

However, to counterbalance this situation, the man who had taken a wife was expected in return to give his semen to a boy. So, when a man was the recipient of a womb-vagina, he donated semen both to the woman (his wife) and to her younger brother (an initiate in the men's house). His wife was expected to produce a baby; her brother was expected to produce the masculinity of physical growth and manliness embodied in the glans penis. In the third-stage initiation that celebrates social puberty, the growth and enlargement of the glans penis was likened to a ritual rebirth, symbolizing culmination of manhood. Sons of arranged marriages were divided in their loyalties and social interests. The offspring of Sambia couples were caught between two social worlds and political networks: sons were to be initiated as future warrior-comrades, and daughters were to be used as commodities in future marriage exchanges for their brothers or other clansmen. These arranged marriages created complex and sometimes contradictory religious and political alliances between hamlets. The symbolism of the secret male initiation ceremonies was intentionally aimed to merge the desires and developmental subjectivity of the growing boy with the larger project of training warriors through boy insemination. Secrecy was vital to create jural authority in the hamlet and hierarchy inside the men's society.

In the precolonial world of the Sambia (especially prior to 1964), the roles of men and women were highly polarized and politically opposed in the condition proverbially described as "sexual antagonism" (Langness 1974). The women who came as brides were from hamlets that were invariably hostile and sometimes enemies in war, and therefore wives were forever regarded alien and mistrusted. The residen-

Sambia women and marriage ceremony, 1975.

tial segregation of unmarried, vulnerable male initiates living in the men's clubhouse (while the women and children were restricted to the women's houses) symbolized this deep structure of perceived social and material difference in village life.

Sexual relations between men and women were loaded with avoidance, ritual, and conflicted feelings. As married couples bore children and aged, however, their interaction in the later years of life improved to the point of even being cordial. In the early years, however, many marital histories reveal jealousies, fears of sorcery and spell-casting, arguments, physical abuse, and sometimes (though rarely) suicide. But it is not as if women simply did whatever their husbands said. A woman had quiet means at her disposal to subvert and resist her husband's demands, such as "forgetting to prepare his food, refusing to make love, shouting and commenting on her husband . . . using sorcery or semen sorcery, and pollution poison in the food" Godelier (1986, 150). But she could also openly criticize him and even castigate him loudly in public, though she risked a beating for doing so. The women could not go beyond a certain point because it infringed upon the men's secret boundary. Men believed sexual intercourse of any kind should be spaced out in time to avoid depletion of masculinity and premature aging or death; yet they typically reacted in frustration, and sometimes anger, when they did not have sex with their wives. Many young men became jealous and vindictive of wrong moves made by their consorts. Couples normatively had sex every few days or as infrequently as once every two or three weeks, depending on age, length of marriage, and other factors. However, the postpartum taboo forbade sexual intercourse for some two years following birth. No overt contact between the sexes was permitted in public—a taboo that has changed radically with increasing westernization.

Social Change and Resistance

Social change has strongly impacted Sambia gender and sexuality. Australian government officers initiated change through a crucial historical episode in the early 1960s when they tricked Sambia war leaders and young adult warriors into capture. The humiliation of the Sambia men was complete when the Australian officers destroyed their weapons, especially their war shields and bows and arrows. For Sambia men, these events disrupted their feelings of mastery and control over their own destinies to such an extent that they forever after lived in the dread of repeated humiliation. Their manhood was tested and they were in this sense emasculated. This subjective experience of social capture led to a new era of modernization and political change by perforating the perceived invincibility of Sambia masculinity. The local community appointees—the tultuls and komiti men—were at first accepted as proxies for the colonial government. Later, however, the sense of collusion with the government began to creep in and has undermined some of their authority. Though not perfect models of the new masculinity for boys to emulate, they do provide alternates to traditional images of men in the village.

The formal end of colonialism brought immediate changes. National independence in 1975 quickly began to shift the government presence and influence around the district capital. A system of independent village councils, constituted of locally elected representatives, serves as the primary link between local communities and the national and district governments. This system (begun in 1973) is only partially successful, and has been increasingly taxed by the absence of regular government visits (such as census patrols) that are no longer conducted.

Missionary activity increased—Lutherans established the first presence in the area, though not directly among the Sambia. They constructed a mission in the Baruya area in the early 1960s (Godelier 1982). Located at Woenara (then the district capital), the mission served as a satellite for Lutheran activities in other parts of the district.

Many local people had been educated at Lutheran missions schools, which sought to convert and "civilize" the indigenous populations. Using a pattern well known from elsewhere in New Guinea, the school's platform aggressively attacked customs such as male initiation, polygyny, and shamanism to successively undermine confidence in traditional systems of belief (see Herdt 2003).

The Seventh-Day Adventists were also active very early in this area. Ironically, although their regional headquarters were located outside the district, and their early influence was not as extensive as that of the Lutherans, they are now dominant in many areas of the region, and their religion is hegemonic among the Sambia. Today, most Sambia consider themselves to be Seventh-Day Adventists and practice their liturgical ceremonies.

The Seventh-Day Adventists established an extensive network of evangelists who, together with their families, lived and worked in villages throughout the district. They preached against boys' initiation and the "heathen ways of ritual and introduced biblical dietary restrictions (based on the book of Leviticus)[2] that dramatically altered the indigenous diet.

Unlike the Seventh-Day Adventists, the Lutherans were quick to display their own material wealth and to demonstrate the benefits of a familiarity with Western marketing practices. The Lutheran mission established its own trade store at Wonenara station in 1968; the store was relocated to Marawaka station

© Gilbert Herdt

Traditional round houses favored by "old" people intermingled with "modern" cornered houses favored by "young" people.

when the district capital was moved there. Backed by a commercial company, and owned by the expatriate-run Lutheran congregation, the store imported trade goods directly from Australia and Japan for sale to locals. The store quickly created a demand for items such as machetes, canned meats and fish, and other commercially produced articles. There is little doubt that the sense of material display undermined the traditional masculinity that figured so prominently with the Sambia and their neighbors. Masculinity could no longer be achieved through the production of local goods.

The new masculinity that could only be produced through the accumulation of Western goods has led to out-migration and coastal work, creating upheavals in traditional social hierarchies. Sambia men began leaving the hamlet areas in the late 1960s and the level of out-migration of male laborers continued apace in the mid 1980s. Under the colonial administrator's Highland Labor Scheme, men were recruited for two-year contracts to work on coastal cocoa, copra, and rubber plantations. The scheme was discontinued in 1974, but many men continue to seek work on coastal plantations. The early cohorts who left the Sambia Valley were the first to see the wider country and to report back the stories of life outside. Some of these men (perhaps a high number of them) never returned to their hamlets. They chose to work and live in the coastal towns. Others returned in the 1970s and early 80s and brought back cash and goods. Still others live on the coast today and send back monies and goods to wives and relatives in the villages. Some of these men have secured marriages and are rearing their children in these distant towns. Their masculinity is now an issue of transition, a liminal betwixt and between tradition and citizenship in the town.

Schools and Gender Change

In Highlands' societies, schooling may be valued for boys because of its perceived relation to the modernization of masculinity: schools promise access to valued opportunities within the larger state society, such as urban jobs in business or government. Traditionally, in many societies, men acquired status through successfully negotiating the various stages of male initiation; this was less emphasized for females. Initiations prepared boys to become warriors, and male war leaders served as models of esteemed masculine behavior. With the cessation of warfare, following Australian pacification of the Highlands, male initiations have declined in importance. Though initiation rites are still performed in some parts of the Highlands, they no longer hold the same promise of status and recognition. Consequently, schools have displaced initiation as a primary means for gaining access to valued positions with the expanding society.

The introduction of schools among the Sambia has followed a similar regional geographical pattern. The first mission school was established at the government station in 1964. Built with the encouragement of the Australian colonial administration, and financed by German and Australian Lutheran churches, the school was attended by children (predominantly boys) from the surrounding Wonenara Valley and other nearby areas. A larger mission school was established in Marawaka when the government outpost was relocated there in 1968. Sons and a few daughters of government employees attended the school. A few local boys also attended. Both schools emphasized religious instruction, and Bible study was a major component of the curriculum. Children were also taught to speak and write in local pidgin, and to perform simple math problems. Both government employees and local villagers initially received the schools well, as they expected concrete results in terms of jobs or further schooling; however, residents became increasingly disillusioned as they began to feel that the school prepared the students only for menial jobs as laborers or clerks. At best, the schools were regarded as training ground for native evangelists (Godelier 1982).

With religious emphasis, the mission schools at Wonenara and Marawaka significantly impacted local communities by offering an alternative to traditional socialization. Nonetheless, by challenging traditional beliefs about how children should be educated, the school helped to create an awareness of diversity in socialization practices. Among the Sambia, the mission school provided the primary alternative to traditional socialization until 1985, when the first government school was created in the Sambia Valley.

The schools directly challenged local ritual customs and beliefs, and broke down gender segregation in a number of ways. First, children who attended the schools came from all tribes in the Wonenara and Marawaka areas, thus disrupting traditional enmity between tribes. Second, the schools admitted girls as well as boys, allowing them access to the same knowledge, and forcing them to mix in the same classroom (albeit on different sides). Thus norms governing sexual segregation and men's privileged access to valued knowledge were violated and ultimately could not be repaired. Third, missionaries were openly critical and aggressively attacked ritual beliefs and customs. Children attending the schools were forbidden to participate in initiation rites or to observe traditional sex-avoidance rules. Those who were shy around the opposite sex could be shamed, for example, into being more aggressive or "Western-like" in cross-sex interactions. Though these practices antagonized many local residents, the school received initial support and approval from mission converts. It seems clear that all of these patterns reinforced internal resistance to ritual initiation norms and opened the way for a much broader form of social challenge that displaced ritual as the structure of authority.

The boys' resistance to initiations was growing (Herdt 1987; Herdt and Stoller 1990). Sambia boys, such as Moodi, traditionally resisted initiation rituals out of fear. They sometimes ran away into the forest, requiring search parties to track them and to bring them forcibly back. The boys were reluctant to go into the areas of warfare and forced nosebleeding. The presence of schools and missions exacerbated this resistance. As Moodi has described this so vividly, he feared that initiation would "change" or "freeze" his thinking, disabling him from going to school, getting an education, or succeeding in the coastal towns (Herdt 1987, 121). In short, he feared the rituals would ruin his chance to become a new man, with a new kind of modernized masculinity. Many boys who followed him have experienced a similar existential dilemma. We might call this the questioning of manhood, a social panic that was a crisis of masculinity among the Sambia in the transition to modernity.

Both the Lutherans and the Seventh-Day Adventists established "bush schools" in isolated parts of the district. These schools were usually small and poorly attended. New government primary schools were opened in the district: the first in 1977 and another in 1985 with more than 300 students from the surrounding villages. Remarkably, they began as male institutions, but within a five-year period, one-third of the students were girls. Both mission and government schools have contributed to changes in traditional socialization practices. Because of these constraints, many parents reject schooling for their children. Much of the evidence, however, suggests that parents value schooling as alternative socialization, particularly for the boys. With the cessation of warfare, and the increase of adolescent and adult male out-migration for work on coastal plantations, male initiation rites have been successfully undermined. Ceremonies that once took months to perform have been reduced to a few short weeks or abandoned. As initiation rites have been increasingly undermined, parents have come to view schooling as a desirable alternative to traditional masculinity.

Although, as elsewhere, schooling is still unequally distributed among boys and girls, more Sambia girls are attending school, both reducing the relationship between the new masculinity and schooling and increasing the social status of the educated woman through acquisition of the "new knowledge." Because the girls' labor in their mothers' gardens is extremely important to the survival of the family (and the status of the mother as a good provider of food), it is difficult to understand why any family would endure the expense of sending a daughter to school. Despite the girls' own assertions that they go to school if they want to, it appears that two major factors drive school attendance: proximity to a school, and proximity to an airstrip that presumably gives the girls (and their parents) greater contact with the outside world, thereby creating the need and the desire to communicate with others in the manner taught in school. These findings suggest that reduced investment (for example, a one-hour daily hike to and from school versus a four-hour hike) is a key factor in determining whether or not to attend school. But girls living furthest from the school, along the airstrip, also have a high rate of school attendance, suggesting social and cultural—as well as pragmatic—forces at work. Not only does the decision to attend school vary by location of the village, once a girl decides to attend school, the number of years she attends significantly correlates with her residence as well. Observed departure from traditional behaviors also follows this same pattern: the location of the village of residence strongly correlates with the level of education and influence of the outside world (Stolpe 2003).

Change Over the Past Decade

As social change sped up, the men's secret society began to lose control of the women, children and the intergenerational transmission of knowledge in Sambia society. The processes of change quickly and strongly impacted the performance of ritual initiation. Within a decade—roughly between 1970 and 1980—the great system of collective initiations known as the mokeiyu was curtailed. The boys were no longer routinely initiated into the men's house. Indeed, by 1979 the boys refused to live in the men's house, in spite of the fierce punishments from their elders. Even many women did not approve of the boys' resistance to male initiation customs, as this had previously assured the reproduction of gender relations, hunting, and marriage arrangements. The end of age-structured homoerotic relations was also at hand, because the out-migration of young bachelors and married men created an imbalance in the men's house. There no longer was a cohort of older males to socially monitor the young boys and serve as their inseminators. The end of warfare also diminished the threat of violence and coercion that was effective in insuring the compliance of boys in the past.

During the period of rapid change in the late 1970s and early to mid-1980s, the elders finally decided they could not trust the boys to keep the secrets of men's society and suspended the ritual of boy insemination. However, other aspects of the ritual teachings continued. For example, the nosebleeding rituals still constituted important ritual purification. The boys were still taught the importance of bleeding at the time of initiation to strengthen themselves and remove their mothers' pollution from their bodies. Also, they were being prepared for when as adults they would bleed themselves as protection during their wives' menstrual periods. However, so much conflict emerged during this period that some men decided not to initiate their sons into the men's secret society. Instead, they sent their sons to the local school, to aim toward future jobs, as well as to avoid the risk of having their ritual secrets revealed and thus destroyed.

These were not only structural changes—they were registered in the lives of individual Sambia as well. Some young boys who were undergoing initiation at this time were adamantly opposed to the old ritual beliefs, whereas others were merely disinterested. The initiates who also attended school openly discussed the decline or collapse of traditional customs. They seemed to point to a real change in the achievement of masculinity outside of the traditional village system of warfare and ritual as necessary and increasingly positive. The more they experienced social change and the longer they attended school, the more aggressive they became in referring to custom as "the old ways" or the "pagan" ways. They also used the disparaging pidgin term *kanaka*, meaning a country bumpkin, yokel, or hick in the English sense, one who is not worldy-wise. Today, they articulate a distinction between the "bad" parts of the traditional initiation ceremonies, those they have eliminated, and the "good" parts, those they have kept.

This discursive exploration of cultural meaning and cultural change is explored in two films from the Sambia area: *Guardians of the Flutes* (1993) and the earlier *Towards Baruya Manhood* (1972). Gender narratives and masculinity are prominent themes in both films. Looking back at *Guardians* now, it is clear that the Sambia view the domination of women as more problematic than they did a generation ago. Likewise, Baruya women do not simply accept male domination in any simple sense. *Towards Baruya Manhood* suggests a more complex picture of the realities of domination. "We must not suppose that women consent at all times and in every way to male domination," Godelier (1986, 149) writes. In addition to the refusal of food and sex, the Sambia women also used gossip, scandal (resulting from suspected adultery for instance), and manipulation of the children to get what they want from their husbands. Sambia women in the BBC film, *Guardians of the Flutes,* strongly hint that women never fully accepted some male beliefs, including the idea that insemination was necessary to produce breast milk. Neither had they demonstrated complete compliance in the oral flexion of their husbands. Men's fears of female semen sorcery and menstrual blood sorcery are always reminders of the powers of women's bodies among the Sambia and indeed are never far from their husbands' minds when they attempt to dominate their wives (Herdt and Stoller 1990).

Beginning in the mid-1970s a new set of social stories (Plummer 1995) on masculinity began to circulate, reaching their peak in the mid-1990s. The new modernizing tradition of masculinity presented two different scenes in which these stories were being played out—in the village and out in the coastal towns. Men who went to the towns saw this as an alternative to ritual initiation, as a means of testing themselves and their manhood to the ordeals and dangers they once faced in the traditions of the men's house. Of course, they did this without the social support of their age-mates or without the collective strategy of secrecy vis-à-vis their enemies and women. The attraction of fast food, alcohol, sex with prostitutes, Western goods, and other elements of "modernity" posed great temptations to these budding young men. When they returned to the village they love, they boasted of their conquests and their survival of the ordeals—proof of their new masculinity.

The men who went away to the towns left a kind of vacuum in the villages necessitating a renegotiation of social structures. Some men have said: "If these men go away, and their wives go to other men, that's their problem! Why can't we men who stay in the village marry all of them? It is more for us! Perhaps as many as three or four wives?" However, other men warned: "Oh, the women are many here, and the men are few; you don't want them to overwhelm you, gobble you up, do you? That's what can result in the loss of all of your semen and strength" (Herdt 1987; Herdt and Stoller 1990). Thus the absence of the men and the availability of their women has introduced a new problem into the social definition of masculinity: Should a man attempt to steal other men's wives to fulfill the ideals of traditional masculinity as in the past? The whole attitude had changed toward this old-fashioned ethic. The new proportion of women to men was one of the components of the new social uncertainty.

Women didn't seem to mind their husbands going away and leaving them, possibly because some of the women had their own means, such as gardens and cash crops, whereas other more modern women didn't want to marry and had designs on attending school. Others were no doubt simply relieved to have one less mouth to feed, and perhaps have a reprieve from frequent beatings from their husbands. Still others joined the Seventh-Day Adventist church and decided to leave or rid themselves of their more traditional or pagan husbands. The women's taste for power grew so much that some men even gasped, "What if the women achieve political office?" This would be the final blow to masculinity.

During this time much was said about the men who remained in the villages, especially the men who were woganya—weak, cowardly, or even "feminine" in their comportment. As one man remarked, "Women don't follow orders very well anymore. And some men don't know who to order them. Those men are woganya. At that time they are afraid of their food being poisoned by their wives. Some of the women only know the old ways, but others are changing." This same man continued, saying the following:

> The younger women, and some of the older ones too, they only want men with money. They "rubbish" [or denigrate] the "poor men." Before in the old days, it was that they only wanted men who could hunt possum and bring home a lot of meat for the women and children. Women would spit on a man who couldn't hunt or bag game. They say that the women want men who have money and will buy them tinned fish and rice from the trade stores. A man without money can't give rice and fish . . . money is possum to them . . . women swallow their spit when thinking about money. For example, Oruko is such a young man. He has fucked the wife of Erumbei and another man. That's because he can offer them rice and fish, and has money. They think he is smart-looking. Some of the women even push their men into going to work on the coast to get money. (pers. comm..)

This man, however, whose wife sometimes pushed him like this, rejected the idea, and told her that she was "behaving in the manner of a sexually loose woman, like a whore, who wants her husband to be gone so that she can play around." (See also Herdt and Stoller 1990 on these points.)

Clearly, out-migration of men was one of the components of the cultural destabilization that resulted in rapid cultural change. Although the effect of these changes has been less dramatic on the everyday lives of women and girls, the stories of exotic places, novel conquests, as well as the material artifacts brought back have left their marks. There is an insurgent discourse among many (especially young) Sambia women regarding traditional beliefs and their societal roles. Today the women's lives are still busy with the hard work of gardening and child care. It is difficult for most Sambia women to shy away from the responsibility of gardening because they and their families will go hungry if they do not harvest enough food throughout the year. However, childbearing and child rearing have become domains in which women can assert some new power. Many young women today do not wish to have more than two children, despite the tremendous social, political, and economic benefit of large broods. With a Western understanding of human reproduction supplied by pamphlets that the missionaries distributed, the young women have eschewed traditional reproductive teachings and are now better able to control their pregnancies. Although monthly birth control shots are now available at the health clinic (up to a six-hour walk for many of the women at the upper end of the Sambia Valley), abstinence is by far the preferred method. Abstinence is also a means for exerting some control over the marital relationship, as well as expressing dislike for spouses whom they were not able to choose. The traditional marriage system of contracted marriages is now contrasted with a new concept, the idea of "love" marriages. No one currently living in the Sambia Valley has such a marriage, thus love marriages remain a highly romanticized ideal. In a larger sense, the mere desire for the agency implied by a love marriage signals a significant departure from the traditional sociocentric cultural devoir and falls under the linguistic umbrella of *laik*, the pidgin word meaning "like" or "want to." To what extent it is appropriate for individuals, especially women, to act upon their "laik" is at the heart of much current debate among the Sambia. In general, the younger people embrace the perceived greater freedoms of the "outside" world by renouncing traditional teachings—*laik* has become metonymic for this freedom. Repudiating cultural mandates requiring many children is a powerful (albeit risky) way for young women to exert their own power, to make their own decisions in such a way as to affect their destinies. It seems likely that in the Sambia Valley, as elsewhere, the young women who attend school will have fewer children in their lifetimes than the women who do not. The reasons for this phenomenon are poorly understood (Bledsoe and Cohen 1993), although within the context of the current discussion, it seems that one source of power—many children—may be supplanted by another—education—while simultaneously displaying newly appropriated power.

But practical reasons drive the desire for fewer children as well. Despite the many perceived benefits of Christian conversion, the biblical dietary restrictions the Seventh-Day Adventists imposed placed an even greater burden of food production on the women. Until the conversions, the Sambia diet consisted of food gathered from the surrounding forest, food the women produced in their gardens, and food the men hunted, as well as pigs slaughtered for ritual and celebratory occasions. The missionaries advocated total restrictions against eating animals with certain traits including those with cloven hooves, animals that perch, and benthic fish (this is, eels and other bottom-feeders found in the local rivers). Almost all of the animals that the Sambia men hunted (as well as the domesticated pigs) fell into one of these categories. Not only did the nutrition of Sambia suffer through the elimination of virtually all sources of animal protein in an already protein-deficient diet, but the proportion of food provided by gardening and gathering increased significantly. Women were now almost the sole providers of food for their families, further emasculating the Sambia men for whom hunting had been an important social and political activity. This increased responsibility also conferred a slight increase in social power on the women. However, with this increased responsibility, each additional child became more and more of a burden, with two seeming to be plenty. "Children are work, work, work," the young women frequently lament.

In the past decade or so, the introduction of coffee as a cash crop has further reorganized the lives of both Sambia men and women. Coffee production presented the Sambia with a dilemma: garden work was women's work; pecuniary and extracultural interests were men's work. Coffee was both. How then should the labor of coffee be divided between the sexes? A similar dilemma occurred in Africa more than a century earlier with the introduction of agricultural tools. Gardening had been the domain of women; tools had been the domain of men (Comaroff and Comaroff 1997). For the time being, the Sambia have blurred gender distinctions and men and women generally work together in their gardens. This may be the first time in Sambia history that gender cooperation has been attempted.

The income from these gardens has both directly and indirectly affected the lives of the women. With monies, they can purchase food, decreasing the stress of daily harvesting in the gardens and the very real fear of disease that can destroy entire gardens and result in starvation. These purchased goods, primarily rice, tinned fish, and Maggi Noodles, also increases the dietetic variation of the family diet. Thus, families with more money to purchase more food have healthier diets. The healthier diet increases the woman's fecundity as well as fertility and, no doubt, reduces the likelihood of infant and child morbidity and mortality. The greater survivability of each child born makes the woman's agency in reducing her number of pregnancies more acceptable.

For most Sambia, these purchased foods constitute less than 10 percent of their diet, but nonetheless the slight decrease in dependency on gardening for survival has significantly impacted the lives of women and girls. With decreased pressure on gardening and with the profits from the coffee gardens, more girls are able to attend school, often filling girls with expectations of lives different than their mothers'. Many of these girls express desires to change the trajectory of their lives—to "do anything but work in the gardens," as one educated young woman laments. These dreams are seldom realized as the women are still

Men and children drying coffee beans.

© Gilbert Herdt

Sambia elders instruct youth.

required to fulfill their social obligations of marriage and reproduction at puberty. The newly realized pecuniary benefit of daughters in terms of brideswealth paid in the local currency (kina) has reconfirmed the importance of women as commodities. Once paid in pigs, other foodstuffs, and weapons, monetary brideswealth (in the amount of 400K for a woman from within the valley, more for an exogenous woman) now constitutes a primary source of family income, and daughters are often talked about in terms of their cash worth. One man in the valley whose wife gave birth to their fifth daughter, was constantly teased that he was now the wealthiest man in the valley – his assets amounted to 2000K. Fear of the loss of the anticipated brideswealth payments is one reason why girls are not often educated beyond grade school. The only woman in the Sambia Valley who had attended high school was "sold" by her parents before she completed her studies because they feared losing their brideswealth payment if she did not return to the valley. Thus, the introduction of cash into the valley has eradicated certain traditional ways of being a Sambia woman and simultaneously strengthened others.

CONCLUSION

As anthropologists have long attested, social change in culture and gender is an uneven, sometimes brittle process, but with possibilities for improvement in the social rights and legal entitlements of some. Throughout Melanesia the process of change that followed colonialism and more recently globalization has brought about a growing recognition of the rights of women in traditional cultures. The end of the men's secret societies (Herdt 2003) is part of this long and relentless process, whereby the conditional masculinity of entrance into male initiation was purchased in part at the subordination and social suppression of women and children. More recently the import of fundamentalist Christianity into Melanesian cultures has come at the price of new restrictions and limitations on the full personhood and citizenship of women, at least in some cases. However, the expansion of cash crops and the opportunities of increased transportation have opened new vistas for younger Sambia, especially women, who aspire to be educated and affirmed in twenty-first-century desires to be more equal to their brothers, father, sons, and husbands. The next chapter of change for the Sambia will come when old and new traditions allow for the companionate gender relations increasingly appearing on Papua New Guinea television programs and commercials that are broadcast for its growing middle class.

REFERENCES

Barth, Frederick 1975. *Ritual and knowledge among the Baktaman of New Guinea*. New Haven: Yale Univ. Press.

Bledsoe, C., and Cohen, B., eds. 1993. *Social dynamics of adolescent fertility in sub-Saharan Africa*. Washington DC. National Academy Press.

Comaroff. J.L., Comaroff, J. 1997. *Of revelation and revolution*. Chicago: Univ. of Chicago Press.

Godelier, Maurice. 1922. Towards Baruya Manhood. Ian Dunlop, filmmaker.

__________. 1982. Social hierarchies among the Baruya of New Guinea. *In Inequality in New Guinea*, ed. Andrew Strathern, 3-34. New York: Cambridge.

__________. 1986. *The making of great men: Male domination and power among the new Guinea Baruya*. Trans. Rupert Swyer, New York: Cambridge Univ. Press.

Herdt, Gilbert, 1981. *Guardians of the flutes: Idioms of masculinity.* Chicago: Univ. of Chicago Press.

_________, ed. 1982a. Fetish and fantasy in Sambia ini tiation. In *Rituals of manhood: Male initiation in Papua New Guinea*, 44-98. Berkeley: Univ. of California Press.

_________. 1982b. Sambia nosebleeding and rites and male proximity to women. *Ethos* 10:189-231.

_________, ed. 1984. Ritualized homosexual behavior in the male cults of Melanesia, 1862-1983: An introduction. In *Ritualized homosexuality in Melanesia*, 1-82. Berkeley: Univ. of California Press.

_________. 1987. *Sambia: Ritual and gender in New Guinea.* NY: Holt, Rinehardt, and Winston.

_________. 1993a. Introduction. *In Ritualized homosexuality in Melanesia,* ed. G. Herdt, vii-xliii, Berkeley: Univ. of California Press.

_________. 1993b. *Guardians of the Flutes.* British Broadcasting Co. Film.

_________. 1999. *Sambia sexual culture.* Chicago: Univ. of Chicago Pres.

_________. 2003. *Ritual secrecy: Perspectives on New Guinea.* Ann Arbor: Univ. of Michigan Press.

Herdt, Gilbert, and Robert J. Stoller. 1990. *Intimate communications: Erotics and the study of the culture.* New York: Columbia Univ. Press.

Langness, Lewis L. 1974. Ritual power and male domination in the New Guinea Highlands. *Ethos* 2:189-212.

Mead, Margaret. 1935/1968. *Sex and temperament in three primitive societies.* Repr. New York: Dell Publishing Co., Inc.

Plummer, Ken. 1995. *Telling sexual stories.* New York: Routledge.

Read, Kenneth E. 1954. Cultures of the Central Highlands. *Southwestern Journal of Anthropology* 10:1-43.

Stoller, Robert J., and Gilbert Herdt.. 1982. The development of masculinity: A cross-cultural contribution. *Journal of the American Psychoanalytic Association* 30:29-59.

Stolpe, Birgitta. 2003. *Cultural endocrinology: Menarche, modernity, and the transformative power of social reconfigurations* Diss. Univ. of Chicago.

NOTES

1. Herdt conducted fieldwork in Sambia 1974-76, 1979, 1981, 1983, 1985, 1987, 1989, 1990, and 1993.

2. The Leviticus book of the Old Testament establishes dietary restrictions against eating pigs, eels, birds that perch, animals with paws, and animals that crawl, all previously important social and nutritional components of Sambia life.

Fieldwork Biography

Leo R. Chavez

Leo R. Chavez conducted his first fieldwork in Otavalo, Ecuador, a small town high in the Andes that was experiencing rural-to-town migration by its indigenous population, the Otavalos, who mostly lived in many small villages in the surrounding countryside. Since 1980, however, Professor Chavez has focused on transnational migration, beginning in San Diego, California. The Ethnography *Shadowed Lives: Undocumented Immigrants in American Society* [1992/1998] was the result of over 10 years interviewing Mexican and Central American immigrants about their lives, integration into U.S. society, and access to medical services. In many ways, finding people to interview was easier in the small town of Otavalo, or in one of the surrounding villages, where all one had to do was walk around and meet people. Immigrants in San Diego, on the other hand, live in a wide range of places, from rural encampments in canyons near farms to apartments and houses in urban centers and suburban neighborhoods. They were not so easy to find! More recently, Professor Chavez has examined cultural, economic, and political issues related to breast and cervical cancer and the use of cancer-screening exams among immigrant women from Latin America in Orange County, California. His current fieldwork is among the adult children of immigrants and how well they are integrating into U.S. society, focusing on the greater Los Angles area. It has now been about 25 years that Professor Chavez has been working to understand the immigrant experience, which he likens to a large jigsaw puzzle. Each research project helps him fill in one small piece of the puzzle.

■ 2/Cultural Change and Cultural Reproduction: Lessons from Research on Transnational Migration

Young Mexican migrant worker in his makeshift campsite next to the fields where he works.

Vignette 1: In San Diego, California, a number of men, recent immigrants from Mexico, stand on a street corner waiting for offers for work from the passing cars. Although they often find work cleaning up construction sites, at flower ranches, or gardening and landscaping, many people find their presence a problem. Complaints about the men's presence are often heard at city council meetings. Sometimes hiring sites are made available for the men and their employers. The men live in makeshift encampments hidden in the bushes and trees not too far from where they look for work. Sometimes their homes are demolished, forcing them to pack up their few belongings and move to another site. What keeps them there is the work and the pay, often seven to ten times what they could make back in Mexico. Women also sometimes live in the campsites. They typically work in homes, as maids or taking care of children. As one woman told me: "I came here because there is no work over there. Oaxaca has no factories, no large businesses to employ people. When you do find work, it's very difficult. You work from nine in the morning to nine at night for little pay and it's hard to find another job. I was told that there were good wages here and that there was plenty of work for women. Right now I do housekeeping, but sometimes I do that and sometimes I don't. It's not stable [work]" (Chavez 1998). Many of these men and women will return to Mexico after a few months to a couple of years

Reprinted from *Globalization and Change in Fifteen Minutes* (2007), Cengage Learning.

working in the United States. Some will stay longer, eventually forming families and settling in the United States. Although they may stay years, they often continue to maintain contacts with family and friends back home, even sending them some of the money they have earned. One of the things that impressed me most about this situation was the level of interdependence between Mexico and the United States, despite the often strong anti-Mexican attitudes expressed in public forums, especially on local talk radio programs.

Vignette 2: In Flushing, New York, Tony Sala, the owner of T.J.s Pizzeria & Restaurant watched as his neighborhood changed from mainly European immigrants and their children to predominantly Korean and Chinese immigrants and their children (Baum 2004). Seeing opportunity, the owner decided to innovate by putting kimchee (hot spicy pickled cabbage favored by Koreans) on his pizzas. The Italian-Korean merger has been quite successful.

Vignette 3: In France, immigrants from the African countries of Senegal, Mali, and Mauritania bring with them the Muslim tradition of polygamy (Simons 1996). However, many of the immigrant's wives have rebelled at continuing this tradition in France, where they find the living conditions no longer tolerable for a man having multiple wives. Back in Africa, if a man could afford more than one wife, he could afford to place her in her own house. Even if they lived close to the other wives, they at least had some measure of separation. However, an immigrant male who manages to save enough money to return home to his village in Africa, acquire a second or third wife, and bring her back to France typically cannot afford to set her up in her own apartment. Consequently, two or three families may pack into a two-room apartment, a situation some wives indicate as difficult, making them feel "trapped" or that they are "losing their minds."

Vignette 4: In Bellflower, California—a 13-square-mile section of Los Angeles—39 languages are spoken (Simmons 2004). A security guard at the local Department of Motor Vehicles speaks to customers with phrases in English, Spanish, Chinese, and Tagalog. Residents find that the cultural diversity makes learning about other cultures a way of life. As one observer in Bellflower put it, "Koreans are among the throng of customers having their eyebrows plucked by Indian beauticians. Japanese housewives have their nails clipped and polished by Vietnamese manicurists. Mexicans and Vietnamese dine on Vietnamese *pho* soup or Mexican *pozole* porridge at each other's eateries. And it is typical to find Indian spices being sold in Latino grocery stores" (Simmons 2004).

Why Is Transnational Migration Important for Anthropologists?

To pick up and move in search of a better life or security from a hostile environment is such an old pattern in human history that it is practically human nature. So is setting down roots in new locations, only to move on again should the opportunity or need arise. In today's theoretical discourse, humans have been deterritorializing and reterriorializing for almost as long as we have been a species (Gupta and Ferguson 1997). *Homo erectus* managed to migrate throughout Europe and Asia beginning more than a million years ago. And yet, despite the fact that migration and settlement are so fundamental a part of what it means to be human, the process itself is fraught with issues for both those who move and those whom migrants encounter.

The contemporary movement of people across national borders raises a whole range of issues, because migration creates the possibility of change in many directions: among those who move, among those where migrants settle, and among those left behind who often continue to communicate and maintain material relations with migrants (Basch, Schiller, and Blanc 1994). About 150 million people live outside the country of their birth (Stalker 2001). Although this accounts for only about 3 percent of the world's population, the importance of that movement is significant for those involved, that is, the migrants, those left behind, and those in the places migrants settle. Importantly, the forces propelling people from their homes and drawing them to live and work in primarily industrial societies will likely continue for most of the twenty-first century (Castles and Miller 1998). Thus, the sheer magnitude of, and the variety of, responses to the movement of people in the world today and in the next few decades makes transnational migration a topic of long-term anthropological interest.

The United States, long considered the preeminent immigrant-receiving nation, is now but one among many nations receiving large numbers of immigrants. For example, in 2003, 11.7 percent of the U.S. population was foreign-born, but the foreign-born accounted for 18.1 percent of Canada's population and 23.1 percent of Australia's population in 2001 (Institute 2004). In the last 25 years, millions of Eastern Europeans, North Africans, Turks, Albanians, and others have migrated into the industrialized nations of Europe. As a result, foreign-born populations in European countries increased, with at least 4.2 percent in the United Kingdom in 2000 (particularly from South Asia and the Caribbean), 2.2 percent in Italy in 1999, and 6.2 percent in Denmark in 2003 (Institute 2004). In 1999, the foreign-born accounted for about 9.8 percent of Germany's population (mainly Turks, Yugoslavs, and Poles),[1]and 7.4 percent of France's population (mainly Algerians, Moroccans, and Portuguese).[2] In 2001, the foreign-born accounted for 2.5 percent of Spain's population (Perez 2004). In 2000, Japan, not known for its openness to immigration, had about 864,000 foreign workers originally from Korea, China, Bangladesh, Pakistan, Iran, the Philippines, Peru, and Brazil, with an estimated 230,000 undocumented immigrants (Yamanaka 2000). In 2001, Russia had as many as 10 million undocumented migrants, mostly from former Soviet republics drawn by economic opportunities (*Los Angeles Times* 2001).

The paradox, however, is that although pressures may exist for more immigration, the presence of immigrants often raises fears associated with epochal change, especially in nations not accustomed to large-scale immigration. The integration of immigrants is not always an easy one. Immigrants pose challenges to dominant notions of what constitutes "the nation," that is, the people. People who had taken for granted that they were the standard bearers of national identity must cope with racial and cultural diversity in their society. Not surprisingly, then, immigrants and immigration often become ground zero in a battle over the perceived implications of change in contemporary societies around the world.

Immigration, and its counterpart, emigration, are often key symbols for a society (Ortner 1973). By this I mean that they are central and important concepts for how a people understand their identity. Some nations explicitly identify themselves as "immigrant nations," for example the United States, Canada, and Australia. Other countries have historically considered themselves "emigrant nations," because they have sent so many of their people to work and live in other countries (for example Italy and Spain). Other nations have not viewed themselves as immigrant nations at all because they have seen their identity as singular and not open to mixing with other people (for example, Japan, Germany, Saudi Arabia, and many others) (Williams 2000a). An important aspect of key symbols is that they can refract multiple meanings. How any individual member of a society perceives the meaning of that symbol depends on that person's own personal status and history. Thus, immigration and being an immigrant nation (or not) can mean different things to different people at the same time. But the centrality of notions about immigration to a nation's identity is at the core of many of the issues raised by transnational migration, and thus a key source of anthropological investigation (Foner 2003).

A Love-Hate Relationship with Immigrants

Vignette 5: In 1996, a black woman, a naturalized citizen who had immigrated from the Dominican Republic four years earlier, won the title of Miss Italy (Bohlen 1996). For a nation that had imagined itself as setting the standard in European beauty with international stars such as Gina Lollobrigida and Sophia Loren, the crowning of Denny Méndez as Miss Italy raised considerable controversy over the appropriate symbol of Italian female beauty. Suddenly, Italians questioned what it means to be Italian. One of the judges of the beauty contest asked "whether China would accept a Miss China without almond-shaped eyes, or if a non-black African could become Miss Senegal" (Bohlen 1996). However, Italy is changing. A nation that until recently sent emigrants out to other nations to work and live now receives many immigrants, mainly from North Africa, Albania, and the Balkans. As one person wrote in the Italian newspaper *La Republica:* "Italy became a land of immigration without ever deciding to, and in some cases, without ever wanting to" (Bohlen 1996). A year after Ms. Méndez was crowned Miss Italy, the guidelines for competing were changed so that at least one parent had to be "full-blooded Italian" (Rodriguez 2004).

Vignette 6: In Japan, Portuguese-speaking Japanese Brazilians find that they are looked down upon by the Japanese (Tsuda 2003). They came to Japan to work in factories, where they can earn more than in Brazil, even though many have experience in business or professional training. The Japanese wanted them because, after all, they are Japanese, and for a nation that values racial similarity rather than diversity, this was a huge plus for a foreign workforce. However, culturally, the Japanese Brazilians stand out because of the way they walk, the way they sit, and the way they express their emotions, all of which are more casual, open, and familiar than is customary in Japan. They also speak Japanese in a way that is noticeably imperfect, if they speak Japanese at all. The Japanese often treat the Japanese Brazilians with suspicion, as culturally inferior, and as people whose families must have been socially and economically unsuccessful if they had to emigrate from Japan in the first place. They are sometimes mocked as "country bumpkins" on television shows. As a result of their experiences, the Japanese Brazilians who migrate to Japan to work often wind up emphasizing their Brazilian, rather than their Japanese, identity. In Brazil they had emphasized their Japaneseness, rarely participating in events such as Mardi Gras parades. Once in Japan, however, it was clear that they had also acquired Brazilian culture, which they came to embrace and exhibit with pride. Japanese Brazilians now put on an annual Mardi Gras parade in Japan, compete with costumes and music.

In the United States, the often heated debate over immigration is about much more than just the number of immigrants coming to our shores and living in our communities (Lamphere 1992). Immigration is a very personal and emotional issue that touches fundamental, and often unconscious, beliefs about how we think of ourselves as a people, as a nation, and how we think of American culture (Chavaz 1998). And despite immigration being central to how we identify ourselves as a nation, America has had a love-hate relationship with immigrants.

Since colonial days, Americans have desired the economic benefits resulting from immigrant labor while at the same time they have often worried about the negative influences of newcomers on American culture and society. In keeping with this love-hate relationship, Americans tend to denigrate this generation's immigrants, while remembering past immigrants fondly. Ironically, the same immigrants in the past were probably just as feared and reviled as some contemporary immigrants. Consider the alarmist sentiments that Benjamin Franklin's made about Germans in 1751:

> Why should the Palatine boors be suffered to swarm into our settlements, and, by herding together, establish their language and manners, to the exclusion of ours? Why should Pennsylvania, founded by the English, become a colony of aliens, who will shortly be so numerous as to Germanize us, instead of our Anglifying them . . .? (Steinberg 1981).

Franklin's statement reflects concern that "Germanizing" would change and destroy what he viewed as a coherent Anglo-American culture in the colonies. This is a view of culture as static and inelastic, and thus as brittle and vulnerable to changes wrought by immigration. But despite such fears, other colonists desired more immigration to the colonies. Indeed, one of the main articles of the Declaration of Independence of July 4, 1776, was a complaint about England's unwillingness to let more immigrants come to the colonies:

> When in the course of human events, it becomes necessary for one people to dissolve the political bands which have connected them with another . . . a decent respect to the opinions of mankind requires that they should declare the causes which impel them to the separation . . . The present King of Great Britain . . . has endeavored to prevent the population of these states; for that purpose obstructing the laws of naturalization of foreigners; refusing to pass others to encourage their migration hither.

Come hither immigrants did. The nineteenth century became *the* century of immigration, first from northern European countries such as the various countries making up the United Kingdom, Ireland, Germany, and Sweden. China and Japan also sent many immigrants beginning in the mid-1800s. By the late 1800s immigrants were overwhelmingly from southern and eastern European countries, such as Italy, Austria, Hungary, Poland, and Russia. Because these "new" immigrants differed from the previous immigrants, they were often viewed with suspicion and ambivalence, as this article in the *Literary Digest* in 1892 strongly indicates:

> Ignorant, unskilled, inert, accustomed to the beastliest conditions, with little social aspirations, with none of the desire for air and light and room, for the decent dress and home comfort, which our native people possess and which our earlier immigrants so speedily acquired, the presence of hundreds of thousands of these laborers constitutes a menace to the rate of wages and the American standard of living, which to my mind is absolutely appalling . . . . Taking whatever they can get in the way of wages, living like swine, crowded into filthy tenement houses, piecing out their miserable existence by systematic begging and by picking over garbage barrels, the arrival on our shores of such masses of degraded peasantry brings the greatest danger that American labor has ever known (Simon 1985).

Despite being thought of as biologically inferior to the stock of Americans at the time and thus unable to fully assimilate into American life, these immigrant groups fared well by today's standards. An Irish American became president (Kennedy), President Reagan liked to joke that his grandfather was an illegal alien from Ireland, and an Italian American is on the U.S. Supreme Court. In short, the descendents of southern and eastern European immigrants are integrated into every aspect of American life. The point is that immigrants once thought to be harbingers of the decline of American culture and people are now considered just plain Americans. Racialized immigrants (Asians, Africans and Afro-Caribbeans, and Latin Americans), however, may find their acceptance in the American mainstream less of a linear process (Pedraza 1996).

The current movement of peoples across national borders raises many of the same concerns as those of earlier periods. But less often is there critical reflection on the underlying causes of transnational migration. A nation can either produce the labor force it needs (by having babies) or import labor. Most of the industrialized nations of Europe, the United States, and Japan are experiencing large numbers of immigrants, partially due to low fertility rates and a demand for unskilled and semiskilled labor. According to the Population Reference Bureau's 2002 Population Data Sheet, the number of children per woman was at a low of 1.2 in eastern Europe, 1.3 in southern Europe, 1.5 in western Europe, and 1.6 in northern Europe. Particularly low fertility rates were the norm in the Czech Republic (1.1 children per woman), Spain (1.2), and Romania (1.2), with slightly higher fertility rates in many countries, including Italy (1.3), Germany (1.3), Austria (1.3) and Russia (1.3) (Bureau 2002). In the United States, 1.23 children are born per woman between ages 18 and 44 (Bean, et al. 2000). Japan's fertility rate is 1.3, the lowest since 1947, and families who produce more than two children receive rewards (French 2000; *Newsweek* 2000).

With such low fertility rates, even modest economic growth can lead to a demand for immigrant labor. But the response to increased immigration has also been ambivalent and, at times, negative. Indeed, right-wing political parties have gained ground in many countries, especially in Europe.[3] For example,

Denmark has witnessed increased anti-immigrant sentiments associated with the rise of Danish People's Party (Williams 2000b). Despite Denmark's being among the 10 richest countries in the world, immigrants are blamed for the few economic ills that exist in that country. Especially troublesome is the need to import labor with computer skills from countries such as India and Russia. In other European countries, as well, right-wing political parties and leaders have gained popularity as a result of pandering to xenophobic sentiments toward foreigners (Los Angeles Times 2000). Examples abound of such sentiment: Jean-Marie Le Pen in France, Joerg Haider in Austria, Pia Kjaersgaard and the Danish People's Party in Denmark, Filip Dewinter in Belgium, the British National Party and the National Front in England, and Pat Buchanan and a number of anti-immigrant organizations in the United States (Brugge 1995; Oakley 2001; Williams 2000b).[4]

Reaction to increased international migration has sharpened the debate over national identity and even the meaning of citizenship in many countries (Ong 2003). Nations that have not included immigration as a core element of their national identity suddenly see their taken-for-granted assumptions challenged. As a spokesman for Denmark's right-wing Danish People's Party commented: "We don't believe in Denmark turning into a multiethnic society. We have never been an immigrant country, and we will never be one" (Williams 2000b). Jean-Marie Le Pen's National Front Party in France views large-scale immigration "as a recipe for cultural suicide" (Tarmann 2001). In March 2001, Tory leader William Hague, speaking at the Tory party's spring conference in Harrogate, said that the United Kingdom was becoming a "foreign land" because of immigration. Hague went on to promise that, if elected, the Tories would "give you back your country" (News 2001a). In a similar vein, Italy's Silvio Berlusconi, leader of the center-right House of Freedom coalition that won a majority of seats in both the Chamber of Deputies and Senate, made reducing immigration one of his campaign themes: "Italy's borders are a sieve. The immigrants sail here across the Adriatic, or get over the border with Slovenia, and then they disappear . . . . That has meant a rise in crime. What we need to ensure is that any illegal aliens arrested for committing crimes are repatriated immediately. They cannot be tolerated" (News 2001b).

Even in countries like the United States that have historically received immigrants, some residents may believe that their national identity is under attack as the number of immigrants increase. For example, Peter Brimelow (1992) holds in disdain America's self-image as a "nation of immigrants," calling it something that children are taught in schools nowadays, "a sort of multicultural Pledge of Allegiance." He calls for an end to immigration into the United States: "It may be time to close the second period of American history with the announcement that the U.S. is no longer an 'immigrant country.'" It should be noted that Brimelow himself is an immigrant, from the United Kingdom.

Brimelow is not alone. Many have expressed concern about the large numbers of immigrants in the United States endangering the common values that defined the American way of life by bringing their plurality of differences, languages, and histories (Geyer 1996; Huntington 2004; Kadetsky 1994; Lamm and Imhoff 1985; Maharidge 1996; Tatalovich 1997). Patrick Buchanan, a nationally recognized conservative politician, provides us with perhaps one of the best articulations of contemporary American nativism (Bosniak 1997; Johnson 1997; Perea 1997). In a *Los Angeles Times* opinion piece, Buchanan (Buchanan 1994) expressed a deep concern for the future of the "American nation." His main anxiety concerned the very real possibility that, sometime in the near future, the majority of "Americans" would trace their roots not to Europe but to Africa, Asia, Latin America, the Middle East, and the Pacific Islands. He thus asked: What would it mean for "America" if, for example, south Texas and Southern California became almost exclusively Latino?[5] He provided the following answer: "Each will have tens of millions of people whose linguistic, historic, and cultural roots are in Mexico," and thus "like Eastern Ukraine, where 10 million Russian-speaking 'Ukrainians' now look impatiently to Moscow, not Kiev, as their cultural capital, America could see, in a decade, demands for Quebec-like status for Southern California" (ibid., B7). For Buchanan, this prospect is not very appealing. He notes that the United States is already suffering for this trend toward cultural differentiation:

> Crowding together immigrant and minority populations in our major cities [is bringing] greater conflict. We saw that in the 1992 [Los Angeles] riots. Blacks and Latinos have lately collided in Washington's Adams-Morgan neighborhood, supposedly the most tolerant and progressive section of the nation's capital. The issue: bilingual education. Unlike 20 years ago, ethnic conflict is today on almost every front page (ibid.).

From Buchanan's perspective, the only solution to this problem of ethnic-cultural conflict is to put a stop to immigration: "If America is to survive as 'one nation, one people,' we need to call a timeout on immigration, to assimilate the tens of millions who have lately arrived. We need to get to know one another, to live together to learn together America's language, history, culture and traditions of tolerance, to become a new national family, before we add a hundred million more" (ibid.). He concluded the article by noting that "Americans" must have the courage to make the decisions that affect "our" lives; otherwise, others will "make those decisions for us, not all of whom share our love of the America that seems to be fading away" (ibid.).

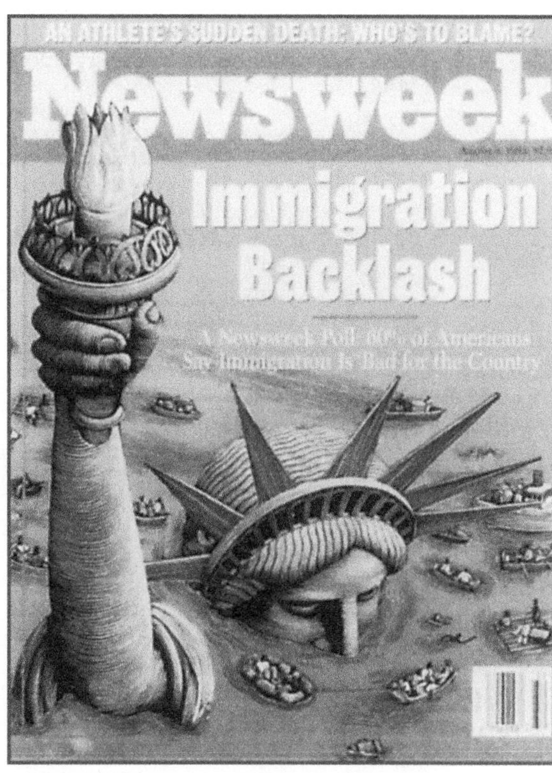

Newsweek's cover illustration on August 9, 1993, captured the image of America dying as a result of immigration. The cover depicts the Statue of Liberty drowning. She is barely visible above a flood of water. Only the top half of her head and her arm holding the torch remain above water. Dark-skinned people circle her in boats, unwilling to leave her alone in her torment. Her eyes are downcast, as if in shock and bewilderment, as she watches the coming peril but is powerless to act.

The meaning of the image is not difficult to read (Chavez 2001). The nation, in the guise of the Statue of Liberty, is in danger. The flood is a common metaphor for the flow of immigrants to the United States. And with floods come danger as the raging waters overwhelm people, land, and nations. The people in the boats represent the immigrants themselves, who are characterized as relentless in their pursuit of America (the Statue of Liberty) and who ultimately destroy that which they so eagerly seek. The image speaks clearly that the nation is at risk because of the uncontrolled movement of large numbers (floods) of immigrants. The text underscores the image's message: "Immigration Backlash: A Newsweek Poll: 60% of Americans Say Immigration Is 'Bad for the Country.'"

The image reflects a common view of culture and draws us to conclude that changes wrought by immigration spell the death of the nation. The theory of culture embedded in this message is that culture is static and nonresilient, that culture should reproduce itself, and that change can destroy a culture. Nothing in the image reflects change being transformative, or of the ability of American culture to absorb that which is new and then to turn the newness into something quintessentially American. Many examples of this process exist in American history. American culture is neither static nor immutable; it has constantly recreated itself. And yet, the message this image conveys is that immigration is causing the impending death of the American nation and culture.

Culture Change and Cultural Reproduction

Vignette 7: In Yolo County, California, Andres Bermudez is a successful tomato farmer (Mena 2001). He is so successful, in fact, that his compatriots call him the "Tomato King." He came to the United States illegally 30 years ago, but has since become a U.S. citizen. Long active in U.S.-based organizations that provided money for projects in his hometown of Jerez, Zacatecas, Mexico, Bermudez ran for mayor of Jerez and won on July 1, 2001. He became the first U.S. citizen to win elected office in Mexico. Mexico has been promoting a "dual nationality" program that allows Mexicans who become citizens in other countries to retain property and nationality rights (Mena 2001). Voting in Mexican elections has been another issue. Although Mexico promotes transnational civic engagement, the country has yet to implement a balloting mechanism for U.S.-based Mexican nationals to vote in Mexican elections. Bermudez's election was later overturned because he failed to meet Mexico's residency requirements, but he finally assumed the position of municipal president of Jerez in September 2004 (Pickel 2004).

Vignette 8: In New York, Indian American college students, both those born in the United States and those who immigrated at an early age, are struggling with issues of identity and Indianness in the American context (Maira 2002). For these second-generation Indian Americans, issues of gender and sexuality are often a point of conflict when it comes to what it means to be "Indian" and what it means to be "Indian American." The tension arises because norms and values that immigrant parents bring with them can become hyper-emphasized, to the point of fossilization, in these immigrant families. For Indian American women, this means that control of their sexuality and public behavior is more important than controlling young men. Immigrant parents view Indian American women as the repositories of the family "izzat," or reputation. Even more, Indian American women are caught in the double bind of representing both tradition and modernity. By adhering to traditional behaviors, they represent authentic Indian ethnic identity. They are the stabilizing factor in cultural reproduction. However, if they change and exhibit "American" cultural behaviors and dress, then they represent change and modernity, and the loss of Indian identity in the American context. Thus, second-generation Indian American women face many pressures from family and community members who expect them to behave in ways that represent ethnic stability and continuity.

Vignette 9: In Long Beach, California, Riem Men, a Cambodian man, reflected on his culture shock at seeing young women taking responsibility in the public sphere. As he so eloquently put it (Yarborough 1996):

> In Cambodia, it was always taught that women must obey and respect men. Many of the old books that some Cambodians still read set out rules for a "good woman." She should always go to bed later than her husband and get up earlier than him, so she can attend to all household tasks. If he is a drunkard or adulterer or gambler, he is still always right. And even if he curses her, she should be quiet and respectful. If she follows these rules she'll be considered the best woman in the community and when she dies she'll go to heaven.
>
> When I grew up in Cambodia no one had any different ideas about that, so it all seemed natural and right. In my mind, women were a group of people who were there to take care of the house and raise children. They were regarded as very weak people, and they certainly had no chance to express opinions on such matters as politics.
>
> Therefore you can imagine my surprise when I first landed in San Francisco with a group of 350 other Asian officers and at our orientation an American girl [who looked] about 19 years old got on stage and talked in front of hundreds of high-ranking officers. She didn't even seem nervous, just normal, and I thought: Oh, my God! I've never seen anything like this before! Yet it was so exciting to see a woman taking that kind of role and I felt admiration for her. Suddenly, it seemed appropriate. And as time went on, all my ideas began to change.

When people migrate they often come into contact with different nations, or people, who also often speak a different language and share different cultural views of the real world and different ways of organizing their social lives. Today, nations are often associated with states with formal political borders. One of the most difficult problems migration raises is how to think about culture and what happens as people move and mix, or migrate and interact with people in different places. Too often culture is conceptualized as a "thing," as something that mechanically gets reproduced from one generation to the next. If novelty is introduced, or change occurs, and the system does not appear to reproduce itself, then fears arise that the culture is broken, failed to function properly, or is about to be destroyed. To parents, this could signal the breakdown of their way of life. Those experiencing rapid in-migration could view the newcomers as unwilling to learn about the welcoming society's culture. Immigrants might also desire that their children reproduce their parents' cultural beliefs and values and this can generate transgenerational tensions and conflicts (Espiritu 2003).

To a certain extent, anthropologists have had a hand in creating this problem of thinking of culture as mechanically reproducing itself. Anthropology became popular in the early twentieth century as part of a discourse on human societies. One of the prominent theories of culture and society at the time was functionalism, which later came to be known as structural-functionalism. In this perspective, the various elements of a society "functioned" in a way that produced or maintained the overall social system. Bronislaw Malinowski (1960 [1944]) believed that "each culture can be understood as an integrated whole of 'partly autonomous, partly coordinated institutions'" (cited in Salzman 2001, 14). Interdependence, maintenance, equilibrium, and continuity of the system as a whole were keys to functionalism and structural-functionalism. In this view, there is not so much change as cultural reproduction with little change.

Radcliffe-Brown, another leading theorist of the time put it this way: "The function of any recurrent activity, such as the punishment of a crime, or a funeral ceremony, is the part it plays in the social life as a whole and therefore the contribution it makes to the maintenance of social structure" (Radcliffe-Brown 1948). Change, in this view, is not as important to understand as the coherent cultural system as a whole. Indeed, change was difficult to even articulate in this theory. Interestingly, functionalism contrasts with an earlier anthropological theory, diffusionism, which focused on the diffusion of cultural traits across wide geographic areas. But functionalism and structural-functionalism described cultures and societies as independent self-sustaining, and autonomous cultures (Salzman 2001).

The arrows in Figure 2.1 represent the way particular cultural domains mutually reinforced the stability and coherence of the overall sociocultural system.

The seeming continuity and mechanical reproduction inherent in functionalism and structural-functionalism lead to the critique of functionalist theories as representing cultures and societies as static and ahistorical. As Eric Wolf (1982) argued, such thinking resulted in many non-Western peoples viewed as "people without history." However, societies and cultures are, or were even then, rarely secluded and cut off from their neighbors and the larger world.

Contemporary anthropological theory conceptualizes culture and change differently. Culture is still the system of meanings that people construct to give order to their world, and the material productions and social relationships that are part of that cultural world. However, cultural reproduction is not cloning. One generation does not transmit a culture in perfect formation to the next generation because the individuals in the next generation are subject to flows of information from many directions at once: from parents, peers, teachers (formal and informal), and the many other interests and institutions in the

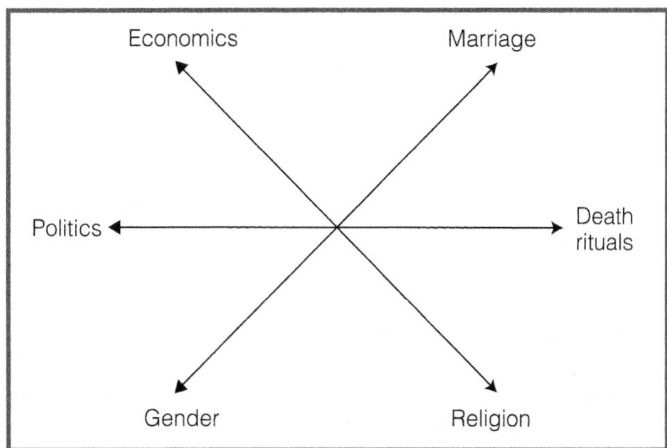

Figure 2.1 Functionalist View of Culture

society and beyond. Therefore, reproduction is never complete; cultural systems are not static. Cultures are dynamic and subject to historical processes, even though culture change is constrained by preexisting cultural understandings and social structures, but these too are subject to change.

Culture is not a fixed, thing-like concept, but is fluid, dynamic, processural, and constructed. Cultural understandings of the world are contested and open to new information so that, although some aspects of culture have continuity, change and even a lack of consensus also exist because of the multiple perspectives found among members of a society. Differences occur because members of social groups differ in terms of gender, age, relationship, where they were born, where they were raised, ethnic/racial identities, and many other ways. Moreover, a sociocultural system is subject to influences for change that originate both internally and externally to the system, which is really a system within systems, as Immanuel Wallerstein (1989 [1974]) argued. A model of culture change along these parameters would look very different from the previous functionalist one (see Figure 2.2).

Cultures and societies can change from internal dynamics, history, and societal pressures. On the other hand, people do not live in isolation. They are often in contact with other people who behave differently and have different ideas about the world. Sometimes people borrow from these others freely. Other times, these outside influences are imposed. Religion was one such transnational force. Whether brought by the sword or diffused more peacefully, major religions have moved from people to people and nation to nation. Conquerors and colonizers often imposed new religions and new ways of living on the people they conquered and colonized. This was as true in the past when "world" religions, such as Christianity and Islam, were spread across national borders, as it is today, when Christian evangelists pursue converts in U.S.-occupied Iraq.

But religion is not the only transnational force in history or in contemporary life. The spread of capitalism in the world today is another such transnational force (Ong 1999). Globalization is a term that refers to how the world and its people are increasingly becoming integrated into one giant economic capitalist system. The spread of world capitalism also carries with it a spread of Western—often American—culture. One thing anyone who travels the world notices is how common American fast-food restaurants have become, a process often referred to as the McDonaldization of the society (Ritzer 2000). But globalization does not just refer to the movement of capital and the search for cheap labor. It is also about the movement of people, ideas, movies, music, "traditional" Chinese Medicine, and a whole host of flows unmoored from fixed national places (Zhan 2001). Jonathan Inda and Renato Rosaldo (2002) define a "world of globalization" as

> . . . a world of motion, of complex interconnections. Here capital traverses frontiers almost effortlessly, drawing more and more places into dense networks of financial interconnections; people readily (although certainly not freely and without difficulty) cut

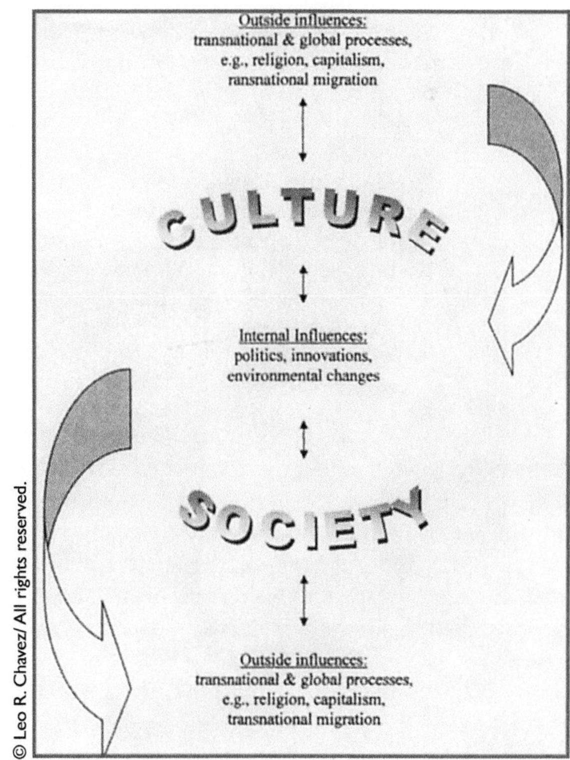

Figure 2.2 Culture change: cultural and social reproduction.

across national boundaries, turning countless territories into spaces where various cultures converge, clash, and struggle with each other, commodities drift briskly from one locality to another, becoming primary mediators in the encounter between culturally distant others; images flicker quickly from screen to screen, providing people with resources from which to fashion new ways of being in the world; and ideologies circulate rapidly through ever-expanding circuits, furnishing fodder for struggles couched in terms of cultural authenticity verses foreign influence.

New technologies that allow rapid electronic communication and faster transportation have made possible the increasing movement of people, capital, ideas, and cultures around the world and across national borders (Appadurai 1996). Although these powerful, worldwide trends may be occurring, they do not simply move around the world unimpeded. People living in local areas often have something to say about how global ideas and ways of life are integrated into local life. However, as some of the vignettes presented here indicate, change often results in backlash, as not everyone is pleased with change, especially if it upsets established relations of power and privilege. Forces for change and those resistant to change lead to a synthesis of new and old cultural beliefs and practices. This new crystallization of local life is not necessarily as hard and durable as the metaphor of a crystal suggests, because here, too, global life continues to influence. But at the same time, the local can effect changes in the global because change can occur in multiple directions, as the arrows in Figure 2.1 indicate.

In this process of change, the movement of people plays an important role. When people move from one social and cultural system to another, changes occur. Immigrants encounter new ideas and behavior while at the same time introducing their ideas and behaviors to the receiving society and culture. The next section examines specific examples of how migration and culture causes change in unanticipated ways. Over time, what was seen as new becomes routine and ordinary.

Immigration and Culture Change

Anthropologists often take the long view of culture change. Immediate reactions to newcomers (immigrants) in a society often focus on difference. New people in the neighborhood speaking a different language, practicing a different religion, and putting up signs on stores in foreign languages all raise ethnocentric responses and even fears. Over time, these differences may not be as pronounced because what was once new can become part of the accepted way things are, and even become central to a nation's identity and symbols of that identity.

Anthropologists are likely to speak of the culture changes that occur in a world of moving people, ideas, and cultural products as a blending, fusion, syncretization, hybridization, and creolization. These concepts reflect the multidimensional, multidirectional, and often unpredictable changes that take place as people and ideas, beliefs and behaviors collide and interweave into new cultural formations. Culture is always an emergent form of life (Fischer 2003). Anthropologists prefer these concepts to the more unidirectional flow of changes represented by models of assimilation, which are often inadequate to capture the complex process of culture change (Foner 2003, 34–35). A few examples make the point.

© Tony Freeman/PhotoEdit

John Wayne's statue at the John Wayne/Orange County airport.

Food is often considered the symbol of a culture's identity and authenticity. Food is so closely associated with particular ethnic and national groups that this relationship is often taken for granted as natural, as if it always existed. People less often consider the history of food and its essential associations. In the United States, for example, burritos are considered Mexican food, but they were really invented in the United States. In Italy, Italianness is represented by food. The very image of tomatoes, tomato sauce, and pasta conjures up connotations about what it means to be Italian (Barthes 1972). Carol Delaney (2004) notes that Italians are particularly identified with tomato sauce, what Americans often refer to as spaghetti sauce. Tomato sauce is a cultural force that holds generations of Italians together. However, before Europeans migrated to the Americas, Europe had no tomato sauce. It took years for the *tomatl* (as the Aztecs called the fruit in the Nahuatl language) to become accepted in European kitchens. Did the introduction of tomatoes destroy Italian culture (or cultures, as the state of Italy did not yet exist)? The introduction of tomatoes to the Italian peninsula actually resulted in tomato sauce eventually becoming the quintessential symbol of what it means to be Italian.

Another example starts close to my home. My local airport is John Wayne Airport in Orange County, California. For years, a statue of John Wayne, dressed as a cowboy, has been displayed prominently at the airport. But where does the "cowboy" come from? The image of the cowboy that John Wayne personifies has not always existed. The cowboy is a far cry from the image of Daniel Boone and the frontiersman of the colonial states in the late eighteenth and early nineteenth centuries. When whites and blacks from the colonial states moved West they encountered people in what is now New Mexico and Texas living a life well adapted to cattle and sheep ranching and herding. They were *vaqueros*, Mexican cowboys, from whom the Americans learned the cowboy way of life. Imagine how foreign the first American cowboys—with their big hats (*sombreros*), bandannas, ponchos, leather leggings over their pants, boots, ropes, and general demeanor—must have looked. And the words these new types of Americans used for the items and the techniques of their trade were essentially foreign, too, because many were words borrowed from Spanish (some of which were in turn borrowed from the Moors in Spain) (Graham 1994). Some cowboy words and their origin include,

Spanish	English
Vaqueros "men who work with cows"	buckaroos (cowboys)
chaparreras (pant leg coverings)	chaps
la reata (rope)	lariat
lazo (noose on rope)	lasso
reinda (ropes riders used to guide horse)	reins
mecate (rope made of horse tail hairs)	McCarty
Jáquima (bitless bridle to tame horses)	hackamore
broncos (wild horses)	broncs
mesteno (trained horses)	mustang
corral (pen)	corral
darle vuelta (roping and stopping cattle in their tracks by quickly snubbing a rope around the saddle horn)	dolly roping
rodeo	rodeo
juzgado (local jail)	hoosegow

But perhaps just as important as the words cowboys borrowed and adapted from the vaqueros was their lifestyle and personal characteristics: the strong, silent type whose time alone on the range made him manly (macho), independent, and self-reliant. Is this not the image John Wayne, the cowboy, exudes? In a few short years, the foreign-looking cowboy became the central figure in the myth of the West, and his qualities and characteristics came to epitomize the quintessential elements of what it means to be American. Did migrating West, encountering Mexican vaquero culture, and constructing the cowboy destroy American culture? Or did American culture change and in the process incorporate novelty? The answer is the statue standing at John Wayne airport.

Another example shows the unanticipated ways culture changes as a result of the immigration. Generations of Mexicans lived in Texas before it became part of the United States. As discussed previously, the cowboy was constructed out of the meeting of Americans and Texans in the early 1800s. However, another group of immigrants, Germans, had a profound and lasting effect on Tejanos (Texans of Mexican descent). Thousands of Germans migrated to Texas in the 1800s (Jordan 1966). They brought with them the accordion and their fondness of the polkas that they played during their parties. Locals heard the music and picked up the accordion, adapting it to fit their needs. Soon Tejanos were playing a new style of music in Texas that came to be known as "conjunto," "Tex-Mex," "Tejano," and "norteno" music (San Miguel 2002). To many Americans, it was "Mexican" music, and yet, this music was a real American invention, blending German polkas, Mexican ballads, and other song styles (see also the excellent PBS documentary *Accordian Dreams*). The late Texas singer, Selena Perez, was one of the most nationally famous performers of this style. In the long run, Tejanos did not lose their culture because they incorporated aspects of German culture into their lives. Their culture changed and was enriched in many ways because of such exchanges.

What are the lessons for anthropologists and others living in today's current world of movement? It is that migrations engender dislocations, opportunities, frictions, fears, and change. Most likely, the changes that occur will be unanticipated because transformations that cultures undergo are difficult to plan and predict. One thing is certain: the sets of cultural practices and understandings about the world that will emerge in the near future will make sense and seem as natural and enduring as the cultures and world we live in today.

References

Appadurai, Arjun. 1996. *Modernity at large: cultural dimensions of globalization.* Minneapolis: Univ. of Minnesota Press.

Bandhauer, Carina A. 2001. *Global trends in racism: The late 20th century anti-immigrant movement in Southern California.* Ph.D., Binghamton Univ.

Barthes, Roland. 1972. *Mythologies.* London: Cape.

Basch, Linda, Nina Glick Schiller, and Cristina Szanton Blanc. 1994. *Nations unbound: Transnational projects, postcolonial predicaments, and deterritorialized nation-states.* Amsterdam: Gordon and Breach.

Baum, Geraldine. 2004. Queens pizzeria sells diversity by the slice. *Los Angeles Times*, May 31, E1.

Bean, Frank D., C. Gray Swicegood, and Ruth Berg. 2000. Mexican-origin fertility: New patterns and fertility: New patterns and interpretations. *Social Science Quarterly* 81:404–420.

Bohlen, Celestine. 1996. Italians contemplate beauty in a Caribbean brow. *The New York Times.* September 10, A3.

Bosniak, Linda S. 1997. 'Nativism' the concept: Some reflections. In *Immigrants out! The new nativism and the anti-immigrant impulse in the United States,* ed. Juan F. Perea, 279–299. New York: New York Univ. Press.

Brimelow, Peter. 1992. Time to rethink immigration? *The National Review,* June 22, 30–46.

Brugge, Doug. 1995. Pulling up the ladder. In *Eyes right! Challenging the right wing backlash*, ed. Chip Berlet, 191–209. Boston: South End Press.

Buchanan, Patrick J. 1994. What will America be in 2050? *Los Angeles Times*, October 28, B7.

Bureau, Population Reference. 2002. 2002 World Population Data Sheet, Vol. 2004: Population Reference Bureau. www.prb.org/pdf/ WorldPopulationDSs02_Eng.pdf.

Castles, Stephen, and Mark J. Miller. 1998. *The age of migration: International population movements in the modern world.* 2nd ed. New York and London: The Guilford Press.

Chavez, Leo R. 1997. Immigration reform and nativism: The nationalist response to the transnationalist challenge. In *Immigrants out! The new nativism and the anti-immigrant impulse in the United States,* ed. Juan F. Perea, 61–77. New York: New York Univ. Press.

_________. 1998. *Shadowed lives: Undocumented immigrants in American society.* 2nd ed. Fort Worth: Harcourt Brace and Jovanovich College Publishers.

_________. 2001. *Covering immigration: Popular images and the politics of the nation.* Berkeley: Univ. of California Press.

Dahlburg, John-Thor. 2000. EU bares its teeth over Austria 'crisis'. *Los Angeles Times* February 3, A1.

Delaney, Carol. 2004. *Investigating culture: An experiential introduction to anthropology.* Malden, MA: Blackwell Publishing.

Espiritu, Yen Le. 2003. *Home bound: Filipino American lives across cultures, communities, and countries.* Berkeley: Univ. of California Press.

Fischer, Michael M.M. 2003. *Emergent forms of life and the anthropological voice.* Durham: Duke Univ. Press.

Foner, Nancy, ed. 2003. *American arrivals: Anthropology engages the new immigration.* Santa Fe: School of American Research.

French, Howard W. 2000. Japan fails to cope with its declining population. *Orange County Register*, March 14, news 19.

Geyer, Georgie Ann. 1996. *Americans no more.* New York: The Atlantic Monthly Press.

Graham, Joe S. 1994. *El Rancho in South Texas; Continuity and change from 1750.* College Station, TX: Texas A&M Univ. Press.

Gupta, Akhil, and James Ferguson, eds. 1997. *Culture, power, place: Ethnography at the end of an era.* Culture, Power, Place: Explorations in Critical Anthropology. Durham: Duke Univ. Press.

Huntington, Samuel P. 2004. The Hispanic challenge. *Foreign Policy* March/April: 30–45.

Inda, Jonathan Xavier, and Renato Rosaldo. 2002. Introduction: A world in motion. In *The anthropology of globalization: A reader,* eds. Jonathan Xavier Inda and Renato Rosaldo, 1–34. Malden, MA: Blackwell Publishers.

Institute, Migration Policy. 2004. Migration Information Source: Migration Policy Institute www.migrationinformation.org. http:/www.migrationinformation.org.

Johnson, Kevin R. 1997. The new nativism: Something old, something new, something borrowed, something blue. In *Immigrants out! The new nativism and the anti-immigrant impulse in the United States,* ed. Juan F. Perea, 165–189. New York: New York Univ. Press.

Jordan, Terry G. 1966. *German seed in Texas soil: Immigrant farmers in nineteenth-century Texas.* Austin: Univ. of Texas Press.

Kadetsky, Elizabeth. 1994. 'Save our state' initiative: Bashing illegals in California. *Nation*, October 17.

Lamm, Richard D., and Gary Imhoff. 1985. *The immigration time bomb.* New York: Truman Talley Books.

Lamphere, Louise, ed. 1992. *Structuring diversity: Ethnographic perspectives on the new immigration.* Chicago: The Univ. of Chicago Press.

Los Angeles Times. 2000. Anti-immigrant nationalist party gains in Flanders. October 10, A4.

_________. 2001. Russia: Illegal migrants number 10 million, official says. 14.

Maharidge, Dale. 1996. *The coming white minority.* New York: Times Books.

Maira, Sunaina M. 2002. *Desis in the house: Indian American youth culture in York City.* Philadelphia: Temple Univ. Press.

Malinowski, Bronislaw. 1944/1960. *A scientific theory of culture.* Chapel Hill: Univ. of North Carolina Press.

Mena, Jennifer. 2001. Expatriates wild about 'Tomato King' mayor. *Los Angeles Times,* July 9, B3.

Migration News. 2001a. Vol. 8, no. 5 (May). Davis, CA: Univ. of California, Davis. http://migration.ucdavis.edu.

_________. 2001b. Vol. 8, no. 6 (June). Davis, CA: Univ. of California, Davis. http://migration.ucdavis.edu.

Migration Policy Institute. 2004. Migration Information Source: Migration Policy Institute www.migrationinformation.org. http://www.migrationinformation.org.

Newsweek. 2000. Perspectives, June 12, 23.

Oakley, Robin. 2001. Europe's tangle over immigration. *CNN.com,* February 20. www.cnn.com/2001/WORLD/europe/02/20/immigration.overview.index.html.

Ong, Aihw. 1999. *Flexible citizenship: The cultural logics of transnationality.* Durham: Duke Univ. Press

_________ 2003. *Buddha is hiding: Refugees, citizenship, the new America.* Berkeley: Univ. of California Press.

Ortner, Sherry. 1973. On key symbols. *American Anthropologist* 75:1228–46.

Pedraza, Silvia. 1996. Origins and destinies: Immigration, race and ethnicity in American history. In *Origins and Destinies: Immigration, Race, and Ethnicity in America,* ed. Silvia Pedraza and Ruben Rumbaut, 1–20. Belmont CA: Wadsworth Publishing Company.

Perea, Juan F., ed. 1997. *Immigrants out! The new nativism and the anti-immigrant impulse in the United States.* New York: New York Univ. Press.

Perez, Nieves Ortega. 2004. *Spain: Forging an Immigration Policy.* Migration Policy Institute. www.migrationinformation.org/Profiles/print.cfm?ID=97.

Pickel, Mary Lou. 2004. Mexican pauper returns to be a president. *Orange County Register.* September 15, news 17.

Radcliffe-Brown, A. R. 1948. *Structure and function in primitive society.* London: Cohen and West.

Reimers, David M. 1998. *Unwelcome strangers: American identity and the turn against immigration.* New York: Columbia Univ. Press.

Ritzer, George. 2000. *The McDonaldization of society.* 3rd ed. Thousand Oaks, CA: Pine Forge Press.

Rodriguez, Gregory. 2004. Europe's Implosion: The EU needs immigrants but feels threatened by them. *Los Angeles Time,* May 5, B13.

Salzman, Philip Carl. 2001. *Understanding culture: An introduction to anthropological theory.* Prospect Heights, Illinois: Waveland Press, Inc.

San Miguel, Guadalupe Jr. 2002. *Tejano proud: Tex-Mex music in the twentieth century.* College Station, TX: Texas A & M Univ. Press.

Simmons, Ann M. 2004. A melting pot that's brimming with alphabet soup. *Los Angeles Times.* July 1, B1.

Simon, Rita J. 1985. *Public opinion and the immigrant.* Lexington MA: Lexington Books.

Simons, Marlise. 1996. In France, Africa women are now fighting polygamy. *New York Times.* January 26, A1.

Stalker, Peter. 2001. *No-nonsense guide to international migration.* London: Verso.

Steinberg, Stephen. 1981. *The ethnic myth: Race, ethnicity, and class in America:* Boston: Beacon Press.

Tarmann, Allison. 2001. *The Flap Over Replacement Migration.* Washington, DC: Population Reference Bureau, June 13. www.prb.org/pt/wooo/MayJune2000/flap_replacement_migration.html.

Tatalovich, Raymond. 1997. Official English as nativist backlash. In *Immigrants out! The new nativism and the anti-immigrant impulse in the United States,* ed. Juan F. Perea, 78–102. New York: New York Univ. Press.

Tsuda, Takeyuki. 2003. *Strangers in the ethnic homeland: Japanese Brazilian return migration in transnational perspective.* New York: Columbia Univ. Press.

Wallerstein, Immanuel. 1974/1989. *The modern world-system.* New York: Academic Press.

Williams, Carol J. 2000a. Citizenship reform has lost its punch. *Los Angeles Times.* January 8, A2.

_________. 2000b. Danes cast cold eye on immigrants. *Los Angeles Times,* April 28, A1.

_________. 2000c. Germans stand up to right-wing violence. *Los Angeles Times.* November 10, A4.

Wolf, Eric R. 1982. *Europe and the people without history.* Berkeley: Univ. of California Press.

Yamanaka, Keiko. 2000. "I will go home, but when?" Labor migration and circular diaspora formation by Japanese Brazilians in Japan. In *Japan and global migration,* eds. Mike Douglas and Glenda S. Roberts, 123–152. London: Routledge.

Yarborough, Trin. 1996. "I saw women go to school and have jobs." *Los Angeles Times,* March 2, B11.

Yee, Sonya. 2002. Far-right freedom party fizzles in Austrian election, *Los Angeles Times,* November 25, A3.

Zhan, Mei. 2001. Does it take a miracle? Negotiating knowledge, identities, and communities of traditional Chinese medicine. *Cultural Anthropology* 16 (4) :453–480.

Notes

1. See Federal Statistical Office Germany, http://www.statistik-bund.de/e_home.htm.
2. See National Institute for Statistics and Economic Studies (INSEE) France in Facts and Figures, http://www.insee.fr/en/home/home_page.asp.
3. There has also been an outcry against anti-immigrant politics and actions (Dahlburg 2000; Williams 2000c; Yee 2002).
4. The list of anti-immigrant organizations in the United States is too numerous to detail here, but includes the Federation for American Immigration Reform, American Citizens Together, Voice of Citizens Together, Stop Immigration Now, and California Coalition for Immigration Reform. See (Bandhauer 2001; Chavez 1997; Maharidge 1996; Reimers 1998) for a more thorough discussion of anti-immigrant organizations in the United States.
5. See Samuel Huntington (2004) for a more recent example of anti-Mexican discourse.

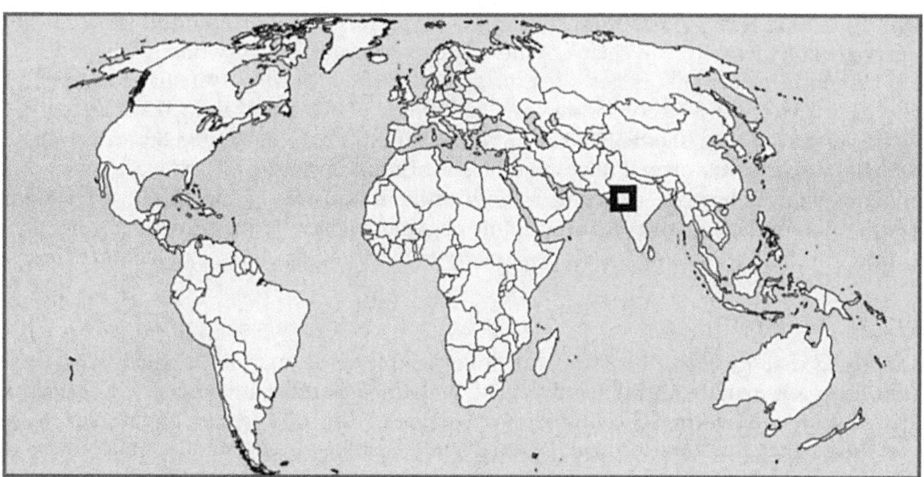

3/Family and Kinship in Village India

David W. McCurdy

Anyone who reads older ethnographic accounts of different cultures will inevitably run across terms such as *clan, lineage, avunculocal, levirate, extended family, polyandry, cross-cousin,* and *Crow* terminology. All these terms and many more were created by anthropologists to describe categories, groups, social arrangements, and roles associated with the complex kinship systems that characterized so many of the groups they studied. The importance of kinship for one of these societies, that found in an Indian village, is the topic of this article by David McCurdy. He argues that kinship forms the core social groups and associations in rural India in a system well adapted to family-centered land-holding and small-scale farming. He concludes by pointing out that Indians have used their close family ties to adapt to life in the emerging cash-labor-oriented modernizing world.

On a hot afternoon in May, 1962, I sat talking with three Bhil men in the village of Ratakote, located in southern Rajasthan, India.[1] We spoke about the results of recent national elections, their worry over a cattle disease that was afflicting the village herds, and predictions about when the monsoon rains would start. But our longest discussion concerned kin—the terms used to refer to them, the responsibilities they had toward one another, and the importance of marrying them off properly. It was toward the end of this conversation that one of the men, Kanji, said, "Now sāb (Bhili for sāhīb), you are finally asking about a good thing. This is what we want you to tell people about us when you go back to America."

As I thought about it later, I was struck by how different this social outlook was from mine. I doubt that I or any of my friends in the United States would say something like this. Americans do have kin. We have parents, although our parents may not always live together, and we often know other relatives, some of whom are likely to play important parts in our lives. We grow up in families and we often create new ones if we have children. But we also live in a social network of other people whom we meet at work or encounter in various "outside" social settings, and these people can be of equal or even greater importance to us than kin. Our social worlds include such non-kin structures as companies and other work organizations, schools, neighborhoods, churches and other religious groups, and voluntary associations, including recreational groups and social clubs. We are not likely to worry much about our obligations to relatives with the notable exceptions of our children and grandchildren (middle-class American parents are notoriously child-centered), and more grudgingly, our aging parents. We are not supposed to "live off" relatives or lean too heavily on them.

[1]Ratakote is a Bhil tribal village located 21 miles southwest of Udaipur, Rajasthan, in the Aravalli hills. I did ethnographic research in the village from 1961 to 1963, and again in 1985, 1991, and 1994 for shorter periods of time.

Conformity and Conflict: Readings in Cultural Anthropology, Thirteenth Edition
by James Spradley and David W. McCurdy

Not so in Ratakote. Ratakote's society, like many agrarian villages around the world, is kinship-centered. Villagers anchor themselves in their families. They spend great energy on creating and maintaining their kinship system. This actually is not so surprising. Elaborate kinship systems work well in agrarian societies where families tend to be corporate units and where peoples' social horizons are often limited to the distance they can walk in a day. For the same reasons, families in the United States were also stronger in the past when more of them owned farms and neighborhood businesses.

What may come as a surprise, however, is how resilient and strong Indian kinship systems such as Ratakote's have been in the face of recent economic changes, especially the growth of wage labor. Let us look more closely at the Bhil kinship system, especially at arranged marriage, to illustrate these ideas.

Arranging a Marriage

If there is anything that my American students have trouble understanding about India, it is arranged marriage. They can not imagine sitting passively by while their parents advertise their charms and evaluate emerging nuptial candidates. The thought of living—to say nothing of having sex with—a total stranger seems out of the question to them. In our country, personal independence takes precedence over loyalty to family.

Not so in India. There, arranged marriage is the norm, and most young people, as well as their elders, accept and support the custom. (They often find it sexually exciting, too.) There are many reasons why this is so, but one stands out for discussion here. Marriage constructs alliances between families, lineages, and clans. The resulting kinship network is a pivotal structure in Indian society. It confers social strength and security. People's personal reputations depend on the quality and number of their allied kin. There is little question in their minds about who should arrange marriages. The decision is too important to leave up to inexperienced and impressionable young people.

As an aside I should note that young Indians play a greater part in the process than they used to. Middle-class boys often visit the families of prospective brides, where they manage to briefly "interview" them. They also tap into their kinship network to find out personal information about prospects. Young women also seek out information about prospective grooms. Bhils are no exception. They often conspire to meet those to whom they have been betrothed, usually at a fair or other public event where their contact is likely to go unnoticed. If they don't like each other, they will begin to pressure their parents to back out of the arrangement.

The importance of arranging a marriage was brought home to me several times during fieldwork in Ratakote, but one instance stands out most clearly. When I arrived in the swvillage for a short stay in 1985, Kanji had just concluded marriage arrangements for his daughter, Rupani.[2] What he told me about the process underscored the important role kinship plays in the life of the village.

Kanji started by saying that he and his wife first discussed Rupani's marriage the previous year when the girl first menstruated. She seemed too young for such a union then so they had waited nine months before committing to the marriage process. Even then, Rupani was still only 15 years old. Kanji explained that everyone preferred early marriage for their children because young people were likely to become sexually active as they grew older and might fall in love and elope, preempting the arrangement process altogether. Now they figured that the time had come, and they began a series of steps to find a suitable spouse that would eventually involve most of their kin.

The first step was to consult the members of Kanji's *lineage*. Lineage is an anthropological term, not one used by Bhils. But Bhils share membership in local groups of relatives that meet the anthropological definition. Lineages (in this case patrilineages) include closely related men who are all descended from a known ancestor. Kanji's lineage consists of his two married brothers, three married sons of his deceased father's brother (his father is also dead), and his own married son when the latter is home. All are the descendants of his grandfather who had migrated to Ratakote many years earlier. He had talked with all of them informally about the possibility of his daughter's marriage before this. Now he called them together for formal approval.

The approval of lineage mates is necessary because they are essential to the marriage process. Each one of them will help spread the word to other villages that Rupani is available for marriage. They will loan money to Kanji for wedding expenses, and when it comes time for the wedding ceremony, they will provide much of the labor needed to prepare food and arrange required activities. Each family belonging to the lineage will host a special meal for the bride (the groom is similarly entertained in his village) during the wedding period, and one or two will help her make offerings to their lineal ancestors. The groom will also experience this ritual.

The lineage also has functions not directly related to marriage. It has the right to redistribute the land of deceased childless, male members, and it provides its members with political support. It sees to memorial feasts for deceased members. Its members may cooperatively plow and sow fields together and combine their animals for herding.

[2]Kanji and Rupani are not real people. Their experiences are a composite of several life histories.

With lineage approval in hand, Kanji announced Rupani's eligibility in other villages. (Bhils are village exogamous, meaning they prefer to marry spouses from other communities.) Kanji and his lineage mates went about this by paying visits to feminal relatives in other villages. These are kin of the women, now living in Ratakote, who have married into his family. They also include the daughters of his family line who have married and gone to live in other villages, along with their husbands and husbands' kin.

Once the word has been spread, news of prospective candidates begins to filter in. It may arrive with feminal kin from other villages when they visit Ratakote. Or it may come from neighbors who are acting as go-betweens in Ratakote for kin who live in other villages and who seek partners for their children. Either way, a process of evaluation starts. Does the family of the suggested boy or girl have a good reputation? Are they hospitable to their in-laws? Do they meet their obligations to others? What is the reputation of the boy or girl they are offering in marriage? Is he or she tall or short, light or dark, robust or frail, cheerful or complaining, hardworking or lazy? What about their level of education? Does the family have sufficient land and animals? Have they treated other sons- and daughters-in-law well?

The most fundamental question to ask, however, is whether the prospective spouse is from the right clan. In anthropology, the term *clan* refers to an aggregate of people who all believe they are descended from a common ancestor. In Ratakote this group is called an *arak*. Araks are named and the names are used as surnames when Bhils identify themselves. Kanji comes from the pargi arak and is thus known as Kanji Pargi. There is Lalu Bodar, Naraji Katara, Dita Hiravat, Nathu Airi—all men named for one of the 36 araks found in Ratakote. Women also belong to their father's clan, but unlike many American women who adopt their husband's surname at marriage, they keep their arak name all their lives.

Araks are based on a rule of patrilineal descent. This means that their members trace ancestry through males only. (Matrilineal descent traces the line through females only, and bilateral descent, which is found in U.S. society, includes both sexes.) Patrilineal descent not only defines arak membership, it governs inheritance. (Sons inherit equally from their fathers in Ratakote; daughters do not inherit despite a national law giving them that right.) It says that the children of divorced parents stay with the father's family. It bolsters the authority of men over their wives and children. It supports the rule of patrilocality. It even defines the village view of conception. Men plant the "seeds" that grow into children; women provide the fields in which the seeds germinate and grow.

The arak symbolizes patrilineal descent. It is not an organized group, although the members of an arak worship the same mother goddess no matter where they live. Instead it is an identity, an indicator that tells people who their lineal blood relatives are. There are pargis in hundreds of other Bhil villages. Most are strangers to Kanji but if he meets pargis elsewhere, he knows they share a common blood heritage with him.

It is this sense of common heritage that affects marriage. Bhils, like most Indians, believe that clan (arak) mates are close relatives even though they may be strangers. Marriage with them is forbidden. To make sure incest is impossible, it is also forbidden to marry anyone from your mother's arak or your father's mother's arak, to say nothing of anyone else you know you are related to.

This point was driven home to me on another occasion when a neighbor of Kanji's, Kamalaji Kharadi, who was sitting smoking with several other men, asked me which arak I belonged to. Instead of letting it go at "McCurdy," I said that I didn't have an arak. I explained that Americans didn't have a kinship group similar to this, and that was why I had to ask questions about kinship.

My listeners didn't believe me. After all, I must have a father and you get your arak automatically from him. It is a matter of birth and all people are born. They looked at each other as if to say, "We wonder why he won't tell us what his arak is?", then tried again to get me to answer. My second denial led them to ask, "OK, then what is your wife's arak?" (If you can't get at it one way, then try another.) I answered that she didn't have an arak either. This caused a mild sensation. "Then how do you know if you have not married your own relative?", they asked, secretly, I think, delighted by the scandalous prospect.

The third step that occurred during the arrangement of Rupani's marriage came after the family had settled on a prospective groom. This step is the betrothal, and it took place when the groom's father and some of his lineage mates and neighbors paid a formal visit to Kanji's house. When they arrive, Kanji must offer his guests a formal meal, usually slaughtering a goat and distilling some liquor for the occasion. The bride, her face covered by her sari, will be brought out for a brief viewing, as well. But most of the time will be spent making arrangements—when will the actual wedding take place?; who will check the couple's horoscopes for fit?; how much will the bride price (also called bride wealth by many anthropologists) be?

Bride price (*dapa*) deserves special comment. It is usually a standard sum of money (about 700 rupees in 1985), although it may also include silver ornaments or other valuables. The dapa is given by the groom's father and his line to the parents of the bride. Bhils view this exchange as a compensation for the loss of the bride's services to her family. It also pays for a shift in her loyalty.

The exchange points up an important strain on families in patrilineal societies, the transfer of a woman from her natal family and line to those of her husband. This transfer includes not only her person, but her loyalty, labor, and children. Although she always will belong to her father's arak, she is now part of her husband's family, not his.

This problem is especially troublesome in India because of the close ties formed there by a girl and her parents. Parents know their daughter will leave when she marries, and they know that in her husband's house and village, she will be at a disadvantage. She will be alone, and out of respect for his parents her husband may not favor her wishes, at least in public. Because of this, they tend to give her extra freedom and support. In addition, they recognize the strain she will be under when she first goes to live with her new husband and his family. To ease her transition, they permit her to visit her parents frequently for a year or two. They also may try to marry her into a village where other women from Ratakote have married, so that she has some kin or at least supporters.

After her marriage, a woman's parents and especially her brothers find it hard not to care about her welfare. Their potential interest presents a built-in structural conflict that could strain relations between the two families if nothing were done about it.

A solution to this problem is to make the marriage into an exchange, and bride price is one result. Bride price also helps to dramatize the change in loyalty and obligation accompanying the bride's entrance into her new family.

Bhils have also devised a number of wedding rituals to dramatize the bride's shift in family membership. The bride must cry to symbolize that she is leaving her home. The groom ritually storms the bride's house at the beginning of the final ceremony. He does so like a conquering hero, drawing his sword to strike a ceremonial arch placed over the entrance while simultaneously stepping on a small fire (he wears a slipper to protect his foot), ritually violating the household's sacred hearth. At the end of the wedding, the groom, with some friends, engages in a mock battle with the bride's brothers and other young men, and symbolically abducts her. The meaning of this ritual is a dramatic equivalent of a father "giving away the bride" at American weddings.

One additional way of managing possible tension between in-laws is the application of respect behavior. The parents of the bride must always treat those of the groom and their relatives with respect. They must not joke in their presence, and they must use respectful language and defer to the groom's parents in normal conversation. In keeping with the strong patrilineal system, a groom may not accept important gifts from his wife's family except on ritual occasions, such as weddings, when exchange is expected. A groom may help support his own father, but he should not do so with his in-laws. That is up to their sons.

Bride price exchange also sets in motion a life-long process of mutual hospitality between the two families. Once the marriage has taken place, the families will become part of each other's feminal kin. They will exchange gifts on some ritual occasions, open their houses to each other, and, of course, help one another make future marriages.

The Future of Indian Kinship

On our last trip to India in 1994, my wife and I learned that Rupani had delivered three children since her wedding. Kanji had visited them a few months before we arrived, and he said that Rupani was happy and that he had wonderful grandchildren. But he also mentioned that her husband now spent most of his time in the nearby city of Udaipur working in construction there. He sent money home, but his absence left Rupani to run the house and raise the children by herself, although she did so with the assistance of his parents and lineage mates.

Rupani's case is not unusual. Every morning 70 or 80 men board one of the 20 or so busses that travel the road, now paved, that runs through Ratakote to the city. There they wait to be recruited by contractors for day labor at a low wage. If they are successful, gain special skills, or make good connections, they may get more permanent, better-paying jobs and live for weeks at a time in the city.

The reason they have to take this kind of work is simple. Ratakote has more than doubled in population since 1962. (The village had a population of 1,184 in 1963. By 1994 an estimate put the number at about 2,600.) There is not enough land for everyone to farm nor can the land produce enough to feed the growing population, even in abundant years. Work in the city is the answer, especially for householders whose land is not irrigated like Kanji's.

Cash labor has a potential to break down the kinship system that Bhils value so highly. It frees men and women from economic dependence on the family (since they make their own money working for someone else). It takes up time, too, making it difficult for them to attend the leisurely eleven-day weddings of relatives or meet other obligations to kin that require their presence. With cash labor, one's reputation is likely to hinge less on family than on work. For some, work means moving the family altogether. Devaji Katara, one of Kanji's neighbors, has a son who has moved with his wife and children to the Central Indian city of Indore. He has a good factory job there, and the move has kept them together. By doing so, however, he and they are largely removed from the kinship loop.

Despite these structural changes, kinship in Ratakote and for India as a whole remains exceptionally strong. Even though they may live farther away, Bhil sons and daughters still visit their families regularly. They send money home, and they try to attend weddings. They talk about their kin, too, and surprisingly, they continue the long process of arranging marriage for their children.

Perhaps one reason for kinship's vitality is the use to which kinship is put by many Indians. The people of Ratakote and other Indians have never given up teaching their children to respect their elders and subordinate their interests to those of the family. Family loyalty is still a paramount value. They use this loyalty to help each other economically. Family members hire each other in business. They take one another in during hard times. They offer hospitality to each other. Unlike Americans who feel guilty about accepting one-sided help from relatives, Indians look to the future. Giving aid now may pay off with a job or a favor later. Even if it doesn't, it is the proper thing to do.

Instead of breaking up the kinship network, work that takes men and families away from the village has simply stretched it out. An Indian student I know has found relatives in every American city he has visited. He knows of kin in Europe and southeast Asia too. Anywhere he goes he is likely to have relatives to stay with and to help him. When he settles down he will be expected to return the favor. Another Indian acquaintance, who went to graduate school in the United States and who continues to work here, has sent his father thousands of dollars to help with the building of a house. This act, which would surprise many Americans, seems perfectly normal to him.

Kanji is not disturbed by the economic changes that are overtaking the quiet agricultural pace of Ratakote. I last left him standing in front of his house with a grandson in his arms. His son, who had left the village in 1982 to be a "wiper" on a truck, returned to run the farm. He will be able to meet the family's obligation to lineage and feminal kin. For Kanji, traditional rules of inheritance have pulled a son and, for the moment at least, a grandson, back into the bosom of the family where they belong.

Review Questions

1. What are the main ways that kinship organizes Bhil society in Ratakote, according to McCurdy?

2. What is meant by the terms *clan, lineage, family, patrilineal descent, patrilocal residence, alliance, and feminal kin group?* Give examples of each.

3. Why do Bhil parents feel that marriage is too important a matter to be left up to their children?

4. What attributes do Bhil parents look for in a prospective bride or groom? How do young people try to influence the marriage partner their parents choose for them?

5. Although the U.S. kinship system seems limited by comparison to India's, many argue that it is more important than most of us think. Can you think of ways this might be true?

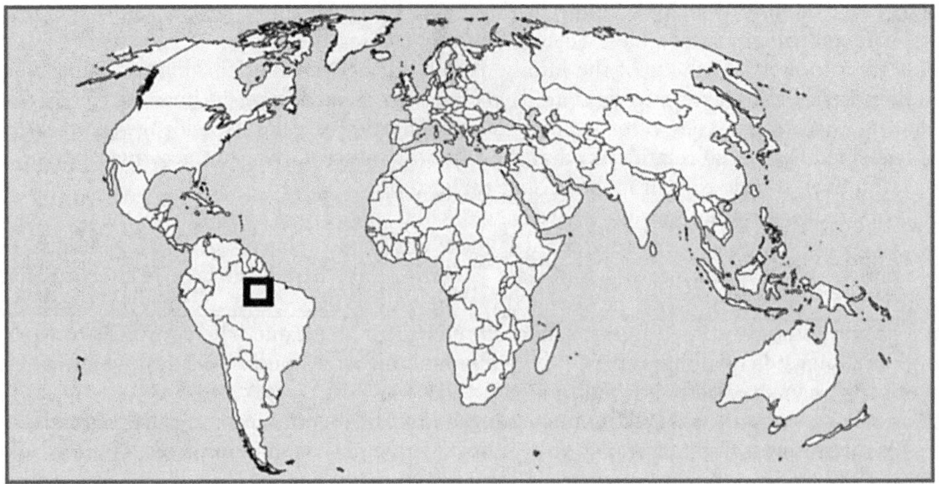

4/ The Kayapo Resistance

Terence Turner

Until about 200 years ago, vast areas of the world were inhabited by native, mostly hunter-gatherer or horticultural, peoples. Few native groups have survived the ravages of colonial and economic expansion, though, and those who are left seem destined to become victims of "progress." In this article, however, Terence Turner argues that "Fourth World" peoples—in this case the Kayapo of the Brazilian Amazon—have acted to conserve their own political autonomy while simultaneously aiding the world conservation movement. Apparently doomed to extinction by the relentless encroachment of Brazilian settlers, loggers, miners, and dam builders, the Kayapo have managed to mobilize not only themselves, but other Indians, environmentalists, legislators, and the world press in a united effort to defend the forest and their right to live in it.

As increasing numbers of people have become aware of the imminence of the destruction of the world's tropical forests and the probable consequences for the atmosphere and climate of the planet, voices have increasingly been heard drawing attention to the need for concern for human populations of forest dwellers, as well as the floral and faunal components of the ecosystem. This has been motivated in part by humanitarian concerns, in part by more specific concerns for indigenous political and legal rights, in part by an awareness that native forest peoples may possess valuable knowledge of their environments, and also, at times, by a realization that the traditional adaptive activities of such peoples may make important functional contributions to the ecosystems in which they live. Whatever their specific point of departure, however, advocates of native forest peoples have tended to assume that recognition of the rights and contributions of the native inhabitants of the forests, as well as their physical and cultural survival, would depend, like the salvation of the forests themselves, upon them. That native forest peoples themselves, many of whom number among the most primitive and remote human societies on earth, should come to play an important role as allies and even leaders in the world struggle to save the forests is a prospect so apparently remote as to seem only a little less improbable than Martians arriving to lend a hand. Yet this is precisely what has been happening in the last few years, nowhere with more impressive scope and success than in the case of the Kayapo Indians of the Brazilian Amazon.

The Kayapo: Ethnographic and Historical Background

The Kayapo are a nation of Ge-speaking Indians who inhabit the middle and lower reaches of the valley of the Xingu River, one of the major southern tributaries of the Amazon. Their total population is cur-

Turner, Terence. The Role of Indigenous Peoples in the Environmental Crisis: The Example of the Kayapo of the Brazilian Amazon. *Perspectives in Biology and Medicine* 36:3 (1993), 526–545.

rently around 2,500, divided among 14 mutually independent communities. The largest of these communities, Gorotire, has about 800 inhabitants, but several others are little more than hamlets. Kayapo country is a mixture of forest and savannah land, with rather more forest than open country around most of the villages. The total area covered by Kayapo communities and their associated land-use patterns is about the size of Scotland.

The massive destruction of the Amazonian environment represented by the cutting and burning of the forest, the cutting of roads, and the soil erosion and river pollution caused by mining and the building of giant hydroelectric dams, have had a shattering impact on the environment and way of life of many forest Indians of the Amazon. Even groups whose lands have not yet been reached by these activities, or are just beginning to be affected by them, now live in the permanent shadow of the threat. To understand the meaning of this threat for indigenous peoples like the Kayapo, one must stand in a Kayapo village under the dense clouds of smoke that now darken the sky over Kayapo country at the end of every dry season, as Brazilian squatters and ranchers burn off vast stretches of previously forested land to the east and south, rapidly approaching the traditional borders of Kayapo territory along a 700-mile front. It is to feel one's world burning, with the ring of fire drawing even tighter.

For members of modern industrial societies, one of the most difficult points to grasp about the relation of native tropical forest peoples to their environment, as articulated through their modes of subsistence production, is that the relationship is not felt or conceived to comprise a separate, "economic" sphere in our sense. Rather, it forms an integral part of the total social process of producing human beings and social life. The threatened annihilation of such a society's environmental base of subsistence is therefore not felt merely as an "economic" threat, nor one that can be located and confined in an external, "environmental" sphere. It is a threat to the continuity and meaning of social life. Understanding this point is essential, not only to appreciate the traumatic effects of wholesale ecological devastation on traditional societies of subsistence producers like the Kayapo, but also to understand the nature of their political response and resistance to such threats.

The Relation of the Kayapo to the Environment through Subsistence Production

For the Kayapo, like most other contemporary Amazonian native peoples, traditional patterns of subsistence adaptation are still the basic way of life. The Kayapo produce their means of subsistence by a combination of slash-and-burn horticulture, hunting, fishing, and foraging. According to the division of labor by gender and generation, men engage in all productive pursuits incompatible with the care of young children, while women perform those which can be carried out while caring for children. This means that men hunt, fish, do the heavy and dangerous work of clearing gardens, and gather certain wild forest products that grow at great distances, requiring overnight journeys. Women do the planting, weeding, and harvesting of gardens; cut firewood; cook the food; build traditional shelters (now done almost exclusively in trekking camps); forage for such wild products as can be found within a day's round-trip walk from the village or camp; and care for children. Girls begin to help their mothers with household and garden chores while still children, but boys do little productive labor until they are inducted into the men's house, a bachelors' dormitory and men's club which stands apart from the family houses in the middle of the round village plaza.

Kayapo gardens must be cleared from fresh forestland and produce for about three years for most crops. The Kayapo raise an impressive variety of garden produce: manioc (both the bitter and sweet varieties), maize, bananas, yams, sweet potatoes, fava beans, squash, *cissus* (a leafy creeper that is a unique domesticate of their own), tobacco, *urucu* (used to make red body paint), and cotton (used to make string, but not woven). In recent years, many Kayapo have added Brazilian-introduced crops such as papaya, rice, various species of beans, pineapples, watermelon, avocado, and mango. Most families maintain about three gardens in production at any one time and clear a new one every year. After a garden is abandoned, it requires about 25 years for reforestation to render it ready for reuse. A sizable village therefore needs an extensive area of forestland for the rotation of its garden plots.

The Kayapo supplement their horticultural diet with large quantities of fish and game. Included among the latter are wild pig, tapir, deer, monkey, tortoise, armadillo, and various species of birds and rodents. Gathered wild produce is also seasonally important, and includes *babassu* coconuts (used for body and hair oil), *piki, tucum,* and brazil nuts, honey, palmito, *acai, bacaba,* and a variety of less important fruits. Hunting or fishing for the men, and gardening for the women, are more or less daily activities while the community is settled in its base village.

For considerable periods of the year, however, the Kayapo abandon their base villages and go off on collective seminomadic treks through the surrounding forest and savannah. These may last from one to three months, and may take one of several forms. Individual age-sets (most frequently, the male bachelors' set) may be sent out to gather seasonally ripening nuts or fruits; the whole village may go together; the individual senior men's societies may trek as separate groups, each with its associated women, children, and bachelor dependents; or only part of the village may go on trek to gather food for a ceremonial feast, while the rest remain behind in the village. A community may go on two or three such treks per year, so that at least some of the village may spend as much as half the year on trek. Large areas may thus be covered by all the treks undertaken by the members of a single village in a given year. In spite of the low population density of Kayapo country, therefore, most of the area is actually used by the mobile trekking groups which continually sally forth from the widely scattered base villages.

The regular alternation between trekking and base village occupation thus appears to be an integral aspect of Kayapo social organization. Why this should be so is not immediately apparent. Trekking by large collective groups is a relatively inefficient way to exploit the wild floral and faunal resources of an area. Only the adult men of the camp do any hunting. The bachelors and younger boys are typically occupied either with clearing the trail to the next day's campsite and the campsite itself, or bringing up horticultural produce from the village gardens, while the women occupy themselves with pitching or breaking camp, cutting firewood, preparing food, and tending children. The camp is moved every one or two days, but usually only for a distance of one or two kilometers, about a 15-minute walk. More game could doubtless be captured by small groups of men working alone, free to move more rapidly over greater distances. Hunting and fishing are routinely done in this way while the community is residing in the base village, and it is certainly no less productive than the hunting done on trek. Trekking by whole communities or large groups, in other words, cannot be accounted for as the most efficient available method of acquiring needed protein or other foodstuffs.

A similar question arises over the frequency with which Kayapo bands moved their village sites in the days before peaceful relations were established with the Brazilians. There is in fact no ecological reason why Kayapo villages as large as two thousand would ever need to move as a group from their permanent village sites to remain supplied with the foods they require. Notwithstanding this fact, Kayapo villages before pacification tended to move as often as every two, or more usually five to ten years. A given community would have as many as a dozen village sites, and occupy most of them over a twenty-year period. This frequency of movement, again, cannot be accounted for simply as a result of material necessity. In common with trekking, it seems part of a dynamic inherent in Kayapo social organization.

The Social Meaning of Subsistence Production

The high mobility of Kayapo society, and the large amount of territory it requires in consequence, thus cannot be understood, as some have attempted to do, as the result of nutritional deficiencies in the soil or lack of protein or other nutrients in the faunal or floral environment. They are, rather, the corollaries and effects of the organization of Kayapo society, with its central tension between female-centered and male-centered forms of social grouping. These forms themselves, however, are articulated in terms of their complementary roles in production, although this is production understood in the Kayapo sense of the social production of human beings and social relations, which includes but is not reducible to, material subsistence. This notion of social production calls for a more extended exegesis as it is essential to an understanding of the Kayapo relationship to their natural environment and their society per se.

Kayapo patterns of environmental adaptation and subsistence production are intricately interwoven with their ways of producing human individuals. This process of human production includes what we call "socializing" children, but continues through the life cycle and the final rites of death. This individual process, in turn, is treated by the Kayapo as an integral part of the process of reproducing collective social units like extended-family households, age-sets, and ceremonial organizations, and thus of society as a whole. As I have already indicated, the division of labor in the production of material subsistence is defined in relation to the division of labor in the production of social persons and relations, with women specializing in the socialization of children. It must be clearly understood that this is not simply a natural result but a culturally imposed social pattern. Women who do not happen to be raising young children nevertheless do not go hunting and fishing. At a higher level of organization, the nuclear family forms the social unit of cooperation in the production and consumption of material subsistence, but as a social unit it owes its form primarily to its role in producing new social persons, not its functions in expediting subsistence activities. Subsistence production thus finds its place as an integral part of the global process of social production, which also includes the socialization of children, the recruitment and reconstitution of families and collective groups, and the celebration of the great communal ceremonies. In these two-to-four month long symbolic dramas, all of these levels of activity are performed in an orchestrated pattern that asserts their essential interdependence as parts of a single whole.

The Kayapo attitude toward the nonhuman natural environment must be understood as a part of this same global pattern. The Kayapo do not oppose "nature" to human society as mutually exclusive, externally related domains; nor can they be said to possess a single, uniform concept of "nature" in our sense. They recognize that the forest and savannah beyond their village clearings are products of forces that are independent of humans and not under social control. They further recognize that they depend upon these natural forces and products for their own social existence, and that social persons are in fact largely "natural" beings, whose physical bodies, senses, and libidinal energies are as extra-social in origin as any forest tree or wild animal. Disease, death, shamanic trance, insanity, and periods of transition in [life]-crisis ritual are seen as moments when the continuity between the internal natural core of human social actors and the external natural environment of the forest and animal world asserts itself, short-circuiting and blacking out the interposed, insulating social veneer. At such times, the social person reverts to a "natural" state, here conceived as one of entropic dissolution of social form. At other times, as in the rituals of initiation at puberty or the everyday bringing in of game, gathered nuts, or garden produce from the forest, displacing or penetrating the boundary between nature and society has the opposite result: an infusion of energy which, directed into social channels, enables society to exist and renew itself. Human beings and society itself, in sum, are seen as partly "natural" entities, dependent on continual infusions of energy from their natural surroundings. The reproduction of human society, the reproduction of socialized human beings, and the reproduction of the natural forest and savannah environment are thus interconnected parts of a single great process.

Society and its members, in sum, are essentially seen as appropriating and channeling natural energy, and are thus dependent on the ability of the natural world (meaning the forest, animals, birds, rivers, and fish) to reproduce itself and continue as a great reservoir and source of the energy society must continually draw upon to live. The destruction of the forest, the killing or driving away of its animals, or the pollution of the rivers and killing of their fish, therefore, are not seen by the Kayapo simply as an attack on "the natural environment" in our sense, but as a direct assault upon them as a society and as individuals.

This view, it should immediately be added, is fully compatible with the destruction of trees and animals on a considerable scale for appropriation by the Kayapo of the energy stored in their flesh, fruits, or the soil on which they stand. The Kayapo operate with a rough rule of thumb derived from millennia of experience, a sense of the ability of the local environment to accommodate a certain level of destruction, inflicted by their traditional modes and levels of subsistence activity, and still regenerate itself. They have no mystical sense of reverence or respect for individual trees or animals and feel no hesitation about chopping them down or taking them as game whenever their interests demand. What concerns the Kayapo is nature in the aggregate, or more specifically, the survival and reproduction of a sufficient slice of the natural environment to support their traditional way of life. It was only when they realized that this aggregate capacity for regeneration was threatened by the vast scale of the destruction now being inflicted on the area that the Kayapo became aroused over the fate of the forest environment as such. Similarly, ecological concerns for tropical rain forests became transformed into urgent political issues in the developed world only when peoples of the developed countries realized the probable consequences of this destruction from the rest of the world's climate and population. Kayapo and First World modes of "ecological" consciousness and concern converged, in short, when, starting from very different premises, the members of both societies realized that the survival of their societies was at stake. The dramatic results of this convergence are the subject of the rest of this paper.

The Kayapo Resistance and the Environmentalist Movement

The Kayapo area of Southern Para state is a representative microcosm of the destructive processes at work in the Amazon as a whole. Beginning in the late 1960s, the Kayapo have been confronted with virtually every major form of environmental destruction and land depredation found elsewhere in the region.

The Kayapo Face the End of Their World

Since the 1960s there has been constant pressure from small squatters and large ranchers attempting to infiltrate Kayapo areas and clear small farms by burning off patches of forest. Land speculators have attempted to build illegal airstrips and to survey and sell off large chunks of Kayapo land to which they did not even hold legal title. In 1971, the Brazilian government built a major road of the Trans-Amazonica highway system through Kayapo country, secretly altering the route so as to amputate the Kayapo area of the Xingu National Park, which it then attempted to sell off to private owners, mostly speculators, would-be ranchers, and farmers. The road brought heavy truck and bus traffic carrying settlers and supplies to the new settlements farther west, bringing with them the perils of infectious disease and the potential for conflict with the Indians. Timber companies interested in the large stands of virgin mahogany within the boundaries of the remaining officially delimited Kayapo reserve, the Kayapo Indigenous Area, sought and obtained logging concessions for large tracts from Kayapo leaders in exchange for sizable money payments and the construction of modern housing and other facilities in Kayapo villages. Most of the money went into communal accounts in banks in neighboring frontier towns. These accounts were either explicitly or tacitly controlled by chiefs or the few literate Kayapo able to keep the accounts. Some of these individuals began to draw heavily on these "communal" funds for personal use, giving rise to tension and resentment by the rest of their communities. Rivalries between competing companies and their respective Kayapo sponsors almost led to war between two Kayapo villages in 1986.

The discovery of gold at the huge mine of Serra Pelada near the eastern border of the Kayapo Indigenous Area led to intense prospecting and exploratory gold-mining activity within the eastern borders of the Kayapo Indigenous Area. This culminated in 1983 with the opening of two large illegal gold mines only ten kilometers from Gorotire village. Three thousand Brazilian miners swarmed onto Kayapo land, and neither the Brazilian Indian Service (FUNAI) nor any other arm of the Brazilian government seemed willing or able to do anything to stop it. Tons of mercury from the mining operations began to pollute the Rio Fresco, the main fishery of several Kayapo communities. Then, in 1986, an even more ominous form of pollution threatened, when radioactive waste from a cancer treatment facility in the city of Goiania caused two dozen fatalities, and the federal government attempted to dump the material on the western border of Kayapo country.

As if all this were not enough, the Kayapo began to hear rumors that the Brazilian government was planning to build a series of hydroelectric dams along the Xingu and its tributaries, which would result in the flooding of large areas of Kayapo land and end the value of most of the river system as a fishery. The scheme was to be funded by loans from the World Bank. Repeated attempts to learn the truth about the government's plans were met with stonewalling and denials that any such plan existed. The rumors persisted, however, and construction sites began to be cleared at certain points along the river. The Kayapo were outraged by the government's disregard for their political and legal rights to be consulted about a project which would so heavily affect their lands and livelihood. They were equally concerned about the ecological effects. While Kayapo leaders strove unsuccessfully to penetrate the government's cover-up about the dam project, however, they were confronted by an even more direct threat to their legal and political rights, as Indians, to challenge governmental or private Brazilian infringements of their land rights, resources, or communal interests. At the convention called to draw up the new Brazilian constitution, a measure was introduced calling for the redefinition of any Indian who demonstrated the capacity to bring a legal action in a Brazilian court as an "acculturated" person who could no longer be considered an Indian, and therefore could no longer represent or bring an action on behalf of an Indian community in court. This "catch-22" provision would have destroyed the possibility of any legal or political resistance by native peoples against abuses of their rights, persons, lands, or environments within the terms of the Brazilian legal and political process.

This daunting array of threats to the Kayapo environment, communal lands and resource base, political and civil rights is a representative sample of the human face of the environmental crisis in the Amazon. The Kayapo confronted this apparently overwhelming onslaught beginning in the early 1970s as a still largely monolingual people of Ge-speakers scattered over a vast area in 14 mutually autonomous and politically uncoordinated settlements. In most of the villages, some of the men (but almost no women) spoke Portuguese, and a handful had learned to read, write, and do simple arithmetic. A few leaders had obtained some experience of Brazilian administrative and political ways through working in the Indian Service or as members of Brazilian expeditions to contact other tribes. They had a few contacts with the outside world through anthropologists and indigenous advocacy groups, and the Brazilian Indian Service (FUNAI) offered some support, although it could not be counted upon to represent the Indians' interests against the more threatening forms of economic development mounted by government or powerful private interests. Aside from this slender array of assets, the Kayapo had no political resources with which to defend themselves and their forest beyond their own largely intact tribal institutions and culture. These, however, were to serve them well in the trials that lay ahead.

The Kayapo Resistance

This is what they did. The two western communities whose land had been severed by the road began an unrelenting campaign of armed attacks on all Brazilian intruders who attempted to open ranches or settle in the separated area. After 15 years and perhaps 50 Brazilian dead, with no Kayapo casualties, no Brazilian settler remained in the entire area. The leaders of the two Kayapo groups meanwhile carried out a campaign of diplomacy, making repeated trips to Brasília to pressure the government to return the stolen land and thus end the violent standoff in the area. The government capitulated in 1985, returning the area to the Kayapo and ceding an additional area immediately to the north of the old area (this became the Capoto Indigenous Area). The two communities of the region joined again into a single large village and have resolutely banned all Brazilian mining, timber, and agricultural interests and settlers from their reclaimed areas.

Also in 1985, the two illegally opened gold mines were assaulted and captured by 200 Kayapo, armed with a mixture of firearms and traditional weapons. The larger mine was accessible only by air, so the Kayapo seized and blockaded the landing strip, confronting the Brazilian government with a choice: either cede title and administrative authority over the mines to the Kayapo, together with a significant percentage of the proceeds (10% was the amount initially demanded), and legally demarcate the boundaries of the Kayapo Indigenous Area (thus making the government unambiguously responsible for the defense of the area against any further such incursions), or the Kayapo would allow no more planes to land or take off, either to supply or evacuate the three thousand miners at the site. After a tense ten-day standoff, the government gave in to the Kayapo demands.

The leaders of Gorotire, the nearest and largest Kayapo village, used the first income from the mine to purchase a light plane and hire a Brazilian pilot. They put the plane to use to patrol their borders from the air to spot intruders and would-be squatters. If any were seen, patrols were dispatched to expel or eliminate the invaders. Within a year, invasions effectively ceased. They have also used the plane to fly to other Kayapo villages and to Brazilian cities to purchase goods and bring people out for medical assistance. In the nearest town of Redencao, and the state capital of Belem, they have bought houses for the use of Kayapo travelers and shoppers, and in the former they have established a tribal office to deal with their bank accounts and official relations with the local office of FUNAI.

All timber concessions on Kayapo land were suspended by the Indian Service (FUNAI) at the end of 1987, at the urging of the most influential Kayapo leaders, Payakan and Ropni. Some concessions, however, were surreptitiously continued by a few other leaders who have lined their own pockets with the fees paid by the companies. Still other communities and leaders not previously involved with lumbering companies are under great pressure from the companies to grant new concessions. Meanwhile, resistance to any new concessions continues to be strong, and one community (A'Ukre) has declared its part of the Kayapo Indigenous Area an "extractive reserve" closed to all ecologically destructive forms of timber and mineral exploitation. This remains a conflicted issue, with the ultimate outcome in doubt. Meanwhile, a substantial area of the Kayapo Indigenous Area has been clear-cut. The fate of the captured gold mines has also proved a divisive issue. Not only have the Kayapo not closed them down, as they originally said they would do within two years of taking them over, but some Kayapo have opened a couple of small new mines on their own land. Other Kayapo vigorously oppose this and have strictly prohibited all mining activity, whether by Brazilians or Kayapo, from their areas of the reserve. Meanwhile, five Gorotire Kayapo have become wealthy enough from the gold and timber revenues to buy private houses for themselves in Redencao, where they live for much of the time, keeping Brazilian servants and, in two cases, acquiring large ranches outside the reserve. This phenomenon has been paralleled by the chief of the village of Kikretum, who owns an airplane, houses, and a hotel in the neighboring town of Tucuma. The rise of this embryonic "new class" has already given rise to significant tensions within Kayapo society and is a factor in the unresolved conflicts over the future form of accommodation between Kayapo society and the Brazilian economy.

Most of the other threats posed by the enveloping national society proved less divisive, and the Kayapo were able to mount concerted, well-organized responses to them without internal dissension or conflict. When the government's plan to dump the radioactive waste on traditional Kayapo land was announced, the Kayapo sent a hundred men to Brasília to demonstrate against the plan. Suitably painted and feathered, they staged a sit-in in the president's palace. Nothing like this had happened in Brazil in the twenty years since the coup d'etat that established the military regime that was then in the process of relinquishing power. The initial incredulity and indignation of the authorities, however, gave way to acquiescence to the Kayapo's demands, and the dumping plan was abandoned. Pressing their advantage, the Kayapo next sent a deputation of some 50 chiefs and leading citizens to the Constitutional Convention to lobby for the defeat of the "catch-22" acculturation clause and other provisions injurious to Indian interests. Presenting themselves as always, in traditional paint and feathers and carrying traditional weapons, they patiently attended the weeks of debates on the sections bearing on indigenous peoples' rights, gave press conferences, and lobbied the deputies. When the acculturation clause was defeated, and surprisingly strong safeguards of indigenous rights, lands, and resources were adopted by the Convention, the Kayapo received much of the credit in the Brazilian press.

In 1988, two Kayapo leaders were invited to the United States to participate in a conference on tropical forest ecology. From there, they traveled to Washington, met with members of Congress, and spoke with World Bank officials about the effects of the proposed Xingu dam scheme on the peoples and environment of the area. They were able to obtain copies of the entire dam proj-ect, the very existence of which the Brazilian government had continued to deny, from the Bank. Shortly after the Kayapos' visit, the World Bank announced that it was deferring action on the Brazilian loan request. Enraged, elements of the Brazilian national security and political establishment had criminal charges brought against them and their American interpreter under a law prohibiting participation in political activity in Brazil by foreigners. The charges were ridiculous in strictly legal terms; since the actions in question had taken place in the United States, the American had been acting in his own country, and the Kayapo were not in any case foreigners. The transparent attempt at legal terrorism boomeranged, as nongovernment organizations (NGOs), anthropologists, and the congressmen whom the Kayapo had met on their tour organized an international outcry.

When one of the Kayapo leaders came to Belem, the capital of the state of Para, where the charges had been brought, to be arraigned, the Kayapo organized a massive protest demonstration. More than five hundred Kayapo men and women danced through the streets and massed in the square before the Palace of Justice to support their kinsman and denounce Brazilian political repression. The defiance turned to ridicule when the judge refused to allow the Kayapo leader to enter the courthouse for arraignment until he changed his paint and feathers for "civilized" (Brazilian) clothes. The Kayapo refused and told the judge he would have to come to the Kayapo village of Gorotire if he wanted another chance to arraign him on the charges. Meanwhile, Kayapo orators unrolled the map of the Xingu dam scheme obtained from the World Bank in Washington on an easel erected in the square and explained the entire secret project in Kayapo and Portuguese for the benefit of the many Brazilian onlookers, who included reporters and TV crews. The government never again dared to try to arraign the Kayapo leader, and eventually dropped all the charges.

With the World Bank still actively considering the Brazilian government's request for a loan to enable the building of the Xingu dams, the proposed multi-dam hydroelectric scheme in the Xingu River valley now appeared to the Kayapo as the greatest threat, not only to their environment, but to their political and legal control over their lands and resources. Since the government still refused to disclose its plans to build the dams, the Kayapo resolved to force it to reveal its intentions and to receive, before an audience of national and world news media, their criticisms of the human and environmental effects of the dams, as well as of its deceit in attempting to conceal and deny its plans. To accomplish this, they decided to convene in great congress of Amazonian peoples at the site of the first of the dams the government hoped to build: Altamira, near the mouth of the Xingu. To the meeting would be invited representatives of the Brazilian government's representatives of the World Bank; representatives of the national and world news media; nongovernmental organizations active in the environmentalist, human rights, and indigenous peoples' support fields; delegates from as many indigenous nations of Amazonia as possible; and as many Kayapo as could be transported and accommodated. At the meeting, the government representatives would be asked to present their plans, to give an account of their probable effects on the environment and the human inhabitants of the region (Brazilian as well as native), and to explain why they had tried for so long to keep their plans secret from those who would be most affected by them.

The Kayapo leaders who envisioned this project saw that its success would depend on international public opinion, press attention, and financial support. Only the attendance of a large number of media and NGO representatives, they felt, would compel the Brazilian government to send its representatives to face certain humiliation at such a meeting. The leader chiefly responsible for the plan, Payakan, therefore embarked on a tour of seven European and North American countries (sponsored and coordinated by Friends of the Earth, the World Wildlife Federation, and the Kayapo Support Group of Chicago) in November, 1988, to publicize the Altamira gathering and appeal for support. At a more general level, Payakan also sought to bring the crisis of the Amazon forest and its native peoples to wider public attention, and to lobby government and international development bank officials against supporting economic development projects (such as the Xingu dam scheme) that would irreversibly damage the environment and require the expropriation or destruction of native lands.

Payakan, at the same time, also sought to bring about greater mutual trust, cooperation, and unity of purpose among the various kinds of nongovernmental organizations and sectors of public opinion involved in supporting the Indians and the environmental struggle. These included human rights, indigenous peoples' advocacy, anthropological, and environmentalist organizations. Among the latter were some groups specifically devoted to defending tropical rain forests, others concerned with saving endangered animal species, and still others dedicated to conservation and environmental quality in a more general sense. Payakan, in his dealings with these groups or their representatives, had quickly realized that they tended to work in isolation from one another, often mistrusted one another's politics, or viewed one another's work as irrelevant to their own concerns. With other Kayapo leaders, Payakan saw this situation as not only damaging the effectiveness of the work of these organizations, but as out of touch with the real interconnections of the issues with which the groups were attempting to deal. For both reasons, they felt, the support of the NGOs was less effective than it might otherwise be. Payakan therefore devoted much effort on his tour to appealing to these groups to join forces and recognize that they were really all involved in a single great struggle. As he put it in a speech at the University of Chicago:

> The forest is one big thing; it has people, animals, and plants. There is no point saving the animals if the forest is burned down; there is no point saving the forest if the people and animals who live in it are killed or driven away. The groups trying to save the races of animals cannot win if the people trying to save the forest lose; the people trying to save the Indians cannot win if either of the others lose; the Indians cannot win without the support of these groups; but the groups cannot win either without the support of the Indians, who know the forest and the animals and can tell what is happening to them. No one of us is strong enough to win alone; together, we can be strong enough to win.

Payakan's message was widely heard. His tour became a concrete example of the intergroup cooperation he preached. For many indigenous advocacy organizations, environmentalist groups, human rights groups, Latin Americanist social scientists and anthropologists, helping to organize Payakan's tour and attending his speeches was their first practical experience of cooperating and coming together around a common set of interests and commitments. This experience has been continually repeated since then in a series of cooperative efforts to support the Altamira meeting, aid new organizational initiatives by the Kayapo and other forest peoples in Brazil, and help with subsequent tours by Payakan and other Kayapo leaders. It is generally recognized by activists of the various support organizations concerned that the Kayapo campaign has become an important catalyst of increased contact and cooperation among them at the national and international level, and that this cooperation has brought increased efficacy in lobbying, fund-raising, and public opinion outreach efforts.

Payakan's tour successfully achieved all its goals. Enough money was raised to defray all the costs of the Altamira gathering (which eventually approached $100,000) without drawing upon any of the funds derived from timber or gold concessions, which Payakan and most of his closest Kayapo supporters opposed. Much publicity and media attention was generated, guaranteeing a strong international media presence at the Altamira gathering itself. The support base of the Kayapo campaign among European and American nongovernmental organizations, public opinion, and politicians was greatly strengthened. The stage was now set for one of the most remarkable events in the history of Amazonia, the environmentalist movement, and modern popular protest politics.

From February 19–24, 1989, 600 Amazonian Indians and a roughly equal number of Brazilian and international journalists, photographers, TV crews, documentary filmmakers, Brazilian and foreign politicians, and representatives of various nongovernmental support organizations converged on the small river town of Altamira. Among the Indians were some 500 Kayapo and 100 members of 40 other indigenous nations, whom the Kayapo had invited to join them in confronting the Brazilian government, and to make their own views on the issues of dams and the destruction of the forest known to the government representatives, the news media, and one another. Five days of meetings, speeches, press conferences, and ritual performances by Kayapo and other indigenous groups were programmed and carried out without a major hitch. The event represented an impressive feat of organization and political coordination. It required the transportation, lodging, and feeding of hundreds of indigenous participants, which involved constructing a large encampment with traditional Kayapo shelters outside the town and daily busing of its inhabitants to the meeting hall in the center. Much of the credit for the event belongs to the Brazilian indigenous peoples' support organization, The Ecumenical Center for Documentation and Information (CEDI), which effectively cooperated with Payakan and the rest of the indigenous leadership in handling many of the logistical tasks essential to the success of the meeting.

Some elements of the regional Brazilian populace, especially those linked with landowning and commercial interests who stood to gain from the construction of the dams, were hostile to the Indians and (even more) their Brazilian and foreign environmentalist supporters. There were fears that violent incidents might occur and spread out of control. That this did not happen can be attributed in part to the foresight and discipline of the Kayapo, who carefully sited their encampment far outside of town and refrained from street demonstrations within the city limits, but also in large measure to the presence of so many foreign and domestic media personnel and observers.

The event took on the aspect of an international media circus. The Pope sent a telegram of support. The rock star Sting flew in for a day and gave a press conference at the Kayapo encampment, denouncing the destruction of the forest and promoting his own project for the creation of a new Kayapo reserve. No doubt because this project depended on the goodwill of the Brazilian government, Sting avoided directly committing himself in support of the Kayapo campaign against the dams. Since this was the whole purpose of the Altamira meeting, his Kayapo hosts roundly criticized him for using their platform for his own project and then skipping off. A British member of Parliament, a Belgian member of the European Parliament, and a half-dozen Brazilian deputies of the National Congress, however, mounted the platform and gave unreserved support. A final communique was issued, on behalf of all native peoples of Amazonia, condemning the dam project. By the time the conference closed with a dance from the Kayapo New Corn ceremony (joined in by assorted Indians of other tribes, European and Brazilian activists and media personnel, momentarily giving it the air of a 1960s hippie love-in), the Altamira gathering had become an international media success of such proportions as to generate serious political pressure against any international funding of the dam scheme, or indeed any attempt to go on with the plan by the Brazilian government. Within two weeks after the end of the meeting, the World Bank announced that it would not grant the Brazilian loan earmarked for the dam project, and the Brazilian National Congress had announced plans for a formal investigation and debate on the whole plan.

The Kayapo have not rested on their laurels since Altamira. One major line of effort was the drive to get a large area of the west bank of the Xingu demarcated as a third major Kayapo reserve, linking the two largest existing reserves (the Capoto and Kayapo Indigenous Areas) in a continuous area the size of Britain. In this effort, the Kayapo were supported by Sting and his recently founded Rainforest Foundation, which raised close to two million dollars to support the project. President Sarney of Brazil made several public statements vaguely in favor of the plan, but in January 1990, when Sting came to Brazil with the money from the Rainforest Foundation to present to the government to start the demarcation of the reserve, Sarney noncommitally passed the buck by merely extending the official period for administrative decision on the proposal into the new administration of President-elect Collor without taking action. Collor finally proclaimed the new reserve in 1991; the actual demarcation of the boundary was finished in September 1992. The demarcation of the new reserve bears witness to the political pressure the Kayapo, and the Rainforest Foundation with its international and Brazilian support, were able to bring to bear. Meanwhile, Payakan established a Kayapo Foundation (the "Fundacao Mebengokre") to administer and raise money for the support of a series of programs, including the establishment of an "extractive reserve" within the Kayapo Indigenous Area. This is an area off-limits to all lumbering and mining operations, devoted exclusively to environmentally sustainable forms of forest exploitation such as the gathering of Brazil nuts and other wild forest products.

The Kayapo also made some attempt to follow up on the links of solidarity with other indigenous Amazonian peoples forged at Altamira. In November 1989, several Kayapo leaders and a Kayapo video-cameraman flew (in a Kayapo plane) to Boa Vista in the northern frontier state of Rondonia to investigate an incident in which Yanomamo villagers had been attacked and driven from their land by Brazilian gold miners. The Kayapo denounced the government policies leading to the incident and declared their support for the survivors. The government had banned the area to all non-Indians after the occurrence, attempting to cover up the affair and keep it out of the press. The government was clearly thinking only of local Yanomamo Indians, but the Kayapo, seizing upon the loophole opened up by the wording of the ban and capitalizing on their undeniable identity as "Indians," were able to penetrate the official smokescreen with their fact-finding and support mission.

Wider Implications: The Kayapo Achievement in World Perspective

The Environmentalist Movement

At the level of international environmentalist politics, the Kayapo are now an established presence. In 1990 alone, Kayapo spokesmen have traveled to various European countries, Canada, the U.S.A., and Japan. They were accorded audiences by heads of state (Mitterand of France), cabinet ministers responsible for loans, aid and financial dealings with Brazil, and members of parliaments and national assemblies (Canada, France, Belgium, England, and the U.S.A.). They have also met with indigenous groups and leaders in North America, notably the Cree of Northern Quebec in 1991 and 1992. All of this notoriety and attention has generated for them a measure of immunity from the cruder forms of abuse and exploitation that have so often been the lot of indigenous peoples in Amazonia and elsewhere.

A mere ten years ago, however, they themselves were the targets of many such abuses, as recounted above. They have succeeded, against fantastic odds, in turning the tables on their would-be exploiters and seizing the political advantage, drawing upon the support of international and urban Brazilian public opinion. The strength of this support owes much to the worldwide wave of concern for the fate of the tropical forests, but the Kayapo would not have been able to capitalize so effectively on the general climate of environmental concern without their shrewd grasp of the possibilities of contemporary news and informational media and their effective presentation of themselves and their cause through them. Other factors in the Kayapo successes have been the effective support of numerous nongovernmental organizations and the impressive capacity of the Kayapo themselves for mass organization and militant but disciplined confrontational tactics, as exemplified by their bold but nonviolent demonstrations in Brasília, Belem, and Altamira.

The success of the Kayapo in furthering their own cause, at the same time, has had an important effect upon the politics of the developed world, and in particular, of the environmentalist movement. The support of environmentalist groups and public opinion has been essential to the Kayapo victories, but it is equally true that the Kayapo have won important victories for the environmentalist movement, and partly as a result have exercised an important influence upon its thinking, strategies, and organizational tactics. Perhaps most importantly, in a few short years they have revolutionized the consciousness of many activists and ordinary persons concerned with the fate of the world's tropical forests, teaching them that indigenous forest-dwelling peoples are not just a passive part of the problem, but an active part of the solution. By their own example, they have demonstrated that native forest peoples, no matter how apparently primitive, remote, or numerically insignificant, can become potent combatants and allies in the struggle to avert ecological disaster. In addition, they have helped bring about working relations of mutual trust and collaboration between members of a number of important organizations, scientific specialists, and politicians, who had previously never considered working together, and in many cases mistrusted one another's politics and policies.

Before the advent of the Kayapo on the international stage, many environmentalists had realized that there could be no solution to the problem of saving the forests that did not include the human inhabitants of the forests. Many who had arrived at this relatively enlightened opinion, however, continued to think of aboriginal forest peoples, and even forest-dwelling members of national societies like the Brazilian rubber-tappers, as historical basket cases, with all the capacity for political action in their own behalf of endangered animal species like the black cayman or the Amazonian giant otter. It has been a humbling, disconcerting, but delightful surprise to many of these same good people suddenly to discover that some of these supposedly hapless victims of progress have assumed a leading role in the struggle environmentalists had thought (perhaps a tad condescendingly) they were leading, and that these same native peoples have even succeeded in bringing to the effort a degree of unity and effectiveness that had previously eluded its familiar leadership.

The Rise of Ecological Resistance in the Fourth World

The Kayapo are not a unique case. Their story, in fact, conforms in its essential features to an emerging pattern of ethnic self-assertiveness and ecological militancy on the part of native forest peoples in the Amazon and other parts of the world. It is not new for native peoples (to refer, by this term, to the tribal societies and ethnic minorities comprising the "Fourth World") to attempt to resist the wholesale appropriation of their lands and resources by the peoples and governments of modern states. What is new is the combination of political, economic, environmental, and ideological pressures with revolutionary new media technologies that has enabled native peoples to take their case directly to the peoples and governments of the world, and to find a receptive hearing because of the convergence of their cause with the new levels of popular concern over the environment.

One major manifestation of this worldwide pattern is the organization, over the past twenty years, of many federations of native peoples, for the most part consisting of groups speaking the same or related languages. Over 50 such groups now exist in the Amazon alone. They typically unite around a program of defense of native land and resources, respect for civil and political rights, and the assertion of traditional values and cultural identity. These groups are increasingly in touch with one another, and in some areas intergroup coordinating organizations, such as the recently organized Coordinating Group of the Amazon Basin, COICA, have begun to appear.

The rise of these organizations and the political consciousness they express has been catalyzed by many factors. Among them are the extension of modern transportation and communications networks to many previously inaccessible areas inhabited by tribal peoples; improved medical technology and assistance; greater availability of manufactured tools and goods; the extension of effective national government administrative control over the contiguous national populations; the increase in the strength and effectiveness of nonindigenous, nongovernmental advocacy and support organizations; the increased interest and ability of national and international media to publicize abuse of native lands, rights and peoples; the increase in international economic and political interdependence, which has made many governments more sensitive to the repercussions of bad publicity over indigenous issues; and last but not least, the influence of a steady trickle of anthropological researchers, who have helped both to catalyze native groups' awareness of the value of their traditional cultures in the eyes of the outside world and to inform them of the existence of potential sources of support in that world for their struggles to resist economic, political, and cultural oppression.

These factors have converged in recent years with growing concern in world public opinion for human rights and environmental issues, which have favored the causes of native groups struggling to defend their traditional lands and resource bases. None of these external factors, however, would have been sufficient by themselves to generate the cultural and social resources, or the political organization and will to act, that have been shown by so many native peoples. This is the part of the story that remains least well known to the world at large. It is important that it become known, as an antidote to the hopelessness induced by apocalyptic but often inaccurate news stories of "genocide" and widespread romantic clichés like the inevitable disappearance of primitive peoples in the path of progress. (The two often have more in common than meets the eye.) These myths have had the harmful effect of discouraging support for the struggles of many native peoples with a fighting chance to win. As the Kayapo case shows, such support can make an enormous difference.

That is the rosy side of a picture which is in the main far from rosy. For every indigenous people who have found the courage, leadership, and ability to respond constructively to the threat of despoliation of their ecological bases or the theft of their lands, others have been or are being decimated, dispossessed, or destroyed. In spite of some shining cases of successful resistance to threats to the ambient life-world, other battles have been, or are being, lost. The sheer volume of environmental destruction, and the variety of its forms and causes, make the struggle appear almost hopeless. Nowhere, however, has this been more true than in the Kayapo area of the Amazon. What the Kayapo have managed to do shows that even the most apparently hopeless odds can be faced and overcome.

Review Questions

1. How do the Kayapo Indians of Brazil subsist in their Amazon forest environment?
2. What forces threaten the livelihood and social existence of the Kayapo as a cultural group?
3. How have the Kayapo reacted to defend their forest environment and their existence as a cultural group?
4. Turner argues that the Kayapo have tried to unite and enlist the aid of several kinds of local and world groups in their fight to preserve their forest and lands. What are these groups? Use the case of the encampment at Altamira to illustrate how they could work together.
5. How have the Kayapo affected the world environmentalist movement?

5/ Wealth and Racial Stratification

Melvin L. Oliver and Thomas M. Shapiro

Income is what the average American family uses to reproduce daily existence in the form of shelter, food, clothing, and other necessities. In contrast, *wealth* is a storehouse of resources, it's what families own and use to produce income. Wealth signifies a control of financial resources that, when combined with income, provides the means and the opportunity to secure the "good life" in whatever form is needed—education, business, training, justice, health, material comfort, and so on. In this sense, wealth is a special form of money not usually used to purchase milk and shoes or other life necessities; rather it is used to create opportunities, secure a desired stature and standard of living, and pass class status along to one's children.

Wealth has been a neglected dimension of social science's concern with the economic and social status of Americans in general and racial minorities in particular. Social scientists have been much more comfortable describing and analyzing occupational, educational, and income distributions than examining the economic bedrock of a capitalist society—"private property." During the past decade, sociologists and economists have begun to pay more attention to the issue of wealth. The growing concentration of wealth at the top, and the growing racial wealth gap, have become important public-policy issues that undergird many political debates but, unfortunately, not many policy discussions. Our work takes up this challenge. This paper begins with a summary of the social science findings on race and wealth. The data are strongest regarding Black–White differences, but reference is made to findings and data that refer to Hispanics, Asians, and American Indians as well.

This paper focuses on three key contributions. First, an indispensable contribution to the current understanding of racial stratification is an examination of wealth, distinct from labor-market indicators, which this paper offers. Second, the paper makes an evidentiary contribution to the theory that current racial trends in inequality result, to a significant extent, from past racial policies and practices; and that the racial inequality of today, if left unattended, will contribute to continued racial stratification for the next generation. Third, by looking at new evidence concerning wealth and racial stratification, this paper contributes an impetus to push forward the research and policy agenda concerned with America's racial wealth gap. Thus, a wealth perspective provides a fresh way to examine the "playing field." Consequently, a standard part of the American credo—that similar accomplishments result in roughly equal rewards—may need reexamination.

Racial Stratification and the Asset Perspective

Understanding racial inequality, with respect to the distribution of power, economic resources, and life chances, is a prime concern of the social sciences. Most empirical research on racial inequality has focused on the economic dimension, which is not surprising considering the centrality of this component for life chances and well-being in an industrial society. The concerted emphasis of this economic component has been labor-market processes and their outcomes, especially earnings, occupational prestige, and social mobility. Until recently, the social sciences and the policy arena neglected wealth, intergenerational transfers, and policy processes that result in differential life chances based on racial criteria. Our ongoing work attempts to redress this severe imbalance.

The data and the social science understanding are strongest for income inequality in relation to race. For most, income is a quintessential labor-market outcome indicator. It refers to a flow of resources over time, representing the value of labor in the contemporary labor market and the value of social assistance and pensions. As such, income is a tidy and valuable gauge of the state of present economic inequality. Indeed, a strong case can be made that reducing racial discrimination in the labor market has resulted in increasing the income of racial minorities and, thus, narrowing the hourly wage gap between minorities and Whites. The command of resources that wealth entails, however, is more encompassing than income or education, and closer in meaning and theoretical significance to the traditional connotation of economic well-being and access to life chances as depicted in the classic conceptualizations of Marx, Weber, Simmel, and Tawney.[1]

[1]See Marx, K., and F. Engels, 1947, *The German Ideology*, New York: International Publishers; Weber, M., 1958, *The Protestant Ethic and the Spirit of Capitalism*, New York: Scribner's; Simmel, G., 1990, *The Philosophy of Money*, London: Routledge; Tawny, R.H., 1952, *Equality*, London: Allen and Unwin.

As important is the fact that wealth taps not only contemporary resources, but also material assets that have historic origins and future implications. Private wealth thus captures inequality that is the product of the past, often passed down from generation to generation. Conceptualizing racial inequality through wealth revolutionizes the concept of the nature and magnitude of inequality, and of whether it is decreasing or increasing. Although most recent analyses have concluded that contemporary class-based factors are most important in understanding the sources of continuing racial inequality, a focus on wealth sheds light on both the historical and the contemporary impacts not only of class but also of race. Income is an important indicator of racial inequality; wealth allows an examination of racial stratification.

A wealth perspective contends that continued neglect of wealth as a dimension of racial stratification will result in a seriously underestimated racial inequality. Tragically, policies based solely on narrow differences in labor-market factors will fail to close that breach. Taken together, however, asset-building and labor-market approaches open new windows of opportunity.

Historical Trends and Context of Wealth Distribution in the United States

Wealth inequality is today, and always has been, more extreme than income inequality. Wealth inequality is more lopsided in the United States than in Europe. Recent trends in asset ownership do not alleviate inequality concerns or issues. In general, inequality in asset ownership in the United States between the bottom and top of the distribution domain has been growing. Wealth inequality was at a 60-year high in 1989, with the top 1 percent of U.S. citizens controlling 39 percent of total U.S. household wealth. The richest 1 percent owned 48 percent of the total. These themes have been amply described in the work of Wolff (1994, 1996a, 1996b). Household wealth inequality increased sharply between 1983 and 1989. There was a modest attenuation in 1992, but the level of wealth concentration was still greater in 1992 than in 1983.

Until recently, few analyses looked at racial differences in wealth holding. Recent work, however, suggests that inequality is as pronounced—or more pronounced—between racial and ethnic groups in the dimension of wealth than income. The case of Blacks is paradigmatic of this inequality. Eller and Fraser (1995) report that Blacks had only 9.7 percent of the median net worth (all assets minus liabilities) of Whites in 1993 ($4,418 compared to $45,740); in contrast, their comparable figure for median family income was 62 percent of White income. Using 1988 data from the same source, Oliver and Shapiro (1995a) established that these differences are not the result of social-class factors. Even among the Black middle class, levels of net worth and net financial assets (all assets minus liabilities excluding home and vehicle equity) are drastically lower than for Whites. The comparable ratio of net worth for college-educated Blacks is only 0.24; even for two-income Black couples, the ratio is just 0.37. Clearly there are factors other than what we understand as "class" that led to these low levels of asset accumulation.

Black Wealth/White Wealth (Oliver and Shapiro, 1995a) decomposed the results of a regression analysis to give Blacks and Whites the same level of income, human capital, demographic, family, and other characteristics. The rationale for this was to examine the extent to which the huge racial wealth gap was a product of other differences between Whites and Blacks. Given the skewness of the wealth distribution, researchers agree that median figures best represent a typical American family; however, it should be noted, that regressions conventionally use means. A potent $43,143 difference in mean net worth remains, with 71 percent of the difference left unexplained. Only about 25 percent of the difference in net financial assets is explained. Taking the average Black household and endowing it with the same income, age, occupational, educational, and other attributes as the average White household still leaves a $25,794 racial gap in mean net financial assets. These residual gaps should not be cast wholly to racial dynamics; nonetheless, the regression analyses offer a powerful argument to directly link race in the American experience to the wealth-creation process.

As important is the finding that more than two-thirds of Blacks have no net financial assets, compared to less than one-third of Whites. This near absence of assets has extreme consequences for the economic and social well-being of the Black community, and of the ability of families to plan for future social mobility. If the average Black household were to lose an income stream, the family would not be able to support itself without access to public support. At their current levels of net financial assets, nearly 80 percent of Black families would not be able to survive at poverty-level consumption for three months. Comparable figures for Whites—although large in their own right—are one-half that of Blacks. Thinking about the social welfare of children, these figures take on more urgency. Nine out of ten Black children live in households that have less than three months of poverty-level net financial assets; nearly two-thirds live in households with zero or negative net financial assets (Oliver and Shapiro, 1989, 1990, 1995a, 1995b).

Because home ownership plays such a large role in the wealth portfolios of American families, it is a prime source of the differences between Black and White net worth. Home ownership rates for Blacks are 20 percent lower than rates for Whites; hence, Blacks possess less of this important source of equity. Discrimination in the process of securing home ownership plays a significant role in how assets are generated and accumulated. The reality of residential segregation also plays an important role in the way home ownership figures in the wealth portfolio of Blacks. Because Blacks live, for the most part, in segregated areas, the value of their homes is less, demand for them is less, and thus their equity is less (Oliver and

Shapiro, 1995b; Massey and Denton, 1994). (Because the area of home ownership is so central to the wealth accumulation process, the most current data will be analyzed in a later section of this paper.)

Similar findings on gross differences between Hispanics and Whites also have been uncovered (Eller and Fraser, 1995; Flippen and Tienda, 1997; O'Toole, 1998; Grant, 2000). Hispanics have slightly higher, but not statistically different, net worth figures than Blacks, based on the 1993 Survey of Income and Program Participation (SIPP); however, these findings are not sufficiently nuanced to capture the diversity of the Hispanic population. Data from the Los Angeles Survey of Urban Inequality show substantial differences in assets and net financial assets between recent immigrants who are primarily from Mexico and Central America and U.S.-born Hispanics (Grant, 2000).

Likewise, place of birth and regional differences among Hispanic groups also complicate a straightforward interpretation of this national-level finding. For example, Cuban Americans, we would hypothesize, have net worth figures comparable to Whites because of their dominance in an ethnic economy in which they own small and medium-sized businesses (Portes and Rumbaut, 1990). They have a far different set of economic life chances than Blacks and other recent Hispanic immigrants by way of their more significant wealth accumulation. For recent Hispanic immigrants, these figures suggest real vulnerability for the economic security of their households and children.

Finally, it is important to point out findings by Flippen and Tienda (1997) that attempt to explain the Black-White and Hispanic-White gap in wealth. Substituting White means for all the variables in a complex Tobit model, Flippen and Tienda found that the model "reduces asset inequality more for Hispanics than for Blacks." This is particularly the case for housing equity; for Hispanics, mean substitution reduced the gap by 80 percent, compared to only 62 percent for Blacks. As Flippen and Tienda note, "This suggests the importance of residential segregation and discrimination in the housing and lending market in hindering the accumulation of housing assets for Black households" (1997:18). Although their findings for Hispanics may be true for "White Hispanics," they may not apply to Black Puerto Ricans, who share social space with non-Hispanic Blacks and, therefore, may also be targeted for institutionalized racism in housing markets and financial institutions. Preliminary data from the Greater Boston Social Survey suggest that Hispanics in that region, the majority of whom are Puerto Rican, have even lower levels of net worth and financial assets than Blacks (O'Toole, 1998).

The case of Asians is quite similar to that for Hispanics, in that it is necessary to be mindful of their diversity, in terms of both national origin and immigrant status. Changes in immigration rules have favored those who bring assets into the country over those without assets; as a consequence, recent immigrants, from Korea, for example, are primarily individuals and families with assets, and once they arrive, they convert these assets into other asset-producing activities—e.g., small businesses. Bates' (1998) analysis of SIPP points out that Koreans who started businesses had significant assets and were able to use those assets to secure loans for business startups. Data from Los Angeles again underscore the importance of immigrant status and place of birth. U.S.-born Asians have both net worth and net financial assets approaching those of White Los Angelenos; foreign-born Asians, however, report lower wealth than U.S.-born Asians but higher wealth than all other ethnic and racial groups (Grant, 2000).

American Indians form a unique case when it comes to assets. They are asset rich but control little of these assets. Most Indian assets are held in tribal or individual Indian trust (Office of Trust Responsibilities, 1995). Thus, any accounting of the assets of individual Indian households is nearly impossible to calculate, given their small population and these "hidden" assets.

The dearth of studies of wealth in the United States has hampered efforts to develop both wealth theory and information. For more than 100 years, the prime sources concerning wealth status came from estate tax records, biographies of the super rich, various listings of the wealthiest, and like sources. In other words, something was known about those who possessed abundant amounts of wealth, but virtually nothing was known about the wealth status of average American families. During the 1980s, several data sources were developed based on field surveys of the American population. Most notable are SIPP, the Panel Study of Income Dynamics (PSID), the Federal Reserve Board's Survey of Consumer Finances (SCF), and the Health and Retirement Study (HRS). Thus, it is only relatively recently that any data at all were available to characterize the asset well-being of American families.

Race, Income, and Wealth

The empirical presentation begins with a fundamental examination of the most current income and wealth data for Whites, Blacks, Hispanics, and Asians. The data displayed in Table 1 are taken from the 1993 SIPP, Wave 7. Drawing attention first to income comparisons, the household income ratio of Blacks, compared to Whites, is 0.61:1, and the Hispanic ratio, 0.67:1. Asians fare considerably better in this comparison, earning close to 125 percent of White income. (It is important, here, to mind the caution from the literature review: the Hispanic and Asian data are aggregated, subsuming important dimensions of country of origin and immigrant status.) These income comparisons closely match other national data and pro-

TABLE 1 Income, Wealth, Race, and Ethnicity: 1994

	Median Income	Median NW[a]	Mean NW	Median NFA[b]	Mean NFA
White	$33,600	$52,944	$109,511	$7,400	$56,199
Black	$20,508	$6,127	$28,643	$100	$7,611
Ratio to White	0.61	0.12	0.26	0.01	0.14
Hispanic	$22,644	$6,723	$40,033	$300	$15,709
Ratio to White	0.67	0.13	0.37	0.03	0.27
Asian	$40,998	$39,846	$117,916	$4,898	$57,782
Ratio to White	1.22	0.67	1.02	0.51	0.98

[a]Net worth.
[b]Net financial assets.
Source: 1993 SIPP, Wave 7.

vide an effective indicator of current racial and ethnic material inequality. Changing the lens of analysis to wealth dramatically shifts the perspective. Black families possess only 14 cents for every dollar of wealth (median net worth) held by White families. The issue is no longer how to think about closing the gap from 0.61 but how to think about going from 14 cents on the dollar to something approaching parity. Nearly half of all Black families do not possess any net financial assets, compared to $7,400 for the average White family. These figures represent some asset accumulation for both Whites and Blacks between 1988 and 1994; nonetheless, the wealth perspective reveals an economic fragility for the entire American population, as it demonstrates the continuing racial wealth gap.

The data for Hispanics resemble the Black–White comparisons in one important respect and diverge in another. The median figures for both net worth and net financial assets reveal similar gaps in comparison with Whites, but the mean figures for net worth and net financial assets bump Hispanics "ahead" of Blacks. This apparent peculiarity most likely illustrates differences in experiences, country of origin, and immigrant status referred to earlier.

Mindful that the Asian data also are grouped, the figures for Asian wealth show an even more exaggerated pattern. The median-wealth figures indicate that Asians possess about three-quarters of the net worth and two-thirds of the net financial assets that Whites own. Commentators could seize on this piece of the story, noting that Asian family income is greater than Whites', and wonder why the wealth gap exists. An examination of mean wealth figures proves this exercise unnecessary—indeed, the data indicate parity in wealth between White and Asian families. Like the Hispanic data, but to an even greater extent, the Asian aggregate data mask different historical immigrant experiences, country of origin, and immigration status. The divergence between median and mean figures also most likely indicates that a sizable portion of the Asian community is relatively well off alongside a sizable portion of the community whose asset resources are far less than the average White family's. In other words, in parts of the Asian community, the wealth resources more closely resemble Black and Hispanic wealth profiles, while some segments of the Asian community virtually mirror the White profile.

These data provide a baseline of information regarding racial and ethnic differences in income and wealth resources. Not only do they update previous analyses in a simple way, they also bolster the previous findings. More important, the wealth data consistently indicate a far greater chasm in and pattern of racial and ethnic inequality than when income alone is examined.

Income and Wealth

A starting point for building on the basic analysis is a further examination of the connection between income and wealth. One leading economic perspective contends that the racial wealth gap predominantly results from income inequality. Do differences in income explain nearly all the racial differences in wealth? If so, then policies need to continue a primarily labor-market orientation that further narrows income inequality. If not, however, then social policy must address dynamics outside the labor market as well as income-generating, labor-market dynamics. Thus, it is critically important to address whether the wealth of Blacks is similar to Whites with similar incomes.

The strong income-wealth relationship is recognized in previous analysis of the 1984 SIPP data. *Black Wealth/White Wealth* (Oliver and Shapiro, 1995a) identified income as a significant variable determining wealth accumulation, next only to age in the wealth regressions. Looking at wealth by income ranges, however, showed that a powerful racial wealth gap remained. A regression analysis similarly indicated a highly significant differential wealth return to Whites and Blacks from income. The idea that wealth is quite similar when controlling for income, nonetheless, still holds some currency; so a direct empirical examination that uses the most recently available data should provide some evidence of, and resolution of, this issue. An empirical examination can be done in two ways.

TABLE 2 Wealth by Race and Hispanic Origin and Income Quintiles: 1994

	Total		White		Black		Hispanic	
	NW[a]	NFA[b]	NW	NFA	NW	NFA	NW	NFA
All households								
Median	$40,172		$52,944	$7,400	$7,400	$100	$ 6,723	$ 300
Ratio to white:					0.14		0.13	
Lowest income quintile								
Median	8,032	185	17,066	551	2,500		1,298	0
Ratio to white:					0.15		0.08	
Second income quintile								
Median	27,638	1,848	39,908	3,599	6,879	249	5,250	250
Ratio to white:					0.17	0.07	0.13	0.07
Third income quintile								
Median	40,665	4,599	50,350	6,800	14,902	800	12,555	1,000
Ratio to white:					0.30	0.12	0.25	0.15
Fourth income quintile								
Median	59,599	10,339	65,998	13,362	29,851	2,699	26,328	2,125
Ratio to white:					0.45	0.20	0.4	0.16
Highest income quintile								
Median	126,923	36,851	133,607	40,465	43,806	7,448	91,102	11,485
Ratio to white:					0.33	0.18	0.68	0.28

[a]Net worth.
[b]Net financial assets.
Source: 1993 SIPP, Wave 7.

The first way to address this issue can be demonstrated by using the data in Table 2, which show median measured net worth and net financial assets by income quintile, race, and Hispanic origin. White households in every income quintile had significantly higher levels of median wealth than Black and Hispanic households in the same income quintiles. In the lowest quintile, the median net worth for White households was $17,066, while that of Black and Hispanic households was $2,500 and $1,298, respectively. For the highest quintile households, median net worth for White households was $133,607; significantly lower was the median for Black households, $43,806. The median net financial assets data are just as revealing. At the middle quintile, for example, the median net financial assets for White households were $6,800, which was markedly higher than for Black ($800) and Hispanic ($1,000) households.

It is important to observe that controlling for income in this manner does, indeed, significantly lessen the Black-White/Hispanic-White wealth ratios. The overall median Black-White net worth ratio was 0.14:1, but this narrows when comparing White and Black households in similar income quintiles. The gap, as expressed in ratios, stays about the same for the two lowest income quintiles but narrows to 0.3:1, 0.45:1, and 0.33:1 for the next three income quintiles. In brief, as shown by this comparative procedure, controlling for income narrows the gap; but a significantly large gap persists, even when incomes are roughly equal. This evidence does not support the proposition that Whites and Blacks at similar income levels possess similar wealth.

Another way to address the income and wealth connection is to examine wealth at precisely similar income points for Whites and Blacks. New worth for Whites and Blacks is examined first at distribution percentiles—i.e., leaving income uncontrolled. Figures 1 and 2, drawn from 1994 SIPP data, show that median White wealth totaled $7,671 and Black wealth totaled $0 at the 25th percentile of each distribution. At the 50th percentile, White net worth was $52,944, compared with $6,126 for Blacks. At the 75th

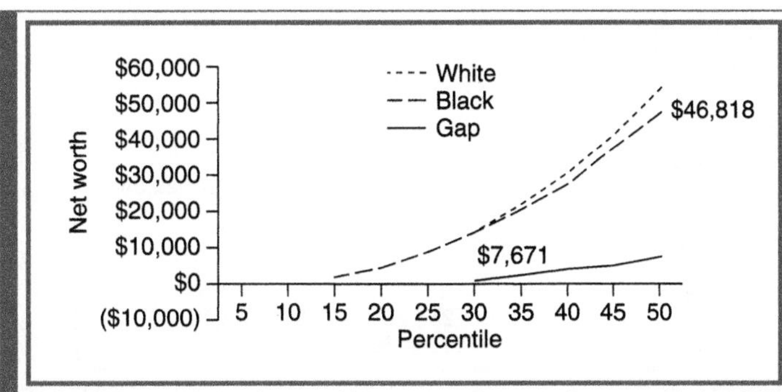

FIGURE 1 Wealth Gap in 1994 with No Control of Income: $0–$60,000.
Source: 1993 SIPP, Wave 7.

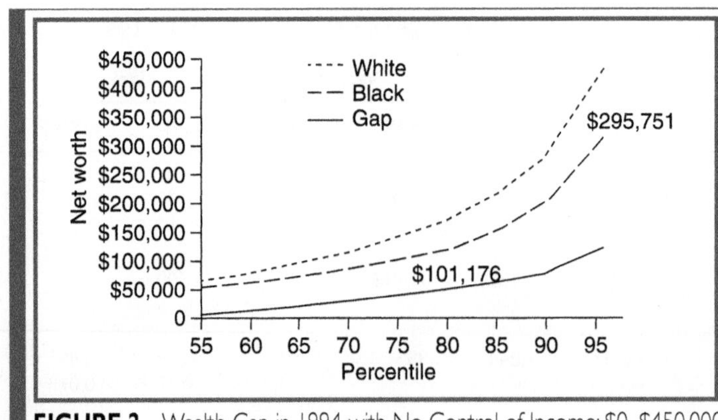

FIGURE 2 Wealth Gap in 1994 with No Control of Income: $0–$450,000.
Source: 1993 SIPP, Wave 7.

percentile, White net worth was $141,491 versus $40,315 for Blacks. How much of this gap is closed by controlling for income? Will Black–White wealth become actually quite similar, or will substantial, dramatic racial wealth inequality persist? At stake here is a test of two contending claims—(1) wealth inequality fundamentally derives from income inequality versus (2) wealth inequality derives from accumulations within historically and racially structured contexts. The claim is that Black wealth would be near parity with Whites' if incomes were equal; therefore, the logic is to compare net worth while controlling for income. Calibrating the White-to-Black income distributions means, for example, comparing the 25th percentile of the White wealth data to the 45th percentile of the Black distribution, the 50th White to the 70th Black, and the 75th White to the 88th Black.

Figure 3 graph this income-wealth relationship. A summary that captures some major data points should guide any interpretation. At the 25th percentile for Whites, median net worth is $7,671; controlling for income, the Black net worth adjusts upward to $3,548. At the 50th percentile for Whites, net worth is $52,944, compared to $30,000 for Blacks earning equivalent incomes. At the 75th percentile for Whites, wealth stands at $141,491 versus $72,761 for Blacks.

At the 50th percentile, then, the original uncontrolled gap weighs in at $46,817 with a ratio of 0.12:1. Controlling for income reduces this gap to $22,944. The Black/White wealth ratio closes as well to 0.57. Let us be clear: controlling for income significantly reduces the wealth gap; at the same time, however, even if incomes are equal, a consequential racial wealth gap remains. Indeed, after controlling for income, it is prudent to note that the remaining wealth gap is about as large as the racial income inequality gap. So if this exercise is correct, something akin to the original racial income gap remains unexplained after equalizing incomes.

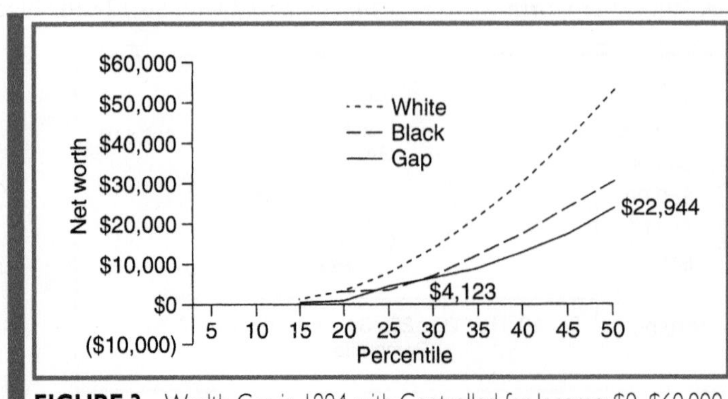

FIGURE 3 Wealth Gap in 1994 with Controlled for Income: $0–$60,000.
Source: 1993 SIPP, Wave 7.

References

Avery, R., and M. Rendell. 1993. Estimating the size and distribution of the baby boomers' prospective inheritances. Pp. 11–19 in *American Statistical Association: 1993 Proceedings of the Social Science Section.* Alexandria, Va.: American Statistical Association.

Bates, T. 1998. *Race, Self-Employment, and Upward Mobility: An Illusive American Dream.* Baltimore: Johns Hopkins University Press.

Butler, J. 1991. *Entrepreneurship and Self-Help Among Black Americans: A Reconsideration of Race and Economics.* Albany, N.Y.: State University of New York Press.

Corporation for Enterprise Development 1996. *Universal Savings Accounts—USAs: A Route to National Economic Growth and Family Economic Security.* Washington, D.C.: Corporation for Enterprise Development.

Darity, W., Jr., and P. Mason. 1998. Evidence on discrimination in employment: Codes of color, codes of gender. *Journal of Economic Perspectives* 12(2): 63–90.

Eller, T., and W. Fraser. 1995. Asset Ownership of Households: 1993. *U.S. Bureau of the Census. Current Population Reports, P70–47.* Washington, D.C.: U.S. Government Printing Office.

Flippen, C., and M. Tienda. 1997. Racial and Ethnic Differences in Wealth Among the Elderly. Paper presented at the 1997 Annual Meeting of the Population Association of America, Washington, D.C.

Gale, W., and J. Scholz. 1994. Intergenerational transfers and the accumulation of wealth. *Journal of Economic Perspectives* 8(4): 145–160.

Grant, D. 2000. A demographic portrait of Los Angeles, 1970–1990. *In Prismatic Metropolis: Analyzing Inequality in Los Angeles,* L. Bobo, M. Oliver, J. Johnson Jr., and A. Valenzuela, eds. New York: Russell Sage Foundation.

Howard, C. 1997. *The Hidden Welfare State: Tax Expenditures and Social Policy in the United States.* Princeton: Princeton University Press.

Jackman, M., and R. Jackman. 1980. Racial inequalities in home ownership. *Social Forces* 58: 1221–1233.

Jackson, K. 1985. *Crabgrass Frontier: The Suburbanization of the United States.* New York: Oxford University Press.

Koltikoff, L., and L. Sommers. 1981. The role of intergenerational transfers in aggregate capital accumulation. *Journal of Political Economy* 89:706–732.

Ladd, H. 1998. Evidence on discrimination in mortgage lending. *Journal of Economic Perspectives* 12(2):41–62.

Leiberson, S. 1980. *A Piece of the Pie.* Berkeley: University of California Press.

Massey, D., and N. Denton. 1994. *American Apartheid: Segregation and the Making of the Underclass.* Cambridge: Harvard University Press.

McNamee, S., and R. Miller, Jr. 1998. Inheritance and stratification. In *Inheritance and Wealth in America,* R. Miller, Jr., and S. McNamee, eds. New York: Plenum Press.

Mink, G. 1990. The lady and the tramp: Gender, race, and the origins of the American welfare state. Pp. 92–122 in *Women, the State, and Welfare,* L. Gordon, ed. Madison: University of Wisconsin Press.

Modigliana, F., and R. Brumberg. 1954. Utility analysis and the consumption function: An interpretation of cross-section data. In *Post-Keynesian Economics,* K. Kurihara, ed. New Brunswick: Rutgers University Press.

National Research Council 1989. *A Common Destiny: Blacks and American Society,* G. Jaynes and R. Williams, eds. Washington, D.C.: National Academy Press.

O'Toole, B. 1998. Family net asset levels in the greater Boston region. Paper presented at the Greater Boston Social Survey Community Conference, John F. Kennedy Library, Boston, Mass., November.

Office of Trust Responsibilities 1995. *Annual Report of Indian Lands.* Washington, D.C.: U.S. Department of the Interior.

Oliver, M., and T. Shapiro. 1989. Race and wealth. *Review of Black Political Economy* 17: 5–25.

———. 1990. Wealth of a nation: At least one-third of households are asset poor. *American Journal of Economics and Sociology* 49: 129–151.

———. 1995a. *Black Wealth/White Wealth: A New Perspective on Racial Inequality.* New York: Routledge.

———. 1995b. Them that's got shall get. In *Research in Politics and Society,* M. Oliver, R. Ratcliff, and T. Shapiro, eds. Greenwich, Conn.: JAI Press Vol. 5.

Ong, P. and E. Grigsby. 1988. Race and life cycle effects on home ownership in Los Angeles, 1970 to 1980. *Urban Affairs Quarterly* 23: 601–615.

Oubre, C. 1978. *Forty Acres and a Mule: The Freedman's Bureau and Black Land Ownership.* Baton Rouge: Louisiana State University Press.

Portes, A., and Rumbaut, R. 1990. *Immigrant America.* Berkeley: University of California Press.

Quadagno, J. 1994. *The Color of Welfare.* New York: Oxford University Press.

Sherraden, M. 1991. *Assets and the Poor: A New American Welfare Policy.* New York: Sharpe.

Wilhelm, M. 1998. The role of intergenerational transfers in spreading asset ownership. *Prepared for Ford Foundation Conference on The Benefits and Mechanisms for Spreading Assets,* New York, December 10–12.

Wolff, E. 1994. Trends in household wealth in the United States, 1962–1983 and 1983–1989. *Review of Income and Wealth* 40: 143–174.

———. 1996a. *Top Heavy: A Study of Increasing Inequality of Wealth in America.* Updated and expanded edition. New York: Free Press.

———. 1996b. International comparisons of wealth inequality. *Review of Income and Wealth* 42: 433–451.

Yinger, J.1995. *Closed Doors, Opportunities Lost: The Continuing Costs of Housing Discrimination.* New York: Russell Sage Foundation.

———. 1998. Evidence on discrimination in consumer markets. *Journal of Economic Perspectives* 12(2): 23–40.

6/ The Meaning and Significance of Race

William Julius Wilson

Many inner-city residents have a strong sense of the negative attitudes which employers tend to have toward them. A 33-year-old employed janitor from a poor South Side neighborhood had this observation: "I went to a coupla jobs where a couple of the receptionists told me in confidence: 'You know what they do with these applications from blacks as soon as the day is over?' Say 'we rip them and throw 'em in the garbage.'" In addition to concerns about being rejected because of race, the fears that some inner-city residents have of being denied employment simply because of their inner-city address or neighborhood are not unfounded. A welfare mother who lives in a large public housing project put it this way:

> Honestly, I believe they look at the address and the—your attitudes, your address, your surround—you know, your environment has a lot to do with your employment status. The people with the best addresses have the best chances, I feel so, I feel so.

Another welfare mother of two children from a South Side neighborhood expressed a similar view:

> I think that a lot of peoples don't get jobs over here because they lives—they live in the projects. They think that just 'cause people living in the projects they no good. Yes, yes. I think so! I think so! I think a lot of people might judge a person because you out—because they got a project address. You know, when you put it on an application, they might not even hire you because you live over here.

A 34-year-old single and unemployed black man put it this way: "If you're from a nice neighborhood I believe it's easier for you to get a job and stuff. I have been on jobs and such and gotten looks from folks and such, 'I wonder if he is the type who do those things that happen in that neighborhood.' "

Although the employers' perceptions of inner-city workers make it difficult for low-income blacks to find or retain employment, it is interesting to note that there is one area where the views of employers and those of many inner-city residents converge—namely, in their attitudes toward inner-city black males. Inner-city residents are aware of the problems of male joblessness in their neighborhoods. For example, more than half the black UPFLS survey respondents from neighborhoods with poverty rates of at least 40 percent felt that very few or none of the men in their neighborhood were working steadily. More than one-third of the respondents from neighborhoods with poverty rates of at least 30 percent expressed that view as well. Forty percent of the black respondents in all neighborhoods in the UPFLS felt that the number of men with jobs has steadily decreased over the past ten years. However, responses to the open-ended questions in our Social Opportunity Survey and data from our ethnographic field interviews reveal a consistent pattern of negative views among the respondents concerning inner-city black males, especially young black males.

Some provided explanations in which they acknowledged the constraints that black men face. An employed 25-year-old unmarried father of one child from North Lawndale stated:

> I know a lot of guys that's my age, that don't work and I know some that works temporary, but wanna work, they just can't get the jobs. You know, they got a high school diploma and that . . . but the thing is, these jobs always say: Not enough experience. How can you get some experience if you never had a chance to get any experience?

Others, however, expressed views that echoed those of the employers. For example, a 30-year-old married father of three children who lives in North Lawndale and works the night shift in a factory stated:

> I say about 65 percent—of black males, I say, don't wanna work, and when I say don't wanna work I say don't wanna work hard—they want a real easy job, making big bucks—see? And, and when you start talking about hard labor and earning your money with sweat or just once in a while you gotta put out a little bit—you know, that extra effort, I don't, I don't think the guys really wanna do that. And sometimes it comes from, really, not having a, a steady job or, really, not being out in the work field and just been sittin' back, being comfortable all the time and hanging out.

A 35-year-old welfare mother of eight children from the Englewood neighborhood on the South Side agreed:

> Well, I mean see you got all these dudes around here, they don't even work, they don't even try, they don't wanna work. You know what I mean, I wanna work, but I can't work. Then you got people here that, in this neighborhood, can get up and do somethin', they just don't wanna do nothin'—they really don't.

Intersecting Inequalities: Class, Race, Sex, and Sexualities
by Peter Kivisto and Elizabeth Hartung

The deterioration of the socioeconomic status of black men may have led to the negative perceptions of both the employers and the inner-city residents. Are these perceptions merely stereotypical or do they have any basis in fact? Data from the UPFLS survey show that variables measuring differences in social context (neighborhoods, social networks, and households) accounted for substantially more of the gap in the employment rates of black and Mexican men than did variables measuring individual attitudes. Also, data from the survey reveal that jobless black men have a lower "reservation wage" than the jobless men in the other ethnic groups. They were willing to work for less than $6.00 per hour, whereas Mexican and Puerto Rican jobless men expected $6.20 and $7.20, respectively, as a condition for working; white men, on the other hand, expected over $9.00 per hour. This would appear to cast some doubt on the characterization of black inner-city men as wanting "something for nothing," of holding out for high pay.

But surveys are not the best way to get at underlying attitudes and values. Accordingly, to gain a better grasp of the cultural issues, I examined the UPFLS ethnographic research that involved establishing long-term contacts and conducting interviews with residents from several neighborhoods. Richard Taub points out:

> Anybody who studies subgroups within the American population knows that there are cultural patterns which are distinctive to the subgroups and which have consequences for social outcomes. The challenge for those concerned about poverty and cultural variation is to link cultural arrangements to larger structural realities and to understand the interaction between the consequences of one's structural position on the one hand and pattern group behavior on the other. It is important to understand that the process works both ways. Cultures are forged in part on the basis of adaptation to both structural and material environments.

Analysis of the ethnographic data reveals identifiable and consistent patterns of attitudes and beliefs among inner-city ethnic groups. The data, systematically analyzed by Taub, reveal that the black men are more hostile than the Mexican men with respect to the low-paying jobs they hold, less willing to be flexible in taking assignments or tasks not considered part of their job, and less willing to work as hard for the same low wages. These contrasts in the behavior of the two groups of men are sharp because many of the Mexicans interviewed were recent immigrants.

"Immigrants, particularly Third World immigrants," will often "tolerate harsher conditions, lower pay, fewer upward trajectories, and other job related characteristics that deter native workers, and thereby exhibit a better 'work ethic' than others." The ethnographic data from the UPFLS suggest that the Mexican immigrants are harder workers because they "come from areas of intense poverty and that even boring, hard, dead-end jobs look, by contrast, good to them." They also fear being deported if they fail to find employment.

Once again, it should be emphasized that the contrasts between blacks and Mexicans in our ethnographic sample are sharp because most of the latter in our sample were recent immigrants. Our ethnographic research was conducted mainly in black and Latino inner-city neighborhoods, and the ethnographic data that were sufficient to draw systematic comparisons concerning work attitudes were those based on intensive field interviews with Mexican men and African-American men. However, as indicated earlier, the large UPFLS survey revealed that white men in the inner city have a much higher reservation wage than either African-American or Latino inner-city men. Accordingly, there is no reason to assume that their attitude toward dead-end menial jobs is any less negative than that of black men.

Since our sample was largely drawn from poverty areas, it includes a disproportionate number of immigrants, who tend to settle initially in poverty areas. As previous research has consistently shown, migrants who leave a poorer economy for a more developed economy in the hope of improving their standard of living tend to accept, willingly, the kinds of employment that the indigenous workers detest or have come to reject. It is reasonable to hypothesize that the more "Americanized" they become, the less inclined they will be to accept menial low-wage and hazardous jobs.

In contrast to the Mexican men, the inner-city black men complained that they get assigned the heaviest or dirtiest work on the job, are overworked, and are paid less than nonblacks. They strongly feel that they are victims of discrimination. "The Mexican-American men also report that they feel exploited," states Taub, "but somehow that comes with the territory." Taub argues that the inner-city black men have a greater sense of "honor" and often see the work, pay, and treatment from bosses as insulting and degrading. Accordingly, a heightened sensitivity to exploitation fuels their anger and gives rise to a tendency to "just walk off the job."

One has to look at the growing exclusion of black men from higher-paying blue-collar jobs in manufacturing and other industries and their increasing confinement to low-paying service laboring jobs to understand these attitudes and how they developed. Many low-paying jobs have predictably low retention rates. For example, one of the respondents in the UPFLS employer survey reported turnover rates at his firm that exceeded 50 percent. When asked if he had considered doing anything about this problem, the employer acknowledged that the company had made a rational decision to tolerate a high turnover rather than increasing the starting salary and improving working conditions to attract higher-caliber workers:

"Our practice has been that we'll keep hiring and, hopefully, one or two of them are going to wind up being good."

As Kathryn Neckerman points out, "This employer, and others like him, can afford such high turnover because the work is simple and can be taught in a couple of days. On average, jobs paying under \$5.00 or \$6.00 an hour were characterized by high quit rates. In higher-paying jobs, by contrast, the proportion of employees resigning fell to less than 20 percent per year." Yet UPFLS data show that the proportion of inner-city black males in the higher-paying blue-collar positions has declined far more sharply than that of Latinos and whites. Increasingly displaced from manufacturing industries, inner-city black males are more confined to low-paying service work. Annual turnover rates of 50 to 100 percent are common in low-skill service jobs in Chicago, regardless of the race or ethnicity of the employees.

Thus, the attitudes that many inner-city black males express about their jobs and job prospects reflect their plummeting position in a changing labor market. The more they complain and manifest their dissatisfaction, the less desirable they seem to employers. They therefore experience greater rejection when they seek employment and clash more often with supervisors when they secure employment.

Residence in highly concentrated poverty neighborhoods aggravates the weak labor-force attachment of black males. The absence of effective informal job networks and the frequency of many illegal activities increases nonmainstream behavior such as hustling. As Sharon Hicks-Bartlett, another member of the UPFLS research team, points out, "Hustling is making money by doing whatever is necessary to survive or simply make ends meet. It can be legal or extra-legal work and may transpire in the formal or informal economy. While both men and women hustle, men are more conspicuous in the illegal arena of hustling."

In a review of the research literature on the experiences of black men in the labor market, Philip Moss and Christopher Tilly point out that criminal activity in urban areas has become more attractive because of the disappearance of legitimate jobs. They refer to a recent study in Boston that showed that while "black youth in Boston were evenly split on whether they could make more money in a straight job or on the street, by 1989 a three-to-one majority of young black people expressed the opinion that they could make more on the street."

The restructuring of the economy will continue to compound the negative effects of the prevailing perceptions of inner-city black males. Because of the increasing shift away from manufacturing and toward service industries, employers have a greater need for workers who can effectively serve and relate to the consumer. Inner-city black men are not perceived as having these qualities.

The restructuring of the urban economy could also have long-term consequences for inner-city black women. Neckerman argues that a change in work cultures accompanied the transformation of the economy, resulting in a mismatch between the old and new ways of succeeding in the labor market. In other words, there is a growing difference between the practices of blue-collar and service employers and the practices of white-collar employers. This mismatch is important in assessing the labor-market success of inner-city workers.

Low-skilled individuals from the inner city tend to be the children of blue-collar workers or service workers, and their work experience is thus largely confined to blue-collar or service jobs. What happens "when employees socialized to approach jobs and careers in ways that make sense in a blue-collar or service context enter the white-collar world?" The employer interviews suggest that workers from blue-collar or service settings seek positions that carry high entry-level salaries that provide all the necessary training on the job and that grant privileges and promotion in accordance with both seniority and performance. But in a white-collar setting, inner-city workers face entry-level positions that require more and continuous training and employers who are looking for people who are energetic, intelligent, and possess good language skills. Promotions in this environment seldom depend on seniority. Accordingly, "their advancement may depend on fairly subtle standards of evaluation, and on behavior that is irrelevant or even negatively sanctioned in the blue-collar and service settings." Interviews with inner-city workers revealed that most recognize the changing nature of the labor market and that a greater premium is placed on education and training for success, but many "did indeed espouse blue-collar ways of getting ahead."

In summary, the issue of race in the labor market cannot simply be reduced to the presence of discrimination. Although our data suggest that inner-city blacks, especially African-American males, are experiencing increasing problems in the labor market, the reasons for those problems are seen in a complex web of interrelated factors, including those that are race-neutral.

The loss of traditional manufacturing and other blue-collar jobs in Chicago resulted in increased joblessness among inner-city black males and a concentration in low-wage, high-turnover laborer and service-sector jobs. Embedded in ghetto neighborhoods, social networks, and households that are not conducive to employment, inner-city black males fall further behind their white and Hispanic counterparts, especially when the labor market is slack. Hispanics "continue to funnel into manufacturing because employers prefer Hispanics over blacks and they like to hire by referrals from current employees, which Hispanics can readily furnish, being already embedded in migration networks." Inner-city black men grow bitter and resentful in the face of their employment prospects and often manifest or express these feelings in their harsh, often dehumanizing, low-wage work settings.

Their attitudes and actions, combined with erratic work histories in high-turnover jobs, create the widely shared perception that they are undesirable workers. The perception in turn becomes the basis for employers' negative hiring decisions, which sharply increase when the economy is weak. The rejection of inner-city black male workers gradually grows over the long term not only because employers are turning more to the expanding immigrant and female labor force, but also because the number of jobs that require contact with the public continues to climb.

The position of inner-city black women in the labor market is also problematic. Their high degree of social isolation in impoverished neighborhoods reduces their employment prospects. Although Chicago employers consider them more acceptable as workers than the inner-city black men, their social isolation is likely to strengthen involvement in a work culture that has few supports allowing a move into white-collar employment. Also, impoverished neighborhoods, weak networks, and weak household supports decrease their ability to develop language and other job-related skills necessary in an economy that increasingly rewards employees who can work and communicate effectively with the public.

Despite the attitudes of employers, joblessness in inner-city ghetto neighborhoods would decline if the U.S. economy could sustain high levels of employment over a long period of time. In a slack labor market—a labor market with high unemployment—employers are—and indeed, can afford to be—more selective in recruiting and in granting promotions. They overemphasize job prerequisites and exaggerate the value of experience. In such an economic climate, disadvantaged minorities suffer disproportionately and the level of employer discrimination rises. In a tight labor market, job vacancies are numerous, unemployment is of short duration, and wages are higher. Moreover, in a tight labor market the labor force expands because increased job opportunities not only reduce unemployment but also draw into the labor force those workers who, in periods when the labor market is slack, respond to fading job prospects by dropping out of the labor force altogether. Conversely, in a tight labor market the status of all workers—including disadvantaged minorities—improves because of lower unemployment, higher wages, and better jobs.

The economic recovery during the first half of the 1990s lowered the unemployment rates among blacks in general. For the first time in more than two decades, the unemployment rate for African-Americans dipped below 10 percent in December 1994. Indeed, "the unemployment rate for black adults dropped faster in 1994 than it did for white adults." This was in part due to a brief expansion of manufacturing jobs. By contrast, the economy saw a slight decrease in manufacturing jobs during the economic recovery period in the late 1980s and more than 1.5 million positions were eliminated from January 1989 to September 1993. However, 301,000 manufacturing jobs were created during the next sixteen months, significantly benefiting black workers who are heavily concentrated in manufacturing.

Nonetheless, the unemployment rate represents only the percentage of workers in the labor force—that is, those who are actively looking for work. A more significant measure is the employment-to-population ratio, which corresponds to the percentage of adult workers 16 and older who are working. For example, whereas the unemployment rate for black youths 16 years old and older was 34.6 percent in December of 1994, compared with a white youth unemployment rate of 14.7 percent, only 23.9 percent of all black youths were actually working, compared with 48.5 percent of white youths. In previous years, labor-market demand stimulated by fiscal or monetary policy not only absorbed the technically unemployed (that is, those jobless workers who are in the official labor force) but also enlarged the employment ranks by drawing back workers who were not in or had dropped out of the labor force. Today, it appears that inner-city residents who are not in the labor force tend to be beyond the reach of monetary or fiscal policy. The problem is that in recent years tight labor markets have been of relatively short duration, frequently followed by a recession which either wiped out previous gains for many workers or did not allow others to fully recover from a previous period of economic stagnation. It would take sustained tight labor markets over many years to draw back those discouraged inner-city workers who have dropped out of the labor market altogether, some for very long periods of time. The disappearance of work in the inner-city ghetto presents a serious challenge to society. The consequences of such joblessness are not restricted to the inner-city ghettos, they affect the quality of life and race relations in the larger city as well.

Index

C

D

E

F